European Politics

PAUL KUBICEK

Oakland University

Longman

Boston Columbus Indianapolis New York San Francisco Upper Saddle River
Amsterdam Cape Town Dubai London Madrid Milan Munich Paris Montreal Toronto
Delhi Mexico City São Paulo Sydney Hong Kong Seoul Singapore Taipei Tokyo

Senior Acquisition Editor: Vikram Mukhija
Editorial Assistant: Beverly Fong
Senior Marketing Manager: Lindsey Prudhomme
Production Project Manager: Clara Bartunek
Project Coordination, Text Design, and Electronic Page Makeup: Aptara®, Inc.
Cover Design Manager: Jayne Conte
Cover Designer: Suzanne Duda
Cover Illustration/Photo: Corbis Images
Manufacturing Manager: Clara Bartunek
Printer and Binder: Courier/Stoughton
Cover Printer: Courier/Stoughton

Library of Congress Cataloging-in-Publication Data
Kubicek, Paul.
European politics / Paul Kubicek.
p. cm.
Includes index.
ISBN-13: 978-0-205-56205-3
ISBN-10: 0-205-56205-1
1. Europe—Politics and government. I. Title.
JN5.K83 2012
320.94—dc22 2010050032

1 2 3 4 5 6 7 8 9 10—CRS—14 13 12 11

Longman
is an imprint of

www.pearsonhighered.com

ISBN-10: 0-205-56205-1
ISBN-13: 978-0-205-56205-3

BRIEF CONTENTS

CONTENTS

PREFACE

I was fortunate to be a senior in college in the fall of 1989, that *annus mirabilis* when the Berlin Wall fell and the peoples of Eastern Europe were liberated from communism. In my US-Soviet relations class, the professor, who had distinguished herself both in academia and in government service, at times seemed bewildered by the speed and nature of events, as communist governments fell, like dominoes, throughout the course of the semester. At one point she informed us—and here I have to paraphrase—that the world that she knew, a world predicated on the divisions of the Cold War, was ending, and that we, members of a new generation, might be better placed to look upon the emerging European and world order with a fresh set of eyes. Over the course of the next several years, the notion sensed in that momentous fall that the world had changed began to take on more tangible forms. Within Europe, democratic institutions spread eastward; new countries formed out of the collapse of the Soviet Union, Yugoslavia, and Czechoslovakia; market forces and globalization seemed triumphant; and the European Union (EU) acquired more powers—best seen with the emergence of the euro—and a greater geographic reach, adding many former communist states in expansions in 2004 and 2007.

During the two decades since I graduated from college, I have followed developments in European politics closely, including extended stays on the continent for research and teaching in Turkey, Ukraine, Poland, Austria, and Slovenia. Most of my work has been on post-communist states, on Turkey, and on countries that have eagerly been trying to validate their European credentials by gaining entry into the EU. Over the course of time, Europe has become more unified, leading some to speculate about an emerging "United States of Europe." While that might be taking things too far—there is no European central government and various divisions are still manifest in Europe today—it is nonetheless true that "Europe," as an idea and in the institutional form of the EU, has taken on new meanings and importance. At the same time, European states face a host of challenges, including immigration, debt and the need to generate economic growth, and competitive pressures from economic globalization. While the great issue of the previous generation—the Cold War—becomes a historical memory, the growth of the EU together with the rise of new concerns such as managing cultural diversity, terrorism, and challenges to the welfare state and the "European social model" make European politics a dynamic field.

This book is, in some respects, an attempt to look upon Europe with a "fresh set of eyes." It was conceived after the introduction of the euro in 2002 and the expansion of the EU to ten states in 2004. Obviously, it also originated in the post 9/11 world, and recognizes that 9/11 has its own echoes in Europe, which has seen its own terror attacks and where some fear Muslim citizens and immigrants.

It was completed in the midst of an economic crisis in 2010 that threatened both the euro and, in a larger sense, the broader project of the EU to unify the continent. How this crisis plays out will no doubt be a major issue in any course in which this book is used.

FEATURES

European Politics boasts several features that make it an easy-to-use yet informative text.

- *Approach:* This book is thematic in its approach, eschewing a focus on institutions or developments in a handful of countries. This allows not only for wider coverage across the continent, but makes comparison across countries more explicit. The goal is to give the student an appreciation for Europe as a whole, not one of specific countries in isolation from each other and from broader European or global developments. In particular, it includes consideration of states in "Eastern" or post-communist Europe, recognizing that the old division between Western and Eastern Europe—divisions that in many places meant separate courses for the two parts of the continent—are less and less relevant today. The book also gives importance to "Europe" as an idea, not simply a geographically defined entity. In this regard, it recognizes that the EU has a central, if contested, role in contemporary European politics. This is not to downplay domestic political institutions, which receive their due coverage, but to note that the reality of politics in Europe often includes both traditional concerns of comparative politics (e.g., national-level structures and policies) and those of international relations (e.g., the role and power of international institutions and norms). Finally, it recognizes that the study of politics needs to be more than about the nuts and bolts of how political institutions work. A complete picture of European politics should also look at the more contentious and important political issues, those that color elections and are the subjects of discussion when Europeans talk about politics. Thus, the final chapters of the book examine issues that have the greatest relevance for Europe as it enters the second decade of the twenty-first century.
- *Organization:* As noted, this book is organized thematically. Broadly speaking, it consists of three sections. First, it covers important historical developments, including the history of the EU. Second, it looks at political institutions and actors, both within countries and at the EU level. Finally, it looks at various policy realms, assessing actions both of individual countries as well as the EU as a whole.
- *Pedagogy:* While providing a basic introduction to European politics—including terminology and core concepts—this book explicitly and implicitly includes many features and asks many questions to develop critical thinking skills. Each chapter begins with an anecdote about a contemporary European event or issue to capture the reader's interest and introduce the broader topic at hand. Each chapter contains an annotated glossary, with useful terms defined in the margins of the text for easy reference. At the end of the each

chapter, these terms are listed again, as are several "application questions" that ask students to apply or expand upon the material. A short annotated bibliography may also be useful to instructors or students alike. Tables, photos, and charts supplement the text with interesting and useful images and data, and various web links are provided for students to pursue their own data analysis or to view materials, including videos, relevant to the subject matter.

To foster critical thinking and to help students understand how European politics has evolved over time and remains dynamic, the text exposes students to information about how various factors and forces (e.g., history, culture, demographics, economics, globalization, the EU) shape European politics. These give rise to basic questions that can be asked in many places in the text, such as "how does history matter?" or "why have institutions evolved over time?". Many issues of comparative analysis, such as the differences between presidential and parliamentary systems, are explored in the **In Focus** sections. In addition to comparisons across Europe, many comparisons are drawn with the US in mind (e.g., the role of religion in politics). Each chapter also contains a **Is Europe One?** section that asks students to reflect critically upon the idea of a "single" or "united" Europe, weighing its empirical reality as well as its advantages and disadvantages.

European Politics begins with a reflection upon the fall of the Berlin Wall, an event that ended one era and opened up possibilities for individual European countries and for Europe as a whole. It focuses on the contested issue of what "Europe" is today, emphasizing that "Europe" is a political idea shaped by history. Its **In Focus** section supports the notion that Europe is, at least by some measures and in some quarters, viewed as a political community. It also discusses Europeanization and raises the question of how united Europe really is, using the case of the Iraq War in the **Is Europe One?** feature to note that "Europe" often has a problem acting as a single actor in international politics.

Chapter 2 is a brief exploration of European political history, split into two parts: Western Europe and Eastern Europe. Core concepts include the formation of the state, nationalism, the emergence (or lack thereof) of democratic institutions, and economic development. The **In Focus** section compares the differing post–World War II economic experiences of West Germany and Great Britain, setting up a later discussion of Thatcherism and the challenges of the welfare state. This chapter includes information on the post-communist transformation of Eastern Europe, which creates the possibility of a more politically united Europe. On this front, the particular problems of reunifying Germany, explored in the **Is Europe One?** feature, illustrate that unification of a single country, let alone an entire continent, is far from a simple process.

Chapter 3 covers the history of the EU, which began initially after World War II as a much more limited project than it is today. Nonetheless, over time the EU has both "deepened" to cover a greater range of issues and "widened" to include more countries. This chapter includes post-Masstricht developments such as the creation of the euro and expansion. The **Is Europe One?** feature compares older and newer members of the EU while the **In Focus** section examines the content of and debates over the Lisbon Treaty.

Chapter 4 begins formal discussion of political institutions, starting with the EU, which plays an important role in many issue areas. This chapter describes the workings of institutions such as the European Commission, the Council of the EU, and the European Parliament, as well as issue areas (e.g., trade, agriculture, the environment) where the EU plays a key role. The **In Focus** section takes up the contentious Common Agricultural Policy (CAP) of the EU, while the **Is Europe One?** feature asks the question of what the EU hopes to and/or will be able to become.

Chapter 5 begins consideration of domestic political institutions by exploring the role and functions of European parliaments. In addition to basic considerations such as parliamentary powers and unicameralism versus bicameralism, the chapter also examines the various ways parliaments are elected in Europe. The **In Focus** section examines a question of broad interest to comparativists—the relative merits of plurality voting systems and those of proportional representation—while the **Is Europe One?** feature weaves the EU back into the discussion by looking at the relationship between the EU and national parliaments.

Chapter 6 takes up executive power, in particular how it differs among parliamentary, presidential, and semi presidential systems. The chapter considers examples from numerous states, as well as discussions on the structure and performance of the civil service. Like the previous chapter, the **In Focus** section explores an issue of broader interest in political science—the relative merits of presidential and parliamentary systems. The **Is One Europe One?** feature takes up the more recent phenomenon of the "presidentialization" of European political systems.

Chapter 7 considers a host of constitutional and legal issues, including the content of constitutions themselves, federal versus unitary systems, and the structure, powers, and performance of court systems. The **In Focus** section looks at devolution and separatism within several European states, while the **Is Europe One?** feature examines the important but often complex issue of the role of EU law in national courts.

Chapter 8 is the last chapter to look at political institutions. It examines political parties in Europe, grouping parties into party families. It notes how the proportional electoral systems in Europe tend to produce multiparty systems in most states. It explores voter turnout across countries and across time, as well as looking in depth at elections in four European states (France, Poland, Italy, and Great Britain) from 2007 to 2010. **In Focus** looks at stability and volatility in party systems—another issue of wider interest in political science—while **Is Europe One?** asks whether political parties are subjects of Europeanization.

Chapter 9 looks at political culture and aspects of political behavior beyond voting. Much of the discussion of political culture is drawn from public opinion research, and highlights the emergence of post-materialist concerns such as the environment and women's rights. Consideration of political behavior looks in particular at the role of interest groups (e.g., labor unions) and social movements in advocating for particular policies and promoting political change. **In Focus** asks whether changes in attitudes and behavior, particularly the decline of confidence in institutions, is a sign of a crisis of democracy—an echo relevant to both sides of the Atlantic, if not beyond—and **Is Europe One?** looks at questions of identity and feelings of "Europeanness."

Chapter 10 is the first of the policy-oriented chapters, and it examines economic issues across Europe. A major theme is how the welfare state has been challenged on numerous fronts, including by the forces of globalization. While some states can be counted as success stories, the chapter devotes much attention to the economic crisis that began in 2008 and is on-going as of this writing, including the Greek and Irish debt crises that some fear threaten the entire eurozone. The **In Focus** section looks at the past success of Ireland and Finland, small countries that until the end of the 2000s had two of the strongest economies in the world, whereas **Is Europe One?** asks what, if anything, the EU can do to help foster growth and economic competitiveness in Europe.

Chapter 11 is devoted to foreign policy, in particular efforts to forge a common foreign policy among European countries. Various issues include security, the environment, use of aid and "soft power," and relations with countries such as Russia and China. The **In Focus** section compares European and American responses to September 11, 2001, and conduct in the "war on terror." The **Is Europe One?** feature examines with a skeptical eye the broader question of whether there really is, beyond pronouncements on paper, a Common Foreign and Security Policy for Europe.

Chapter 12 takes up cultural issues, including immigration and the difficulties many states have had in assimilating immigrants. Among many recent events that highlight problems in managing cultural diversity, the **Is Europe One?** feature looks at the fallout from the Danish cartoon controversy in 2005. The chapter then discusses the decline in religiosity among many Europeans, comparing in its **In Focus** section the public role of religion and the level of religious belief between Americans and Europeans. It concludes by discussing Turkey's bid to join the EU, an issue that challenges Europe on many fronts but will go a long way in defining what "Europe" is or can become.

SUPPLEMENTS

Longman is pleased to offer several resources to qualified adopters of *European Politics* and their students that will make teaching and learning from this book even more effective and enjoyable. Several of the supplements for this book are available at the Instructor Resource Center (IRC), an online hub that allows instructors to quickly download book-specific supplements. Please visit the IRC welcome page at **www.pearsonhighered.com/irc** to register for access.

PASSPORT FOR COMPARATIVE POLITICS With Passport, choose the resources you want from MyPoliSciKit and put links to them into your course management system. If there is assessment associated with those resources, it also can be uploaded, allowing the results to feed directly into your course management system's gradebook. With more than 150 MyPoliSciKit assets like video case studies, mapping exercises, comparative exercises, simulations, podcasts, *Financial Times* newsfeeds, current events quizzes, politics blog, and much more, Passport is available for any Pearson introductory or upper-level political science book. Use ISBN 0-205-10925-X to order Passport with this book. To learn more, please contact your Pearson representative.

MYSEARCHLAB Need help with a paper? MySearchLab saves time and improves results by offering start-to-finish guidance on the research/writing process and full-text access to academic journals and periodicals. Use ISBN 0-205-10908-X to order MySearchLab with this book. To learn more, please visit http://www.mysearchlab.com or contact your Pearson representative.

TEST BANK This resource includes multiple-choice questions, true/false questions, and essay questions for each chapter. Available exclusively on the IRC.

THE ECONOMIST Every week, *The Economist* analyzes the important happenings around the globe. From business to politics, to the arts and science, its coverage connects seemingly unrelated events in unexpected ways. Use ISBN 0-205-00267-6 to order a fifteen-week subscription with this book for a small additional charge. To learn more, please contact your Pearson representative.

THE FINANCIAL TIMES Featuring international news and analysis from journalists in more than fifty countries, *The Financial Times* provides insights and perspectives on political and economic a developments around the world. Use ISBN 0-205-00250-1 to order a fifteen-week subscription with this book for a small additional charge. To learn more, please contact your Pearson representative.

ACKNOWLEDGMENTS

When I began my academic career, I did not consider myself a "Europeanist." "*East* Europeanist," perhaps, but not one with continent-wide expertise. To the extent that I am a bona fide "Europeanist" today, I became so only with time and often through teaching. Thus, thanks must first go to my former students (in Turkey, Ukraine, Slovenia, and the US), as this book is in part an outgrowth of how I learned to teach various classes on European and EU politics, often incorporating insights and feedback from students. Among my academic colleagues, numerous individuals stimulated my interest in European political issues and provided me with opportunities or inspiration to pursue research in the field. I would like to make special mention of Ilter Turan, Zvi Gitelman, Ronald Suny, Kevin Deegan-Krause, Amie Kreppel, Rudi Rizman, and Frank Schimmelfennig. For this particular project, thanks must be given to the numerous reviewers who read early drafts of the manuscript: Juan M. Arroyo, Ithaca College; Terence Casey, Rose-Hulman Institute of Technology; Paola Cesarini, Providence College; Clay Clemens, College of William and Mary; Neil Scott Cole, Longwood University; John Easley, Western Connecticut University; Scott Erb, University of Maine Farmington; Karl Kalthenthaler, University of Akron; Brian Kessel, Columbia College; Petia Kostadinova, University of Florida; Paulette Kurzer, University of Arizona; Shane Martin, Penn State University; Daniel Masters, University of North Carolina-Wilmington; Vladimir Matic, Temple University; Heather Mbaye, University of West Georgia; Shannon Peterson, Utah State University; John Scherpereel, James Madison University; Kerstin Sorensen, Elon University; Jae-Jae Spoon, University of Iowa; Thorsten Spehn, University of Colorado-Denver; and Rebecca Steffenson, DePaul University. I have tried to incorporate many of their suggestions, which no doubt resulted in an improved project. Vikram Mukhija at Pearson Longman provided encouragement and wealth of useful suggestions from start to finish.

Lastly, thanks to Alyce, Jonah, and Asher. Work in earnest for this book began during our wonderful stay in Slovenia, where I was awarded a Fulbright. Completion took longer than I thought, and their backing and patience in helping see it through is much appreciated.

PAUL KUBICEK

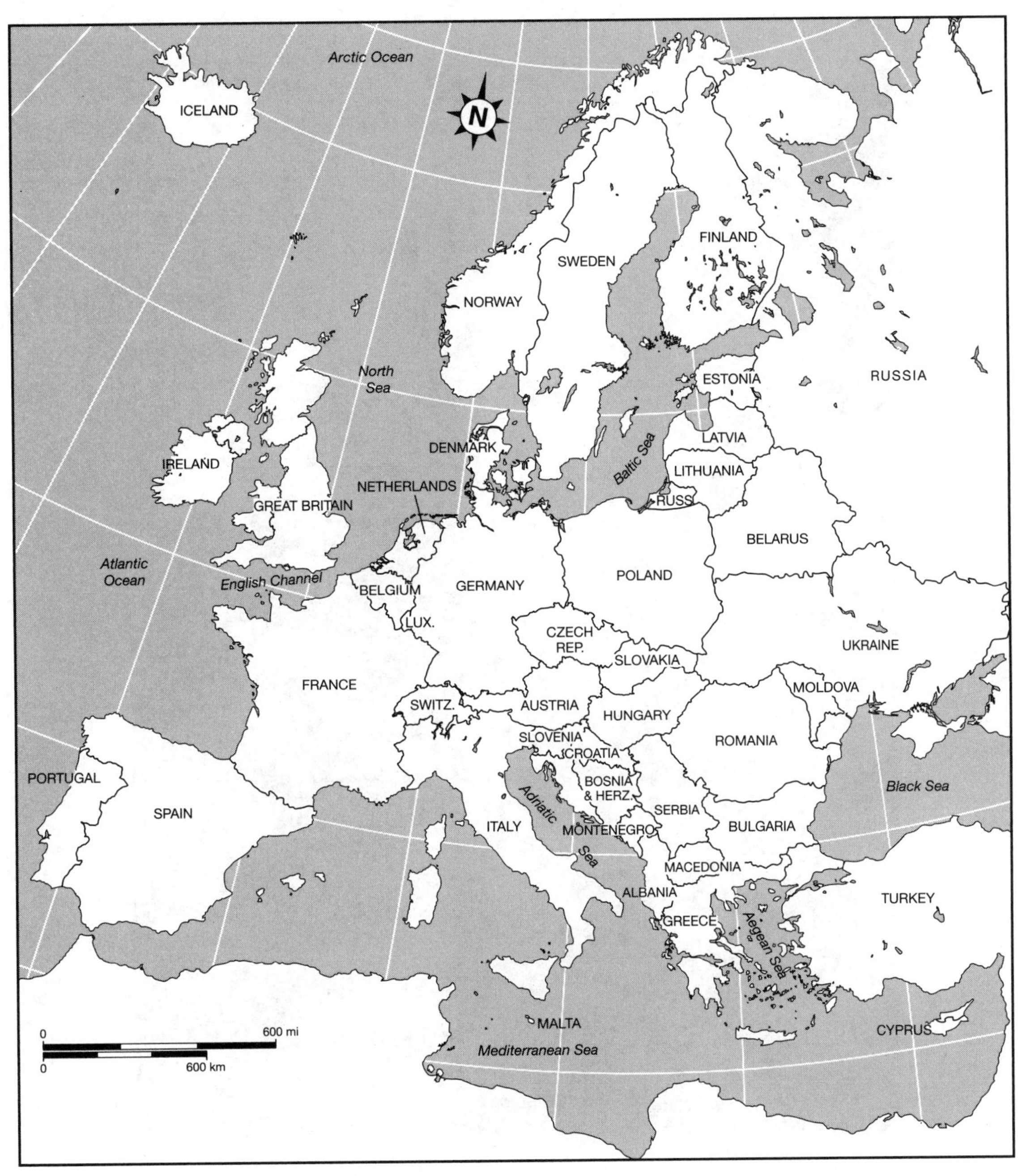
Arctic Ocean
N
ICELAND
FINLAND
SWEDEN
NORWAY
North Sea
ESTONIA
RUSSIA
LATVIA
DENMARK
IRELAND
Baltic Sea
LITHUANIA
NETHERLANDS
RUSS.
GREAT BRITAIN
BELARUS
Atlantic Ocean
POLAND
English Channel
BELGIUM
GERMANY
LUX.
CZECH REP.
UKRAINE
SLOVAKIA
FRANCE
MOLDOVA
SWITZ.
AUSTRIA
HUNGARY
SLOVENIA
ROMANIA
CROATIA
PORTUGAL
BOSNIA & HERZ.
Black Sea
Adriatic Sea
SPAIN
SERBIA
ITALY
MONTENEGRO
BULGARIA
MACEDONIA
ALBANIA
TURKEY
GREECE
Aegean Sea
MALTA
CYPRUS
0
600 mi
0
600 km
Mediterranean Sea

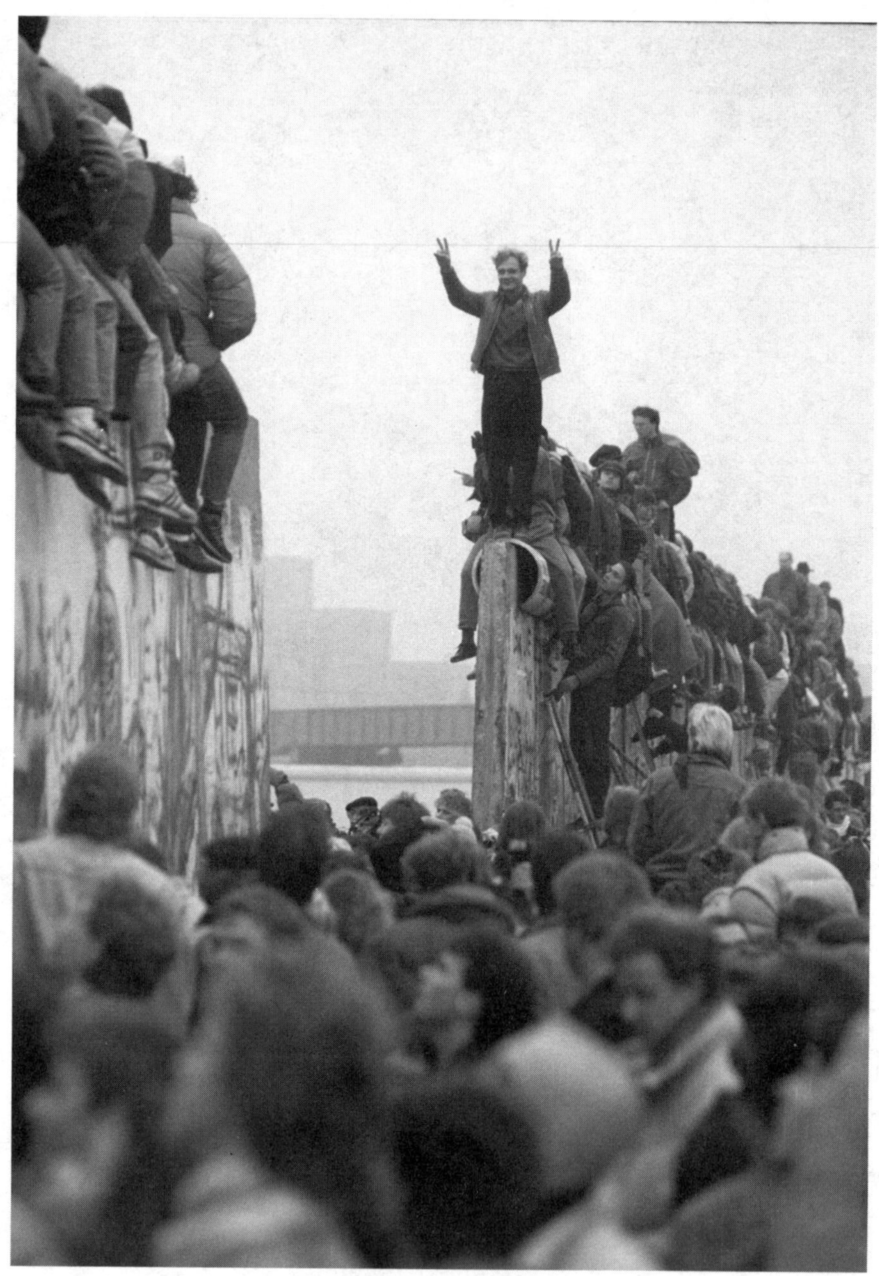

The Fall of the Berlin Wall: A Transformative Moment for Europe

CHAPTER 1

Introduction

What Is Europe?

In my view, the best place to begin an examination of European politics is with an anecdote from a trip to Berlin, a city that has been the locale of world-altering events throughout the past century and is once again the capital of Germany. I am standing in the center of the city, just outside the Brandenburg Gate. Although it has long been a symbol of the city, Brandenburg Gate is perhaps best known for the events that occurred there in November 1989. The Berlin Wall, the icon of the Cold War and a divided Europe, stretched in front of its western façade. In that month, the Berlin Wall fell, and Berliners from both the western and eastern halves of the city scaled the wall to celebrate the end of communism. The scene of jubilant crowds celebrating on top of a structure that was associated with violence and repression was one of the defining images of the end of the Cold War and of the twentieth century.

A tourist approaches me, asking, "Where is the Wall?" Ironically, he is from the divided island of Cyprus, which has a wall through the middle of its capital city. I tell him that it has been removed from here and one has to look elsewhere in the city to see areas where it still stands. He walks away disappointed, and I reflect on the fact that indeed, if one did not know the history, one could easily walk around and through the Brandenburg Gate and never know what had transpired here. Perhaps this is a good thing, a reflection of how Eastern and Western Europe have been brought together after the end of the Cold War. Yet, as a friend of mine remarked, the fact that Berlin chooses to downplay its history—which has both an ugly as well as an uplifting side—disturbed him.

Yet, the history is there if one wants to look. Just north of the Brandenburg Gate is the refurbished Reichstag, the German parliament building, which the Nazis purposefully set on fire in 1933 to justify repression of their opponents. South of the gate is Hitler's bunker, where, presumably, he committed suicide in the waning days of World War II. Adjacent is a memorial to victims of the Holocaust, a square city block of giant coffin-like boxes laid out in rows. There are not many old buildings of the type one would find in central Paris, Prague, or Porto, a reminder that Berlin was subjected to massive bombing by the Allies in World War II. Just east of the gate is the hulking Soviet (now Russian) embassy, a vivid reminder of the Cold War. A couple of blocks further one sees concrete barriers reminiscent of the Wall, but these now surround the US Embassy, structures that are now *de rigueur* in the post-9/11 world.

Perhaps such physical reminders of Berlin's past are beside the point. Since the fall of the Wall, Berlin has turned into a giant construction site, and the symbol of the new Berlin arguably is a sparkling new, if garish to some, commercial complex on Potsdamer Platz. Asking young Berliners to reflect upon their past may elicit the response *Wir sind jetzt alle Deutsche* ("We are now all Germans") or, even, *Wir sind jetzt alle Europäer* ("We are now all Europeans"). These young Berliners did not experience the Cold War and the division of their city.

Look closer, however, at two older ladies chatting amicably on the park bench. Despite sharing a common language, they grew up in two different countries (West and East Germany) with diametrically opposed political systems. The aged pensioner walking with a cane is a veteran of Hitler's army, although, becoming a citizen of West Berlin after the war, he says he completely embraces democratic values and his wartime allegiance to the Third Reich is no longer relevant.[1] The businessman rushing to a meeting—could he have been, as hundreds of thousands of East Germans were, employed by the *Stasi*, the communist secret police? Further along you see a group of dark-haired young men speaking a language that is clearly not German. Perhaps they are refugees from Bosnia, where they witnessed unspeakable horrors, or, more likely, they are of Turkish descent. Like many Turks in Germany today, they may have been born in Germany and can speak fluent German, but they, like their ancestral homeland, have difficulty gaining acceptance as full-fledged Europeans.

ESTABLISHING THE MAIN THEME

European Union (EU) ■ collection of twenty-seven countries (as of 2011) that aims for economic, political, and social integration in Europe. The EU possesses its own political structure and assumes an important role in formulating public policies.

The breaching of the Berlin Wall, the end of communism, and the subsequent expansion of the **European Union** (EU) to post-communist states in 2004 and 2007 has fostered the idea of an undivided or single Europe. This view scraps the notion of dividing Europe into various parts (e.g., "Eastern" or "Southern" Europe) and stresses the common features of European societies today and the drive to unify the continent in political, economic, and even social and cultural terms. One can point to a number of issues and problems—such as immigration and multi-culturalism, worries about the pace and scope of European integration, and the need to manage globalization and promote economic growth—that are common throughout the continent. Discussion of "one Europe" also has social numerous dimensions, ranging from mass tourism to the ubiquitous Irish pubs, Spanish tapas bars, Italian pizzerias, and French bistros throughout Europe to the multinational composition of European football (*soccer*, in American parlance) teams and the wildly popular Eurovision pop music contest to formation of a common "European" identity. Looking at various aspects of European unity today and how they could have geopolitical significance, some speak of Europe as the new "superpower."[2]

This book explores the notion of "one Europe," both how it can help describe, analyze, and explain contemporary European politics and its limitations. Of course, a complete understanding of the drive for European unity would weave together various cultural, economic, historical, and sociological threads into a complex fabric. This book gives attention to each, but, as a text for a course in European politics, it focuses on political institutions, political culture, and domestic and international political challenges facing European states and citizens today. Entertaining the idea of "one Europe," it searches for commonalities and devotes much attention to the EU, arguably the main institutional driving force behind a single Europe. It assesses how **Europeanization**—the process by which EU political and economic dynamics become part of the logic of national-level politics and policy-making—affects states throughout the continent.[3] One example of Europeanization is the adoption of a common currency, the euro, which dramatically affects economic policy and takes away powers traditionally exercised at the state level. In this sense, the study of today's Europe necessitates consideration of both traditional, state-level concerns of comparative politics and of international relations as reflected in the EU and in other actors and forces that promote globalization. Looking beyond the concerns within Europe itself, one should also note that the quest to transform Europe—historically a region of intense conflict and bitter national rivalries—into a more coherent, stable, and peaceful entity is one of the great issues in international politics and it makes Europe an exciting and dynamic region to study.

Europeanization ■ the process by which EU political and economic dynamics become part of the logic of national-level politics and policy-making.

Yet, recognizing the validity of the EU's motto, "Unity in Diversity," it is also worth remembering the different historical experiences of European peoples and the peculiarities of their domestic political institutions and socio-economic systems. The EU, while important, has not made the nation-state obsolete. Despite Europeanization in a number of fields (e.g., media markets, environmental policy, orientations of interest organizations), "one Europe" is a contested idea that has yet not been realized and is not a given for the future. It is not an empirical reality, and for many it is not and should not be a normative goal. Schisms in Europe—both between countries and within them—are real, and often Europe does not speak with a single authoritative voice or act like a superpower. For example, despite vowing "never again" in the wake of the Holocaust and asserting that the managing the disintegration of Yugoslavia would be the "hour of Europe,"[4] European countries sat largely idly by while genocide occurred in the Balkans in the 1990s. "One Europe" also does not mean that Europe has or will ever have a single government. Indeed, scholars refer to **multi-level governance** within Europe, meaning that political power in Europe is territorially dispersed among European-level decision-makers in the EU, national-level political leaders and institutions, and, in many countries, sub-national or regional actors. The idea of multi-level governance does not wholly contradict the idea of "one Europe." Rather, multi-level governance recognizes that European-level institutions and rules are *one* of the defining characteristics—but not the *only* characteristic—of political life in Europe today. In this way, use of multi-level governance requires one to take approaches that bridge the disciplinary divide between comparative and international politics, as "states no longer serve as the exclusive nexus between domestic politics and international relations."[5]

multi-level governance ■ idea that political power in Europe is territorially dispersed among European-level decision-makers in the EU, national-level political leaders and institutions, and, in many countries, sub-national, or regional actors.

This book embraces the idea of multi-level governance, in particular how political authority has, in various issue areas, moved from the national-level to the European level. While not a text on the EU, it recognizes that the EU has autonomous powers and plays a central role in European politics. The rise of multi-level governance is a "watershed in European political development."[6] Traditional approaches rooted exclusively in domestic political institutions or that tack on brief consideration of the EU as a sort of after-thought thus do not capture the reality of Europe today. At the same time, however, national governments still matter. Because of Europeanization and the multi-level governance present in Europe, the study of European politics should, as suggested above, weave together comparative and international politics in a way that the study of Middle East or Latin American politics (where the Arab League and Organization of American States, respectively, are relatively weak actors) would not. This might make more a more complex presentation, but such is political life in contemporary Europe.

Defining Europe

Before proceeding further, one should address a central definitional question: What is Europe? While the question appears simple enough, it can elicit a number of different answers.

Geography At a most basic level, Europe is a continent defined by geography. However, the borders of Europe, unlike those of Africa or South America, are not clearly delineated. Excluding islands, one can say that Europe stretches from Scandinavia in the north to the Mediterranean Sea in the south and from Portugal and Spain in the west to . . . well, therein lies the problem. Students in elementary school may learn that Europe stretches eastwards to the Ural Mountains, thereby encompassing part of Russia. Many in Europe would dispute Russia's European credentials, but by this definition several other post-Soviet states, including Armenia, Azerbaijan, and Georgia, would be European by virtue of lying west of the Urals. By similar logic, Iraq and Syria could even be considered part of Europe. Perhaps one could follow another long-standing tradition[7] and argue that the border between Europe and the Middle East (usually defined as part of Asia) is the Bosphorus Strait, which bisects sprawling Istanbul, the largest city in Turkey and at one time the capital of the Byzantine (Greek) Empire. Yet, Turkey has been declared eligible to join the EU, which, in crucial ways, trumps mere geography in defining Europe. Of course, many oppose Turkish membership in the EU, and, if Turkey is allowed to join, the boundaries of Europe might stretch further: on what grounds could Georgia and Armenia then be excluded? For that matter, what of Israel, which, even though it has been deemed ineligible to join the EU, participates in the European basketball and football championships and the Eurovision music competition? Suffice to say that consensus on Europe's geographical borders remains elusive.

Europe as an Idea Perhaps, one might say, Europe today is best conceived as an idea, or even as a political or social *project*. Put in the jargon of social science, Europe is a construction, not a geographical entity but a product of human agency.[8] Notably, during the **Cold War**, "Europe" as a political or social unit did not exist. Instead, Europe had to be modified by adjectives. Western Europe not only had clear geographic borders but was also defined by its democratic political systems and opposition to Soviet-inspired communism.[9] Most classes and textbooks on "European politics" were overwhelmingly devoted to this part of Europe. Eastern Europe, in contrast, was defined by its communist political and economic systems and in opposition, in its ideological orientation at any rate, to the "decadent," "imperialist" capitalist West. Since the end of the Cold War, the division of the continent into two opposing ideological camps is over, although the old West/East division still has some meaning and some are beginning to speak of an emerging North/South division on the continent.[10] Such observations, however, do

Cold War ■ ideological conflict from the end of World War II to the late 1980s–early 1990s between the US and its allies and the Soviet Union and its allies. As a consequence of the Cold War, most of Europe was divided into two ideological-military blocs.

not undermine the claim that today's Europe is more unified than at any previous time in modern history. Still, however, one could ask, what is this "Europe"?

Note that citizens of most nation-states would not normally ask this question of their own countries. Most Americans, Britons, Poles, Germans, Italians, Spaniards, and so on, beset as they might be with internal divisions in their own countries (think "red states" versus "blue states," English versus Scots, or northern versus southern Italians), could nonetheless agree on a set of values or traditions—regardless of how vague or banal—that help define their national identity. Countries usually have a history with a set of narratives or myths on which they can draw. Europe, with a history of conflict and populated by diverse peoples living in dozens of national states, has no such luxury. There is no "founding father" of Europe that resonates like George Washington does for Americans or a unifying cultural figure like Shakespeare for the English or Cervantes for the Spanish. How then can one define Europe? Or, to put it differently, what is Europe for?

Europe as an Economic Community Helene Sjursen, a Norwegian political scientist, suggested that there are three possible answers to this question.[11] First, one could view Europe—best epitomized by the early history of the EU—as a "problem-solving entity," based on economic citizenship and material economic interests. Arguably, this was the main basis for European legitimacy in the formative years of the EU. However, as we'll see in Chapter 3, in the 1990s the EU and concomitant processes of Europeanization began to move beyond mere economic concerns, and in discussions of EU expansion to former communist countries an economic definition or conception of Europe was far less pronounced and compelling, giving way to moral, cultural, and political claims.[12] In other words, as Europe has grown in recent years, its definition and mission have changed.

Europe as a Cultural Community An alternative conception of Europe, according to Sjursen, would be a value-based community, based upon social and cultural citizenship and drawing a firm line between Europe and other states and actors. From this perspective, Europe would be a geographically defined entity that seeks to revitalize traditions and memories of distinctly "European" values, to forge a "we-feeling" as a basis for integration. Ironically, Mikhail Gorbachev, the last leader of the Soviet Union (1985–1991), advanced this type of argument, maintaining, "Europe from the Atlantic to the Urals [a phrase used by French President Charles de Gaulle in the 1960s] is a cultural-historical entity united by the common heritage of the Renaissance and the Enlightenment."[13] What precisely that "we-feeling" is would be a subject of dispute and may crucially depend upon what Europe is trying to define itself against. Former West German Chancellor Helmut Schmidt wrote an interesting essay entitled, "Who Doesn't Belong in Europe," where he argued that for cultural reasons Russia, Ukraine, Belarus, and Turkey lie outside.[14] Since Turkey has applied to join the EU, it is the Turkish case that elicits the most debate on the questions or "what" or "where" is Europe. According to Pat Cox, former President of the European Parliament, "This [Turkish membership in the EU] is the most difficult question of all . . . It's about how we define Europe."[15] On the other hand, some Europeans, as we will note below, define "European values" in a way that distinguishes them from those of the US. Some of these values would be a commitment

Istanbul, Turkey: Does this Look Like Europe to You?

to social solidarity, a welfare state, supranational governance through the EU, and multi-lateral international institutions. Of course, not all Europeans would want to draw such a sharp distinction with the US, and some would even suggest that Europe needs to embrace many aspects of the American system.

Europe as a Political Community Finally, one can imagine Europe in more inclusive terms, defined not culturally but as, in Sjursen's words, a "rights-based post-national union" based upon political citizenship and appeals to universal standards and rights. In this vein, political legitimacy within states and within the EU would rest upon political support and legally entrenched fundamental rights and fealty to democratic procedures. In contrast to a cultural model, this rests upon universal values. This sentiment was captured in the 1990s with the assertion that the repressiveness and violence associated with the rule of Slobodan Milošević in Serbia somehow was not befitting of a "European" country and made Serbia a justifiable target of European political and economic sanctions. As noted in the **In Focus** boxed feature, expression of a more political idea of Europe has been included in various EU documents. From examination of these materials, one definitely gets a sense that Europe stands for something universal, and although, naturally enough, Europe would have to have some geographic parameters (e.g., Mexico or Canada are not part of Europe), all

IN FOCUS

European Political Values

Individual countries, one might say, rest upon core political values. These values are usually promulgated in their constitutions. "Europe," of course, is not a single country, and it lacks a common constitution. If, therefore, one is to conceive of "Europe" as an already existing or at least a potential political community, on what values does it rest? What documents would express these values?

To the extent that the EU is the most powerful expression of European unity, one should expect that if "Europe" rests on political values, they could be found in EU documents. Indeed, this is the case. As you'll learn in Chapter 3, the EU is built on a foundation of various treaties that date to the 1950s. Each of these treaties—while focusing on construction of institutions or development of policies in particular issue areas—includes statements of political vision and values. Specific rhetoric and the overall emphasis of these statements have changed over time. For example, the 1957 Treaty of Rome, which sets the goal of "an ever closer union" of peoples in its first preambulatory clause, does not mention the terms "democracy" or "human rights" in its entire preamble, emphasizing instead elimination of trade barriers, balanced trade, and coordination of commercial policy. In contrast, the 1992 Maastricht Treaty confirms Europeans' "attachment to the principles of liberty, democracy and respect for human rights and fundamental freedoms and of the rule of law" in its third preambulatory clause, subjugating economic issues to later in the document. The ill-fated Constitutional Treaty of 2004 stated in its first preambulatory clause that it draws inspiration from "the cultural, religious and humanist inheritance of Europe, from which have developed the universal values of the inviolable and inalienable rights of the human person, freedom, democracy, equality and the rule of law," and goes on to mention the goal of "peace, justice and solidarity throughout the world" (second clause) Europeans' "common destiny" (third clause) and the continent as a "special area of human hope" (fourth clause). This document, ambitious as it was, was not approved, but the 2009 Lisbon Treaty, its replacement-of-sorts, puts democracy and freedom front and center, including—at the risk of sounding a bit repetitive—both the clauses from the Maastricht Treaty on the attachment to democracy and human rights and the first clause from the Constitutional Treaty linking such values to historical and cultural inheritances.

While one can debate both how effectively these documents and the EU as a whole work in practice—issues we'll return to several times in the text—as well as their eloquence or coherence compared to national constitutions, the overall message is clear—the EU, whose goal is to eliminate divisions in Europe, is built on political values. Given the EU's importance in the construction of "Europe," it makes it easier to view the later as more than mere geography or an economic arrangement to bolster trade and more as a political community.

Critical Thinking Questions

1. Do you think common values such as commitment to democracy and human rights are enough to form a cohesive political community among countries with different histories and political experiences?
2. The US started as thirteen separate states but over time evolved into a more cohesive political community. What factors facilitated this? Do you think conditions to form such a community in contemporary Europe are as propitious as those in early US history?

humanity could, vicariously at least, embrace Europe's vision and values. Such a conception would obviously benefit states like Turkey who seek to join Europe (here defining the parameters of Europe as the EU) but arguably do not meet cultural criteria. Turkish Prime Minster Recep Tayyip Erdoğan has made this argument to press the Turkish case, noting that "the EU is neither a union of coal and steel, not of geography, nor only of economies. It is a community of political values."[16]

Why it Matters

One might suggest that such debates over the definition of Europe seem too abstract or are mere rhetoric. However, they do matter for several reasons. First, as noted in Chapter 12, many European states, thanks to immigration, are already culturally diverse and the need for immigrants will grow in coming years, so narrower definitions of the EU as a cultural-based entity will poorly serve a dynamic, multi-cultural Europe. Second, as noted, they have great relevance when considering both possible EU expansion to Turkey, Bosnia (another predominantly Muslim state), and beyond and Europe's relations with neighboring states that clearly do not meet minimal geographic definitions to qualify as "European." In particular, a rights-based, universalist conception of Europe could be used to advance replication of the "European model" far beyond the boundaries of Europe whereas adherents of a culturally defined Europe would argue that Europe could not export its values or institutions. Finally, and perhaps most importantly, a rights-based identity would best serve those interested both in "deepening" European integration (e.g., such as adopting a single constitution for the EU or re-structuring of EU institutions to better involve European publics) as it expressly views Europe in political terms. If Europe is primarily about economics or culture/values (the latter narrowly defined), then the rationales for both deepening and widening the EU to other states may be essentially over and the "European project" largely complete with Europe's "*re*-unification" in 2004 and 2007, when most of the post-communist states of Eastern Europe joined the EU. If, however, there is to be a broader, more ambitious European *political* project, then the EU could advance a more political or rights-based identity for itself. As Thierry de Montrbrial of the French Institute of International Relations argued, the core concepts of the EU are democracy, rule of law, human rights, secularism, market economy, security, and solidarity. "What we want to achieve in Europe," he claims, "is a new kind of political unit, whose identity is based on these concepts."[17]

A Provisional Definition

For now, we'll let these debates lie, although they will be taken up throughout this text. Clearly, it is hard to reach a clear verdict on what Europe is or what it seeks to become. At present, the safest route is to note that the substantive meaning of Europe is subject to much debate and is still evolving. Europe and European are, in short, constructed and contested terms. However, this caveat of sorts does not solve the present problem of how to delineate the subject of study for this volume. For a solution, I defer to the EU, which declares that only "European" states are eligible for membership. Obviously, therefore, all twenty-seven members of the EU are European, as are candidate countries (e.g., Turkey, Croatia, Macedonia) and countries of the Western Balkans (e.g., Serbia, Bosnia, Albania) whose potential eligibility to join the EU has been recognized. Countries that have been invited to join the EU but have chosen to stay out—Norway, Switzerland, and Iceland[18]—are also, by this standard, European, and will be periodically mentioned in this text. However, most of the post-Soviet states, including Ukraine, Armenia, Georgia, and, most significantly, Russia, have not been explicitly recognized as potential members of the EU and therefore, by the paradigm I adopt, they will not be covered as European countries in this text.

WHY STUDY EUROPE?

In the not-so-distant past, few would have asked the above question. However, at the dawn of the twenty-first century, some—particularly in the US—might argue that Europe is outmoded or passé and that other regions of the world deserve more of our attention. Some speculate that this century will be the Chinese century, and there is little question that China—and that other Asian giant, India—are rising powers in the global economy. After 9/11 and the invasion of Iraq, the Middle East has been *the* area of focus, particularly for Americans.

Europe Is a World Power

Europe, however, is no peripheral player in either the world economy or in the global battle against terrorism. True, the individual countries within Europe are at best medium-sized states. The days of a world dominated by European "Great Powers" such as Great Britain, France, Spain, and Venice are long gone. However, when Europe is regarded as a collective entity, which reflects in part the accomplishments of the EU, a different picture emerges. The EU has created a single economic market among its members. Comprising twenty-seven countries and 500 million people, the total EU economy is the largest in the world, as seen in Figure 1.1. Moreover, even though China and India are important and growing countries, their impact on the world economy is primarily a function of their sheer size (1.3 billion and 1.1 billion people, respectively), not *per capita* income of each individual citizen. When one looks at this variable, as seen in Figure 1.2, one clearly sees that Europe ranks as one of the wealthiest and most highly developed areas in the world, a point confirmed by other data such as educational achievement and public health.[19] Europe is also the dominant actor in terms of international trade, and Germany has a larger trade surplus with the rest of the world than China or Japan.[20]

While **globalization** and "Americanization" are almost used interchangeably—with McDonalds becoming the literal (and often despised) symbol of globalization[21]—one should recall that there are a number of important European firms in the world economy that compete and often out-compete their American or Japanese rivals—Nokia, Siemens, Bosch, BMW, Daimler-Benz, Ericsson, Cadbury-Schweppes,

globalization ■ multi-faceted process with both fans and detractors that refers to the diminishing importance of national borders and increasing ties that connect countries and peoples of the world.

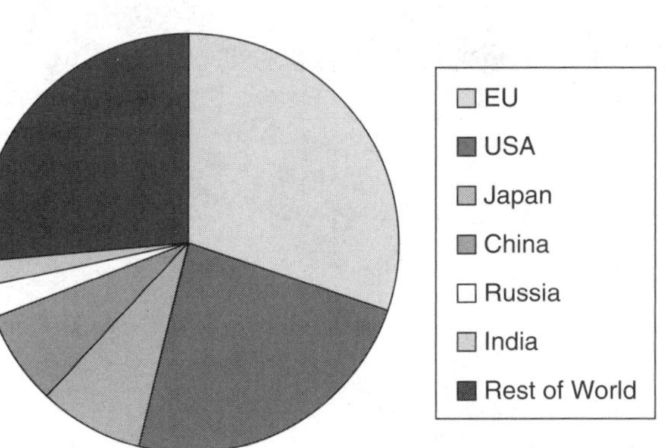

FIGURE 1.1
Distribution of 2008 World Gross National Product (GNP), by Country/Region.
World Bank Data from 2008, available at http://www.worldbank.org

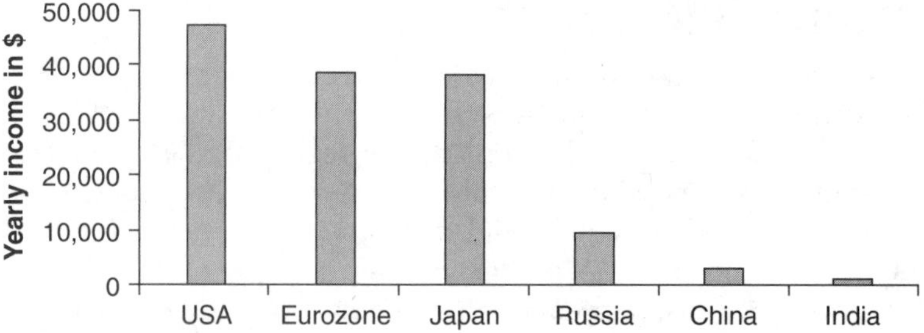

FIGURE 1.2
Income Per Person in Selected Countries/Regions, in Dollars.
World Bank Data from 2008, available at http://www.worldbank.org

Airbus, British Airways, Vivendi, DHL, Pearson, Fiat, Royal Dutch Shell, Vodafone, Carrefour, Nestle, Renault, British Petroleum, Novartis, Unilever, and British-American Tobacco, just to name a few. One hundred seventy-nine European companies are in the 2009 Global Fortune 500, whereas only 140 are American, and many recognizable "American" brands are now part of European companies.[22] Defining globalization differently—by tourism, Internet traffic, or investment flows—Europe similarly comes out on top.

However, as Table 1.1 reveals, Europe is not a fully fledged superpower, at least when one looks at military aspects of power. Even though no EU member ranks in the top fifteen in terms of number of people in the military,[23] collectively EU countries do have a sizeable number of men and women in their militaries. However, the EU is no military superpower: EU countries as a whole spend much less than the US and only about a third as much *per capita*. Europeans cannot come close to the Americans in terms of projecting military power or employing the most technologically advanced weapons. The main nuclear powers remain the

TABLE 1.1

Military Capabilities of Various Global Powers

Country or Region	Active Duty Military, 2009	Military Spending in 2007 $ billion	Military Spending per person	Deployed Nuclear Warheads	Aircraft Carriers	Combat Aircraft
EU	2,014,000	288.6	$598	460	8	2497
Germany	244,000	42.1	$511	0	0	243
Great Britain	160,000	63.3	$1041	160	4	341
France	353,000	60.7	$993	300	2	368
US	1,540,000	552	$1835	2702	22	4000
Russia	1,027,000	32.2	$228	4834	1	2295
China	2,185,000	46.2	$35	186	0	1700
Japan	230,000	41.0	$322	0	0	360
India	1,281,000	26.5	$23	60–70	0	796

Source: Stockholm Institute Peace Research Institute (SIPRI) Yearbook, 2009, available at http://www.sipri.org/yearbook/2009/05/05A, accessed November 26, 2010; and International Institute of Strategic Studies, *The Military Balance 2009* (London: Routledge, 2009).

US and Russia. As for the EU itself, as opposed the individual militaries of European countries, it possesses only a 60,000 person rapid-reaction force. An all-out military conflict between America and Europe—a fear that I hear frequently from my own students—seems both far-fetched and, should it come, likely to be very one-sided. Moreover, one could argue that even if Europe has the capability to act militarily, it has little will to do so alone (e.g., the war in Iraq) and even in cases to stop genocide, as in Bosnia and Rwanda in the 1990s or Darfur in the 2000s, Europe refused to take the military initiative.

This is not to say Europe is not a powerful force in international affairs. Instead, it relies far more on "**soft power**" (e.g., economic assistance and trade policy, diplomacy, multilateral institutions, moral authority, culture) than on "**hard power**", exemplified by military might. As defined by Joseph Nye, "soft power" suggests that "a country may obtain the outcomes it wants in world politics because other countries want to follow it, admiring its values, emulating its example, aspiring to its level of prosperity and openness."[24] To the extent that Europe can market itself as a democratic zone of peace, be more generous in foreign assistance than the US, engage in more public diplomacy, and is less intent than Americans upon using military muscle to bully states to comply with its preferences, it is, at least according to Europhiles, becoming more and more influential around the world. Some maintain that Europe is a "transformative power," having great economic and political influence across one hundred countries in the "Eurosphere," a collection of states in Europe, Africa, and the Middle East that are connected together by sizable economic, and, in many cases, historical and cultural ties.[25] Across a wide range of issues—corporate mergers, genetically modified food, data privacy, airplane engine emissions, human rights—Europeans set the standard, forcing others to abide by European law and norms (or regulations). One writer claims that "Europe's weapon is the law," meaning that the EU's regulations and use of conditionality for aid and trade are producing an invisible but unstoppable "Europeanization" of laws and economic practices throughout this "Eurosphere."[26]

soft power ■ use of non-coercive and non-military instruments of power, such as diplomacy, economic assistance, and power of example, to exert influence in world affairs.

hard power ■ use of the military and other coercive measures such as economic sanctions to exert influence in world affairs.

As for being eclipsed by the struggle against terrorism, one should note that in the 2000s European troops were on the front lines with Americans in both in Afghanistan and (more controversially and less universally) in Iraq. Moreover, Europeans have been the victim of terrorist acts (e.g., in Madrid in March 2004, in London in July 2005) and homegrown, Islamic terrorist cells composed of immigrants to Europe or even European citizens are a grave worry. In this respect, Europe is a major theater in the "war on terror," and some speculate that extremist groups that could emerge in democratic European states actually present a larger threat than groups based in the Middle East or South Asia.[27] Chapter 11 takes up this important issue.

Europe as a Source of Political Ideas and Institutions

There has always been a powerful philosophical and historical argument for the study of Europe. Europe was the birthplace of democracy—both in its ancient Greek variants and in more "modern" forms that arose in Great Britain centuries before the creation of the US. Europe was also home to the **Enlightenment**, an intellectual movement that began in the seventeenth century that sought, in broadest terms, the political and intellectual liberation of humanity by emphasizing the power of human reason (over that of religious dogma), material progress, and enlightened individual

Enlightenment ■ intellectual movement that began in the seventeenth century in Western Europe and emphasized human reason, material progress, and individual self-interest.

self-interest. The Enlightenment spawned a search for new ideas in the sciences, arts, and social life. The most fundamental ideas on which contemporary democracies are based—limited government, separation of powers, rule of law, religious tolerance, capitalist economic systems, civil rights—found earliest expression during the Enlightenment among various European thinkers. For example, the bases of **liberalism**, the ideology that animates the US system of government,[28] were articulated by the English writers such as John Locke (1632–1704), John Stuart Mill (1806–1873), and the Scottish economist Adam Smith (1723–1790), whose *Wealth of Nations* (1776) is considered the classic exposition of capitalist thought. The French Revolution of 1789, with its slogan of *liberté, egalité, fraternité*, was an inspiration to millions around the globe and is often argued to be the one of the foundations for the still-potent ideology of nationalism.[29] The study of European politics is thus, in part, how the rise of democratic ideas gave rise to democratic institutions and how those institutions have adapted to new challenges over time. This has relevance for a wide audience in today's world.

liberalism ■ ideology that emphasizes the rights of the individual and limited government; a basic idea behind modern democracy and capitalism.

It is also worth mentioning that the two greatest ideological challengers to liberal democracy—**fascism** and **communism**—arose in Europe and made Europe central to American security interests. Fascism is most associated with Hitler's Third Reich in Germany (1933–1945), but it was first put into practice by Benito Mussolini in Italy (1922–1943). It rejected the very premises of individual rights, preferring instead to invest authority in an all-powerful, militaristic state. Fascism was defeated in World War II by an alliance of democratic and communist states (an alliance that is at times forgotten), and the post-war period through the late 1980s was defined by the Cold War, a struggle between democratic capitalist states and their erstwhile communist allies, led by the Soviet Union. Communists rejected capitalism as inherently unjust, preferring state ownership and planning of the economy to secure economic equality. Communism's moral and utopian impulse, however, could not be realized because in practice communism produced an all-powerful, repressive state that denied basic democratic rights to citizens. In literal and figurative terms, Europe was the front line in the Cold War, which divided the continent into two antagonistic halves. Communism ended in Eastern Europe in 1989–1991, and since then major steps have been taken to foster democracy in Eastern Europe and integrate the entire continent.

fascism ■ ideology associated with Hitler and Mussolini that glorifies the state and rejects ideas of democracy and individual rights.

communism ■ ideology associated with the Soviet Union that aspires to create utopia but it practice led to state domination over economic and political life.

While the end of the Cold War has, in some ways, reduced Europe's strategic significance, there is little question that Europe remains a vital region for the US. Even though there has been a surge of anti-American feeling in the first years of the twenty-first century due, in large part, to the war in Iraq, it is also safe to say that most of the US's most important and trusted allies are found in Europe.[30]

Europe as Case Study for Political Science

It is also worthwhile to study Europe as part of broader study of comparative politics and international relations. While every region or country of the world offers something to these sub-fields of political science, Europe represents a great laboratory to illustrate political concepts and test numerous theories of the discipline. As noted, Europe is central in any study of democratic practices. On this score, one could also add that the study of European democratic systems should be of interest to students of US politics, as various European institutional arrangements (e.g., parliamentary systems, proportional representation, corporatism) provide a contrast to American practices and reveal that there is more than one way to organize a democratic system. The recent movement to democracy in post-communist Europe also figures prominently in the so-called "transitions literature" that looks as recent waves of global democratization. Thus several of the European countries may offer lessons to would-be democratizing states elsewhere. While on-balance capitalist, the different mix of free market and statist economic orientations among European states offers a great opportunity to compare varieties of capitalism. Because Europeans enjoy free and open political systems that are based upon popular participation, one can see how political culture matters in shaping political institutions and outcomes. Thanks to the success of the EU, Europe is the primary focus for theories of regional integration. On the other hand, ethnic conflict, most recently in the former Yugoslavia, reveals the continued power of nationalism in a supposedly "post-national" continent. Numerous issues connected to globalization—immigration and adjustments to a more multicultural political environment, structural economic reform to enhance competitiveness, and the search for solutions to transnational problems (e.g., climate change, organized crime)—figure prominently in Europe. Where possible, this book tries to connect our discussion of Europe to larger debates and theories in political science.

A European Model?

Lastly, and certainly most controversially, one could suggest that Europe not only presents an empirical field for the study of politics but also a normative (values-based) one. In other words, Europe represents a model of how political, economic, and social life *should* be organized. We have already mentioned how some writers regard contemporary Europe as a new superpower. This normative line of argument, however, goes even further and suggests that Europe is not only powerful but also a type of moral exemplar, worthy of study *and* emulation. Jeremy Rifkin, for example, develops this argument by referring to the "European dream" that, in his view, is more compelling than the better-known "American dream" as a source of inspiration both for Europeans and for a wider global audience.[31] Paradoxically, he argues that Europe today is abandoning the emphasis on individualism and material progress spawned by the Enlightenment and is instead focusing on sustainable development, community, and quality of life issues.

Much of his argument rests on claims about what might be called the **European social model**, which emphasizes the role of the state in providing social welfare for its citizens. For example, most European states have nationalized and universal health care,[32] free or very low-cost universities, paid maternity benefits,[33] and generous unemployment and child support provisions. Europeans also work far less each year than Americans or Japanese do,[34] and they are allowed to retire earlier. Whereas some might contend this is just a reflection of laziness, the fact is that in the 2000s workers in several European states were more productive than their American peers. True, taxes are higher in Europe than in the US and there are signs that this system is in need of a major overhaul in several countries. Whether the European social model can survive in today's globalized world is an important subject we will consider in Chapter 10.

European social model ■ the highly developed welfare state found in many European countries that is funded by high taxes and provides numerous economic and social benefits to citizens.

Some in Europe would go even further, however, and posit that various aspects of the European social model *define* Europe today. More often then not, this point is framed not only in terms of institutions but as part of modern-day European culture, a feature that distinguishes Europe from the US. For example, Jürgen Habermas, the well-known German philosopher, argues that European identity is built upon a separation of religion from politics, a belief in the power of the state to correct the failures of the market, a party system that explicitly confronts the negative results of capitalist modernization, an ethos of solidarity, a moral sensibility (part of which, according to him, has resulted in a continent-wide ban on the death penalty), and deference to supranational and international authority.[35] Habermas and those that adhere to this view would argue that on these fronts not only is Europe different from the US—a country that Europeans associate with intense religiosity, unbridled patriotism, widespread violence, and an obsession for individual wealth—but also better.

Euro-skeptics ■ those that doubt or fear the prospect of greater European unity and a stronger role for the EU.

One should note that not all would agree with Habermas or have taken kindly to the idea of a single Europe. Many on both sides of the Atlantic reject any suggestion that Europe offers model for others to follow. **Euro-skeptics** abound in Europe, especially in countries such as Denmark and Great Britain. Many Britons, in particular, recoil from the idea of getting too close to Europe, preferring to believe, as former Prime Minister Margaret Thatcher (1979–1990) asserted, that all British problems have come from across the English Channel and all the solutions from across the Atlantic.[36] Recall that even the supposedly Europhile French and Dutch in 2005 rejected a Constitutional Treaty for the EU that was designed to strengthen EU institutions. On the other side of the Atlantic, the idea of a European superpower has rung some alarm bells. One British journalist, appealing to an American audience, wrote in 2003 that "it is not too late for the United States to help stop the European superstate from becoming a reality."[37] Robert Kagan, a prominent American neo-conservative writer, acknowledges the numerous differences between Europe and America, maintaining, "Americans are from Mars and Europeans are from Venus," which, in his view, compliments Americans as stronger and "real men."[38] Charles Kupchan, a liberal American scholar, goes even further, suggesting that the coming "clash of civilizations" will not be the West versus Islam or China but, instead, could be Europe versus the US.[39]

Fears of open, hostile conflict between Europe and the US can be easily exaggerated. Madeline Albright, the former US secretary of state, offered an addendum to Kagan's points, noting that Mars and Venus—as Roman gods—got along well and even produced children together, including Harmonia, the Goddess of Concord.[40] Despite real differences on a number of important issues during the presidency of George W. Bush—Iraq, climate change, the US prison camp at Guantanamo Bay, Cuba—Europeans and Americans share a number of basic values, including a commitment to democracy and human rights, and Bush's successor, Barack Obama, is extremely popular in Europe. Moreover, as noted above, Europe offers no military threat to the US. Focus on differences overlooks the numerous projects—democracy promotion, anti-poverty and anti-AIDS programs, nuclear non-proliferation, international peacekeeping operations—in which Americans and Europeans have worked together.

Moreover, one would be unwise to dismiss the broader European project. After World War II, who would have imagined that France and Great Britain would be allies of Germany within less than a generation? In the 1980s, who could have imagined that the Berlin Wall would fall, prompting dramatic yet peaceful changes that would allow previously Western European institutions such as the EU and NATO (North Atlantic Treaty Organization) to expand eastward? In the 1990s, many—including Henry Kissinger, the worldly and eminent former US secretary of state—expressed doubts that the euro would ever exist, and yet, in 2002, euros replaced the national currencies of twelve countries and more countries are lining up to join the eurozone. This is not to say that we will see, in Winston Churchill's words in 1946, a "United States of Europe" in our lifetimes. Nonetheless, given Europe's accomplishments, would one want to bet against it?

ONE EUROPE, OR MANY?

Much of this chapter has discussed the idea that European states and societies are moving closer together and that there is utility in looking at commonalities across individual countries. In each chapter, there is an **Is Europe One?** section that illustrates the extent of European unity on a particular issue. However, the question is not purely rhetorical. Please be mindful of the question mark. In other words, while the idea of a single Europe helps set up a narrative for the text, it is not a pre-judgment on either the empirical reality or on what Europe should become. One therefore can and often should look critically at the very idea of "one Europe." Europe is, after all, made up of more than thirty countries, each with its own history, system of government, cultural and sub-cultural traditions, and, in most cases, unique language.

True, historians might discuss Christianity as a common cultural tradition in Europe or feudalism as a common feature of the region's socio-economic development, but one can argue whether either retains relevance today. Christianity has been tore by schisms, some of which led to violence (e.g., the Thirty Years' War in Europe, 1618–1648), and, debates over Turkey's place in Europe not withstanding, it is less and less salient as a political or cultural force in most of Europe today. Feudalism has long been eclipsed by industrial development, either in its capitalist or communist forms, and it makes little sense to invoke this as a unifying force in Europe today. As opposed to unity, in modern times Europe has known far more conflict, prompting Jean Monnet, often thought of as the father of European integration, to remark that "Europe has never existed; one has genuinely to create Europe."[41] Perhaps the greatest common denominator in Europe today—at least politically speaking—is the universal establishment of democracy (a factor that by the late-2000s serves to leave Russia out of discussions of "Europe"), but, as we shall see, European democratic institutions differ from country to country and many are of recent origin.

Thus, in contrast to the discourse on European unity, one can also speak of numerous divisions that are a source of conflict or at least potential conflict among European countries. Obviously there have been numerous wars among European states. A partial listing of major conflicts since the seventeenth century would include the Thirty Years' War; the Ottoman conquests in the Balkans and subsequent siege of Vienna (1683); the Seven Years' War (1756–1763) fought globally between France and Britain; the Napoleonic Wars (1803–1815); the Crimean War (1853–1856); the Prussian-Austrian War (1866); the Franco-Prussian War (1870–1871); the First and Second Balkan Wars (1912–1913); World War I (1914–1918); the Polish-Soviet War (1919–1921); World War II (1939–1945); the Cold War (1940s–1991); and the wars after the breakup of Yugoslavia

(1991–1999). A student of modern European history could thus argue, with only slight exaggeration, that for more than three hundred years major European states were either at war, preparing for war, or recovering from war. Today, war among the larger European states seems impossible, even inconceivable—France, for example, is not preparing for war with Great Britain or Germany.[42] In historical perspective, then, the geo-political situation in today's Europe is the exception, albeit one for which we can be grateful. While some Europeans would like to say that this past is behind them, or, perhaps, that historic conflicts are now manifested in jokes about one's erstwhile enemies or played out on the football pitch, occasionally one does see vestiges of Europe's past wars rear their head. For example, when Germans began to talk seriously of reunification in early 1990, many French, Polish, and British figures were apprehensive, remembering what a previously strong and united Germany had done a half century earlier.[43]

Moreover, even though a major war between large European states seems inconceivable, there are still divisions and important differences among countries in Europe. In most general terms, one can point to four distinct peoples, cultures, or linguistic groups in Europe: a Germanic one (e.g., German, Swedish, Dutch) in the north, Slavic (e.g., Polish, Bulgarian, Slovak) in the east, Latin (e.g., Italian, French, Portuguese) in the south, and Celtic (e.g., Irish, Scottish, Breton) on the western fringe. Stereotypes regarding each abound (e.g., the hardworking and stoic German, the amorous and passionate Italian, the fatalistic Pole), and, perhaps, these do capture some real differences. There are also a variety of religious traditions: Catholic, Protestant, and Orthodox Christians (and numerous variants with respect to the latter two categories), Jews, and, increasingly, Muslims. This has been both a source of past conflict and of current tensions. Ideological divides may seem less salient today than during the Cold War, but one can still speak of how vestiges of communist rule account for sociological, cultural, and economic differences between West European and former communist states. The fact that the very definition of Europe is contested has led to some conflict as some countries, such as Serbia and Turkey, are excluded from the most grandiose incarnation of Europe—the EU—on the grounds that they do not, as yet, fully embrace "European" standards or principles.

Even within the EU—with members committed to common values—there are regular battles over the budget and the distribution of power between larger and smaller countries and between richer and poorer ones, the latter of which became particularly salient during the economic crisis of the late 2000s. On various foreign policy matters, including the war in Iraq, featured in the **Is Europe One?** box, there are splits between those states that harbor more goodwill towards America or see their interests align with those of the US (e.g., Great Britain, Poland) and those that, for historical, ideological, or purely pragmatic reasons, are more apt to oppose some of Washington's initiatives (e.g., France, Greece). In economic orientation, one can identify differences between states that have a more free market approach (e.g., Great Britain, Ireland, Finland, post-communist Poland) and those that have more of a socialist tradition with a large state sector and state regulation over the economy (e.g., France, Italy, Slovenia). Even though most European states do have well-developed social welfare programs, there are variations across countries and regions. Among the citizens of Europe, one can also point to differences in political culture defined by national lines, economic conditions, or historical experiences, a topic we shall explore in more detail in Chapter 9. One can argue whether all of these types of differences are more salient

IS EUROPE ONE?

European Involvement in the War in Iraq

Although Europeans and Americans both espouse freedom and democracy, and most European countries are in NATO with the US, Europeans and Americans have not always seen eye to eye on foreign policy matters. This was made most clear in the 2000s, when the US, with the American peoples' support, invaded Iraq, whereas the war was wildly unpopular in Europe and several European countries chose not to send their troops to support the Americans.

While this phenomenon might be offered as evidence of a schism between the US and Europe—an issue explored more fully in Chapter 11—it also revealed schisms within Europe. Many countries—some of whom were praised by then-US Secretary of Defense Donald Rumsfeld as the "new Europe"—did send troops to Iraq. The list of participating European countries includes Great Britain, Italy, Spain, the Netherlands, Denmark, Portugal, Norway, Poland, Romania, the Czech Republic, Slovakia, Latvia, Estonia, Bulgaria, Albania, Hungary, and Bosnia. Of the current twenty-seven members in the EU, more than half (fifteen) sent troops—hardly evidence that Europe refused to support the US. True, only a few countries deployed a large number of troops: the British sent 46,000 men and women; Italian forces peaked at 3,200; Poland's at 2,500; Spain and the Netherlands sent roughly 1,300 troops each. In contrast, Estonia sent only forty (about a tenth of the per capita US commitment of troops) and Slovakia and Lithuania just over a hundred each.[44] Still, this was more than France or Germany—"old Europe" in Rumsfeld's terms—which refused to send any troops at all.

European publics had less stomach for the war than Americans, and by the summer of 2009 all non-US forces were withdrawn from Iraq. Still, the fact that many governments sided with the US—even, in some cases, in face of large public protests against the war—was testimony to the strength of the Atlantic alliance. On the other hand, the fact that Europe was so divided, with two of the largest EU members opposing the war while many "old" (e.g., Britain, Italy, and the Netherlands) or soon-to-be or "new" EU members (e.g., Poland and Slovakia) sent troops, provided further evidence that the quest to forge a united Europe, at least on some important foreign policy matters, remains a chimera. We'll explore more fully efforts to create a common foreign and security policy for Europe in Chapter 11.

Critical Thinking Questions

1. What factors do you think best account for why some European countries supported the war in Iraq and others did not? Is there a common denominator among the countries that sent troops?
2. Why do you think Americans tend to be more supportive of overseas military campaigns—Iraq is but one example—whereas Europeans frequently are not?

than the common features across European countries today, but the simple point is that one cannot and should not uncritically treat Europe as an undifferentiated whole.

Equally significantly, one must recognize that there are important divisions or **social cleavages** within countries. In other words, just as it would be mistaken to focus exclusively on the commonalities of Czechs and Germans as Europeans, one should also recognize that there are notable differences among people within the Czech Republic or Germany. Many of these cleavages are well known to social scientists: class, occupation, urban/rural divides, age, region (e.g. West versus East Germany), and ethnicity (e.g., ethnic Czech versus a Czech citizen of Roma [Gypsy] heritage). Sometimes, these differences have manifested themselves in open, armed conflict or terrorism, as has been the case in Northern Ireland,

social cleavages ■ lines of division within a given society, produced by socio-demographic factors such as class, region, ethnicity, and age.

Turkey, and Spain. Most of the time, these cleavages do not garner headlines (e.g., divisions in Poland between the older generation and a younger generation that never knew communism, an urban/rural divide in Norway), but in many respects they are the stuff of politics, contributing to the formation of competing political parties, social movements, and interest organizations.[45] One would be remiss not to discuss these features within various European polities.

This text takes up many of themes suggested in this opening chapter. In contrast to many treatments of today's Europe that are rooted exclusively in comparative politics at the state level, this book devotes more attention to the EU, processes of Europeanization, and the workings of multi-level governance. The next two chapters provide brief historical background. One focuses on domestic political developments, particularly the continent-wide emergence of democratic, capitalist systems, while another traces the development of the EU, the main institutional form for a "one Europe." The next set of chapters (Chapters 4 through 9) focuses on political institutions and political culture. It begins, however, with consideration of the institutions and policies of the EU, recognizing that the EU is central to much of European politics today and that and processes of Europeanization emanating from the EU have a great impact on domestic political institutions. Coverage of domestic political institutions (e.g., parliaments, executives, courts, parties) follows and these chapters largely eschew country-by-country analysis, looking instead at patterns across the continent and comparing and contrasting various features. Within these chapters we shall also consider how Europeanization affects state-level institutions and decision-making. Finally, the last three chapters take up a variety of contemporary issues that have relevance across a wide number of countries, looking for factors that are helping to pull European states closer together and those that create problems of governance at both the national and international levels.

The fall of the Berlin Wall, as noted at the outset of the chapter, was a key event in opening up possibilities for a freer, more united Europe. Germany and Europe as a whole have changed dramatically in the past twenty years. Over this period, Europeans have had other events to celebrate, but, for those pushing for an institutionally more capable EU or a more dynamic, competitive economic environment on the continent, much work remains to be done. The expectation is that after reading this book you will gain insights into these contemporary issues, as well as the history, political institutions, and complex political, economic, and social forces that define European politics today.

APPLICATION QUESTIONS

1. What characteristics do you associate with the term "Europe"? What makes Europe distinctive from, say, the US or Canada?
2. Some have asserted that Europe or the EU should not have physical boundaries. What does this mean? If Europe has no boundaries, how would one define Europe?
3. Do you see Europe as a successful actor on the world stage? If so, how? Where? If not, what prevents Europe from being a "superpower"?
4. How could an American make counterarguments, like those made by Habermas, about the superiority of the "European model"?
5. In your lifetime, do you think Europe and the US will move closer together or move further apart? What factors would be most important to consider?

KEY TERMS

Cold War 6
communism 14
Enlightenment 13
European social model 15
European Union (EU) 4
Europeanization 5
Euro-skeptics 16
fascism 14
globalization 11
hard power 13
liberalism 14
multi-level governance 5
social cleavages 19
soft power 13

ADDITIONAL READING

Calleo, David. 2003. *Rethinking Europe's Future.* Princeton: Princeton University Press.

Utilizing perspectives from history, economics, politics, and philosophy, this book traces the development of Europe's political economy. It also raises important questions about whether and how Europe can build on its past achievements and overcome contemporary challenges. Although intended for a scholarly audience more so than other books mentioned here, it would be very useful to students taking classes on modern Europe.

Delanty, Gerard. 1995. *Inventing Europe: Idea, Identity, Reality.* New York: St. Martin's Press.

An oft-cited source that takes up, from a historical and constructivist position, the question, "What is Europe?". Delanty's core argument is that the definition of Europe has changed over time, and that is a reflection of particular economic, social, international, and ideological contexts.

Hooghe, Liesbet, and Marks, Gary. 2001. *Multi-Level Governance and European Integration.* Lanham MD: Rowman and Littlefield.

Important source on how the growing power of the EU and delegation of authority to sub-national (regional) governments is eroding the power of the nation-state. This presents a more nuanced picture of governance in Europe, particularly how the different levels (pan-European, state, sub-state) interact with each other.

Reid, T.R. 2004. *The United States of Europe: The New Superpower and the End of American Supremacy.* New York: Penguin.

This book, written by a journalist who was stationed in Europe, compares the US and Europe on a number of fronts and argues that Europe is eclipsing the US in several key respects, including economic performance and international influence.

Rifkin, Jeremy. 2004. *The European Dream: How Europe's Vision of the Future is Quietly Eclipsing the American Dream.* New York: Penguin.

Perhaps one of the strongest "pro-Europe" manifestos, this book examines the development of a particular European "model" and why this is more compelling, both within Europe and as a global model, than the American "dream."

END NOTES

1. Lest one think this is completely hypothetical, in 2006 Günter Grass, Germany's most famous post–World War II author, admitted that he had served in the German army in the later stages of the war. This revelation puts a shadow on Grass's moral authority within Germany and as a world literary figure. Pope Benedict XVI was also compelled to join Hitler Youth during World War II.
2. T.R. Reid, The *United States of Europe: The New Superpower and the End of American Supremacy* (New York: Penguin, 2004).
3. For more on this concept, see Maria Green Cowles, James Caporaso, and Thomas Risse, eds. *Transforming Europe: Europeanization and Domestic Change* (Ithaca NY: Cornell University Press, 2001), and Kevin Featherstone and Claudio Radaelli, eds. *The Politics of Europeanization* (Oxford: Oxford University Press, 2003).
4. This was the phrase of Jacques Poos, the Foreign Minister of Luxembourg, rebuffing possible American intervention in the early stages of the conflict. Quoted in Noel Malcolm, "The Case Against Europe," *Foreign Affairs* 74:2, March/April 1995, p. 68.
5. Gary Marks, Liesbet Hooghe, and Kermit Blank, "European Integration from the 1980s: State-

Centric vs. Multi-Level Governance," *Journal of Common Market Studies* 34:3, September 1996, p. 372. See also Hooghe and Marks, *Multi-Level Governance and European Integration* (Lanham MD: Rowman and Littlefield, 2001).

6. Hooghe and Marks, *Multi-Level Governance*, p. xi.
7. Pocock argues that the first delineation of Europe was made by ancient peoples who plied the waters of the Bosphorus. They developed myths and folktales that in effect gave the name "Europa" to the lands to the West and "Asia" to the lands to the East. From J.G.A. Pocock, "Some Europes and Their History," in Anthony Pagden, ed. *The Idea of Europe* (Washington: Woodrow Wilson Center Press, 2002), p. 56.
8. See Gerard Delanty, *Inventing Europe: Idea, Identity, Reality* (New York: St. Martin's Press, 1995), and Pagden, *The Idea of Europe*.
9. Some states, such as Switzerland and Austria, were officially neutral in the Cold War, but their political systems would qualify them as western European. Arguably, it was Turkey's alignment with the West in the Cold War—Turkey joined NATO in 1952—that helped it gain recognition in 1963 as geographically eligible to join the fledgling European Economic Community
10. Charlemagne, "The Myth of the Periphery," *The Economist*, March 27, 2010.
11. Helene Sjursen, "Introduction—Enlargement in Perspective," in Sjursen, ed. *Enlargement in Perspective* (Oslo: ARENA, 2005), p. 8. See also Sjursen, "Why expand? The Question of Legitimacy and Justification in the EU's Enlargement Policy," *Journal of Common Market Studies* 40:3, 2002, pp. 491–513.
12. Jose I. Torreblanca, *The Reuniting of Europe: Promises, Negotiations and Compromises* (Aldershot: Ashgate, 2001).
13. Mikhail Gorbachev, *Perestroika: New Thinking for Our Country and the World* (New York: Harper and Row, 1987), p. 190. The irony, of course, is that many Europeans saw the Soviet Union separate from Europe and Gorbachev himself, although a reformer, was leader of an undemocratic state.
14. Helmut Schmidt, "Wer nicht zu Europa gehört," *Die Zeit*, October 11, 2000.
15. "Turkey's EU Bid: Resistance is on the Rise," *Business Week*, 9 February 2004.
16. *New York Times*, October 3, 2004, p. 13.
17. Thierry de Montbrial, "Debating the borders of Europe," *International Herald Tribune*, May 21, 2004.
18. In 2009, after a severe economic crisis, the parliament of Iceland approved a measure to make an application to join the EU. It is highly uncertain whether Icelandic voters, however, will eventually approve EU membership.
19. Europe has achieved near universal literacy, as compared with 93 percent in China and 66 percent in India (World Bank data, from 2007). As for health, average life expectancy in the EU is seventy-eight, compared to seventy-three in China and sixty-five in India (World Bank data, 2008).
20. In its December 18-31 2010 issue, *The Economist* reported that Germany ($211.6 billion) had the world's largest annual trade surplus, eclipsing China ($189.9 billion), Japan ($91.9 billion), and Saudi Arabia ($105.2 billion). In contrast, the US trade deficit was $639.6 billion.
21. As an example, even *The Economist* employs a Big Mac index to gauge prices and purchasing power across countries.
22. Such brands include Texaco, Amoco, Budwesier, Snapple, A&W Root Beer, Dr. Pepper, Random House, Dunkin Donuts, Holiday Inn, Dial soap, Bazooka bubble gum, Baskin-Robbins, and even Ben and Jerry's, now owned by Unilever, a Dutch company. See Jeremy Rifkin, *The European Dream: How Europe's Vision of the Future is Quietly Eclipsing the American Dream* (New York: Penguin, 2004).
23. Germany, with 250,000 active duty personnel, ranks nineteenth, after countries such as Ukraine, Vietnam, South Korea, and Egypt. Turkey (ninth largest at 617,000 people) has the largest force in Europe, excluding Russia. See http://www.docstoc.com/docs/6345430/List_of_countries_by_size_of_armed_forces, accessed April 5, 2010.
24. Joseph S. Nye, *The Paradox of American Power* (Oxford: Oxford University Press, 2002), p. 8.
25. Mark Leonard, *Why Europe Will Run the 21st Century* (London: Fourth Estate, 2005).
26. Leonard, *Why Europe*, p. 35.
27. Zachary Shore, *Breeding Bin Ladens: America, Islam, and the Future of Europe* (Baltimore: Johns Hopkins University Press, 2006).
28. I use liberalism here in its classic and European sense, meaning a belief in limited government, individual rights and choice, and tolerance toward differing views. In this view, liberalism is associated with democratic governments and free-market economies and virtually all Americans, whether they recognize it or not, are liberals. I recognize

that Americans often define the term liberal differently, denoting a political position left of center than often endorses a more interventionist role of the state in the economy. However, any reader of the conservative British publication *The Economist* will immediately notice how it generally praises "liberal" policies and programs.

29. Classic works on nationalism that identify it as a modern phenomenon arising at the time of the French Revolution include Ernest Gellner, *Nations and Nationalism* (Ithaca: Cornell University Press, 1983) and Eric Hobsbawm, *Nations and Nationalism Since 1780* (Cambridge: Cambridge University Press, 1992).
30. The schism between Europe and the US has captured attention on both sides of the Atlantic, with the usual suspects pointing fingers at their adversaries. For an attempt to chart a path to a stronger transatlantic alliance, see Timothy Garton Ash, *Free World: America, Europe, and the Surprising Future of the West* (New York: Vintage, 2004).
31. Rifkin, *The European Dream*.
32. Whereas some would contend that the quality of health care in the US is superior, the fact is that the US spends more on health as a percentage of its national wealth (about 15 percent, twice as much as Sweden or France), and has a lower life expectancy than most Western European countries.
33. Whereas in the US new parents gained the right in the 1990s to take twelve weeks of unpaid leave, Swedish mothers get up to sixty-four weeks off at two-thirds pay.
34. Reid claims that in 2003 Americans worked on average 1976 hours, 400 more than German or French workers and 200 more than British workers. See Reid, *The United States of Europe*, p. 155.
35. From Ash, *Free World*, pp. 47-48.
36. Ash, *Free World*, pp. 25–26. As he notes, anyone wanting to familiarize herself with the British Euroskeptic position need only pick up a copy of a British tabloid newspaper such as *The Sun* or *The Daily Telegraph*. A more erudite Euro-skeptic account can be found in Malcolm, "The Case Against Europe," and in Christopher Booker and Richard North, *The Great Deception: Can the European Union Survive?*, 2nd edition (London: Continuum, 2005).
37. Gerard Baker, "Against United Europe," *Weekly Standard*, September 22, 2003.
38. Robert Kagan, *Of Paradise and Power: America and Europe in the New World Order* (New York: Alfred Knopf, 2003), p. 3. This reference draws the 1992 book *Men Are from Mars, Women Are from Venus* by John Gray.
39. Charles Kupchan, *The End of the American Era* (New York: Vintage, 2003).
40. Taken from remarks made at the William Davidson Institute at the University of Michigan, March 24, 2004.
41. Quoted in Rifkin, *The European Dream*, p. 200.
42. There are, of course, security issues in the Balkans and growing worries in some quarters of a resurgent Russia, but conflict between major powers in Europe—as opposed to local, secessionist conflicts such as Kosovo, Abkhazia, or Chechnya—is not a major worry.
43. Margaret Thatcher wrote that she had conversations with French President Francois Mitterand (1981–1995) about how to "check the German juggernaut." Quoted in Tony Judt, *Postwar: A History of Europe Since 1945* (New York: Penguin, 2005), p. 639.
44. Data come from http://en.wikipedia.org/wiki/Multi-National_Force_%E2%80%93_Iraq#Troop_deployment_in_Iraq_2003-2009, accessed July 13, 2010.
45. The classic work on social cleavages in advanced industrial states in Seymour M. Lipset and Stein Rokkan, *Party Systems and Voter Alignments: Cross-National Perspectives* (New York: Free Press, 1967).

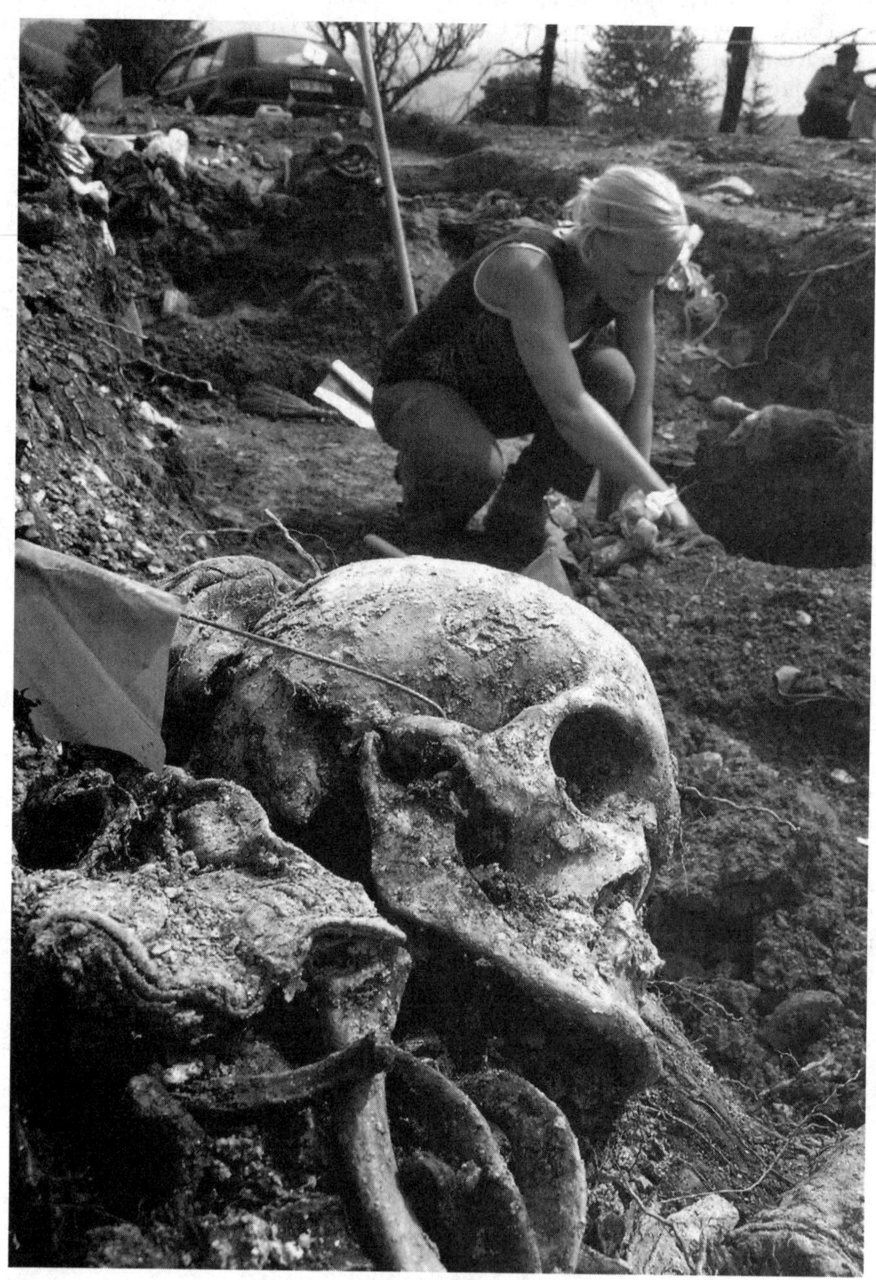

Srebrenica 1995: Fifty Years after World War II, Another Genocide in Europe

CHAPTER 2

Political and Economic Development in Western and Eastern Europe

On March 30, 2010, the Serbian parliament voted to express "condolences and apologies" to the victims of the July 2005 massacre of 8,000 Muslim men and boys in Srebrenica, Bosnia, the worst war crime committed in Europe since World War II. This action was newsworthy because that atrocity was committed by ethnic Serbs who were fighting to gain control of parts of Bosnia after the breakup of Yugoslavia. For years, many Serbs had denied that the massacre had even occurred, despite findings by international tribunals that it was an act of genocide.[1] The Serbian apology—which called Srebrenica a "crime" and a "tragedy" but stopped short of using the word genocide—was welcomed by the European Union, which many Serbs hope to join in the near future.[2]

This event illustrates a number of important points. First, history affects contemporary life and politics. Whether it be past wars, the Holocaust, the communist past in Eastern Europe, centuries-long national rivalries or experience of empires, history casts a long shadow over the European present, coloring political debates, accounting for economic development (or lack thereof), and shaping culture and values. Second, history is contested. This apology passed the parliament with a bare majority (127 of 250) of votes, and many victims complained that it was insincere, aimed more at Serb aspirations to join the EU than to offer solace or justice to victims. One can find numerous examples of how history, or, more accurately, arguments over history affect both relations among countries in Europe and among groups within individual countries. Finally, in some cases, history is something to be overcome. Certainly this was the case with Germany after World War II, and one could say that in order to fully join Europe, today's Serbia, like Germany before it and post-communist countries in the 1990s, must put many of its historical ghosts to rest and embrace new values such as democracy, rule of law, and respect for human rights, features that themselves evolved over time and today increasingly define what it is to be European.

This chapter serves as a historical overview of Europe, recognizing that in order to understand many of the contemporary political issues and debates in Europe and to discuss where Europe might be heading, it is imperative to have some idea of where Europe has been and how, through various means, certain "European" ideas and practices developed and took root. It will focus on broad trends, in particular the development of states, democratic institutions, and economic systems. It is intended to be more a cursory treatment than a comprehensive history. It is difficult, of course, to isolate a single European history. Thus, for the sake of narrative flow, it is divided into two sections, Western and Eastern Europe.

WESTERN EUROPEAN DEVELOPMENT

The countries of Western and Eastern Europe developed differently in several key respects, and one could argue that the Western European experience defines in substantive terms what Europe "means" today. Thus when Eastern Europeans stated in the 1990s that they wanted to rejoin Europe, they were asserting that they wanted to enjoy what *Western* Europe already had, as democratic, capitalist systems had become the norm for the continent. Understanding how Western European states evolved is thus a logical first step in understanding contemporary discussions of "Europe."

The Emergence of Nation-States

state ■ a political association that exercises authority over a territory and its inhabitants.

A fundamental institution in the study of political science is the **state**, a political association that exercises authority over a territory and its inhabitants. In English, state and country are often used interchangeably, although one can distinguish the two by noting that it is the state, as an organization, that rules over a given country/territory. Although other political associations (e.g., tribes, empires) have existed throughout human history, modern states first arose in Western Europe. Whereas there were more than a thousand different European mini-kingdoms or principalities in the fourteenth century, by the end of the nineteenth century one could speak of a dozen major states in Western Europe.

State Formation How did states form? Although some might want to harbor more romantic notions, examination of European history reveals that today's European states are, in essence, winners in a brutal survival-of-the-fittest conflict among competing political entities. In simple terms, today's states with their territorial boundaries are largely the result of military conflict. In Charles Tilly's well-known formulation, "War made the state and the state made war."[3] In the case of Great Britain, for example, most date the emergence of the current English state to 1066, when William the Conqueror (from Normandy, part of today's France) invaded and won the English crown. In France, early French rulers in the Middle Ages subdued provincial rulers in regions such as Brittany and Burgundy. Switzerland, one of Europe's oldest states, traces its foundation to 1291 with the creation of a confederacy among three Swiss cantons (regions) that fought against foreign rule. In Scandinavia, Denmark, due to military prowess and dynastic unions, gained dominance by the time of the Kalmar Union in 1397, but Swedish revolts in the 1500s led to the creation of a separate Swedish kingdom, which eventually extended its dominion to Norway (independent only since 1905) and Finland (independent since 1917). Spain was united in 1492, when the last Moors (Muslims) were driven out of southern Spain, but the Spanish government, even with its vast wealth thanks to its colonies in the New World, exercised weak authority over its many disparate regions.

Other states in Europe are more recent creations. The Netherlands, which was part of the Spanish Kingdom, gained independence in 1648 after an eighty-year struggle. In 1830, Belgium, which had been incorporated into the Netherlands in 1815, revolted against Dutch rule and, thanks to international support, became an independent state. Italy and Germany were the last two major Western European states to form. Both had well-established cultures and economically vibrant regions but lacked political unity. Italy, divided into a host of regions and city-states (e.g., Naples, Florence, Venice, Rome), was unified only in 1861 thanks to the combined military efforts of the rulers of the region of Piedmont and the revolutionary Giuseppe Garibaldi. In the early 1800s there was an effort to unite the numerous German principalities, but a single Germany did not exist until 1871, when various German regions were unified thanks to the military victories of Prussia (one such German region, centered in Berlin) over Denmark, Austria-Hungary, and France. Austria, where German is also the primary language, became a separate state only in 1918 after the dismemberment of the multi-ethnic Austro-Hungarian Empire.

Intense military competition on continental Western Europe prompted the formation of more centralized governments. State power in turn led to technological, administrative, and economic growth.[4] Early European states, of course, did not perform all the functions of states today. However, their primary activities—taxation and military recruitment—put resources into their hands so that they could consolidate their power in Europe and, eventually, globally, as they established colonies in the Western Hemisphere, Asia, and Africa.

The Doctrine of Sovereignty Two features distinguish modern European states from their predecessors: the doctrines of **sovereignty** and nationalism. Sovereignty refers to the exclusive right of a ruler to exercise political authority over a territory and people. It suggests that the ruler is supreme, that is, not needing to share power with any other social or political entity. Put forward initially as a legal doctrine by Jean Bodin (1530–1596), sovereignty suggested that the ruler (a king) was not subject to any human law, answering only to God or natural law. As it evolved, sovereignty included the principle of non-interference in the affairs of other states. States were therefore sovereign, able to do whatever they wanted over the territory they ruled. As ideas of democracy expanded, the notion of popular sovereignty developed, meaning that it was the people or nation that was sovereign, not an individual monarch. To the extent that supranational organizations such as the EU and global economic forces are undermining the "power of the people," many worry about how democracy will fare as European states draw closer together.

sovereignty ■ the exclusive right of a ruler or state to exercise political authority over a territory and people; in various, this doctrine is being challenged by today's EU.

Nationalism: Fostering a Sense of Identity Establishing sovereign control over a territory was but a part of state formation in Western Europe. States also had to rule over people. In order to facilitate political control, they needed to gain legitimacy, a sense among the population that state authorities have a right to rule. Previously, rulers had attempted to legitimize their rule and claim sovereignty through use of religion, claiming a divine right to rule. As the power of the religious establishment, however, came under assault and, in some cases, monarchies were overthrown or were forced to make compromises with groups in society, notions of "divine right" became untenable. Instead, leaders attempted to foster a sense of loyalty, an affective link between the state and the people under its control. In most European countries, this was accomplished by the development of **nationalism**.

nationalism ■ belief that primary source of an individual's identity belongs with a broader collective, the nation; often used to argue for the independence and power of the nation.

Nationalism has many possible definitions.[5] For our purposes, we can define it as a belief that locates the source of individual identity within a broader collective, the **nation**, which is also the central object for loyalty. The nation can be defined in various ways. Some endow it with more objective, observable traits (e.g., a common language, religion, history) that unify its various members and give a nation political and social coherence. Others would emphasize that nations are constructed, built upon myths or imaginations of the past or of a common destiny. For nationalists, the boundaries of the state (an organization) should correspond to with those of the nation (a people). Nationalism, in other words, posits that nations should have their own states, and state power is legitimate to the extent that it fulfills the need for the nation to rule itself. The push for a more united Europe in many respects seeks to transcend nationalism and create a pan-European identity. Suffice to say that this project is controversial among those still beholden to more conventional ideas of nationalism.

nation ■ a group of people united by various traits (e.g., language, culture, history) that often aspire for a state of their own.

Not all nationalisms, however, are the same. Obviously, the particulars of French, Danish, Italian, and so on, nationalism will differ. Broadly speaking, however, one can point to two different types of nationalism: **civic nationalism** and **ethnic nationalism**. Civic nationalism defines the nation on the basis of common citizenship and/or acquired characteristics such as acceptance of certain political values. It tends to be more inclusive. Most Western European states have a predominantly civic view of the nation. Whereas citizenship might be defined by birth, one can also "become" British or French, for example, by moving to the country, accepting its basic political values, and becoming naturalized citizens. To the extent that civic nationalism emphasizes membership in a political community, it is rather similar to patriotism, love of one's country. The American notion of a "melting pot" rests on the principles of civic nationalism, that anyone can become an American. Ethnic nationalism, on the other hand, stresses features such as heredity and religion that are allegedly intrinsic to the people. It tends to be reactive and less inclusive, positing clearer divisions between "us" and "them," the latter of which cannot truly become part of "us." Although more common in Eastern Europe, it does have one Western European variant worth mentioning: Germany. Because Germany existed as a cultural entity long before it was politically unified, it could not have a nationalism based upon a common citizenship. Its earliest nationalists tended to be intellectuals who emphasized the cultural uniqueness, if not superiority, of the German people. According to Wilhelm von Humboldt (1767–1835), a relative liberal and the founder of the University of Berlin,

civic nationalism ■ a more inclusive idea that defines the nation on the basis of common citizenship and/or acquired characteristics such as acceptance of certain political values; examples include Great Britain, France, and the US.

ethnic nationalism: ■ a more exclusive form of identity that stresses features such as heredity and religion that are allegedly intrinsic to the people; a historical example is German nationalism.

> There is perhaps no country that deserves to be free and independent as Germany, because none is so disposed to devote its freedom so single-mindedly to the welfare of all. The German genius is among all nations the one which is least destructive, which always nourishes itself, and when freedom is secured Germany will certainly attain an outstanding place in every form of culture and thought.[6]

Understanding the roots of German nationalism, which even in the nineteenth century was directed against the British, French, and Jews, goes a long way toward explaining some of the darker moments in twentieth-century Europe.

One might also note that many states had trouble establishing any form of state-centered nationalism. This was especially true in multi-ethnic states such as Belgium (split between Dutch speakers and French speakers) and Spain (with sizeable non-Spanish peoples such as Basques, Catalans, and Galicians).

Nationalization of Politics Nationalism was put forward as an objective and ideology by political elites and intellectuals. Its goal was to create a more coherent, homogeneous nation-state, one in which the political boundaries of the state would correspond with the cultural boundaries of the nation. This was not an easy task. In the words of Massimo D'Azeglio, a leading figure in the drive to unite Italy in the 1860s, "Now that we have made Italy, we have to make Italians."

The nationalization of politics was thus an important theme in many states, lasting at least into the early part of the twentieth century.[7] More parochial, peripheral, or local identities had to give way to a national identity. In nationalization's initial stages, center-periphery cleavages predominated, with state elites interested in consolidating their authority by forging a coherent national whole. Particulars varied from state to state: in Germany, the main battles were in overcoming longstanding local identities; in the Netherlands, the division was between Catholics and Protestants; in Scandinavia, the urban/rural divide was important.

Over the course of the nineteenth and twentieth centuries, nationalism's hold grew stronger throughout Europe. Much of this was the result of the expansion of state power, meaning that the state made nations.[8] Common curricula in public education helped spread the national idea and standardize language. Media such as radio and newspapers also played a role, as people began to connect, however vicariously, with other citizens in the state. Economic growth contributed to the growth of more cosmopolitan cities, where people from different parts of the country interacted with each other. The growth of transportation networks led to the development of national economies. Over time, the development of capitalism contributed to the growth of class antagonisms, meaning that left-right political cleavages between workers and owners increasingly defined political life, as territorial or ethno-linguistic divisions receded in importance. Diversity gave way to standardization. Whereas in the 1700s multiple languages were spoken in France and Germany was a collection of small princely kingdoms, by the early twentieth century, one could speak without hesitation of a French or German nation that was both culturally and politically unified.

Origins of Democracy

Europe is not only the birthplace of the modern state. Europeans were also the first to develop democratic forms of government. Indeed, one of the main themes of European history has been the expansion of democracy, both in terms of its spread to more states and in terms of creating a more inclusive citizenry with political rights. Today, **democracy**, defined in simplest terms as a system of government based upon free and fair elections with universal suffrage and respect for civil and human rights, is fundamental to the political idea of Europe.

democracy ■ a system of government based upon free and fair elections with universal suffrage and respect for civil and human rights.

The Genesis of Democracy in Great Britain Several European countries claim a long democratic history. Iceland maintains that its parliament, the *Althing*, which dates to 930, is the world's oldest legislature. Other Scandinavians such as the Danes and Swedes point to their experience with their own *tings* (assemblies) among various tribes in the Middle Ages as precursors to their own democracies. The Swiss date their democracy back to the first formation of a Swiss Confederacy in 1291.

Most accounts, however, focus on Great Britain as the birthplace of modern democracy. Britons refer to their parliament, which dates from 1265, as the "mother of all parliaments." The origins of British democracy are usually traced to 1215 with the signing of the Magna Carta, an agreement between the king and feudal barons that protected the latter from abuses by the King. However, the unelected monarch still enjoyed great power, and the earliest English parliaments were also unelected bodies of wealthy, landowning nobility. In the 1600s, the power of the monarch was more directly and seriously challenged, thanks in part to the growth of an urban merchant class that wanted political power to go along with its wealth.[9] The English Civil War of the 1640s, which had both political and religious dimensions, led to the overthrow and eventual beheading of King Charles I. In 1688, the (Protestant) monarchy was restored, but the king was allowed to assume the throne provided he recognized the supremacy of parliament, limiting the power of the Crown still further and making Britain the first constitutional monarchy. This event, together with passage in 1689 of a Bill of Rights, was an important milestone toward the development of British democracy, although, because voting rights were severely limited, it is problematic to refer to Great Britain in the 1700s or 1800s as democratic in the contemporary sense. Political and civil rights were only gradually extended to most Britons in the late nineteenth and early twentieth centuries.

Enlightenment and the Democratic Idea Whereas the first stirrings of limited government and constitutionalism in Europe date to the Middle Ages, democracy remained both spatially and substantively limited. Most states were monarchies, and most residents could not participate in politics. While democracy often emerged as a consequence of economic growth and modernization, its philosophical roots lie in the intellectual revolution of the Enlightenment.[10]

The core idea of democracy dates back to ancient Greece. However, ancient Greeks did not have any well-developed notion of individual rights or political equality, all of which underpin modern democratic states. These basic notions arose during the Enlightenment in the seventeenth and eighteenth centuries. As noted in Chapter 1, the Enlightenment and its ideals distinguish Europe from other regions of the world. Enlightenment thinkers elaborated ideas of natural freedom and that government should be limited and based upon a **social contract** between the rulers and the ruled, with the rulers enjoying the right to rule only as long as they protected individuals' political and civil rights. They also argued for the liberation of people from both state and religious authority. Denis Diderot, the editor of the famous *Encyclopedia* (1751–1765), the gospel of sorts for the Enlightenment, stated that salvation would arrive "when the last King was strangled with the entrails of the last priest."[11] The Enlightenment provided inspiration for the French Revolution in 1789, which overthrew one of Europe's strongest monarchies and had ripple effects across the continent, as more and more people were drawn to its

social contract ■ idea from various thinkers of the Enlightenment that government rests on a contract, with rulers having the right to rule only as long as they protect peoples' political and civil rights.

slogan of "*liberté, egalité, fraternité*" (liberty, equality, solidarity) and its proclamation of universal manhood suffrage.

Democracy Expands The idea of giving the people a say in their government was put into practice in several European states in the nineteenth century. True, definitions of "the people" were usually limited to the upper classes, but one should recognize that even a narrow application of popular sovereignty constituted a major break with the past, when kings were subject to no law and people were subjects of the crown rather than citizens. Voting in competitive elections, the *sine qua non* of democracy, became widespread, and most states featured some sort of parliamentary institution that was supposed to reflect the popular will. Again, this should not be equated with modern democratic practice. Only a minority of the people could vote. Civil and human rights were not universally respected. However, political power was gradually transferred from monarchs and put in the hands of assemblies that made some sort of claim to represent "the people." The dates in which parliamentary representation and universal manhood suffrage were established are presented in Table 2.1.

A few comments are in order. First, the path to democracy varied from state to state. Whereas in some states such as Britain, Sweden, and Denmark, democracy evolved in a relatively peaceful fashion, in states such as France, Italy, and Spain it was the product of wars and domestic upheavals. As Charles Tilly notes, there is no singular path to democracy.[12] Secondly, the degree of democracy—as measured by parliamentary supremacy—varied throughout Europe. Whereas in Britain and the Netherlands elected parliaments and prime ministers became the main political

TABLE 2.1

Development of Parliamentary Representation and Voting in Western Europe

Country	1810	1820	1830	1840	1850	1860	1870	1880	1890	1900	1910
Norway	A									B	
Great Britain			A								B
Switzerland				AB							
Belgium			A						B		
Netherlands				A							B
Italy						A					B
Denmark				A							B
Spain						AB					
France							AB				
Germany							AB				
Sweden						A					B
Finland										AB	
Portugal											AB

A: Start of continuous parliamentary representation; B: First universal manhood suffrage

Source: Adapted from Tilly, 2004, p. 214.

players, in Germany executive authority in the figure of the Chancellor (Prime Minister) was accountable to the Kaiser (Emperor), not the parliament. In Belgium, King Leopold II (1865–1909) was able to use his position to establish a brutally repressive and murderous regime in the Congo in Africa. Lastly, not all "democracies" functioned very well. Italy's was (and still is) marked by corruption, and ostensibly democratic governments in Spain and Portugal were wracked by instability throughout the 1800s and in practice functioned more like oligarchies that concentrated power into the hands of very few individuals.

Expansion of Suffrage The final stage in the growth of European democracy was the expansion of the vote to groups that were previously disenfranchised. Whereas by the mid-1800s men—usually men of property—enjoyed the vote in most European states, no state was democratic in the modern sense of that term. For example, in the 1830s less than 5 percent of the population enjoyed the right to vote in Switzerland, the Netherlands, and Great Britain. At this time, urban industrial workers and ordinary peasants and farmers, not to mention all women, were often deemed unfit to participate in politics by their social "betters." In the middle and late 1800s these disenfranchised groups advocated for voting rights in several European countries. It was largely due to pressures "from below," particularly from the working class, not the goodwill of elites or a culture of equality, that more people were given basic democratic political rights.[13]

The first restrictions to go were those that discriminated by economic standing or literacy. As seen in Table 2.1, from the mid-1800s to the early 1900s, property restrictions and literacy tests were lowered and eventually removed, leading to universal male suffrage. Age restrictions were also gradually lowered, so that by after World War II, eighteen became the usual age for voting eligibility in Europe. The last disenfranchised group to win the vote was women. Women had lobbied aggressively for the right to vote, especially in Great Britain and the Netherlands, but they were unable to achieve success until after World War I. As seen in Table 2.2, Scandinavian states tended to be the first to expand suffrage to women. Italy, Belgium, and Greece granted women equal voting rights only in the aftermath of World War II, and in Switzerland, it was not until 1971 that Swiss men, in a referendum, agreed to give the vote to their wives, mothers, and daughters.

The table shows the year that women gained equal voting rights with men. In some cases, women were allowed to vote in local elections or subject to different age qualifications prior to gaining full equality with men.

Economic Development

The Industrial Revolution and Early Capitalism Western Europe's ascendance to world economic dominance, which it would maintain until the end of World War II, can be dated to the Industrial Revolution of the 1700s. True, there were important antecedents to Europe's economic takeoff: the discovery of the "New World," which supplied markets, raw materials, and precious metals; profits from the slave trade, which was intimately tied to agricultural production in colonies in the Americas; technological change; and urbanization.

TABLE 2.2

Granting of Female Suffrage in Western Europe

Country	Year
Finland	1906
Norway	1913
Denmark	1915
Iceland	1915
Austria	1918
Germany	1918
Netherlands	1919
Sweden	1921
Ireland	1922
Great Britain	1928
France	1944
Italy	1946
Belgium	1948
Greece	1955
Switzerland	1971

As with constitutional government, Britain was a leader, developing a textile industry in the early 1700s.[14] Development of the steam engine led to breakthroughs in both transportation and early industrial production. Mechanized power contributed to the growth of factories, which were both economically more efficient and fostered more urbanization. By the early 1800s France, the Netherlands, Belgium, and German states, particularly Prussia, also became industrial powers. By the end of the 1800s, factory towns popped up across the continent.

Without a doubt, the industrial revolution led to great economic progress, at least measured in terms of gross output and the development of new products. While the specifics of each economic system varied from state to state, early industrialization was based on **capitalism**, which rested on private ownership, competition among economic producers, and minimal state intervention in the economy. The father of capitalist thought, the Scottish Enlightenment thinker Adam Smith, wrote in *Wealth of Nations* in 1776 that the pursuit of individual self-interest would lead to an improvement in general welfare.

capitalism ■ the economic system that rests on private ownership, competition among economic producers, and minimal state intervention in the economy; developed in much of Western Europe in the 1700s and 1800s.

Despite the enormous technological progress and immense social change wrought by capitalism, many critics emerged to advocate a different path. Industrialization, while producing immense profits for the owners of capital, also created a working class that worked long days in dangerous conditions and lived in squalor. Child labor was commonplace; the drive for profits kept wages low. Righting the perceived wrongs of capitalism thus became a major political struggle. The best known critic of capitalism was the German political economist Karl Marx (1818–1883), who argued that it dehumanized workers and needed to be thrown off by a workers' revolution, which would lead to the development of communism, a classless society in which there was no private property and all people were equal. Marx's ideas would be the inspiration for revolutionary activity throughout Europe—most notably in 1848 and 1870—and, after his death, a version of his vision was put into place in the Soviet Union.

The Rise of National Economies Capitalism, at least envisioned by its early advocates, rested upon the actions of individuals. Later industrializers tended to rely more upon state planning or financing for economic development. This was best exemplified in Germany, where Friedrich List (1789–1846), pressed for the economic unification of German states and urged protectionist measures (e.g., imposition of tariffs) to shield German industry from competition from Great Britain and other more developed states.[15] Although List did not live to see it, the unified German state would grow rapidly thanks to economic nationalism and state encouragement of construction of modern industries, particularly iron, steel, and chemicals. By the early twentieth century, the state was taking the lead in the economic life of many European states. Nationalism, however, was tempered by growing cross-national economic ties. Ultimately, however, national competition—in economics, armaments, and imperial expansion—spilled over in military conflict.

TURMOIL IN EUROPE, 1914–1945

While European history is marked by a variety of political, economic, and technological accomplishments, Europe had a nightmarish first half of the twentieth century. Wars, genocide, and repressive governments caused some 60 million deaths.[16] Economic depression led many to doubt the virtues of capitalism and democracy. Although advocates of a united Europe might emphasize, as did the draft Constitutional Treaty of the EU in 2005, that Europe is a region of "special area of human hope," one should be mindful of the darker side of Europe's past.

This turmoil affected both Western and Eastern Europe. Indeed, both World Wars started in Eastern Europe, and the majority of the military casualties, civilian deaths, and victims of the Holocaust were from Eastern Europe. Politically, however, some of the most important developments in this period occurred in Western Europe. In particular, after World War I (1914–1918), weak democratic governments in Italy and Germany fell to mass movements espousing a militant form of nationalism and a cult of a powerful leader. This was fascism, which explicitly rejected the norms of liberal democracy by emphasizing the nation over the individual and rejecting ideas of equality and tolerance. The first Fascist leader to come to power was Benito Mussolini (1883–1945) in Italy, who organized his "blackshirts" in a struggle against communists and socialists and, promising to restore order, was appointed Prime Minister in 1922. Within a few years, Mussolini stripped the Italian parliament of powers, banned opposition parties, and put the press under government control.

Far more dangerous was Adolf Hitler (1889–1945), who modeled Mussolini's tactics while adding elements of Social Darwinism, eugenics, and anti-Semitism (which was far from unique to Germany) in an effort to cultivate his German "master race" and a new *Reich* that would last a thousand years. After 1930, when the Great Depression hit Germany, sparking hyperinflation, massive unemployment, labor unrest, and the possibility of a communist seizure of power, Hitler emerged as a popular figure. His Nazi Party gained 18 percent of the vote in 1930 parliamentary elections and 37 percent in 1932. Conservatives, thinking they could control Hitler, supported his appointment to Chancellor (Prime Minister) in 1933. Afterwards, however, he passed laws banning other political parties and trade unions, passed a series of anti-Jewish laws, and, as *Der Führer* (The Leader), he demanded the unquestioned obedience of the German people. He began to re-arm Germany in an effort to secure more *Lebensraum* (living space) for Germany.

Germany's invasion of Poland in September 1939 marked the beginning of World War II, which engulfed most of the continent. It was during the war that Hitler committed his greatest crime, the Holocaust, as millions of European Jews (as well as Roma [Gypsies], Soviet prisoners of war, ordinary Poles, homosexuals, and socialists and communists) were sent to labor and death camps. It is worth mentioning as well that others—in France, the Netherlands, in Poland, in Austria, and elsewhere—collaborated with Hitler, although thousands of people also tried to save Jews from the gas chambers.

The invasion of the Soviet Union, as well as the declaration of war against the United States in December 1941 after Pearl Harbor, proved to be Hitler's greatest mistakes. Eventually, the alliance of the Soviet Union, Great Britain, and the US pushed the armies of Germany and Italy back. Hitler committed suicide as the Soviet army advanced on Berlin. His thousand-year *Reich* lasted just over twelve years, but was responsible for the deaths of millions, including the genocide against 6 million European Jews.

POST-WAR DEVELOPMENT

The end of World War II opened an important new chapter in European history. Whereas the Cold War division between Western and Eastern Europe dominated international politics, within Western Europe democratic governments took hold. Capitalism was tempered with the emergence of a welfare state and, in order to prevent future conflicts, states began the process of economic and political integration.

Cold War Divisions

After World War II, the two superpowers—the US and the Soviet Union—divided Europe into spheres of influence. In Western Europe, the US, with economic assistance delivered under the **Marshall Plan**, helped rebuild countries devastated by war and fostered democratic, capitalist systems. In Eastern Europe, behind what Winston Churchill called the "Iron Curtain," the Soviets imposed communism. The two former allies viewed each other with suspicion and formed rival military blocs. Germany, occupied by both the Soviets and the Western powers (the US, Great Britain, and France) was divided into two states. West Germany, as we shall see in the In Focus section, became both a political and economic success story. East Germany, on the other hand, became a repressive police state under communist authority. The competition of the Cold War—which occasionally turned "hot" in places such as Korea and Vietnam—lasted for more than forty years, ending with the collapse of communist regimes in Eastern Europe in 1989 and the reunification of Germany in 1990. But, as noted in the **Is Europe One?** section with respect to today's Germany, vestiges of Cold War divisions remain.

Marshall Plan ■ US economic assistance program directed to Western Europe after World War II; often credited with the post-war economic recovery in Western Europe and helped cement ties between the US and European governments.

(Re)Democratization

Consolidating democracy became a major political project in post-war Western Europe. Indeed, the existence of democracy would become, in many respects, *the* distinguishing feature of the region and an indicator of its successful political development.

For democratic states that prevailed in the war (Great Britain) or that were neutral and escaped conflict (Ireland, Switzerland, and Sweden), democratization was not a pressing issue. Similarly, many previously democratic states that were occupied by the Germans (e.g., the Netherlands, Norway, Finland, Belgium, Denmark), were able to reestablish themselves with relative ease, often with their pre-war political leaders returning from exile and resuming leadership. In many of these countries, a high degree of consensus on basic policies (e.g., the welfare state) and the general moderate orientation of the parties on the left and the right facilitated coalition governments and, for the most part, post-war political stability.

Some countries had more difficulties in establishing democratic governments. In Italy, fascism had been defeated, but the nineteenth-century constitution, which established Italy as a constitutional monarchy, was no longer tenable because the monarchy had been discredited by its association with Mussolini. A popular referendum turned Italy into a republic in 1946. In 1948 Italy adopted a new constitution that guaranteed individual rights, and in elections that year the Christian Democrats, benefiting from covert US support, defeated their communist rivals. The Christian Democrats would dominate Italian politics for the next four decades, but Italian governments were troubled by problems of corruption and were typically fragile coalitions that had an average lifespan of one year.

One would have thought the West German case would be difficult as well. Germany's attempt to install democracy after World War I failed. Overcoming the legacy of Hitler—recalling that millions of Germans voted for him and presumably supported him during the war—obviously presented many problems. The Western allies helped oversee a process of de-Nazification, but clearly not every Nazi Party member could (or, perhaps, even should) be punished for political affiliation. The allies also helped draft a new constitution that included federalism, judicial review, and a higher electoral threshold for parties to enter parliament, thus creating a more coherent party system. As in Italy, the Christian Democrats, led by Konrad Adenauer, dominated political life, but there was no specter of a communist takeover. Emphasizing moral renewal—a welcome message for many—and the need for Germans to both confront their past and move forward with a new stronger, democracy, Adenauer ruled Germany until 1963. Thanks to the government's ability to provide stability, the German "economic miracle," discussed more in the In Focus section, European economic integration, and reach a great deal of consensus within German society on basic priorities, democracy succeeded.

Ironically, France, with a longer democratic tradition and nominally on the winning side in World War II, was more problematic. France was left between groups on the political right and left, with more nationalist and conservative forces allied with Charles de Gaulle, leader of the anti-Nazi French Resistance, opposed by those on the political left, particularly the communists, who also had contributed heavily to the Resistance. All the main actors wanted a new constitution, but they could not agree on particulars. De Gaulle opposed the 1946 Constitution, which established the principle of parliamentary supremacy, but, as proportional representation voting led to growth of many parties, it was hard to form stable coalition governments. The final straw was a colonial crisis in French-ruled Algeria. With French paramilitary forces in Algeria threatening to invade France itself, the government turned to de Gaulle, the only man deemed to have the credibility with the military to end the crisis. He agreed to serve, but only if France adopted a new constitution with a stronger presidency, which he saw as his rightful position. Thus, in 1958, the French Fifth Republic, with its semi-presidentialism system (a strong president but also a prime minister) was born.

A few West European countries had a more arduous path to democracy. Spain had suffered under the military dictatorship of Francisco Franco since 1939, when his forces, with the help of Nazi Germany and Fascist Italy, prevailed in a brutal civil war. It was only after Franco's death in 1975 that Spain was able to democratize. Portugal, the poorest country in Western Europe, similarly suffered under the dictatorship of Antonio Salazar (1932–1970). Like Spain, Portugal democratized in the 1970s. In Greece, elections had been held in 1946, even as the country was embroiled in civil war, but sharp political divisions (between left and right, monarchists and republicans) made governance difficult, contributing to a military coup in 1967. Civilian, democratic rule was reestablished in 1974. Thanks in part to the assistance of the European Community (forerunner of the EU), all three states became stable democracies in the 1980s.

Reconstruction and the Rise of the Welfare State

After World War II, economic reconstruction was a top priority, necessary for the survival of democratic governments. Rebuilding would not be easy. The devastation from the war was enormous, and there was a political imperative to get economic life back to normal as quickly as possible.

The economic recovery in Western Europe was predicated upon several policies. First, because of the lack of private resources, the state took the lead in investment, planning, and often exercising ownership over industries. Reliance on the state as the engine for growth was driven both by necessity and a widespread feeling (one not felt in the US) that *laissez-faire*, free-market capitalism had to be managed and/or constrained in order to avoid the economic dislocations that preceded World War II. In the words of the famous Austrian economist Joseph Schumpeter, "The all but general opinion seems to be that capitalist methods will be unequal to the task of reconstruction."[17] Second, the US provided $13 billion in economic assistance—over $100 billion in today's dollars—to Europe to assist in rebuilding through the Marshall Plan. Third, by the 1950s several European states began to push for freer trade and economic integration. These early efforts—which were the first steps toward creation of the EU—are covered more in the next chapter.

There was, it should be noted, no single economic model, although in all states, state spending—for both investments and for social welfare—rose far above pre-war levels, and millions of workers moved off the farms and into manufacturing and service jobs in the cities. France went furthest with state planning, which

IN FOCUS

The Post-War Miracle in West Germany versus Relative Decline in Great Britain

Great Britain was on the winning side in World War II. Germany lost and was divided into two. These facts are well known. As seen in Figure 2.1, at the end of the war *per capita* income in Britain was more than 50 percent higher than that in West Germany. However, by 1958 the total West German economy was larger than that of Great Britain and by 1973 its *per capita* income eclipsed that in Britain. In the wake of the German "economic miracle," Britain, with one of the lowest economic growth rates in Europe in the 1960s and 1970s, looked like the new "sick man of Europe." Britons began to wonder who really won the war. How does one explain the different experiences of these two states?[19]

Note first their similarities. In both states, state spending represented a sizeable part of the economy. For example, between 1950 and 1973 government spending rose from 30.4 percent to 42 percent of GDP in West Germany and from 34.2 percent to 41.5 percent in Great Britain.[20] Many of these funds went to social welfare programs—health care, pensions, education, and housing. Moreover, in both countries the state pursued interventionist policies to help equalize incomes and regulate private enterprise. Tax rates, reaching more than 80 percent, were high. In the immediate post-war years, both states had rapid recoveries. Within a decade, however, the two countries were on separate paths.

The roots of Germany's "economic miracle," ironically, go back to the 1930s, when the Nazis invested heavily in communications, chemicals and metallurgy, and vehicle manufacture. Much of its economic infrastructure, including many of its manufacturers and banks, survived the war. The destruction that did occur allowed the Germans to build from scratch, constructing new, more efficient factories. Britain, which had less damage, had an older industrial core. Relative to Germany, it was declining *before* World War II, and after 1945 Britain continued its pre-war policies of under-investment, limited research and development, and low-risk, low-reward business strategies. It also emerged from war heavily in debt, had higher defense expenditures, and, through the 1960s, supported several colonies in the developing world. The famed British economic John Maynard Keynes observed during the war itself

> If by some sad geographical slip the American Air Force (it is now too late to hope for much from the enemy) were to destroy every factory on the North East coast and in Lancashire (at an hour when the Directors were sitting there and no one else) we should have nothing to fear. How else are we to regain the exuberant inexperience which is necessary, it seems, for success, I cannot surmise.[21]

Similar arguments can be made with respect to labor relations.[22] The British trade unions, which survived the war, were strong players in the economy, eventually becoming a burden on the economy as their resistance to change and insistence upon full employment at any price hampered economic growth. In the 1970s, when the government advanced tepid reform plans, the unions wielded the strike weapon and created multiple political crises. In contrast, the West German trade unions, while strong in membership, were essentially new creations, lacking the institutional ability to flex their muscles independently in the post–war period. Instead, the key aspect to Germany's social market economy was cooperation among the state, employers, and workers, with workers agreeing to be less militant and to hold down wages (thereby freeing up funds for investment) in return for steady employment. The fact that West Germany was also willing to import cheaper labor—from southern Italy, Turkey, and Yugoslavia—also helped keep German companies more competitive.

Government policies also differed. The Germans, as had been the case in the late 1800s, developed close and productive ties between private business and the state, which helped guarantee favorable loans for businesses and supplied much of the capital for investment and research. The high value of the Deutschmark meant that imported raw materials were relatively cheap. Even though German exports were costly, they quickly developed a reputation for quality that allowed them to compete extremely well in global markets. In contrast, British companies did not enjoy positive state patronage in terms of access to needed capital. Instead, political pressures often forced them to build plants and distribution centers in uneconomic parts of the country in order to appease local politicians and unions. Whereas state ownership of business was far more prevalent in Britain than in Germany, the British economy remained far less planned than elsewhere in Europe. This was not necessarily a good thing, as the economy lacked any sort of strategic ambition. For example, while German car companies—Volkswagen, BMW, and Mercedes—became world champions thanks in part to pragmatic state policy, the British car companies, which had been dominant in Europe in the early 1950s, collapsed, with the remains of the last independent British car maker, British Leyland, purchased by . . . BMW.

Why this discussion of "ancient history?" First, the German success (in addition to that in France, Italy, Scandinavia, and elsewhere) points to the fact that "big government" can work. Indeed, the recovery in post-war Europe was attributable in large part to an activist state. Secondly, this history helps explain the condition of both Britain and Germany today. Ironically, however, today their roles are reversed. As we'll see in Chapter 10, Britain's decline fueled the rise of Margaret Thatcher, whose tenure in office (1979–1990) witnessed the unraveling of Britain's collectivist consensus and the introduction of a more free-market approach. Because of Germany's success, there was no such reform impulse. By the 1990s, chronic double-digit unemployment and sluggish growth had made Germany's "economic miracle" seem, indeed, like ancient history. Pushing through reforms, however, has proven to be extremely difficult, thanks in part to the power of German unions and their unwillingness to abandon a system that has served their interests for so long. Those familiar with British experience might ask: could Chancellor Angela Merkel, first elected in 2005, be Germany's Thatcher?

Critical Thinking Questions

1. What lessons (if any) does the West German "economic miracle" have for contemporary Europe and the US?
2. What lessons (if any) does the successful consolidation of democracy in West Germany have for efforts to construct democracy in countries such as Iraq and Afghanistan?

included nationalization of industries, an interventionist industrial policy, state promotion of exports, and economic programs that set national goals and techniques of production.[18] In Italy, pre-existing ties between the state and businesses were revitalized, with the state providing credits to priority sectors and (less productively) favored clients. In Britain, state takeover of many economic enterprises (e.g., transport, utilities, mining) was at the heart of the program of the Labour Party, which defeated Churchill's Conservatives in elections in 1945. In West Germany, there was little state ownership and explicit planning, but the state did play a role as mediator between workers and employers to ensure economic stability. As noted in the **In Focus** section, the result was an economic "miracle."

TABLE 2.3

Economic Growth in Post-War Western Europe

Country	Average Annual Growth Rates				
	1950–1958	1958–1966	1966–1973	1973–1980	1980–1990
Austria	6.1	4.4	4.9	2.5	2.1
Belgium	2.4	4.3	4.8	2.3	1.6
Denmark	2.3	4.9	3.2	1.0	1.7
Finland	4.0	5.0	5.1	2.2	2.9
France	4.2	5.3	4.9	2.2	2.1
West Germany	8.7	5.3	3.9	1.8	2.0
Great Britain	1.8	3.1	2.9	0.9	2.4
Greece	6.7	6.9	7.7	3.0	1.4
Ireland	0.8	3.3	5.0	4.3	3.4
Italy	6.1	5.7	4.6	3.1	2.0
Netherlands	3.8	4.8	4.9	2.1	1.9
Spain	5.4	7.3	7.1	3.3	3.0
Sweden	2.7	4.3	3.3	1.5	1.8
Switzerland	3.8	5.0	3.8	0.3	1.8

Source: Data are Total GDP converted at Purchasing Power Parity (PPP). Taken from Groningen Growth and Development Centre at http://www.ggdc.net, accessed on 10 June 2007.

European economies began to rebound quickly.[23] Growth rates in the 1950s and 1960s—the so-called post-war "Golden Age"—exceeded those in the US. Data are presented in Table 2.3 and in Figure 2.1. As one can see, growth rates remained impressive in most states into the 1960s, producing, as seen in Figure 2.1, a steep increase in *per capita* GDP (gross domestic product) by 1973. Moreover, even with various economic crises and the decline in average growth in the 1970s and 1980s, West Europeans in 1990 were still markedly richer on a *per capita* basis than in 1973. The best performers were West Germany as well as poorer states such as Greece and Spain, which started from a lower base. Economic growth, in addition to providing a better quality of life for citizens—flush toilets, refrigerators, color television, automobiles and washing machines were the norm for a growing middle class—also contributed to the preservation of democratic systems of government.

welfare state ■ a feature of Western Europe after World War II that featured government provisions for free health care and education, state-provided pensions, unemployment insurance, subsidized housing, and other goods; paid for by higher taxes, but often supported by parties both on the right and left.

Finally, one should mention one other component of the socio-economic system that developed in post-war Western Europe: an extensive **welfare state**. The recognition in the post-war years that the state would have to take a leading role to ensure public health and provide support to the infirm, aged, and orphaned spurred the creation of new government programs, such as Britain's National Health Service, established in 1948. The state thus played a role in the economy not only to facilitate growth but also, in the words of John Maynard Keynes, to satisfy the "craving for social and personal security."[24] As the historian Tony Judt observed, many believed the state could foster "social cohesion, moral sustenance and cultural vitality.[25]

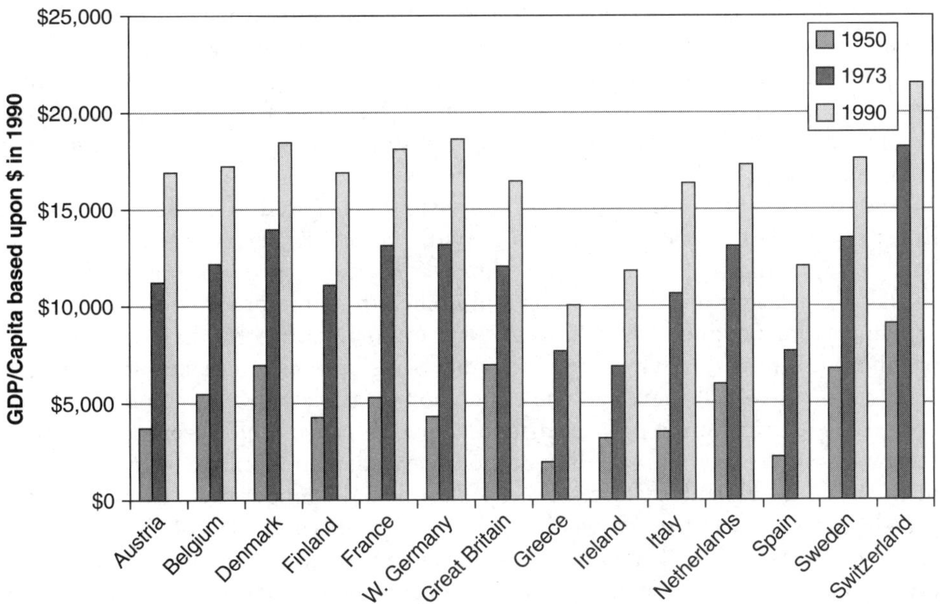

FIGURE 2.1
GDP/Capita in Post–war Western Europe.
Source: Data are GDP/Capita based upon 1990 dollars at Purchasing Power Parity. Taken from Groningen Growth and Development Centre at http://www.ggdc.net, accessed on 10 June 2007.

The welfare state encompassed many policies, including free health care and education, subsidized housing, state-provided pensions, generous vacation allowances, unemployment insurance, and daycare and maternity leave. State spending rose in each successive decade from the 1950s to the 1990s, reaching by the late 1980s more than 50 percent of the total GDP in Sweden, the Netherlands, France, and Italy. In order to pay for it, marginal tax rates were set high (often over 80 percent), which meant that many elements of the welfare state helped redistribute income from the rich to the middle class and poor. As a result, inequality declined in Western Europe.

The welfare state had an ideological edge, with growing parties on the Left typically advocating more extensive social welfare programs. However, even Winston Churchill, hardly a socialist, conceded that "there is no firmer investment for any community than putting milk into babies."[26] In Britain, a so-called collectivist consensus between Labour and the Conservatives oversaw construction of a generous welfare state throughout the 1950s and 1960s. Speaking of the British case, one writer noted that

> British capitalism has been compelled, by the sheer pressure of the British people, acting through our effective democratic institutions, to do what we used to say it would never, by definition, do; it has been forced to devote its productive resources to raising the standard of life of the population as a whole.[27]

In West Germany, the social-market economy, which saw a pronounced redistributive role for the state, was developed under center-right Christian

Democratic governments. France's statist economic system was furthered by de Gaulle, ostensibly a right-wing political figure. Parties on the Right in Austria, Belgium, the Netherlands, Norway, Italy, and elsewhere championed welfare policies. Bargaining among the government, business associations, and trade unions often provided the underpinning for state policy. Few parties advocated *laissez-faire* capitalism.

What were the consequences of this system? As noted in Table 2.3, Western Europe saw high levels of economic growth, especially before 1973. While it is hard to argue that the welfare state "caused" economic growth, one could point to rising education levels and better public health as factors that contributed to growing labor productivity. Although Britain, as noted in the In Focus section, began to fall into relative stagnation, numerous studies confirmed through the 1970s a positive link between the expansion of the state sector and economic growth.[28] Redistributive policies also cut poverty rates, which were far lower in most parts of Western Europe than in the US. Sweden and Finland, which had two of the most developed welfare states—ruling Social Democratic parties tolerated private ownership but taxed wealth very heavily—became two of the wealthiest countries in the world, a remarkable achievement for countries that as recently as the 1930s were undeveloped by Western European standards.[29] Aside from the bottom line, Europeans would point to quality of life issues (e.g., leisure time, cleaner and well-planned cities, social cohesion) to argue for the superiority of the European social model.

In many respects, then, post-war Western Europe was a success story. Most countries in the region had stable democratic governments and were generating respectable figures in terms of economic growth. By the 1970s, however, in several countries growth began to decline. While this did not threaten democracy, it did lead some to call for overhauling aspects of the socio-economic model and the welfare state. These challenges—which continue through today—are reserved for later discussion in Chapter 10.

EASTERN EUROPEAN DEVELOPMENT

The political history of Eastern Europe, as we shall see, differs in many ways from that of Western Europe. Whereas Western Europe has built upon centuries of political and economic development, particularly the emergence of democracy and capitalism, Eastern Europe, in many ways, has in recent years tried to overcome its more troubled past in order to establish institutions and policies similar to those in Western Europe.

Eastern Europe as a Land of Empires

Whereas, similar to Western Europe, several independent kingdoms appeared in Eastern Europe in the medieval period, in the more modern period, as seen in Figure 2.2, much of the region was encompassed by larger empires, political structures that grouped together a variety of nations or peoples in which one nation or group tended to have political dominance. These were empires of the Germans (Prussians), Russians, Turks (Ottomans), and Austria-Hungary (Habsburgs). These empires controlled much of the region until the end of World War I.

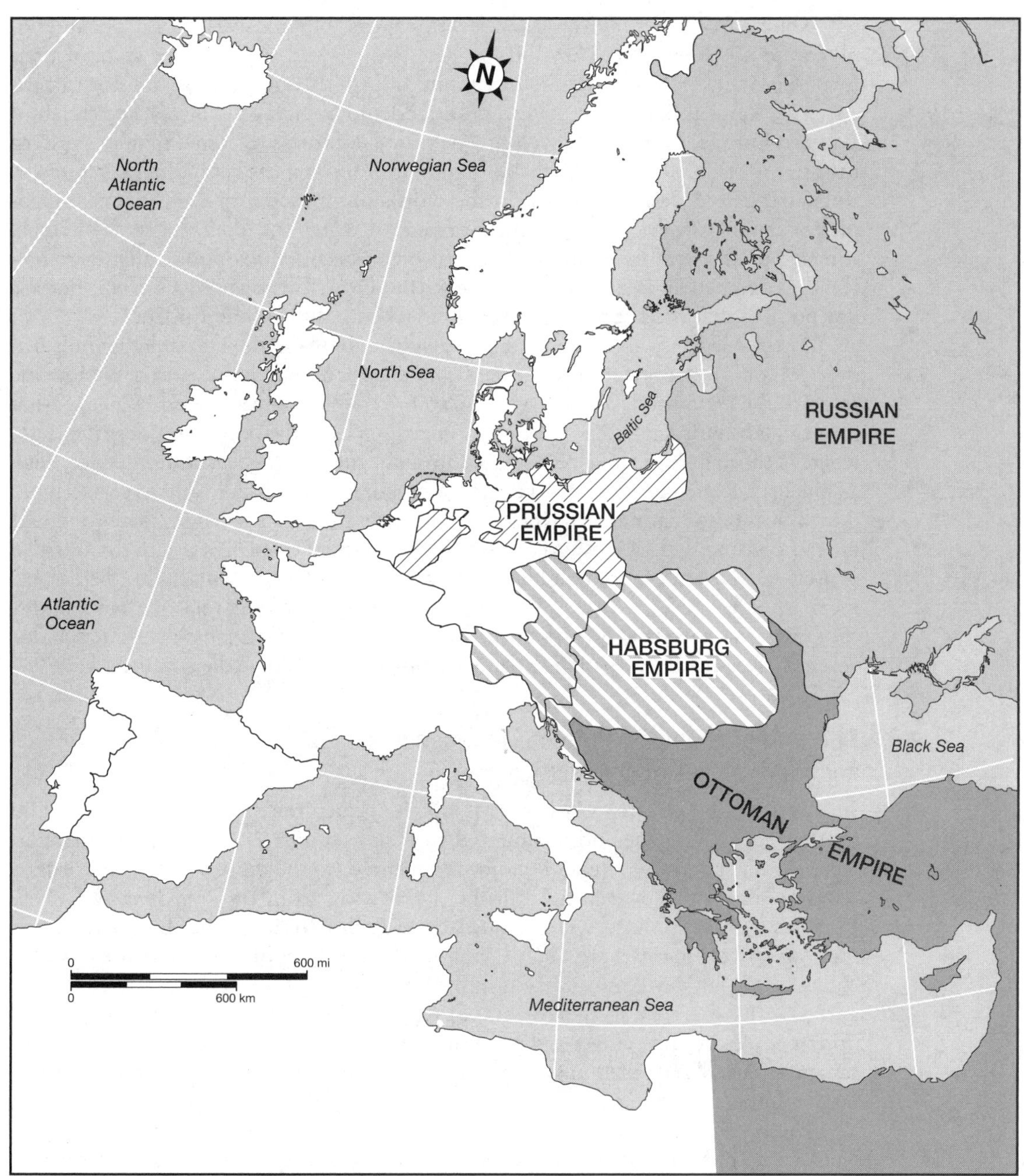

FIGURE 2.2
Eastern Europe in 1825.

Being part of an empire meant several things. Obviously, East European peoples were not sovereign. They did not rule themselves. They had no state of their own. Civil and political rights were limited. Eastern Europe thus did not experience the political liberalization and gradual democratization that marked much of Western Europe. Economic development was also far less dynamic than in Western Europe. Most of the people in the region were poor peasants. Illiteracy rates in some areas exceeded 90 percent. In the words of one scholar, East European peoples became "hewers of wood and drawers of water for alien masters."[30] True, some empires, in terms of political repression and economic opportunity, were better (e.g., the Habsburgs) than others (e.g., the Ottomans or the Russians), but the key point is that the peoples of the region lacked political independence.

Imperial legacies arguably matter today. In a simple sense, it mattered who ruled over you. It is no accident, many would contend, that the most advanced, democratic states in the region today—such as the Czech Republic, Slovenia, and Hungary—are former Habsburg lands that were economically more advanced over a century ago, whereas those that experienced longer Ottoman rule and/or Russian influence, such as Bulgaria, Romania, and Albania, are both poorer economically and have had more difficulties consolidating effective democratic governments. In Poland, there were vast differences among the Habsburg, Russian, and German ruled areas, with the German regions far more urbanized and industrialized, especially compared with the eastern regions controlled by Russia.[31] Poles will sometimes even note that one can still discern differences in their own political culture among a "Germanic" west and Baltic coast, a "Russified" east, and the former Habsburg lands of Galicia in the south.

The End of Empires, Political Independence, and the Failures of Democracy

That would change after World War I, which marked the defeat and collapse of all four empires. With the end of imperial rule, new countries (e.g., Czechoslovakia) were formed and others (e.g., Poland) reappeared on the map. The watchwords in redesigning post–World War I Europe, borrowing from US President Woodrow Wilson's Fourteen Points, were democracy and self-determination. Democratic systems of government were established with the help of the victorious Allies. Significantly, however, not every group of people was given its own state: Czechs and Slovaks shared Czechoslovakia; Slovenes, Croats, Serbs, Macedonians, and other peoples became citizens of the Kingdom of Serbs, Croats, and Slovenes (later renamed Yugoslavia, meaning "land of the Southern Slavs"). Many states also had large numbers of ethnic minorities, including Jews, who had no state of their own.

The hopes that some had for the region were, for the most part, not realized. Democracy did not take root, save in Czechoslovakia. In general, democratic governments lacked stability and a strong sense of legitimacy from the populace and they could not solve challenging socio-economic issues. More controversially, one might suggest that the peoples of the region—poorly educated, with little tradition of self-rule or tolerance and often holding grievances against ethnic minorities or other states—did not possess a democratic political culture. Democratic governments fell to military coups in several states, including Poland, Bulgaria, and Lithuania. In Yugoslavia, tensions among Serbs, Croats, and other nationalities—

dramatically leading to the assassination of Croatian leaders on the floor of the national parliament—led the king to disband the Yugoslav parliament and establish a royal dictatorship in 1929. The king of Romania declared himself royal dictator in 1938. In several states, pro-fascist movements, taking inspiration from Italy and Germany, challenged democracy and whipped up animosity toward Jews and other minorities. Only in Czechoslovakia, blessed by higher levels of economic development and led by Westernized intellectuals Tomas Masaryk and Eduard Benes, did democracy survive, even though within the country Slovaks complained of discrimination and arrogance from the more numerous and better-off Czechs.

World War II and the Communist Takeover

On top of the domestic challenges, there were also international tensions in the region. The peace treaties of World War I did not create homogeneous nation-states, meaning that political borders did not correspond with ethnic or cultural borders. The desire to redraw the borders thus became great rallying cries in "revisionist" states such as Hungary and Bulgaria, not to mention Germany, where grievances against the Treaty of Versailles contributed to the rise of Hitler.

World War II started in Eastern Europe. In 1938, Germany occupied part of Czechoslovakia, eventually taking over much of the country by early 1939. That fall, Germany and the Soviet Union attacked and dismembered Poland, which led Britain and France to declare war on Germany. In 1941, Germany attacked the Soviet Union, and much of the fighting in World War II occurred along the Eastern Front. Germany found some allies (e.g., Hungary and Bulgaria) in the region. Most of the Holocaust's infamous death camps—such as Auschwitz, Treblinka, Belzec, and Majdanek—were in Poland. Of the 6 million Jews killed in the Holocaust, half were Polish citizens. Most of the others also came from Eastern Europe.[32] The memory of the Holocaust is an important—and at times highly charged—issue in the region, and only after the fall of communism have some states looked closely at what happened and the role of their own citizens in this genocide. During World War II, Yugoslavia was also engulfed in a three-way civil war among Nazi-backed Croats, Serbs, and communist fighters.

The war was far more devastating in Eastern Europe than in Western Europe. Poland lost 6 million people, a fifth of its population; more than a million perished in Yugoslavia; Romania lost half a million soldiers and civilians combined; the Soviet Union lost up to 20 million people to fighting, disease, and death camps. Economic losses were also staggering:[33]

While there was some homegrown resistance against the Germans, most of Eastern Europe was "liberated" by the Soviet Union. Despite promises made in the Yalta Agreement of February 1945 to the Americans and British to hold "free and unfettered elections," the Soviets did not allow democracy to take root in the countries and regions they occupied.[34] Non-communist politicians were harassed, often driven from the country. Secret police forces were established to root out "unreliable elements." Communist parties "won" rigged elections. The communist economic system was established. By the end of the 1940s, Germany was divided into two countries, mirroring the political division of Europe between a democratic, capitalist West and a communist East.

COMMUNISM IN EASTERN EUROPE 1945–1989

Communism lasted in Eastern Europe for more than forty years. Most of the region adopted the Soviet model of communism and remained allied with the Soviet Union. The major exceptions to this pattern were in Yugoslavia and Albania, where local communist leaders—Jozef Tito and Enver Hoxha—prevailed in their wartime conflicts and imposed their own versions of communism upon their states. Some East Europeans may have supported communism because of its promises of a better life and social equality—appealing given the region's recent past history—but the imposition of communism owed more to Soviet force than popular demand. Vladimir Tismaneanu reflected that

> The new structures erected on the ruins of those smashed and increasingly atomized societies had to be carbon copies of the Soviet ones: rubber-stamp parliaments, communist control over all spheres of life, establishment of concentration camps for the extermination of politically unreliable elements, and the institution of a command economy, where private property was virtually eliminated and replaced by state ownership of all resources.[35]

Those who dissented risked loss of a job, imprisonment, even death.

Communism transformed Eastern Europe. The economic priority was industrialization, which meant that new factories and cities were constructed. Literacy became near universal as these states experienced socio-economic modernization. Living standards for many went up, as there was substantial economic growth in the 1950s and 1960s.[36]

This is not to say that communism was a paradise. It was not. Political freedoms were virtually non-existent. Farmers were pushed off their land into collective farms. Living conditions for many workers were squalid. Consumer goods were in short supply, and people had to wait years to obtain an apartment, car, or goods such as a washing machine. Despite promises to overtake the Western model, communism never did. East European economies never acquired a reputation for making quality products (as did West Germany, for example), were cut off from most of the world, and were not driven by consumer demand. For a relatively advanced economy like that of Czechoslovakia, the results were particularly dire. Whereas in 1938 Czechoslovakia's standard of living was comparable to that of Belgium and higher than in Austria or Italy, by 1960 Czechoslovakia had not only fallen behind all of these states but was poorer than in had been in 1938.[37]

When given a change, there were efforts to reform and/or escape from communism. These occurred in Hungary in 1956, Czechoslovakia in 1968, and Poland in 1980 and 1981. The first two reform efforts were crushed by Soviet invasion. The last, given inspiration by the Catholic Church and Pope John Paul II, formerly a bishop in Poland, and spearheaded by the independent trade union Solidarity, ended with a declaration of martial law by the Polish government. Many tried to leave communist Eastern Europe; more than a hundred were killed trying to get over, around or under the Berlin Wall, which was built in 1961. There were some brave individuals, labeled dissidents, who lived under communism and campaigned for human rights and freedoms. However, many of these people were jailed and seemed, at the time, to be politically marginalized.

THE END OF COMMUNISM

Despite a veneer of stability, Eastern European regimes were never fully secure. They failed to win widespread legitimacy. Economic problems made it clear that the regimes would never deliver on promises of a material paradise. Although most citizens did not face daily violence or coercion, most knew that they were not free and, thanks to the efforts of institutions such as American-supported Radio Free Europe, they knew that life in the West was better. Lastly, many citizens resented the presence of Soviet troops in their countries. It was not until 1989, however, that they were able to throw off the yoke of communism.

Why did communism collapse in 1989? Note the two parts of this question. The first part—communism's collapse—could be answered by invoking several of the factors mentioned above (e.g., low legitimacy, economic problems, repression). By focusing on these factors, one might conclude that the collapse of communism was simply inevitable. In retrospect, this might be true, yet few saw it coming, and it is important to remember that these factors had existed for years and communism survived.

By 1989, however, several factors converged that made the overthrow of communism possible. First, economic problems were becoming more acute, whether measured by overall growth rates or shortages of products. Average citizens and elites increasingly lost faith in the system. Corruption was increasingly a problem as well. However, this discontent had no sizeable outlet until the Soviet leader, Mikhail Gorbachev, began to encourage political and economic reform, both within the Soviet Union and in Eastern Europe. Gorbachev encouraged greater freedom of expression and economic experimentation, and, crucially, he did not send Soviet troops into the region to suppress reform efforts.

Gorbachev's reforms helped activate **civil society** within Eastern Europe.[38] By civil society, one refers to networks and associations of citizens that are independent of the state. Organizations in civil society campaigned for greater freedom and respect for human rights. Civil society did not seek to battle with authorities with violence. Rather, the point was to confront the regimes with moral claims and to develop an "alternative society" composed of those who rejected the official ideology and create new forms of media, culture, and informal educational institutions. Many were led by dissidents. Obvious examples would be Solidarity, "flying universities" (*ad hoc* lectures on political topics in private homes) and the Catholic Church in Poland, the Charter 77 citizens' initiative in Czechoslovakia, and human rights and environmental groups that emerged in the late 1980s in Hungary.

civil society ■ networks and associations of citizens that are independent of the state, argued by some to be instrumental in the collapse of communism and development of democracy in Eastern Europe.

The collapse of communist governments throughout the region occurred very quickly, within a matter of months in the second half of 1989. Poland was, in many respects, the leader, thanks to its well-formed civil society centered on Solidarity. With the economy in deep crisis, the government reached out to Solidarity and the Catholic Church in negotiations in February 1989. Lech Wałesa, the leader of Solidarity who had been placed under house arrest earlier in the decade, said he would be willing to talk to devil himself if it would save Poland. These negotiations led to elections in June of that year, in which the communists were decisively defeated. By September 1989, Poland had a new, non-communist

Solidarity Leader Lech Wałesa, a Key Figure in Communism's Collapse in Eastern Europe.

government led by Solidarity. In Hungary, talks between the government and opposition led to various reforms (including the opening of the border with Austria) and an agreement to hold new elections. In East Germany, protesters from religious, human rights, and environmental organizations, openly supporting Gorbachev when he visited East Berlin, put more and more pressure on the government. On November 9, 1989, a government spokesman—mistakenly it turned out—announced that citizens now had the freedom to travel and leave the country. That night, East Germans began to pour over and through the Berlin Wall, as East German border guards were confused about their orders and did not stop them. Within a year East Germany would cease to exist as a separate state. In Czechoslovakia, protests and strikes in late November 1989 led to the "Velvet Revolution"[39] and the installation of Václav Havel, a playwright and leading dissident who had been dismissed two months earlier as "morally insignificant" by the government, as president.[40] In Bulgaria, the government also agreed to new elections. Only in Romania, which suffered under perhaps the most brutal and megalomaniac dictator in the region, Nicolae Ceausescu, was there violence as government troops clashed with protesters in December 1989 and, after his fall from power and flight from the capital, Ceausescu and his wife were executed after a brief trial.

IS EUROPE ONE?

Bridging the Gap Between East and West Germany

The reunification of Germany in 1990 can be considered a microcosm for the idea of a single Europe. Borders were torn down as people, separated by political arrangements made after World War II, agreed to live in a common state. Democracy and capitalism spread eastward. The adjectives "West" and "East," it was assumed, would soon become a thing of the past.

Two decades later, the euphoria of reunification is long faded. Whereas the stark divide of the Cold War era is no more, some Germans refer to a continued "wall of the mind" between the *Ossis* (those in East Germany) and the *Wessis* (those in West Germany). One German politician suggested that, "We might be the first country which has, by unifying, created two peoples."[41]

Each side has a host of complaints to make about the other. From 1990 to 2007, West Germany gave some $2 trillion (about $30,000 for every West German) to the East to assist in the construction of new housing and infrastructure, social welfare, and environmental cleanup. No one expected the costs to be this high. Not only did West Germans see a tax increase, but the entire economy experienced a deep crisis in the 1990s because of the financial costs of reunification. Many areas of the former East Germany now have newer and better roads, rail terminals, hospitals, and airports than in the West. To the extent that economic performance of much of the former East Germany still lags behind West Germany, many West Germans wonder where their money has gone. The answer, according to many, is for generous social welfare programs for the "lazy," "unskilled," and—most gallingly—"ungrateful" *Ossis*. Shockingly, in 2004 a poll found that 24 percent of *Wessis* believe it would be better if the Berlin Wall was still up.[42]

Despite the money spent in the East, many *Ossis* feel shortchanged. The installation of capitalism in the former East Germany meant that many of the East German companies went bankrupt. The unemployment rate in the former East Germany hovers above 15 percent, twice that in West Germany. *Ossis* on average also receive about two-thirds the wages of *Wessis*. Many *Wessis* came to East and bought cheap property, and they are resented for their wealth and perceived arrogance. An idea (later scrapped) by one West German entrepreneur to build a theme park outside of Berlin that would "recreate" the East German experience—grey buildings, police watchtowers, bad food and service, tin-can East German cars, crumbling infrastructure, arbitrary "arrests" of patrons—was not well received by those who had actually lived under such conditions. Many East Germans report that they feel like second-class citizens and report feelings of *Ostalgie*, nostalgia for aspects of East Germany. True, one of their own—former physics professor Angela Merkel—became chancellor in 2005, but Merkel's ideas to cut subsidies for the East did not win her much support in her home region.

Public opinion polls reveal the gap that still exists between West and East. For example, Eurobarometers from 2005 to 2006 find that Easterners are more likely than Westerners to claim that they are dissatisfied with their lives, that the country is headed in the wrong direction, that more equality and justice is desirable even if restrictions have to be placed on freedom, and, overwhelmingly (65 percent versus 38 percent) that they are dissatisfied with the state of democracy in Germany. On balance, those in eastern Germany also express lower levels of trust in the government and in political parties.[43]

What are the political effects? The former East German communists, renamed first the Party of Democratic Socialism and now the *Linke* (Left) Party and anathema to mainstream German political parties, receives more than 20 percent of the vote in the former East Germany. Some East Germans are also turning to the far right. In the 1990s, "skinhead" attacks on ethnic Turks were a major cause for concern, and the 2000s far-right parties—which are inevitably compared to the Nazis—won seats in local and regional elections in parts of eastern Germany.

(*continued*)

With *Wessis* now arguing they need to pull back their support for the East—government subsidies to eastern Germany still account for 4 percent of total West German GDP—it is clear that regional divisions within Germany will be a festering problem.

The fate of Germany may be cautionary. One could fairly ask, if Germany is still not truly "reunited" twenty years after the fall of the Berlin Wall, how long will it be before one can speak of an undivided or single Europe?

Critical Thinking Questions

1. Who would you expect to be most nostalgic about the old East Germany? Why would they feel that way?
2. Should West Germans continue to transfer money to the East to make economic conditions in Germany more equal?

THE POST-COMMUNIST TRANSFORMATION

The collapse of communism in Eastern Europe in 1989 was a cause for massive celebration. With the end of Soviet domination and authoritarian rule, many hoped that the division of Europe would end and that East Europeans would quickly be able to overcome the communist past and enjoy democracy, peace, and prosperity. However, elation gave way to a hangover as people began to realize that the road ahead would not be easy. In some places, as noted in the **Is Europe One?** section on reunified Germany, there is even a nostalgia for the past as citizens of former communist countries have had trouble adjusting to a democratic, free-market system.

A prevailing issue in Eastern Europe since 1989 has been the transition from communist rule toward a more democratic polity and more market-based economic system. The challenges to this dual transition—creating democracy *and* a market—seemed formidable. There was no tried-and-true formula that states could adopt and no guarantee of success. As the decade unfolded, it became clear that states would pursue a different mix of policies and that there were reform leaders (e.g., Hungary, Estonia, Czech Republic, Slovenia), reform laggards (e.g., Romania, Slovakia), and states or regions engulfed by widespread violence (e.g., Croatia, Bosnia, Kosovo). By 2000, most states could claim success, meaning that democratic systems worked relatively well and that their economies had mostly recovered from an arduous reform period. By 2007, ten post-communist states had joined the EU and several more were clamoring for closer ties and eventual membership.

Establishing Democracy

Whether the states of Eastern Europe could establish stable, democratic governments in the wake of communism's collapse was a major question in the region for much of the 1990s. Whereas there was widespread support for creation of democratic governments, there were concerns that the transition to democracy would not be easy. Few of the states had prior success with democracy. Economic dislocations in movement to capitalism would be severe. The specter of nationalism could reemerge and thwart political liberalization. The international environment was uncertain. Ralf Dahrendorf suggested that the most challenging part of the transition would be the "hour of the citizen,"[44] which would take more time to develop than new political and economic institutions. Some alarmists feared that over a generation of communist rule had created a "Leninist" political culture among both elites and masses that did not possess the levels of public trust and tolerance and willingness to compromise necessary for democratic politics.[45] President Havel, speaking to fellow Czechoslovaks in 1990, lamented that "the worst enemy" of reform was "our own bad qualities—indifference to public affairs, conceit, ambition, selfishness, the pursuit of personal advancement and rivalry."[46]

Ultimately, most states succeeded in building democratic systems. Elections were held, and many parties ran, offering voters a genuine choice. Most parties ran on platforms to preserve civil and political freedoms, and many explicitly looked to Western Europe as a positive example. In several states, such as Poland, Estonia, Czechoslovakia, and Hungary, voters immediately embraced anti-communist parties rooted in the dissident movement. These states became leaders in the reform process. New constitutions were adopted or previous ones were amended to guarantee democratic freedoms. A lively, if at times low-quality, media developed. Public opinion surveys found publics in most states thought having democracy was good, and support for non-democratic alternatives—military rule, a dictatorship, a return to communism—was low throughout most of East-Central Europe, especially among Slovenes, Czechs, and Hungarians.[47] Post-communist publics were not always enamored with their governments, but rather than turn to non-democratic actors, they voted out incumbents when given a chance. This was the pattern in a number of states, including Poland, Hungary, Lithuania, and Bulgaria.

Western assistance to post-communist Europe was also substantial. From 1989 to 1995, Western countries pledged $86 billion to assist post-communist Europe, and the largest donor was the European Union.[48] Both NATO and EU expansion was undertaken with the idea of supporting and encouraging democratization. Non-governmental actors in Western Europe (e.g., universities, businesses, women's groups, human rights groups) also invested and partnered with actors in Eastern Europe to encourage political, economic, and broader social change.

This is not to say there were no problems along the way. Establishing an independent and capable judiciary was one of the top challenges, as well as developing a civil society supportive of democratic institutions. Nationalist politicians in a number of countries, taking advantage of economic uncertainty and making various historical claims, tried to stoke conflict by making claims against minorities and/or other states.[49] With the exception of the former Yugoslavia, however, this did not lead to widespread violence or derail the democratization project. Czechoslovakia did split up, peacefully, into two countries (the Czech Republic and Slovakia) in 1993, and some states, such as Romania and Slovakia, led by former communist parties or by leaders who presided over corrupt, nationalistic governments, remained "reluctant democratizers" throughout much of the 1990s. In many of these states, the EU and other international organizations played a positive role, offering material incentives for reforms, monitoring the environment (in particular with regard to media and minority rights), and strengthening the hand of minorities and opposition parties against political incumbents that were ambivalent or hostile to reforms.[50] Table 2.4 reports "freedom scores" for several states in the region in the 1990s, reflecting the different pace of reform. These data, compiled by Freedom House, judge states based upon political rights (PR) and civic liberties (CL) on a scale from one to seven, with one being the most free. These data allow us to classify states as leaders or laggards, although one can see that over time, thanks in large part to international encouragement as well as an improving economic environment some of the laggards have managed to catch up to the "leaders."

TABLE 2.4

Freedom House Scores for Selected Post-Communist States

Country	1989		1991		1993		1995		1999		2005	
	PR	CL	PR	CL	PR	CL	PR	CL	PR	CL	PR	CL
Poland	4	3	2	2	2	2	1	2	1	2	1	1
Hungary	4	3	2	2	1	2	1	2	1	2	1	1
Czechoslovakia/Czech Republic	6	6	2	2	1	2	1	2	1	2	1	1
Slovakia	n/a	n/a	n/a	n/a	3	4	2	3	1	2	1	1
Bulgaria	7	7	2	3	2	2	2	2	2	3	1	2
Romania	7	7	5	5	4	4	4	3	2	2	2	2
Yugoslavia/Serbia and Montenegro	5	4	6	5	6	6	6	6	5	5	3	2
Croatia	n/a	n/a	3	4	4	4	4	4	4	4	2	2
Albania	7	7	4	4	2	4	3	4	4	5	3	3
Estonia	n/a	n/a	2	3	3	2	2	2	1	2	1	1
Latvia	n/a	n/a	2	3	3	3	2	2	1	2	1	1
Russia/Soviet Union	6	5	4	4	3	4	3	4	4	5	6	5

Source: Freedom House, at http://www.freedomhouse.org, or see Freedom House's annual publication, *Nations in Transit.*

One is tempted to suggest, in fact, that by the 2000s political life in most of East Central Europe had become "normal." True, there were some interesting developments:[51] the election of twin brothers as President and Prime Minister of Poland in 2005; the inability of Czech parties to form a government for half a year after 2006 elections; and the return of Bulgarian Tsar (King) Simeon II, who served as Prime Minister from 2001 to 2005 and became the first monarch in history to ever be elected head of government in democratic elections. However, the main political patterns are similar to what you would find in Western Europe: a social democratic left that was progressively becoming further and further removed from the communist past, a conservative right that was either tied to the Church or a free-market ideology, a liberal—in the European sense—center, and a few extremists haunting the political margins and winning the votes of the disaffected. But the big debates and questions—Will post-communist states become democratic? Can economic and political reform be dome simultaneously? Will they make enough progress to join the EU?—have been resolved.

Establishing Capitalism

In addition to creating democratic political systems, post-communist leaders in Eastern Europe also faced the task of creating a new economic system, one that would not be state-directed but instead rely upon free markets, entrepreneurship, and private property. There was no blueprint for dismantling the communist economic system, and, more so than on the issue of democratization, the pace and scope of economic reform generated great controversy.[52]

The reason for this is that economic reform would be painful. Guarantees created by the old system (e.g., state-determined prices, subsidies for enterprises) would be taken away. Freeing prices would mean inflation. Taking away state subsidies and direction would create chaos and possibly bankrupt many enterprises. Some of the communist welfare state would also be dismantled. Many individuals would be, in the short term at least, "losers" during the transition. Living standards would decline, and many individuals would feel far less economically secure in the free-market system.

The precise mix of reforms varied from country to country. Poland, eager to shed its communist past, launched "**shock therapy**" economic reforms designed to make a rapid break with the past. The political rationale for shock therapy was that publics might become frustrated with economic reforms and vote to undo reforms created the impression among many reformers that political reality meant that they only had a limited amount of time to reform. Better then, in this view, to do as much as possible.

shock therapy ■ name for economic reform programs in post-communist Europe that emphasized a rapid move from communism to capitalism.

Other states, such as Hungary and Romania, undertook more gradual reforms. Advocates of gradualism sought to minimize the pain of reforms. Moving too fast, they thought, would be too costly. Moreover, by moving slower, one could wait until one set of reforms was consolidated and then move on to another reform, creating less chaos. Whereas the recognized the risks of lengthening the reform period, their position was that the fragile democracies in the region could not survive the "shock" of shock therapy.

In all cases, however, economic reform entailed taking the state out of the economy and allowing the market to function. This meant freeing prices, allowing private business and ownership of land, fostering competition, encouraging foreign investment, ending state planning and letting individual producers make economic decisions, and, most controversially of all, privatizing enterprises owned by the state by either selling them at auction, distributing shares of companies to their workers and managers, or giving all citizens vouchers with which they could buy shares of companies on newly formed stock markets, all to make a rapid break with the communist system.

privatization ■ process by which state-owned enterprises in Eastern Europe were sold or otherwise transferred to private individuals; it was often controversial as it produced inequality and was subject to corruption.

Each type of **privatization** had its pluses and minuses (e.g., vouchers were more "democratic" but, unlike auctions, did not raise money for the state) and this issue was one of the most controversial of all, as individuals and groups made various political, economic, and even moral claims to obtain economically valuable assets. There was no single model of privatization. The Czechs were famous for their vouchers, which seemed like an effective strategy until revelations of corruption were brought to light in 1997. The Poles, given the heritage of Solidarity, preferred management-employee buyouts, which was a very protracted process and ultimately left many Polish workers unhappy. The Hungarians sold off their enterprises—often to foreigners—which allowed them to generate more revenue but left many wondering who in the end benefited from the process. Ultimately, by whatever strategy and whether it was done quickly or slowly, most of the state's assets were privatized. Throughout the region, however, ordinary workers expressed frustration with the outcome, and few felt that privatization had delivered on its promises.[53]

What were the results? Certainly, as seen in Table 2.5, there was pain: inflation, unemployment, economic decline. The retreat of the state and the nebulous legal environment meant corruption flourished. Inequality increased. Some—younger, better-skilled workers—fared well, and many of these individuals found jobs in the newly expanding service economy or with international companies. Others, especially older workers in blue-collar jobs, fared far less well, as their factories shut down and they lacked skills to find work in the new economy. "Losers" protested against government policy, which, in the cases of Romania in 1991, Poland in 1993, and Bulgaria in 1997, helped bring about the collapse of governments.

As seen in Table 2.5, there is evidence to suggest that the "shock therapy" approach in those states that reformed more rapidly such as Poland and the Czech Republic, was a superior strategy, as these states saw growth by the mid-1990s. Anders Aslund, who advised several governments in the region, argues that the record conclusively shows that those who were slower to adopt reforms or moved more gradually (e.g., Romania, Bulgaria, and, further east, Ukraine and Russia) did worse.[54] The World Bank, assessing the experience in the region, argues that focusing solely on the speed or sequence of reforms ignores other factors (e.g., initial starting points, country-specific variables) that also matter. The general picture is that a commitment to reforms is key and that reforms needed to build momentum to begin to produce positive results. Vacillating between one course or another or adopting only partial reforms (as occurred early on in Romania and Bulgaria or later in Russia) was not the recipe for success.[55]

TABLE 2.5

Results of Economic Reforms in Post-Communist Europe

Country	Avg. Annual Inflation, 1990–1996, %	Avg. Unemployment, 1990–1996, %	First Year of Economic Growth	Real GDP 2000 (1990 = 100)	Private Sector Share of GDP, 1999	Foreign Investment, 1991–1998, $ *per capita*	GDP/*Capita*, 2005, Atlas Method, $
Poland	116.3	13.2	1992	144	65	386	7,160
Czech Republic	30.9	2.9	1994	99	80	995	11,220
Hungary	25.7	9.9	1994	109	80	1,666	10,070
Romania	121.4	8.1	1993	82	60	215	3,910
Bulgaria	115.5	11.5	1994	81	60	n/a	3,450
Estonia	47.4*	4.1*	1995	85	75	1279	9,060
Lithuania	136.5*	5.4*	1994	67	65	n/a	7,210
Slovenia	64.0	12.5	1993	120	55	n/a	17,440

Source: World Bank, *Transition: The First Ten Years* (Washington: The World Bank, 2002), and online data from http://www.worldbank.org, United Nations Conference on Trade and Development (UNCTAD), on-line at http://www.unctad.org, Austrian National Bank (Osterreichische Nationalbank), *Focus on Transition*, no, 1, 1997, available at htp://www.oenb.at.

*Data available only from 1993–1996.

Regardless, as the case with democratization, the laggards did catch up. By the mid-1990s, most states could claim the "worst" was over. Return to the communist past was politically and practically impossible. Shops in cities such as Prague, Budapest, and Riga were full of all sorts of goods, including luxury products. New factories of all sorts were being built. Slovakia, for example, on a *per capita* basis had by 2010 the most autoworkers in the world. Although in terms of *per capita* income post-communist Europe still lags behind Western Europe, growth rates in the mid-2000s approaching 10 percent a year in countries such as Slovakia, Estonia, and Latvia would make the average German or Italian quite jealous. Some, as noted in Chapter 10, even suggested that Eastern Europe, economically speaking, had important lessons to offer for Western Europe.

This is not to say all is fine. As seen in Table 2.5, some countries, such as Albania and Bosnia, remain quite poor by European standards. Unemployment is still a major problem, ranging from about 6 percent in more successful states such as Slovenia and Hungary to more than 17 percent in Poland and Slovakia to over 37 percent in Macedonia.[56] The gap between the capital cities and the countryside is very pronounced in most states, with thousands migrating to the cities in search of work, even at low wages. The economic crisis of 2007 to 2010 also hit the region hard, a topic covered more in-depth in Chapter 10.

THE TRAGEDY OF YUGOSLAVIA

While nobody would claim the post-communist transition was easy in East Central Europe, the worst-case scenarios were largely averted. The great exception, of course, was the former Yugoslavia, whose constituent parts and peoples became embroiled in several wars, resulting in over 200,000 deaths, some 2 million refugees, and, on a continent where most thought such things could never happen again, genocide.

Explaining the Breakup of Yugoslavia

In retrospect, such a development does not seem entirely surprising. As seen in Table 2.6, Yugoslavia was an amalgam of seven main different national groups representing three religions who, prior to 1919, had never before lived in a single country. Levels of economic development varied widely—with Slovenia and Croatia far more advanced than Kosovo or Macedonia. Most republics had sizeable numbers of ethnic minorities (e.g., Serbs in Croatia, Albanians in Serbia and in Macedonia). To top it all off, many of the groups had histories of conflict with the other, and many in each national group felt that the idea of a "South Slav" union denied their own nationality its right to self-determination. Jozef Tito, the communist leader, managed to keep a lid on potential conflicts, but after his death in 1980, economic decline and nationalist politicians—chief among them the Serb leader Slobodan Milošević—began to pull Yugoslavia apart. Warren Zimmerman, the last American ambassador to Yugoslavia, argues that

> The breakup of Yugoslavia is a classic example of nationalism from the top down—a manipulated nationalism in a region where peace has historically

TABLE 2.6

Ethnic Composition of Yugoslavia

Ethnic Group	Main Religious Affiliation	Population	% of national total	% of total in Bosnia*
Serbs	Orthodox	8,140,000	36.3	37
Croats	Catholic	4,428,000	19.8	20
Muslims**	Islam	2,000,000	8.9	40
Slovenes	Catholic	1,754,000	7.8	n/a
Albanians	Islam	1,730,000	7.7	n/a
Macedonians	Orthodox	1,340,000	6.0	n/a
"Yugoslavs"	Mixed	1,219,000	5.4	n/a
Montenegrins	Orthodox	579,000	2.6	n/a
Hungarians	Catholic	427,000	1.9	n/a

*Full name is Bosnia and Herzegovnia
**This category refers to ethnic Slavs who speak Serbo-Croatian, not Albanians, Turks, or Roma.

Source: 1981 Census Data (last full census in Yugoslavia, presented in Denitch, *Ethnic Nationalism: The Tragic Death of Yugoslavia* (Minneapolis: University of Minnesota Press, 1996), pp. 29, 234.

prevailed more than war and in which a quarter of the population were in [ethnically] mixed marriages. The manipulators condoned and even provoked ethnic violence in order to engender animosities that could then be magnified by the press, leading to further violence.[57]

The End of Yugoslavia

After Tito's death, rumblings of discontent and manifestations of nationalism emerged in Yugoslavia. The first activity was in Kosovo, a region within Serbia that is considered the birthplace of the Serbian people but by the 1980s had a population that was 90 percent ethnically Albanian. As Albanians began to mobilize to assert their rights, Serbs responded with their own claims, including a memorandum in 1986 published by the Serbian Academy of Sciences that referred to a "genocide" occurring against Serbs in Kosovo. Milošević seized upon this idea, and employed authoritarian methods to strip Kosovo of its autonomy. Other national groups became nervous about Milošević and the possibility that he would try to create a "Greater Serbia."[58] When Yugoslavia held regional elections in 1990—a result in part of the wave of reform that occurred elsewhere in the region in 1989—nationalist politicians fared well. Fearing both Serb nationalism and tired of subsidizing poorer regions of the country, many Slovenes and Croats clamored for independence. Efforts to save federal Yugoslavia—both internally and internationally—failed. US Secretary of State James Baker famously declared that "we have no dog in this fight."[59] The final straws were the declaration of independence in June 1991 by the Slovenian and Croatian legislatures, moves that were widely supported within both republics—with the obvious exception of the ethnic Serb communities in Croatia.

War and "Ethnic Cleansing"

The breakup of Yugoslavia led to violence. Slovenia, where there were few ethnic Serbs, fought a brief ten-day war and secured its independence. In Croatia, where there were areas with Serb majorities, local Serbs declared themselves separate from Croatia and were supported by the Serb-dominated Yugoslav National Army. Serbs seized control of large areas of Croatia and shelled cities such as Dubrovnik, Vukovar, and the Croatian capital, Zagreb. In early 1992 UN peacekeepers were sent to enforce a ceasefire.

The worst fighting, however, occurred in Bosnia-Herzegovina (hereafter Bosnia), which was the most heterogeneous of all the regions of Yugoslavia and had territory claimed by both Serbs and Croats. The main division among the three groups in Bosnia (Bosnian Muslims [or Bosniacs], Serbs, and Croats) was religion, but it is perhaps worth mentioning that the Muslims in Bosnia had to rank as among the most secular of all Muslims in the world. In January 1992, Serbs in Bosnia proclaimed their own Republic of the Serb People. On March 24, 1992, Milošević and the Croatian leader Franjo Tudjman, ostensibly enemies, met and agreed to divide up Bosnia.[60]

Although one could foresee that Bosnia would be engulfed by fighting, international peacekeepers did not arrive, making the claim in 1991 by Jacques Poos, Luxembourg's Foreign Minister, that Yugoslavia would be "Europe's hour," utterly fatuous.[61] As had occurred in Croatia, local Serb forces mobilized and drove non-Serbs—mainly Muslims—from their homes in what would be euphemistically called "**ethnic cleansing.**" Ethnic Croats did the same, and by the end of 1992 Muslims controlled only a small percentage of Bosnia's territory. Efforts to negotiate a peace agreement led nowhere, and the bleeding wound of Bosnia—a six-hour drive from Vienna or Venice—created a moral crisis for Western governments. In the summer of 1992, images of Muslims in Serb "concentration camps" were transmitted on television, invoking memories of Auschwitz and prompting many to label the violence a genocide and call for international intervention. Sarajevo, the multi-ethnic Bosnian capital, was put under siege and its residents targeted by snipers.[62] As noted at the outset of this chapter, the worst single massacre during the war occurred in Srebrenica, where 8,000 unarmed Bosnian men were killed by Serb forces. This event so shocked the world that at last NATO was compelled to do something.

ethnic cleansing ■ euphemism used to refer to ethnic-based violence which occurred in the former Yugoslavia, including the massacre of civilians in Srebrenica in 1995.

The conflict in Bosnia came to an end after NATO began bombing Serb positions. In November 1995, US President Bill Clinton managed to get Milošević, Tudjman, and Bosnian President Alija Izetbegović to come to Dayton, Ohio to negotiate and finally sign a peace agreement. The Dayton Accord put a NATO-led force of over 40,000 international peacekeepers into Bosnia and Croatia, and agreed to create a single Bosnian state with two "entities"—a Muslim-Croat Federation and the *Republika Srpska* (Serb Republic). It also required all governments to cooperate in the hunt for war criminals, allow refugees to return to their homes, and it set up a means for international financial assistance for rebuilding in both Croatia and Bosnia.

The Fighting in Kosovo

The next major conflict was in Kosovo, where the process of Yugoslavia's breakup started in the 1980s. Interestingly, while fighting raged in Bosnia, Kosovo was tranquil, in large part because the leader of the Kosovar Albanians, Ibrahim Rugova, an admirer of Gandhi, believed that Albanians should follow for both moral and practical reasons a strategy of non-violent resistance against the more powerful Serbs. Rugova was pointedly *not* invited to Dayton, however, leading many Kosovar Albanians to question his approach. By 1997, insurgents in the Kosovo Liberation Army (KLA), supported by some of their co-ethnics in Albania proper, emerged to attack Serbs in Kosovo. In reprisal, Serbs began to attack Kosovar civilians.

In March 1999, NATO began a bombing campaign against Serb positions both in Kosovo and in Serbia itself. This action lacked authorization from the United Nations and aroused great international controversy. Tens of thousands of refugees fled to Macedonia and Albania, and a large-scale humanitarian crisis loomed. After six weeks of bombing, which inflicted heavy damage in Serbia and produced at minimum hundreds (Serbs claimed several thousand) of civilian casualties, Milošević agreed to pull out of Kosovo, which became a UN protectorate and was occupied by 50,000 peacekeepers. Since the conflict, international administrators have overseen reconstruction efforts, helped conduct elections, and prevented conflict, although Serbs—perhaps 5 percent of the population—claim that they have been the targets of violence from Albanians.

Endgame: Milošević's Defeat

The final denouement of the conflict, however, occurred in Serbia itself. Opposition to Milošević had been growing throughout the 1990s, not only because he championed an aggressive foreign policy but also because the conflict and international sanctions were devastating to the economy. Corruption thrived, whereas the average Serbs were hit hard by an unemployment rate of over 50 percent and inflation that topped 5,000,000,000,000,000 percent (that is *not* a typo) between October 1993 and January 1995.[63] In October 2000, many believed that opposition leader Vojislav Kostunica defeated Milošević in Serbian presidential elections, prompting widespread protests when it was clear the government falsified voting returns. Facing massive civil unrest, Milošević resigned, and in March 2001, after an armed stand-off, he was arrested by Serbian police on a corruption charge and subsequently turned over to international authorities to stand trial for war crimes. His trial began in 2002, but he died in his prison cell in March 2006, before the court could render a verdict.

Within Serbia in the 2000s, there has been intermittent progress toward a more liberal democracy, even as Montenegro, the one Yugoslav republic that remained united with Serbia, declared independence in 2006 and Kosovo declared independence in 2008. Taking action to purge the military and government of those who were parties to war crimes and allowed corruption to flourish has been a major challenge for post-Milošević Serbian governments. A pro-Western prime minister was assassinated in March 2003 by rogue policeman with ties to nationalist groups, and nationalist parties continue to do well at the polls. Serbia's apology on Srebrenica, noted at the outset of this chapter, was thus a major development that was welcomed in Europe and the broader international community, albeit one that generated great debate within Serbia itself as some nationalist groups refuse to own up to the war crimes committed in the name of Serbian nationalism in the 1990s. The Balkans thus remain a flashpoint for potential conflict and a major concern of the EU. More recent developments in the region are taken up in Chapter 11.

APPLICATION QUESTIONS

1. Why did Europe, as opposed to another region of the world, rise to global pre-eminence? Does this early history make Europe unique and therefore make it less likely that ideas such as democracy and limited government, which developed in Europe, can take root elsewhere?
2. Most Americans would claim that they are patriotic or nationalistic. Most would argue that these are positive traits. How can one explain why some countries have more positive manifestations of nationalism and others—particularly in Eastern Europe—tend to have more negative ones? Do you think globalization and economic integration will allow Europe or other parts of the world to "overcome" nationalism?
3. Given widespread belief today in the superiority of free and open markets, what relevance does the post–war success of statist welfare policies have today?
4. How specifically might the legacy of empire matter for countries in Eastern Europe today? Are there still important political, social, or cultural differences that make this region somehow less "European"? Given the different historical experiences of peoples of Europe, what is your understanding of the term, "European"?
5. Why do you think the international community did not act preemptively to prevent conflict in Bosnia? What do the atrocities there show about the idea of "Europe"?

KEY TERMS

capitalism 33
civic nationalism 28
civil society 47
democracy 29
ethnic cleansing 58
ethnic nationalism 28
Marshall Plan 35
nation 28
nationalism 28
privatization 54
shock therapy 53
social contract 30
sovereignty 27
state 26
welfare state 40

ADDITIONAL READING

Davies, Norman, 1998. *Europe: A History*. New York: HarperCollins.

An account of Europe from its prehistory to modern times, with most of the focus on the twentieth century. Extremely lengthy (more than 1,000 pages long), but a very handy reference work.

Judt, Tony. 2005. *Postwar; A History of Europe Since 1945*. New York: Penguin.

An encyclopedic account of developments in both Western and Eastern Europe since World War II. Judt's work covers both major political and economic developments as well as social history and popular culture. Judt is particularly useful on the issue of the development of the welfare state.

Mason, David S. 2005. *Revolutionary Europe 1789–1989: Liberty, Equality, Solidarity*. Lanham MD: Rowman and Littlefield.

Examines intellectual and ideological trends in Europe since the French Revolution, including nationalism, fascism, communism, and liberalism.

Schopflin. George. 1993. *Politics in Eastern Europe*. Oxford: Blackwell.

A relatively short treatment of the region, focusing on developments since 1945 as well as the revolutions of 1989.

Tilly, Charles. 2004. *Contention and Democracy in Europe, 1650–2000*. Cambridge: Cambridge University Press.

A major scholarly work that examines how states and democratic governance arose in Europe. One of its major themes is that social conflict, including outbreaks of internal and inter-state violence, has been an important force for political development in Europe.

END NOTES

1. Some disputed whether the atrocities in the region, especially in Bosnia, amounted to genocide. A premier source on this issue is Samantha Power, *A Problem from Hell: America and the Age of Genocide* (New York: Basic Books, 2002), Chapters 9 and 11. In 2006, the International Criminal Tribunal for the former Yugoslavia concluded that genocide did occur in Bosnia, at least during the 2005 Srebrenica massacre, but in 2007 the International Court of Justice ruled that the state of Serbia and Montenegro, while failing to prevent genocide, could not held accountable for it.
2. For commentary on this event, see Tim Judah, "Serbia's Honest Apology," *New York Times*, April 2, 2010.
3. Charles Tilly, "Reflections on the History of European State-Making," in Charles Tilly, ed., *The Formation of National States in Western Europe* (Princeton: Princeton University Press, 1975), p. 42.
4. See Paul Kennedy, *The Rise and Fall of the Great Powers* (New York: Random House, 1987), and Charles Tilly, *Contention and Democracy in Europe, 1650–2000* (Cambridge: Cambridge University Press, 2004).
5. For an excellent collection of works on nationalism, see Anthony Smith and John Hutchinson, eds., *Nationalism* (Oxford: Oxford University Press, 1995).
6. Quoted in Liah Greenfeld, *Nationalism: Five Roads to Modernity* (Cambridge: Harvard University Press, 1992), p. 276.
7. Daniele Caramani, *The Nationalization of Politics: The Formation of National Electorates and Party Systems* (Cambridge: Cambridge University Press, 2004).
8. Ernest Gellner, *Nations and Nationalism* (Ithaca: Cornell University Press, 1983), and Benedict Anderson, *Imagined Communities: Reflections on the Origin and Spread of Nationalism* (London: Verso, 1991).
9. The classic source is Barrington Moore, *Social Origins of Dictatorship and Democracy* (Boston: Beacon Press, 1966).
10. For general works on this topic, see Roy Porter, *The Enlightenment* (New York: Palgrave, 2001), and Dorinda Outram, ed. *The Enlightenment* (Cambridge: Cambridge University Press, 1995).
11. David Mason, *Revolutionary Europe 1789–1989: Liberty, Equality, Solidarity* (Lanham MD: Rowman and Littlefield, 2005), p. 21.
12. Tilly, *Contention and Democracy in Europe*, pp. 34–41. His analogy is that democracy is like a lake, which can form in a limited number of contrasting ways. It is not, in his view, like an oil field (unique to very special conditions) or a garden (which can be cultivated by anyone with the proper skill).
13. Dietrich Rueschmeyer, Evelyne Huber Stephens, and John Stephens, *Capitalist Development and Democracy* (Cambridge: Polity Press, 1992) and Tilly, *Contention and Democracy in Europe*.
14. For more on the British case, see Robert Allen, *The British Industrial Revolution in Global Perspective* (Cambridge: Cambridge University Press, 2009).
15. Roman Szporluk, *Communism and Nationalism: Karl Marx versus Friedrich List* (Oxford: Oxford University Press, 1991).
16. Mark Mazower, *The Dark Continent: Europe's Twentieth Century* (London: Penguin, 1998).
17. Tony Judt, *Postwar: A History of Europe Since 1945* (New York: Penguin, 2005), p. 63.
18. Peter Hall, *Governing the Economy: The Politics of State Intervention in Britain and France* (Cambridge: Polity Press, 1986), Chapter 6.
19. This account draws heavily from Judt, *Postwar,* pp. 354–359.
20. Judt, *Postwar,* p. 360.
21. Judt, *Postwar,* p. 358.
22. Mancur Olson, *The Rise and Decline of Nations* (New Haven: Yale University Press, 1982)
23. Barry Eichengreen, ed. *Europe's Postwar Recovery* (Cambridge: Cambridge University Press, 2003).
24. Quoted in Judt, *Postwar*, p. 73.
25. Judt, *Postwar*, p. 361.
26. Quoted in Judt, *Postwar*, p. 538.
27. Alan Warde, *Consensus and Beyond* (Manchester: Manchester University Press, 1982), p. 26.
28. See Hall, *Governing the Economy*, pp. 29–30.
29. Judt, *Postwar*, pp. 364–367.
30. Robin Okey, *The Demise of Communist East Europe: 1989 in Context*, (Oxford: Oxford University Press, 2005), p. 4.
31. David Turnock, *The Economy of East Central Europe 1815–1989* (London: Routledge, 2006), p. 76, 88.
32. Interestingly, even though Bulgaria was allied with Germany, it did not surrender its Jews to Hitler and the SS. One wonders how the fate of Jews would have been different if other states did not

cave in to Hitler's demands to turn over their Jews for annihilation.

33. Tony Judt, *Postwar*, pp. 18–19. For comparison, Poland lost 20 percent of its pre-war population; Germany lost only one-fifteenth and France one in seventy-seven.
34. When Roosevelt told Stalin he wanted the Polish election to be pure like Caesar's wife, Stalin responded, "They said that about her but in fact she had her sins." Charles Bohlen, *Witness to History*, quoted in Gale Stokes, ed. *From Stalinism to Pluralism: A Documentary History of Eastern Europe Since 1945*, 2nd edition (Oxford: Oxford University Press, 1996), p. 23.
35. Vladimir Tismaneanu, *Reinventing Politics: Eastern Europe from Stalin to Havel* (New York: Free Press, 1992), p. 24.
36. See data in J.F. Brown, *Eastern Europe and Communist Rule* (Durham: Duke University Press, 1988), pp. 504–505.
37. Judt, *Postwar*, pp. 171–172.
38. Excellent treatment of civil society in the region can be found in Tismaneanu, *Reinventing Politics*, Chapters 4 to 6.
39. The exact derivation of the term is disputed. Many allege that it arose because the important meetings of the Czechoslovak opposition occurred in the Magic Lantern Theater in Prague, which has velvet curtains and carpeting. Others contend that the name simply implies softness and non-violence. Indeed, in Slovak the event is simply known as the "Gentle Revolution."
40. Quoted in Stokes, *From Stalinism to Pluralism*, p. 154.
41. Wolfgang Nowak, a former minister in the government of Saxony (region in formerly East Germany) in "Getting back together is so hard," *The Economist*, September 18, 2004, p. 58.
42. "Getting back together is so hard."
43. Data from Eurobarometers 64, 65, 66, from 2005–2006, available online at http://ec.europa.eu/public_opinion/index_en.htm.
44. Ralf Dahrendorf, *Reflections on the Revolution in Europe* (London: Verso, 1990).
45. Vladimir Tismaneanu, *Fantasies of Salvation: Democracy, Nationalism, and Myth in Post-Communist Europe* (Princeton: Princeton University Press, 1998), and Ken Jowitt, *New World Disorder: The Leninist Extinction* (Berkeley: University of California Press, 1992).
46. Valcav Havel, "New Year's Day, 1990," in Stokes, *From Stalinism to Pluralism*, p. 252.
47. According to the 1999 World Values Survey, over 70 percent of those in Hungary, Poland, Romania, Estonia, and Slovenia thought having democracy was a good thing. Serbia and Croatia ranked as primary exceptions, and further to the east in Russia and Ukraine non-democratic attitudes were more prevalent. Online analysis from http://www.worldvaluessurvey.org. For more on public opinion in the region, see Richard Rose, *Understanding Post-Communist Transformation: A Bottom Up Approach* (London: Routledge, 2009).
48. Okey, *The Demise of Communist East Europe*, p. 181.
49. For example, in Romania, the government courted the support of openly anti-Semitic, anti-Hungarian, and anti-Roma forces, some of which openly expressed admiration for both communist dictator Nicolae Ceaucescu and the World War II fascist leader Ion Antonescu. In Hungary, Ivan Csurka, vice-chair of the Hungarian Democratic Forum, wrote in 1992 about the need for Hungarians—implicitly referring to Hungarian minorities in Slovakia and Romania—to create their own "*Lebensraum*," a term most famously associated with the Nazis.
50. Paul Kubicek, ed. *The European Union and Democratization* (London: Routledge, 2003), and Milada Vachudova, *Europe Undivided: Democracy, Leverage, and European Integration* (Oxford: Oxford University Press, 2005).
51. Many of these fears stem from the rise of "populism," an admitted nebulous term, in the region. See collections of articles devoted to this topic in *Journal of Democracy* 18:4, October 2007, and *Problems of Post-Communism* 55:3, May/June 2008.
52. Excellent sources on the economic reforms in the region are The World Bank, *World Development Report 1996: From Plan to Market* (Oxford: Oxford University Press, 1996); Anders Aslund, *Building Capitalism: The Transformation of the Former Soviet Bloc* (Cambridge: Cambridge University Press, 2002); and The World Bank, *Transition: The First Ten Years* (Washington: World Bank, 2002)
53. Paul Kubicek, *Organized Labor in Postcommunist States* (Pittsburgh: University of Pittsburgh Press, 2004).
54. Anders Aslund, "The Advantages of Radical Reform," *Journal of Democracy* 12:4, October 2001, pp. 42–48.

55. World Bank, *Transition*, p. 16.
56. Data from the World Bank, online at http://www.worldbank.org.
57. Warren Zimmerman, "Origins of a Catastrophe," *Foreign Affairs* 74:2, March–April 1995, p. 12. See also Bogdan Denitch, *Ethnic Nationalism: The Tragic Death of Yugoslavia* (Minneapolis: University of Minnesota Press, 1996).
58. Good books on Kosovo are Julie Mertus, *Kosovo: How Myths and Truths Started a War* (Berkeley: University of California Press, 1999), and Tim Judah, *Kosovo: War and Revenge* (New Haven: Yale University Press, 2002).
59. Quoted in Richard Holbrooke, *To End a War* (New York: Random House, 1998), p. 27.
60. Misha Glenny, *The Balkans: Nationalism, War, and the Great Powers* (New York: Penguin, 2001), p. 633.
61. Quoted in Noel Malcolm, "The Case Against Europe," *Foreign Affairs*, 74:2, March/April 1995, p. 68.
62. For accounts, see Zlata Filipovic, *Zlata's Diary: A Child's Life in Sarajevo* (New York: Penguin, 1995), and Tom Gjelten, *Sarajevo Daily: A City and Its Newspaper Under Siege* (New York: Harper, 1997).
63. James Lyon, "Yugoslavia's Hyperinflation, 1993–1994: A Social History," *East European Politics and Societies* 10(2), Spring 1996: 293–327.

Irish get a second chance to vote for the Lisbon Treaty.

CHAPTER 3

The Development of the European Union

For most Europeans, October 2, 2009 was just a typical Friday, but it proved to be exceptional in Ireland and in the history of European integration. On that day, by a margin of two-to-one, Irish voters approved the Lisbon Treaty, a major reform effort that promised a stronger and more efficient EU. Ireland was the only country in which voters' consent was necessary. The treaty's approval, however, was far from a foregone conclusion, as a majority of Irish voters had rejected it an earlier vote in June 2008. The Irish veto of the Lisbon Treaty subsequently prevented its adoption by the EU as a whole, and it made many in Europe worry about whether European integration could continue to move forward. In a heated campaign prior to the second vote, as seen in the photo opposite, the Irish were pressed by their European partners as well as their own government to give their blessing to the treaty, which they duly did. This vote removed a major hurdle for the Lisbon Treaty, which came into force on December 1, 2009. The Lisbon Treaty makes a number of reforms in the EU, including the creation of posts of a *de facto* president and foreign minister of "Europe."

The Lisbon Treaty, however, is only the most recent of a series of treaties in the history of the EU. As suggested in the opening chapter, the idea of a single Europe may be best embodied in the EU, an organization that includes twenty-seven European countries—with further expansion possible—committed to the goals of economic, political, and social integration of the continent. Created after World War II with a limited mandate and perhaps idealistic aspirations, the EU has grown in scope, taking on paramount importance across Europe. Today, discussion of every major political issue in Europe has some dimension that includes the EU, which makes it difficult to examine European politics by exclusively focusing on institutions or issues within individual states.

Despite its significance, the EU is not always well understood or appreciated. Former US Secretary of State Madeline Albright said that one must be "a genius or French" to decipher its workings,[1] and even the French no doubt have problems comprehending its Byzantine-like bureaucracy and myriad of rules and regulations. Entire courses could easily be taught just on the EU or on some of its policies. Our task is far more modest. This chapter will cover the historical development of the EU, providing a building block for the subsequent chapter that examines the institutional structure and some of the most crucial functions carried out by the EU.

WHAT IS THE EUROPEAN UNION?

Before jumping into the origins of today's EU, a good starting point might be to define what the EU is and how it differs both from national states and from other international organizations. Although the EU has its own flag, anthem (Beethoven's "Ode to Joy"), holiday ("Europe Day" on May 9), motto ("Unity in Diversity"),[2] laws, regulations, and governing structures, the EU is not a single state, as is France or Germany. It is an organization made up of national states. As of 2011, it has twenty-seven members and twenty-three official languages.[3] While these states are said to have "pooled" their authority or sovereignty together in the EU, they are free to leave it at any time. The EU exists, in a basic sense, only because its members allow it to function. It thus has, unlike states that establish their own control and sovereignty over a territory, no life of its own. Viewed in this light, the EU is not that much different from other international organizations, and its actions can be understood as policies that conform to the interests of states. Such a perspective is known as **inter-governmentalism,** which stresses the powers of the member states within the EU.

inter-governmentalism ■ view of European integration that argues that the guiding force behind integration is the interest and power of individual nation-states.

Yet, one can clearly see that the EU is not just another international organization. Not only does it cover a wide number of issues (e.g., trade, social policy, environment, security), but it also offers to those who reside within its borders rights as citizens, all of whom carry an EU passport. It taxes its member-states to give it financial means. It has its own military force and issues its own currency, both competencies that traditionally have been the sole prerogative of nation-states. Most importantly, it possesses power above that of member-states. In other words, on a host of issues enumerated in EU treaties and legislation, it has sovereign authority so that its decisions trump those of national governments. The UN Security Council can make a decision and demand that members accede to UN demands, but enforcement is sporadic at best, and five major states (the US, Russia, China, Great Britain, and France) have a veto on the UN Security Council, so the UN cannot compel them to do anything. In contrast, on most issues in the EU, no state has a veto, there is a court to arbitrate disputes and enforce decisions, and states are required to adopt EU laws and directives into their national law. The UN has no such equivalent. This aspect of the EU—the power that it has above that of its member-states—is referred to as **supranationalism,** and the goal of those who want to see a stronger EU is to strengthen its supranational elements.

supranationalism ■ view of European integration that emphasizes the powers the EU has gained over nation-states so that it can compel them to act in certain ways.

There is, of course, a tension between inter-governmentalism, which emphasizes the interests, rights, and powers of states, and supranationalism, which essentially wants to take power away from states and invest the EU with greater authority. This tension has played itself out historically, with the two perspectives ascendant at different times, and in the institutional make-up of the EU, which includes elements of both. Over time, the EU has become more and more supranational, although it is still far from the point where one could talk about the irrelevance of nation-states in Europe. The EU does matter as an independent institution—it now has *de facto* a life of its own—but individual countries in Europe continue to matter as well. At present, one might best think of the EU as something in between a federal government such as the US or Canada and an international organization, with its final stage of development still unknown.

What is the EU designed to do? The key term here is **integration.** Integration is not merely cooperation, which occurs all the time in the international arena. Integration suggests something wider than an agreement on a limited set of issues (e.g., arms control). Rather, it refers to a process of sustained and institutionalized interaction among states and social actors that fosters a harmonization of policies. Integration requires institutional arrangements, and it implies as well that states pool their powers or sovereignty together in such a way to create a larger whole (the EU) out of the sum of its parts (member-states). One can imagine different levels of integration, such as moving from a free-trade zone to a common market to economic and monetary union. In less than fifty years, the EU has traversed this territory. One can also discuss different types of integration, such as economic, political, and social. Although there are a number of organizations in the world that may aspire to foster some level of integration (e.g., Arab League, Organization of American States), few have made much progress or have real powers. There are various regional trading blocs, such as the North American Free Trade Agreement (NAFTA), but none come close to the EU in the level of economic and political integration. Ultimately, the EU serves to create a common set of policies throughout Europe and promote "ever closer union" among its peoples

integration ■ sustained and institutionalized interaction among states and social actors that fosters a harmonization of policies; usually rests upon creation of an international organization such as the EU.

RATIONALE FOR EUROPEAN INTEGRATION

Why would one want to pursue European integration? Realist theory—which stresses the desire for states to maintain sovereignty—has some difficulties explaining it,[4] and, in broad historical perspective, European integration sounds like an idealistic, fanciful, perhaps impossible notion. Europe, after all, had been the scene of two horrific wars in the first half of the twentieth century, not to mention previous centuries of strife and warfare.

Political Goals

Yet, it was precisely those wars and the desire for peace that inspired post-war European leaders to search for new, pan-European solutions to Europe's problems. When Robert Schuman, the post-World War II French foreign minister considered one of the founding fathers of today's EU, first proposed a limited plan of economic integration, his stated goal was make future wars "not merely unthinkable but materially impossible."[5] The core idea was that by fostering economic **interdependence**—that is, strong ties among states so that they rely upon each other for their individual well-being—the need and incentive to go to war would be removed. If by destroying your enemy you also destroy the basis for your own livelihood, war becomes less desirable. As integration and interdependence take root, one could also argue that such sustained cooperation would weaken feelings of nationalism, which were viewed by many as the cause of World War II. The goal, which was truly ambitious and in some ways revolutionary, was to create a peaceful continent. Regardless of what one may think of the EU—and it has plenty of critics—there is little doubt that it has succeeded in attaining this over-arching goal. War today among Great Britain, France, Spain, and Germany—previously bitter rivals—is inconceivable.

interdependence ■ the idea that connections (e.g., political, economic, social) between countries make them dependent on each other; often attributed to globalization; many argue this has decreased the likelihood of war.

Economic Goals

Above and beyond creating a more peaceful Europe, proponents of integration would point to concrete economic benefits. Andrew Moravcsik argues that integration has been driven largely by the economic interests of states and social actors, not pure idealism.[6] The economic arguments in favor of integration are several. Free trade, which was the point of emphasis in the first decades of the European project, would allow states to specialize in areas where they had comparative advantage, and all states would benefit through the trade of more efficiently produced goods. Indeed, one could argue that much of the post–World War II recovery in Europe was trade-driven, and exports in all EU countries increased after economic integration began. By building a common market, the middle- and small-sized European states could also take advantage of economies of scale and pool resources and thus better compete economically with larger states like the US and Japan. Moreover, certain aspects of integration (e.g., the Common Agricultural Policy or CAP) were deemed essential to states to develop and support sectors of their national economies. For poorer member-states, EU development, cohesion, and regional funds have been important sources of revenue in national budgets.

Other Objectives

euro ■ common currency used by most members of the EU; came into being in the late 1990s.

With most aspects of the common market achieved by 1992 and monetary union launched with the common currency or **euro** (€), European integration is no longer just about economics. It has, as argued below, "spilled over" in a host of other concerns. Many transnational issues (e.g., pollution, crime, immigration, security) require international cooperation, and the EU has taken on responsibilities in these fields. European integration also allows Europe to pursue collective goals in foreign affairs, ranging from fostering democracy in neighboring states or deploying peacekeepers to troubled regions. Within Europe, as the EU has deepened its authority into new fields (e.g., social policy, education, good governance practices), some believe the EU can socially integrate Europe and help laggards in some fields meet higher standards. Some even see a united Europe as a means to balance US power or to present an alternative vision to American-style capitalism and its values.[7] In short, as idealistic as the EU may seem, one can fashion a realist-style argument that EU integration should be pursued so that European states can be more powerful than they would be on their own.

Arguments Against the European Union

Of course, European integration has numerous critics. "Euro-skeptics" point to a number of problems such as inefficient and costly EU bureaucracies, lack of openness and democracy, and the transfer of funds from richer states to poorer ones.[8] Certain EU policies foster passionate critiques. One core issue is that the EU requires states to surrender decision-making authority, and in turn the EU may make decisions that are unpopular with member-states and their publics. In other words, the EU has become too supranational for some, and its excessive rules and regulations worry those who want states (and voters) to have the freedom to pursue policies as they see fit. Whereas Euro-skeptics are traditionally more associated with states such as Great Britain and Denmark—states that notably do not use the euro—it was the rejection of the proposed EU Constitutional Treaty by French and Dutch voters in 2005 and Irish rejections of the Nice Treaty in 2001 and the Lisbon Treaty in 2008 that revealed that European publics may not have unlimited enthusiasm for the further EU deepening and expansion.

ORIGINS OF THE EUROPEAN COMMUNITY

The original idea for a united Europe goes back several centuries. The German philosopher Immanuel Kant (1724–1804) argued in *Perpetual Peace* for a confederation of European democratic states that would help secure peaceful international relations. Nineteenth-century communist leaders envisioned working-class revolutions that would do away with national states. After World War I, the idea of pan-European integration took on new life, with the French foreign minister Aristide Briand proposing a European Confederation of States and various British intellectuals supporting a European socialist confederation. World War II obviously obliterated any plans for European unity, but during the war anti-Fascist groups kept the dream of a united Europe alive.

Post-War Roots

The devastation of World War II convinced many that new political arrangements would have to take hold in Europe. Every country in Western Europe had some sort of federalist movement, and those favoring a united Europe found a prominent spokesman in British wartime leader Winston Churchill. In a famous speech delivered in Zurich in September 1946, he called on Europeans to replace "rivers of blood" with "a kind of United States of Europe" that would give people a "sense of enlarged patriotism and common citizenship."[9] This goal received the backing of the US, which was worried about the spread of Soviet influence and wanted West Germany reintegrated into Europe. Specifically, the US encouraged those states receiving Marshall Plan money to work together and embrace free trade, and various international bodies were put together to help with distribution of aid and reconstruction.

Immediately after the war, there were numerous efforts to promote European integration. In 1948, various organizations sponsored a Congress of Europe, which attracted over 1,200 political figures to discuss European unity. The Congress produced a number of recommendations, including a call for "economic and political union" as an "urgent duty." In 1949, the inter-governmental Council of Europe was created, which was essentially a consultative body, although it did create in 1950 a European Court of Human Rights, which has frequently been used by individuals to defend their rights against abusive governments. In 1952, a treaty was signed for a European Defence Community (EDC), which envisioned a pan-European security organization. It failed to take root, however, because the French National Assembly refused to ratify it, citing concerns about West German remilitarization and encroachments on French sovereignty.

Despite problems with more grandiose schemes for European unity, there was one success. In 1950, Jean Monnet and Robert Schuman, French officials, proposed a "High Authority" to integrate and oversee the development of French and German coal and steel industries, two key sectors for the military and for general economic development. Konrad Adenauer, chancellor of West Germany, accepted what is known as the Schuman Plan, which had been developed secretly and without British input. France and West Germany invited others to participate in this scheme. The result was the **European Coal and Steel Community** (**ECSC**), formed in 1951 and the precursor to today's EU.

European Coal and Steel Community (ECSC) ■ a precursor to today's EU; formed in 1951 among six countries, it was a supranational organization that integrated coal and steel production and distribution.

The ECSC was limited. It covered only two industries and had only six members—France, West Germany, Italy, Belgium, the Netherlands, and Luxembourg. Great Britain was invited to join, but, preferring to emphasize its relations with its colonies and with a history of wanting to remain apart from political ventures on the continent, it stayed out. Scandinavian countries also refused to join, and no offer was made to Spain or Portugal, which had nondemocratic governments at the time. Monnet, who assumed the leadership of the organization, wanted it to be a purely supranational and centralized organization with a High Authority (later called the Commission), assembly, and court, but, because states were unwilling to cede total authority to this new entity, an inter-governmental Council of Ministers was added as well. All of these institutions are found in today's EU.

The Formation of the European Economic Community

The ECSC's economic impact was limited, but its importance was in providing a "psychological space for Europe to move forward" and serving as a "political vehicle" to overcome French-German hostility and put European integration in motion.[10] Paul Henri-Spaak, the Belgian foreign minister, took the lead in organizing a conference in Messina 1955 to consider further integration. The result was the **Treaty of Rome**, signed in March 1957, which created the Euratom (which sought cooperation in the field of nuclear power) and the **European Economic Community (EEC)**.[11]

Treaty of Rome ■ signed in 1957, this expanded early integration efforts with the a goal of a common market and an "ever closer union" of European countries.

European Economic Community (EEC) ■ another earlier version of the EU, created in 1957, which was charged with lowering trade barriers and creating a common market for goods, labor, and capital.

The EEC joined together the members of the ECSC in a far more ambitious project. Its stated goal was creation of an "ever closer union" of European countries that would be realized in the first instance with a common market, in which goods, labor, services, and capital could move without hindrance across national borders. This was a momentous break with the past, which had been dominated by economic nationalism.

Reaching this goal would not be easy, and several stages were envisioned. First, states would have to lower trade barriers, eventually removing all barriers to trade in goods. The six countries would also form a customs union, meaning they would have a common trade policy vis-à-vis the rest of the world. Certain policies, such as a competition policy, freeing of internal markets, tax harmonization, coordination of state planning, and mutual recognition of product standards, would have to be in place to help ensure a level playing field among the actors. To protect agriculture, a major concern of the French, the EEC agreed to create the CAP, which would ensure a higher price for agricultural products. The emphasis was overwhelmingly on economic goals. The Treaty of Rome functioned largely as an "economic constitution," not one with explicit political elements.[12] However, the implications of the Treaty were clearly political. In the words of Spaak, "Those

TABLE 3.1

The Evolution of the European Union

Year	Event
1950	Schuman Plan for Franco-German integration
1951	Treaty of Paris forms the six-member ECSC
1957	Treaty of Rome establishes EEC
1966	Luxembourg Compromise allows national vetoes
1967	EEC, ECSC, and Euratom form European Community (EC)
1973	Great Britain, Demark, and Ireland join EC
1979	First direct elections for European Parliament
1981	Greece joins EC
1986	Spain and Portugal join EC
1986	Single European Act (SEA)
1992	Common Market created
1993	Maastricht Treaty approved by all members; EU formally created
1995	Austria, Finland, Sweden join EU
2002	Euro introduced in twelve countries
2003	Nice Treaty enters into force; EU Convention publishes draft Constitutional Treaty
2004	Cyprus, Czech Republic, Estonia, Hungary, Latvia, Lithuania, Malta, Poland, Slovakia, and Slovenia join EU
2005	EU Constitutional Treaty rejected in France and the Netherlands
2007	Bulgaria and Romania join EU
2009	Lisbon Treaty Ratified by All Member-States

who drew up the Rome Treaty . . . did not think of it as essentially economic; they thought of it as a stage on the road to political union."[13]

The Functional Approach

Why did economics predominate the early years of European integration? What theories can one employ to explain this process? Most discussions of European integration invoke the idea of **functionalism**, meaning that successful European integration would have to rest on functional, tangible goals and programs and not over-arching idealistic schemes. Schuman was clear about this, acknowledging that "Europe will not be made all at once, or according to a single, general plan. It will be built through concrete achievements, which first create a *de facto* solidarity."[14] Economic issues were more amenable to integration because states could find common ground, and they did not touch upon items like foreign policy or cultural issues seen to be the sole prerogative of states. In particular, one could argue that issues outside of view of the wider public—the technical elements of economic integration—would be less subject to nationalistic pressure. In short, it would be easier to begin with agreements on coal and steel than on war and peace. This notion is supported by the failure of the more ambitious and supranational EDC. Rather than creating a supranational body among Europeans, the American-led NATO alliance became the key structure for West European security.

functionalism ■ idea that integration would move slowly, step-by-step, based upon pragmatic, functional goals, not idealistic schemes.

Proponents of integration, however, did not intend to stop just with economic integration. From the beginning there was a political impulse, one designed to foster deeper political integration as well. The idea, known as **neo-functionalism,** was that economic integration would incrementally "spillover" into other issues.[15] In other words, as states drew closer together economically and began to integrate in certain areas, they would see greater need for integration in other areas. The logic of "spillover" would produce more and more integration. Monnet put the matter best.

neo-functionalism ■ idea that economic integration would build momentum and gradually "spillover" into political and other realms.

> Once nation-states and their leaders find themselves bound by rules, infringement of which will destroy common policies that are to their own advantage, these institutional bonds will serve not only to inhibit the occurrence of conflict, but also to mediate it if it does occur. Little by little this method of conducting policy in common will spread to all sectors of interstate relations until the members of the Community no longer deal with each other on a bilateral basis. At this point they will have become a federation just as the provinces of France were assembled in a national state at a moment favorable to a change in this status.[16]

Monnet's adherents—known as **federalists**—sought to expand the power of the institutions of the EEC and give them a more supranational orientation.

federalists ■ those who sought to expand the powers and supranational orientation of institutions of European integration.

This (neo-)functionalist perspective long dominated discussions of the EU, but it has been challenged by differing perspectives. Andrew Moravcsik grounds his explanation of EU development on liberal inter-governmental theory, stressing, as noted above, the economic interests of states and actors (e.g., business and labor groups) within states. The overlying notion is to focus on the interests and decisions of states, not on automatic processes of spillover or the role of technocratic elites within the EU to shape policy. The precise arrangements of the EU, in his view, are the result of bargaining among various actors with various amounts of power.[17]

Obstacles to Integration

After the signing of the Treaty of Rome, the federalists had trouble realizing even their more limited vision of a common market. Part of the problem was technocratic, meaning the sheer task of coordinating a myriad of economic policies was difficult. Politics, however, also entered into the picture, as states wanted to ensure that they were being treated fairly by the EEC and, more broadly, that the EEC served their interests. In this respect, Moravcsik's analysis is persuasive in pointing out how *states* held up or forwarded the progress of European integration, which did not automatically or magically occur.

The power of states—and their leaders—to slow down the process of integration was manifested most clearly during the rule of French President Charles de Gaulle (1958–1969). De Gaulle was in favor of European integration—as a means to contain Germany and counter American power—but only insofar as it served French interests. In particular, de Gaulle favored the CAP as a means for other European states to support French agriculture.[18] He twice vetoed a British bid to join the EEC, arguing it would disrupt the cohesion of the existing organization and lead to unwanted US influence. He also favored an inter-governmental approach—a "Europe of nation-states"—and vehemently objected to efforts by

EEC to acquire its own revenue and reduce national veto powers. In 1965, France boycotted the work of the EEC, paralyzing the organization. The result was the "Luxembourg Compromise" of 1966, which noted that the EEC would work for unanimity if "very important interests" were at stake, *de facto* preserving states' vetoes on matters they chose to view as "very important." De Gaulle, however, was not the only problem. By the 1970s, as many European economies began to slow and the world economy experienced oil and currency shocks, states looked to national, not European solutions. Integration stalled, and many began to speak of "Eurosclerosis."

Early Accomplishments

This is not to suggest that the Treaty of Rome was a failure. There were some notable accomplishments. In 1967, the ECSC, the EEC, and Euratom merged, forming the European Community (EC). By 1968, tariffs on industrial products were eliminated, and the EC formed a customs union for purposes of international trade. Intra-European trade increased dramatically. In 1970, the EC acquired its own independent source of revenue, secured from a portion of tariffs levied on non-EC goods and a portion of a value-added tax (a type of sales tax) employed by member states. In 1974, the EC established a Regional Development Fund, which was used to promote economic development in less well-off areas (e.g., southern Italy and Ireland, later Spain, Greece, and Portugal). In 1979, voters directly elected the European Parliament for the first time. In the 1970s the EC also took early steps toward monetary union by creating the European Exchange Rate Mechanism (later called the European Monetary System) to lower inflation and end dramatic currency fluctuations, both of which had become problems. Most significantly, perhaps, the EC expanded to more countries. First, after its two rebuffs by de Gaulle, Great Britain was admitted in 1973, taking the plunge on a larger, more supranational organization after spearheading the creation of the inter-governmental European Free Trade Association (EFTA) with Scandinavian states. Ireland and Denmark joined with Britain, and the British and the Danes would become prominent voices for more inter-governmentalism within the EC. Greece, Spain, and Portugal joined the 1980s once they had thrown off the shackles of authoritarian rule.

THE ROAD TO MAASTRICHT AND FORMATION OF THE EUROPEAN UNION

The first few decades of European integration included some notable accomplishments, namely that states that have once been bitter rivals decided to pool their sovereignty and cooperate on a host of issues. This very fact should not be underestimated. Progress on several key issues, however, did remain modest. The goal of a common market was not achieved. Inter-governmentalism remained the norm. Other issue areas, such as foreign policy and the environment, received only modest levels of attention at a pan-European level. For many, "Eurosclerosis" seemed to better describe the status of the EC than the vision of an "ever closer union" articulated in the Treaty of Rome.

By the end of the 1990s, however, the European integration project had new momentum. The Maastricht Treaty, signed in 1991, transformed the EC into the EU, and the EU assumed powers over a host of issues. The end of the Cold War opened up possibilities for further expansion and the unification of the continent. Many countries gave up their currency and adopted the euro. The vision of Monnet, Schuman, and other early advocates of European integration, which had looked utopian only a few decades before, looked closer and closer to being realized.

More Impetus for Integration

European integration gained renewed vigor in the late 1980s, thanks to the efforts of an unlikely duo: British Prime Minister Margaret Thatcher (1979–1990), who was suspicious of the EC as a socialist project, and the Frenchman Jacques Delors, a federalist and supranationalist *par excellence* who served as the head of the European Commission from 1985 to 1995.

Thatcher viewed the EC as ideologically suspect and hopelessly inefficient, and she launched many attacks on the EC, extracting concessions in 1984 on budgetary issues because of British "over-payments" to the EC budget. However, she did support open markets and competition. To the extent that the proposed and delayed common market would advance free markets on a European level, she was in favor of fulfilling the terms of the Treaty of Rome. The EU Commission under Jacques Delors agreed, stating that "Europe stands at the crossroads. We either go ahead—with resolution and determination—or we drop back into mediocrity."[19] The result was the **Single European Act (SEA)**, adopted in 1986. It contained a strict timetable to remove all trade barriers (e.g., non-tariff trade barriers, differential tax rates, lack of standard regulations) and create a common market by 1992. The common market would ensure not only free movement of goods, but also of capital (money for investment) and of people. Customs regulations essentially ended, border checks became minimal, and individuals living within the EC were free to reside, work, or study in any EC country.[20]

Single European Act (SEA) ■ adopted in 1986, it put forth a timetable to remove all barriers to trade and create a common market by 1992 and expanded the powers of the European Community to new areas, such as the environment.

The SEA contained other measures—expanding the role of the EC to areas such as the environment and research and development, adding powers to the European Parliament, and limiting use of national vetoes by introducing qualified majority voting—that were not to Thtacher's liking, but she agreed to it for the sake of forging a freer and common market. The SEA also mentioned the goal of monetary union, to which Thatcher vehemently objected, but she believed that it would never happen.[21] As noted below, it did, thanks in no small part to the efforts of Jacques Delors, who made creation of a single currency a top priority.

As if that were not enough, international events, namely the collapse of communism, opened up more opportunities for the EC. Delors, emphasizing his role as a "policy entrepreneur," suggested that Europe also move closer to political union, which would necessitate an expansion of EC power in a variety of fields. In 1990, Delors, backed by France and Germany, announced an Inter-Governmental Conference (IGC) on European Political Union, which had a broad mandate to suggest internal reforms and expansion of EC powers.

THE MAASTRICHT TREATY

The result was the Treaty on the European Union or, as it as better known, the **Maastricht Treaty,** so named because a draft version of it was approved in 1991 in Maastricht, a city in the Netherlands. This document ranks as important as the Treaty of Rome in the annals of European integration, perhaps even "one of the most important developments in world politics in the latter half of the twentieth century."[22] It made many changes. First, it formally created the European Union, a three-pillared organization that includes the old EC (the economic pillar), a pillar for a new Common Foreign and Security Policy (the so-called second pillar), and a third pillar on Justice and Home Affairs, which covers issues like immigration and criminal activity. Each pillar would have its own rules, with the latter two more inter-governmental in design.[23] Second, the treaty spelled out a timetable for monetary union and criteria under which states could join it. The Maastricht Treaty led to the birth of the euro. Third, the treaty established EU citizenship, which took on a physical manifestation with the distribution of EU passports.[24] Fourth, it made several institutional reforms: it strengthened the powers of the European Parliament; it gave the European Council an explicit agenda-setting role; it expanded the use of qualified majority-voting in the Council of the European Union; and it established a Committee of the Regions. All of these institutions are discussed in the next chapter. Lastly, within the EC pillar, the EU, as a neo-functionalist might have expected, expanded into new domains: education, culture, public health, infrastructure, labor market policy, and consumer protection.

Maastricht Treaty ■ signed in 1991, it formally created the EU and expanded the scope of European integration, including creation of the euro and a Common Foreign and Security Policy.

The Maastricht Treaty was not popular in all quarters of Europe, and even as it was drawn up one could see that it was the result of various compromises: Spain, Portugal, and Greece, among the poorer members, demanded more financial assistance; France was adamant that monetary union have a set schedule; Germany insisted on strict criteria to join a single currency; Britain rejected any reference to a "federal union," thus leaving the Maastricht Treaty to assert that it was "a new stage in the process of creating an ever closer union among the people of Europe." Still, this was not enough to satisfy all critics. Thatcher, no longer Prime Minister but Baroness Thatcher of Kesteven in the British House of Lords, railed against it, but the British House of Commons, after much debate, ratified it. The Danes, Euroskeptics like the British, rejected it, with just over 50 percent voting no in a referendum in March 1992. Six months later, only 51 percent of French voters, long thought to be Europhiles, voted in favor. On a second attempt, after Denmark secured opt-outs on the common currency and defense, Danes approved it. In 1993, Germany, where the public remained unsold on the euro, became the last to ratify the treaty, where it had been challenged in court by Germany's *Land* governments.

POST-MAASTRICHT DEVELOPMENTS

Since the mid-1990s, the pace of European integration has quickened. Not content to establish simply a common market in which goods, capital, labor, and services could move freely, advocates of a more united Europe pushed forward new projects: the euro, which replaced the currencies of twelve countries in 2002; institutional reforms designed to make the EU stronger, more efficient, and more accountable to

IN FOCUS

The Adoption of the Lisbon Treaty

In 2005, French and Dutch voters rejected the EU's Constitutional Treaty, a document that was three years in the making and designed to replace all existing EU treaties with a single document. The word "constitution" indicated that this was a far more explicitly political document than previous treaties, one that some feared would create a European superstate and spell the end of each country's sovereignty. Its rejection was therefore hailed in many quarters. *The Economist,* a British newsweekly that was never particularly keen on the Treaty, claimed that the "dream of deeper political integration and, in the 1957 Treaty of Rome's famous phrase, 'ever closer union', is over."[25] However, European leaders did not abandon the notion that major reforms of the EU were needed. Eighteen of the twenty-seven states had ratified the Constitutional Treaty, and many wanted to salvage something, although they were more reluctant to employ the term "constitution."

In December 2007, the leaders of the EU met in Portugal and signed a new treaty, known as the Lisbon Treaty. Unlike the Constitutional Treaty, the Lisbon Treaty would not replace earlier EU treaties with a single document; rather, it would amend existing EU treaties. According to José Sócrates, the Portuguese Prime Minister, the Lisbon Treaty "is not a treaty for the past. This is a treaty that will make Europe more modern, more efficient, and more democratic."[26] Similarly, according to a statement on the EU's website, the Lisbon Treaty will "provide the EU with modern institutions and optimized working methods to tackle both efficiently and effectively today's challenges in today's world."[27]

The Lisbon Treaty is not markedly different from the Constitutional Treaty. Angela Merkel, Germany's Chancellor, acknowledged that "the substance of the Constitution is preserved. That is a fact."[28] It changes voting procedures within EU institutions (discussed more in the next chapter) and increases the powers of the European Parliament. It includes a provision for a Citizens' Initiative in order to connect the EU to the population. Perhaps its most visible change is the creation of the post of President of the European Council, a *de facto* President of Europe, who would be selected by the heads of European governments. Some of the differences with the Constitutional Treaty are of a more symbolic nature: there is no reference to the term "constitution"; it makes no mention of EU symbols such as the anthem and flag; the Charter of Fundamental Rights is referenced but not formally included; opt-outs (Great Britain and Ireland for Justice and Home Affairs, Poland and Great Britain for the Charter of Fundamental Rights) are recognized; and the EU will not have a "Foreign Minister" but instead a "High Representative in Foreign Affairs and Security Policy," although this individual will have the same role envisioned in the Constitutional Treaty. A few changes are more substantive. National parliaments will have a greater role in EU decision-making, including a mechanism whereby they can challenge the legitimacy of EU proposals. While the old pillar structure is formally abolished, there is explicit recognition that the Common Foreign and Security Policy will remain subject to its own rules, including unanimous decision-making.[29]

Overall, though, the most important difference was that the Lisbon Treaty, as noted, amended, but did not wholly replace, existing treaties. Thanks to that provision, its drafters hoped that member states would not feel an obligation to submit its ratification to popular referendums, which doomed the Constitutional Treaty. José Manuel Barroso, President of European Commission, noted that referendums were "more complicated" and "less predictable" and asked (rhetorically?), "If a referendum had to be held on the creation of the European Community, or the introduction of the euro, do you think these would have passed?"[30] Valéry d'Estaing, the former French President who was responsible for drafting the Constitutional Treaty, confessed that the Lisbon Treaty differed little from the earlier document but that "subtle changes" were adopted to "head off any threat of referenda by avoiding any form of constitutional vocabulary." He also noted that the earlier proposals were "hidden or disguised in some way," hardly reassuring given that greater transparency was supposed to be one of the aims of the reforms.[31] The Belgian foreign minister acknowledged that, "The aim of the Constitutional Treaty was to be more readable; the aim of this treaty [Lisbon] is to be unreadable... The Constitution aimed to be clear, whereas this treaty had to be unclear. It is a success."[32] Needless to say, such statements cannot be found on the EU's website that purports to explain and answer questions about the Lisbon Treaty.

Initially, the Lisbon Treaty seemed destined to suffer the fate of the Constitutional Treaty. Although most states—included France and the Netherlands—ratified it by overwhelming majority vote in parliament,[33] in Ireland a popular referendum is required to ratify new EU treaties. In June 2008, as they had done seven years before with the Nice Treaty, Irish voters voted "No" (53.4 percent against), despite the fact that all three major parties in Ireland lobbied for it and Ireland had been historically a major beneficiary of EU largesse. Various reasons were put forward for its rejection, including Irish fears of loss of sovereignty, military neutrality, and EU tax harmonization policies. Others noted that at five hundred pages, the Lisbon Treaty was simply too long, a collection of "unintelligible drivel" put forward by the "dictatorship" of Brussels that, in the words of Ireland's representative on the European Commission, "no sane or sensible person" would read in full. Research conducted by the Irish government indeed found ignorance among both "yes" and "no" voters, but this may simply reflect that voters do not want to understand the "fiendish complexity of the EU."[34]

The Irish vote made it impossible for the Lisbon Treaty to go into force in early 2009 (as was planned) and threw the EU into a new crisis. Luxembourg's Jean-Claude Juncker stated, "This vote doesn't resolve any of the European problems, it almost makes every European problem bigger. It was a bad choice for Europe. There is no Plan B."[35] Although a few leaders, such Václav Klaus, the Euroskeptic president of the Czech Republic, declared the treaty dead, other states went ahead with the ratification process. By May 2009, all EU members, save Ireland, had approved it through parliamentary ratification.[36]

Could Ireland, compromising approximately one percent of the EU population, stand alone? Although some suggested that the Irish could perhaps try to argue that voter approval was in fact not necessary, it was politically impossible to simply have a revote in parliament after the measure had been submitted to and rejected by voters. Demanding a revote (which had also been done after the Irish rejected the Nice Treaty in 2001) risked the perception of "bullying" the Irish prime minister and, according to *The Economist*, could amount to "leaving whisky and a loaded revolver in the study and expecting him to do the decent thing for Europe."[37] To placate the Irish, other European states agreed to some modifications in the Treaty (e.g., removing a provision that meant some EU countries would not have an EU commissioner), and a new referendum was scheduled. This time, the Irish government took great pains to educate voters and stressed that the Lisbon Treaty would not end Irish neutrality, legalize abortion, or mean Irishmen would be drafted into a European army, fears that were expressed during the first referendum. Feeling pressure from other countries as well as humbled by an acute economic crisis, in October 2009, as noted at the outset of this chapter, the Irish gave their blessing to the Lisbon Treaty, with 67.1 percent voting in favor. The following month, the Czech Republic's Klaus reluctantly gave the treaty his blessing, meaning it was now ratified by all member states. Herman Van Rompuy, former prime minister of Belgium, and Catherine Ashton, the EU Trade Commissioner from Britain, became the first President and "High Representative" under the Lisbon Treaty.

Some hailed passage of the Lisbon Treaty as a great victory, and, as will be noted in other parts of this text, it will have a real impact on the machinery of the EU. However, the saga of the Lisbon Treaty is in many ways cautionary. Like the Constitutional

(*continued*)

Treaty, it fell victim (at least at first) to voters less than enamored with the idea of giving more power to Brussels. Moreover, given the fact that Ireland was the only state where it was put before voters, it makes it difficult to argue that the adoption of the Lisbon Treaty is a means, among other things, to remedy the EU's perceived "democratic deficit." Skepticism and, in some cases, fear of the EU is widespread. In order to move forward—whether it be with institutional reforms ("deepening") or further expansion ("widening"), the EU will need public support. How to win over increasingly Euro-skeptical voters is something that proponents of EU reforms must figure out.

Critical Thinking Questions

1. How significant are the changes made by the Lisbon Treaty?
2. How do the debates about the Lisbon Treaty illustrate the tension between supranationalism and inter-governmentalism?

European citizens; expansion of the EU to more countries, so that by 2007 contained more than twice (twenty-seven to twelve) the number of members it had in 1992; and, last but certainly not least, a Constitutional Treaty designed to consolidate all previous treaties, build a stronger connection between EU institutions and citizens, and, perhaps, provide a basis for still further integration.

Because EU institutions are covered more fully in the next chapter, discussions of institutional reforms, including the EU's alleged "democratic deficit," are largely covered there, although the **In Focus** section of this chapter reviews the **Lisbon Treaty,** mentioned at the outset of this chapter and probably the most important EU treaty of the 2000s. Among the many important new EU policies and initiatives in the 2000s, we shall focus here on two of the most consequential: the adoption of the euro and expansion of the EU in the 2000s.

Lisbon Treaty ■ a reform treaty that, among other things, changes the voting rules within the EU and creates a de facto EU "president" and "foreign minister"; came into force in 2009.

The Euro

According to Robert Mundell, an American Nobel Prize–winning economist, "The introduction of the euro is one of those epochal events that can only be understood in the context of long periods of history."[38] Volatility in exchange rates threatened the European trading system, prompting the creation of mechanisms to tie the value of European currencies together. By the late 1980s, full monetary union—which had been discussed in the early 1970s but left undone—appeared to many, including EU Commission President Delors, a logical extension of the common market. In 1988, he chaired a committee to examine the question of monetary union, which a year proposed a three-stage process to bring it to fruition. Still, the idea was highly controversial. Thatcher said that "it confirmed our worst fears" and was full of "Delorism socialism,"[39] and the Germans were loathe to part with their beloved *Deutschemark*. However, once provisions were put in place to create an independent central bank and enforce strict criteria to join the currency—together with French support for German reunification in 1990—the Germans, perhaps reluctantly, acceded. Monetary union could be hailed as "victory" of sorts for neo-functionalists, as it was a logical outgrowth, a "spillover" of a common market, but was also, particularly for Delors and French President Francois Mitterand, a political project, an affirmation of the unity of Europe.

Rationale for a Single Currency Advocates of the euro, which in 1995 became the somewhat uninspiring name for the single currency, pointed to several advantages of having a single currency.[40] Most obviously, it would make travel and business easier. Tourists would no longer have to exchange money (and pay sizeable commission fees) when traveling among European countries, and businesses would no longer have to keep multiple accounts in different currencies and exchange money as a consequence of intra-European trade and investment. Put another way, having to exchange money at the border or convert prices from one currency to another cut against the grain of a single, common market. Imagine the US—a common economic market of fifty states—with fifty different currencies! The EU estimated that elimination of currency exchange expenses alone would save some $10 billion annually.[41] In addition, businesses would no longer be subject to exchange rate risk. Businesses prefer predictability to volatility. A single currency was thus seen as a boon to business, encouraging more trade and investment across borders, and, consequently, generating jobs.

There were also less obvious economic advantages to the euro. A common currency, it was argued, would allow Europeans to compare prices easier and find better bargains. Additionally, many alleged that making the necessary reforms to join the euro—discussed more below—would especially benefit countries such as Italy and Greece that had chronic inflation and high budget deficits. The euro would thus inject a measure of fiscal responsibility into states where it had been, to say the least, rare. The euro was designed as well as an expression of European power, to give medium-sized European economies a means to compete globally with the almighty dollar, which was the world's preferred reserve currency and standard unit of exchange for international transactions. Lastly, it was advocated as an important symbolic reflection of European integration and even European identity. As the French economist Jacques Rueff wrote in the 1950s, "Europe shall be made through the currency, or it shall not be made."[42] As national governments could put their design on one side of the euro coins (the bills are standardized), one could argue that as a Dutch woman reaches into her pocket and pulls out coins graced by the images of an Irish harp, the Slovenian poet France Prešeren, and Vienna's Belvedere Palace, she *feels* more European. In the words of Wim Duisenberg, the first head of the European Central Bank, "The euro is much more than just a currency. It is a symbol of European integration in every sense of the word."[43]

Meeting the Requirements One could not, however, simply sign up for the euro. A multi-national conversion of multiple currencies involving millions of people and literally trillions of euros was historically unprecedented. It could not happen overnight. Nor, for that matter, would it succeed if just anyone could join. Each aspirant to join the eurozone had to demonstrate that it was economically solvent and thus not bring the value of the euro down or generate monetary instability. In this respect, joining the euro was like a marriage. Love may be most important, but it might still be worth looking at your prospective partner's financial situation before making a commitment, because upon the exchange of vows his debt becomes your debt. For countries that prided themselves upon fiscal responsibility—chiefly the Germans—this meant that chronic debtors and spendthrifts such as the Italians had to get their fiscal house in order.

convergence criteria ■ rules on inflation, interest rates, and debt that countries had to meet in order to join the euro.

The Maastricht Treaty laid out **convergence criteria** countries had to meet to join the euro. These were low inflation, low interest rates, exchange rate stability, a budget deficit of less than 3 percent of gross domestic product (GDP), and a total debt ratio of 60 percent to the country's total GDP. These last two criteria proved to be the hardest for several states to meet. The Italians, Greeks, French, and Spanish had to cut government spending and even privatize companies to raise revenue and cut their debt. By 1997—the year before exchange rates were to be permanently fixed—eleven states met the criteria, although the EU showed remarkable flexibility in claiming that states such as Belgium (122 percent debt/GDP ratio) and Italy (121 percent debt/GDP ratio) made enough progress to be included.[44] Greece, which had not met the criteria in 1997, was allowed into the eurozone in 2001, although many speculated at the time (with good cause, as it turned out) that Greek claims of meeting the criteria were at best dubious. In an effort to prevent future problems, prospective euro members agreed in 1997 to a **Stability and Growth Pact,** whose key provision is that states using the euro pledge to keep their annual budget deficits under 3 percent of GDP. To employ the marriage analogy again, this "vow" meant that the new spouse could not, after being wed, run up a big credit card debt.

Stability and Growth Pact ■ agreement among countries using the euro that is aimed to keep the euro stable; its primary provisions concern budget deficits, which must remain under 3 percent of GDP.

Arguments against the Euro Not all Europeans were enamored with the euro. Arguments against its introduction fell into three broad categories.

First, there was the nationalistic argument. The euro would be managed by the European Central Bank (ECB, formally created in 1998), with oversight from various EU bodies. By "pooling" their sovereignty together in the euro, states surrendered the ability to conduct their own monetary policy—meaning setting exchange rates, interest rates, and the money supply. All of these can be employed by states to spur or slow down economic growth. Many feared giving control to the ECB, thinking that their own national level central banks should remain in charge of monetary policy. On a less technical, but nonetheless important, level, people tend to like "their" money. It is a reflection of their history, part of their identity. Replacing colorful bills with images of national heroes for the bland euro was, for many, not a good trade. Largely because of economic nationalism, as well as confidence that their economy would out-perform the eurozone, the British opted to retain their pounds and pence.

Those on the political left were nervous about the euro because of the above-mentioned constraints put on euro members via the Stability and Growth Pact. By limiting the ability of states to run budget deficits, some leftists—especially in Sweden and Denmark with their sizeable welfare states—feared that the ECB would order Stockholm or Copenhagen to cut generous health care, pension, and education benefits in order to meet euro criteria. Both the Danes (in 2000) and the Swedes (in 2003) in referenda rejected participation in the euro. Notably, these were the only two instances when Europeans were able to vote directly on joining the euro.

Finally, economists made technical arguments against the euro. Chief among them was the notion that the eurozone was not an "optimum currency area." What does this mean? In brief, the eurozone has a functional lack of labor mobility, does not have much wage flexibility, and does not have a strong central government able to dispense funds to areas affected by adverse local economic conditions or "asymmetric shocks." For example, if Spain were to experience economic problems due to a country-specific problem (e.g., natural disaster, a downturn in the business cycle, a bust in the local real estate market [which did occur in 2008–2009]), one could not expect Spaniards to move *en masse* to another country with better prospects or the European Union to be able to devote enough resources to pull Spain out of the crisis. Moreover, the Stability and Growth Pact—if strictly enforced—would limit the ability of Spain itself to do much about the problem. Although this type of argument seems hypothetical, it manifested itself in 2010, when Greece and Ireland, because of severe debt crises made worse by the global economic downturn, required a bailout from their European partners and made some doubt the very viability of the euro.[45] This important development is taken up more fully in Chapter 10.

These arguments, however, did not prevail prior to the adoption of the euro. The economic and *political* rationale in favor of the euro proved too strong to overcome in twelve of the EU states. Unlike in the 1970s, in the 1990s European leaders fulfilled their pledge to create a monetary union.

The Launch of the Euro The euro was officially launched as a medium of exchange on January 1, 1999, after exchange rates among all of the participating euro countries were permanently fixed in December 1998. Combining the values of, at that time, all eleven currencies, the euro was born with a value of $1.168. At this stage, the euro was only a virtual currency; one could keep a bank account or credit card in euros and even purchase euros electronically, but there were no euro coins or bills. Many stores, however, priced products both in euros and in local currency so that people would get used to "thinking" in euros.

The physical currency was introduced in January 2002. In the years before its appearance, there was extensive debate on what or who should appear on euro notes (generic representations of "European architecture" prevailed over depictions of actual [meaning "national"] people or places); whether the money should include Greek lettering spelling out "euro" (it does); and whether the Italians could form a plural for euros (*euri*) more in line with Italian (they could not). Despite fears of confusion and money shortages, the transition was incredibly smooth—ATMs dispensed euros, clerks were able to calculate prices and make change, and banks had enough money on hand. After a two-month transition period in which both older currencies and the euro qualified as legal tender, venerable currencies such as the French franc and Greek drachma had value only for collectors of obsolete money.

The Effects and Future of the Euro Like it or not, the euro is a reality. One can, however, ask a number of questions: How has the euro fared? Can its adoption be judged a success? What is its future?

In strictly economic terms, the euro has largely been a success. Initially, it did fall in value—reaching a nadir of $0.83 in October 2000, losing nearly a third of its value after less than two years of existence. However, as seen in Figure 3.1, it bounced back, reaching a high of $1.60 in April 2008, although it later fell rather precipitously due in part to the world economic crisis and fears in 2010 that a Greek debt default would have ramifications throughout the eurozone, issues covered more fully in Chapter 10. For most of the 2000s, the euro remained high compared to the dollar, a development not welcomed by European exporters (or by

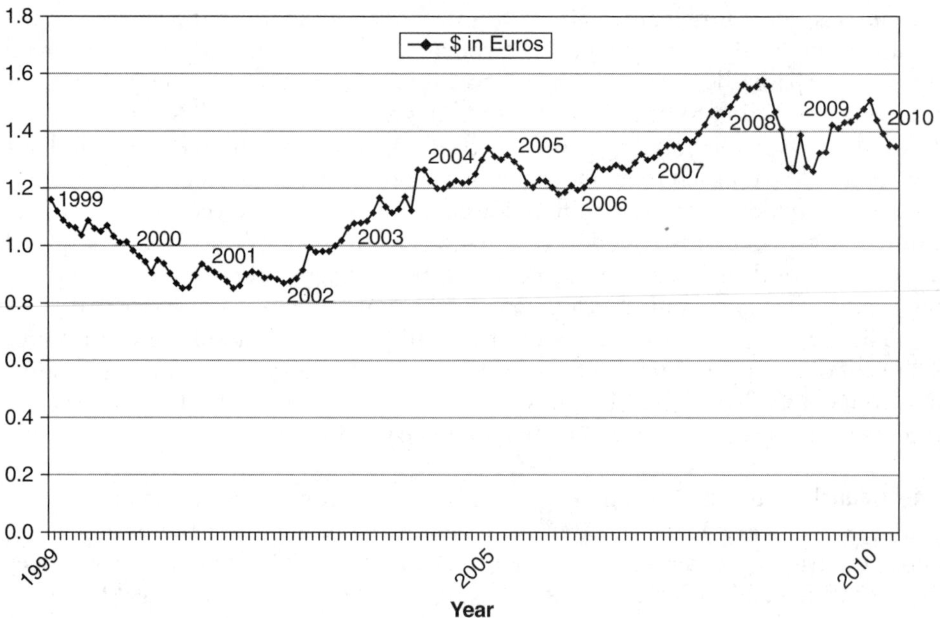

FIGURE 3.1
Dollar/Euro Exchange Rate, 1999–2010
Source: http://www.x-rates.com

American tourists!), but one that did make imported products in Europe cheaper for local buyers and signaled market confidence in European economic stability.

Whether the euro has delivered on all of its promises is a subject of debate. Cross-border trade and investment have increased. The overall inflation in the eurozone has been low—about 2 percent a year.[46] However, France, Italy, and Germany—the largest euro economies—continued to have sluggish growth and high unemployment. Overall, growth in the eurozone from 2002 to 2006 averaged less than 1.4 percent, compared to 2.3 percent in Great Britain and 2.5 percent in Sweden,[47] and in 2008 most European economies went into recession. Whether or not economic problems in Europe in the 2000s were the "fault" of the euro can be debated—all three of the biggest euro economies have chronic problems that predate the euro and it was problems in the US that triggered the global economic crisis in 2008—but many remain unsold on the promise that the euro will bring jobs and growth.

Since its introduction, however, the eurozone has expanded, albeit slowly. Micro-states such as Andorra, Monaco, and Andorra were *de facto* forced to adopt the euro after the currencies they had previously used (e.g., Spanish pesetas, French francs, and Italian lira) disappeared. On January 1, 2007, Slovenia, which joined the EU in 2004, became the first post-communist country to adopt the euro. Cyprus and Malta joined the eurozone a year later, followed by Slovakia in 2009. Some countries that recently declared their independence, such as Montenegro and Kosovo, use the euro as their currency even though they do not belong to the EU.

More EU members are expected to join the euro—indeed, prior to joining all new EU members in Eastern Europe pledged to join the eurozone—and, in the wake of the 2008 to 2010 economic crisis, which hit Eastern Europe very hard, several states redoubled efforts to qualify for the euro to insulate them in the future from international financial pressures. Estonia succeeded in this venture, joining the eurozone in 2011. Iceland, whose economy collapsed in 2008, has also expressed interest in joining both the EU and the eurozone.

The largest debates over the euro within the eurozone concern the terms of the Stability and Growth Pact. Many states, particularly France and Italy, have complained that the 3 percent cap on budget deficits is too constraining. In 2001, the European Commission issued a warning against Portugal, threatening the imposition of fines. More seriously, in 2004 chronic poor economic performance pushed Greece, Italy, France, and, ironically, Germany above the limit. The European Commission sought a reprimand and possible fines, but the Council of the European Union, where member states vote, refused to act. Ultimately, the EU agreed to loosen the Stability and Growth Pact, allowing states to exceed the 3 percent limit for a host of reasons, including public investments, pension reforms, and "any other functions, which, in the opinion of the Member State concerned, are relevant." In wake of the global financial crisis from 2008 to 2010, many states that use the euro began to run budget deficits well in excess of the 3 percent cap. The overall budget deficit in the eurozone in 2009 was 5.3 percent of GDP, with Greece's the highest at well over 10 percent, leading some to wonder if the Stability and Growth Pact is truly dead and what would be the future stability of the euro.[48]

Expansion—Where Is the Border of Europe?

As noted in the previous chapter, one of the slogans of the 1989 revolutions in Eastern Europe was "Return to Europe," and many post-communist political figures soon began clamoring for membership. Finding the case for expansion hard to resist (if still controversial in some circles) the EU-15 (the member states after the trouble-free accession of Sweden, Austria, and Finland in 1995) agreed to take in the newly democratic, albeit poorer, countries to the east. Making preparations for them to join the EU was a major preoccupation in the 1990s on both sides of the continent. By 2007, as seen in Figure 3.2, the EU did expand to include twelve new members.

Motivations for Expansion Why Eastern Europeans sought membership in the EU is easy to understand. The EU could be a major source of aid, it would help secure international peace and democracy, its influence would be helpful on more technocratic and legal matters of the post-communist transition, and, perhaps above all else, membership would be a potent symbol that these states were indeed European—for all that implied—and that they had "made it." In simple terms, the EU was a club of successful, secure, democratic, wealthy states. Who would not want to belong to such an organization?

The motivations of the EU are perhaps more difficult to decipher. After all, if you are in "the club," why would you want—to put the matter crassly—the "riff-raff" to join? Indeed, as noted below, there were potent arguments

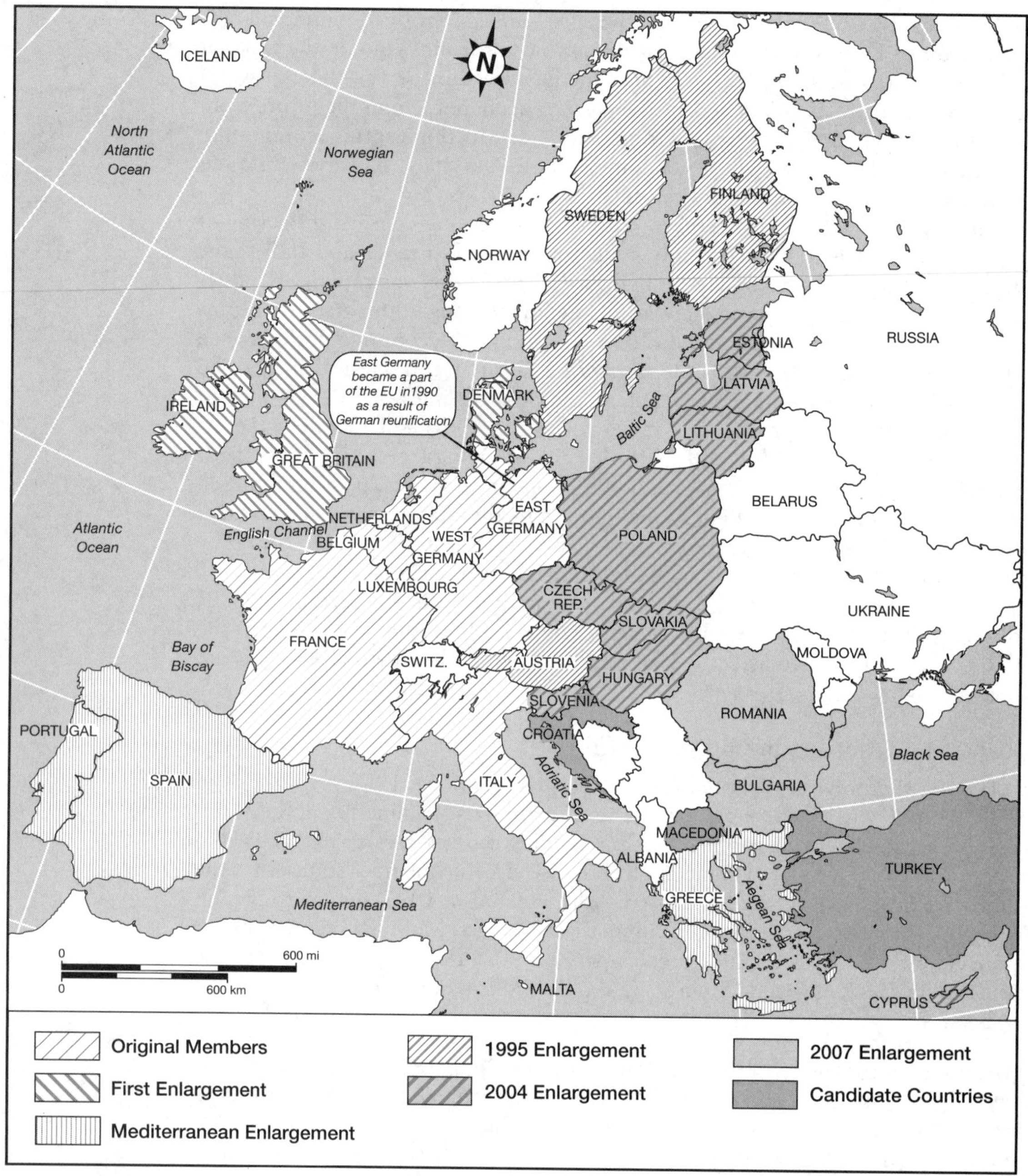

FIGURE 3.2
The Expansion of the EU Over Time

against expansion. Nonetheless, the EU decided, after some hesitation, that post-communist countries could join the organization. Why?

One might cite an economic rationale: the need to find new markets and trade partners. While at first this seems a compelling argument, the EU could have achieved this goal via free-trade agreements or by using various incentives (e.g., aid, access to the EU market) to encourage post-communist states to liberalize their markets to accommodate EU trade and investment. The EU has a host of such arrangements with other countries (e.g., a Customs Union that went into effect with Turkey in 1996). These arrangements would be a far simpler and less expensive option for the EU: new members would not complicate EU decision-making and place demands on EU Structural, Regional, and Cohesion funds.

Perhaps the main goal was to spread democracy and peace to a region with a troublesome past—remember that both World Wars started in Eastern Europe, and the wars in the former Yugoslavia in the 1990s alarmed many in Europe. Certainly, this was a stated objective, and it explains in part why Germany (bordering post-communist Europe) was more enthusiastic about expansion than, for example, France. According to former German Chancellor Helmut Kohl, "the policy of European integration [including expansion] is in reality a question of war and peace in the twenty-first century."[49] However, by the time the EU actually expanded, all of the new member states were stable democracies, and, arguably, the EU could have employed other mechanisms besides expansion to encourage peace and security. Moreover, NATO expanded in 1999 (to Poland, the Czech Republic, and Hungary) and to the other post-communist EU members in 2004. These moves were probably sufficient to provide security to those countries.

Several analysts have suggested that purely materialistic or practical concerns are not sufficient to explain the EU decision to expand.[50] Instead, moral claims played a large role. Eastern European states were European. Article 237 of the Treaty of Rome states that any European state can join (a clause that was applied in 1963 to affirm that Turkey is eligible for membership). These states wanted to "Return to Europe." They had suffered under communist repression. They were now building democracies and market economies. They looked to Europe for inspiration. In terms of material costs and benefits, the case for expansion was arguably somewhat thin. In terms of morality—and to some extent guilt—there was little that the EU could do but agree to expand.

The roadmap to expansion was first laid out with promulgation of the **Copenhagen Criteria** of 1993, which stated that those who wished to join must be stable democracies (with establishment of rule of law and protection for minorities), have a predominantly free-market economic system, and agree to incorporate all aspects of the 90,000 odd pages of EU law and policies, often referred to as the **acquis communautaire** or simply the *acquis*, into their national legislation. In the meantime, the EU would provide aid to help with economic restructuring, democratic development, and technical assistance. In 1998 the EU finally agreed to open accession talks with (at that time) six aspiring members. As more states (e.g., Slovakia, Romania) met the basic political and economic requirements of Copenhagen, the EU opened talks with them as well. By the end of the 1990s, a "big bang" expansion to a dozen states—including the small island nations of Malta and Cyprus—seemed imminent. Still, the process took some time and often

Copenhagen Criteria ■ agreed upon in 1993, these specify that a country wishing to join the EU must be democratic, have a predominantly free-market system, and adopt all pre-existing EU laws and directives into their national legislation.

acquis communautaire ■ the existing body of EU laws, regulations, directives, and policies, which must be adopted by aspiring member states; by 2010, it numbered some 90,000 pages.

TABLE 3.2

Chapters of the *Acquis* (EU Law and Policies)

Chapter 1: Free movement of goods
Chapter 2: Freedom of movement for workers
Chapter 3: Right of establishment and freedom to provide services
Chapter 4: Free movement of capital
Chapter 5: Public procurement
Chapter 6: Company law
Chapter 7: Intellectual property law
Chapter 8: Competition policy
Chapter 9: Financial services
Chapter 10: Information society and media
Chapter 11: Agriculture and rural development
Chapter 12: Food safety, veterinary, and phytosanitary policy
Chapter 13: Fisheries
Chapter 14: Transport policy
Chapter 15: Energy
Chapter 16: Taxation
Chapter 17: Economic and monetary policy
Chapter 18: Statistics
Chapter 19: Social policy and employment
Chapter 20: Enterprise and industrial policy
Chapter 21: Trans-European networks
Chapter 22: Regional policy and coordination of structural instruments
Chapter 23: Judiciary and fundamental rights
Chapter 24: Justice, freedom and security
Chapter 25: Science and research
Chapter 26: Education and culture
Chapter 27: Environment
Chapter 28: Consumer and health protection
Chapter 29: Customs union
Chapter 30: External relations
Chapter 31: Foreign, security, and defense policy
Chapter 32: Financial control
Chapter 33: Financial and budgetary provisions
Chapter 34: Institutions
Chapter 35: Other issues

Note: Negotiations on all chapters must be successfully concluded prior to a state gaining admission to the EU.

was highly technical. As seen in Table 3.2, the EU and aspiring members had to conclude negotiations on thirty-five chapters of the *acquis*. For each, the EU had to be satisfied that the new member's laws were in accordance with EU policies and practices. This table also gives one a good idea of the reach of the EU in various policy realms.

The Costs of Expansion

This is not to say that all were pleased with the EU's plans or that the EU could easily absorb all the prospective members. The post-communist expansion would be far more difficult than the addition of Austria, Finland, and Sweden in 1995. This time, the EU was looking to add many more states and more than 100 million people. In terms of languages, cultures, and historical experience, the EU would become much more diverse. The sheer size of the new EU would complicate EU decision-making. Because each prospective new member (Poland, and, to some degree, Romania excepted) was relatively small, there was no overcoming the fact that their accession would tilt the balance of power in the EU toward smaller states and away from the traditional powers of France, Germany, and Great Britain.

Most significantly, however, was the fact that post-communist states, unlike the entrants in 1995, were far poorer than the EU average, as seen in Table 3.3. Put in aggregate terms, what this meant was that the planned EU expansion to ten post-communist states—forgetting for a moment about tiny Malta and Cyprus—would increase the EU population by 28 percent, but its economic output by only about 5 percent. They would, without question, require massive amounts of EU assistance—tens of billions of euros—to meet EU standards in a number of areas (e.g., environmental protection, social policy). They would henceforth qualify for the bulk of EU Regional Funds, much to the consternation of Greece, Portugal, Spain, and Italy, which had previously been the primary beneficiaries of EU largesse. Thus, prior to their admission there was a reworking of the EU budget to help wean older members off the EU dole gradually. Many of these states are very agricultural, with rates of agricultural employment particularly in Romania (44 percent), Bulgaria (26 percent), and Poland (25 percent) well above the EU average of about 5 percent.[51] Overall, the proposed expansions would double the number of farmers in the EU and put the CAP, already accused by its critics of ending up too much of the EU budget, under great strain. Lastly, the prospect of millions of relatively poor people having the right to move and work anywhere in Europe (this

TABLE 3.3

Economic Comparisons: East vs. West

Country	GDP/Capita	GDP Growth, 2005
Slovenia	$17,700	3.7%
Czech Republic	$11,960	4.1%
Hungary	$11,210	4.0%
Estonia	$9,310	6.0%
Slovakia	$8,940	5.1%
Poland	$7,300	4.5%
Lithuania	$7,110	6.5%
Latvia	$5,800	5.5%
EU-15	$34,520	2.7%

Source: "Countries: The World in Figures," *The World in 2005,* The Economist Intelligence Unit.

being one of the basic freedoms of the EU, freedom of labor) led to fears of a wave of western immigration. Germany and Austria, as "front-line states" were particularly worried. Imagine, many would tell me, if the US opened its border to any Mexican who wanted a job in the US!

To limit some of these costs, the EU placed certain conditions on the applicants from Central and Eastern Europe. First, older EU members were given the right to restrict labor mobility from the new member states for up to seven years. Great Britain, Ireland, and Sweden chose to let their labor markets remain open to those who joined in 2004 (but not, interestingly, for Bulgaria and Romania which joined later). As a consequence, hundreds of thousands of people from Central and Eastern Europe have moved to these states—half of the 600,000 migrants to Great Britain from 2004 to 2006 were Poles.[52] While this phenomenon is changing the complexion of British, Irish, and (to a lesser extent) Swedish societies—which now have dozens of Polish groceries, bars, churches, and civic associations in addition to Polish waiters, hotel maids, and construction workers—their economies have continued to grow and unemployment has not gone up. Secondly, CAP support to new states will be phased in over a ten year period, giving the EU time to make more reforms to CAP. In addition, the EU-15 were allowed to put protectionist measures in place to guard against any risk of unsafe food from the east. Ironically, these actions—which people in applicant countries saw as discriminatory—were occurring at the same time that the EU-15 enjoyed, because of CAP subsidies, a trade surplus against the lower cost farmers in post-communist Europe.[53]

Fulfilling the Criteria

As can be inferred from the above discussion, once the nitty-gritty of accession negotiations began, the luster of EU membership began to fade away. People in post-communist countries felt like they would be second-class citizens in the EU and that the EU was simply dictating terms to them. Some complained that adopting EU regulations (e.g., particularly in employment policy) would undermine their comparative advantage of lower labor costs on international markets and ultimately cost them jobs. Others began to talk of the EU as a new empire, which, like the Soviet Union, would cost states their sovereignty. By 2002, the percentage of respondents who thought EU membership would be a good thing fell to under 50 percent in Estonia (32 percent), Latvia (35 percent), Slovenia and the Czech Republic (43 percent), and Lithuania (45 percent).[54]

Despite some frustration on both sides, accession talks made progress. Democracy became consolidated, even in laggards like Romania. As seen in Table 3.3, post-communist economies were growing faster than most within the EU, mitigating fears that these states would be hopeless economic burdens. As the technical chapters of the accession talks (e.g., industrial policy, competition policy, taxation) were gradually concluded, the question about expansion no longer was *if* or *who* but *when*. Ten countries—Estonia, Latvia, Lithuania, Poland, Czech Republic, Slovakia, Hungary, Slovenia, Malta, and Cyprus—were admitted on May 1, 2004, and EU flags, as seen in the Photo 3.2, were proudly displayed along with national ones. Bulgaria and Romania, which had more "catching up" to do, were let in on January 1, 2007.

EU flag is raised alongside Slovenia's during the 2004 EU expansion to post-communist Europe.

In the 2004 expansion, the most problematic case turned out to be Cyprus. The island of Cyprus has been divided since 1974 between the internationally recognized Republic of Cyprus, sometimes known as "Greek" or "Southern" Cyprus, and the Turkish Republic of Northern Cyprus, created as a result of the 1974 invasion of Turkish armed forces and recognized by no state except Turkey. The EU and the United Nations (UN) have hoped that the prospect of EU accession would further reunification talks, but a UN reunification plan, accepted by the Turkish side, was rejected in 2004 by voters in "Greek" Cyprus.[55] This outcome was seen as a defeat both to the EU and the UN, and now that they are ensconced in the EU, the Greek Cypriots are in an even stronger bargaining positions vis-à-vis Turkish Cypriots should reunification talks resume.

The expansion to Romania and Bulgaria in 2007 proved difficult mainly because on certain key issues—particularly corruption and judicial reform—it was clear that they did not meet EU standards. Nonetheless, in a move that honestly left some in Brussels scratching their heads, they were admitted anyway because little was thought to be gained by pushing back the accession date and dragging on negotiations indefinitely. In part recognizing what some would call a mistake, the EU, fearing that reforms would stop once they were in, has made aid to both conditional on continued progress.[56]

There is little doubt that the EU's expansion to the east will create new challenges for the union, as real differences exist between older and newer members of the EU, a point developed in this chapter's **Is Europe One?** section. Among other concerns, observers note that throughout post-communist Europe corruption remains a problem, one that is arguably worse now that "joining the European Union has produced temptingly large puddles of money to steal." One head of an anti-corruption agency laments, "Before accession, governments were under close

IS EUROPE ONE?

Comparing New and Old Members of the European Union

The expansion of the EU to primarily post-communist countries in 2004 and 2007 radically altered its composition. The newest members have very different histories and are much poorer than the EU-15. Their addition has forced changes in the EU budget and in the EU's institutional structure. Beyond these basic and obvious issues, however, how much has expansion changed the EU? Do the new member states have different policy preferences compared to older members? Does the widening of Europe somehow dilute the European project?

In certain respects there is little question that the countries of Central and Eastern Europe *are* different. For example, on foreign policy questions they generally tend to be much more Euro-Atlantic in orientation, meaning they value good relations with the US and are not—much to the consternation of former French President Jacques Chirac, who suggested that they should know their place—willing to follow the French or German lead. This has been clearest with respect to the US-led invasion of Iraq in 2003, which France and Germany opposed and most post-communist governments (if not their publics) supported, but it extends to other questions as well (e.g., planned placement of bases for a US missile-shield in Poland and the Czech Republic).[58] On economic policy, many post-communist states, particularly the Poles, Czechs, and Estonians, have, by many measures, more liberalized economies than states such as France and Italy and, like the British, are not amenable to efforts to construct a more "social Europe." Poland and the Baltic states are eager to expand the EU further to the east, whereas France, Austria, and others complain of "expansion fatigue."

Moreover, the inclusion of post-communist countries has brought history back into the European Union.[59] Whereas Western Europeans, thanks to the EU, have overcome much of their tragic past and, for the most part, do not linger on the past (although the British arguably still get some pleasure out of aggravating the French), Eastern Europeans brought a fair amount of historical baggage into the EU. Examples include a difficult relationship with Russia, tensions among Slovakia, Hungary, and Romania on treatment of ethnic Hungarians, and disputes with Germany on the treatment of ethnic Germans after World War II. The possible expansion to the western Balkans (e.g., Bosnia) and Turkey (consider its troubled relationship with Greece) would add more historically based intra-EU tensions.

In terms of public opinion, one can point to some differences. However, for the most part they reveal that publics in new member states tend to be *more* enthusiastic about the European project. For example, Eurobarometer surveys from the fall of 2006[60] show that those in new member states (not counting Bulgaria and Romania, which joined in 2007) were more supportive of further enlargement (72 percent in favor in the new states, 41 percent in the EU-15), a common defense and foreign policy (84 percent to 73 percent) and a European Constitution (60 percent to 50 percent), exhibited more trust toward the European Commission (59 percent to 46 percent) and European Parliament (61 percent to 50 percent), and were more likely (52 percent to 45 percent) to have positive views of the EU. Cynics might suggest that they have not yet had time to become jaded about "Europe" and that they are not the ones paying for the 2004 and 2007 expansions. Indeed, those in new member states are considerably more likely (67 percent to 52 percent in older members) to claim that their country has benefited from membership in the EU. Lastly, even though there are real differences across European countries on key issues (e.g., foreign policy, the Constitution, economic policies), the East-West divide is only one of the many cleavages in Europe, not even the most visible or important one (think of problems from

"Euro-skeptics" such as the British and Danes, or tensions in 2010 when richer Germany balked at bailing out poor and troubled Greece). Reassuringly, surveys reveal that publics on both sides of the continent rank order the values of the EU similarly: human rights, democracy, peace, rule of law, and respect for other cultures. On this crucial measure, Europeans stand united.

Critical Thinking Questions

1. If you were a citizen in France or Germany, would you have favored EU expansion to post-communist states?
2. Has EU expansion strengthened or weakened the EU? Be able to employ specific evidence to support your case.

scrutiny. Now the fight against corruption is not a priority."[57] Not only are chronic corruption issues eroding Eastern Europeans' confidence in political institutions, but they also temper EU enthusiasm for additional expansion.

Who's Next?

The expansion of the EU to Bulgaria and Romania in 2007 will not be the last expansion of the EU, although many EU members have stated that they would like to take a break and concentrate on internal reforms and absorbing the newest members. Some might also add that given the above-mentioned concerns with the 2007 expansion, the EU should be extra careful before additional states joined. Nonetheless, formal accession procedures with additional candidate countries have been launched. The EU began accession talks with both Croatia and Turkey in 2005 and with Macedonia in 2008. Croatia and Macedonia are relatively small countries and their applications are widely supported in Europe. Turkey, however, is a far more difficult case for a number of reasons, not the least of which is that most Turks are Muslims. Some European governments, including France and Germany, as well as a large share of European public opinion, are against Turkish membership. This highly controversial issue is covered in more detail in the final chapter of this book. Beyond these states, which, as of 2010, are official candidate countries, one could also list Bosnia, Serbia, Montenegro, Albania, and Kosovo, all of which have aspirations to join the EU. To the east, Ukraine, Moldova, Belarus, and, conceivably, Russia, could join, although the EU has yet to give any of these states a green light by saying that they would be geographically eligible for membership.

In the long term, one could imagine the EU expanding even further. After all, if one hails the EU is a great success story, why must it remain only European? Why could it not—indeed why *would* it not—want to extend the belt of peace and prosperity? Indeed, if Turkey is accepted, the boundaries of "Europe" could expand—to Georgia and Armenia (both Christian countries) on the eastern border of Turkey, perhaps to Lebanon, even to North Africa (Morocco's application in the 1980s was rejected on geographic grounds, but this could be revisited). *The Economist*, speculating on what the EU would look like on its hundredth anniversary in 2057, suggested that Israel and Palestine joined as its forty-ninth and fiftieth members (!) and negotiations over Russian entry were in the works.[61]

Inconceivable? Imagine the highest hopes of Europe's architects in the 1950s compared to the reality today: a common market, single currency, twenty-seven members, cooperation in a myriad of fields, and, most recently, passage of the Lisbon Treaty which should improve EU decision-making in a number of fields. European integration, despite the views of Euro-skeptics, continues to move forward. In this respect, despite various controversies and setbacks, the EU has much to celebrate over the past half-century.

APPLICATION QUESTIONS

1. Give an example of how supranationalism can conflict with national sovereignty. Overall, what do states gain through the EU? Why do they need an organization like the EU to reap the benefits of closer integration?
2. Some envision the EU as a potential alternative to the traditional sovereign state. Would you agree? What does this mean, precisely? What might this say about not only the EU but also about politics in an era of globalization?
3. Given the history of Europe, few would have believed European integration could go as far as it has. How much further might it go? What might slow it down or stop it?
4. How does the EU fit into realist perspectives of international relations? Does its growth and success fundamentally disprove or undermine realism?
5. Some think the EU is like a bicycle, meaning you have to be pedaling and moving forward or you fall off. Others retort that you can stop and park a bicycle from time to time without getting off it. Which makes more sense? In other words, could Europe just "stop" and abandon grandiose reform projects?

KEY TERMS

acquis communautaire 85
convergence criteria 80
Copenhagen Criteria 85
euro 69
European Coal and Steel Community (ECSC) 70
European Economic Community (EEC) 70
federalists 72
functionalism 71
integration 67
interdependence 67
inter-governmentalism 66
Lisbon Treaty 78
Maastricht Treaty 75
neo-functionalism 72
Single European Act (SEA) 74
Stability and Growth Pact 80
supranationalism 66
Treaty of Rome 70

ADDITIONAL READING

Europa (http://europa.eu)

Main portal to the EU's website. Excellent source of information and documents on the EU.

Gilbert, Mark. 2003. *Surpassing Realism: The Politics of European Integration since 1945*. Lanham MD: Rowman and Littlefield.

This book suggests how the emergence of the EU challenges the basic assumptions of realism, which has been the dominant theory in international politics. According to the author, other approaches may be more useful for understanding both the EU and global politics more generally.

Moravcsik, Andrew. 1998. *The Choice for Europe: Social Purpose and State Power from Messina to Maastricht*. Ithaca: Cornell University Press.

A classic source for European integration theory. Moravcsik is particularly interested in how realist perspectives about power can be used to explain the EU.

Nelsen, Brett, and Stubb, Alexander. 2003. *The European Union: Readings on the Theory and Practice of European Integration*, 3rd edition. London: Lynne Rienner.

This book contains historical documents related to European integration as well as reviews of the basic theories (e.g., functionalism, neo-functionalism) that have been invoked to explain the development of the EU.

Rosamond, Ben. 2000. *Theories of European Integration.* New York: Palgrave.

One of the shorter and more accessible texts that wades through what can be a very difficult topic to understand fully. This book lays out both the initial theories of integration and how they have been challenged and amended over time.

END NOTES

1. *The Economist*, October 21, 1999.
2. None of these, it might be worth adding, are mentioned in the body of the Lisbon Treaty, whereas they were formally enshrined as EU symbols in the ill-fated Constitutional Treaty, which was rejected by French and Dutch voters in 2005. Some thus might dispute calling them official EU symbols, but a statement of sixteen member states included in the final act of the Lisbon Treaty said that for them these will "continue as symbols to express the sense of community of the people in the European Union and their allegiance to it." They remain widely used within the EU.
3. The EU employs over 3,000 translators and translation costs in 2006 were $1.3 billion. From *The New York Times*, December 6, 2006, p. A10.
4. Realists have tried to explain European integration by focusing on the calculation of costs and benefits to member states. However, one should also recognize that integration has been about values and a new way of viewing international relations. According to one observer—who gives some credence to realist interpretations—the states of the EU have "turned the theory and practice of nation-state behavior on its head." See Mark Gilbert, *Surpassing Realism: The Politics of European Integration since 1945* (Lanham MD: Rowman and Littlefield, 2003), p. 10.
5. Quoted in John Pinder, *The Building of the European Union* (Oxford: Oxford University Press, 1998) p. 3
6. Andrew Moravcsik, *The Choice for Europe: Social Purpose and State Power from Messina to Maastricht* (Ithaca: Cornell University Press, 1998).
7. T.R. Reid, *The United States of Europe: The New Superpower and the End of American Supremacy* (New York: Penguin, 2004) and Jeremy Rifkin, *The European Dream: How Europe's Vision of the Future is Quietly Eclipsing the American Dream* (New York: Penguin, 2004).
8. An excellent and multi-faceted critique of the European project is Noel Malcolm, "The Case Against Europe," *Foreign Affairs* 74, March/April: 52–68.
9. Randolph Churchill, ed. *The Sinews of Peace: Post-War Speeches by Winston S. Churchill* (London: Cassell, 1948), pp. 198–202. Notably, however, he noted that Britain would not the basis for such a scheme, which would have to rest upon France recovering "the moral leadership of Europe."
10. Tony Judt, *Postwar: A History of Europe Since 1945* (New York: Penguin, 2005), p. 158.
11. On the same day, a second Treaty of Rome created the European Atomic Energy Community (Euratom), which was structured like the ECSC.
12. James A. Caporaso, *The European Union: Dilemmas of Regional Integration*. (Boulder: Westview, 2000), p. 4.
13. Quoted in Derek Unwin, *The Community of Europe*, (New York: Longman, 1991), p. 76.
14. Quoted in Uwe Kitzinger, *European Common Market and Community* (New York: Barnes and Noble, 1967) pp. 37–39.
15. The classic reference for neo-functionalism is Ernst Haas, *The Uniting of Europe: Political, Social, and Economic Forces 1950–1957* (Stanford: Stanford University Press, 1958).
16. Quoted in Anonymous, "What Jean Monnet Wrought" *Foreign Affairs*, April 1977.
17. Moravcsik, *The Choice for Europe*.
18. Moravcsik, *The Choice for Europe*, pp. 181–196.
19. Commission of the European Communities, "Completing the Internal Market," *White Paper*

from the Commission to the European Council, Brussels, 1985, p. 55.

20. Sometimes one hears reference to the "four freedoms," which includes the free movement and exchange of services. This, however, has proven to be more problematic to implement.
21. Margaret Thatcher, *The Downing Street Years* (London: HarperCollins, 1993), p.555.
22. Gilbert, *Surpassing Realism*, p. 220.
23. Foreign and Security Policy is typically formulated within the Council of the European Union by unanimous voting, with the Commission and European Parliament playing minor roles. Similarly, matters under the Justice and Home Affairs pillar are primarily the responsibility of the Council of the European Union. Proposals in the Constitutional Treaty, devised in 2003–2004, would have changed decision-making in both of these pillars, in particular by making Justice and Home Affairs subject to first pillar institutions. This document, however, was not ratified by all member states
24. Passports are issued by national governments and include on their covers the name of the both the individual country and the EU.
25. "The Europe That Died," *The Economist*, June 4, 2005.
26. Quoted in *The Irish Times*, May 12, 2008.
27. For more on what the Lisbon Treaty does, see information on the EU's website at http://europa.eu/Lisbon-treaty/index-en.htm.
28. Speech before European Parliament on June 27, 2007, quoted in *Brussels Journal*, December 11, 2007.
29. Sebastian Kurpas, "The Treaty of Lisbon: How Much of the Constitution is Left?" Centre for European Union Policy Studies, Brussels, December 2007.
30. Quoted in *The Irish Times*, February 8, 2007.
31. Quoted from *The Independent*, October 30, 2007, and *The Irish Times*, May 12, 2008.
32. *Brussels Journal*, December 11, 2007.
33. The Lisbon Treaty was actually approved unanimously by both house of parliament in Italy!
34. *The Irish Times*, August 23, 2008, and Charlemagne, "Who cares about Europe?," *The Economist*, September 20, 2008.
35. Quoted on http://www.bloomberg.com, June 14, 2008.
36. The greatest challenges to Lisbon, besides Ireland, were in the German court system (over its effects on German federalism) and Czech President Vaclav Klaus, a strong Euro-skeptic who resisted granting his approval, thus delaying Czech ratification.
37. "Vote early, vote often," *The Economist*, July 26, 2008, and Charlemagne, "Bad times ahead," *The Economist*, October 18, 2008.
38. Quoted in T.R. Reid, *The United States of Europe*, p. 63.
39. Thatcher, *The Downing Street Years*, p. 708.
40. Good sources on the euro include Barry Eichengreen, *European Money Unification* (Cambridge: MIT Press, 1997), and Paul de Grauwe, *Economics of Monetary Union* (Oxford: Oxford University Press, 2000).
41. Reid, *The United States of Europe*, p. 67.
42. Quoted in "Holding Together: Special Report on the Euro Area," *The Economist*, June 13, 2009, p. 4.
43. Quoted in Reid, *The United States of Europe*, p. 66.
44. "Holding together," *The Economist*, June 13, 2009, has excellent background on the euro. See also Werner Atweiler, "The Euro: Europe's New Currency," at http://fx.sauder.ubc.ca/euro/euro.html, accessed April 11, 2010.
45. For a piece that discusses precisely this problem with respect to Spain, see Paul Krugman, "The Spanish Prisoner," *The New York Times*, November 28, 2010.
46. "Holding together," *The Economist*, June 13, 2009.
47. European Commission, *Economic Forecasts*, Autumn 2005.
48. "Holding Together," *The Economist*, June 13, 2009, p. 11. For an analysis of this issues prior to the financial meltdown, see William Buiter, "The 'Sense and Nonsense of Maastricht' Revisited: What Have We Learned About Stabilization in EMU," *Journal of Common Market Studies*, 44:4, November 2006, pp. 689–690.
49. Quoted in Steven Haseler, *Super-State: The New Europe and Its Challenge to America* (London: I.B. Tauris, 2004), p. 80.
50. See José I. Torreblanca, *The Reuniting of Europe: Promises, Negotiations, and Compromises* (Aldershot: Ashgate, 2001), and Helene Sjursen, ed. *Questioning EU Enlargement* (London: Routledge, 2006).
51. BBC News, "Brussels Plans Bulgaria-Romania Aid," February 9, 2004, online from http://news.bbc.co.uk.
52. "Romania and Bulgaria Join EU," *International Herald Tribune*, January 1, 2007.

53. Marian Tupy, "EU Enlargement: Costs, Benefits, and Strategies for Central and East European Countries," Cato Institute, *Policy Analysis*, no, 489, September 18, 2003.
54. EU Candidate Eurobarometer Surveys, cited in Tupy, "EU Enlargment."
55. Elie Kedourie, "The Cyprus Problem and its Solution," *Middle Eastern Studies*, 41:4, September 2005: 649–660, and *The Economist*, "A Greek Wrecker," April 17, 2004.
56. "Romania and Bulgaria Join EU," 2007.
57. "Talking of Virtue, Counting the Spoons," *The Economist*, May 24, 2008.
58. A good review of the foreign policy of new EU member states is Janusz Bugajski and Ilona Teleki, *Atlantic Bridges: America's New European Allies* (Lanham MD: Rowman and Littlefield, 2007).
59. Charlemagne, "The burden of history," *The Economist*, May 19, 2007.
60. Eurobarometer 66, October–November 2006, available at http://ec.europa.eu/public_opinion/archives/eb/eb66/eb66_en.htm.
61. "The European Union at 100: A Special Report on the European Union," *The Economist*, March 17, 2007.

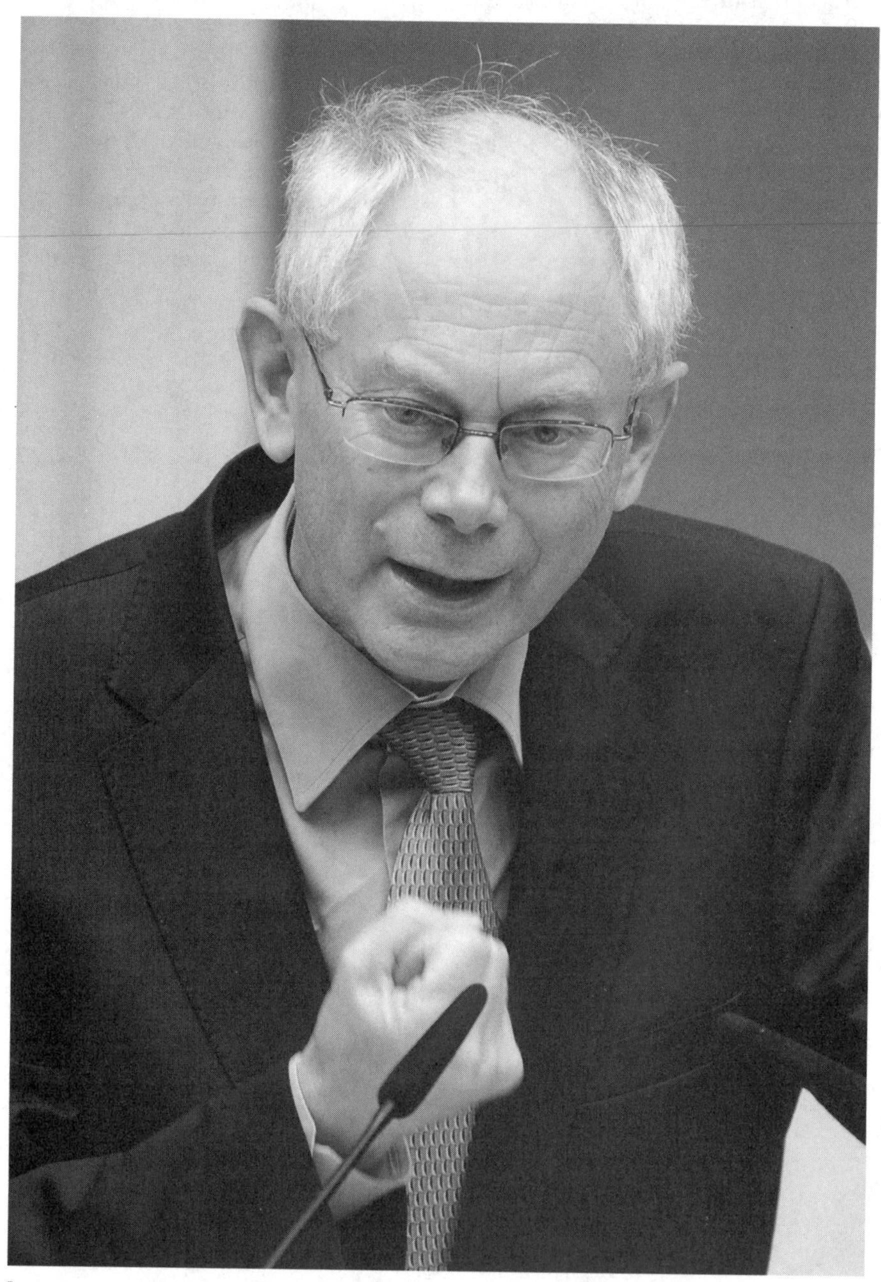

Herman Van Rompuy: "President" of Europe.

CHAPTER 4

Institutions and Policies of the European Union

According to several accounts, in the 1970s former US Secretary of State Henry Kissinger asked, "If I want to speak to Europe, who do I call?" In 2009, the question was finally answered: Herman Van Rompuy. "Herman Van Who?" might in turn have been the response of many Europeans, who had heretofore never heard of him. Van Rompuy was a Belgian parliamentarian and became Belgian prime minister in 2008. He became a figure of European and global prominence, however, in November 2009, when he was selected to become the first president of the European Council, a new position in the EU created by the Lisbon Treaty. Tasked with chairing the meetings of the European Council, the biannual gathering of European leaders, Van Rompuy could, with some plausibility, be labeled the "president" of Europe.

His appointment was not without controversy. Some thought that the EU would be better served with a well-known leader in this post, and former British Prime Minister Tony Blair made little secret of his desire for the job. One British political figure accused Van Rompuy of coming from a non-country, looking like a low-grade bank clerk, and having the charisma of a damp rag.[1] A further accusation—that he had no legitimacy to represent the 500 million people of the EU—has more substance, given that he was not elected by voters but chosen by the European leaders who sit on the European Council. Van Rompuy's low-key demeanor, however, was seen as a positive by others who believed he would be unlikely to press an ambitious agenda of his own or upstage other European leaders such as French President Nicolas Sarkozy or German Chancellor Angela Merkel, both of whom backed his selection. Whether or not he can lead the EU, energized by final ratification of the Lisbon Treaty but reeling from economic crisis and declining public confidence, remains to be seen.

This chapter continues our discussion of the EU, building upon the previous one that covered many of its important historical milestones. As noted in the opening chapter, the EU is the main institutional force behind Europeanization and, perhaps, "One Europe." Since the signing of the Maastricht Treaty in 1991, the EU has taken numerous initiatives both to "widen" (expand to more countries) and "deepen" (integrate in more policy areas). Today, Europeanization in a variety of fields—economics, the environment, justice, social policy, culture—means that the EU helps shape policies that are then enacted in its member states. Put differently, the locus of political decision-making in Europe frequently is at the EU level.

The political institutions of the EU—those bodies that make and enforce decisions—are therefore of foremost importance for a student of European politics. This is not to say that domestic political institutions—parliaments, prime ministers, and courts—do not matter. They do, but in many cases these institutions are either enacting EU policy or directives or are constrained from acting in a certain direction because of EU authority in that area. Scholars and observers of the EU debate how much weight one should put on the supranational and the intergovernmental aspects of the EU. The issue, in essence, boils down to where political power in Europe presently lies and which institutions matter the most.

This chapter focuses on EU institutions, leaving national level ones for subsequent development. This is not meant as a statement that the EU somehow matters more than national governments. Many treatments of European politics, especially those rooted more in comparative politics than in international politics, would reverse the order, or even include the EU only as a sort of afterthought. However, as mentioned earlier, the boundaries between comparative and international politics are blurred, not only within the discipline of political science but also in Europe itself. We cover the institutional "nuts and bolts" of the EU first because they have continent-wide relevance and by necessity will appear in discussions of how domestic institutions operate in a Europe that is increasingly characterized by Europeanization and multi-level governance.

The EU has a complex decision-making structure. Like any government, one can point to legislative, executive, and judicial organs. These are identified in Figure 4.1. However, one must remember that the EU is not a national government. Its structures blend together elements of inter-governmentalism, in which states are represented, and supranationalism, which empowers EU structures and citizens directly, bypassing national governments. One issue to keep in mind is that while the supranational powers of the EU make it unique among international organizations and provide the basis for multi-level governance in Europe, intergovernmentalism remains a powerful force within the EU.

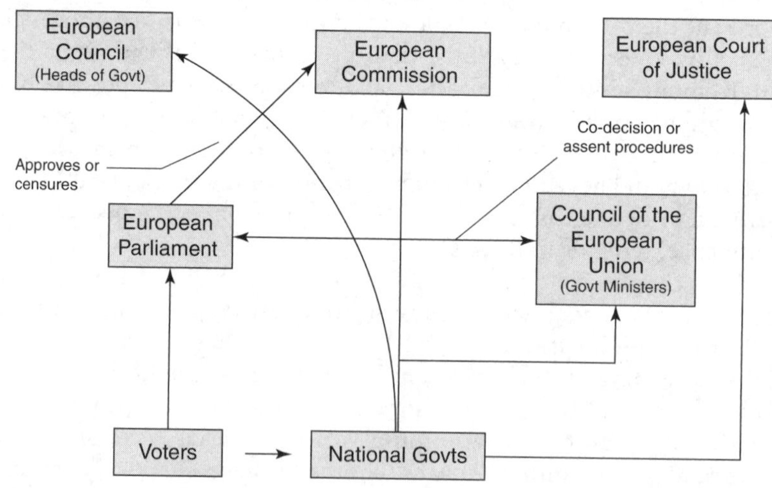

FIGURE 4.1
Institutions of the European Union

INSTITUTIONS OF THE EUROPEAN UNION

The European Commission

The **European Commission** is commonly viewed as the supranational executive body of the EU. It is responsible for overseeing the implementation of EU laws and directives, but—unlike most national executives—it is also responsible for developing the ordinary, day-to-day agenda of the EU and initiating legislation. It oversees the bureaucracy of some 25,000 "Eurocrats." Its headquarters is in Brussels. The commission's work is divided up into thirty-seven service institutions and departments called **Directorate Generals (DG)**, roughly similar to what might be a cabinet portfolio or division with a national-level executive branch. Each DG has its own staff and is overseen by an EU commissioner. Each country receives one commissioner, and some of the twenty-seven commissioners oversee more than one DG. The Lisbon Treaty, as originally formulated, envisioned reducing the number of commissioners to two-thirds the number of member states, but after the Irish voters initially rejected the treaty, this provision was dropped. States will continue to receive one commissioner each.

European Commission ■ executive body of the EU charged with drafting legislation and directives and overseeing implementation of EU policy.

Directorate Generals (DG) ■ departments within the European Commission akin to executive departments or ministries in a national government.

The European Parliament must approve the slate of nominated commissioners. Commissioners serve five-year terms, and they take an oath of loyalty to the EU, pledging to accept no national instructions on EU policy. In other words, the European Commissioner from Hungary, for example, is supposed to cease being "Hungarian" upon appointment to the Commission. He or she is supposed to think of the common good of the EU and all its members, not just Hungary. In practice, of course, this may be difficult to do. Therefore commission seats are typically divided up on the basis of the country's interests, although the most visible slots (e.g., foreign relations, industry, trade) are often given to larger countries.

The head of the European Commission, its president, is nominated by the Council of the EU. Presidents of the Commission, unlike the typical commissioner, usually have some political prominence: Jacques Delors (1985–1995) had served as French finance minister; Jacques Santer (1995–1999) had been prime minister of Luxembourg; Romano Prodi (1999–2004) was the former prime minister of Italy (a post to which he returned in 2006); and José Manuel Barroso (2004–) is former prime minister of Portugal and was reappointed to his second five-year term in 2009. The president of the Commission, however, is only *primus inter pares* (first among equals). Notably, unlike a prime minister in a parliamentary system, he or she is not responsible for the selection of the other commissioners, as they are selected by their own national governments. Seven commissioners also serve as vice presidents, including the new post of High Representative for Foreign Affairs and Security Policy created by the Lisbon Treaty. The composition of the European Commission as of 2011 is presented in Table 4.1

The Commission is expected to work in close concert with other EU institutions and national governments. Ideally, DGs have the political, legal, and technical expertise to run the day-to-day affairs of the EU. The Commission debates ideas for draft legislation, which often originate in the DGs. Decisions are usually made by consensus, although a majority vote can be sufficient to pass proposals onwards to decision-making bodies. The Commission is not a legislative body, but it is intimately involved in the legislative process, drafting laws, regulations, and

TABLE 4.1

Commissioners of the European Union, 2010–2014

Portfolio	Commissioner	Country
President	José Manuel Barroso	Portugal
VP, High Representative for Foreign Affairs and Security	Catherine Ashton	Great Britain
VP, Justice, Rights, and Citizenship	Viviane Reding	Luxembourg
VP, Competition	Joaquín Almunia	Spain
VP, Transport	Siim Kallas	Estonia
VP, Digital Agenda	Neelie Kroes	Netherlands
VP, Industry and Entrepreneurship	Antonio Tajani	Italy
VP, Interinstitutional Relations and Administration	Maroš Šefčovič	Slovakia
Economic and Monetary Affairs	Olli Rehn	Finland
Environment	Janez Potočnik	Slovenia
Trade	Karel De Gucht	Belgium
Regional Policy	Johannes Hahn	Austria
Enlargement and European Neighborhood Policy	Stefan Fule	Czech Republic
Agriculture and Rural Development	Dacian Cioloş	Romania
Employment, Social Affairs	László Andor	Hungary
Energy	Günther Oettinger	Germany
Internal Market and Services	Michel Barnier	France
Climate Action	Connie Hedegaard	Denmark
Taxation, Customs Union, Audit	Algirdas Šemeta	Lithuania
Development	Andris Piebalgs	Latvia
Health and Consumer Policy	John Dalli	Malta
Research and Innovation	Maire Geoghegan-Quinn	Romania
Education, Culture, Multi-lingualism and Youth	Androulla Vassiliou	Cyprus
International Cooperation and Humanitarian Aid	Kristalina Georgieva	Bulgaria
Financial Programming and Budget	Janusz Lewandowski	Poland
Fisheries and Maritime Affairs	Maria Damanaki	Greece
Home Affairs	Cecilia Malmstrom	Sweden

directives, issuing opinions on proposed amendments, suggesting amendments of its own, and, if necessary, withdrawing a proposal prior to a vote by the Council of the European Union or the European Parliament. The Commission also oversees the implementation of EU law, as the EU requires that member states transpose EU directives and policies into their own national legislation, an important mechanism in how Europeanization actually works. This gives the Commission a lot of power over national governments, as it sort of stands over the shoulder of national-level parliamentarians and bureaucrats to ensure that national laws are drawn up and enforced in accordance with the Commission's expectations. If states do not adopt or fail to implement EU laws and directives properly, the Commission then has the power to take offending states, institutions, or individuals to the European Court of Justice. In this respect, national governments surrender their sovereignty to the EU.

However, the Commission is not all-powerful. It must work within parameters defined by EU law and, above all else, is circumscribed by the more inter-governmental Council of the European Union (discussed below). However, the Commission has much *de facto* power to interpret matters as it sees fit, and its own interest is usually in expanding the competencies and supranational aspects of the EU.[2] For this reason, the Commission is a target for those opposed to deeper EU integration, and it is often accused for being too technocratic and opaque in its work. Notably, in the wake of corruption scandals in the 1990s, the power of the European Parliament to oversee the work of the Commission has been expanded with visible effect.

The Council of the European Union

Among all EU institutions, the **Council of the European Union** (formerly referred to as the Council of Ministers and not to be confused with the European Council, discussed later in the chapter) is arguably the most powerful, as it is the body that is most empowered to decide what the EU should and should not do. Unlike the Commission, it is inter-governmental, and functions like a legislature insofar as it votes to approve laws, regulations, and directives. However, the Council is not a single institution with a set membership. Rather, it is more like a collection of specialist subcommittees, whose composition changes depending upon the issue at hand. In other words, the Council of the EU is not a single council; it is a series of issue-specific councils, and it meets, in one form or another, about ninety times a year.

Council of the European Union ■ inter-governmental body made up of national-level ministers that reviews and approves Commission proposals; also called the Council of Ministers.

Each version of the Council is made up of representatives from the governments of each member-state. The actual person occupying the seat, however, changes with the issue. For example, if the Council is discussing economic issues, then ministers of finance would typically represent their governments; if the issue is the environment, it would be environmental ministers; health ministers for health issues, and so on. There is no set term of office for those on the Council; individuals serve as long as they hold onto their national-level cabinet post. As governments change, however, the composition of the council inevitably is altered. Formal meetings of the Council occur in Brussels and under the Lisbon Treaty its meetings must be open to the public when it votes on legislative proposals. Leadership of the Council rotates every six months according to a pre-determined order of countries. The selected country, not a particular individual, is said to assume the presidency of the Council of the EU, which gives it greater visibility and ability to shape the EU's agenda. Some argue that a six month rotating presidency is not particularly efficient. In practice, three successive Council presidencies, often referred to as a *troika*, cooperate to ensure some policy coordination.

The Council of the EU takes decisions on proposed legislation, which includes both directives that must be transposed into national law and regulations that are automatically binding on member states without any action by national parliaments. Its approval is required for anything to become EU law, although, as noted below, the European Parliament also has a voice in many areas of legislation. How the Council of the European Union makes decisions, though, is rather complicated and has been the subject of numerous disputes and changes. Traditionally, decisions were taken by unanimity. Unanimous voting on every piece of legislation, however, could cripple the decision-making capacity of the EU, as even the smallest

qualified-majority voting (QMV) ■ procedure used in the Council of the EU based upon weighted votes for each country; supermajority of votes required to pass legislation; will be phased out under Lisbon Treaty.

state could kill a proposal. For this reason, the EU adopted a procedure of **qualified-majority voting (QMV).** QMV prevents any one state from vetoing policy, but unlike simple majority voting, it is designed to ensure that a large majority of states favor an approved proposal. QMV was originally established with the Single European Act of 1986, but its voting weights were altered by the Nice Treaty (which went into effect in 2003), and its scope has expanded as a result of several EU treaties and agreements.

Under QMV each country is assigned a number of votes. The precise figures based upon EU membership as of 2011 are presented in Table 4.2. As one sees, larger countries get more votes. However, the votes are not directly proportional,

TABLE 4.2

Representation in the Council of the EU and European Parliament

Country	Population in millions	# of Votes under QMV	Vote per million people	# of MEPs (2009)	MEP per million people
Germany	82.4	29	0.35	99	1.20
France	62.9	29	0.46	72	1.14
Great Britain	60.4	29	0.48	72	1.19
Italy	58.8	29	0.49	72	1.22
Spain	43.8	27	0.62	50	1.14
Poland	38.2	27	0.71	50	1.31
Romania	21.6	14	0.65	33	1.53
Netherlands	16.3	13	0.80	25	1.53
Greece	11.1	12	1.08	22	1.90
Portugal	10.6	12	1.13	22	2.08
Belgium	10.5	12	1.14	22	2.10
Czech Republic	10.3	12	1.17	22	2.14
Hungary	10.1	12	1.19	22	2.18
Sweden	9.0	10	1.11	18	2.00
Austria	8.3	10	1.20	17	2.05
Bulgaria	7.7	10	1.30	17	2.21
Slovakia	5.4	7	1.30	13	2.41
Denmark	5.4	7	1.30	13	2.41
Finland	5.3	7	1.32	13	2.45
Ireland	4.2	7	1.67	12	2.86
Lithuania	3.4	7	2.06	12	3.53
Latvia	2.3	4	1.74	8	3.48
Slovenia	2.0	4	2.00	7	3.50
Estonia	1.3	4	3.08	6	4.62
Cyprus	0.8	4	5.00	6	7.50
Luxembourg	0.5	4	8.00	6	12.00
Malta	0.4	3	7.50	5	12.50
Total	492.8	345	.70	736	1.49

Source: 2006 population figures from Eurostat.

meaning that Germany, with more than 200 times the population of Malta, receives fewer than 10 times the number of votes. If anything, small countries are actually over-represented. For a proposal to pass, it must meet three criteria. First, it must have 255 of the 345 votes (73.9 percent), which is a "super-majority" of the votes. Secondly, under pure majoritarian logic, it must have the support of majority (fourteen of twenty-seven) of the member states.[3] Finally, to prevent the smaller states from ganging up and imposing their will on the larger ones, the total votes in favor of a proposal must come from countries representing at least 62 percent of the EU's population. This final procedure helps ensure a degree of democracy: those that represent a minority of the population cannot impose their will on the majority.[4] By comparison, note that in the US Senate a bill could pass with fifty-two votes from senators representing the smallest twenty-six states, whose population is less than 20 percent of the national total. In this respect, the EU procedures, although cumbersome, might look more "democratic" by ensuring that the requisite number of votes represents the majority of EU voters.

This system of QMV has been subject to disputes and proposed revisions, and, with the adoption of the Lisbon Treaty, it will be eliminated in November 2014, although a state can still request that QMV be applied until March 2017. After 2014, the Council of the EU will use a **double majority** voting procedure. Under double majority, a proposal would be adopted if 55 percent of the states (fifteen of twenty-seven as of 2011) representing 65 percent of EU citizens approved it. An additional provision is that any blocking minority must compose at least four member states. Under these provisions, the various weighted votes assigned to each country would be entirely scrapped. Instead, Malta and Germany will have equal votes out of the twenty-seven for the first criterion in the double majority scheme, but Germany's size would be recognized in the second criterion. Whether this is "fairer" or not is subject to some dispute and one must still wait to see how it plays out, but at minimum the double majority plan is far simpler than QMV.

double majority ■ voting procedure for the Council of the European Union established by Lisbon Treaty; requires 55 percent of states representing 65 percent of population to pass proposals.

Lastly, one should recognize that the Council of the European Union does not always use QMV. True, there has been a gradual expansion of QMV, and one could argue that with EU expansion to more states potentially in the works, there should be more use of QMV (or, after 2014, double majority) to facilitate decision-making. Nonetheless, there are still various areas (taxes, culture, expansion, regional funds, foreign policy) that require unanimous voting. These issues are often considered more important or more sensitive to concerns about sovereignty, and thus by requiring unanimity, each state retains a veto over EU policy. In this way, the very voting system used by the Council of the EU combines—awkwardly perhaps—inter-governmentalism with supranationalism, although, as with much in the EU, the push is toward more supranationalism that would take away the power of any individual member state.

The European Parliament

European Parliament ■ the popularly-elected legislature of the EU, which shares much decision-making power with the Council of the EU; only EU body elected by voters.

The **European Parliament** (EP) is the other legislative body within the EU and is the only EU institution directly elected by EU citizens. Because member-states are not directly represented in the EP, it functions more as a supranational institution than an inter-governmental one. Housed both in Brussels and in Strasbourg, France, it is elected every five years in European-wide elections by proportional representation.[5] However, there is no single European party-list. Instead, each member state receives a certain number of MEPs (Members of the European Parliament) based roughly on its population, although again smaller states are disproportionately represented (see Table 4.2). MEPs receive the same salary as members of their respective national parliaments, as well as a generous €262 per diem when they are in Brussels or Strasbourg. For the most part, MEPs are second-tier politicians, as those with more possibilities would be more prone to serve in their national parliaments.

Once elected, members of the various national parties (e.g., the British Labour Party, the Spanish Socialist Party, the Czech Christian Democratic Party) form blocs within the EP based upon party affinity. As of 2009, there were seven such groups. The largest are the European Peoples' Party (264 seats out of the 736 in the 2009 elections), composed of representatives of various conservative and Christian Democratic parties from the center-right, and the Party of European Socialists (161 seats), uniting Socialist and Social Democratic parties on the center-left.[6] Interestingly, anti-EU parties such as the British Independence Party, the True Finns, and the Danish People's Party won seats in the 2009 EP elections and formed their own bloc, Europe of Freedom and Democracy, but a larger, anti-EU campaign slate under the heading "Libertas," which ran 500 candidates across Europe, won only one seat.[7] Because no single grouping commands a majority in the EP, coalitions are necessary to pass proposals. Interestingly, studies have shown that MEPs do vote more along party/partisan lines than on national lines, showing perhaps that supranationalism has taken hold.[8] Like national legislatures, the workload of the EP is assigned to committees in policy-specific areas. EU Commissioners frequently appear before EP committees, and there is much cooperation between the specialized DGs and their EP counterparts. MEPs can speak in any of the twenty-three official languages, which can make its proceedings cumbersome.

The EP shares its legislative power with the Council of the EU. This is not, however, an equal partnership. In the early days of European integration, the EP—then appointed—had purely advisory powers. Since 1979, however, when voters first elected it, the EP has steadily gained power vis-à-vis the Council. The SEA introduced a cooperation procedure, which gives the EP the right to review the Council of the EU's common position before a final decision is officially made. At this stage, the EP can reject or amend the Council's common position, and the Commission is also allowed to weigh in on the process. Ultimately, however, under cooperation procedures, Council had the final say as it could override any action of the EP with a unanimous vote.

co-decision ■ increasingly used mechanism in which EU actions and proposals must be approved both by the EP and the Council of the EU.

The cooperation procedure has largely been superseded by **co-decision,** created by the Maastricht Treaty and expanded in use by the 1997 Amsterdam Treaty and the 2009 Lisbon Treaty. The co-decision procedure is rather complicated, involving multiple readings of proposals in both the EP and the Council, but the gist of it is that for a proposal to pass it must be approved both by the Council (in this case, at present, by QMV) and by an absolute majority vote in the EP. If the two sides cannot reach agreement, a conciliation procedure is employed to hammer out differences. If there is no compromise, the act is not adopted. Thus, under co-decision, the EP has real legislative power, as its agreement is necessary for legislation to pass. There is also an assent procedure, usually used for the ratification of agreements, including expansion, reached by the EU. Under assent, the EP's approval is necessary, but it cannot offer amendments. In addition, the EP's approval is necessary for all non-compulsory items in the EU budget. Amie Kreppel argues that the EP is no longer a weak "multinational chamber of Babel" but instead a "transformative" legislature that plays a powerful role in EU decision-making.[9] Significantly, however, there are certain issues (e.g., foreign policy, some justice and home affairs issues) where the EP's powers remain purely consultative or advisory. Thus, while the EP is certainly more empowered than before, it is not yet co-equal to the Council.

The EP has also gained powers over the European Commission, although only the Commission has the right to actually propose legislation. In 1999, it forced Jacques Santer, then head of the European Commission, to form an investigatory body to examine charges of corruption within the Commission. The committee confirmed most of the allegations, and the EP was prepared to censure (in effect dismiss) the European Commission. Before the EP could do so, Santer and the rest of the Commission resigned. In 2004, the EP forced two nominated Commissioners to withdraw from consideration. The principle of the EP as a check on the power of the Commission has thus been enshrined.

As noted, the EP is the only body directly elected by voters, although elections to the EP have occurred only since 1979. The fact that the other EU bodies are not directly elected has led some to complain of a democratic deficit within the EU. Some even joke that measured against the EU's criteria for membership—a prospective member must be a democracy—the EU could not join itself! Despite such complaints, however, one cannot say that European voters have made the most of their opportunity to influence the EU, as turnout in EP elections is far lower than turnout in national elections. In 1979, for example, 63 percent of those eligible to vote turned out to vote for MEPs. In 2009, the figure was only 43.2 percent, the lowest turnout ever for EP elections, with very low turnout in some new EU members. Table 4.3 shows the turnout rates in select countries in the past four elections.

The European Court of Justice

The **European Court of Justice** (ECJ) is the highest judicial organ in the EU and one that is clearly supranational in orientation. Housed in Luxembourg, the ECJ is composed of twenty-seven judges, one appointed by each of the member states for six-year terms by common concord among member states. The ECJ is empowered to hear cases that involve states, corporations, or individuals, and makes rulings on a range of issues, including provisions of the common market, rights of EU citizens, social policy, and interpretation of EU treaties. It also issues preliminary opinions on matters sent to it by national courts. It ruled on more than five hundred cases a year from 2000 to 2005. Decisions usually require only a majority of the judges, and many cases are heard before a panel of only three or five judges. There is also a subsidiary Court of First Instance to handle initial rulings on less complex cases. The role of the ECJ is crucial for the functioning of the EU. Without a body of law that is subject to interpretation by an EU institution, the EU's decisions and policies

European Court of Justice (ECJ) ■ highest judicial institution in the EU, it upholds EU law and has the power to enforce decisions against member-states.

TABLE 4.3

Turnout in European Parliament Elections 1994–2009

Country	1994	1999	2004	2009	+/− 1994 (or 2004)–2009
Great Britain	36.4	24.0	38.3	34.5	−1.9
Germany	60.0	45.2	43.0	43.3	−16.7
France	52.7	47.0	42.8	40.5	−12.2
Spain	59.1	64.4	45.1	46.0	−13.1
Italy	74.8	70.8	73.1	72.0	−2.8
Greece	71.2	70.2	63.4	52.6	−18.6
Netherlands	35.7	29.9	39.3	36.9	+1.2
Cyprus	n/a	n/a	71.2	58.9	−12.3
Czech Republic	n/a	n/a	28.3	28.2	−.1
Poland	n/a	n/a	20.9	24.5	+3.6
Slovakia	n/a	n/a	17.0	19.6	+2.6
Total EU	56.8	49.4	45.7	43.2	−13.6

Source: Web pages of the European Parliament, http://www.europarl.europa.eu

would appear to be arbitrary and be subject to numerous disputes. If a state is found in violation of EU law, the ECJ has the power to issue fines, which it has had to do only once, when Greece failed to comply with a directive to quit dumping hazardous waste.

While the procedures of appointment are reminiscent of inter-governmentalism, the judges are expected to abandon their national identities and act to interpret and apply EU law. Since the 1960s, the ECJ has become an important supranational institution. The primary elements of EU supranationalism—that EU provisions directly apply to individuals and that EU law supercedes national law—has been a guiding principle of the ECJ.[10] Writing in 1978 in *Simmenthal v. Commission*, the ECJ ruled that "every national court must . . . apply Community law in its entirety . . . and must accordingly set aside any provisions of national law which may conflict with it." Thus, the ECJ enjoys the power of judicial review at a supranational level and can void national laws if they are conflict with EU law.

Overall, the ECJ has been an important player in propelling European integration forward. Its ruling in the *Cassis de Dijon* case of 1979—involving the importation into West Germany of a French liqueur—established the principle of mutual recognition of product standards, considered to be essential for the functioning of a common market. Analysts have suggested that the growing power and relevance of the ECJ shows functionalism in practice. In other words, the ECJ has helped expand EU powers by supporting the European Commission with expansive readings of EU treaties and by being sympathetic to interests and actors that have sought to acquire EU protections and privileges that are denied to them by member states.[11]

The ECJ has thus been a site of "judicial activism," and worries about the powers of the un-elected ECJ and its bias toward promoting supranationalism led to special provisions being inserted into the Maastricht Treaty that would prohibit the ECJ for ruling in policy areas such as Justice and Home Affairs. National courts, especially in Germany, have also challenged the ECJ by asserting their rights to determine whether or not EU treaties accord with the national constitutions. Battles over the powers of the ECJ are a primary example of ongoing tensions between competing visions of the EU.

The European Council

The **European Council** (again, not to be confused with the Council of the EU) is where heads of government or state participate directly in the EU. It is therefore the quintessential inter-governmental body. It is a newer institution, created in 1974 as a forum for discussions among European leaders. It was formally incorporated into the EC in the 1986 SEA, and the Maastricht Treaty specifies that the European Council "shall provide the Union with the necessary impetus for development and shall define the general political guidelines thereof."

European Council ■ EU body comprised of leaders of member states that sets broad goals for the EU; headed by president of the European Council.

It meets at least twice a year and sets the general agenda for the EU as well as discussing the most important and controversial issues of the day. The more particular and technocratic issues concerning the EU are generally left to the expertise of the Commission. The European Council strives to reach decisions by consensus. Indeed, one of its main functions has been to smooth over major disagreements before divisive issues come to a vote before the Council of the European Union. Prior to adoption of the Lisbon Treaty, the presidency of the European Council rotated every six months (in accordance with the previously mentioned presidency of the Council of the EU), and the incumbent's country was therefore said to have the presidency of the EU. This has now changed. Under the terms of the Lisbon Treaty, the European Council appoints an individual to serve as president of the European Council for a two-and-a-half-year term. As noted, Herman Van Rompuy of Belgium was the first person to assume this post in 2009.

Already in the 2000s, European Council meetings became increasingly important to set goals and new initiatives for the EU, and some would argue that the energy for policy generation increasingly comes from the more high-profile European Council (whose meetings are well publicized and occasionally dramatic[12]) as opposed to the more technocratic European Commission. The creation of the post of president of the European Council, even in the person of the uncharismatic Van Rompuy, will likely serve to elevate the importance of the European Council even further.

Other Bodies

The EU is far more than the institutions discussed above. It includes a host of more specialized agencies, think tanks, and service providers. Examples include the European Environmental Agency, the Office for Harmonization in the Internal Market, and the European Training Foundation. Agencies such as these are headquartered throughout Europe in an effort to spread out the EU bureaucracy, and most of these are unknown to European publics.

European Central Bank (ECB) ■ ostensibly politically independent body of the EU responsible for management of the euro.

The most important specialized institution within the EU is the **European Central Bank** (ECB), located in Frankfurt, Germany. This institution functions as the central bank for those states using the euro as their currency. Like the US Federal Reserve, it is politically independent, with a mandate to "maintain price stability" and "promote the smooth operation of payment systems," and it is expressly prohibited in Article 108 of the Maastricht Treaty from taking instructions from EU institutions or national governments. It was formally created in 1998, just before the euro was born, but evolved out of the European Monetary Institute, which was founded in 1994. The ECB's financial holdings are determined by subscriptions from member states, with largest economies (Germany, France, Great Britain, and Italy) making the largest contributions. The ECB is managed by a Governing Council and an Executive Board. As noted, the ECB is supposed to be entirely independent and professional in its operations. However, management of the euro, particularly its Stability and Growth Pact, which places a limit on states' budget deficits, has been a political issue, particularly in France and Italy.

Other bodies deserve brief mention. The Court of Auditors was established in 1977 to monitor the EU's financial affairs. It publishes an Annual Report, and, given widespread belief in the wastefulness and inefficiency of the EU, it has assumed a prominent role as a sort of watchdog. The European Economic and Social Committee (EESC) was established by the Treaty of Rome and consists of 344 representatives of trade unions, employers, professional, and civic organizations appointed to four-year terms by national governments. The purpose of this body is to consult with other EU institutions and to provide a forum for "participative democracy" and "Europe with a human face."[13] The Committee of the Regions (COR), created by the Maastricht Treaty, consists of 344 representatives of regional and local governments, such as the *Länder* of Germany or the *voivodeships* (provinces) of Poland. It is purely a consultative body, providing a means for local officials to have their voice heard at the EU. It is also a nod to the principle of **subsidiarity,** explicitly mentioned in the Maastricht Treaty and meaning that decisions in the EU should be taken at the closest practical level of governance to the citizen. In other words, if it is strictly a local issue, it is not the business of the EU as a whole, and the COR provides a means for regions and municipalities not only to lobby the EU for particular items but also to tell it when not to rule in certain fields. Both the COR and the EESC are designed to put more democratic input into EU decision-making, although the fact that these two bodies have no binding authority is held up by some as proof of the overly technocratic, anti-democratic orientation of the EU.

subsidiarity ■ principle that decisions within the EU should be taken at the closest practical level to the citizen; often used to defend national or regional powers and argue against EU action in a given area.

HOW DEMOCRATIC IS THE EUROPEAN UNION?

One of the longstanding criticisms of the EU is that it does not function democratically. In other words, it has a "**democratic deficit.**" As noted above, the only EU institution elected by voters is the EP, but even in this case interest in EP elections is low, as evidenced by voter turnout. A common complaint is that the EU is too distant and too complex for voters to understand, meaning that it does not "connect" with the citizens it purports to serve.

democratic deficit ■ idea that the EU suffers from a lack of democracy and connections to its citizens.

The democratic deficit of the EU actually has several dimensions.[14] First, the EU as a whole is rather isolated and not very well accountable to national parliaments, which are the primary bodies that represent voters. According to one set of observers, "governments can effectively ignore their parliaments when making decisions in Brussels."[15] Unfortunately, when up to 80 percent of the laws passed at the national level originate from the EU, one begins to wonder what purpose national parliaments even serve.[16] Second, as noted the EP has historically been rather weak, not a co-equal legislature to the inter-governmental Council of the European Union, particularly with respect to the budget. It also lacks the ability to propose legislation (which is bestowed exclusively to the European Commission). Third, there are no real European-wide elections. EP elections are contested by national political parties, usually revolve around national-level political issues, and often draw people to the polls only so they can register a protest vote against their governments.[17] A prime example of this was in Great Britain in 2009, when the anti-EU British Independence Party placed second, as voters registered disgust both at the EU and the governing Labour Party. Fourth, the EU, institutionally, cognitively, and psychologically, is too distant from voters, who often do not understand it or identify with it.

Not all agree that there is a sizeable democratic deficit. Andrew Moravcsik, a well-regarded scholar who has a very inter-governmental perspective on how the EU works, notes that national governments, accountable to voters, still call the shots within the EU and that the EP has acquired substantial power over time. Moreover, the EU is quite transparent for a political institution (consider how easy it is to acquire all sorts of information from the EU's website, http://europa.eu.int) and includes mechanisms for input from local and regional governments and civic organizations.[18] Others would argue that the EU should not be so concerned about democracy. Instead, it is and should remain a technocratic, regulatory state that, rather than doing what is popular, should focus on adopting policies to foster more effective and efficient international cooperation.[19]

Discussions in the 1990s by and large reflected concerns about the perceived democratic deficit. The Amsterdam Treaty established the procedure of co-decision that gave, in some areas, the EP equal powers with the Council of the European Union. It also made the president of the European Commission accountable to the EP. However, it did not make the EP fully co-equal and did nothing to create a system of European-wide elections (e.g., popular election for the president of the Commission). There is no EU government for the EP (or voters) to hold accountable and the EU still lacks a means for voters to choose between rival policy agendas.[20] Yes, voters are linked to the EU through their national governments, but this tie to the EU seems tenuous to many in Europe. In 2009, the EP made extraordinary efforts to increase voter turnout (e.g., media messages to encourage voting, use of Twitter and YouTube to communicate with younger voters). Voter turnout, however, continued to decline, demonstrating that the EP has yet to connect with its ostensible constituents.[21] Further ideas of strengthen the EU and its connections with citizens include more funding for the Euronews television station and creation of Europe-wide electoral districts to get away from the tendency that EP elections are, in effect, a collection of various national campaigns.

Interestingly, when voters are given a say, they frequently opt against decisions made at the EU level. Consider Denmark's initial rejection of the Maastricht Treaty as well as the Irish rejection of the Nice Treaty in 2001, the French and Dutch voters "no" votes on the Constitutional Treaty in 2005, and the Irish rejection of the Lisbon Treaty in 2008, which was "undone" when they voted for it on a second attempt in 2009. The 2005 votes in particular, coming from original members of the European Community, may embolden more Euro-skeptical populations in countries such as Great Britain, Denmark, and Poland to both demand a vote on future EU reforms and to put the brake on Brussels's plans for deeper integration and expansion. The fact that public opinion polls find declining confidence in the EU institutions is evidence that the EU needs to do more to connect with citizens. For example, one poll in 2007, which found that 44 percent of respondents in Great Britain, Spain, France, Germany, and Spain think that life is worse since their countries joined the EU, is strong evidence of the EU's malaise.[22] Polls in Great Britain, perhaps the most Euro-skeptic country, in 2009 found that those Britons who thought EU membership had been bad for Britain outnumbered those who thought it had been good (37 percent vs. 31 percent).[23] Throughout Europe in 2009, anti-EU or protest parties of various types (e.g., the Dutch Freedom Party, the British Independence Party, Jobbik in Hungary) did well in EP elections, showing increasing disaffection with the EU.[24]

Antipathy towards the EU is not due solely or even primarily to perceptions of a "democratic deficit." As noted in the previous chapter, some may object to the very idea of a supranational organization making decisions that they think should be made at a national or even local level. However, the proposition, which arguably has guided the EU since its inception, that the EU does not really need to be democratic because integration should be purely technocratic in nature and/or that the process of integration would automatically win popular support, is no longer tenable.

WHAT DOES THE EUROPEAN UNION DO? PUBLIC POLICIES OF THE EU

The EU plays an important role on many political, economic, and social issues in Europe and, over time, has acquired competencies in new areas. What it ultimately hopes to achieve or what it will ultimately become remain open questions, as explained in the **Is Europe One?** feature. Casting aside concerns about the future, however, today one might reasonably ask what current EU policies typically entail. The simplest answer is "a lot," although EU policy itself often tends to be extraordinarily technocratic and complex. As noted in Chapter 3, there are over 90,000 pages of EU directives, regulations, and case law (referred to as the *acquis communautaire*), and one can easily get bogged down in the minutiae of EU activity. EU regulations extend into a wide variety of areas. Governments, of course, typically have a wide variety of detailed and sometimes arcane regulations, but critics of the EU suggest that in many areas the EU's rules are overly restrictive, unnecessary, or just plain ridiculous. For example, the EU has rules and regulations on the height of playground swings, the curvature of bananas, the trade of fresh and frozen bovine semen, and ratings of the quality of pig carcasses.[25] The discussion in this chapter is therefore not meant to be exhaustive. It focuses on several of the most contested and important EU policies.

IS EUROPE ONE?

What is the Final Goal of the European Union?

Will Winston Churchill's stated aspiration in 1946 of a "United States of Europe" ever be realized? What will be EU become? Or, more precisely, what does it *intend* to become?

Natural as these questions are, they are very difficult to answer. Part of the reason is simply that they are speculative, and no one can know the future. However, a larger problem is that the final goal of the EU has never been spelled out. True, the Schuman Plan of 1950 envisioned itself as "the first concrete foundation for a European Federation," but, rhetoric of federalists such as Robert Schuman and Jean Monnet to the contrary, the subsequent treaty creating the European Coal and Steel Community only mentioned a "broader and deeper community among peoples." The Treaty of Rome and the Maastricht Treaty state an "ever closer union of peoples" as an objective, but such language purposefully avoids defining how "close" this union would ultimately be. The proposed Constitutional Treaty of the European Union, notably, was even more vague, making reference to a "common destiny" or the goal of building a "common future." Nonetheless, it clearly was a step toward political union, and some compared its crafting to the constitutional convention in Philadelphia that ultimately formed the US.[26] However, its rejection in 2005 by French and Dutch voters left the whole idea of a European constitution up in the air.

Where then does Europe go? Neo-functionalist theories, of course, would argue that integration builds upon integration, and, one imagines, successive spillovers stop only once full political union has been achieved. Less charitably, one could invoke Robert Michels's "iron law of oligarchy" to argue that political institutions always seek to expand the scope of their influence, become more complex, and, for Michels, less democratic.[27] In other words, political actors and bureaucracies are never satisfied; they seek new missions for themselves, regardless of whether there is any objective need for them to do so. Euro-skeptics would argue that the expansion of EU authority through the Single European Act, the Maastricht Treaty, and other more recent treaties exemplify this tendency, and that the creeping authority of the EU has gone beyond reason. After the adoption of the Nice Treaty, the decision to expand in 2004, and promulgation of a draft Constitutional Treaty, Europhiles appeared to be ascendant. The apparently unstoppable EU, however, ran into a more powerful force: its own citizens, as Dutch and French voters in 2005 and Irish voters in 2008 put a brake on treaties that would reform and presumably strengthen EU institutions.

By the end of the 2000s, the EU was at a crossroads. While the Lisbon Treaty, after great controversy in several states—including Poland, the Czech Republic, Great Britain, and, obviously, Ireland—was finally ratified by all member states, it remains unclear what its impact will be. Despite fears by its critics, it does not create a European superstate. The EU remains a hybrid organization, containing elements of both inter-governmentalism and supranationalism. While some would no doubt like to scale back EU powers, it is clear that the most important policies of the EU—the common market, the euro, common policies on a host of transnational issues—are here to stay. Some policies, such as the CAP, as noted in the **In Focus** feature, may have to be scaled back or even scrapped. Others, particularly foreign policy, may have to be left to individual states, or, at best, rely upon inter-governmental cooperation. However, barring a major shift in international affairs, the EU is not going away.

But it is clear that, for the foreseeable future at any rate, there are limits to European integration. Europeans are apprehensive about a host of issues—immigration, terrorism, threats from global economic

(*continued*)

forces, chronic unemployment. These issues are taken up in subsequent chapters. While some of these issues may point to the need for more integration, there is little doubt that in many countries there is more emphasis on national-level solutions and a disdain for the EU. Nationalist sentiments are on the rise across Europe—in Britain, Denmark, Austria, Italy, Poland, and Slovakia, among others. Whereas the thirteen colonies could form the US, Europe, with its linguistic, economic, historical, and religious divisions, will not easily merge into a single state.

In this respect, it is easy to be skeptical of the future of the EU. Europe is not yet "one" and may never be. Nonetheless, there is little doubt that globalization is making the world a smaller place and compels international cooperation. No country is seriously talking about pulling out of the EU or substantially revising past treaties. Europe may be taking a breather, giving itself time to overcome its "enlargement fatigue." If the EU will not be a single state, it may be able to create a somewhat decentralized federation—modeled perhaps ironically on Switzerland, which has rejected EU membership—that would make decisions in a broad array of fields independently of member states. In the economic arena, one could say that Europe is already largely there. It could assume powers to cover all pan-European issues.

If this strikes you as too optimistic, imagine attending Churchill's speech in Zurich in 1946. Talk of a "United States of Europe" a year after World War II could easily have been dismissed as utopian. More than sixty years later, look how far Europe as come. In another sixty years, who knows what might be achieved?

Critical Thinking Questions

1. Looking ahead ten to twenty years, do you think European integration will deepen? In what ways?
2. In what policy area do you think EU integration has been least effective? Do you think the EU will abandon or retreat from efforts to pursue integration in this area?

The Budget of the EU

A good place to start a discussion of EU policy is to look at its budget, which gives one some idea of its priorities and resources. As one can imagine, the budget is a source of contention, with some states, especially Great Britain, arguing that the EU spends too much money. Reforming the EU budget is thus a constant item of debate.

Common Agricultural Policy (CAP) ■ controversial agricultural policy of the EU that helps insure farmers' income, protects EU agriculture from foreign competition, and eats up a sizeable part of the EU budget.

structural funds ■ monies distributed within the EU from richer members to poorer member states to help the latter develop economically and meet EU standards.

Figure 4.2 presents a breakdown of the proposed 2007–2013 EU budget, which reflects the fact that the EU operates on a six-year budget cycle. Several items are worth noting. First, the overall budget of the EU, given its size and scope, is actually rather modest—€123.5 billion in 2006.[28] This works out to about 1 percent of the output of all EU countries, which pales in comparison to the budgets of member-states, which often consume over 40 percent of the country's gross domestic product and is far less than the nearly $3 trillion annual budget of the US.[29] Second, one sees that a large portion of the EU funds are spent on the **Common Agricultural Policy,** which is discussed in the **In Focus** section. The 36 percent figure from Figure 4.2 actually represents a sizeable decrease in the CAP, which consumed 70 percent of the budget in the early 1980s and 45 percent of the 2006 budget. Next to the CAP, one sees a sizeable amount of money for **structural funds,** which are used to help poorer states develop economically and meet EU standards on such issues as social policy and environment. Money for competitiveness is devoted to research and development, education, and support for common

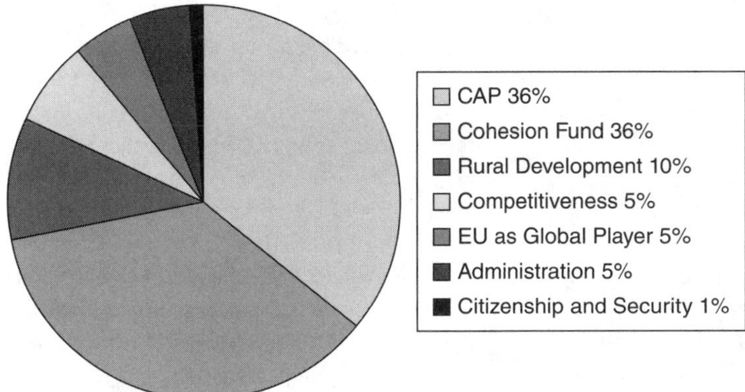

FIGURE 4.2
EU Budget Projections.
Source: European Commission, reported at http://www.2007-2013.eu/by_scope.php

IN FOCUS

The Common Agricultural Policy

The Common Agricultural Policy (CAP) is one of the largest and most controversial of all the EU's programs. Traditionally, it has consumed the vast share of the EU's budget, and debates over how to reform the CAP—or to scrap it altogether—figure prominently both within the EU and in international trade talks.

CAP's origins lie with the 1957 Treaty of Rome, which set the "common organization of agricultural markets" as a goal that would serve five objectives: increase productivity in agriculture, create a sufficient level of income for farmers, stabilize markets, guarantee a secure food supply, and deliver reasonable prices to consumers (Articles 39–40). Initial discussions on the CAP began in 1958, and most of its provisions were codified in the early 1960s. It replaced national agricultural support systems with a Europe-wide one, and established free trade in agriculture with common prices for products across Europe. CAP provided export subsidies to allow European farmers to be competitive with lower cost producers in international markets, and it set a target price for most agricultural goods (e.g., cereals, meat, dairy products), which guaranteed farmers a higher price for their products than what they would garner on a purely open, competitive market. In this way, CAP was a protectionist policy, insulating European farmers from world market forces and explicitly encouraging European consumers to buy European products. In its early years, the CAP's primary backer was France, which had relatively large agricultural sector, envisioned agriculture as part of its national heritage, and viewed CAP as a trade-off for allowing the free trade of German industrial goods. For the French, the CAP was a means to make the rest of Europe pay for its agricultural subsidies. Put differently, Dutch and Belgian and German taxpayers were helping to ensure a good income for French farmers. However, to the extent that rural populations were a sizeable voting bloc—about 25 percent in many countries—CAP proved to be a political "winner" for many European leaders.[30]

It should be obvious that the objectives of CAP were contradictory. In particular, consumers were not served very well because without the CAP they would enjoy lower prices for food, as cheaper imported food from, for example, the US or North Africa would be allowed into Europe. However, with CAP setting an

(*continued*)

artificially higher price for products, there was no cost advantage to potential imported products such as US wheat or Tunisian olive oil. Instead, Europeans consumed French wheat and Italian olive oil, and, predictably, farm lobbies emerged to lobby both national governments and Brussels for continued subsidies.

In certain respects, the CAP worked remarkably well. Because farmers were encouraged to produce and offered a high price for their goods, production soared, so that by the 1980s the EC had mountains of surplus butter, cheese, and meat that it could not consume or even unload. Large portions of each year's grain harvest were turned into fertilizer. However, thanks to export subsidies, European farmers could also sell their produce on world markets, even though producers elsewhere had lower costs because land and labor was more expensive in Europe.

While all looked great from the farmers' perspective, CAP had many critics. It consumed most of the EC's budget, and as fewer and fewer people worked the land—by the 1990s only about 4 percent of the workforce was employed in agriculture—transferring a vast amount of money to a small minority caused many to look twice at CAP. This was especially true in states that were less agricultural or had more efficient farms that did not need CAP support. Great Britain, particularly under Thatcher, became the primary critic of CAP, but others, including the Germans and the Dutch, began to ask why their taxpayers were supporting French, Italian, or Spanish agriculture. Moreover, consumers began to recognize that CAP was costly to them, as they would end up saving money if they could buy lower cost agricultural goods. At present, estimates are that CAP costs the average consumer in Europe about €250 a year in terms of higher food costs and financial transfers to farmers and leads to such absurdities that the EU ends up granting each cow a $913 subsidy![31] Lastly, data revealed that CAP overwhelmingly benefited large landowners who really did not need additional income. For example, in budget year 2003–2004, the queen of England received €360,000 from CAP. Data revealed that only six percent of the farms received 53 percent of the benefits, with 60 percent of the smallest farms getting only 10 percent of CAP funds.[32] Audits in 2009 found—in addition to Queen Elizabeth—German gummy bear manufacturers, Italian luxury cruise caterers, Prince Albert II of Monaco, and Spanish brandy distillers were recipients of CAP largesse.[33]

Reforming CAP is thus a major topic within the EU. The first serious efforts to reform CAP began in the 1980s, when the EC reduced price supports for many products and committed itself to budgetary discipline on the CAP. More concerted efforts to reform CAP occurred in the early 1990s under the leadership of Ray MacSherry, the Irish commissioner for agriculture. His reforms helped modify CAP so that it relied less and less upon price supports and instead gave a direct payment to farmers. Moreover, he proposed that CAP monies be better targeted to those farmers that really needed support, typically owners of smaller farms, not giant agri-businesses. The EC's trading partners also sought CAP reform, as they argued that export subsidies and tariffs prohibited free trade in agriculture and hurt poorer developing-world farmers who could not sell their products in the giant European market. Export subsidies were cut as part of the Uruguay Round of international trade talks. Paradoxically, however, the new compensation packages for European farmers, which included direct payments and monies for taking land out of production (which helped eliminate the mountains of butter), actually added to the cost of CAP.[34]

New efforts to reform CAP were launched in the 1990s. One impetus was the outbreak of mad cow disease in Britain, which focused attention on food safety and environmental issues. These issues received additional attention thanks to the contamination of poultry products in Belgium in 1999 and in Germany in 2002 and the avian flu scare in 2005. Moreover, as the EU looked to expand to Eastern Europe—which is far more agricultural—it was clear that current levels of CAP spending were unsustainable. Germany, which in the past had deferred to the French on the CAP, also became more vociferous on the need for reform.[35] After often-acrimonious debate, proposals were put forward in the EU's Agenda 2000 reform program. They envisioned less money for price support and more utilization of direct payments to farmers. By 2003, CAP market support schemes, which had composed two-thirds of the CAP in 1990, were reduced to a fifth of CAP spending. More monies were also to be set aside for rural development and environmental protection, which is turning CAP more into a structural and aid policy than a market support scheme. As for expansion, the post-communist countries, some of which, like Poland and Romania, have almost 20 percent of the population employed in agriculture, were offered only partial CAP support. Polish farmers, for example, would only get 25 percent of their CAP entitlement in 2004, 30 percent in 2005, and so on, until full CAP payments would be given in 2013.

CAP, however, remains under great pressure. Part of the problem is the 2004 expansion, which has doubled the number of farmers in the EU. According to the Court of Auditors, in 2005 over 1,400,000 Polish farms applied for CAP support, more than France, Spain, and Italy (three of the largest CAP recipients) combined.[36] While many in Brussels (and now doubt Paris and Madrid) hope that many of these Polish farmers will go bankrupt and find other employment by 2013, it is clear that post-communist countries will eat up more and more of the CAP. For the 2007–2013 budget cycle, Great Britain, together with Sweden, the Netherlands, and Germany, all net contributors to the CAP, faced off against more agricultural countries such as France, Spain, and Italy, which together received half of the CAP funds in 2004 and are concerned that without CAP many of their farms would no longer be economically viable. In the end, however, the British position largely prevailed: price supports for cereals were cut and more CAP money will go to sustainable development, food safety programs, and efforts to promote alternatives to farming such as tourism. As seen on Figure 4.2, rural development funds now consume 10 percent of the entire EU budget; in 2008 rural development consumed nearly €10 billion.[37] Interestingly, surveys from 2005 reveal that European publics are not virulently anti-CAP (even though it does hurt their pocketbooks), but they like CAP more for what they believe it does to ensure food safety, quality of food products, and environmental protection than as a means to promote farmers' incomes.[38] This may be a harbinger of more changes in the CAP. At present, CAP funds in real terms will be frozen from 2007 to 2013. The EU also wants to simplify CAP to cut down on red tape. Lastly, the World Trade Organization (WTO) has put a lot of pressure on the richer regions—particularly the EU and the US—to end or reduce their farm support programs in order to help the developing world. However, the Doha Round of WTO trade negotiations failed in 2008 precisely because the EU and the US would not make sufficient changes in agricultural policy.

Critical Thinking Questions

1. Has CAP outlived its usefulness and original justification?
2. How might CAP conflict with other policies and goals of the EU and create tensions within the EU?

market policies. Despite sizeable EU aid efforts in neighboring countries such as Ukraine, its foreign assistance/international affairs budget is relatively modest, as are its administrative costs.

Revenue for the EU comes from three main sources: a portion from tariffs of goods entering the EU (15 percent of the budget), part of the base of each state's value-added tax on consumers (15 percent of the budget), and, since 1988, assessments based upon the state's total gross domestic income (70 percent of the budget). Note that most of the EU's budget is dependent upon funds transferred from member states and thus is a source of tension between national governments and Brussels. Because of how funds are spent—overwhelming on agriculture and economic development—some states are net contributors to the EU, whereas others, mainly poorer states, are net beneficiaries. Table 4.4 provides data from the 2007–2013 estimated budget. As one could expect, there are disagreements between the better-off contributors and beneficiaries on the size and shape of the EU budget.

TABLE 4.4

Net Contributors and Beneficiaries of EU Spending

Estimated Budgetary Balances 2007–2013*

	Net Contribution/Benefit from the EU as % of Gross National Income	Income/person at Purchasing Power Parity, 2007 EU avg = 100
Contributors		
Netherlands	−0.56%	126
Germany	−0.54%	108
Sweden	−0.50%	117
Italy	−0.41%	100
Austria	−0.38%	123
France	−0.37%	107
Cyprus	−0.37%	84
Denmark	−0.31%	125
Great Britain	−0.25%	116
Finland	−0.25%	117
Beneficiaries		
Spain	0.23%	99
Ireland	0.47%	139
Malta	1.06%	68
Belgium**	1.21%	118
Slovenia	1.31%	84
Portugal	1.50%	69
Greece	2.16%	84
Hungary	3.06%	63
Czech Republic	3.17%	78
Slovakia	3.27%	60
Estonia	3.76%	70
Poland	3.76%	53
Latvia	4.40%	55
Lithuania	4.41%	58
Luxembourg**	5.80%	257

*Based on assumption that the current funding schemes do not change and that funds are actually disbursed as planned. This is taken from Commission of the European Communities, COM(2004) 501 final/2, Proposal for a Council Decision on the system of the European Communities own Resources, available at http://eur-lex.europa.eu/LexUriServ/site/en/com/2004/com2004_0501en02.pdf, accessed on 6 December 2006. Bulgaria and Romania were not included. GNP/capita figures from Eurostat.

**Without administrative expenditures, Belgium and Luxembourg would be net contributors.

Policies of the Common Market

The most developed area of EU policy is in the vast number of laws and regulations necessary to establish and maintain a common market. This makes up the bulk of the pre-Lisbon Treaty "first" or "community" pillar of the EU, and important steps in the development of the common market were highlighted in the previous chapter. While one might think that creating a common market is easy—after all, one simply allows people, goods, services, and capital to move freely—it requires much policy harmonization in order for it to work effectively. In other words, it is not enough to remove a tariff and say that one can sell a French car in Germany. Among other items, one would want to ensure that the French car meets safety and emissions standards, that the French carmaker does not receive subsidies or other benefits that give it an unfair edge over its German competitors, and, perhaps, that French workers are free to form unions, receive a decent wage (or at least are not clearly exploited), and have good working conditions. In other words, there needs to be some assurance that trade is both free and *fair*.

Reducing Barriers to Trade The policies of the common market thus reach into a number of areas. On the most basic level, physical barriers to trade and labor and capital flows have been removed: tariffs, quotas, customs offices, and border checks. One area of concern on this front is importation of products that are legal in one state into another where they are illegal. Such importation (e.g., marijuana legally purchased in the Netherlands) is prohibited, as states are empowered to enforce their own laws on banned or illegal goods.

In addition, the EU has moved to reduce fiscal barriers that can be barriers to trade and distort prices. An obvious example would be differential tax policies, which can make the same products more expensive in different states. The EU has thus made tax harmonization—particularly of the VAT, in effect the sales tax—a priority, setting a 15 percent minimum and working toward a single VAT across Europe. Excise taxes on alcohol and tobacco are also regulated under EU rules. And, of course, adoption of the euro makes it impossible for states to use exchange rates to gain trade advantages vis-à-vis others.

More difficult have been technical barriers to trade. These include items such as safety standards on products and even how products can be defined or labeled. As noted above, the *Cassis de Dijon* case of 1979 was crucial in setting the precedent of mutual recognition of standards, meaning that states must accept products that meet the minimum technical standards of the country of origin. Prior to this, there had been haggling over various points, including whether the cocoa content in British chocolate met the Belgian or Dutch standards to be called chocolate and whether or not Italian or French beer met the standards of German beer as defined by its famous 1516 purity law. In addition to mutual recognition, the EU has devised its own standards and regulations on a range of products, such as depth of automobile tire treads and allowable noise levels from lawnmower engines. EU regulations can be quite detailed and cumbersome. A proposal in 2006 required companies to register the use of 30,000 different chemicals, and the EU Commissioner for Enterprise and Industry estimates that the *annual cost* to European companies of complying with all EU regulations is €600 billion.[39]

Regulation Many laws, however, do make life easier for businesses. As part of the single market, the EU passed directives to streamline and harmonize national legislation so that banks and insurance companies can set up businesses in other EU countries. Education operates under the principle of mutual recognition of diplomas and certification. The key notion in all areas of EU law is that of nondiscrimination, meaning that all EU products and all EU citizens must be treated equally without regard for national origin. Previous policies that favored one's own national companies (as was the norm in government procurement, for example) have been abolished. These measures can be controversial. For example, Austrian universities, now less expensive than their German counterparts, have been, according to some, overrun with German students. However, under EU rules, Austria cannot favor its own citizens over foreigners.

The EU has set standards to maintain fair competition among European firms. Government support for particular enterprises is now regulated and cannot create unfair advantages for some firms over others. Of course, this is hard to enforce when many companies are owned wholly or in part by the state, but the idea is to create a more equal playing field and end the practice of state support for so-called "national champions." This has been felt most keenly in the airline industry, which used to be dominated by the flag carriers of various states (e.g., Air France, Iberia, Austrian Airlines), which could charge high prices because they had near monopolies on various routes. Air travel in Europe has been deregulated, and new, low-cost carriers (e.g., EasyJet, Air Berlin, Wizz Air) are now offering services. The EU's competition policy has also prevented the merger of various companies, including in 2001 the proposed merger of the American companies General Electric and Honeywell, both of whom, because they do business in Europe, are subject to EU regulations. This decision provoked outrage across the political spectrum in the US, but, as Jack Welch, chairman of General Electric noted, one could not simply say "to hell with Europe." Instead, he maintained that "we have to do business with Europe, so we have no choice but to respect their law."[40] In 2004, the EU took on the juggernaut of Microsoft, fining the company €497 million for using its near-monopoly in operating systems to corner the market on operating software and work group servers. In addition to paying fines, Microsoft was forced to unbundle its Windows XP system from Media Player and to open up its operating system to goods provided by other companies.

Trade in Services Over a decade after the creation of a common market, free movement of services remained a problem. Even though labor, capital, and goods moved, with few exceptions, freely, there were still various licensing barriers that prevented free trade in services. Part of the worry related to recognition of standards (e.g., could a Portuguese-licensed doctor practice in Germany?), and, after the 2004 expansion in particular, there were widespread fears that cheap service providers from post-communist countries would flood the more advanced countries. The "Polish plumber" was the archetypical figure, who, it was alleged, would, for example, move to France, charge less than French plumbers, and put French plumbers out of work. Campaigns for and against the "Polish plumber" raged inside the EU and among the mass public,

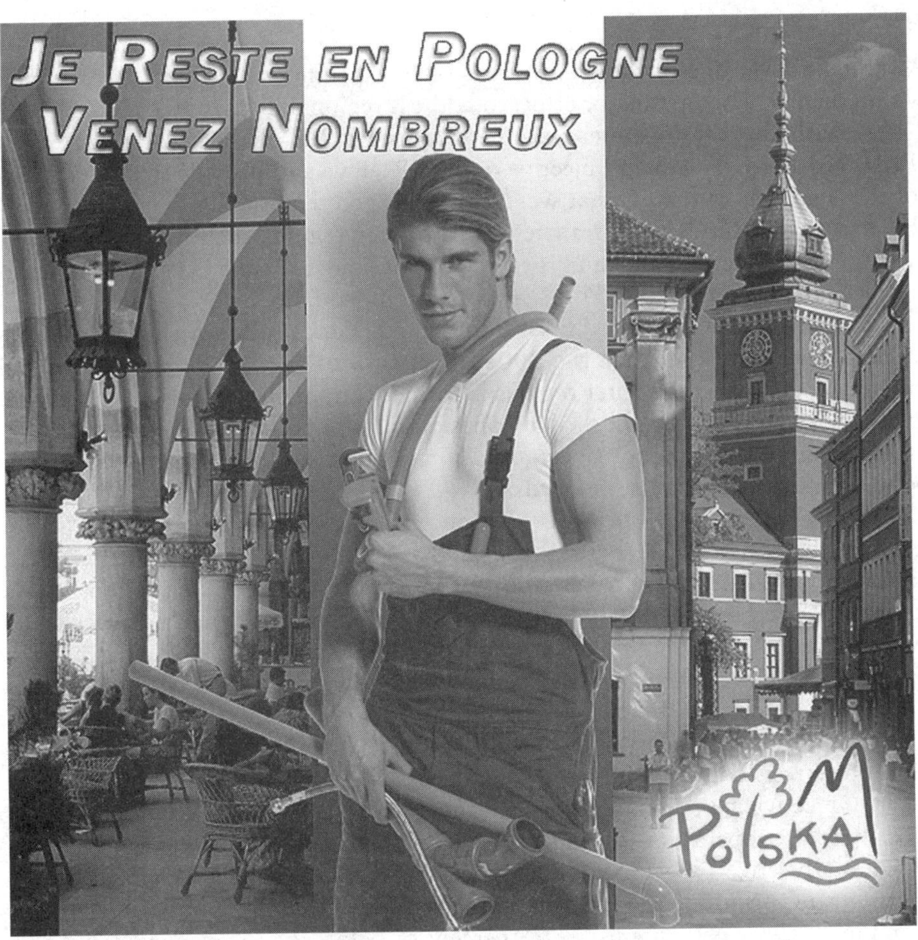

Poland presents its new face to Europe.

with the Polish tourist board, as seen in the photograph above, even displaying a large billboard in Paris that featured a handsome Polish plumber (no doubt with French women in mind) inviting people for a visit. In 2006, the EU adopted a compromise plan to liberalize trade in services, but service providers would have to meet the standards of the host country, not their country of origin, and some professions (e.g., health care, public transport, legal services) were exempted and provisions were also added to put restrictions for the sake of national security or the public interest.

Thus, whereas the EU claims to be a common market, it is clear that it is not yet a single economic space in the same way, for example, as the US. That said, the EU has adopted literally thousands of regulations and directives to break down the myriad barriers to unfettered movement and competition among economic actors and movement is toward closer and closer economic integration. Although the idea of a single market is today almost taken for granted, it bears emphasis that its creation is arguably the greatest accomplishment of the EU.

Regional Policy

As noted above, one of the major areas of EU spending is regional development within the EU. The first major effort to address regional disparities occurred in the 1970s with the establishment of the European Regional Development Fund (ERDF) in 1975. The main objective of the ERDF was to provide structural funds for those regions of the EC that were less developed than the EC average. Initially, this meant that funds were transferred to poorer regions such as southern Italy, Scotland and Wales, Ireland, and rural regions of France. As the EC expanded, other regions—mainly in Greece, Portugal, and Spain—qualified for assistance. In the 1990s, a reunified Germany dipped into regional funds to assist in the rebuilding of East Germany, and after the 2004 expansion of the EU most of the ERDF monies are going to the poorer regions in former communist countries. In addition, the Maastricht Treaty established a Cohesion Fund, which is devoted to providing assistance in the areas of transportation, competition, and the environment so that poorer states can meet EU standards.

The vast majority of intra-EU assistance occurs via the regional or structural funds of the ERDF. In the period from 2000 to 2006, the ERDF disbursed €195 billion; for the 2007 to 2013 period, €336 billion has been committed, the increase reflecting in part the addition of a large number of relatively poorer states. Whereas in 1975 regional policy consumed only 5 percent of the budget, its share has grown as the EU became more economically diverse. It grew to 15 percent by 1988 and 36 percent in 2006. Starting in 2006, the ERDF, the ESF, and the Cohesion Fund, although still technically separate, are all committed to three common objectives: convergence to EU standards by promoting sustainable development (Objective 1); regional competitiveness and employment (Objective 2); and cross-border cooperation (Objective 3). Over three-quarters of the funds are devoted to Objective 1, and include such fields as research and development, health, energy, transportation, and information technology. To qualify under ERDF, a region's income per person must be 75 percent or below the EU average; the threshold for the Cohesion Fund in 90 percent. It is important to note that the funds are devoted to regional, meaning primarily sub-national development. For example, regions in southern Italy or eastern Germany have qualified for EU assistance even though Italy or Germany as a whole would not. Regions must apply for the funds, and the EU's COR helps oversee EU regional policy. These are not complete giveaways, as EU monies are expected to be matched by funding by national or regional governments.

As might be expected, the EU's structural funds are a subject of some controversy. Taxpayers in richer states do not relish the idea that their money is being taken from them and given to others. On the other hand, those who receive EU structural funds have fought hard to maintain their level of support. In this respect, the 2004 and 2007 expansions changed the calculus, meaning that many regions of Spain, Italy, Greece, and Portugal—formerly the main beneficiaries of EU largesse—no longer qualify for ERDF monies. To remedy this, some money has been set aside so that these regions will be gradually weaned off the EU, and small amounts of money remain available to sparsely-populated regions of the EU (e.g., northern Finland and Sweden) and to the outermost regions of the EU, such as the Azores Islands of Portugal and French New Caledonia in the western Pacific.

Environmental Policy

Environmental issues are now a top concern of the EU. Notably, the environment was not mentioned at all in the original Treaty of Rome. Initial discussion of environment policy occurred only in the early 1970s. In 1981, the EU established a separate DG on environmental issues, and the SEA devoted considerable attention to environmental policy. Spurred in part by European publics that are very concerned about environmental issues, the EU has made environmental assessment an issue across a wide range of policy areas, including economics, transport, agriculture and energy. The EU's commitment to environmental protection was reiterated in numerous documents in the 1990s, and in 1994 the European Environmental Agency (EEA) began operations. As amended by the 2003 Nice Treaty, the Treaty of the European Community now commits itself to preserving the quality of the environment and sustainable development (Article 2) and devotes Article 174 to environmental priorities.

In 2001, the EU adopted its Sixth Environment Action Programme, which governs EU policy for 2001–2010. It states a number of priorities: climate change, biodiversity, human health, and sustainable development. In addition, the EU advanced a Sustainable Development Strategy in 2001, which was renewed in 2006. This document makes an explicit effort to link environmental concerns with the 2000 Lisbon Strategy on growth and jobs, envisioning a "green" future for Europe. Specific EU environmental competencies include policies regulating air quality, pesticides, waste management, "ecolabeling" for consumers, habitat preservation, adoption of the Kyoto Protocol, emissions trading to reduce greenhouse gases, encouragement of organic farming, and a ban on genetically modified organisms. The thrust of EU environmental policy, which has often been driven by "greener" countries such as Denmark, Germany, Finland, and the Netherlands, has been to boost standards across Europe, and the EU has taken a leading global role on environmental issues.

Despite EU interest on the environment, implementation has been a problem. EU directives are not always transposed into national legislation, and the EU has had to take member states to the ECJ to compel them to take action. Even on such a high-profile issue as the Kyoto Treaty, most EU states had not met the target greenhouse gas reductions, and the EU continues to monitor the laggards' compliance.

Justice and Home Affairs

One of the most rapidly evolving areas of EU policy is **Justice and Home Affairs,** which in the pre–Lisbon Treaty EU constituted a separate "pillar" of the union. This area covers a host of issues, most of which are managed by the DG on Justice, Freedom, and Security. Issues under its purview include standard law-and-order issues (e.g., immigration, fight against organized crime, terrorism, human trafficking, drug policy, Internet crime), but also the defense of rights granted to all EU citizens. Among these rights are free movement across EU borders, the right to stand and vote in European and municipal elections,[41] rights of legal redress at the European level, and the rights against discrimination. The EU has set up bodies to monitor and combat instances of racism, xenophobia, and anti-Semitism. The EU also tries to promote "active

Justice and Home Affairs ■ growing area of EU competence, including border control, crime, terrorism, and provision of EU-wide rights to all citizens.

citizenship," which includes sponsorship of international youth programs, sister-city relationships, and EU-wide non-governmental organizations. Within the rubric of Justice and Home Affairs, there have been some notable accomplishments: the creation of Europol (European Police Office) in 1995; a European Arrest Warrant; the Schengen Agreement (originally signed in 1985 but incorporated into the EU in 1997), which eliminates border controls across several EU countries[42]; and a Charter of Fundamental Rights adopted by EU leaders in 2000. The EU has repeatedly advanced a goal of a common visa and asylum policy and more coordination on immigration, and it has adopted an Action Programme for 2005–2010 on a host of issues covered under the rubric of Justice, Freedom, and Security.

Whereas cooperation on criminal activity has been forthcoming, some issues have been far less amenable to cooperation or harmonization as states have resisted a common, EU-wide standard. For example, despite repeated statements emphasizing the need for political guidelines in areas such as immigration and asylum, states have continued to maintain their own policies. Additionally, it is hard to imagine all EU countries adopting a common standard on citizenship and naturalization, let alone the EU creating a comprehensive bill of rights for all EU citizens that would supersede protections and responsibilities defined in national constitutions. In short, it is in this sphere, as well as in foreign policy, where inter-governmentalism remains strong and the integrationist impulse is far weaker.

As seen throughout this chapter, the EU aspires to do many things and has an ambitious agenda to become an even more powerful and effective actor. While many are skeptical about its future, it has already come further than many of its doubters could ever have imagined. The Lisbon Treaty and the appointment of Herman Van Rompuy to a newly created office hardly represent an endpoint of the European project. It will continue to entrench itself into the lives of Europeans and affect its member-states in profound ways. Without wholly abandoning consideration of the EU—which impinges upon national-level politics in numerous forms—we now turn to fuller consideration of political institutions and practices within individual states.

APPLICATION QUESTIONS

1. What is the rationale for QMV or double majority voting? Are these practices examples of inter-governmentalism or supranationalism? What alternatives might there be to these schemes?
2. Why doesn't the EU adopt a purely parliamentary style of government, in which an elected parliament selects a prime minister and cabinet? Who would object to such an arrangement?
3. Do you agree that the EU has a "democratic deficit"? What could realistically be done to make the EU more democratic?
4. From your understanding of EU institutions, can you give several examples of how the tensions between inter-governmentalism and supranationalism play out?
5. The EU spends a great deal of money redistributing money from richer countries to poorer ones. Whereas one might be able to understand how regional redistribution is plausible within a single country (e.g., "rich" Connecticut contributes more to the federal budget than it receives and "poor" South Carolina takes more out than it contributes), how does such a scheme work in a multinational environment? Why would richer states agree to this?

KEY TERMS

co-decision 104
Common Agricultural Policy (CAP) 112
Council of the European Union (Council of Ministers) 101
democratic deficit 108
Directorates General (DGs) 99
double majority 103
European Central Bank 108
European Council 107
European Commission 99
European Court of Justice (ECJ) 105
European Parliament (EP) 103
Justice and Home Affairs 121
Qualified-majority voting (QMV) 102
structural funds 112
subsidiarity 108

ADDITIONAL READING

Bomberg, Elizabeth, Peterson, John, and Stubb, Alexander, eds. 2008. *The European Union: How Does it Work?*, 2nd edition. Oxford: Oxford University Press.

Edited volume that focuses on the actors and policy-process of the EU. In addition to detailed information about specific EU institutions, includes chapters on democracy within the EU and how organized interests and lobbying impact EU policy.

Ginsberg, Roy. 2010. *Demystifying the European Union: The Enduring Logic of Regional Integration*, 2nd edition. Lanham MD: Rowman and Littlefield.

This book covers the historical development, institutions, and more contemporary policies of the EU. It is written with students in mind, meaning that most of its focus is more descriptive about the nuts and bolts of the EU, but it also includes some discussions about theories of EU integration and policy-making.

Hix, Simon. 2008. *What's Wrong with the European Union and How to Fix It.* Cambridge: Polity.

A provocative and lively text that does far more than simply describe how the EU works. Rather, it diagnoses problems both in the processes and outputs of policy-making in the EU, with particular attention to the question of garnering more public support and making EU institutions work more efficiently.

Journal of Common Market Studies, published by Wiley-Blackwell, website at http://www.blackwellpublishing.com/jcms

Premier academic journal on the EU, with many articles on the functions and dynamics of EU institutions and on the evolution and effectiveness of EU policies. An excellent resource for research papers on the EU.

Wallace, Helen, and Wallace, William, eds. 2005. *Policy-Making in the European Union*, 5th edition. Oxford: Oxford University Press.

With contributions by leading scholars in the field, this book looks in detail at sectoral policies (e.g., agriculture, immigration) of the EU. A very good reference for those looking for more detail at particular features of what the EU actually does.

END NOTES

1. See the tirade of Nigel Farage of the British Independence Party against Van Rompuy on YouTube at http://www.youtube.com/watch?v=lqovTGjYjM4, accessed April 26, 2010.
2. Jonas Tallberg, "Delegation to Supranational Institutions: Why, How, and with What Consequences?" *West European Politics* 25, January 2002, 23–46.
3. When acting on its own (e.g., not in response to a proposal from the Commission), a two-thirds majority is required.
4. This stipulation is almost always met by the weighted voting requirement, but it is possible that a proposal backed by all but three of the largest states would not meet this population criterion.
5. As a concession to the French, the EU agreed to hold the EP's plenary sessions once a month in Strasbourg. The "monthly move" of MEPs and staff to Strasbourg costs upwards of €200 million a year, and the EP itself has voted to hold sessions and regular committee work henceforth only in Brussels. However, the EP has no power to amend the agreement to hold sessions in Strasbourg. Thus, one can see how the EP is a weaker institution within the EU—it cannot even decide where it meets! See Rockwell Schnabel and Francis Rocca,

The Next Superpower: The Rise of Europe and Its Challenge to the United States (Lanham MD: Rowman and Littlefield, 2005), pp. 151–152.
6. The most up-to-date information on the EP can be found at its website, http://www.europarl.europa.eu.
7. Charlemagne, "Liberta or freedom?" *The Economist*, May 23, 2009. This group, funded by Declan Ganley, a wealthy Irishman, won a seat only in France.
8. Amie Kreppel, *The European Parliament and the Supranational Party System* (Cambridge: Cambridge University Press, 2002).
9. Kreppel, *The European Parliament*, p. 1.
10. Key cases are those in 1963 that ruled that the Treaty of Rome placed constitutional obligations on members above that of their own laws and the *Costa v. ENEL* ruling (1964), which confirmed the primacy of EU law over national law.
11. Anne-Marie Burley and Walter Mattli, "Europe before the Court: A Political Theory of Legal Integration," *International Organization* 47, Winter 1993: 41–76.
12. The best example of this was in 2007, when, during discussion about re-weighting votes in the Council of the European Union, the Poles suggested they should have more votes because if it were not for Nazi Germany, there would be millions of more Poles. Suffice to say this did not sit well with the Germans.
13. More information on this institution is available at http://www.eesc.europa.eu.
14. Andres Follesdal and Simon Hix, "Why There is a Democratic Deficit in the EU," *Journal of Common Market Studies* 44:3, September 2006, 533–562.
15. Ibid, p. 535.
16. *The Economist*, "Four Ds for Europe," March 17, 2007.
17. Mikko. Mattila, "Why Bother? Determinants of Turnout in European Elections," *Electoral Studies* 22:3, 2003, 449–465. For the 2009 EP elections, see *The Economist*, June 13, 2009.
18. Andrew Moravcsik, "In Defense of the Democratic Deficit: Reassessing the Legitimacy of the European Union," *Journal of Common Market Studies* 40:4, 2002, 603–634.
19. Giandomenico Majone, *Regulating Europe* (London: Routledge, 1996).
20. Follesdal and Hix, "Why There is a Democratic Deficit," and Charlemagne, "Not Normal," *The Economist*, January 20, 2007.
21. Charlemagne, "The Endless Election Round," *The Economist*, June 13, 2009.
22. *Financial Times*, March 19, 2007. More than 50 percent of Britons thought life was worse; more than 40 percent of French, Italians, and Germans thought so. Only in the Spain did a majority think life has gotten better.
23. "More Want Less," *The Economist*, May 30, 2009.
24. *The New York Times*, June 8, 2009.
25. These examples were culled from a project in my class asking students to find the strangest EU regulation.
26. See *The Economist*, "The EU's Would-Be Founding Fathers," February 21, 2002, and Ben Crum, "Politics and Power in the European Convention," *Politics* 24, 2004, 1–11.
27. Robert Michels, *Political Parties: A Sociological Study of the Oligarchical Tendencies of Modern Democracy* (New York: Hearst's International Library, 1915).
28. European Commission, *General Budget of the European Union for the Financial Year 2006*, Brussels, 2006.
29. By agreement, the budget of the EU is capped at 1.24 percent of the EU's Gross Income. In the 2007–2013 budget cycle, the EU's budget is projected to be 1.05 percent of gross output.
30. German farms, typically rather small and not particularly efficient, also benefited from CAP and the German farm lobby, although not as well known as its French counterpart, nonetheless would help ensure German support for CAP for many years. See Tony Judt, *Postwar: A History of Europe since 1945* (New York: Penguin, 2005), p. 306.
31. Jack Thurston, *How to Reform the Common Agricultural Policy* (London: Foreign Policy Centre, 2002), and Timothy Garton Ash, *Free World: America, Europe, and the Surprising Future of the West* (New York: Vintage, 2005), p. 155. More critiques of the CAP can be found in Noel Malcolm, "The Case Against Europe," Foreign Affairs 74:2, March–April 1995, pp. 52–68, who calls it a "colossal waste of money."
32. Richard Baldwin, "Who Finances the Queen's CAP Payments," Paper from the Graduate Institute of International Studies, Geneva, December 2005.
33. *New York Times*, July 17, 2009.
34. Desmond Dinan, *Ever Closer Union: An Introduction to European Integration*, 2nd edition (Boulder: Lynne Reiner, 1999), p. 344.
35. Christilla Roederer-Rynning, "Impregnable Citadel or Leaning Tower? Europe's Common Agricultural Policy at Forty," *SAIS Review* 23, Winter/Spring 2003, 133–151

36. Court of Auditors, Audit of 2005 Budget, available through http://www.eca.europa.eu, accessed December 13, 2006.
37. *New York Times*, July 17, 2007.
38. "Europeans and the Common Agricultural Policy," Special Eurobarometer, published in January 2006, available through Eurostat.
39. "Regulatory over-reach?" *The Economist*, December 9, 2006, p. 70.
40. Quoted in T.R. Reid, *The United States of Europe: The New Superpower and the End of American Supremacy* (New York: Penguin, 2004), p. 105.
41. Any EU citizen can run for the European Parliament or run in local elections, regardless of one's national citizenship.
42. Great Britain and Ireland did not sign on to the Schengen Treaty, and restrictions on free movement of peoples from the ten new members added to the EU in 2004 are in place until 2011. Norway and Iceland, not EU members, participate in this treaty.

Will David Cameron and Nick Clegg usher in a "new era" for British politics?

CHAPTER 5

Parliaments and Electoral Systems

British politicians will often claim that their parliament is "the mother of all Parliaments."[1] Whether that is historically accurate or not—as noted in Chapter 2, Iceland may have a stronger claim—many would argue that the British Parliament has done little to distinguish itself in recent years. Many parliamentarians were embroiled in an expense account scandal in 2009, and, given the economic crisis that began in 2008 along with a widespread feeling that Tony Blair lied in order to justify British involvement in the war in Iraq, trust in government and in the ability of political leaders to solve the country's problems has plummeted. Within the august halls of Westminster Palace (the home of the British Parliament), members of parliament typically vote as their party leaders tell them to, and, since one party typically has the majority, there is little suspense about the outcome of the vote or even meaningful parliamentary debate. According to one critic, British parliamentarians "have little power or purpose—they sit out their lives in tearooms, gossiping and making trouble," with many having safe seats so "they barely need to turn up."[2]

The results of the 2010 elections may change much of the style and substance of British politics. For the first time since the 1970s, no party received a majority of the seats in parliament, and for the first time since World War II, Britain will have a coalition government, which will be composed of the Conservatives and the Liberal-Democrats. New laws will now require the agreement of both parties, which may make governance both more unpredictable and interesting. Backbenchers—members of parliament not in the party's leadership—may become more involved in legislative debates, and the government may not be able to count reliably upon getting all it wants passed. Meanwhile, as part of the coalition deal, Britain will have a referendum in 2011 to change its electoral system, meaning that a political system that favors two dominant parties, the Conservatives and Labour, may be effectively scrapped for one that gives more prospects for smaller parties like the Liberal-Democrats.[3] Incoming Prime Minister David Cameron from the Conservatives and Deputy Prime Minister Nick Clegg from the Liberal-Democrats, pictured in the photo on the opposite page, have pledged that their coalition will produce a "new era" of "new politics" in Britain. Whether or not this is merely rhetoric to soothe the feelings of alienated voters or a harbinger of real change remains to be seen.

The example above is but one of many in contemporary Europe that point to the importance of political institutions, including bodies that make decisions (e.g., parliaments), the rules of the political game (e.g., type of electoral system), and organizations that participate in political life (e.g., parties). The next several chapters of this book examine political institutions, the actors and structures that determine how political power is distributed and exercised. This is one of the core areas of political science. Aristotle, whom many consider the first political scientist, based his *Politics* on a comparative study of government in Greek city-states. By analyzing political institutions, he classified various types of government: monarchies, tyrannies, aristocracies, oligarchies, and democracies. We still classify governments based upon how political institutions are designed, often employing the same terms used by Aristotle. In today's Europe, all countries have democratic forms of government. The modern form of democracy[4] is a system of government in which political leaders are chosen through free competitive elections and citizens have a variety of civil and political rights (e.g., freedom of speech, of assembly) that allow them to gain information from different sources, express alternative viewpoints, and organize opposition to the government. Examples of democratic political institutions include elected parliaments and executives as well as courts and constitutions that help guarantee respect for political and civil rights and the rule of law.

These institutions, however, will vary from state to state, both in their organizational design on paper and in their actual practice. Whereas all democracies in a most general sense give people the power to determine their government, various forms of political institutions help determine *how* people's preferences are represented and translated into policy. How these institutions are designed matters, and knowing how they function is crucial to understanding how the political system in a given state operates. This chapter will introduce you to features of parliaments (often known better in American English as legislatures) in Europe, with subsequent chapters taking up executives, constitutions and legal systems, and political parties.

FUNCTIONS OF PARLIAMENTS

National parliaments are the centerpieces of democratic governance in Europe, responsible for many important political tasks and often the only branch of government elected by voters. They are made up of individuals—often labeled members of parliament or simply MPs—who typically are given two general tasks that at times may contradict each other. On the one hand, MPs, as representatives of the people who voted them into office, are supposed to articulate and support the goals of their constituency, whether they be voters in a particular district or supporters of a certain political party. On the other hand, as public servants they are also charged with being responsible for the country as a whole. At times, it may be difficult to decide what should take priority—to defend the narrow interests of their constituency or to act in a manner that they think would be better for the country. This conundrum—who or what should elected representatives represent—has been an important concern in democratic theory.[5]

party discipline ■ practice whereby elected officials and would-be candidates for office adhere to the party line, voting or endorsing programs backed by the party leadership.

In actual practice in most European democracies, MPs are expected to adhere to **party discipline**, meaning that they vote in accordance with the preferences of their party. This gives political parties a great deal of power, and it is easier and usually more accurate to think of the workings of parliament as more the interaction of a small number of political parties than as the activities of dozens or hundreds of individual MPs. Parliaments are organized around party blocs or factions. The leaders of the various party blocs structure the agenda and debates within parliament, in many cases micromanaging the details to include who should speak and for how long. This type of structure severely limits the powers and prerogatives of individual MPs. Relatively junior members of the party bloc that habitually break party discipline may risk losing the nomination of their party to run in future elections.

Parliaments are typically assigned a variety of tasks. Above all else, they are charged with making laws. Insofar as elected representatives of the people make laws, it is this lawmaking authority that, ultimately, makes European states democratic. Draft legislative proposals are debated in parliamentary sessions, and in several countries parliamentary committees play an important role in amending proposals before they are voted on by the whole parliament.

However, one should recognize that the lawmaking functions of most European parliaments are often rather *pro forma*. The reason for this is that most European states are parliamentary democracies, a feature we explore more in Chapter 6. For now, however, it is important to understand that, unlike in the US presidential system, in most European states the parliament is responsible for choosing the executive authority (e.g., the prime minister and the cabinet), which is often referred to as the government. The government draws up legislative proposals and submits them to parliament for formal approval. Because of party discipline, MPs are expected to vote along party lines. Since, in most cases, the government commands the allegiance of the majority of the MPs, it is able to push through legislation because those parliamentarians from the ruling party or parties are expected to support the government's initiatives. In this way, MPs in Europe are not like their American counterparts, who often take the lead in drafting legislation and guiding it through Congress, or, in some cases (e.g., the "blue dog" Democrats) may break with the party's leadership on particular issues. As noted in the above critique of the British system, MPs in Europe typically show much less individual initiative, and if they do draw up their own proposals—known as a "private bill" in the British system—it stands little chance of passing unless it garners the support of the government.

Thus, despite the fact that European parliaments possess, on paper at any rate, supreme lawmaking authority, some argue that parliaments have become "reactive" or "rubberstamps."[6] In addition to constraints imposed by party discipline, parliaments also typically lack the staff or expertise to be able to take the legislative initiative. Thus, in most of Europe, proposals are drafted within government ministries, approved by the cabinet, prime minister, and requisite party leaders, and then submitted to parliament for formal approval. True, in some states, as we'll note below, legislation can be subject to amendments and real substantive debate, but the driver of the legislative process is not parliament itself. Again, this is in stark contrast to the US system, where legislators themselves must sponsor bills and a stronger committee system within Congress gives more of a role for legislators in the lawmaking process. In addition, some argue that national-level parliaments have been significantly weakened by Europeanization, as more and more power is being transferred to the EU and that national parliaments increasingly do Brussels's bidding, not that of their own constituents. This contention is taken up in the **Is Europe One?** feature.

IS EUROPE ONE?

National Parliaments and the European Union

In this chapter, we will largely isolate national-level European parliaments from issues surrounding Europeanization, assuming that parliaments' primary interplay is with voters who elect MPs and the government that presents proposals to parliament. We should not realize, however, that one cannot easily isolate domestic politics from the European-level, as the EU has more and more influence over lawmaking in EU member states. Thus, in addition to debating and approving proposal drafted governments, European parliaments are also expected to pass legislation required by the EU. What percentage of domestic-level legislation actually originates in Brussels—in the form of an EU regulation or a directive to transpose EU rules into national law—is difficult to say, as it depends how one counts individual legislative actions and varies considerably from country to country. For example, whereas critics of the EU in Britain claim that half or more all laws in Britain originate with the EU, a study by the House of Commons put the figure at 9 percent.[7] Other counts of EU actions compared with adoption of national legislation in Ireland and Germany argue that, in these states, up to 80 percent of national-level legislation originates with the EU.[8]

Regardless of the precise figures, many see this as troubling. As noted in the previous chapters, some object to this on sovereignty grounds (e.g., national states lose power), but several observers have suggested that the real "losers" in the process are national parliaments (NPs). Some argue that Europeanization means "deparliamentization," as real legislative authority is being taken away from NPs and given to the EU, where the European Commission typically drafts proposals that are then approved by the Council of Ministers and European Parliament. Much of the work of NPs is then in formally passing legislation to conform to decisions taken by the EU. One author concluded that because of the strong role of the EU, NPs "lack authoritative power over transnational policy-making."[9] True, national governments, via the European Council and the Council of the EU, are involved in EU policy-making, but those two forums include the executive branch (e.g., prime ministers and cabinet officials), not NPs. The net result is that NPs are no longer the locus of decision-making. NPs are, at times, deprived of the right to deliberate over legislation and even represent voters. The lack of involvement of NPs in the EU is seen by some as another example of the "democratic deficit" of the EU.

NPs have attempted to remedy this situation. NPs have European affairs committees that attempt to influence or even control national decision-making within the EU. Some, such as those in Great Britain and Ireland, are advisory. In other cases, such as Germany, Austria, and Denmark, these committees have more power and can effectively order ministers to vote a certain way on EU proposals in the Council of the EU.[10] In this way, NPs can ensure that their preferences are represented in Brussels, although, because the EU employs qualified-majority voting for many of its actions, it is possible that a NP can express an opinion against a proposal but then be forced to adopt legislation in order to see it implemented on the national level.

The EU itself recognizes that the lack of involvement of NPs in decision-making is a problem and has taken some steps to remedy the situation.[11] Since 1989, the EU has had a Conference of Community and European Affairs Committees of the Parliaments of the EU (COSAC, its French-language acronym), which meets twice yearly. This is a consultative body that provides a forum for communication and information, and it was formally recognized in a protocol to the 1997 Amsterdam Treaty.[12] According to that protocol, the COSAC can address to EU institutions any "contributions" that it deems necessary. The Amsterdam Treaty also stipulated that all European Commission consultative (e.g., research and background papers) documents be forwarded to national parliaments. Moreover, since 2006, as part of its "Citizens Agenda" to involve more actors in EU decision-making, the European Commission has agreed to provide copies of all proposals to NPs for feedback. In 2006, the EU received 53 opinions from various NPs. By 2008, the EU received 200, indicating that NPs are trying to involve themselves more in the EU's work.[13] In particular, NPs have been interested in enforcing the principle of subsidiarity, maintaining that certain decisions are best left to national-level, not EU-level, action. Between 2005 and 2009, there were also more than five hundred meetings involving European Commissioners and NPs. There is also an Interparliamentary Forum between NPs and the European Parliament, as well as an electronic Interparliamentary Information Exchange, allowing MPs in any state to learn about the work of other NPs on EU issues. The Lisbon Treaty would involve NPs even more in the EU, giving them enhanced rights to information and to scrutinize EU proposals. Specifically, NPs would have the right to raise objections on the grounds of subsidiarity through the so-called "yellow and orange card procedure." If one-third of NPs agree that a proposal violates subsidiarity, this means it has a "yellow card" and the Commission is obligated to reconsider it. If a majority of NPs issue an objection, the proposal acquires an "orange card" and must then by submitted to the Council of the EU and the European Parliament. These powers, however, are purely advisory, as NPs cannot veto an EU proposal. Suggestions for an even stronger role for NPs, for example, a second chamber of the European Parliament that would include MPs from NPs, have met stiff resistance from national governments.

While most observers do concede that deparliamentization, to a certain degree, is occurring and is a natural result of Europeanization, some scholars have tried to find a silver lining for NPs.[14] EU action in certain areas may create precedents for new policies, functioning as a "catalyst for parliamentary activity in those areas traditionally not subject to domestic legislation."[15] For example, prior to EU attention to gender equality or the environment, several states (especially in Southern Europe) had few laws on these issues. Because of EU involvement in these spheres, NPs understand that legislative action for these issues is desirable and necessary. NPs may then extend the principles of EU rules (e.g., pay equity in the workplace) to new national-level legislation (e.g., gender equity in paternal leave benefits). Moreover, EU involvement may facilitate policy transfer, as pan-European action on a particular issue may lead NPs to share data, learn about a particular field, and borrow "best practices" from others. The idea is that Europeanization will not only lead to legal uniformity across Europe but that the quality of legislation will actually improve across the continent.

Critical Thinking Questions

1. Has the EU taken any too much power from national parliaments and individual countries?
2. Do you view the existence of "European level" decision-making more as a necessity and logical outgrowth of common, transnational problems that require concerted action or more as a deliberate usurpation of national power?

But, let us not push these positions too far. Most European governments—cabinet officials and prime ministers—answer to parliaments and individual parliaments continue to matter. Just as parliaments vote in a government, they can vote them out with a **vote of no confidence**, meaning that a majority of MPs indicate that they will no longer support the actions of the government. This provides an important check on power, as parliaments can, if pushed, say no. Votes of confidence are actually rare events, as governments would prefer not to push things to that point,

vote of no confidence ■ a parliamentary vote against the existing government that forces the government either to resign or call for new elections.

and on controversial measures (e.g., raising of university fees in Britain, maintenance of German or Dutch troops in Afghanistan), governments will work with individual MPs for their support to ensure that the ruling bloc in parliament will not be subject to individual MP defections. Parliaments also possess means to check or oversee governmental actions. These include "**question time,**" in which government ministers are called before parliament to answer questions and are often subjected to close scrutiny, particularly from opposition parties. Parliaments also possess committees (e.g., an environmental committee, an agricultural committee) charged with working with and, to some extent, keeping an eye on corresponding ministry of the government. These committees also serve as place where interest associations or even individual citizens can present their case for reform in policy or against possible abuses of power by the government.

question time ■ practice in which government ministers are called before parliament to answer questions and are often subjected to close scrutiny, particularly from opposition parties.

While the general points made above apply across the continent, one should recognize that there are measurable differences in power among European parliaments. The Parliamentary Powers Index (PPI), developed by M. Steven Fish and Matthew Kroenig, measures the powers of legislatures on thirty-two dimensions, including the scope of the legislature's authority, its control over the executive branch, its administrative resources, and the power of courts to review legislation. Scores are from zero to one. In general, as one can see in Table 5.1, most European parliaments are

TABLE 5.1

Parliamentary Powers Index (PPI) for Select Countries

Country	PPI Score
Germany	0.84
Italy	0.84
Czech Rep.	0.81
Great Britain	0.78
Poland	0.75
Hungary	0.75
Finland	0.72
Austria	0.72
Sweden	0.72
Romania	0.72
Portugal	0.63
France	0.56
Cyprus	0.41
US	0.63
Ukraine	0.50
Russia	0.44
Kazakhstan	0.31
Belarus	0.28

Source: M. Steven Fish and Matthew Kroenig, *The Power of National Legislatures: A Global Survey* (forthcoming). Data were gathered from 2002–2004, based upon a questionnaire administered to at least five country experts. The score is based upon parliamentary powers on thirty-two dimensions and can range from 0 to 1.

relatively powerful—especially when compared to legislatures in post-Soviet states with stronger presidencies and weaker or non-existent democracies—reflecting the fact that they are the primary decision-making bodies, although in those European states with stronger presidents (e.g., Cyprus, France, Portugal, discussed in the next chapter), legislative powers are weaker. Indeed, in Table 5.1 one sees that the allegedly powerful US Congress is far weaker than most European legislatures, reflecting the powerful role of the president and Supreme Court in limiting Congress's authority. True, this index measures formal powers—e.g., the British House of Commons is constitutionally supreme, free of any checks by courts or a written constitution, hence it scores relatively high—whereas actual practice may temper the powers of parliaments. However, when one takes into account that under parliamentary democracy parliaments possess ultimate power over the executive—a feature not found, for example in the US where there is more separation of power—it remains true that European parliaments are powerful institutions.

That said, it bears mentioning that the process of producing legislation and the actual ability to exercise power differs from parliament to parliament. One obvious source of difference is whether a single-party controls the majority of seats in the legislature or whether a coalition of parties must form in order to achieve a majority of votes necessary pass legislation. Greek and British politics, for example, are dominated by two main parties, virtually assuring one party a majority in the parliament.[16] This is known as a **majoritarian system** of governance.[17] In Great Britain, Prime Minister Tony Blair of the Labour Party (1997–2007) enjoyed large (greater than 60 percent) majorities in the House of Commons from 1997–2005.[18] Because of party discipline, members of the Labour Party typically backed the government on its legislative proposals—controversial issues such as the war in Iraq and education reforms were the exceptions in which some Labour MPs voted against the government—Tony Blair managed to get most all of his legislation through the Parliament.

majoritarian system ■ political system that features two dominant parties, insuring that one party has the majority of seats in parliament.

Because of its majoritarian features, the British Parliament *looks* relatively weak. Despite the at-times theatrical sessions of the House of Commons (particularly during question time), in which Blair would be booed by the opposition Conservative Party, the outcome of parliamentary "debate" was rarely in doubt. Blair's government had already lined up the necessary majority, making the passage of his proposals almost a foregone conclusion. However, even though the House of Commons might have looked, at times, like a rubberstamp, it bears reminding that Blair possessed political authority only because he was selected by the majority in Parliament. That same majority could remove him at any time with a vote of no confidence, meaning that supreme or ultimate power continued to lay with the parliament.

The legislative process can be much more complex when a **coalition** is required to pass legislation. This means that two or more parties need to form an alliance in order to produce a parliamentary majority, which is often labeled a **consensus system** of governance because it rests on compromises between or among various political parties who are included in the legislative process. Unlike the British or Greek case, no one party can impose its will upon parliament. Under a consensus system, the members of the parliamentary coalition share both legislative and executive authority, with the latter submitting proposals to the ordinary parliamentarians for their approval. Examples of coalitional governments can be found in Germany. As seen in Figure 5.1, no German political party secured a majority of seats in the *Bundestag*

coalition ■ an alliance of two or more parties in a parliament that together produces a majority that can pass legislation and elect a government.

consensus system ■ a political system in which governance depends upon coalitions among political parties because no one party has a majority.

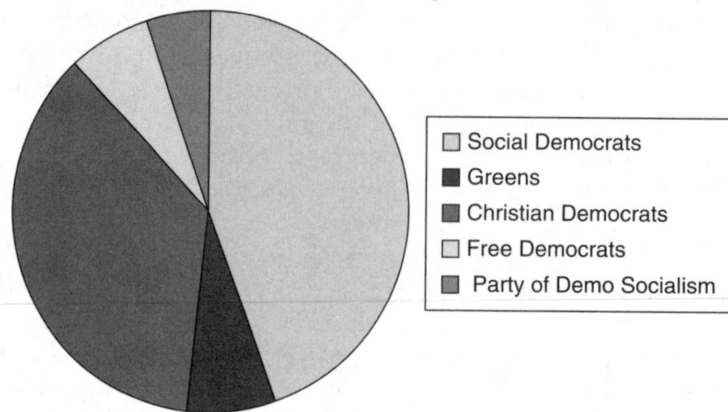

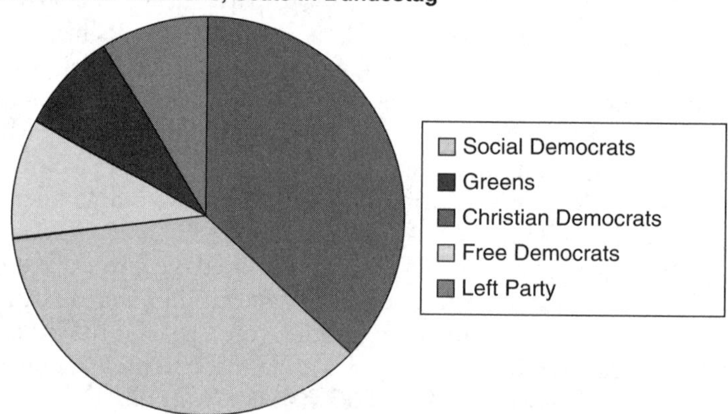

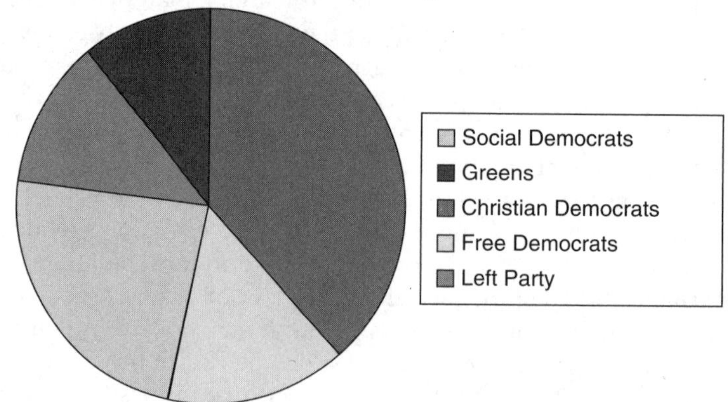

FIGURE 5.1

2002, 2005 and 2009 German Elections, Seats in Bundestag

Source: Election results as reported on Wikipedia

(lower house of parliament) in the 2002, 2005, or 2009 elections. As a consequence, parties had to make coalitions in order to form a government. In 2002, the Social Democratic Party (SDP) and the Greens, both on the political left, which had governed Germany since 1998, were able to resecure their majority. In 2005, the situation was more complex. With the parties on the Center-Right (the Free Democrats [FDP] and the Christian Democrats) and the parties on the Center-Left (the SDP and the Greens) pledging only to cooperate with each other and no party willing to make a deal with the far-left *Linke* [Left] (former East German Communist Party) Party, there was no obvious coalition. After weeks of haggling, the SDP and the Christian Democrats agreed to forge a grand coalition of the two largest parties, making Angela Merkel of the Christian Democratic Union (CDU) Germany's first female chancellor. In 2009, when the SDP suffered a major setback at the polls and the FDP gained seats, Merkel refashioned the governing coalition, jettisoning the SDP in favor of the FDP, which, as free market champions, are ideologically closer to the Christian Democrats.

Because of the necessity to maintain a coalition in order to pass proposals through parliament, political life in countries with a consensus system is subject to more compromises than, for example, in Great Britain. Consider, for example, the period of the German "grand coalition" from 2005 to 2009, when Chancellor Merkel had to work with her center-left coalition partner (and erstwhile opponent), the SDP, to pass legislation. Parliamentary committees in the German *Bundestag* also play a far more active role than in Britain, as the coalition partners and, at times, even the opposition have come together to make amendments to the government's proposals. On the one hand, this makes the process of passing laws more cumbersome. Parties have to negotiate and make deals, and Merkel or any German chancellor will not get everything she might want. In some cases during the period of the CDP-SDP grand coalition, the two parties were unable to agree on substantive proposals in areas such as on taxes, health care, and labor market reform. Legislation deemed too controversial was watered down or put off for another day. Some decried this, even suggesting that Merkel was locked in a "cage" with the SDP,[19] and certainly this leads to more uncertainty than in a purely two-party, majoritarian system, where the ruling party does not have to worry about securing a majority vote on proposed legislation. However, one might retort that politics in Germany—and in other states such as the Netherlands, Sweden, and Finland that typically have parliamentary coalitions—will rest more on consensus than in cases where parties do not have to work with each other in other to get things done.

Coalitions are not always successful, however. For example, twenty-nine parties won seats to the Polish *Sejm* in 1991 elections, necessitating the formation of a six-party "minimal" winning coalition. Needless to say, balancing the interests and positions of six different parties was difficult, although Poland did manage to continue with its course of post-communist economic reforms for two years before the coalition collapsed and new elections had to be held. In 2006, the Czech Republic went without a government for several months because there was 100-100 tie between the right and left parties in parliament, making it impossible to even produce a coalition. In 2009, the Dutch government collapsed because one of the coalition partners withdrew from the government. The same thing happened in Belgium in

2010. This introduces more instability and unpredictability than, for example, in the US system. However, these countries manage—parties simply renegotiate their coalition partners or the country has new elections and forms a new parliament and the process of building coalitions starts anew.

Whether or not a country requires coalitions is likely to be a function of how many political parties are present in parliament. The number of parties, as we shall see below, is in turn determined, in part, by how parliaments are elected.

ONE PARLIAMENT OR TWO?

unicameralism ■ a system with only one parliamentary (legislative) body.

bicameralism ■ a system with two parliamentary bodies.

Before examining that topic, however, it is worth noting one other obvious structural difference in European parliaments. Parliaments may be either **unicameral** (having only one "house" or legislative body) or **bicameral** (possessing two legislative bodies). Unicameralism is far simpler, as legislation must pass through only one body. Unicameralism tends to be associated with smaller countries and those without sizeable minority groups or regional divides. As seen in Table 5.2, most European states, particularly those with fewer people, are unicameral. Bicameralism is by definition more complicated, as bills must pass through two legislative chambers, making the process of legislation are more difficult, especially if different parties or coalitions control each legislative chamber. One could argue, however, that the presence of another legislative body serves as a check on abuse of power, or, as is the case in federal systems such as Germany and Austria, that a second chamber provides a means for regions or sub-national governments to be represented.

Bicameralism, however, does not work the same in all states. In Great Britain, the unelected House of Lords—whose members are appointed or inherit their positions—has very limited power, able to at most delay legislation. Similarly, in France the indirectly elected Senate, chosen by an electoral college of regional councils, is inferior to the National Assembly, which has the final say on all legislation. In Italy, in contrast, the Chamber of Deputies and Senate are coequal in legislative powers, with the Senate (uniquely among bicameral systems) even enjoying the right to remove the government with a vote of no confidence. Other cases, such as the Netherlands, Belgium, and Germany, fall somewhere in the middle, with the "upper house" of the legislature possessing some real power

TABLE 5.2

Unicameralism and Bicameralism in Europe

Unicameral States:	Albania, Bulgaria, Croatia, Cyprus, Denmark, Estonia, Finland, Greece, Hungary, Iceland, Latvia, Lithuania, Luxembourg, Macedonia, Malta, Montenegro, Norway, Portugal, Serbia, Slovakia, Sweden, Turkey.
Bicameral States:	Austria,* Belgium,* Bosnia and Herzegovina,* Czech Republic, France, Germany,* Great Britain, Italy, Ireland, Netherlands, Poland, Romania, Slovenia, Spain,* Switzerland.*

*Federal State
Source: Author's compilation

but subordinate to the "lower house," which, among other items, enjoys the right to name the prime minister (note how these labels can lead to confusion). The precise division of power between the two chambers is often complex. For example, in Germany, the "upper house" of the legislature, the *Bundesrat*, is where Germany's sixteen regions (*Länder*) are represented, with each *Land* sending members to the *Bundesrat* based upon its population. Legislation that is deemed to affect the *Länder* is put on a separate track, meaning that in these cases the *Bundesrat*'s power equal to that of the *Bundestag*, the "lower house" of the German parliament. In other words, on these questions that are ruled to affect the *Länder* (e.g., transportation, health, education; typically most questions fall on this track), both chambers must give their approval. If different parties control the *Bundestag* and the *Bundesrat*—which has often been the case and occurred again in 2010—passing legislation can be very difficult. Even if the same party controls both chambers, it could be that the members of the *Bundesrat*—less accountable to the executive branch and perhaps more independently minded as they represent a distinct region—would complicate the passage of legislation. For this reason, bicameralism inherently puts the German chancellor in a weaker legislative position than the Norwegian, Bulgarian, or Swedish prime ministers, who work with unicameral legislatures. For matters that are deemed not to be of direct interest to the regions (e.g., foreign policy), the *Bundesrat* enjoys only a suspensive veto over policy, meaning that if it rejects a measure it can be overridden by the *Bundestag*, which has the final say.

One additional structural issue concerns the size of parliament. As one would expect, larger countries have larger parliaments, so that the ratio of voters to an MP is not unmanageably high. For example, the French National Assembly has 577 members, the German Bundestag has 598,[20] and the Italian Chamber of Deputies has 630. In contrast, the Estonian State Council has only 101 members, the Slovenian National Assembly has 90, and the Icelandic *Althing* a mere 63.

HOW ARE PARLIAMENTS ELECTED?

Knowing that parliaments are elected bodies, one natural question would be how they are elected? **Electoral systems**, meaning the rules and mechanisms that determine how candidates or parties win elections and thereby gain positions in government, vary from country to country. The nature of a country's electoral system can have a profound effect on its overall political structure, and the study of the design and consequences of electoral systems is a major topic in comparative politics.

electoral systems ■ rules and mechanisms that determine how candidates or parties win elections.

One issue to consider is the term of office of parliamentarians. Put another way, the question is how often are parliamentary elections? The short answers are that it varies and that it depends. It varies because the term of parliamentary office is different from country to country. In most European states it is four (as in Germany, Sweden, Spain, Romania, and Poland) or five (as in France, Great Britain, Italy, and Turkey) years. It depends because most European parliaments do not have fixed terms of office, unlike the US Congress. Elections can be called before the term actually ends, necessitated either by a vote of no confidence in the government or the prime minister choosing to dissolve parliament and have early

TABLE 5.3

Plurality and Proportional Representation Systems Compared

Plurality	Proportional Representation
Country divided up into districts.	Country may (e.g., Spain) or may not (e.g., Netherlands) be divided up into districts.
One person represents each district.	Districts have multiple members.
Parties nominate a single candidate to run in a district.	Parties present voters a list of several candidates.
Voters vote for a candidate.	In closed list systems, voters vote for a party; in open list, STV, or mixed systems, they can vote for a candidate.
Candidate with most votes—plurality—wins; "winner take all."	Seats divided up based upon proportion of votes received; more than one "winner."
Used in Great Britain and variation used in France.	Used elsewhere, in various forms.

elections. These are features of parliamentary systems of government, explored more in the next chapter.

Under what rules are elections held? Whereas all European countries are democracies, meaning that elections are free and fair and voters have a meaningful choice among parties and/or candidates, they do not all have the same type of electoral system. Here we will discuss mechanisms for parliamentary elections, leaving consideration of presidential elections—important in countries such as France, Poland, and Romania—to the subsequent chapter. In general terms, legislatures can be elected through one of two methods: **plurality systems** (sometimes called, erroneously, majoritarian systems) and **proportional representation.** Both are, in the broadest sense, democratic because they offer voters a choice of candidates or parties. Their fundamental logic, however, is very different. Each system has its own advocates who argue for its superiority over the other one. The most essential features and differences between these systems are displayed in Table 5.3.

plurality systems ■ voting system in which voters vote for candidates and whichever candidate gets the most votes wins.

proportional representation ■ voting system in which voters typically vote parties and parliamentary seats are divided based on the proportion of votes each party receives.

single-member district plurality system (SMDP) ■ used in Great Britain, a plurality system in which the country is divided into districts and voters choose one representative per district; winner-take-all system.

Plurality Voting Systems

Only two European countries—Great Britain and France—use plurality voting, although, thanks to British influence, it is used elsewhere, such as the US, Canada, India, and Australia. The British system is often upheld as the "purest" type of plurality voting. It is called a **single-member district plurality system (SMDP)**, sometimes referred to as first-past-the-post. The basics are relatively simple. The country is divided up into electoral districts (646 at present in Great Britain), ideally with each roughly the same in terms of population. Candidates run for office hoping to represent a particular district. Voters vote for a candidate. Within each district, the candidate with the most votes—in other words, the one with a plurality—wins.

There is only one winner in each district, making it a winner-take-all system as the winner wins the seat and the other candidates get nothing.

In these respects, elections in Britain look very similar to US congressional elections. It is important emphasize, however, a core difference. Because the British have a parliamentary form of governance, the vote for a particular candidate is both a vote for an individual and a vote designed to tip the balance of power in parliament in favor of a particular party so that it may select the prime minister and cabinet. In the US, legislative and presidential elections are separate, so the choice of one's representative in Congress has no bearing on who is elected president.

The French electoral system works a little differently. Again, the country is divided into districts (577) and voters vote for a candidate. However, in order to win the election in the first round a candidate must get a majority of the vote. If there are several candidates and no one wins a majority, all the candidates that poll over 12.5 percent of the vote are entitled to enter a **run-off election,** held a few weeks later. The candidate who gains the plurality of the vote—not necessarily the majority—in the second round wins the seat, making this method of voting a **two-ballot plurality system.**

run-off election ■ a second-round election in which candidates that receive a certain number of votes in the first round are allowed to run; used in France.

two-ballot plurality system ■ used in France, it requires a run-off election under plurality rules if no candidate in a given district receives a majority of the vote in the first round of voting.

This system is more complex that the British one, and it functions in a matter that is not obvious at first glance. Consider hypothetical cases for two districts, as displayed in Table 5.4. In each case, several candidates have the right to advance to the second round of voting. The question is who wins in the second round. In District 1, three candidates—the Communist, the Socialist, and one from the center-right UMP (Union for a Popular Movement)—advance, whereas one from the Greens does not. If voting in round 2 repeated the results of round 1, the UMP would win (even assuming the Greens vote for the Socialists in round 2). If all the non-UMP parties combine their votes, however, this coalition will defeat the UMP.

TABLE 5.4

Illustration of French Two-Ballot Plurality System

Candidate/Party	% vote Round 1	% vote Round 2
District 1		
Michel Rivard Communist	20%	
Maria Vert Greens	5%	
Caroline Bodin Socialist	33%	58%
Laurent Monet UMP	42%	42%
District 2		
Sophia Blanc Communist	13%	
Maurice Zidane Socialist	32%	45%
Amie Govier UMP	35%	42%?? w/o FN 55%?? w/ FN
Jonah Cohen UDF	7%	
Jacques Charlot FN	13%	13%? or does it vote for UMP?

Thus, parties make a deal, with one throwing support to the other—presumably the Socialists would support a Communist candidate in another district—and, in this case, the Socialists take the seat, even though the UMP candidate won the most votes in round 1. District 2 is more complex. Here four candidates advance, and if one followed the same logic as in District 1, the parties on the Left—the Socialists and Communists—would get 45 percent of the vote in the second round, enough for it to win over an easily predictable alliance of the UMP and Union of French Democrats (UDF), both center-right parties. The wild card here, though, is the far-right National Front (FN), viewed as a pariah by other political parties, which officially have refused to cooperate with it on the national level. The question, though, is whether the UMP will make an appeal to try to court FN voters (e.g., by proposing crackdowns on immigration or cuts in public assistance to minority groups) to persuade the FN candidate to drop out of the race and throw his support to the UMP. If the FN keeps its candidate in the race and FN voters vote for him, the Left wins. If the UMP makes some sort of deal with the devil of the FN, it wins. Thus, even though the FN is a relatively small party—and it does have the capacity to win seats on its own under plurality rules—it still can play an important role in French elections.

Proportional Representation

Proportional representation (PR) in various forms is far more common in Europe. The purest form of proportional representation is found in the Netherlands. There are no separate electoral districts. Instead, the entire country is treated as a single district, and parties rank-order a list of candidates to fill the 150 seats of the *Tweede Kamer* (Second Chamber of the Dutch Parliament). Most countries with PR employ a closed-list system—meaning voters vote for a party only (this occurs, for example, in Turkey, Portugal and Spain). In other countries such as Sweden, the Czech Republic, Estonia, and the Netherlands, there is an open-list system, meaning voters have the option to vote for an individual candidate, not merely a party, although in fact most voters simply check off a party's name and individual votes for a candidate rarely make a major difference.[21] Seats are then doled out in proportion to the percentage of votes the party receives. If, for example, the Dutch Labour Party gets 20 percent of the vote, it would win 30 seats, 20 percent of the total of 150 seats. In this case, the candidates ranked 1 to 30 on the **party list**—a ranked list of candidates developed by each party—would gain seats. The unlucky soul at number 31 would not. Obviously, those at the top of the list have the best chance of winning seats, and are chosen by the party for their ability, experience, and loyalty. Party-list voting—particularly a closed-list system where voters have no say over candidates—thus discourages maverick or upstart candidacies.

party list ■ rank-order list of a party's candidates for office; used in a proportional representation system to determine which individuals will end up serving in parliament.

Other countries have variants of this basic PR system. Most commonly, the country is broken up into multi-member districts (as in Sweden [29], Poland [41], Spain [52], Turkey [79], Slovenia [9], and even tiny Malta [13], among others), parties present a list in each district—which can vary from district to district or be exactly the same across districts—and seats are then determined based upon the proportion of vote received in each multi-member district. This allows for some geographic representation—although a voter still cannot identify his/her individual representative, as under plurality voting where each representative is connected to a unique district—and gives smaller, regional parties a chance a greater chance to win seats. In addition, some countries, such as Sweden, Denmark, and Austria, reserve a proportion (roughly 12 percent in the Swedish case) of seats that are held-back as a "top-off" to ensure that the final distribution of seats mirrors the national vote as closely as possible.

Significantly, electoral systems also vary in terms of the minimal **electoral threshold** of votes needed to gain seats in parliament. The Netherlands has the lowest, with a party needing only 0.67 percent of the vote to win a seat in parliament. Turkey has the highest, at 10 percent, which could produce a highly skewed electoral result if too many small parties fail to meet the threshold. Most countries have a threshold somewhere in the middle, at 4 to 5 percent, which eliminates the smallest parties from gaining seats. Table 5.5 shows the electoral results for recent elections in the Netherlands, Turkey, and Sweden, the last of which has a 4 percent electoral threshold. Clearly, the electoral threshold has an impact on both the number of parties that gain entry into parliament and on the overall proportionality of the system.[22] In particular, one sees that the higher the threshold, the larger number of "wasted votes," votes cast for a party that, because it fails to meet the threshold, does not win any seats in parliament. Voters for these parties are not represented in parliament.

electoral threshold ■ the minimum percentage of votes necessary to win seats in a proportional representation system; varies from country to country.

Some countries go further with their adaptations. Germany and Hungary (and Italy from 1993–2001) have a mixed system, in which some seats are determined by plurality voting and some are determined by PR, but the overall logic of the system is such that the total number of seats are distributed proportionately. In Germany, this is known as **personalized proportional representation**. German voters get to vote twice. On one side of the ballot, as seen in the picture below, they vote for a candidate that represents an electoral district, similar to how Britons vote. Half of the *Bundestag* is elected this way. On the other side of the ballot, voters choose a party, with each *Land* serving as a multi-member district for purposes of proportional representation. The percentage of votes a party receives on the second side of the ballot determines its total number of seats per *Land*, meaning the overall logic of the system is in accordance with PR. For example, let's say that Green Party wins 10 percent of the nation-wide vote, meaning it is entitled to roughly 60 (10 percent of the *Bundestag*'s 598) seats. If the Greens won 10 seats outright in district voting, they would then get 50 more from their party list. If they won 20 seats outright, they would receive 40 from the list. Occasionally, a party will win more direct mandates in first vote than they are entitled to in the second (proportional vote). If this happens, the party keeps their direct mandates and the extra or "overhang" seats are simply added to the total in the *Bundestag*. In a simplified version based on the hypothetical results above, if the Greens won 65 seats in district voting, they would be entitled to all 65, not 60 as would be the case based on proportionality, and 5 seats would be added to the *Bundestag*. In each of the recent German elections there have been several "overhang" seats, meaning that the actual number of seats is higher than 598 and will change after each election. Lest one get bogged down in minutiae, the key point is that the overall outcome of the German system in terms of the number of seats awarded to parties looks as if it was PR. District-voting, in addition to providing geographic representation, only helps determine the actual individuals who will serve in the legislature.

personalized proportional representation ■ used in Germany, whereby half the seats are determined by votes for a candidate in a district and half the seats are determined by nation-wide proportional representation; voters therefore vote twice in each election, one for a candidate, once for a party.

TABLE 5.5

Effect of Electoral Thresholds on Representation

Country/Party	% votes, nationally	% seats in parliament
Netherlands, 2010		
People's Party for Freedom and Democracy	20.5	20.7
Labour Party	19.6	20.0
Party for Freedom	15.5	16.0
Christian Democratic Appeal	13.6	14.0
Socialist Party	9.0	10.0
Democrats 66	7.0	6.7
Green Left	6.7	6.7
Christian Union	3.2	3.3
Reformed Political Party	1.7	1.3
Party for the Animals	1.3	1.3
Proud of the Netherlands	0.6	0
Sweden, 2010		
Social Democrats	30.7	32.1
Moderate Party	30.1	30.7
Green Party	7.3	7.2
Liberal People's Party	7.1	6.9
Center Party	6.6	6.6
Sweden Democrats	5.7	5.7
Christian Democrats	5.6	5.4
Left Party	5.6	5.4
Pirate Party	0.7	0
Turkey, 2007		
Justice and Development Party	46.7	61.8
Republican Peoples' Party	20.9	20.3
Nationalist Movement Party	14.3	12.9
Democratic Party	5.4	0
Youth Party	3.0	0
"Wasted Votes"		
Netherlands	1.2	
Sweden	1.5	
Turkey	18.1	

Source: Electoral outcomes as reported on Wikipedia.

single transferable vote [STV] ■ used in Ireland and Malta, a complex form of PR in which voters rank-order candidates under candidates must win a certain threshold of votes and ranked votes may be transferred to other candidates.

There is a still more complex system, which is used in Malta and in Ireland: the **single transferable vote (STV)**. Under this system, for example, Ireland is broken up into forty-two districts, and voters rank-order candidates, meaning they assign one as their first choice, one as a second choice, and so on. The votes are tallied for each candidate. If a candidate receives a certain minimum number of first-place votes (e.g., 25 percent +1 in a four-candidate race, 20 percent + 1

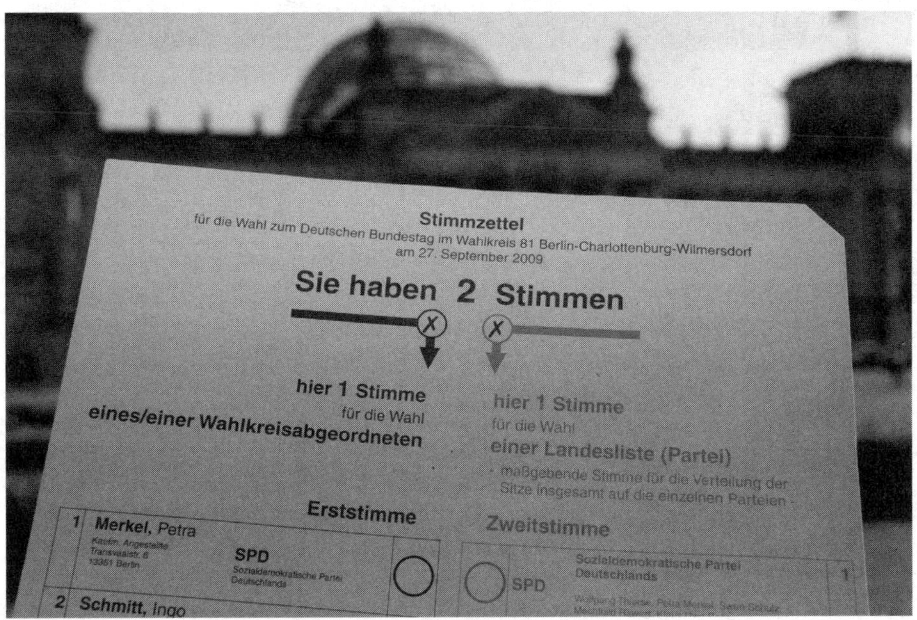

A German election ballot: Voters select both a candidate and a party.

in a five-candidate race) she is elected. Her "extra votes"—those she did not need to be elected are then given to the candidates ranked second on the ballot of those "extra" voters. Once a second candidate meets the threshold, his second-place (or, possibly, third-place) votes are assigned to other candidates until all the seats in the district are filled. If no candidate has a surplus after the first count, the candidate with the lowest number of votes is eliminated and his/her votes are transferred to other candidates in accordance with the preferences marked on the ballot. Without question, this system is complex.[23] However, when some in Britain suggested that changing to an **alternative vote** system (proposed as part of the 2010 coalition deal and discussed in the **In Focus** section) would be too complex, others retorted that even the Irish could manage the more complex STV system—and have done so even before use of computers and electronic voting!

alternative vote ■ a type of SMDP in which voters rank-order candidates, and second- and third-choices from voters of losing candidates are considered until one candidate gets a majority of votes; under consideration in Great Britain.

Consequences of Electoral Systems

Does any of this matter, or is it only of academic interest? Many would argue that the choice of electoral system has great consequences. Each system has pluses and minuses and its own defenders, and further discussion on these particulars is provided in the **In Focus** section. For now, however, one should understand and appreciate arguably the greatest consequence of an electoral system: its effect on the number of parties in a political system. In a famous pronouncement called **Duverger's Law**, French political scientist Maurice Duverger suggested that SMDP systems like the British tend to produce a two-party system, that PR tends to produce a multi-party system, and that France, with its two-ballot plurality system, would produce a multi-party system characterized by party alliances.[24]

Duverger's Law ■ idea that the type of electoral system will help determine the number of political parties.

IN FOCUS

The Relative Merits of Plurality Systems versus Proportional Representation

Earlier in this chapter we discussed the mechanics of different electoral systems and made only a brief reference to some of their consequences. The importance of electoral systems, as well as the relative merit of one type of system over another, are contested topics both in academic circles and in many European countries (e.g., Great Britain, Italy, Turkey) that have considered or have actually changed their electoral system in recent years.

Those favoring plurality systems make several points.[25] First, many would echo the claims of Duverger and note that plurality systems tend to produce two-party (or, more accurately, perhaps, predominantly two-party) systems, as seen in Great Britain, France (which, although it is technically multi-party, has had two relatively solid center-right and center-left blocs), and, beyond Europe, in Canada, Australia, and the US. Two-party systems ensure that one party will be able to form a majority, obviating any need to form a potentially messy and unstable coalition government. In addition to being cumbersome to manage, coalitions are also problematic from the standpoint of democratic theory. As noted earlier, they are often created through a process of bargaining or "horse-trading" among political elites, behind the scenes and beyond the power of voters. In addition, coalition government make give undue influence to small parties (e.g., historically the case with the Free Democrats in Germany), who become the "kingmakers," creating or destroying government by throwing their support to one party or another. Coalitions can therefore be held captive by the interests of a small group, complicating the efforts of the government to adopt policies that may have wide support among the population.

A two-party system also makes parties compete for the "median voter," the hypothetical voter occupying the middle of the political spectrum. In other words, plurality systems encourage moderate, large, catch-all parties. In contrast, under proportional representation, more extremist parties can gain seats and, as seen with the case of the *Linke* (former Communist) Party in Germany in 2005, complicate the formation of a government. In France, in contrast, the two-ballot plurality system has prevented the extreme right FN from winning a large number of seats. Moreover, historically speaking, some would argue that the PR system in Weimar Germany (1919–1933) facilitated the rise of extremist politics, epitomized by the emergence of the National Socialist (Nazi) Party.

In addition, plurality systems ensure geographical representation (although PR systems can make some accommodation for this), making individual members of parliament are more clearly accountable to a particular constituency. Moreover, by getting to vote for a candidate—not merely a party as with a closed list PR system—voters can weigh the particular merits of individuals (e.g., ethics, experience) and not just the party's ideology.

Advocates of PR point to several flaws with plurality systems. Under plurality systems, election results tend to be skewed, meaning the number of seats a party wins does not match the number of votes it receives. For example, in British elections in 2001 and 2005, the Labour Party won a clear majority (63 percent in 2001, 55 percent in 2005) of seats in the House of Commons, allowing Tony Blair to remain prime minister. In each case, however, the Labour Party received a minority (41 percent in 2001, 35 percent in 2005) of votes. On the other side, the third-place Liberal Democratic Party received 22 percent of all votes in 2005 but only 9.6 percent of the seats. A similar outcome (23 percent of the vote, 8.8 percent of the seats) befell the Liberal-Democrats in 2010. The reason lies in the winner-take-all nature of SMDP: it does not matter how much you win by, as long as you receive more votes than other candidates. Smaller parties with a sizeable fraction of the vote, for example, 20 percent in several districts, will not win seats in those districts, so, adding up votes and seats across districts, the percentage of vote they receive will not correspond to the percentage of seats. In France, which uses a different version of plurality voting, there are also skewed results. For example, in 2007 the UMP received 39.5 percent of votes in the first round of voting, but ended up (after the second round) with 54.2 percent of the seats. Thus, even though the majority of French voters did not, when given initial choice, vote for the UMP, it won the majority of the seats.

Compare these results to those in Table 5.5. There is much more proportionality between votes received and seats won. The greatest proportionality is in the Netherlands, where the threshold of entering parliament is under one percent of the vote, meaning that even the smallest parties can win seats and few votes are "wasted" on parties that win no seats. The proportionality is less in the Turkish case, in large part because of the ten percent threshold requirement. In most PR systems, though, there is a closer correspondence between votes and seats. In the 2007 Polish elections, for example, the leading vote-getter was Civic Platform, which won 41.5 percent of the vote. In the British case, such a result would almost assuredly produce a majority in parliament. In the Polish case, however, Civic Platform won only 45.4 percent of the seats, meaning that there was not an immense discrepancy between the percent of votes and percent of seats.

For defenders of PR, this is an issue of fairness. How "fair" is it, they would assert, that a majority of voters in Britain vote against Labour in 2005, but Labour wins a majority of seats? From their perspective, the results of elections under PR—meaning the number of seats won by a party—more closely resemble the preferences of the voters. Advocates of PR would thus claim it is more "representative," and that, unlike plurality systems, every vote counts.[26] Under a plurality system, many votes are "wasted," making no difference whatsoever to the final outcome. Moreover, because voters in two-party plurality systems have fewer meaningful choices,[27] it is alleged they are unable to vote their true convictions, settling instead for the lesser of two evils. PR, then, in short, is more representative, offer more choices, and, it is also argued, results in higher voter turnout.

What of the argument against coalitions and in favor of more moderate, two-party systems? True, sometimes coalitions are difficult to manage, but they require a more consensual form of politics, ensuring that the policies that area adopted have broad political support. Moreover, the expectation that parties will have to form coalitions with each other may lead to less adversarial politics. As for governability, the political scientist Arend Lijphart maintains that PR systems perform better in terms of economic performance and in minority and female representation. Additionally, although cabinets under PR may be less durable, the changes from government to government are less radical than under plurality systems, when one party tends to wholly displace the other.[28] As for small parties having too much power, one could say the same about factions or unelected interest groups in two-party systems. Geographic representation may sound nice in principle, but we know that parties can gerrymander districts, drawing lines in such a way that they can ensure their candidates will be elected by friendly electorates. Although this is often considered a problem in the US, there are plenty of "rotten boroughs" in Great Britain that are so overwhelmingly oriented to one party that elections are essentially meaningless.

Many of these points solicit rebuttals. Why should parliament reflect all the divisions in society? Might it be better to force the disparate elements of a country to transcend their differences and join larger, more moderate catch-all parties instead of offering separate parties for, example, Catalans or Northern Italians or women or communists or racists? True, PR may work well for prosperous Sweden or Finland, but Lijphart does not discuss Weimar Germany (1919–1933) or the failed French Fourth Republic (1946–1958), which had a PR system and high levels of political polarization and instability. As for turnout, any number of factors can account for that aside from type of electoral system (meaning correlation

(*continued*)

does not mean causation), and gerrymandering can be thwarted if the drawing of districts is left to more neutral parties (e.g., courts or non-partisan commissions).

How might one resolve these points? Obviously, one can compare cases and look and see which system is "better" on the basis of certain criteria. Another means may be to look and see who is clamoring for change, thereby revealing dissatisfaction with one system over another. France, for example, controversially switched to PR in 1986—albeit for only one election once the governing party calculated that would actually do better under the previous system, with which French voters were more accustomed. In Great Britain, the Liberal Democratic Party—not surprisingly—has made electoral reform, specifically adoption of PR, its top issue, and in the late 1990s the Labour Party appointed a commission to make suggestions. Several ideas were floated, including a mixed plurality/PR system as in Germany and an alternative vote system, a version of plurality voting which is used in Australia. Under alternative vote, winner-take-all single-member districts are retained, but, like STV, voters get to rank-order the candidates. If no one gets majority, the last place candidate is eliminated, and his or her second-place votes are transferred to other candidates. The process continues until one candidate gets a majority, ensuring that the winner has majority support compared to other candidates and reducing the number of "wasted votes." This system, which is criticized as too confusing, has been adopted for mayoral elections in London, and will be put to British voters in a referendum, as part of the coalition deal between the Conservatives and the Liberal Democrats in 2010.

However, proving perhaps that the grass is always greener on the other side, the Italians in 1993 switched from a pure PR system to a mixed system that was primarily (75 percent) based upon district-voting. This was done with the desire to eliminate smaller parties and introduce some rare stability into Italian politics. Alas, neither happened, and as regional parties such as the *Lega Nord* benefited from district voting Italian politics became arguably even more polarized. In 2006, Italy returned to a pure PR system, resulting in a nine-party coalition government. One might suggest that the problem in Italy is less PR or plurality than, simply, Italy itself.

Interestingly, most of the new democracies in Europe have adopted a PR system or, as in the case of Hungary, a mixed system. One could muster this as evidence that institutional designers in these countries concluded that PR is better or more democratic, but, with an increasingly authoritarian Russia abandoning a mixed system in favor of pure PR, one might make the simple observation that choice of electoral system is not the decisive factor in judging the quality of democracy. Both systems can work and both offer a version of democracy. Echoing Ken Gladdish, one might simply argue that the advantages of one system over the other hinges upon the particular circumstances (e.g., cleavage structures, economic stability) in a given country.[29]

Critical Thinking Questions

1. Can you say that one type of electoral system (plurality or proportional representation) is more "democratic" than the other?
2. Why do plurality electoral systems tend to produce a two-party system? Why does such a system work against "third" or smaller parties?

One can easily see how some aspects of this might work. For example, in the Netherlands even if a party wins only 2 percent of the vote, it still wins seats (three), and can use these seats as a basis to champion certain positions, win further support, and perhaps even serve in a coalition government. In short, under PR smaller parties survive and get some representation. They "matter" more, and individuals will vote for them feeling that a vote for them counts and is not "wasted," as arguably happens when people vote for the Green or Libertarian Party in the US. Look at Table 5.5 again, and compare this with the classic two-party system of the US, which uses SMDP. Parties that win only a small percentage of the national vote in the US do not win many—or any—seats in the legislature, and they tend to disappear. This feature of the US—and not any particular preference Americans have for the two-party system—explains why the US does not have a strong third party on the national level.

The logic underpinning Duverger's Law may be sound, but does the evidence support it? Malta has the purest two-party system in Europe—and uses PR-STV. Greece has, more or less, a two-party system, and it also uses PR. In contrast, whereas Great Britain in the past largely had a two-party system, the Liberal-Democrats have established a solid niche, having parliamentary representation for more than twenty years and even winning over 20 percent of the vote in 2005 and 2010 elections. True, they won fewer than 10 percent of the seats—which raises a different issue—but they have survived. Britain no longer has a pure two-party system. Critics have suggested that Duverger got cause and effect backwards, and that the true story is not that PR produces many parties but that a highly fractured polity, with multiple lines of division or cleavage (e.g., religion, class, ethnicity, region, nationalism) led political elites to choose a PR system that would facilitate power-sharing.[30] Indeed, when Italy adopted a more plurality-based system in 1993, it did not appreciably reduce the number of parties. Still, rather than use the term "law," perhaps one could refer to this as a tendency, one that is supported by evidence outside of Europe.[31]

HOW REPRESENTATIVE ARE EUROPEAN PARLIAMENTS?

In addition to knowing about electoral systems and their consequences on party systems, one might also wonder what sort of people are elected to parliament. This gets to the important question of representativeness: Do representatives reflect—literally—their constituents and/or the make-up of the country? This question can be answered in several ways by looking at the composition of European parliaments. For example, one might wonder about the representation of women, who are typically—because women live longer than men—the majority in most countries. Data on this issue are presented in Figure 5.2. Women are best represented in Scandinavian countries, the Netherlands, and Spain, where as of 2010 over a third of all MPs in all of these countries were female.[32] Some countries, such as France, have tried to redress gender inequality through quota laws, requiring political parties to nominate a certain percentage of women for office, whereas in Great Britain, the Labour Party since the 1990s has made an explicit effort to nominate more women for office, albeit for "safe" seats. The results of both efforts, as seen in Figure 5.2, were not particularly impressive. In general, studies have found that systems that use proportional representation are likely to have more female representation, whereas countries that do not, such as France, Great Britain, and the US rank among the lowest in the developed world. In Europe, the lowest percentage of female parliamentarians is found in post-communist Europe and in Turkey.

In other ways, one also finds that MPs do not accurately mirror the country in which they serve. For example, while "European" minority groups—for example,

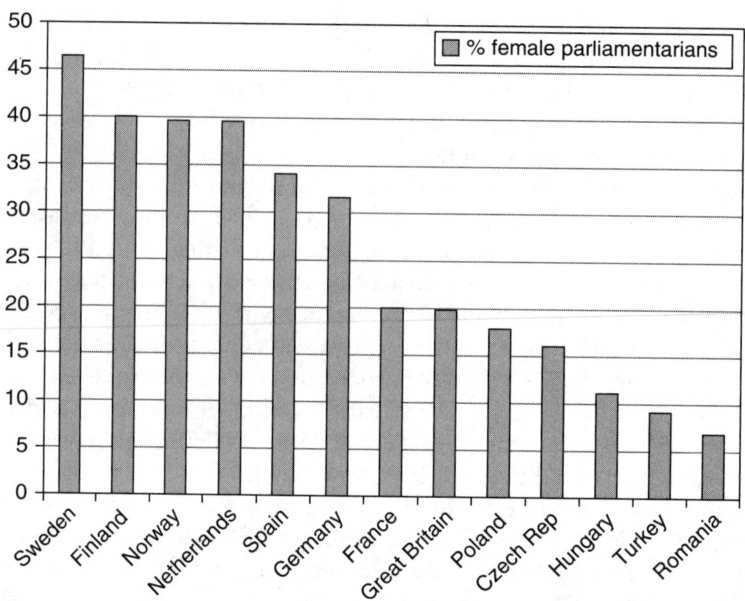

FIGURE 5.2
"Percentages of Female Parliamentarians by Country"
Source: Inter-Parliamentary Union, at http://www.ipu.org/wmn-e/classif.htm, accessed on 3 May 2010. Data are as of 28 February 2010. Data are for both houses of parliament if the country has a bicameral system.

Scots in Great Britain, Catalans in Spain, Hungarians in Romania—are usually represented roughly proportionally to their numbers, other minorities (e.g., Turks in Germany, North Africans in France, Africans and South Asians in Great Britain) fare less well. For example, despite the fact perhaps as many as 10 percent of all people in France are Muslims, only one Muslim was elected in 2007 from mainland France to serve in the National Assembly. Turks in Germany have fared almost as poorly, although in 2008 the Green Party elected a German of Turkish heritage as its party leader. In terms of social class, most parliamentarians, as one would expect are well-educated professionals. Lawyers, business people, and academics are typically "over-represented" compared to blue-collar workers, housewives, and (perhaps most obviously) the unemployed, although parties on the political left, particularly those with strong ties to trade unions, have made efforts to recruit candidates from the working class. Some countries (e.g., Romania, Serbia, Turkey), one might add, buck this pattern and have a reputation of electing a large number of "thugs" to parliament. Fistfights among legislators, for example, were sadly not uncommon events in Turkey in the 1990s.

Most parliaments, of course, do not witness such dramas, and the more mundane day-to-day operations of European parliaments rarely grab headlines. However, they are essential players in European democracies, and typically play a role very different from that of the US Congress. While focus is often on prime ministers and presidents, the composition and actions of parliaments matter greatly, and, as underscored by the British case in 2010, shifts in power within parliament can shake up the entire political system. Whether the coalition government in Britain is a one-off affair or a harbinger of larger changes in the British political system remains to be seen. However, this example demonstrates quite vividly the key role parliaments play in shaping European governments.

APPLICATION QUESTIONS

1. Most European countries have a parliamentary system of governance. In what ways do most European parliaments function differently than the US Congress?
2. If the US were to adopt a proportional representation system, what do you think would happen? What sort of parties would form? Who might benefit? Who would lose? Would this system be workable?
3. Why are women better represented in the parliaments of Scandinavian countries than in Britain, France, or post-communist states? Should parties adopt "affirmative action" style policies or quotas to ensure better female representation?
4. Can you think of several reasons why a SMDP system produces "skewed" electoral results?
5. Why would a country have a bicameral legislature? Are there advantages/disadvantages to bicameralism?

KEY TERMS

alternative vote 143
bicameralism 136
coalition 133
consensus system 133
Duverger's Law 143
electoral systems 137
electoral threshold 141
majoritarian system 133
party discipline 128
party-list 140
personalized proportional representation 141
plurality systems 138
proportional representation (PR) 138
question time 132
run-off election 139
single-member district plurality (SMDP) 138
single transferable vote 142
two-ballot plurality 139
unicameralism 136
vote of no confidence 131

ADDITIONAL READING

Doring, Herbert, ed. 1995. *Parliaments and Majority Rule in Western Europe*. New York: St. Martin's.

A comparative treatment of how Western European parliaments function. Unlike most works, it is organized around topical themes (e.g., relations between ministers and MPs, use of question time) than a country-by-country description.

Gallagher, Michael, and Mitchell, Paul, eds. 2006. *The Politics of Electoral Systems*. Oxford: Oxford University Press.

A survey of the design and effects of electoral systems in twenty-two countries (twelve in Europe), as well as general information on how different types of systems function.

Lijphart, Arend. 1999. *Patterns of Democracy: Government Forms and Performance in Thirty-Six Countries*. New Haven: Yale University Press.

This is a classic source that contrasts majoritarian and consociational forms of democracy. Many of the theories about why political institutions matter and how they might be better designed come from Lijphart's work.

Norris, Pippa. 2004. *Electoral Engineering: Voting Rules and Political Behavior*. Cambridge: Cambridge University Press.

This book looks at the interplay between electoral systems and political behavior, especially voting. In particular, it looks at how the choice between plurality and proportional representation systems affect the behavior of parties and voters.

O'Brennan, John, and Raunio, Tapio, eds. 2007. *National Parliaments within the Enlarged European Union*. London: Routledge.

Provides both an overview of interactions between the EU and national parliaments as well as several case studies on how individual parliaments, including those in new EU member states, work with the EU.

END NOTES

1. The original quotation of John Bright, a radical Quaker politician, is that "England is the mother of Parliaments" (1865).
2. A.A. Gill, "In Britain, Change You Can Bereave In," *The New York Times*, May 2, 2010.
3. "There is an Alternative," *The Economist*, December 29, 2010.
4. In Aristotle's time, Greek city-states practiced direct democracy, where citizens themselves made or approved many of the laws. Assemblies were chosen by lot, not competitive election. Today, because populations are larger, representative democracy—in which voters select people to represent them—is the norm, although, in some cases (e.g., use of referenda in countries such as Switzerland), one finds use of direct democracy in Europe.
5. A classic source on this question is Edmund Burke, Speech to the Electors of Bristol (1774), available in E.J. Payne, ed. *Select Works of Edmund Burke* (Indianapolis: Liberty Fund, 1990).
6. Michael Mezey, *Comparative Legislatures* (Durham NC: Duke University Press, 1979), p. 36.
7. Briefing paper by Vaughne Miller, "EU Legislation," at http://www.parliament.uk/commons/lib/research/notes/snia-02888.pdf, accessed 26 April 2010.
8. For a calculation on Ireland, see http://eulaws.freetzi.com. For a report on Germany co-authored by Roman Herzog, the former German president, see http://www.openeurope.org.uk/analysis/herzog.pdf, both accessed 27 April 2010.
9. Vivian Schmidt, "European 'Federalism' and Its Encroachment on National Institutions," *Publius* 29:1, 1999, p. 25. See also John O'Brennan and Tapio Raunio, eds. *National Parliaments within the Enlarged European Union* (London: Routledge, 2007).
10. Tapio Raunio and Simon Hix, "Backbenchers Learn to Fight Back: European Integration and Parliamentary Government," *West European Politics* 23:4, 2000, 142–168.
11. Summary of actions on this issue can be found in "National Parliaments and the EU," Euractiv.com, August 1, 2008, at http://www.euractiv.com/en/eu-elections/national-parliaments-eu/article-174732, accessed 4 December 2009.
12. The website for COSAC is http://www.cosac.eu/en/
13. See reports of the European Commission on its interactions with NPs. Available at http://ec.europa.eu/dgs/secretariat_general/relations/relations_other/npo/index_en.htm, accessed 4 December 2009. The most opinions were issued by the French Senate, German *Bundesrat* (which represents German *Länder*), and, interestingly, Britain's House of Lords.
14. See Sonia Mazery, "The European Union and Women's Rights: From the Europeanization of National Agendas to the Nationalization of a European Agenda," *Journal of European Public Policy* 5:1, 1999, 131–152, and Francesco Duina and Michael Oliver, "National Parliaments in the European Union: Are There Any Benefits to Integration?" *European Law Journal* 11:2, March 2005, 173–195.
15. Duina and Oliver, "National Parliaments," p. 176.
16. Both countries do have other parties, with the Liberal-Democrats in Great Britain winning a significant share of the vote, reaching 22 percent in 2005. They have not, however, for reasons we shall explore below, typically been able to translate success at the ballot box to a sizeable presence in Parliament.
17. This terminology comes from Arend Lijphart, *Democracies: Patterns of Majoritarian and Consensus Government in Twenty-One Countries* (New Haven, CT: Yale University Press, 1984).
18. Blair's Labour Party retained its majority in 2005 elections, but it lost fifty-seven seats, giving it a mere 55 percent of the seats in the House of Commons.
19. "Set Angela Free," *The Economist*, September 19, 2009.
20. Or, more accurately, at least 598, as peculiarities of the German election law allow for additional members of parliament to be elected and seated in the *Bundestag*.
21. In 2006, one candidate—supported by Turkish immigrants—moved up on the party list thanks to individual votes and won election to parliament.
22. Proportionality is also determined by the mathematical formula used to determine winners of seats (e.g., the d'Hondt method versus Sanite-Lague). These issues are rather technical. For more details on proportional representation systems, see David Farrell, *Electoral Systems: A Comparative Introduction* (New York: Palgrave, 2001), and Michael Gallagher and Paul Mitchell, eds. *The Politics of Electoral Systems* (Oxford: Oxford University Press, 2006).
23. Details as well as arguments for and against can be found in Gallagher and Mitchell, *The Politics of Electoral Systems*, Chapter 25.

24. Maurice Duverger, *Political Parties: Their Organization and Activity in the Modern State* (London: Methuen, 1954).
25. This discussion borrows heavily from the contributions of Arend Lijphart—a well-known defender of proportional representation—as well as Guy Lardeyret and Quentin Quade in Larry Diamond and Marc Plattner, eds. *Electoral Systems and Democracy* (Baltimore: Johns Hopkins University Press, 2006).
26. Shocking as it might be to some, not *every* vote counts in a plurality system. Consider, for example, an election in which Candidate A, two hours before the polls close, has already won more than 50 percent of the votes from all eligible voters in a district. True, no one knows the results until the votes are tallied, but in this case the votes of all who vote in the last two hours of voting, after A has already "won," have no effect on the outcome. Put another way, why should a Labour voter turn out to vote in a "safe" Conservative district if she is certain the Conservative candidate will win? In contrast, under PR, hypothetically at least one extra vote could make a difference in terms of the proportional distribution of seats. There are fewer "wasted" votes.
27. Tiny parties, such as the British Monster Raving Loony Party, which among other things, advocates a 99 pence coin to save on change, may appear on the ballot, but everyone knows they have no chance of winning. Candidates from this party—really—actually received 6,311 votes in the 2005 elections. In order to cast a vote that "matters," voters may be compelled to vote for a party that is not their first or second choice.
28. Lijphart, "Constitutional Choice for New Democracies," in Diamond and Plattner, *Electoral Systems*.
29. Ken Gladdish, "The Primacy of the Particular," in Diamond and Plattner, *Electoral Systems*.
30. Stein Rokkan, *Citizens, Elections, Parties* (Oslo: Universitetsforlaget, 1970), pp. 147–168, and Lijphart, *Democracies*.
31. Canada and India, which use SMDP, have more than two parties, but this is largely a consequence of religious, linguistic, and/or ethnic diversity. The US and Australia remain two-party systems, although they use different types of plurality systems.
32. Data from Inter-Parliamentary Union, available at http://www.ipu.org/wmn-e/classif.htm, accessed on 22 September 2009.

Czech President Václav Klaus: A staunch opponent of the European Union.

CHAPTER 6

Executive Authority in Europe

The Irish vote in October 2009 to approve the Lisbon Treaty, discussed in Chapter 3, removed a major hurdle to its adoption by the EU as a whole, but a final one remained: President Václav Klaus of the Czech Republic. Klaus, an admirer of Margaret Thatcher and free-market economists such as Milton Friedman, believed the EU imposed too many economic regulations and was steadfastly opposed to the Lisbon Treaty, which he believed would create a European super-state with little democratic control. Even though the Czech parliament had ratified the treaty in May 2009, Klaus, whose signature under the Czech constitution was required for international treaties, refused to sign the document, pending the Irish vote and a ruling by the Czech Constitutional Court that it did not violate Czech sovereignty.

After the Irish vote, the question became whether Klaus, by himself, could stand in the way of Lisbon. Some Czechs feared that Klaus's intransigence would isolate the Czech Republic from the rest of Europe. Klaus began to talk about changes he wanted in the treaty, including guarantees that Germans expelled from Czechoslovakia after World War II could not make property claims against Czechs. He largely conceded, however, that Lisbon was a done deal, saying "the train has already traveled so far and so fast that I guess it will not be possible to stop it or turn it around, however much we would wish to."[1] Ultimately, he did secure a British-style opt-out from the treaty's Charter of Fundamental Rights, and, after the Czech Constitutional Court gave its approval to the document, he signed it on November 3, 2009, allowing it to enter into force the following month.

Klaus's holdout against Lisbon created some tensions and drama, both between the Czech Republic and her EU partners and between himself and Czech Prime Minister Jan Fischer, who supported it. It highlighted particular features of the Czech system, namely a president who is separate from parliament and can, on certain issues, wield real authority. Even though Klaus withdrew his opposition, this saga also reveals that individual leaders, even in small countries, are important players on pan-European issues.

This chapter examines the role and power of the executive branch of government, such as the Czech presidency, in contemporary Europe. Because in many European states, parliamentary and executive authority are linked together, this chapter builds upon the previous one. However, one can, at least for analytical purposes, separate the parliament or the legislative "branch" (to employ the American term) from the executive branch of government, which can be defined as the one responsible for implementing or administering the law. Executive authorities in modern Europe, however, often do much more than that, and, as suggested in Chapter 5, some think executives have eclipsed parliaments. Individual chief executives, acting as heads of state and/or heads of government, are responsible for representing their country overseas, for crafting legislation and setting the legislative agenda, and for shepherding their proposals through parliaments. They oversee vast bureaucracies. Some can issue executive orders with the force of law. They represent their country at the EU level. Typically, they are leaders of a political party. Chief executives are also often better able than parliaments to rally public opinion one way or another, and in some states they can call referenda to have the public vote on a favored proposal.

Because European states are democratic, the top executive authority with real, effective political power—the president, prime minister, or chancellor—is elected (directly or indirectly) and is accountable to voters. As with parliaments, however, the nature of executive authority varies from country to country. This chapter highlights the main patterns of how executive authority is organized and how it functions in various settings in contemporary Europe.

HEAD OF STATE VERSUS HEAD OF GOVERNMENT

head of state ■ individual that is the chief public representative or symbol of the state; can be elected or unelected.

In the US, supreme executive authority at the federal level of government is vested in the singular person of the president, who serves as both head of state and head of government. **Head of state** refers to the individual who serves as the chief public representative of the state. This role includes personifying the legitimacy of the state itself. Charles de Gaulle, former French president and architect of France's current constitutional order, stated that a head of state, as he envisaged it for France, would embody the spirit of the nation. The head of state is thus a living symbol, and in this role he or she is removed from day-to-day political squabbles. Americans might think of this as the office of presidency versus the actual person of the president. The office of head of state, although it may be granted various political duties, can be thought of mainly as a symbolic or affective power that is designed to unite all the people of the country.

head of government ■ individual who holds executive authority in the government and is responsible for running the government; this post is elected in European states.

cabinet ■ collection of ministers who oversee departments of the government.

The **head of government,** in contrast, is the individual who is responsible for the running of the government. He or she is empowered to direct the activities of the government and typically oversees a **cabinet** composed of government ministers who in turn oversee various departments or ministries (e.g., foreign affairs, defense, transportation, the environment). The head of government does not, as a head of state would, represent the country primarily in a symbolic fashion. Rather, he or she exercises real political authority.

Because most European countries do not have a presidential system of government like the US, these two offices, head of state and head of government, are often separated. In parliamentary systems—discussed more below—there is typically a largely symbolic executive head of state. In eight European states[2]—Great Britain, the Netherlands, Sweden, Norway, Spain, Denmark, Luxembourg, and Belgium—this takes the form of a monarch (king or queen). These states are

constitutional monarchies, meaning that the monarch, although often powerful in the past, is constrained by major constitutional limits on his or her authority. These figures usually serve symbolic or ceremonial roles, at times with great fanfare (e.g., as with the royal family in Great Britain) but sometimes in a more low-key manner (e.g., as in the Netherlands, Sweden, and Norway). At times, monarchs exercise *de jure* political power—meaning that they are given formal, legal power to approve laws and appoint government officials—but *de facto*—in actuality—they are merely signing off on decisions taken by elected officials that exercise real political power. For example, the Dutch monarch is responsible for naming the country's prime minister, but the king or queen of the Netherlands could not impose his or her own selection as prime minister on an unwilling parliament. In such cases, the symbolic head of state delegates her or his political power to the elected head of government. Any monarch who attempted to overrule or even influence democratic institutions to exercise real political authority would rapidly lose much of his or her public standing in today's Europe. A curious episode occurred in Belgium in 1990, when the king, a practicing Catholic, refused to sign a law that would permit abortion. In response, the parliament temporarily suspended the king, promulgated the law, then reinstated him.

constitutional monarchy ■ form of government in which a monarch serves as head of state but his or her power is severely limited, with real political authority vested in an elected head of government.

In several parliamentary republics (e.g., Germany, Italy, Austria, Hungary) that lack a symbolic monarch, there is a president who serves a similar function. Whether elected directly by voters (as in Austria) or by some type of electoral college involving parliamentary and/or regional authorities (as in Germany, Hungary, and Italy), this individual fulfills ceremonial roles (e.g., recognizing and receiving ambassadors, formally opening parliament). Some of these figures possess, in theory, wide powers. For example, the Austrian president is empowered to appoint cabinet ministers, judges, and military officers and can dismiss parliament. Like European monarchs, however, the Austrian president is constrained by traditions not to interfere in political decision-making. He or she in effect rubberstamps decisions made by the chancellor or parliament. Similarly, in Italy, the president has a variety of powers, including nominating judges to the Supreme Court, calling referendums, declaring a state of war, and issuing decrees with the force of law. Any act of the president, however, must be countersigned by a minister from the government, meaning that the Italian president's political autonomy is limited. These symbolic presidents are thus largely figureheads, nothing like the US president in terms of actual political power. They are supposed to represent national unity rather than a particular political tendency. At times, however, these leaders can play important mediating roles in the political life of their country. For example, the president of Italy was called upon in early 2007 to broker talks among factions within parliament to hobble together a continuation of its coalition government. For the most part, however, such symbolic figures are rarely politically relevant. Thus, when we discuss executive authority in states such as these, we are talking about politically empowered actors (heads of government), not the affective, symbolic ones (heads of state).

Several countries with parliamentary systems (e.g., the Czech Republic, Turkey) have presidents who serve as head of state but also can exercise some real power (e.g., by vetoing laws, conducting foreign policy). More political authority in these states, however, is vested in the prime minister, who serves as head of government. In states (e.g., France, Poland) with semi-presidential systems—discussed later in this chapter—matters are still more complex, as power is, in various configurations, shared between an elected president (head of state) and a prime minister (head of government) who emerges from the parliamentary body.

ORGANIZATION OF EXECUTIVE AUTHORITY

The exact form of executive authority will not be the same from country to country. Some items that vary include length of term of office for chief executives, how they are elected, their precise constitutional powers, and the size and effectiveness of the bureaucracy that administers the law. More relevant in terms of categorizing types of executive authority is how executive authority relates to parliamentary bodies. Thinking about pure, ideal types with respect to the last factor, one can envision a system in which executive and parliamentary power are linked or fused together, one in which they are separated, and one that combines these types, with one executive separate from parliament and one connected to it in some fashion. These are, respectively, a parliamentary system, a presidential system, and a semi-presidential system.

Parliamentary Systems

parliamentary system ■ form of government in which the executive authority (the prime minister) is chosen by the parliament, not directly by voters.

vote of no confidence ■ procedure by which a parliament can remove the executive authority from office.

As noted in the previous chapter, most European democracies have parliamentary forms of governance, with executive power vested in the prime minister (or chancellor in Germany and Austria) and his or her cabinet. The essence of the **parliamentary system** of government is that the prime minister is chosen by the parliament (not the voters) and he or she is a member of the legislative body. The executive and the parliamentary bodies are thus said to be fused together. The prime minister is directly accountable to the legislature, which not only voted him/her into office but retains the power to oust the prime minister at any time by a **vote of no confidence.** In this way, although there are clear lines of accountability, there is no separation of powers as understood in the US system and election cycles are less predictable than in a presidential system with a fixed term of office. Table 6.1 lists key differences between a parliamentary system and a presidential system, the later of which is likely to be more familiar to US students but is, as we shall see, very rare in Europe.

In states with bicameral legislatures, the prime minister is selected by the "lower house"—for example, the House of Commons in Great Britain, the *Bundestag* in Germany, the *Sejm* in Poland. If one party has a majority in the legislature, then the leader of that party is typically selected to be prime minister, and he or she then names cabinet ministers, who frequently are members of parliament from the same party of the prime minister. Such has been the norm in Great Britain (at least until the 2010 elections, as noted in Chapter 5) and in Greece, whose parliamentary composition in shown in Table 6.2. Together, the prime minister and cabinet—in effect the executive branch but more commonly referred to in parliamentary system as simply "the government"—are charged with presenting proposals to the parliament and ensuring that laws passed by the legislature are duly implemented.

TABLE 6.1

Features of Parliamentary and Presidential Systems

Features	Parliamentary Systems	Presidential Systems
Head of Government	Prime minister, selected by legislature	President, elected by voters
Head of State	Separate individual; largely symbolic office	President; both roles are fused together
Head of Govt Part of Legislature?	Yes	No
Can Legislature Remove Head of Govt?	Yes	No (except for impeachment)
Can Head of Govt Dissolve the Legislature?	Yes	No
Separation of Powers?	No—"Fused Government"	Yes
Set Term of Office?	No	Yes
Divided Govt Possible?	No	Yes
Can Executive be a Coalition?	Yes—Cabinet positions can be divided among parties	No—president is sole executive body
Examples	Great Britain, Italy, Germany, Netherlands, Sweden, Hungary, Estonia	Cyprus (pure presidential); France, Poland, Portugal, and Romania are semi-presidential

Single party governments, as of 2010, also ruled in Turkey, Spain, Hungary, and Portugal.

Because most European countries have multi-party (three or more significant parties) systems—in large part due to the proportional representation electoral system, discussed in the previous chapter—it is difficult for one party to win a majority in the parliament. Most countries therefore are ruled by a coalition of parties, meaning that a group of two or more parties within the parliament form an alliance for the purpose of constituting a majority and selecting a prime minister and cabinet, whose members will come from the coalition partners. Typically, the formation of a coalition is subject to negotiation, both in terms of the individuals who will serve in the government positions and in terms of the policy priorities to be pursued by the government. Because the coalition should be based on some sort of common political ground, they are often based upon ideological affinity, meaning parties that share similar outlooks join together and elect the leader of one of the parties (typically the larger or largest party) as the prime minister. For example, as seen in Table 6.2, as of 2010 Sweden and Ireland had coalition governments: Sweden's was center-right in orientation and Ireland's was more center-left. Note that in the Swedish case it took more parties to form a coalition to achieve a majority in parliament than in the Irish case (because there are so many more parties in the Swedish parliament) and that the largest party in Sweden after the 2010 elections, the Social Democratic Party, was *not* in the coalition as its opponents

TABLE 6.2

Governing Parties in Various European Countries

	Greece (2009)	Sweden (2010)	Ireland (2007)	Germany (2009)	Denmark (2007)
Party/ Orientation/ Seats	**Pan-Hellenic Socialist Movement (center-left) 160**	Social Democrats 112	**Fianna Fail (center) 78**	**Christian Democrats (right) 239**	**Venstre (center-right) 46**
	New Democracy (center-right) 91	**Moderate Party (center) 107**	Fine Gael (right) 51	Social Democrats (left) 146	Social Democrats (left) 45
	Communists (left) 21	Green Party (center-left) 25	Labour (left) 20	**Free Democrats (center-right) 93**	Danish People's Party* (right) 25
	Popular Orthodox Rally (right) 15	**Liberal Peoples' Party (center) 24**	**Green (left) 6**	Left Party (far-left) 76	Socialist People's Party (left) 23
	Coalition of the Radical Left (left) 13	**Center Party 23**	Sinn Fein (left) 4	Greens (left) 68	**Conservative People's Party (right) 18**
		Sweden Democrats (far-right) 20			Radical Left 9
		Christian-Democrats (center-right) 19			
		Left Party 19			
Total Seats	300	349	166	622	179
Prime Minister or Chancellor	George Papandreou (PSM)	Fredrik Reinfeldt (Moderate)	Brian Cowen (FF)	Angela Merkel (CD)	Lars Rasmussen (V)

Governing parties are in **bold**. Smaller parties and independents are not listed. *Party offers support to minority government.
Source: Parties and Elections in Europe (http://www.parties-and-elections.de, accessed on 20 May 2009) and reports from the British election in 2010.

banded together and controlled more votes. Usually, coalitions contain only the necessary number of parties to obtain a majority; there is no need to add an "extra" party to the coalition, as this would only make governing more difficult. At times, when other possibilities do not exist, one may see the formation of a grand coalition, an alliance of the two largest parties, usually on opposite sides of the political spectrum, that will command the overwhelmingly majority of votes in parliament. As noted in the previous chapter, this occurred in Germany in 2005, because no one would form a coalition with the pariah Left (*Linke*) Party, the neither of the smaller parties on the left (Greens) or the center-right (Free Democrats) would join in a coalition with parties on the other side of the spectrum. After protracted negotiations, the Christian Democrats (center-right) and the Social Democrats (center-left) agreed on a grand coalition. In 2009, as seen in Table 6.2, the grand coalition in Germany ended, but in the late 2000s grand coalitions could also be found in the Czech Republic, the Netherlands, and Romania.

It is possible that a **minority government**, one that does not possess a majority of votes in the legislature, can form if the majority in the legislature does not actively oppose it. For example, in post–World War II Sweden and Denmark, most governments have been minority governments, with the Social Democratic Party in both states able to pass measures thanks to *ad hoc* deals with centrists or far-left parties, with these parties preferring to eschew the formal creation of a coalition government. After the 2007 elections in Denmark, as seen in Table 6.2, Danish parties formed a minority government, with the liberal (centrist) Venstre Party and the Conservative People's Party (which together only had 64 of the 179 seats in the Danish parliament) relying upon the support of the far-right (and very controversial) Danish People's Party (DPP), which elected not to formally enter the government but is a reliable partner to vote in favor of the most of the government's initiatives. With the DPP, the government can count on eighty-nine votes, enough for a majority to pass legislation. Sweden after 2010 elections had a minority government of the center-right, as the four-party coalition controlled 173 of the 349 seats, two short of a majority. The government expects to be able to pass legislation, working on an ad hoc basis with center-left parties or with the far-right, anti-immigrant Sweden Democrats on some issues. Minority governments, because they are not based on a formal coalition, are often more unstable compared to those with a majority coalition.

minority government ■ a government that relies upon the permanent support of only a minority of members of parliament but that can survive with case-by-case support from other parties.

Note that prime ministers or chancellors do not "run" for office in the same way that US presidents do. They are not elected directly by the country's voters. Typically, they are the head of a party, elected to parliament either from a party-list or, as in the British case, from a particular district. Most European voters thus do not vote for their chief executive. They vote for his or her party or for another representative from that party. Ideally, however, voters know that their votes will contribute to the possibility of the leader of a party to become prime minister. The central point though is that voters, in parliamentary systems, do not directly elect the executive. If voters want to change the chief executive in a parliamentary system, they must do so by voting in legislative elections.

In between elections, the prime minister remains accountable to the legislature in a fashion completely unlike that of an American president. Just as prime ministers are selected by the legislature (or, more accurately, parties within the legislature), they can also be removed by a vote of no confidence, meaning that a majority in the legislature votes, in essence, to "fire" the prime minister. This vote can either be an explicit one on the future tenure of the prime minister or a vote on a matter of such importance that, should the prime minister lose, he or she would feel it impossible to continue serving and would thus resign. In practice, this means prime ministers, despite all of their authority, can be ousted from office if only a few members of parliament decide to vote against them. For example, looking at Table 6.2, one can see that if only two members of the Irish Green Party defect from the coalition with the Fianna Fail party, the government would lose its majority. While Irish politicians under normal circumstances would not likely be cavalier with their votes, the Greens did defect from the government in November 2010 in the midst of Ireland's economic crisis, necessitating new elections in 2011. Similarly, in early 2010, both the Belgian and Dutch governments collapsed because coalition partners withdrew their support. After trying unsuccessfully to form a new coalition with different parties, the governments in both countries called for new elections, hoping that a new parliament will produce a more workable government. As seen in Figure 6.1, across the multi-party parliamentary systems in Europe, where coalition governments are frequently the norm, the average duration of governments varies considerably, with some (e.g., Poland and Italy) countries prone to more fragile coalitions than those in Scandinavia, where governments frequently manage to serve their entire term of office. In Germany, government longevity is enhanced

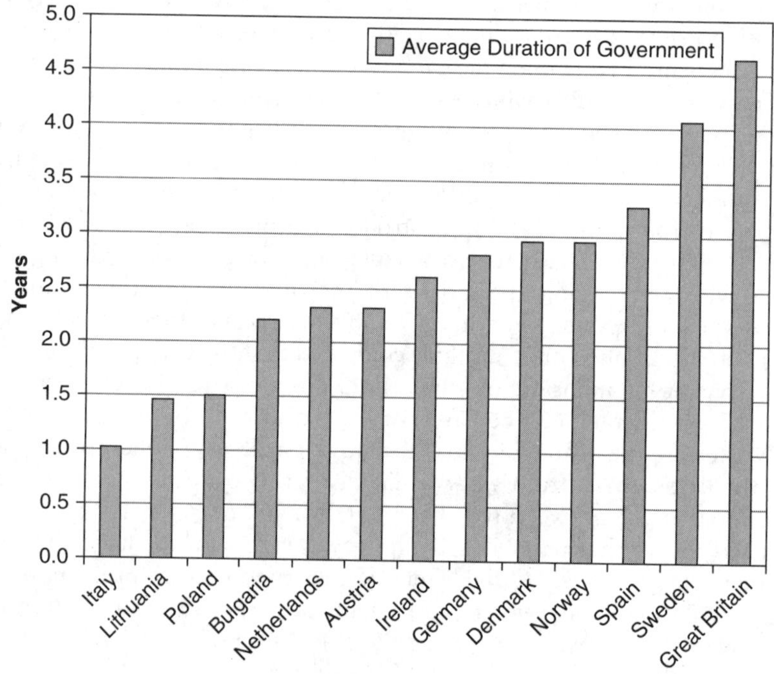

FIGURE 6.1

Average Duration of Parliamentary Governments

Source: Author's calculations, primarily from list of governments and cabinets from Wikipedia. If government is reelected, it only counts as one government. Years are 1945–2010, except for Ireland (1937–2010), Poland (1990–2010), Bulgaria (1990–2010), and Lithuania (1991–2010)

by a provision that requires the *Bundestag* is to pass a constructive vote of no confidence, meaning that a majority must not only reject the chancellor but also vote in favor of an alternative candidate.

In Great Britain, one-party governments have been the norm, and, as seen in Figure 6.1, British governments tend to be among the most stable in Europe. However, governments can, potentially at any rate, fall in countries with parliamentary systems in which only one party serves in government. For example, in the 2000s, both Tony Blair and Gordon Brown in Great Britain faced opposition on important questions (e.g., the Iraq War, education reform, economic policy) from members of their own Labour Party, who threatened at times to vote against the prime minister and potentially necessitate new elections. In Greece, the economic crisis of 2010 produced some uncertainty about whether the one-party government of the Socialists would be able to pass painful austerity measures and weather the storm.

Typically, if a prime minister is removed by a vote of no confidence, the legislature either selects another individual—from the same or from another party—to serve or the country holds new elections. If a prime minister resigns voluntarily—as Tony Blair did in Great Britain in June 2007 or Anders Fogh Rasmussen did in Denmark in April 2009—new elections are not necessary; the parliament has the prerogative to select a new person as prime minister (in these cases Gordon Brown and Lars Rasmussen [no relation], respectively). In addition, in a parliamentary system the prime minister can, at his or her discretion, dissolve the legislature and call for new elections. This is an important power, as the prime minister can time an election at the height of his or her popularity in order to gain a fresh term of office. Thus, election cycles are irregular as new elections can be held at any time, although each state has a maximum term (typically four or five years) after which new elections must be held. Provided that the prime minister's party wins elections—"winning" meaning that the party gains a majority of seats or can organize a coalition to form a government—the prime minister can stay in office for multiple terms.

Because the chief executive is responsible to the legislature (not directly to voters) and is a member of the legislature, the executive and legislative branches are in effect fused together. The composition of the executive—either a single-party executive or a coalition—reflects the will of the majority in the legislature, making divided government, in which one party controls the executive and one the legislature, impossible. Thus, in parliamentary systems, it is usually easier to the government to pass its proposals through the legislature, although managing coalitions, minority governments, or bicameralism can at times be complicated because the prime minister will be less certain that he or she will command a majority of votes at all times. For example, many in the German government in 2010 wanted to make substantial reforms in health care, but this was problematic, given disputes among the coalition partners, interest associations, and the federal and regional governments.[3] Whether this topic proves to be as divisive as it was in the US in 2009 to 2010 remains to be seen.

In most parliamentary systems, the initiative to propose legislation is assumed by the government, with relevant cabinet ministers (and, at times, the prime minister) appearing before the legislature for question time, during which they can be grilled by members of the opposition. Although question time provides some form of accountability, is often entertaining to watch (in the British case during heated sessions insults are hurled across the political aisle), and requires government ministers to be able to speak extemporaneously and defend their policies in a rough-and-tumble forum, the outcome of the final vote is usually known in advance.

Although parliamentary systems are structured similarly, the actual power wielded by prime ministers varies. The British prime minister, for example, tends to be very powerful. Because Great Britain has—more or less—a two-party system, the prime minister, at least until the 2010 elections, could count on a majority in the House of Commons. Party discipline is also high, meaning that members of his or her party will usually cast their votes as they are instructed. The House of Lords, if it wants to stop a measure proposed by the prime minister, can only delay legislation. Lastly, there is no judicial review to overturn any act of parliament. Parliament can do, in a strictly legal sense, whatever it wants, which gives the party that controls parliament a political blank check. For some, this may amount to little more than "elected dictatorship," but in practice the prime minister is constrained by what is politically acceptable to his own cabinet, the majority of his party, and, ultimately, the British public. For example, in the early 2000s Tony Blair on numerous occasions expressed some support for Britain joining the euro. However, powerful figures in the Cabinet opposed this, including Gordon Brown when he was chancellor of the exchequer (minister of finance) during Blair's tenure as prime minister. Blair thus did not push the issue, either in parliament or in a referendum among the larger public.

In contrast, the Italian prime minister has traditionally been far weaker. Italy has several parties represented in parliament, and the typical Italian prime minister has had to manage a coalition of several parties. Finding common ground to get agreement on many policies is difficult. If the prime minister cannot maintain the support of his or her coalition partners, he or she risks losing office. In addition, the Senate has co-equal legislative powers with the Chamber of Deputies, meaning that even if the prime minister and the government get a bill through the Chamber of Deputies, they may encounter opposition in the Senate. Lastly, there is a Constitutional Court, to which the opposition may appeal, claiming that proposals violate the constitution.

Thus, even though the two countries both have parliamentary systems, they function quite differently. The consequences are clear for all to see: Great Britain generally has had stable, powerful, durable governments, whereas governments in Italy have been politically weak and fragile. Italy went through fifty-six governments in fifty-six years between 1945 and 2001. Silvio Berlusconi, the richest man in Italy and the melodramatic, arguably megalomaniac leader of the *Forza Italia* (Go Italy) party, was the first Italian prime minister to serve a full term of office (2001–2006) in fifty years. Italy's problems are sometimes trotted out by those who would argue that parliamentary systems are too unstable. After all, they might say, the government in a parliamentary system can be voted out at any time, and this can be chaotic—look at Italy! However, Italian politics suffer from a number of problems: a high degree of political polarization, the fact that some parties (e.g., the traditionally large Communist Party) have been treated as pariahs by other parties (thereby constraining possibilities for coalition governments), and a proportional electoral system that encouraged the proliferation of small parties.

Changes in the electoral law in 1993 to reduce the number of seats decided by proportional representation did not appreciably reduce the number of parties, and Italian politics today remains far more unstable than British politics. For example, whereas Tony Blair, after serving as prime minister for ten years, managed to hand power over to Gordon Brown in 2007 without much difficulty, in Italy Prime Minister Romano Prodi, leader of a nine-party center-left coalition, tendered his resignation in February 2007, less than a year after his razor-thin victory over the right-wing government of Silvio Berlusconi, who had changed the electoral law again in a misplaced hope that such a change would contribute to his victory. Prodi was reinstated the following week, but a year later, in February 2008, after a small party in the Senate withdrew support from the coalition, Prodi narrowly lost a vote of confidence in the Senate and was forced to resign. Italy held new elections, and Berlusconi, whose popularity had increased since his 2006 defeat, became prime minister (for a third time) in a center-right coalition government.

In addition to managing the government, prime ministers or chancellors also have other duties. Although they are not nominally head of state, in practice they represent the country in international affairs and make important decisions with respect to foreign policy. The prime minister, in most cases, is also the head of a political party, giving him or her discretion in managing the affairs of that party, including how to assign members of his or her party to cabinet positions.

Varieties of Presidentialism in Europe

Although most governments in Europe are parliamentary and thus headed by prime ministers or chancellors, many countries also have presidents, although many of these, as noted above, tend to have only symbolic powers. While they do serve as head of state, most European presidents (with a few exceptions) co-exist with more powerful prime ministers. In general terms, one can identify three different types of presidentialism in Europe, and some features of all European countries with presidents is presented in Table 6.3.

presidential system ■ form of government in which executive authority is vested in an individual who is typically elected by voters separately from the parliament.

Pure Presidentialism

When most people speak of a **presidential system**, they would be referring to a "pure" presidential system are like those found in the US and in much of Latin America, in which a directly elected president[4] is the undisputed head of the executive branch, not sharing power with a prime minister and serving as both head of state and head of government. Presidential power is entirely separated from the legislature, meaning that the two branches have distinct powers, are elected separately, and a person cannot simultaneously serve as president and in the legislature. Usually, there is a system of checks and balances (e.g., presidential veto, right of the legislature to approve presidential appointments) that, in theory at least, are designed to foster limited government. Note as well that a presidential system can have a divided government, meaning that the executive branch and the legislative branch are controlled by two different parties (e.g., the situation in the US from 2006 to 2008 when the Democrats won control of the House of Representatives and Senate while Republicans retained the White House). This would be impossible in a parliamentary system, in which the majority party or coalition of parties in the parliament chooses the leaders of the executive branch from its own members. Differences with

TABLE 6.3

Forms of Presidentialism in Europe

Country	Who elects?	Substantial Powers?	Prime Minister?	Type of Presidentialism
Cyprus	Voters	Yes	No	Pure presidentialism
France	Voters	Yes	Yes	Semi-presidentialism
Finland	Voters	Some	Yes	Semi-presidentialism
Lithuania	Voters	Some	Yes	Semi-presidentialism
Poland	Voters	Some	Yes	Semi-presidentialism
Portugal	Voters	Some	Yes	Semi-presidentialism
Romania	Voters	Some	Yes	Semi-presidentialism
Czech Republic	2 Houses of Parliament	Some	Yes	Semi-presidentialism
Austria	Voters	No	Yes	Symbolic
Bosnia and Herzegovina[a]	Voters	No	Yes	Symbolic
Bulgaria	Voters	No	Yes	Symbolic
Croatia	Voters	Some	Yes	Symbolic
Ireland	Voters	No	Yes	Symbolic
Macedonia	Voters	No	Yes	Symbolic
Montenegro	Voters	No	Yes	Symbolic
Serbia	Voters	No	Yes	Symbolic
Slovakia	Voters	No	Yes	Symbolic
Slovenia	Voters	No	Yes	Symbolic
Albania	Parliament	No	Yes	Symbolic
Estonia	Parliament	No	Yes	Symbolic
Germany	Parliament	No	Yes	Symbolic
Greece	Parliament	No	Yes	Symbolic
Hungary	Parliament	No	Yes	Symbolic
Latvia	Parliament	No	Yes	Symbolic
Malta	Parliament	No	Yes	Symbolic
Switzerland[b]	Parliament	No	Yes	Symbolic
Turkey	Parliament	Some	Yes	Semi-Presidential

Source: Author's compilation, drawing from the state's constitution and political practice.

[a]In Bosnia and Herzegovina, the presidency consists of a three person council composed of one Serb, One Croat, and one Bosniac (Muslim). The chair of this body rotates every eight months.

[b]The Swiss president is a member of the seven-member Federation Council, which as a collective body functions as the head of state. The president rotates among the members of the Council on a yearly basis.

the more common parliamentary system were presented earlier in Table 6.1, and an extended discussion about the relative merits of presidential and parliamentary systems can be found in the **In Focus** feature.

The only example of "pure" presidentialism in Europe is in Cyprus, where the president is elected by voters for a five-year term, is both head of state and head of government, and has numerous political powers, including veto power over legislation. The fact that Cyprus—under British control from 1878 until gaining

IN FOCUS

The Relative Merits of Presidential and Parliamentary Forms of Government

Earlier in the chapter we discussed general differences between presidential and parliamentary forms of governance. As noted in Chapter 6, there is a long-standing focus in political science on the study of institutions. The goal typically is not just description or classification but to demonstrate how institutions matter. In other words, there are consequences to how institutions are set up, and implicitly there is a normative argument as well: some designs are better than others. This is not just an exercise in abstract argument. In the 1980s and 1990s, when numerous states—including those in Eastern Europe—began to move towards democracy, a lively debate emerged how which types of institutions should be adopted. One of the core areas of argument revolved around the choice between parliamentarism and presidentialism.

Each has its defenders.[5] Those favoring presidential systems of governance would claim that it has several advantages[6]: first, because the term of office of a president is fixed, whereas in a parliamentary system the prime minister can lose office at any time through a vote of no confidence, presidential systems are said to be more stable and facilitate predictable policy planning. Americans, for example, know literally centuries in advance when presidential elections will be held (in early November every four years), whereas elections in European states with parliamentary systems could occur, literally, at any time. Second, a president (forgetting for a second about the vagaries of the Electoral College in the US) is directly elected, and thus can claim a mandate from the people, whereas a prime minister is elected by parliament and does not therefore stand before all of the country's voters. Third, presidential systems are said to have a more effective system of checks and balances, as the executive and legislative branches are independent of each other. Fourth, one could also argue—in somewhat of a contrast to the point just made—that presidential systems, because the executive branch is controlled by a single individual not beholden to maintaining parliamentary approval, will produce more decisive executive leadership than prime ministers whose hold on power depends upon their ability to manage complex coalitions.[7]

Those favoring a parliamentary system offer different arguments. First, they would maintain that presidential government, with all of its checks and balances, can lead to "gridlock" when the executive and legislative branches are controlled by different parties. This is not only inefficient, but also makes political accountability difficult, as each branch blames the other if they cannot agree on what policy to adopt. This has been an issue in France, which has seen "cohabitation" between its president and prime minister, and it can make governance more complicated. In contrast, parliamentary systems—particularly those in which a single party is able to form the government—can be very efficient and have clear lines of accountability for policy. Second, one could argue that presidential systems are too rigid. Presidents having a fixed term of office can turn into "lame ducks," whereas a parliamentary system can make more rapid adjustments to respond to changing circumstances or public opinion. True, in extreme cases—such as Italy with its fifty-six governments in fifty-six years after World War II—this can lead to instability; in more moderate cases, one might deem such "flexibility" a positive feature. Third, presidential systems rest on a "winner-take-all" logic, meaning that only one individual can be president. Although one could argue that the president thus represents the entire nation, this may be problematic in ethnically divided societies, where the minority group would find it difficult to have one of its own elected president. A power-sharing arrangement that would allow for the possibility of executives made up of coalitions of parties might therefore be more inclusive. Fourth,

(*continued*)

there is a problem of representation. For example, in the first round of French presidential elections in 2002, when sixteen candidates ran for office, Jacques Chirac, the eventual winner, polled only 20 percent of the vote. True, he prevailed with 82 percent of the vote in the run-off against the extreme xenophobe Jean Marie Le Pen, but, given his low vote total in round one, can one really say that Chirac's election represents the will of the people of France? Lastly, one could argue that presidential elections are often akin to celebrity beauty contests and hinge too much on personalities and personal lives and not enough on the issues (e.g., this is a chronic complaint in every US election). Because voters in a parliamentary system are typically not voting for the prime minister directly, they may focus more on the party platforms than the personalities.

In a simple sense, then, there are trade-offs between the two systems. Moreover, one could argue that each system can work: parliamentarism has a successful track record in Great Britain, the Netherlands, Sweden, and many other countries; presidentialism works in the US, and few Americans would even dream of the idea of adopting a parliamentary form of government; and semi-presidentialism, despite some its complexities, has succeeded in France. Does this demonstrate that all systems are equal?

Not quite. In empirical work looking at the performance of "new democracies" since World War II, several analysts have noted that parliamentary systems perform better: They both more stable governments and are far more likely to become consolidated, successful democracies.[8] Why? Alfred Stepan and Cindy Skach suggest that a major problem is that the mutual independence of presidents and legislatures can produce political impasses for which there are no easy remedies. The consequences are military coups, suspension of the constitution, and instability—an dramatic example being the stand-off in 1993 in Russia between President Yeltsin and the Russian parliament, which was "resolved" only after Yeltsin ordered tanks to fire on the parliament building. In contrast, the mutual dependence between prime ministers and parliaments provide a means to break political impasses and ultimately contribute to the stability of the democratic system.[9]

What does one find in Europe? In a recent study of post-communist countries, Steven Fish examined how the powers of legislative branches—as opposed to presidents—affect democracy. He concludes that there is a relationship, with presidential systems, such as Belarus, Ukraine, and Russia—far less democratic by 2002 than countries with parliamentary systems or semi-presidential systems with stronger parliaments, such as Slovenia, Hungary, and Slovakia.[10] Moreover, one can argue that the adoption of semi-presidentialism in countries like Poland and Romania complicated governance in both countries in the 1990s, with, for example, President Lech Walesa in Poland trying to gain more powers by pushing a "Little Constitution" and undermining parliament by using his status as a heroic figure to appeal directly to public opinion.[11] In Romania, disputes between President Emil Constantinescu (1996–2000) and parliament led to the collapse of several cabinets and slowed the course of reform.

Critical Thinking Questions

1. Can you make an argument that one type of system (presidential or parliamentary) is more "democratic" than the other?
2. Why might it be that parliamentary systems are more common than presidential ones in Europe?

independence in 1960—adopted presidentialism may seem peculiar, but it developed as a means of power-sharing between the island's majority Greek population (which elects the president) and minority Turkish population (which is supposed to elect a vice president who wields some political power). After the Turkish invasion of Cyprus in 1974, the island has been politically divided, with the Turkish population having their own government (not internationally recognized) on the northern third of the island. Since this time, the office of the vice president has been unfilled.

Semi-Presidentialism More common in Europe is **semi-presidentialism,** sometimes called a "dual executive" system.[12] The classic definition of this arrangement, set forth by Maurice Duverger, has three elements: the president should be elected by direct popular vote; the president should possess considerable political power; and the president must co-exist with a prime minister and cabinet ministers who possess powers over the government and can stay in office only if the parliament does not show opposition to them.[13]

semi-presidentialism: ■ form of government in which executive authority is shared between a president and prime minister; combines features of both the presidential and parliamentary systems.

Among European governments, the best example of semi-presidentialism is found in France. This arrangement evolved as a compromise in 1958 between Charles de Gaulle and forces in the French legislature. After World War II, France adopted a parliamentary form of government, but it was weak and unstable. De Gaulle, hero of the French resistance to the Nazis, was called back to rescue the government from a grave crisis in the French colony of Algeria, but he agreed to serve only if France would adopt a new constitution with strong presidential powers—which, of course, he would be able to use. Forces within the French legislature agreed to accommodate this demand, but were unwilling to cede all power to the office of the presidency. Thus, the Fifth Republic in France—its current constitutional system—has both a president, popularly elected by the people and serving as head of state, and a prime minister, who is accountable to the French National Assembly (the lower house of parliament) and is considered the head of government.

The French president, however, is quite powerful, reflecting de Gaulle's belief that "parliaments should be seen, not heard." The French president, by the Constitution, directs the military and is responsible for foreign policy; he or she, unlike the US president, can dissolve the legislature[14]; he or she can also call referendums declare a state of emergency, force the National Assembly to vote on proposed laws, and appoint numerous bureaucratic, judicial, and military officials. He or she is also charged with naming the prime minister, but, since the National Assembly can censure the prime minister and remove him or her from office, *de facto* the president must name someone acceptable to the majority of the representatives in the legislative branch. The prime minister in turn nominates the other cabinet ministers, who are also accountable to the National Assembly.

The precise division of power between the president and the prime minister is rather vague. Whereas the Constitution enumerates several specific presidential powers, the prime minister is given, in Article 21, more general directives such as directing the action of the government and being "responsible" for national defense. How this squares with the powers of the president—who, after all, directs the military!—is not explicitly stated. When de Gaulle was President (1958–1970), there was little question who was in charge: Prime ministers did the bidding of the president. Indeed, given the fact that the president can dismiss the National Assembly and the prime minister[15] and not vice versa, it is clear that there is a lopsided relationship, with the prime minister and government—in most periods of the Fifth Republic—expected to execute the president's political program and serve as a lightning rod to deflect public criticism away from the president. Indeed, if the president's party commands a majority in the Assembly and thus can count on a reliable prime minister, the French president can in practice exercise more power than virtually any other democratically elected leader.

However, matters have not always been that simple. Naturally, the French prime minister does not want to be the president's lap dog. He or she has a personal interest in carving out an individual political identity, if for no other reason than to gain stature and run for president someday. However, France's semi-presidential form of government creates opportunities for tension and conflict than goes beyond personalities. It is possible that the president and prime minister could be political rivals from different parties, because the president must appoint a prime minister acceptable to the National Assembly.[16] This situation, known as **cohabitation**, has occurred three times: in the periods from 1986 to 1988, from 1993 to 1995, and 1997 to 2002. In these cases, there was rivalry between the two executives, and the president could not expect the prime minister and National Assembly to go along with his initiatives. During cohabitation, there are *de facto* "checks and balances" and the prime minister gains power, although the precise arrangements depend as much upon personalities and willingness to compromise as upon the rather vague prescriptions in the French Constitution. In general, the pattern has been for the president concentrate on foreign policy and representing France in more symbolic ways as the head of state, but with the growing power of the European Union on French domestic issues, the line between foreign and domestic policy is increasingly blurry. In the 1997 to 2002 cohabitation period between President Jacques Chirac (from the political right) and Prime Minister Lionel Jospin (from the Socialist Party), France experienced a weak government that did not or could not take major initiatives. Chirac won 2002 presidential elections, and his party—named at the time the Movement for a Presidential Majority—reflected in its very name a desire to be rid of cohabitation, which may be less likely in the future because the Assembly and the President are now, thanks to a constitutional amendment, on the same five-year election cycle. For example, in 2007 French voters elected as president Nicholas Sarkozy and gave Sarkozy's party, the Union for a Popular Movement (UMP), a majority in the National Assembly, allowing Sarkozy to name François Fillon of the UMP, pictured in the photo (page 169), as prime minister.

cohabitation ■ arrangement in a semi-presidential system in which the president and prime minister come from different political parties.

As seen in Table 6.3, other countries in Europe also have semi-presidential systems, although in most cases their presidents are constitutionally weaker than the French President.[17] Examples include Finland, Poland, and Portugal. Notably, in these cases, the powers of the president have diminished in recent years. In Finland, the president is popularly elected and in the post–World War II era has exercised control over foreign policy and had the power to dissolve the parliament, but constitutional changes in 2000 stripped the president of many of his or her domestic political powers and diminished his or her role in foreign policy. In Poland, from 1992 to 1997 under the so-called "Little Constitution," the president enjoyed a range of powers ranging from a veto over legislation to a designated special role in defense and foreign affairs. The 1997 constitution took away many of the president's powers, although he or she still can still refer bills to the Constitutional Tribunal, nominate state officials, and possesses a veto that requires a 60 percent (as opposed to two-third vote, as before) vote in the Polish lower house to override it. In Portugal, the president enjoys, on paper, a host of powers, although since the transition to democracy the president has generally not exercised them, deferring instead to the prime minister. An exception occurred in 2004, when President Jorge

President Nicholas Sarkozy and Prime Minister François Fillon: Semi-presidentialism at work in France.

Sampaio dismissed the controversial government of Pedro Santana Lopes, despite the fact that Lopes enjoyed the support of the majority in parliament. The Czech Republic could also be called a semi-presidential system, even though it does not mean Duverger's definition because the president is not elected by voters. However, as noted at the outset of this chapter, this post, at least as occupied by Klaus, has not been purely ceremonial; in addition to approving treaties, the president can veto laws passed by parliament, although parliament may override the veto.[18]

In many states of the former Yugoslavia (e.g., Croatia, Bosnia, Serbia), elected presidents exercised great authority (at times undemocratically) in the 1990s. More recently, after the fighting stopped and the wartime leaders were removed from office or died, they have moved closer to parliamentary forms of governance, with the presidential powers more circumscribed by law. Thus, across Europe, the trend has been to move away from stronger presidents, with all semi-presidential systems, including France's, becoming less "presidential."

Symbolic Presidentialism As noted earlier in this chapter, several European republics have a system of **symbolic presidentialism**, in which presidents are heads of state and perform functions similar to those of kings and queens in constitutional monarchies. In these systems, one sees parliamentary forms of governance, with presidents expected to remain above partisan politics and not involve themselves in issues of governance.[19]

symbolic presidentialism ■ form of government in which a president (elected or unelected) has weak powers and serves, like a constitutional monarch, as a largely symbolic head of state.

It is worth noting that not all symbolic presidential systems are structured in the same way. In some cases, the president is popularly elected and thus can claim some democratic legitimacy to insert him- or herself into political debates. This was true, for example, in Ireland in 1994, when President Mary Robinson refused to grant the dissolution of parliament and call for new elections, although in the past the president had always granted such requests.

Other presidents are selected by the legislature, with the president usually some well-respected, older, non-divisive figure. In such cases, the office of the presidency is seen as a political reward for a distinguished career of public service. Whereas one would expect presidents of this type to adhere more closely to the non-political role than those that are elected, such is not always the case. For example, in Italy in the 2000s, Italian presidents challenged Prime Minister Berlusconi, including rejecting some of ministerial nominees and vetoing a measure in 2003 that critics claimed would have strengthened Berlusconi's already substantial control over Italian media.

One exceptional case, Turkey, also merits brief consideration. Although the Turkish president is appointed by the National Assembly and is expected to be strictly non-partisan, he or she enjoys real political power, including the right to veto legislation and the right to refer laws to the Constitutional Court. When the ruling Justice and Development Party (JDP), which has an Islamist orientation, had the votes to name one of its leaders, Abdullah Gül, as President in 2007, it generated a storm of controversy from more secular-oriented Turks. The office, even though it is appointed, is not primarily symbolic. For this reason, it is arguably more accurate to label the Turkish system semi-presidential (as in Table 6.3), although it is clear that the prime minister is the more important political figure.

THE CABINET

Whereas the prime minister or chancellor serves as the political chief executive in European parliamentary democracy, the political executive as a whole—often referred to simply as the government—is the cabinet, which functions like a board of directors. The cabinet—called the Council of Ministers in some countries such as Spain, Belgium, and Albania—comprises a set of ministers, each of whom is typically responsible for overseeing a government department.[20] The precise number of ministers will vary, depending upon the number of executive departments: as of 2009, Germany has sixteen members of the cabinet (including the chancellor); Greece has eighteen; Britain twenty-three. In Switzerland, seven individuals comprise the Federal Council, which also serves as a collective head of state. Ministries can be created (or eliminated) from time to time. Whereas some ministries will be specific to a particular country (e.g., the British minister for Northern Ireland, the Danish minister for Nordic cooperation), many ministries are in common across countries. These include foreign affairs, finance, education, agriculture, culture, defense, health, science, justice, and environment.

The cabinet is appointed by the prime minister or chancellor, but, as noted above, he or she may not have complete discretion in choice. This is especially true in coalition governments, where the coalition partners will negotiate over what party and what individual will assume a cabinet post. Frequently, cabinet positions are political appointments, meaning they are given out to top party officials on the basis of seniority or patronage. In other cases, particularly those ministries that are deemed less "political" (e.g., science, tourism, or health), appointments can be made from civil service officials or academics who have expertise in the area.

Cabinet officials serve two major roles. First, they oversee a particular department or ministry. This means they oversee personnel and the functioning of the department and during cabinet meetings advance agendas emanating from that department. If there is a problem in a department, responsibility rests with the cabinet minister, who may be, depending upon the severity of the problem, be expected to resign from office. Secondly, however, the cabinet official is a member of the government, a collective entity. He or she participates in policy decisions, and, regardless of his or her particular position, each cabinet official is expected to take collective responsibility for decision-making. This means he or she is expected to defend the government's decision in public. If one cannot go along with the decision, one is expected to resign, as British Foreign Secretary Jack Straw did in 2003 over decisions relating to the war in Iraq. This role of collective responsibility distinguishes ministers in parliamentary democracies from those in presidential systems such as the US, where the cabinet minister merely oversees a department and is not typically responsible for collective decision-making. Collective responsibility provides protection for individual ministers for unpopular decisions. All cabinet ministers are expected to sink or swim together.

This does not mean, however, that cabinet ministers actively participate in each and every decision made by the government. Given the thousands of decisions taken by a government in the course of a year, proposals are typically developed within a particular department or ministry that has expertise in a given area. The minister in charge of that department will present the proposal at a cabinet meeting, and other ministers will typically defer to that member, who is more familiar with the proposal. This means that there is a division of labor within cabinets, and ministers typically abide by a policy of non-intervention in the affairs of other ministries. In some countries, ministries may include junior ministers or undersecretaries. In coalition governments, they often come from parties different from those of the minister. For example, the minister of education in Sweden may be from the Center Party, but a junior minister responsible for higher education may be from the Moderate Party. Although the junior minister may answer to the minister, the fact that he or she is from a different party may provide some sort of oversight on the working of the ministry.

Within a cabinet, the prime minister is typically considered *primus inter pares*, first among equals. In point of fact, however, the prime minister—by virtue of his or her control of a political party, ability to dismiss ministers, access of information from all components of government, and political visibility—occupies the commanding position. In some countries—most notoriously Great Britain—the prime minister has become so powerful and dismissive of the cabinet for decision-making that some speak of "prime ministerial" government or the "**presidentialization**" of the system.[21] As noted above with the example of adopting the euro, however, this can be exaggerated, as prime ministers, even in the British system, do not always get their way. This topic of "presidentialization" and concentration of power is explored more fully in the **Is Europe One?** section.

presidentialization ■ term that refers to the growing power of prime ministers in parliamentary systems over both the cabinet and the parliament.

THE CIVIL SERVICE

Most people who serve in the government or work for the state are not prime ministers, cabinet officials, members of parliament, or judges on a Constitutional Court. Moreover, on a day-to-day level, such high-level officials have little contact with the wider public. Most people encounter "government" on a personal level in

IS EUROPE ONE?

Concentration of Power and Movement Toward Informal "Presidentialism"

As noted earlier in this chapter, most European democracies have parliamentary forms of government. In this respect, there is a sort of uniformity across the continent. Parliamentarism also distinguishes "European style" democracy from the US system. The irony, however, is that one can discern movement in numerous European states to something that looks more and more like presidentialism.

This is not to say that the formal, legal institutional arrangements have changed. Instead, presidentialization refers to a "process by which regimes are becoming more presidential in their actual practice without, in most cases, changing their formal structure."[22] "Presidential" in this case means that the core executive (prime minister or chancellor) acquires more power and autonomy vis-à-vis other political actors (cabinets, parties, and parliaments) and that politics as a whole becomes much more centralized and personalized, tied to a leader as opposed to collective entities or an ideology. A "presidential" type of executive would, for example, have more control over the agenda of government, appointments to the cabinet, decisions taken by his or her party, and play a central, very visible role in elections.

Several factors may drive this process. One is the internationalization of politics, meaning, particularly in Europe, that as more and more decisions are subject to inter-governmental negotiations, power is shifted to the head of government. Increasingly, parliaments are called on only to ratify decisions that have been taken elsewhere. Examples include EU treaties but also directives issued from the EU that require parliamentary action. Secondly, one can point to the increasingly complexity of governments and bureaucracies that require more executive oversight and less parliamentary involvement. As the head of government, the prime minister is at the nexus of communication flows and is uniquely empowered to oversee the entire governmental operation. This gives the office of prime minister more power and resources and makes him or her more necessary to coordinate sectoral policy-making, in which the cabinet plays more the role of a rubberstamp than a locus of decision-making. Third, one can point to the erosion of ideology, traditional cleavages, and interest associations, which make voters focus more on specific issues and leaders. Finally, the role of the media, especially television, is central, as prime ministers can gain easier access to the media and parties feel the need to put forward charismatic, media-friendly leaders. According to one study, "presidentialism would appear to be a characteristic of modern parliamentary elections that is unlikely to go away, largely because political parties have become more dependent in their communications with voters on the essentially visual and personality-based medium of television"[23] (2000, 129).

There are numerous examples of European prime ministers exhibiting both the style and substance of presidentialism. These include Margaret Thatcher (1979–1990) and Tony Blair (1997–2007) in Great Britain, Silvio Berlusconi (2001–2006 and 2008–) in Italy, and Václav Klaus (1992–1997) in the Czech Republic. In all of these cases, the movement toward presidentialization was abetted by their outsize personalities, and, in Berlusconi's case, his ownership of a media empire. In the late 2000s, the British Conservative Party, out of office for over a decade, "remade" itself thanks to the selection of a more youthful, camera-friendly David Cameron as its leader, much as the Labour Party did in the 1990s by choosing Blair as its leader. Some in Britain pointed to presidentialization (or, "Americanization") in the 2010 elections, when, for the first time ever, there were televised debates among the three major party leaders. In cases such as these, the focus is more and more on the individual, less and less on policy or ideology. Italy may be the extreme case, where politics (and media) is so dominated by Berlusconi that the main cleavage in Italian politics boils down to one's view of him. Studies have also presented evidence of presidentialization—in terms of the resources at the disposal of prime ministers and diminishing power of cabinets and parliaments—in Spain, Finland, Belgium, Denmark, and the Netherlands, although there is less evidence for this phenomenon in Germany and Sweden. The authors of the leading study on the subject conclude that "it is reasonable to talk of the 'presidentialization' of contemporary democracy."[24]

How much is one to make of this trend? While the specific traits of some leaders may facilitate presidentialization more in some countries than in others—and the more majoritarian British system might foster it even more—some of the factors that promote it, such as bureaucratic complexity, electronic media, and internationalization, will only continue to grow in prominence. Those who favor old-style politics driven by political machines and clear ideological lines and those who worry about centralization of power may decry signs of presidentialization, but such a development may be both functionally necessary for governance and create affective links between the political system and citizens.

Critical Thinking Questions

1. The notion that executive political authority—presidents and prime ministers—has gained at the expense of parliaments is not confined only to Europe. Why might this be the case?
2. Why might be done to prevent concentration of executive power?

the form of the building inspector, policeman, mail carrier, register of deeds, schoolteacher, or the like. Of course, thousands of "faceless bureaucrats"—those that process tax forms, ensure that pension checks are delivered on time, distribute government grant money, and perform countless other tasks—operate behind the scenes, albeit often in little cubicles that give them little contact with real live human beings. These government employees—often referred to as the **civil service** or the bureaucracy—are the human machinery of government, ensuring that government implements the laws and performs the services it is assigned to do. Because most members of the civil service ultimately answer to a government representative at the national or sub-national level and because their primary duty is to execute the laws, they are properly understood as part of the executive branch of government.

civil service ■ government bureaucracy that is considered part of the executive branch.

Government bureaucracies are often criticized. Indeed, the inventor of the very word bureaucracy, the Frenchman Vincent de Gowmey, endowed it in 1765 with a negative connotation, opposing it to the alleged efficiencies of a *laissez-faire* or market-based system. One scholar argues the following:

> In study after study produced from the 1960s on, state bureaucracies have been presented as endlessly demanding, self-serving, prone to lie in order to cover the blunders that they commit, arbitrary, capricious, impersonal, petty, inefficient, resistant to change, and heartless.[25]

Perhaps many of you have your own horror story from an encounter with a government official. However, it is worth asking what one would do in modern states without large government bureaucracies? Who would enforce the laws? Who would administer government programs? Whereas an anarchist or a libertarian would argue for no or very limited government, the fact is that today governments do a lot and require civil servants to administer their duties. Certainly, bureaucracies have problems—many can be inefficient, predatory, or even unnecessary—but given the size of modern states, public administration based upon a bureaucracy is necessary. Max Weber (1864–1920), for example, wrote about how bureaucracy is an inherent and productive component of modern life and how bureaucratic rule engenders its own sense of legitimacy, as it allows political life to move beyond personalized politics—where all depends upon the will of the leader—and instead be based on the rule of law. Perhaps donning some rose-colored glasses, he praised it as a mechanism that provides, among other things, "precision, speed, unambiguity, [and] knowledge . . . ."[26] Updating Weber's terms, bureaucracies produce **state capacity**, endowing them with the resources to perform their essential duties or maintaining law and order and implementing laws. In many parts of the world (e.g., sub-Saharan Africa, Pakistan, Iraq), the problem is *not* "big government" but low state capacity, as governments do not have the means to perform basic tasks, often because they lack well-trained personnel in government bureaucracies.

state capacity ■ the ability of a state to perform its essential duties; depends heavily upon the quality and resources of the civil service.

In contrast, European states have large bureaucracies. From 1950 to 1980, for example, the number of civilian employees of the government grew in Western Europe from 11 percent to 23 percent of the workforce. Communist countries in Eastern Europe had even larger public sectors, as the state owned most of the property and administered a great number of economic and social programs. Despite the rhetoric of "new public management" and various efforts to slim down government—either through, for example, contracting out services to private providers or by employing technology such as the Internet to perform some basic services—in Europe today government, by far, is the largest employer, although there is a lot of variation.[27] For example, according to the Organization for Economic Cooperation and Development (OECD), in 1997 government employment constituted 25 percent of all employment in Finland, 23 percent in Hungary, 21 percent in France, 13 percent in both Great Britain and Germany, and (remarkably given the blowup over the Greek financial crisis in 2010) only 7 percent in Greece.[28] True, not all of these individuals are the "faceless bureaucrats" that are the usual target for derision. These figures include garbage collectors, teachers, mail carriers, and transportation workers, all of which, in most people's view, perform essential tasks. Still, there is little doubt that government is, so to speak, "big business."

Why are civil services so large? Much of the answer has to do with the tasks assumed by European states, particularly after World War II when large social-welfare states became the norm. The state now administers a variety of economic and social programs, and the workers of a number of institutions—hospitals, universities, state-owned firms—can be considered employees of the government. In a broader sense, one could argue that democracy itself is the cause of an expanded bureaucracy, insofar as democratic government produces demands for redistribution of income and social welfare programs.[29] Indeed, in many European states government spending accounts for over 40 percent of the gross domestic product (GDP)—the figure comes closer to 60 percent in Sweden, the Netherlands, and Denmark—and obviously part of that money is the salaries of civil service personnel.[30]

Of course, beyond size, not all European civil services are the same. Some speak of the differing political cultures within the civil service. One can compare, for example, the British tradition of pragmatism based upon a staff of "generalists," meaning that public administration relies upon civil servants that typically possess only general administrative and managerial skills, with most European states that have a more technocratic civil service that relies upon specially trained, more "elite" bureaucrats. This is the case in France, where the administrative corps is recruited, trained, and socialized in higher education system that lies outside of the regular university sector. The two main training grounds both for French bureaucrats and politicians are the École Polytechnique and the École Nationale d'Administration. Both are highly competitive, as the prospect of a well-paying job in the French civil service is an extremely attractive proposition to many young French men and (increasingly so) women. Whereas defenders of this system stress the skills of their graduates, others complain that the upper echelon of the French civil service is too elitist and is composed of "drones" that lack sufficient individualism.

In addition, there are differences in the degree of **politicization** of the bureaucracy. The question here is whether bureaucratic officials—and here we are discussing those serving in the top ranks of the bureaucracy—should be strictly professionals independent of any particular political party or whether they should reflect the partisan composition of the government. Those favoring professionalism—which is well reflected in practices in Great Britain and Sweden—would stress the need for continuity and expertise in the bureaucracy and that the bureaucracy should only faithfully administer the laws, not have a partisan position. In contrast, one could argue that the bureaucracy will work better with elected officials if those elected are allowed to put some of "their people" in top positions. France, Austria, and Belgium, among other countries, have a more politicized civil service with a higher turnover of top officials when governments change. Of course, political appointments can be abused, with plum government jobs going to partisan "hacks" who may have little knowledge about the tasks they are expected to fulfill. In communist Eastern Europe, the entire bureaucratic apparatus was politicized under the ***nomenklatura*** system, which meant that virtually all of the officials appointed to the civil services in these countries were vetted and approved by the Communist authorities, with loyalty to the Communist Party (if not actual membership in the Party) usually a necessary qualification. Depoliticizing the civil service in post-communist states in the 1990s was an important task of democratization, albeit one that rarely captured headlines.[31]

politicization ■ term that refers to whether the government civil service is politically neutral or whether it reflects the partisan composition of the government.

nomenklatura ■ system of appointments in communist countries in which appointments were strictly controlled by the Communist Party.

Finally, there are significant differences among civil services in terms of their performance. Consider for instance corruption—are civil servants fundamentally honest or not? While one could argue that bureaucracies are inherently corrupt, as they are interested in advancing their own political and budgetary agendas, caring little about the broader public interest,[32] there is nonetheless a vast divergence in Europe in terms of corruption. Data for several countries from Transparency International, a non-governmental organization that monitors corruption, are reported in Figure 6.2. Here one sees that countries in Northern Europe, which have both a high level of economic development and a long tradition of democracy, fare quite well, among the very best in the world. In contrast, one sees more corruption in the poorer countries of post-communist Europe such as Bosnia and Romania—but also low scores for Greece and Italy, which have long histories battling against—often unsuccessfully—corruption. If one considers additional data—for

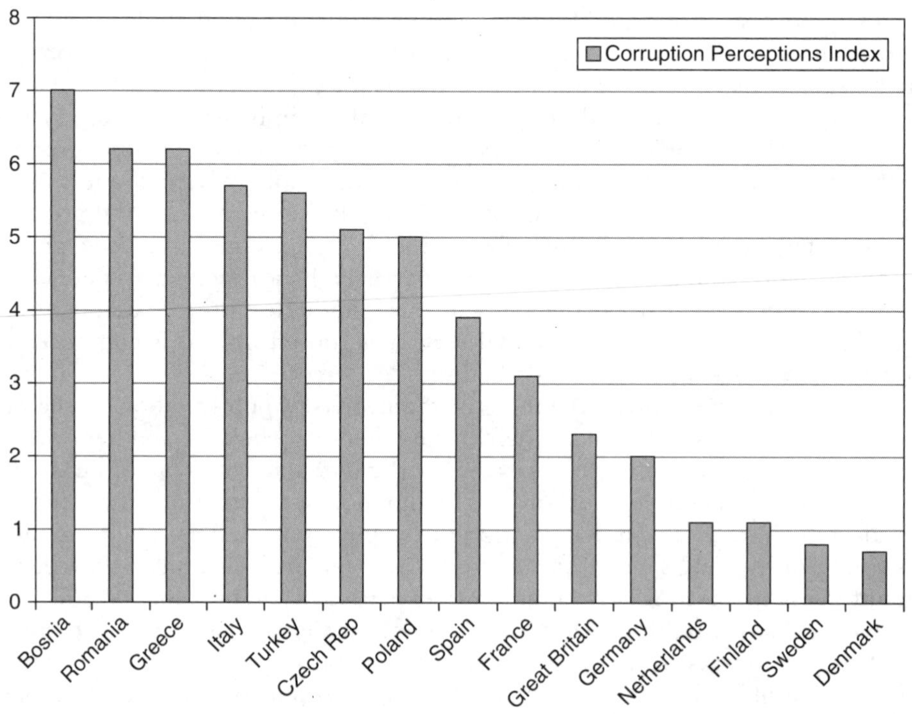

FIGURE 6.2

Corruption Perceptions Index, 2009.

Source: Transparency International (TI), at http://www.transparency.org. Data come from questionnaires completed by experts that interact with each country. Score is inverted score of the original 1–10 index of TI, inverted to make the results more intuitively understandable.

example that 66 percent of Albanians, 20 percent of Romanians, and 17 percent of Greeks personally reported in 2006 of having to bribe a public official in the past year[33]—one can understand that creating an honest—let alone efficient—bureaucracy remains a serious problem in many countries in Europe. While this *per se* does not make these countries undemocratic, it does raise a question about the quality of the democracy.

Although executive authority in Europe is typically beholden to parliaments, there is little doubt that prime ministers, chancellors, and presidents command great authority. More so than parliaments, they are the face of political authority to their own publics and to the outside world. Their actions shape the politics of their own countries and, at times, European politics as a whole. While some leaders are advocates of a stronger and more united Europe, others, such as Czech President Václav Klaus mentioned at the outset of the chapter, are skeptics or even opponents of the EU and efforts to integrate the continent. Klaus ultimately tabled his objections and allowed the Lisbon Treaty to take effect. Given the ongoing debates about the European project and the proper role of the EU, it is unlikely that he will be the last leader to raise a voice against the idea of "one Europe."

APPLICATION QUESTIONS

1. Why have several European states retained a constitutional monarchy? What purpose does a monarch serve? Why are they often popular with their subjects?
2. Coalitions can be hard to manage. What might be some advantages of a coalition government?
3. Data seem to suggest that parliamentary systems perform better than presidential ones. From this record, would you suggest that a country with a presidential system (e.g., the US) adopt a parliamentary system? Can you think of how a presidential system might create problems for the performance of democracy in the US?
4. Why do you think some countries are more corrupt than others? What practical steps can be undertaken to combat corruption?
5. Is "presidentialization" a worrying trend? How might this affect the quality of democracy (e.g., accountability, efficiency) in Europe?

KEY TERMS

cabinet 154
civil service 173
cohabitation 168
constitutional monarchies 155
head of government 154
head of state 154
minority govermment 159
nomenklatura 175
parliamentary system 156
politicization 175
presidentialization 171
presidential system 163
semi-presidentialism 167
state capacity 174
symbolic presidentialism 169
vote of no confidence 156

ADDITIONAL READING

Elgie. Robert, ed. 1999. *Semi-Presidentialism in Europe*. Oxford: Oxford University Press.

The seminal source on the phenomenon of semi-presidentialism, this book examines both what it means in terms of institutional behavior and how it functions in a number of settings.

Lijphart, Arend, ed. 1992. *Presidential versus Parliamentary Government*. Oxford: Oxford University Press.

A collection of essays examining the pros and cons of each form of government, both in theoretical terms and in particular case studies.

Müller, Wolfgang, and Strøm, Kaare, eds. *Coalition Governments in Western Europe*. 2003. Oxford: Oxford University Press.

This book, which examines both theories of coalition formation and how governments have behaved in Western Europe, might be especially helpful for American students, who are less familiar with the premises and practices of coalition governments.

Poguntke, Thomas, and Webb, Paul, eds. 2005. *The Presidentialization of Politics: A Comparative Study of Modern Democracies*. Oxford: Oxford University Press.

An exploration of the development of presidential style and substance in European democracies, based upon examination of this trend in a number of countries, including Great Britain, Italy, Spain, Portugal, Sweden, and Finland.

Shugart, Matthew S., and Carey, John. 1992. *Presidents and Assemblies: Constitutional Design and Electoral Dynamics*. Cambridge: Cambridge University Press, 1992.

Written for a scholarly audience, this book examines the interplay between institutional design and voting, including voter turnout, coalitions, and development of political parties.

END NOTES

1. Interview in *Lidove Noviny* (Prague), October 17, 2009.
2. Small states such as Monaco, Andorra, Liechtenstein, and the Vatican are also properly considered monarchies, but we do not discuss them in the text.
3. "Dr. Rosler's Difficult Prescription," *The Economist*, May 1, 2010.

4. The president of the US is actually indirectly elected through the Electoral College, a feature that is extremely difficult to explain to many Europeans.
5. A good review of arguments can be found in Arend Lijphart, "Introduction," in Lijphart, ed., *Parliamentary vs. Presidential Government* (Oxford: Oxford University Press, 1992).
6. These arguments apply best to a "pure presidential" system such as that in the US, but they can also apply to a semi-presidential system with a strong president, such as France.
7. This argument blends parliamentarism and multi-party systems together. The two do not have to go hand in hand (e.g., Great Britain has in essence a two-party system), but in Europe one frequently encounters multi-party parliamentary democracies.
8. See Alfred Stepan and Cindy Skach, "Constitutional Frameworks and Democratic Consolidation: Parliamentarism versus Presidentialism," *World Politics* 46:1, October 1993, 1–22, and Juan Linz and Arturo Valenzuela, eds., *The Failure of Presidential Democracy* (Baltimore: Johns Hopkins University Press, 1994).
9. Stepan and Skach, "Constitutional Frameworks."
10. M. Steven Fish, *Democracy Derailed in Russia* (Cambridge: Cambridge University Press, 2006), pp. 194–209.
11. Alfred Stepan with Ezra Suleiman, "The French Fifth Republic: A Model for Import? Reflections on Poland and Brazil," in H.E. Chehabi and Alfred Stepan, eds. *Politics, Society, and Democracy* (Boulder: Westview Press, 1995).
12. Some offer different terms to describe the French system. Saalfield, for example, dubs it a "premier-presidential" system, as he emphasizes the fact that *de jure* the French President (unlike the Russian one) cannot fire the Prime Minister (called premier in French) and that governance on most issues—save foreign policy—looks like a parliamentary system. See Thomas Saalfield, "Government and Politics," in Richard Sakwa and Anne Stevens, eds., *Contemporary Europe*, 2nd edition (New York: Palgrave Macmillan, 2006), pp. 90–91.
13. Maurice Duverger, "A New Political System Model: Semi-Presidential Government," *European Journal of Political Research* 8:1, June 1980, 165–187. Note that the definition does not say that the parliament names the prime minister, as *de jure* (and in some cases *de facto*) this is often done by the president.
14. Note that this does not reflect the standard view that presidential systems have a separation of powers between the executive and legislative branches of government. This right applies to the National Assembly, not the Senate, which is a much weaker legislative body.
15. The Constitution does not explicitly give the president this power, but in 1962 de Gaulle asked his first prime minister, Michel Debré, to resign, and Debré did so. Whether a president under cohabitation could succeed in dismissing the prime minister has yet to be tested.
16. Technically the president could nominate anyone he or she wants, but if the assembly censures the selection, it would produce a political crisis, for which the president would likely be blamed. No French president has pressed his authority in such a fashion.
17. Elgie defines semi-presidentialism in such a way that any state with a popularly elected president (e.g., Austria, Ireland, Iceland) would qualify as semi-presidential, even if presidential powers are minimal. See Robert Elgie, ed. *Semi-Presidentialism in Europe* (Oxford: Oxford University Press, 1999). I tend to follow Duverger, with the exception of the Czech Republic and Turkey, and consider how presidents function in the political system.
18. For example, in 2006, Klaus vetoed a measure to legalize same-sex partnerships; the veto was, however, overridden by the Czech Parliament.
19. Some constitutions do give the president the power of commander-in-chief of the military and some authority in foreign affairs, but, in most cases, the norm has been for the president to allow the prime minister to exercise real authority, even in these fields.
20. At times, some members of the cabinet may be a "minister without portfolio," meaning that he or she does not oversee a particular department. Deputy prime ministers with various duties may also be included in the cabinet.
21. Thomas Poguntke and Paul Webb, eds. *The Presidentialization of Politics: A Comparative Study of Modern Democracies* (Oxford: Oxford University Press, 2005).
22. Poguntke and Webb, *The Presidentialization of Politics*, p. 1. This section borrows heavily from this volume.
23. Anthony Mughan, *Media and the Presidentialization of Parliamentary Elections* (New York: Palgrave, 2000), p. 129.

24. Poguntke and Webb, *The Presidentialization of Politics*, p. 347.
25. Martin van Creveld, *The Rise and Decline of the State* (Cambridge: Cambridge University Press, 1999), p. 408.
26. Max Weber, from "Wirtschaft und Gesellschaft," reprinted in Richard Stillman, ed. *Public Administration: Concepts and Cases*, 8th edition (New York: Houghton Mifflin, 2006), p. 59.
27. Van Creveld, *The Rise and Decline of the State*, p.361.
28. OECD, at http://www.oecd.org/dataoecd/37/43/1849079.xls, accessed March 5, 2006. Regular OECD *Labour Force Statistics* publications do not include such data.
29. Margit Tavits, "Size of Government in Majoritarian and Consensus Democracies," *Comparative Political Studies* 37:3, April 2004, 340–359.
30. Data on government spending as percentage of GNP can be found at http://www.oecd.org.
31. Jan-Hinrik Meyer-Sahling, "Civil Service Reform in Post-Communist Europe: The Bumpy Road to Depoliticisation," *West European Politics* 27:1, January 2004, 69–101.
32. A classic view on this question can be found in Aaron Wildavsky, *The Politics of the Budgetary Process* (Boston: Little Brown 1964).
33. 2006 Global Corruption Barometer from Transparency International, available at http://www.transparency.org

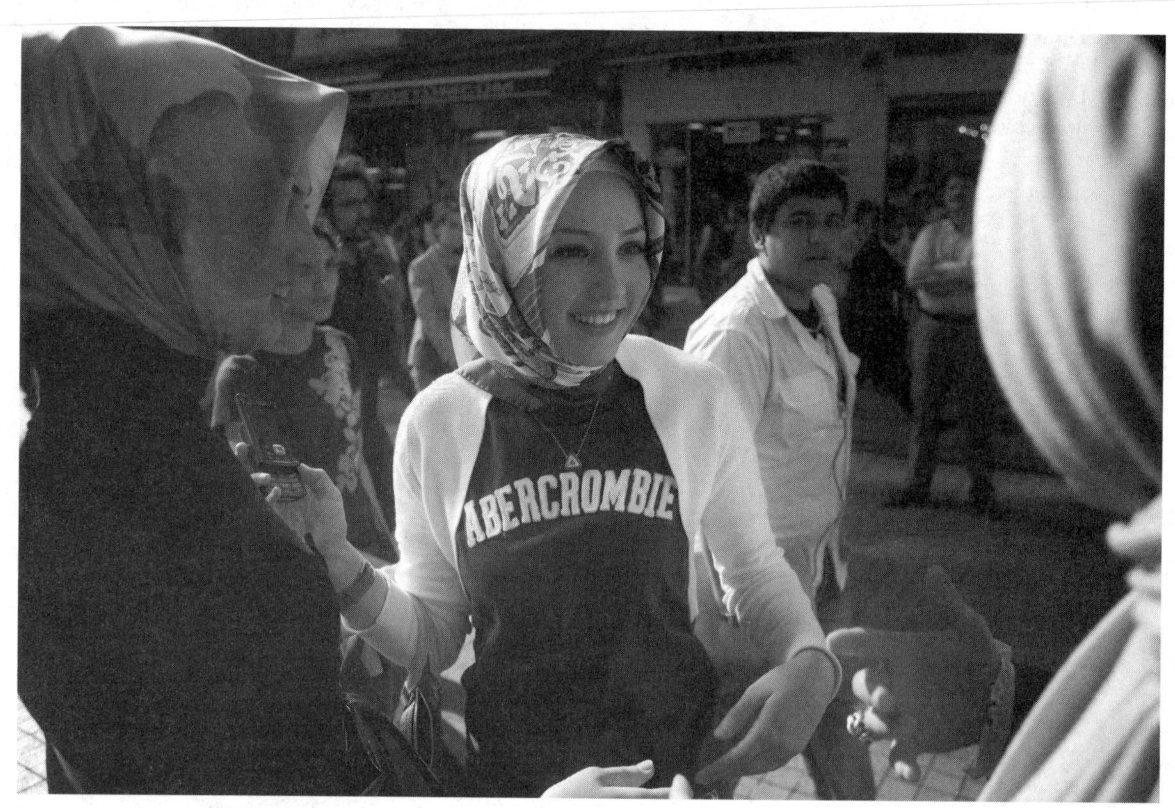

Are they a threat to the Turkish constitution?

CHAPTER

7

Legal Structures and Judicial Systems

On July 30, 2008, the Turkish Constitutional Court issued a ruling that may have profound implications for the future of Europe. The impetus for the court case was a measure, backed by the ruling Islamic-oriented Justice and Development Party (JDP), to allow women to wear Islamic head coverings in Turkish universities, which, its opponents claimed, ran counter to the principles of secularism in the Turkish constitution. In June, the court had found the law itself unconstitutional, but the ruling in July was on the constitutionality of the JDP itself. It found that the JDP had violated the Turkish constitution by being a focal institution for anti-secular activities. In past cases against other Islamic-oriented parties, the court had ordered the parties to disband and barred their leaders from participating in political life for a period of several years. In this instance, however, the sentence was to cut state funding for JDP by half, as the court lacked the required seven out of eleven votes to disband the JDP.

This ruling sparked controversy in Turkey and had importance for Europe as a whole. Within Turkey, this court case represented a major battle between the secular elite in the state bureaucracy and the military, which traditionally have exercised political power, and a popular governing party that claimed an Islamic heritage and had won reelection to office in 2007. It also, however, had repercussions for Europe, as Turkey has been trying to enter the EU, and a ruling that would have banned Turkey's largest party would have raised troubling questions about Turkey's commitment to liberal democracy and seriously jeopardized its longstanding quest for EU membership. Ironically, it was EU pressure that helped change Turkey's law on political parties in 2003. Under the new law, a supermajority of judges must vote to disband a party; this provision saved the JDP from the fate of its predecessors. This 2008 ruling not only saved the JDP but also Turkey's EU bid. Should Turkey one day join the EU—a proposition that is still very much in doubt—this court ruling will be one that profound implications for the fate of Europe.

Not all court decisions are so dramatic, of course, and constitutional questions in individual countries do not always have European import. Nonetheless, one should acknowledge that courts and constitutions can play important roles in structuring political institutions and defining what is and what is not permissible. This chapter takes up the

judiciary ■ institutions of government that are designed to apply and interpret the law and adjudicate legal disputes.

institutions of the **judiciary**, which are designed to apply and interpret the law and to adjudicate in cases where one party is alleged to have broken the law. Often, the judiciary is assumed to be the least political of government institutions in that most courts adjudicate disputes between private parties (e.g., divorce, lawsuits) or try those accused of criminal offenses. Judges in Europe—unlike in many areas of the US—do not run for office, and thus are assumed to be impartial and immune from popular or political pressure. We know, of course, that courts can at times play a political role in numerous ways, such as by ruling on the constitutionality of certain questions, by adjudicating disputes in which the government is a party, or by expanding or constricting individual rights. In Europe, courts play an important role insofar as they are expected to uphold both national and EU-level laws and directives. Because of the growing importance of European-level law, an issue explored in the **Is Europe One?** section of this chapter, the judiciary is the political institution that arguably has witnessed the most Europeanization.

This chapter takes up judicial systems in Europe as well as broader issues relating to the legal structure of power, concerns that did not fit neatly into our previous discussions of parliaments and executives. These questions include the scope of individual rights and the division of powers among national, regional, and local governments.

CONSTITUTIONS

constitution ■ set of rules for a particular country that define how political power is distributed, how political decisions are to be made, and the nature and extent of citizens' rights.

The good starting place to begin examining the overall legal structure of European polities is with **constitutions**, sets of rules that define how power is distributed among political bodies and actors; how political decisions are to be made, applied, and interpreted; and the nature and extent of citizens' rights. In short, constitutions define the rules of the political game. They are not the only source of law, but they serve as a foundation for all laws and rules of governance, an idea nicely captured by the Turkish term for constitution, *Anayasa*, meaning "mother law."

The adoption of a constitution is an exceptional event in a country. No countries in Europe can boast of a written constitution as old as the US's Constitution (1787). The oldest European written constitution that is still functioning, that of the Netherlands, was adopted in 1815, and most states' current constitutions were adopted in the twentieth century. However, the old joke that one had to look for the French Constitution in the periodical section of the library is a bit of an exaggeration. Constitutions are designed to last, although from time to time a state may decide to adopt a new constitution. Typically, there are three main occasions that necessitate adoption of a constitution. First, as one would expect, when a country gains independence, it adopts its own constitution. Such was the case, for example, with Finland in 1919 and Ireland in 1922. Secondly, when there is a major change in political regime, either through revolution, defeat in war, or democratization, a new constitution is usually necessary to define the rules of the new system of government. Thus, Germany and Italy adopted constitutions after World War II, Spain did so in 1978 as it began a transition to democratic government, and most countries in Eastern Europe adopted new constitutions after the collapse of communism. Third, countries may adopt new constitutions as a solution to a political crisis or to facilitate major political adjustments. For example,

France adopted a constitution in 1958 to resolve a crisis that put the country on the brink of civil war, and Denmark adopted a new constitution in 1973, the same year it joined the European Community. In some cases, constitutions are adopted by supermajority (more than 50 percent) votes in the legislature or through some sort of constitutional convention, although in other cases (e.g., Switzerland in 1874, France in 1958, Spain in 1978, and Poland in 1997) constitutions are approved by popular **referendum**, meaning that the people vote directly on the constitution.

referendum ■ procedure by which political questions are put directly to voters; an example of direct democracy.

Constitutions vary widely from country to country, and each state can claim a unique set of constitutional traditions. However, one can identify a number of common tasks served by virtually all constitutions. Typically, they set forth who is to carry out the major functions of politics; how power is divided among different branches of government; who controls the military; how citizenship is defined and acquired; how people occupying positions of authority are to be chosen; areas in which the state is given authority; what rights citizens retain; the role of religion; and how the constitution can be changed. Many constitutions also contain provisions on symbolic aspects of the state, such as the flag, the national anthem, and the national motto.

They can vary in some basic and obvious ways. One is length. Some constitutions are short, focusing only on basic principles of governance. The US Constitution is famously short, as constitutions go, at 4,620 words. In Europe, France's stands out as relatively short (7,686 words).[1] Others are much longer, detailing many specific tasks of government. As a general rule, the more recent constitutions tend to be longer, delving into policy areas that are largely ignored in older constitutions when the state's role in society was more limited. For example, both the Spanish Constitution (17,976 words) and the Polish Constitution (20,750 words) enumerate a number of socio-economic rights that one would not, for example, find in the US Constitution: rights to education, health care, housing, social security, workplace safety, and paid vacations. In addition, both states commit themselves to protect the natural environment, to strive for full employment, and to foster a more equitable distribution of income. These documents, however, are shorter still than Germany's Basic Law (the *de facto* constitution), which was adopted by West Germany in 1949, envisioned as a temporary document (pending long hoped-for reunification) and weighs in at 21,941 words.

Which is better? While some might like a document that is more detailed and specific, it can be a problem if the government cannot fulfill all of its constitutional obligations. No constitution can foresee every political exigency, and shorter and vaguer constitutions have the advantage of flexibility, although their adaptability may depend upon the ability of courts to interpret centuries-old provisions for use in the contemporary world. Indeed, one could say that court decisions, legislation, and traditional understandings make up, albeit in a less formal manner, the constitution in many states. For example, the Spanish Constitution recognizes the right of autonomy of nationalities and regions within a common, unitary "fatherland." What this means in practice for the various regions of Spain (e.g., Catalonia, Valencia, Basque areas) has been the subject of negotiations with the central government and has evolved over time, making up, so to speak, an aspect of the Spanish constitution (little *c*).

judicial review ■ mechanism through which courts can declare legislation or actions of other governmental actors as unconstitutional.

Constitutions also vary in strength. One dimension of strength is whether a political institution—typically a court—can defend the constitution against the actions of another institution. In the US, this is captured in the idea of **judicial review**, the idea that courts can declare legislation or actions of the executive branch unconstitutional. This means that nothing can contravene the Constitution, at least as it is interpreted by the courts. As we shall see later in this chapter, several European states, among them France, Germany, Poland, and Italy, have judicial systems with elements of judicial review. However, in other cases, such as Sweden, the Netherlands, and Great Britain, judicial review is much weaker or non-existent, meaning that legislatures can pass measures without any explicit check on whether they pass constitutional muster.

Another way of defining strength is how easy it is to change the constitution. Obviously, constitutions must be subject to change. If they were not, citizens would be stuck with the arrangements adopted by their forebears, a predicament hardly compatible with popular sovereignty and democratic governance. Constitutional provisions that can be easily changed or annulled, however, are not particularly powerful. In most states, supermajorities of the legislature and/or a popular vote are necessary to change the constitution. These measures make it difficult to change the constitution. However, in some states, a simple majority vote in the legislature is sufficient to alter the constitution. Such is the case in Sweden, where the constitution can be amended by a majority vote in the Swedish parliament, although the parliament must vote twice: once before and once after a general election. Not coincidentally, the Swedish "constitution" is called "The Instrument of Government," a moniker that signifies a lesser status than that of a constitution.

A third way in which constitutions differ is how they are assembled. In most countries, the constitution is a single document. The exception is Great Britain, which is commonly described as having an "unwritten constitution." This is not really accurate, as the British Constitution is composed of numerous written documents, including such famous treaties as the Magna Carta of 1215 and landmark acts of Parliament such as the 1707 Act of Union, which brought Scotland into the United Kingdom, and the Reform Acts of 1832 and 1867 that expanded suffrage. Other elements of the British Constitution include treaties (e.g., EU treaties to which Britain has acceded), common law, tradition and convention, and "works of authority" developed by scholars of the constitution. In general, however, the principle of "parliamentary supremacy" reigns in Britain, meaning that anything passed by the British parliament carries constitutional weight. Thus, one could say that since the mid-1990s Britain has experienced a constitutional revolution, considering the major reforms such as devolution of greater political authority from the central government to the non-English regions of Scotland, Wales, and Northern Ireland, changes in the House of Lords, and adoption of the European Convention on Human Rights.[2] Some, including those in Britain lobbying for a written constitution, worry that parliamentary supremacy could be dangerous, as there is nothing to prevent, for example, the parliament from ending democracy by cancelling future elections. In practice, however, elections are strong enough of a constitutional feature that no British Parliament could, in practice, actually do such a thing.

TABLE 7.1

Constitutional Features in Selected European States

Country	Const. Monarchy/ Republic	Parliamentary/ Presidential	Unicameral/ Bicameral	Federal/ Unitary	Judicial Review?
Germany	Republic	Parliamentary	Bicameral	Federal	Yes
France	Republic	Semi-Presidential	Bicameral	Unitary	Yes
Great Britain	Const. Monarchy	Parliamentary	Bicameral	Unitary*	No
Spain	Const. Monarchy	Parliamentary	Bicameral	Unitary*	Yes
Austria	Republic	Parliamentary	Bicameral	Federal	Yes
Netherlands	Const. Monarchy	Parliamentary	Bicameral	Unitary	No
Sweden	Const. Monarchy	Parliamentary	Unicameral	Unitary	No
Poland	Republic	Semi-Presidential	Bicameral	Unitary	Yes
Hungary	Republic	Parliamentary	Unicameral	Unitary	Yes
Serbia	Republic	Parliamentary	Unicameral	Unitary	Yes
Romania	Republic	Semi-Presidential	Bicameral	Unitary	Yes
Turkey	Republic	Semi-Presidential	Unicameral	Unitary	Yes

*Devolution of authority in Great Britain and Spain has been significant, but most observers would still classify them as unitary.

Finally, constitutions differ in how they define the type of government in a given state. Again, within Europe we are always talking about democratic governments, but among democracies there are various subtypes Table 7.1 highlights some features of the constitutional structures in several European states. Some of these aspects have been covered in earlier chapters, and some will be discussed more in depth below.

SUB-NATIONAL GOVERNANCE

A basic question within any political system is what institution is empowered to act on certain issues. In most countries, different bodies have different political competencies; these can be divided among type of institution (e.g., parliaments versus executives) but also by the level of government. Thus far, we have discussed political institutions at the national level, those that are located in the capital city and make decisions affecting the entire country. However, these are not the only governments in Europe. Voters also get to elect mayors and city councils, and in most countries there are regional or provincial level governments as well. These sub-national governments have a more restricted mandate, typically tending to such issues as road maintenance and transportation, education, sanitation, law and order, public recreation, and housing, and their reach is obviously more geographically constrained. Minutiae of their powers and performance need not concern us here. However, it is worth making distinctions based upon the degree upon which political power is centralized within a given country.

Some countries in Europe are **federal states,** meaning that political powers are formally divided between the national government and regional (sub-national) governments. The precise division of powers is constitutionally defined and varies

federal states ■ countries in which political power is legally and formally divided between the national government and regional (sub-national) government.

among federal states, but the key point is that "some matters are exclusively within the competence of certain local units . . . and are constitutionally *beyond* the scope of the authority of the national government."[3] Of course, sub-national governments are not free to countermand any aspect of national law as they see fit, but federalism does mean that in areas under their purview (e.g., culture, education, housing), the national government is expected not to interfere and sub-national governments have legal recourse to defend their "turf" against encroachments from the national government.

There are several rationales for federalism. One is to give ethnic or linguistic minorities, who are often concentrated in a particular region, group autonomy and powers of self-government on issues (e.g., education, culture) that are important to their self-identity.[4] Within Europe, this type of federalism is exemplified by Switzerland, a very decentralized state made up of German, French, and Italian speakers and twenty-six *cantons* (regions) with long traditions of autonomy, and Belgium, which has a complicated territorial/linguistic federalist system to ameliorate disputes between the Walloons (French speakers) and Flemish (Dutch speakers). After horrific fighting in the early 1990s, Bosnia and Herzegovina also became a federal state, with power divided between the *Republika Srbska* (dominated by ethnic Serbs) and the Confederation of Croats and Bosniacs (Muslims).

Federalism may also be defended as a means to check potential abuse of power by national governments and populist majorities.[5] This, together with a nod to a history of local or regional self-rule, provided the rationale for the creation of a federal state in (West) Germany and Austria after World War II, as it was felt that having a weaker national government would make it less likely for a figure like Hitler to emerge.

subsidiarity ■ principle that political decisions should be taken at the closest level possible to the individual citizen.

Third, one could make an argument for federalism by invoking the principle of **subsidiarity**, meaning that political decisions should be taken, for reasons of democracy and for efficiency, at the closest possible level to the individual citizen. Some issues, such as national defense and management of the national currency, must be left to the national government. Uniformity across the nation, however, is not required in all policy areas. Some issues, such as education, might be better handled at the sub-national level, which can take into account the preferences of citizens in a particular region and provide more accountability. Local experimentation, it could also be argued, might serve as a laboratory to test out new ideas or policies that, if successful, could later be adopted across the entire country.

Federalism can co-exist with a number of different forms of government and electoral systems, but it typically requires two institutional arrangements. One, described in Chapter 5, is bicameralism, as the second chamber of the legislature provides a means for regional governments to be represented at the national level and thus gives, to some degree, regions a say over national policy.[6] Secondly, federal states should have some form of judicial review, discussed more in the next section of this chapter. This is necessary to prevent the national parliament or executive authorities from adopting any measure that it sees fit. Without some sort of credible guarantee that the national government could simply abrogate federalist arrangements, it would be difficult to defend the rights of sub-national governments and make federalism work.[7] In these respects, the German federal system is fairly typical. Each of Germany's seventeen different regions (*Länder*) has responsibility in fields such as education and transportation and is responsible for implementing much of the national legislation adopted by the federal government. *Länder* have a direct say in policy-making, as they are represented in the upper house of the German parliament (the *Bundesrat*), which must give its approval to all legislation affecting the *Länder*, effectively two-thirds of all laws. Lastly, as discussed more below, Germany has a very powerful Constitutional Court, and the *Länder* can appeal to it to rule on the constitutionality of legislation.

unitary states ■ countries in which the national government has exclusive political powers, although it may delegate some of its powers to regional or local governments.

Most states in Europe are non-federal or **unitary states,** meaning that only the central government has exclusive political powers. In many cases, it delegates its authority to sub-national governments; the key point is that the central government is not compelled to share any of its powers with other structures, and it can take away its delegated powers at any time. Perhaps the fact that most European states are unitary can be explained by the fact most federal states in the world (e.g., the US, Canada, Russia, Australia, India, Mexico, Brazil, Nigeria, Malaysia) tend to be very large and/or be ethnically diverse, whereas most European states are small and many are rather ethnically homogeneous. However, the lack of federalism in some states can also be attributed to political choices made by political elites. For example, after the collapse of communism in Eastern Europe, one might have thought, on democratic grounds, that federalism would be appealing, among other reasons, as means to bring government closer to the people and prevent the emergence of another centralized dictatorship. Moreover, as seen in Figure 7.1, many Eastern European states have sizeable ethnic minorities. Moreover, these minorities, unlike the immigrant minorities in countries such as France and the Netherlands, are indigenous. They include ethnic Albanians in Macedonia, ethnic Hungarians in Slovakia and Romania, ethnic Turks in Bulgaria, and ethnic Russians in the Baltic states. The presence of such groups might have augured well for federalist arrangements.

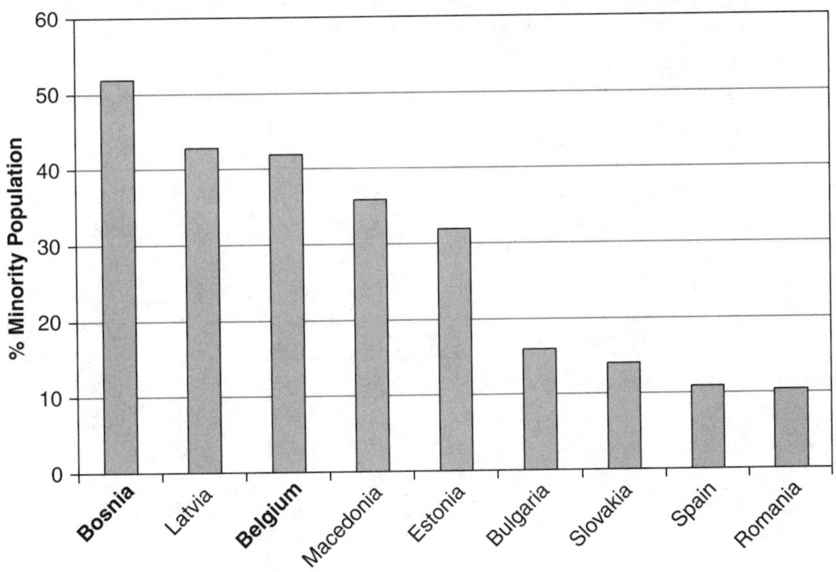

FIGURE 7.1
Minorities in Select European Countries (Federal states are in bold)
Source: Christoph Pan and Beate Sibylle Pfeil, *National Minorities in Europe* (West Lafayette IN: Purdue University Press, 2004).

IN FOCUS

Devolution and Separatist Impulses in Europe

The idea of a single Europe is often equated with movement to a federal Europe that is bringing European states closely together. However, federalism can evolve not only as a means to bind political units closer together. It also can emerge to devolve political authority to lower-level political structures (e.g., regions, provinces). Indeed, while Europe as a whole is drawing closer together, devolution is occurring in a number of European states. Some formerly unitary states are looking more and more federal, stoking the fears (or hopes) that they make break apart into several states. In this respect, some national governments are being squeezed in both directions, with pressures to surrender sovereignty both to European institutions and to sub-national governments. These issues are acute in Italy, Great Britain, and Spain.

Italy was unified as a single state only in 1861, and vast economic and cultural differences remain between a more prosperous north and a poorer south.[8] The *Lega Nord* (Northern League), a right-wing political party, has emerged to champion the cause of *Padania*, part of northern Italy that claims to be a separate nation united by its own history and culture. Many would argue that *Padania* is pure invention, but there is no denying that since the 1990s the *Lega Nord* has been an important force in Italian politics, gaining more seats than any other party in 1994 elections and withdrawing its support in the next year from the government thereby ending the tenure (at least until his return to power in 2001) of Prime Minister Silvio Berlusconi. In 2002, the government adopted reforms to devolve authority over health, education, and police to the regions, and some actors in Italy's regions want to take matters further by making Italy a federal state.

The government of Prime Minister Tony Blair pursued devolution in Great Britain as part of an ambitious constitutional reform agenda.[9] Scotland now has its own parliament, enjoying control over police, culture, education, and housing, and it also has the right to levy its own taxes. Wales has an assembly, albeit one without the ability to tax. London and other localities now elect their own mayors. Northern Ireland, a land troubled since the 1970s by violence between its Catholic and Protestant communities, also has its own assembly, although power-sharing arrangements envisioned by the 1998 Good Friday Accord have not been easy to implement, with Northern Irish leaders finally agreeing on a power-sharing government in 2007. Some have even broached the idea of regional assemblies within England—where most of the population lives—but this was rejected by voters in 2004. The endpoint of devolution in Great Britain is unclear, particularly with regard to Scotland. Many in England resent the fact that Scots, with their own parliament, are not covered by all national legislation but still have representation in the House of Commons. The victory of the pro-independence Scottish Nationalist Party in regional elections in 2007 makes the idea of a Scottish vote for independence more possible than ever before.

All seventeen of Spain's regions are officially "autonomous communities," although the precise set of rights enjoyed by each region is subject to negotiations with the central government and varies from region to region. The desire for independence from Madrid is strongest among the Basques, an ancient people who speak a language unrelated to Spanish, and Catalans, who have their own language (related to Spanish and French), culture, and cosmopolitan "capital," Barcelona. As a consequence, these regions enjoy a wide range of rights, including their own police forces, civil law, official status for their languages, and, for the Basque Country and neighboring Navarre, the right to raise revenue. Moreover, general devolution in Spain has allowed all the regions broad powers over health and education, and 60 percent of public spending in Spain is now at the sub-national level.[10] Some already list Spain as a "semi-federal" state or one with "asymmetric federalism,"[11] although some in Spain would like to take matters further. One survey suggested eleven of the seventeen regions desire more autonomy.[12] For example, Catalonia, which is Spain's richest region, wants to win recognition for Catalan as an official language of the EU and in 2006 passed a declaration declaring Catalonia a "nation," a move the Spanish Constitutional Court declared had no legal value as the Constitution recognizes the "unity of the Spanish nation." Many in Spain are upset at what they perceive as the arrogance of the Catalans, prompting in other regions of Spain a well-publicized boycott of *cava*, a sparkling wine produced in Catalonia. Many Basques support separatism, and the Spanish government has battled against the group ETA (Basque Homeland and Liberty), generally considered a terrorist organization, whose attacks since the 1960s have claimed more than eight hundred lives, including those of prominent Spanish politicians.[13] Basque political parties, while distancing themselves from violence, nonetheless seek as much power as they can obtain from Madrid, with the Basque government led by the Basque Nationalist Party in 2003 calling for the Basque Country to be a "freely associated state" with Spain and to have its own representation in the EU. The government has tried to reach accommodation with the Basques, including negotiating with ETA, but with ETA resuming its campaign of violence in 2007 with a bombing at the Madrid airport, the Spanish government is less inclined to meet the demands of Basque nationalists.

Critical Thinking Questions

1. How should countries beset by regional or ethnic divisions try to preserve their unity? What are the advantages/disadvantages of policies such as federalism and devolution?
2. Some have suggested that the growth of the EU has encouraged regionalism within European countries (think of Scotland or Catalonia). Why might there be such a connection?

However, the example of Czechoslovakia and Yugoslavia—authoritarian federal states that broke up, in part, due to ethnic-based separatism—as well as the desire to create a strong national government to serve the interests of the titular (dominant) nationality, made federalism less attractive to most states.

However, in several non-federal states things have been moving in a "federal direction," although as of yet they are not, by most accounts, truly federal. Most European countries guarantee language and cultural rights for their ethnic minorities, although, as in Slovakia, and Macedonia, they may lack a territorially defined federal unit. Sometimes, as with the case of France's island of Corsica, Sicily and Sardinia in Italy, or the Åland islands of Finland (dominated by Swedish speakers), a territorial unit is granted a measure of autonomy or a special status. This is closer to federalism, but in France, Italy, and Finland other regions do not enjoy autonomy and political authority ultimately is in the hands of the national government. Matters have gone further in Great Britain, where since the 1990s the central government pursued a policy of **devolution,** granting more authority to regional governments in Scotland, Wales, and Northern Ireland.

devolution ■ process by which more authority is granted to regional or sub-national governments, although the powers of these governments are not constitutionally protected as they are in federal state.

In some states, such as Spain, regions are pushing for even greater power, including independence from the central government. An irony of sorts is that as Europe is coming closer together through economic, political, and social integration, separatist impulses are present in many countries. This issue is taken up in the **In Focus** section.

LEGAL TRADITIONS

Because laws vary widely from state to state—despite the growth of EU law—it is hard to make comprehensive comparisons about each state's legal system. True, as noted in the **Is Europe One?** section, there has been a certain amount of Europeanization of legal codes, as EU directives and regulations have been adopted in all member states and must be applied in an equivalent manner. However, laws on a variety of topics such as freedom of expression, government surveillance, abortion, gay marriage, drug use (just to take a few controversial topics) vary across the continent, although there are some commonalities, including a ban on capital punishment. Rather than focus on individual issues, some of which are covered elsewhere in this book, we can speak more generally about the bases for the legal system as a whole.

common law ■ system of law developed in Great Britain in which judicial precedents obtain the status of law; judges have more power and discretion under this system.

There are two primary legal traditions in Europe.[17] In England, Wales, and Ireland (but, interestingly enough, not Scotland), Anglo-Saxon or "**common law**" legal traditions prevail. This system also exists in the US and Canada, as they were subject to English influence. Under this system, laws are comprised of include statutory law enacted by a legislature, regulatory law promulgated by executive branch agencies, and common law or "case law," which are decisions issued by courts or quasi-judicial tribunals within government agencies. Put another way, the law contains not only explicit provisions approved by the government but also is composed of judicial precedents that are binding on lower courts. Often, enacted statutes generally give only terse statements of general principle, and for the fine boundaries and definitions necessary to apply the law, one must consult previous judicial decisions on the topic and reason from those by analogy. From time to time, precedents may be overturned (e.g., think of the 1954 decision *Brown v. Board of Education* in the US that outlawed racial segregation of the public schools, which previously had been legal), meaning that the law can evolve over time thanks to discretion and judgment offered by individual judges. In England and Ireland today, however, the common law traditions are weaker than they were in the past, thanks in large measure to the body of EU law—which must be applied by English and Irish judges—and their governments' accession to the European Convention of Human Rights.

code law ■ system of law in which laws are defined exclusively as statutes adopted by the government and courts and judges merely apply the law.

Most European states—as well as Scotland—rely upon Roman or "**code" law**. This means that law is codified in detail by the government and then expected to be applied by qualified judges. The classical code law was adopted by Napoleon in France—the Napoleonic Code—and under French influence this system spread to many parts of Europe. In systems based on code law, judges do not enjoy much discretion. They are merely civil servants who determine the relevant facts to which codified laws are they applied. Judicial precedent plays much less of a role, as the judiciary becomes "merely an administrative tool for the implementation of legislatively determined policies."[18] In addition, defendants typically do not enjoy the presumption of innocence—although France adopted such a provision in 1999—or protection against self-incrimination. In this tradition, the judge is also not a neutral arbiter; he or she is an agent of the state, frequently entering into arguments during trial. In contemporary practice, this means working to determine the pertinent facts, not siding with the state, although in Eastern Europe under

IS EUROPE ONE?

Europeanization of Judicial Systems

Europeanization requires that national-level political institutions work with the EU and coordinate some of their activities. As we saw in Chapter 5, national parliaments are increasingly tied to the EU. Heads of government work through the European Council to set EU priorities. However, coordination between EU-level and national-level institutions may go furthest in the court system, reflecting the supranational reach of the EU into its members' legal systems.[14]

As we learned in Chapter 4, European-level law is extensively developed. Application of this law is often through national court systems. Europeanization of the legal system thus means that national-level judges must apply European-level law in an identical manner. In order to facilitate uniform application of the law, Article 177 of the 1957 Treaty of Rome provides the European Court of Justice (ECJ) with power to make preliminary rulings on questions raised by national courts concerning the interpretation of EU law. In other words, one responsibility of the ECJ is to make sure courts apply EU law similarly throughout the union. National level courts as operate as *de facto* European courts when they interpret EU directives that have been transposed into national law and can, in principle, request legislatures to "re-do" legislation that does not meet EU requirements. In this way, via national courts, European-level rules can be introduced into domestic legal orders.

Additionally, the ECJ requires national courts to enforce European law. By the doctrine of direct effect of Article 189 of the Treaty of Rome, provisions of EU law confer rights and impose obligations on individuals and public authorities. National courts can apply these directly, without the need for national-level legislation. Litigants in court can appeal to these EU-level measures, which, due to the doctrine of supremacy that holds that EU law is supreme to national law, means that if EU law contradicts national-level law, EU law prevails. This later principle was established in the case of *Costa v. ENEL* in 1964, in which an Italian citizen invoked European law to sue his government when the Italian government nationalized ENEL, an energy company. Although the ECJ ruled against Mr. Costa, it noted that he did have a right to invoke EU law, and, if there were a conflict between European law and Italian law, the former would prevail. In the ECJ's words,

> [i]t follows from all these observations [in the case] that the law stemming from the treaty, an independent source of law, could not, because of its special and original nature, be overridden by domestic legal provisions, however framed, without being deprived of its character as community law and without the legal basis of the community itself being called into question.[15]

In practice, this means that there is judicial review at the EU level, which can be done both at the ECJ if a case comes before it but also at the national-level, as courts are expected to override domestic level law where it conflicts with EU law. National level courts can even order compensation in cases where individuals suffer losses from inadequate implementation of EU law.

In effect, what this means is a legal hierarchy has taken hold in Europe, with EU law at its pinnacle. The EU, however, does not have the resources to oversee an entire legal structure. Whereas the ECJ does adjudicate some disputes, it relies upon national-level courts to do part of its job. The courts thus partner up in a manner far more extensively than do executives or parliaments, and, because the doctrine of supremacy is well established, the turf battles and disputes over subsidiarity that might affect relations between national parliaments and the EU are relatively absent.

This does not necessarily mean, however, that all functions smoothly all the time. Examination of how national courts interact with the ECJ reveal that links between the ECJ and the French and British courts,

(*continued*)

are, in comparison with the Dutch, Italian, Belgian, and German courts, not very extensive. In the French case, the lack of strong judicial review as well as concentration of power works against litigants trying to appeal to EU law. In the British case, judges may, as they can under common law, cite EU law as precedent, but many of the direct appeals to the ECJ for preliminary rulings concern social issues, an arena in which British law is relatively undeveloped and/or in conflict with prevailing EU law, and thus British litigants are more able to make appeals for the use of EU law. In contrast, German use of EU law is facilitated by its decentralized federal system and stronger judicial review, which provides more opportunity for litigation. In the words of one writer,

> German courts are the most active participants in the European judicial dialogue, and German political structure provides the best "institutional fit" with European political structure. The dispersion of power in both systems promotes the organization of societal interests into groups that can pursue legal action. German society has long been prepared to seize the opportunities of Europeanization through judicial forums.[16]

Critical Thinking Questions

1. Countries typically accept judgments against them at the European Court of Justice. Why would they do so instead of simply ignoring the ECJ?
2. "Europeanization" of judicial systems is fairly extensive, yet the ECJ is typically viewed more favorably and is less controversial than the European Commission or European Parliament. Why might this be?

communism judges were clearly on the side of the authorities, rendering the judicial system fundamentally unfair. Even though judges are not supposed to be biased with respect to the outcome of cases, there can be real difficulties with this type of system when the state itself is the defendant (e.g., sued by a citizen for violating her rights). To handle questions like these, many states with code law systems have created a whole separate system of administrative courts, and these courts do make laws by precedent.

COURT SYSTEMS

Most European states have a hierarchical court system, in which the decisions of local or lower-level courts can be subject to appeal to higher courts, culminating in some sort of supreme court. Federal states have their own courts to administer laws passed at the sub-national level, and there are often courts for civil and criminal matters as well as separate juvenile and tax courts. In Turkey, military courts have played a role in prosecuting those deemed to be threatening to the state, although this feature of the Turkish state has been subjected to criticism by the EU, compelling the Turkish government to curtail their role.

Judges are expected to be well-trained professionals, and thus the naming of judges is typically not left to voters. In most states, the president and/or parliament appoints the judges, although rules are established that create a minimum level of qualification (e.g., law degree) for judges. In many states (e.g., Italy, Spain, Hungary), a non-political judicial committee made up of judges and/or lawyers screens and recommends potential judges to the authorities. Although judges are supposed to be above politics, a strict separation is often impossible to maintain as political actors or bodies are prone to appoint judges that share their general orien-

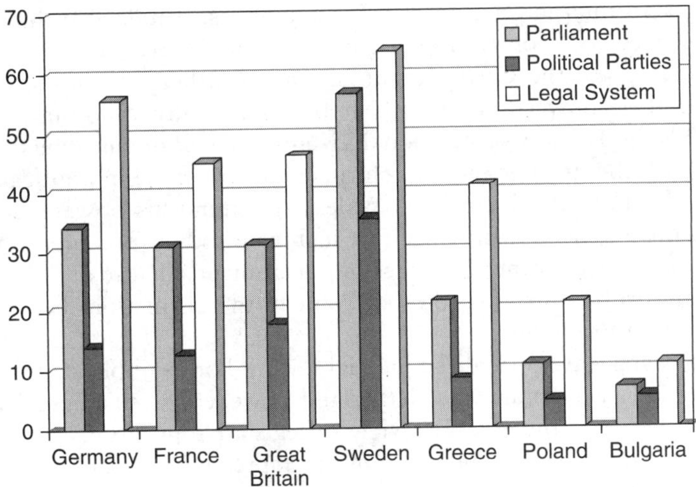

FIGURE 7.2
Trust in Legal Systems and Other Political Actors
Source: European Social Survey Round 4, 2008, online analysis at http://ess.nsd.uib.no/ess/round4. Question was level on trust on a scale from 0 (no trust) to 10 (complete trust). Responses are percentage of those indicating 6 or higher on this scale.

tation. The independence of the courts from interference by other branches and the expectation of political impartiality in judicial decisions are enshrined in many constitutions and are crucial to maintaining the integrity of the court system. If the courts seem packed with political cronies—a problem at times in states such as Spain and Italy, hence generating a system whereby appointments to courts are made by fellow judges—the credibility of the court system suffers. However, as seen in Figure 7.2, surveys from many countries reveal that the judiciary is typically far more trusted by citizens than more "politicized" institutions such as parliament or political parties.

The most explicit political role normally undertaken by courts is to exercise judicial review, meaning that the courts can nullify or declare invalid a law or regulation passed by parliament or an action taken by the executive branch. Although generally thought of as a US innovation and at odds with principles of code law that served to constrain judges, judicial review has spread throughout Europe. Reflecting in part the tradition of code law, constitutional questions are usually reserved for special **constitutional courts** or constitutional councils. Some courts, such as France's Constitutional Council and Romania's Constitutional Court, only have the power of *a priori* review, meaning they can consider the constitutionality of a measure only *before* it is adopted into law. Most constitutional courts have the power of *posterior* review, meaning they review the constitutionality of legislation after it becomes law. In these cases, for example, an individual may argue that a law violates his or her constitutional rights and take the matter to court or to an **ombudsman**, an office usually attached to parliament that is expressly designed to handle citizen complaints about government abuse of power. Cases may also be brought before a constitutional court if one believes a law

constitutional courts ■ special courts whose primary purpose is to rule on the constitutionality of proposed or adopted legislation; they are the main agents who exercise judicial review.

ombudsman ■ government official charged with handling citizen complaints about governmental abuse of power.

contravenes an international treaty. These matters, if judged to have merit, can then be referred to a constitutional court for a definitive ruling. Germany, Italy, Poland, Spain, and the Czech Republic, among others, all have constitutional courts with these powers, and they have been politically important. For example, in the 1990s the Polish Constitutional Tribunal struck down some of the government's "shock therapy" economic reforms and intervened in political disputes by declaring efforts to President Lech Walesa to extend his powers as unconstitutional. To the extent that these rulings such as these set precedents and give the courts power over the other branches of government, the use of judicial review in continental Europe is helping to erode some of the distinctions between common law and code law systems.

Not all states have formalized judicial review. For example, courts do not have such power in Great Britain, the Netherlands, Sweden, and Finland. This does not mean, however, that there is no review of legislative proposals. For example, in Sweden, a Legal Council of judges from the Supreme Court can be asked whether controversial measures are compatible with the constitution and its judgment carries considerable weight. In Great Britain, the highest court for normal civil and criminal appeals is composed of Law Lords from the House of Lords. Judges ensure that political entities follow existing law, but they are not empowered to review the laws themselves and declare the acts of the House of Commons as unconstitutional. Similarly, in the Netherlands Article 120 of the constitution expressly prohibits courts from considering the constitutionality of laws. However, because both Great Britain and the Netherlands have ratified treaties such as the European Convention of Human Rights, the courts can now ask that laws be considered in light of their respect for such treaties. This is not merely theoretical: Issues such as granting of political asylum, a controversial in issue in the wake of terrorist attacks in London in 2005, have involved the British courts ruling that government proposals run afoul of its international commitments.

The Swiss case deserves special mention because constitutional questions are often decided not by courts but by voters themselves in a referendum. Referendums, an example of direct democracy, give people a direct say in the adoption of laws. In Switzerland, questions can be put to voters if 50,000 signatures are put on a petition. Any bill decided by parliament can be subject to referenda, and all constitutional amendments must be submitted to voters. A referendum passes if it is approved by the majority of voters and by voters in a majority of the twenty-six cantons. If voters wish to amend the constitution, neither parliament nor the courts can stand in their way.[19] Swiss voters have decided a number of important issues, including granting women the right to vote (1971), joining the UN (2002), and acceding to the Schengen Agreement (2005).

In order to gain more understanding of the importance of the judiciary and, in particular, judicial review, let us turn to a few examples in contemporary Europe.

Germany: The Growing Importance of the Constitutional Court

Germany has one of the strongest constitutional courts in Europe. It is separate from the regular system of civil, criminal, and administrative courts, ruling only on the constitutionality of legislation and international treaties. Cases can come before it by referral from members of the *Bundestag*, regional governments, ordinary courts, or individuals. Notably, there was no such court prior to World War II, which meant that no institution could overturn Hitler's laws and decrees. Much of the rationale for creating this court after the war therefore was a desire to avoid a repeat of this experience. Members of the court are nominated by political parties and appointed to a twelve-year term by a two-thirds vote in both houses of parliament. The court is comprised of two eight-member Senates, one of which is for issues arising out of ordinary litigation and one is for disputes between branches of government. The federal government, *Länder* governments, and a collection of one-third of *Bundestag* members can request an abstract review of any existing law, and individual citizens can request a concrete review of suspect law if they believe they have been harmed by it. The constitutional court is based not in Berlin but in Karlsruhe, a medium-sized city in southwestern Germany.

This court has made many noteworthy rulings and exerts real influence both in Germany and within the EU as a whole.[20] In the first fifty years of its existence, it declared about 5 percent of the bills passed by the *Bundestag* to be unconstitutional.[21] Alone among German institutions, it can ban a political party, which it did in the 1950s in the case of neo-Nazi and communist parties. Since the 1990s, the German Constitutional Court has ruled on such diverse issues as public financing of political parties; the liberalization of abortion laws; religious symbols in the schools; allowing German military units to participate in international operations; approval of the euro; granting equal legal treatment to homosexual unions; and ruling on the constitutionality of the EU's Maastricht Treaty. In some cases, as with

The German Constitutional Court in session.

rulings on whether smoking can be allowed in bars or whether commuters can deduct transport costs from their taxes, the Court has waded into minutiae of public policy, leading some to call it the third chamber of the legislature. Nonetheless, there is no evidence that Germans are dissatisfied with such "judicial activism." The Constitutional Court is trusted by over 80 percent of Germans, double the number who trust the federal government and the *Bundestag*.

Germany's Constitution Court is also powerful beyond the country's borders, as it has ruled on the constitutionality of EU treaties, specifically whether those treaties violate German principles of federalism and individual rights of Germans. Since 1974, the German Constitutional Court has made the transfer of powers to the EU conditional on the protection of Germans' basic rights; if they are infringed, Germany could, therefore, reclaim them. Because it has asserted itself in this manner, the German Constitutional Court is often the last legal hurdle needing to be overcome when the EU adopts major reforms. This was the case with the Lisbon Treaty, which was held up by a court ruling in June 2009 that said that the EU was not democratic enough to support more integration. In this case, the Constitutional Court asked the German parliament to pass new laws to give itself more say over EU affairs so that Germany will retain power to shape "citizens' circumstances of life" in areas such as education, religion, and criminal law.[22] This ruling delayed final German ratification of the treaty, which finally occurred in September 2009. This feature of the German judiciary is interesting because Europeanization is often conceived as a one-way process, with power and influence flowing from the EU to member states; here is a case of a domestic political body ruling on the legitimacy of EU actions. In this way, the German Constitutional Court becomes an important arbiter of future EU integration.

France: Abstract, *A Priori* Review

Judicial review in France functions very differently than in Germany, or, for that matter, in the US. France's equivalent of a constitutional court is a Constitutional Council, created in the 1958 constitution of the Fifth Republic. The Council is composed of nine regular members,[23] who are appointed to a nine-year term. Three each are appointed by the president, the president of the National Assembly, and the president of the Senate.

France has abstract and *a priori* judicial review, a system that some would not consider to be a true system of judicial review.[24] This means that the Council reviews a law or executive order *before* it is enacted into law, not afterwards (as in the US) and that it reviews the law without having a specific complainant (again, as in the US). "Organic bills," those which fundamentally affect government and treaties, must be vetted by the Council. Other proposed measures may be brought before it, but, unlike in Germany or the US, only certain individuals can bring a case before it: the president, prime minister, president of the National Assembly, president of the Senate, or (since 1974) a group of sixty individuals from either legislative body.[25] Ordinary citizens who feel they might be harmed by the legislation, in other words, cannot take a case to the Constitutional Council. If the proposal does not meet with the Council's approval, it goes back to the legislature or president for revisions. Interestingly, in addition to the 1958 Constitution and international treaties (e.g., the European Convention on Human Rights), the

Council has stated it may void measures that violate the 1789 Declaration of Rights of Man, which dates to the French Revolution. In this way, the Council can exercise real power, but, because only elected officials can make appeals to it, it reviews fewer cases than the German Constitutional Court and traditionally has been far less likely to issue rulings against the government's wishes. Since the 1980s, however, the Council has been both more active and been more politicized: Members of the opposition party in the National Assembly now regularly bring controversial bills before it, and, if the political makeup of the Council differs from that of the incumbent government, disputes are more likely.[26] Some of its more controversial decisions have touched on bills to limit immigration and government funding for church-run schools. The Constitutional Council also supervises and certifies elections and referenda.

Post-Communist Europe: Ensuring an Independent Judiciary

Whereas several West European states adopted judicial review after World War II, in Eastern Europe the court system, like all political and social institutions, was subjugated to the Communist Party. Courts were not independent, and often they enforced measures (e.g., censorship, imprisonment for public dissent) that were not compatible with democratic governance. Judges were servants of the government, and rather than having independent powers, they were expected to fall into line with the demands of the communist authorities. In the words of one writer, communism "translated into corruption and 'telephone' justice," the latter phrase meaning decisions were made with the help of a phone call to a Party official.[27]

One of the priorities, therefore, in post-communist Europe has been the establishment of a well-functioning, independent judiciary that will uphold principles of democracy and the rule of law. Eastern European states, inspired in part by the French and German systems, also established constitutional courts with the power of judicial review. New measures—either in statutes or in new constitutions—were passed relatively quickly to create these courts and uphold the principles of separation of powers and judicial independence. Appointment of judges for the regular civil and criminal court system is either by the executive authority (as in the Czech Republic), an expert judicial committee (as in Bulgaria), or a combination of the two (as in Poland). Appointment procedures for constitutional courts are more similar, usually involving legislative and executive authority and putting judges on the court for a fixed term of seven to ten years.

Whereas putting changes on paper was relatively easy, creating well-functioning courts, in some cases, has been more problematic. Communist-era judges, for example, were frequently disqualified from continued service on the bench, and finding new, qualified individuals willing to work as a judge on a civil servant's salary has not always been easy. Although judges are supposed to be politically independent, the fact that they are, in many cases, appointed by presidents or parliaments has made some question their independence. In some cases, such as Bulgaria, the parliament has tried to interfere in the workings of courts. This interference took various forms: changing the qualification of judges in order to get rid of certain troublesome (from the perspective of the parliamentary majority) judges; cutting the budget of the courts; even trying to evict the Constitutional Court from its building![28] Throughout the region, connections between judges and political and/or business figures has led to accusations of corruption, and judicial reform and the elimination of corruption were major concerns of the European Union in the 2000s in accession talks with Romania, Bulgaria, and Croatia. Whereas in some countries, notably Hungary, Constitutional Courts have been very active in asserting their powers—one observer suggested that Hungarian Constitutional Court, which rules on approximately a thousand motions a year, may be the "most powerful constitutional court in the world"[29]—in other cases the culture of judicial review has been harder to establish, as parliaments have tried to ignore or override the courts.

Spanish Courts and Universal Jurisdiction

universal jurisdiction ■ controversial idea established by Spanish courts that they have the ability to try human rights crimes regardless of where such crimes allegedly occurred.

The Spanish court system is structured and functions similarly to those elsewhere on the continent. However, it has one special feature: its courts claim **universal jurisdiction** over human rights crimes. What this means is that one does not have to commit such a crime in Spain in order to be tried by Spanish courts. Spanish law allows Spanish courts to investigate and try these cases wherever they occur in the world.

Spaniards who would defend this provision would argue that it helps to ensure justice. If human rights crimes (e.g., genocide, mass murder) are "crimes against humanity," then there is no logical reason why those who commit such crimes must be tried only by one certain country. Moreover, in some cases—think of government officials in Sudan accused of genocide or Saddam Hussein when he ruled Iraq—it would be impossible to bring the accused to justice in their home countries. This does not mean that Spanish courts seek indictments against all alleged human rights abusers. However, they have sought such indictments in a couple of high-profile cases. One involved Augusto Pinochet, who ruled Chile from 1973 to 1990 and was accused of being complicit in the murder and torture of thousands of civilians, including Spanish citizens living in Chile. Spain's arrest warrant against Pinochet led to his arrest in Great Britain in 1998, as Britain was obligated by European law to honor it. This was a watershed event in the history of international law as no previous head of state had been arrested on the principle of universal jurisdiction.[30] Cases have also been opened against officials in Israel and China for human rights abuses in Gaza and Tibet, respectively. Perhaps even more controversially, in 2009, Baltasar Garzón, a Spanish judge, opened an investigation against six former officials in the Bush Administration—including Alberto Gonzales, the former US attorney general—for providing legal cover for torture allegedly committed at the prison in Guantanamo Bay, Cuba. Because of the fallout of this action, the Spanish parliament passed a measure to change the law that allows the courts to claim universal jurisdiction.[31] Beginning in 2010, the accused will have to be arrested in Spain, a victim will have to be a Spaniard, or there will have to be some other clear connection to Spain before the court will be allowed to proceed. There will also have to be proof that no other national court system has taken up a given case. Interestingly as well, Garzón was indicted in 2010 for opening up examination of crimes committed under the dictatorship of Francisco Franco (1936 to 1975) in Spain that were, according to those who sought his indictment, covered by an amnesty law that forbids prosecution of anyone for these actions.[32]

Constitutional arrangements and court systems rarely capture political headlines, although there are some exceptions, including Judge Garzón in Spain and the Constitutional Court in Turkey, noted at the outset of this chapter. For the most part, constitutions and legal systems are accepted as givens, the neutral "rules of the game" for political actors as well as the citizenry as a whole. However, as we've seen in this and in other chapters, these rules have real consequences and help account for differences in institutions and policies across Europe. Moreover, as actors question the fairness or legitimacy of these rules, courts can take on real political importance and become a source of both controversy and change.

APPLICATION QUESTIONS

1. Do you think a constitution should include socio-economic rights, such as right to education and right to health care?
2. Why do you think judicial review has become common in Europe? Why might some be against it?
3. What are the advantages and disadvantages of extensive use of referenda? Should some matters be reserved for decisions by referenda?
4. Should a constitution prevent something that a majority of people wants to see adopted as a law or policy?
5. How seriously, in your view, does the power of the ECJ erode the sovereignty of states and their voters?

KEY TERMS

code law 190
common law 190
constitution 182
constitutional courts 193
devolution 189
federal state 185
judiciary 182
judicial review 184
ombudsman 193
referendum 183
subsidiarity 186
unitary states 187
universal jurisdiction 198

ADDITIONAL READING

Bell, John. 2006. *Judiciaries within Europe: A Comparative Review*. Cambridge: Cambridge University Press.

This book presents an overview of the workings of court systems in France, Germany, Spain, Sweden, and Great Britain, with an effort to make comparisons across these cases.

International Constitutional Law website, sponsored by University of Bern, at http://www.servat.unibe.ch/law/icl/index.html.

This is a portal through which one can view constitutions (in English) of many countries in the world, as well as retrieve basic information about elections and party systems; an excellent resource.

Sweet, Alec Stone. 2004. *The Judicial Construction of Europe*. Oxford: Oxford University Press.

This work focuses on the legal development of the EU and how this has affected national-level legislation and judicial systems.

Sweet, Alec Stone. 2000. *Governing with Judges: Constitutional Politics in Europe*. Oxford: Oxford University Press.

This work examines constitutional courts function in a number of countries, as well as the workings of the ECJ.

Swenden, Wilifried. 2005. *Federalism and Regionalism on Western Europe*. New York: Palgrave Macmillan.

This book, a thematic treatment of how sub-national governments work in European states such as Germany, Spain, and Austria, focuses on political decision-making and the allocation of resources among levels of government.

END NOTES

1. Calculations come from English translations found through a website sponsored by the University of Bern (Switzerland) at http://www.oefre.unibe.ch/law/icl/index.html, accessed on 5 April 2010. This website is an excellent site to view and compare constitutions.
2. For more on the unique features of Great Britain, see Anthony King, *Does the United Kingdom Still Have a Constitution?* (London: Sweet and Maxwell, 2001).
3. Robert Dahl, *Democracy, Identity, and Equality* (Oslo: Norwegian University Press, 1986), p. 114.
4. Federalism is thus part of a "consociational" system, long advocated by the political scientist Arend Lijphart, to make democratic governance easier in ethnically divided societies. See Arend Lijphart, *Democracy in Plural Societies* (New Haven: Yale University Press, 1997), and Andrew Reynolds, ed., *The Architecture of Democracy: Constitutional Design, Conflict Management, and Democracy* (Oxford: Oxford University Press, 2002).
5. For a classic treatment of federalism on this front, see William Riker, *Federalism: Origin, Operation, Significance* (Boston: Little Brown, 1964).
6. Exceptions are the tiny Federated States of Micronesia and Canada, which has an appointed Senate as its upper legislative chamber.
7. By this definition, non-democratic systems such as the Soviet Union and Yugoslavia, despite the façade of federalism, could be said not to have true federal governments, since, particularly in the Soviet case, sub-national governments did not have effective means to defend themselves against the political center.
8. Robert Putnam with Robert Leonardi and Raffaella Nanetti, *Making Democracy Work: Civic Traditions in Modern Italy* (Princeton: Princeton University Press, 1993).
9. Colin Pilkington, *Devolution in Britain Today* (Manchester: Manchester University Press, 2003).
10. James Graff, "Regional Ruckus," *Time*, February 29, 2004, and "All Must Have Prizes," *The Economist*, August 1, 2009.
11. John Gibbons, "Spain: A Semi Federal State," in D. McIver, ed. *The Multinational State* (London: Macmillan, 1999), and Kenneth McRoberts, *Catalonia: Nation-Building without a State* (Oxford: Oxford University Press, 2001).
12. "Homage to Barcelona," *The Economist*, June 18, 2005.
13. "Survey of Spain," *The Economist*, May 19, 2001.
14. This section relies heavily on Paul Mullen, "Legitimate Options: National Courts and the Power of the European Court of Justice," *European Community Studies Association Review* 11:1, Winter 1998, 2–7; and Lisa Conant, "Europeanization and the Courts: Variable Patterns of Adaptation among National Judiciaries," in Maria Green Cowles, *et al*, *Transforming Europe: Europeanization and Domestic Change* (Ithaca: Cornell University Press, 2001).
15. European Court of Justice, Case 6/64, *Falminio Costa v. ENEL* [1964] ECR 585, 593.
16. Conant, "Europeanization and the Courts," p. 113.
17. Prior to the collapse of communism, one could speak of principles of "socialist law" that animated legal systems in Eastern Europe. These have largely been eradicated.
18. Robert Utter and David Lundesgaard, "Comparative Aspects of Judicial Review: Issues Facing the New European States," *Judicature* 77 (1994), p. 241.
19. An exception occurs if a proposed measure violates international law. Such was the case in 1996 with an anti-asylum measure.
20. Much of this section comes from "Judgment days," *The Economist*, March 28, 2009, pp. 59–60.
21. Manfred Schmidt, *Political Institutions in the Federal Republic of Germany* (Oxford: Oxford University Press, 2003), p. 120.
22. "Constitutional Concerns," *The Economist*, July 25, 2009, p. 51.
23. Former French presidents are *de jure* members of this council, but they do not always participate in its proceedings.
24. Such is the presentation in Michael Gallagher, *et al.*, *Representative Government in Modern Europe*, 4th ed. (New York: McGraw-Hill, 2006), p. 99.
25. Constitutional reforms in 2008 provide for appeals to the Council from lower courts, but statutory law to spell out how this would function have not been adopted as of 2010.
26. For more on developments in France, see Paul F. Mullen, "Legitimate Options."
27. A.E. Dick Howard, "Judicial Independence in Post-Communist Central and Eastern Europe," in Peter Russell and David O'Brien, eds. *Judicial Independence in the Age of Democracy* (Charlottesville: University of Virginia Press, 2001), p. 91. Much of this section borrows from this chapter.

28. Albert Melone, "The struggle for judicial independence and the transition toward democracy in Bulgaria," *Communist and Post-Communist Studies* 29:2, June 1996, 231–243.
29. Jon Elster, "On Majoritarianism and Rights," *East European Constitutional Review* 1, 1992, p. 11.
30. Pinochet was eventually taken back to Chile to stand trial, where, up until his death in 2006, he was in and out of house arrest and fought prosecution by claiming legal immunity and health problems, including dementia.
31. "Push in Spain to Limit Reach of the Courts," *New York Times*, May 21, 2009.
32. *New York Times*, March 26, 2010.

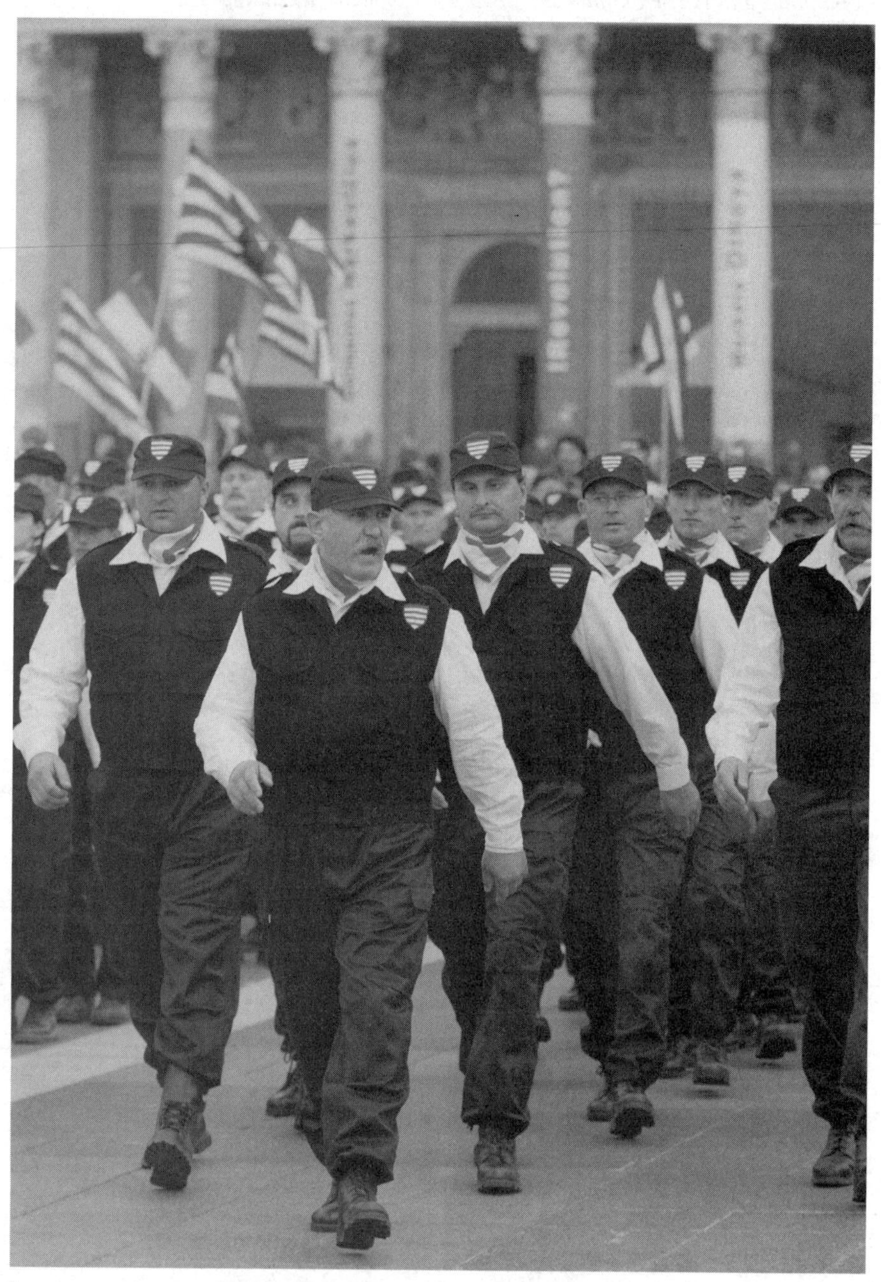

The far-right Jobbik Party: What does it demonstrate about democracy in Hungary?

CHAPTER

8

Political Parties and Elections

A European political party that campaigns against Jewish control of the world's financial system and a party leader who instructs Jews to "go back to playing with their tiny circumcised tails." A party with a militia dressed in black that patrols Roma [Gypsy] ghettoes and threatens to deport or send the Roma to prison. Attacks on a rabbi's house and defacement of a Jewish memorial occur during the political campaign.[1] When the votes are counted, the party is claimed the big winner of the elections, threatening to upend the established political order. Could this be Germany in the 1930s, perhaps Italy in the 1920s? No, this is Hungary in 2010, where the Jobbik Party,[2] which warns voters against the rise of "Judapest", surprised observers by winning 16.7 percent of the vote in the first round of the April 2010 parliamentary elections and became the third-largest party in the Hungarian parliament with forty-seven seats.

Is this a cause for alarm? Perhaps not. Jobbik's supporters claim that it is merely principled and patriotic, and it is not a coalition partner in the Hungarian government, so its actual political influence is limited. Hungary's economy also suffered a severe blow during the 2008–2009 economic crisis, and many may have voted for Jobbik, which campaigned extensively in areas with high unemployment, as a means to protest. However, far-right parties such as Jobbik are not a purely Hungarian or Eastern European phenomenon. Parties with barely concealed racist platforms have done well in several Western European countries such as France, Switzerland, Austria, and Denmark, and they may enjoy greater electoral success in coming years. Moreover, radical or "anti-system" parties on the Left have done well in some European elections in recent years, including in Germany in 2009. At minimum, issues of whether fringe parties threaten democracy aside, what these phenomena demonstrate is that the political spectrum in Europe, with parties representing highly controversial and combative views, is far more diverse and dynamic than that found in the two-party system of the US.

This chapter takes up the topics of political parties and elections, subjects that have been mentioned at various points in the text but have yet to receive concerted, systemic treatment. These are, of course, core subjects in European politics and in consideration of democratic governments more generally. After all, the main attributes that distinguish democracies from other forms of government are political competition among various groups or parties and that power is won through free and fair elections. All governments have some form of executive, legislative, and judicial power—even if in extreme cases powers are fused and all held by a single individual—but only in democracies do elections determine who holds power and only in democracies are people given a meaningful choice when they vote.[3] The choices that are presented to voters are usually determined by political parties, which are the principle organizations that nominate candidates for public office and contest elections. Political parties are thus a necessary component of modern democracies, and, insofar as parties structure political life and provide the key personnel for government, they are often considered a political institution.

FUNCTIONS OF POLITICAL PARTIES

The key actors in any democratic electoral system are political parties. Political parties serve several essential roles in modern democracies, making politics as we know it today "unthinkable" without them.[4] Indeed, political parties arose with the expansion of suffrage and introduction of democratic politics, first in the US in the early 1800s and later in Europe in the late 1800s through early 1900s.[5] Their primary function is to contest elections and nominate candidates for public office. This activity distinguishes political parties from other organizations such as interest groups, which are involved in political life but do not nominate candidates and seek formal governmental authority. In Europe, there are few US-style primaries, meaning that party organizations have a great deal of control in recruiting and nominating candidates for office. Typically, they choose individuals that they believe will be loyal to the goals and top leadership of the party, thus helping to ensure a higher degree of **party discipline** among elected officials in Europe than one finds in the US.[6] Mavericks rarely buck the party line, knowing that they risk losing their party's nomination in the next election cycle.

party discipline ■ practice whereby elected officials and would-be candidates for office adhere to the party line, voting or endorsing programs backed by the party leadership.

In addition to nominating candidates to stand for office, parties also hope, obviously, to win elections. This implies several things. First, they need to motivate and mobilize voters to get them to the polls. Indeed, near election time, parties care about little else. Between elections, though, parties must also stake out positions to attract members and sympathizers. This means they must develop programs and try to voice and represent the interests of a wide number of individuals. Most parties therefore aim to be **catch-all parties** (e.g., the British Conservative Party or the German Social Democratic Party), meaning that they try to broaden their base as far as possible to attract the most supporters. Others, though, are **single-issue parties** (e.g., the Dutch Party for Animals or the now-defunct Polish Beer-Lovers Party), seeking to generate support by emphasizing an issue that they hope will be popular and/or drawing attention to an issue otherwise ignored by other parties. In some cases (e.g., the Greens) single-issue parties can broaden their base by moving beyond just a single issue and developing a wider political platform. In either case, parties help to organize the political life of a country, provide individuals with a sense of political identity, and make a potentially myriad of possible choices simpler and more intelligible to voters. Whether in or out of government, they also can provide input to policymakers and organize actions (e.g., protests, petition campaigns) to influence state leaders.

catch-all parties ■ parties whose platforms and programs try to appeal to the broadest range of voters.

single-issue parties ■ parties whose programs typically are restricted to a single or a very narrow set of issues.

Parties are organizations, and as such have their own internal structures and rules. Most parties are hierarchical, having a national, regional, and local branches, as well as, in many cases, special youth bureaus to recruit the next generation. With only some insignificant exceptions, European political parties embrace democracy, and thus one would expect parties themselves to function democratically. Although most parties do give local bodies and the general membership some sort of say (e.g., through a national convention), ensuring intra-party democracy is a problem. Nearly a century ago, Robert Michels, in a study of the German Social Democratic Party, developed his **iron law of oligarchy,** noting the propensity of any organization, even those committed to democracy, to produce bureaucratic, elite leaders, who, by virtue of control over finances and information, tend to gain control of the organization and use it to promote their own interests.[7] Rather than serving as democratic vehicles, many parties become corrupt, or at least are perceived to be so, using their power to dispense patronage (e.g., jobs, government contracts, access to public housing) to their supporters. These phenomena are captured in the German term *Parteibuchwirtschaft* and the Italian term *Partitocrazia.* Although most political parties in Europe receive public (government) funding, many also rely upon private funding. The corrosive effect of money on politics is a concern in many European states, although the cost of campaigning in Europe has yet to reach the tens of billions of dollars as in the US.

iron law of oligarchy ■ idea that all organizations will produce bureaucratic, elite leaders who tend to gain control of an organization and thereby limit internal democracy.

Perhaps for these reasons—as well as diminishing ideological polarization in many European states—party membership in most European states has declined. Accurate membership figures are hard to come by—parties have an incentive to exaggerate their membership—but many surveys have confirmed that fewer and fewer Europeans belong to political parties. Party membership figures from several countries—as taken from the 2008 European Social Survey—are presented in Table 8.1. This table also shows the percentage of respondents who say they tend to trust political parties. Both figures must be troubling to party leaders. The drop

TABLE 8.1

Membership and Trust in Political Parties

Country	% Party Members	% Trust Political Parties*
Germany	3.1	6.0
France	2.2	5.4
Great Britain	2.9	9.2
Spain	1.3	7.9
Netherlands	5.0	21.4
Sweden	6.7	18.7
Denmark	9.0	**36.4**
Cyprus	**12.7**	15.9
Greece	7.5	4.2
Hungary	**0.7**	**2.8**
Czech Republic	4.2	6.4
Slovakia	2.3	9.9
Turkey	4.3	11.6
Total (25 states)	4.6	10.0

Source: European Social Survey, 2008, online analysis available at http://ess.nsd.uib.no/ess/round4.
*Scores of 7–10 on 10-point scale of trust, with 10 being completely trust. Results in bold are lows and highs for the entire survey.

in membership since peaks in the 1950s and 1960s ranges, depending upon the country, from 30 to 80 percent.[8] In post-communist Europe, the newness of the party system and "partyphobia"—a disgust with political parties thanks to the negative experience of living under communist rule—is invoked to explain the particularly low figures of party membership. In the British case, the decline has been so precipitous that by 2005 more Britons belonged to birdwatching clubs than all political parties combined![9] Party identification is also on the decline, making it less likely that parties can rely upon a base of loyalists. The term **dealignment** is used to refer both to the failure of individuals to attach themselves to a particular party and the general mistrust towards political parties. Indeed, given the rise of single-issue interest groups and blogging, not to mention a more general withdrawal from political life, one might wonder if the traditional idea of a mass-based party makes any sense today. Because of declining membership subscriptions, parties are relying more and more on public financing and/or large donations, and some worry about growing reliance in campaigns on professional consultants and the mass media instead of grassroots mobilization of the membership.

dealignment ■ declining attachment to and increasing distrust of established political parties.

PARTY FAMILIES IN EUROPE

There are literally hundreds of political parties in Europe, and no two are exactly alike. Obviously, they differ in size, power, and particulars in their party platforms. In a broad comparative perspective, however, today most European political parties are similar insofar as they accept the basic tenets of individual rights and democratic government, although there are some (e.g., the National Front [FN] in France, the Freedom Party in Austria, the Radical Party in Serbia, the aforementioned Jobbik in Hungary) that espouse racist or extreme xenophobic views and, according to their critics, would endanger democracy if they would come to power.

How should one try to classify the myriad of parties in Europe? The simplest way is delineate party families, based upon a combination of shared origins and ideological or policy orientation. In the broadest terms, one can speak of parties of the Left and parties of the Right. The division between Left and Right dates to the French Revolution and refers to how members of the post-revolutionary French assembly seated themselves according to their ideological viewpoints.

Historically speaking, the Left and the Right have been defined on the basis of several social or **political cleavages,** divisions within a society that acquire political importance and become political markers that divide supporters of one party from those of another.[10] Historically, probably the most important political cleavage has been class, meaning a group defined by its social standing and relative economic and political power. The parties of the **Left** have traditionally catered to those in the lower and working-class (manual or industrial laborers), arguing for (among other items) higher tax rates on the wealthy to help re-distribute wealth, more government intervention in the economy to create more economic equality, and a welfare state to provide basic needs (e.g., education, health care) to the population. The parties of the **Right** tend to appeal to the middle or upper classes, and favor, compared to the Left, less government involvement in the economy, emphasizing the responsibility of the individual to provide for his or her own needs and the greater efficiency achieved by free markets. Class voting—meaning that voters

political cleavages ■ divisions within a society that acquire political importance and become political markers that divide supporters of one party from those of another.

Left ■ political orientation that tends to appeal to those from lower classes and minorities and is more secular and cosmopolitan in outlook.

Right ■ political orientation that tends to appeal to upper classes, is often concerned with preserving traditions, and frequently puts priority on religion and/or nationalism.

chose parties on the basis of their own class position—has traditionally been the primary prism to view electoral behavior and party systems in Europe, although in the past two decades many analysts have suggested that class voting is on the decline and that other cleavages matter more both in terms of defining parties and in terms of explaining voting behavior.[11]

Another cleavage that has been important historically is religion. The Left tends to be more secular, favoring less involvement of religious authorities in political and social questions. The Left also tends to be less "traditional," endorsing measures that make it easier to divorce, obtain an abortion, or (most recently) allow homosexuals to marry. Parties of the Right, in contrast, tend to espouse "traditional values" and often, as in the case of Christian Democratic parties, adopt an explicitly religious moniker. Even though most European states today are very secular—especially by US standards—the individual voter's level of religiosity remains a potent predictor of her vote in many countries. For example, Russell Dalton, utilizing survey evidence from 1999 to 2002, finds that frequency of church attendance is a more powerful explanatory factor in voting than class in countries such as the Netherlands, Belgium, Finland, Denmark, Italy, and France.[12]

Finally, one can identify a cleavage between those who are more cosmopolitan and those who are more nationalist in orientation. **Cosmopolitanism** refers to the degree to which a person is interested in the wider world and sees him- or herself as part of a wider community outside of his or her own country. Those who are more cosmopolitan would, for example, be more likely to embrace the EU, economic and cultural globalization, and the rights of immigrants and ethnic minorities. **Nationalists,** on the other hand, are more suspicious of the outside world, put priority on the interests of their particular country and/or national group, and worry that the EU, globalization, and immigrants are changing their country in negative ways.

cosmopolitanism ■ the degree to which a person is interested in the wider world and sees him- or herself as part of a wider community outside of his or her own country; usually associated with the political left.

nationalists ■ those who are suspicious of the outside world and tend to put priority on the interests of their particular country; usually associated with the political right.

More recently, Ronald Inglehart and his collaborators have argued for the existence of a different sort of cleavage in Europe, between "post-materialists" and "materialists."[13] Post-materialists are most interested in quality of life issues, such as expansion of political and social freedoms and in protection of the environment, and tend to gravitate towards the political Left. The Greens, discussed below, are the archetype of a "post-materialist" party. Post-materialists tend to be younger, wealthier, and better educated. Materialists, in contrast, emphasize economic and physical security, putting emphasis on achieving the most basic needs. Greater discussion of manifestations of post-materialism within Europe can be found in the next chapter.

There are other cleavages in Europe, although some are less salient than before. The pioneering study on political cleavages by Seymour Lipset and Stein Rokkan, who based their work on how parties emerged in the 1920s, pointed to the existence of an urban-rural divide and a center-periphery one.[14] Urbanization in most European countries has made the urban-rural cleavage less salient. The center-periphery cleavage refers to battles over the consolidation of the nation and of state authority. In most states, as noted in Chapter 2, the center prevailed, imposing its rule over the disparate regions of the country, but, the push for decentralization, federalism, and even separatism in some European states reveals that this cleavage has not wholly disappeared. However, it is hard to put this dimension on a traditional Left-Right spectrum. Scots and Catalans, for example, might be more leftist in their general orientation, but the *Lega Nord* in Italy would be better classified as on the political right.[15]

Note that although some social cleavages may appear to be similar and thus reinforce each other (e.g., secularism may be correlated with post-materialism or cosmopolitanism as all three may arise thanks to education), they can also "cross-cut," meaning that they work in such a way that individuals do not fall on one side on all dimensions. Consider, for example, an unemployed, worker in the French city of Marseilles. Is he, based upon social class, likely to vote for the Communist or Socialist Party (left-wing parties in France)? Or, because he may believe a North African immigrant has "stolen" his job and/or that France is becoming too "Americanized" due to globalization, will he vote for a far-right, nationalist party such as the National Front? Electoral politics often boils down to how parties pitch their programs and whether and how they can persuade voters that a particular cleavage matters more than others and thus earn their votes.

Let us now examine in brief the main party families in Europe, moving from Left to Right across the spectrum. Not all states have all types of parties. Party systems will vary in terms of the number of parties, their relative strength, and their volatility from election to election.

Communist Parties

Communists ■ parties on the far Left that try to appeal mostly to urban, blue-collar workers and emphasize government ownership of industry and generous social welfare policies.

Communist parties occupy the far Left of the spectrum. They have been in sharp decline since the collapse of communism in Eastern Europe and the Soviet Union in 1989 through 1991, but they have been important forces in European politics. Obviously, they were the ruling parties in all of the communist countries in Eastern Europe,[16] although their "success" depended upon their ability to outlaw or suppress any form of political opposition. In Western Europe, Communist parties emerged as the largest parties immediately after World War II in both France and Italy, although in both states they were unable to capture a majority of the votes and form the government. Nonetheless, they were the dominant party on the Left in both states for several decades. In Greece, the Communist Party was also a sizeable force and fought a civil war after World War II against its centrist and right-wing opponents to win power. It lost the war and was banned until 1974. Communist parties have also had a sizeable presence in (Greek) Cyprus. In Sweden and Finland, communist parties regularly won parliamentary seats and at times offered their support to left-wing governments. Elsewhere, Communist parties did not fare so well, either because their ideas never caught on with voters (e.g., in Great Britain and West Germany) or because they were actively suppressed by right-wing, anti-communist governments (e.g., in Spain, Greece, and Turkey).

All Communist parties claim fealty to the ideas of Karl Marx (1818 to 1883), who railed against the injustices of the capitalist system. The actual program of Communists, taken from Karl Marx, includes state ownership of the "means of production" (meaning factories and land), government planning of the economy, and generous provision of social welfare benefits. Over the years, communism acquired an unsavory reputation thanks to its association with the Soviet Union and Eastern Europe, where some of Marx's core ideas—state ownership and planning—were implemented but were accompanied by political repression and eventually economic stagnation. After 1989, most of the Communist parties in Eastern Europe changed their names, usually dropping any reference to communism in favor of a less-tainted socialist or social democratic label. Some of these reformed communist parties have returned to power (e.g., in Lithuania, Poland, Slovenia, Hungary, Romania), but they have abandoned the core communist program of government control over the economy, and they have agreed to play the game of democratic politics.

In Western Europe, the once-mighty Communist parties in France and Italy are no more. Although popular among urban workers and some intellectuals, they were always burdened with an association with the repressive Soviet state, even though from the 1950s onward they condemned numerous actions of the Soviet government and tried to fashion their own "Euro-communism." Whereas they were able to appeal to more than 20 percent of voters even through the 1980s, the collapse of communism in Eastern Europe left many wondering about the feasibility or attractiveness of communism. In 2007 French parliamentary elections, the Communists won less than 5 percent of the vote—compared with 10 percent in 1997—and in the 2006 Italian elections the Communists—now split into two groups—collectively polled only 8 percent of the vote. Elsewhere, the Communist parties of Finland and Sweden have renamed themselves (the Left Alliance and Left Party) and abandoned much of the hard-core communist program, joining the Nordic Green Left Alliance cross-national group as a reflection of their desire to maintain respectability. They still win enough of the vote (8.8 percent in 2007 Finnish elections and 5.6 percent in 2010 Swedish elections) to make a difference, and both parties served in coalition governments in the 1990s and 2000s.

Green Parties

Greens ■ parties on the left of the political spectrum that emphasize environmentalism as well as peaceful approaches to international relations and minority rights.

Green parties, so named for their focus on environmental protection, emerged in the 1970s and 1980s. Green parties typically grew out of Socialist, Communist, or other left-wing parties, but they are less concerned about social class issues and more about quality of life issues. As such, they are a prototypical post-materialist phenomenon. As one would expect, environmental concerns—nuclear power, alternative energy, water and air quality, species protection, recycling—figure prominently in their platforms. Many of them also have a pacifist streak, growing out of the nuclear disarmament movement. Green parties have thus been critical of the deployment of European troops overseas (e.g., Afghanistan, Iraq) and favor cuts in their own states' military budgets. As left-wing parties, they also tend to support government regulation over aspects of the economy, the welfare state, grassroots democracy, women and minority rights (including those for homosexuals), and, controversially in some cases, the legalization of marijuana. Some—such as those in Germany and the Netherlands—are decidedly pro–European integration, whereas others, such as those in Sweden and Great Britain, are far less keen on the idea.

Green parties have fared best in northern European countries such as Sweden, the Netherlands, Finland, Germany, and Belgium, all of which also have strong environmental movements and multi-party political systems. In these states, Greens since the early 1980s have averaged 7 to 8 percent of the vote, giving them, potentially at least, a great deal of power in the formation of government coalitions. In 1995, the Finnish Green Party became the first Green party to enter into government, and in 1998 through 2005 the German Green Party served as a coalition to the Social Democrats in a "Red-Green Coalition." Joshka Fischer, leader of the

German Greens, became German foreign minister and Germany's most popular political figure, in part due to his arguments against the war in Iraq, which was widely unpopular in Germany. Greens have also served in governments in France, Sweden, Belgium, and Italy. Whereas some in the 1980s might have thought of the Greens as a short-term, "protest" type of development, it is clear that they will be a fixture in European politics, and, thanks in part to their efforts in drawing attention to environmental concerns, European states have gone "green" in terms of their environmental laws and regulations.

Green parties elsewhere are small, either because the electoral system works against small, start-up parties (as in Britain) or because there is not such a strong environmental consciousness (arguably true in Greece, Spain, and much of post-communist Europe). Nonetheless, they do exist in virtually every country, winning a few seats in national elections or those for the European Parliament. In February 2004, Indulis Emsis of the Latvian Green Party became the first Prime Minister from any European Green Party, although he managed to hold his coalition government together for less than a year.

Social Democratic Parties

The largest parties on the Left are Social Democratic parties. They go by different names (Social Democratic, Socialist, the Labour Party in the British or Dutch cases) and some countries (e.g., Portugal) have more than one, but most trace their roots back to the mid-late 1800s and the emergence of a social-democratic movement in Europe. Although influenced by Marx, their primary intellectual forebears are so-called Marxist "revisionists" such as the Germans Karl Kautsky and Edward Bernstein. They endorsed a more moderate perspective than revolutionary communists, rejecting the need for a violent revolution or complete government control over the economy. Instead they believed that the lower and working class could take advantage of the democratic process to elect parties that would serve their interests and reform capitalism to create a more just economic and social system. Trade unions were historically a crucial ally of Social Democratic parties, supplying funds, reliable voters, and party officials and solidifying the identity of **Social Democrats** as the party of the working class.

Social Democrats ■ term used to refer to a variety of parties on the Left that have traditionally embraced a strong role for government in the economy and generous welfare policies.

Although Social Democratic parties did come to power in some European states in the 1920s and 1930s, they really emerged as a powerful electoral force after World War II, best shown with the victory of the Labour Party over Winston Churchill's Conservatives in Great Britain in 1945, months after Churchill had played such a heroic role in the defeat of Hitler. In office, Social Democrats in many states established sizeable welfare states, expanded workers' rights, and set up corporatist systems of governance that gave unions a voice in setting economic policy. Although many Social Democratic parties were skeptical of European integration in the 1950s and 1960s, today most embrace the EU as a positive economic and political institution. In post-communist Europe, Social Democratic parties are frequently successors to the former Communist parties, moderating themselves and pledging to work for social and economic reforms within a democratic and capitalist framework. Today, parties from the Social Democratic "family" dominate the Left side of the European political spectrum across Europe, and in the

2000s they led governments in countries as diverse as Spain, Great Britain, Sweden, Germany, Poland, Romania, Italy, Greece, Turkey, and Slovakia.

Although these parties have a tradition as a party of the working class and a party of "big government," that has changed in recent years as the number of blue-collar manufacturing jobs has shrunk in favor of more white-collar jobs in the service sector, where employees are less likely to view themselves as members of the "working class."[17] As a consequence, Social Democratic parties have broadened their base, appealing in particular to state employees, workers in the arts and in education, and students, and they are the overwhelming choice of voters in European urban centers such as London, Paris, Madrid, Vienna, Berlin, and Rome. One challenge for Social Democrats, as we shall examine in greater detail in Chapter 10, is that the welfare state is under assault across Europe due to demographic and global economic pressures, making it harder for parties on the left to advocate "tax and spend" policies as they did in the past. Thus, since the 1990s, many parties on the Left have moved towards the political center in search of a so-called **Third Way** between capitalism and communism.

Third Way ■ term used to refer a middle ground between capitalism and communism and embraced by some on the political Left who moved toward the political center in the 1990s.

This phenomenon can be seen in many countries, and, as noted in the **Is Europe One?** feature, has even taken on pan-European dimensions in an effort to force greater transnational links among like-minded parties. In Great Britain, Tony Blair, who became leader of the Labour Party in 1994, argued for a "New Labour," one that would move to the center to appeal to more middle-class British voters. Under Blair, the Labour Party renounced previous policies such as state ownership of economic enterprises and curtailed the powers of the trade unions. Blair became Prime Minister in 1997, and pushed through so many economic programs associated with the Right (e.g., tax cuts, welfare reform) that critics accused him of being Margaret Thatcher in a suit. In Germany, Gerhard Schröder of the Social Democratic Party became Chancellor in 1998 and, like Blair, advocated a series of reforms such as tax cuts for businesses and less generous welfare policies. In France, which has a long tradition of state intervention in the economy, François Mitterand, elected in 1981 as the first Socialist President, turned away from a left-wing platform and oversaw numerous privatizations of state-owned firms.[18] His successor as head of the Socialist Party, Lionel Jospin, ran for president in 2002 claiming that, "My program is not socialist."[19] In the 1990s in Poland and Hungary, left-wing Social Democratic parties, which were the reformed successor organizations of the old, discredited communist parties, continued the free-market economic reforms pursued by right-wing governments after the collapse of communism.

This is not to say that all Social Democratic parties have abandoned their beliefs. There are still real differences between the Left and Right on economic questions, and "big government" can still win votes, especially as some people want some protections from globalization and free market capitalism. For example, in 2007 in France, Ségolène Royal, the presidential candidate of the Socialist Party, launched her campaign with proposals that included increases in the minimum wage, unemployment benefits, and pensions, interest-free loans for eighteen-year-olds, and renationalizing some French companies.[23] However, with France already deeply in debt and with some of the highest taxes in Europe, it is unclear how any elected French leader could deliver on such promises. She lost, making, at least to the time being, such a question moot.

IS EUROPE ONE?

The Europeanization of Political Parties

Political parties are quintessentially national organizations, succeeding or failing on the basis of their ability to appeal to national-level voters. Even within party families, one finds significant differences in both style and substance among different national parties. At the same time, however, as European countries face a host of common problems (e.g., immigration, pressures on the welfare state, globalization) and the power of the EU is growing, might one see greater convergence or coordination among political parties? In other words, are parties becoming "Europeanized," adapting to the demands, constraints, and opportunities of European integration?

Evidence is mixed, and in many ways one could say that parties—as opposed to courts, parliaments, and executives—are the least Europeanized of all political institutions in Europe. True, as explained in Chapter 4, similar political parties form groups within the European Parliament and parties sit and caucus on a pan-European, not national, level. For example, most Christian Democratic parties belong to the European Peoples' Party, most Social Democrats belong to the Party of European Socialists, and Greens belong to the European Federation of Green Parties. These umbrella organizations provide a means for different national political parties to consult with each other and forge common positions on European issues. However, these groups do not always vote as a bloc, and MEPs (Members of the European Parliament) are far more accountable to their national parties than any pan-European organization. Moreover, because elections to the European Parliament are conducted on a national level with national parties, national-level issues (e.g., is the government popular? is unemployment falling?) often figure more than cross-national, European issues. Just as there is no "European" electorate, there are no "European"—as opposed to national—political parties.[20]

Additionally, there is little to suggest that European issues have significantly changed the organizational structure of most European political parties. Surveys among parties reveal that there has been little structural adaptation to pan-European or EU concerns. Moreover, MEPs are not usually not particularly influential within their respective political parties, which serves to minimize any sort of socialization effect one might hope is provided by work in the European Parliament.[21]

This is not to suggest that party leaders are unaware of the need for more cooperation on the pan-European level. This is arguably gone furthest with the Greens and the center-left parties, which are among the keenest for European integration. For example, in the 1990s Tony Blair and Gerhard Schröder, then leaders of Great Britain and Germany, together with former US President Bill Clinton, sponsored a series of high-level meetings to discuss the previously mentioned "Third Way." They issued a well-publicized manifesto ("Europe: The Third Way/The New Middle") on this concept in 1999, and subsequent meetings involved leaders from the political left in Sweden, Italy, the Netherlands, as well as Latin American and African countries. The aim was to fashion a common response among left-wing parties to social and economic challenges of globalization and how best to reform welfare states. Blair even reached out to the Conservative leader of Spain, José María Anzar (1996–2004), for his input into how to transform European social democracies. Many, however, were skeptical that these efforts had any lasting impact, and some political parties (e.g., the French Socialist Party) clearly had little enthusiasm for the idea.[22] In short, although many European political parties are supporters for more European integration, it is too early to say that parties are forging links in such a way that would be congruent with the notion of a single European polity.

Critical Thinking Questions

1. Assuming one wanted greater "Europeanization" among political parties, how might one accomplish that goal? Think about how in the US parties often tend to have more of a national than regional or local focus.
2. Is the relative lack of "Europeanization" among political parties evidence that the powers of the EU are exaggerated? Or does it tend to reflect more on *how* the EU has acquired power?

The Liberals

In the American view, "liberal" is associated with the Left. In Europe, however, **Liberals** occupy what could best be described as the political center. By "liberal," they refer back to the classic expositions of European liberalism by, among others, John Locke, Alexis de Tocqueville, Adam Smith, and John Stuart Mill. The common thread for all liberals is a belief in limited government and individual freedom, making many European liberals similar to US Libertarians. Their primary political basis is businesspeople and urban professionals, although, in Scandinavia, the Liberals (or Centrists, as they are frequently known) are successors to the most powerful Agrarian Parties and do try to appeal to rural voters. Most Liberal parties tend to be pro-European integration.

Liberals ■ parties of the political center that combine a commitment to free markets with a belief for social tolerance and individual rights.

Liberalism, however, contains two main components. One is free-market liberalism, a belief that the state should minimize interference with the market. Liberal parties are often the loudest champions of free markets in Europe, although most European Liberals accept the need for some sort of welfare state as a social safety net. The other strand of liberalism is social-liberalism, a more post-materialist orientation that emphasizes the need for individual rights and more progressive state policies. These include civil rights, legalized abortion, more opportunities for political participation, and, frequently, government spending in areas such as education to expand opportunities. Examples of Liberal parties that emphasize the first component are the Free Democratic Party in Germany, the People's Party for Freedom and Justice in the Netherlands, the Civic Platform in Poland, and the Estonian Reform Party. Examples of those more focused on social-liberalism include the Liberal-Democratic Party in Great Britain, Democrats 66 in the Netherlands, and the Center Party in Finland.

Liberals are rarely the dominant political party in any European country, but, because in many respects they occupy a middle ground between the Left and Right, they have been attractive coalition partners. For example, the German Free Democratic Party and the Dutch People's Party for Freedom and Justice have served in several post–World War II coalition governments, allying themselves at times with Social Democrats and at other times with Christian Democratic parties on the Right. In the 2000s, Liberals supplied the Prime Minister in Finland, Denmark, Estonia, Iceland, and Romania, and served in coalition governments in Belgium, Germany, the Netherlands, and Sweden.

The Christian Democrats

The center-right portion of the political spectrum in Europe is represented by two groups of parties. One is the **Christian Democrats.** The Christian Democrats have

Christian Democrats ■ parties on the center-right that tend to favor a mixed economy while making some appeals on the basis of traditional "value" issues.

been the dominant political party on the Right in Germany, the Netherlands, Austria, Malta, Switzerland, and Belgium, and, until 1992, Italy.[24] Some—those in Austria, Italy, Belgium, and (formerly) Italy—are Roman Catholic in origin, whereas Scandinavian Christian Democratic Parties—strongest in Norway—are Protestant in origin. In Germany, there are technically two Christian Democratic Parties (the Christian Democratic Union and Christian Social Union, the latter centered in the overwhelmingly Catholic region of Bavaria) and the Netherlands, with a history of separate parties based upon religion, has a bi-confessional party alliance, the Dutch Christian Democratic Appeal.

Obvious question about these parties is what they mean by "Christian" and what place they have in a secular Europe? These are not easy questions to answer. Many of these parties—particularly the Catholic ones—originally appeared as a response to secular, left-wing Social Democratic parties, and they stood for (among other things) defending the interests of the Church. Today, they are more secular in their orientation, although they still campaign for traditional values such as restrictions on abortion, against gay marriage and euthanasia (the latter very sensitive in Germany due to Nazi policies), and even engage in quixotic campaigns to restrict alcohol and pornography in famously liberal, permissive countries such as Sweden. Some of their Christian inclinations, however, have also pushed them (compared to Conservative parties on the right) toward the Left, as most Christian Democratic parties accept the need for consensual politics between different class interests and accept the idea that society has an obligation toward the poor and less advantaged. Consequently, they not only accept many aspects of the welfare state but actually oversaw construction of strong welfare states and mixed forms of economic statism and capitalism (e.g., the "social market economy" in Germany, strong corporatist institutions in Austria that give a voice to trade unions and try to promote social consensus) when they were in government in the 1950s and 1960s. Many social-welfare policies (e.g., maternity leaves, subsidized child care) are also supported by Christian Democrats as "pro-family." While it would be fair to say that Christian Democratic parties are to the Right (meaning more pro-market) than Social Democratic parties, the former have not rushed to embrace radical neo-liberalism that seeks to remove the state from the economy. Indeed, in one of her first initiatives after becoming Chancellor of Germany in 2005, Angela Merkel of the Christian Democratic Union supported an increase in the value-added-tax in Germany, a move that Prime Margaret Thatcher of the British Conservative Party (1979–1990) would have found anathema. Christian Democrats also tend to be in favor of European integration.

Christian Democrats were strong—one might even say dominant—in many Western European countries in the years immediately following World War II. Since the 1980s, their share of vote has dropped in many countries, including former strongholds such as Germany, the Netherlands, and Belgium, reflecting in large part the rise of both Liberal and far-right parties. In post-communist Europe, Christian Democratic parties—typically embracing a combination of nationalism, market economics, and at times economic populism—have done best in Slovakia, Hungary, and Poland, all countries with a Catholic tradition. Smaller Christian Democratic parties exist in the Czech Republic, Romania, and Slovenia.

Although it may seem peculiar, one could place Turkey's Justice and Development Party (JDP) in the Christian Democratic family. True, the JDP has

Islamic roots, thereby obviously meaning it is not a *Christian* Democratic party. However, it won election in 2002 and reelection in 2007 emphasizing not only a more public role for religion in a state which since the 1920s has enforced secularism, but also a communitarianism rooted in social responsibility. To the extent that the JDP advocates "traditional values" and more open markets tempered with policies to help the disadvantaged, it is, ironically, closer to the Christian Democratic tradition than any other party in Turkey, and aligns itself with the Christian Democratic–dominated European People's Party in pan-European party forums.

The Conservatives

The other center-right parties in Europe belong to a family that might best be described as **Conservatives.** Although they may make reference to defending "traditional values" and appeal to more religious voters, Conservative parties do not carry a religious label. Conservatives are generally associated with pro-business policies and traditionally received most of their support from the upper and middle classes, although, as class-based voting has dissipated throughout Europe, many Conservative parties try to appeal to lower-class voters by touting the ability of freer markets to be both more efficient than state intervention and to create economic opportunities for all members of society. Conservatives in general tend to be more skeptical of the EU than parties on the Left, perhaps because they associate the EU with excessive regulation and assaults on the traditional prerogatives of the state. Many conservative parties emphasize the need for a strong national defense and "law and order" issues. As immigration and multi-culturalism have emerged as major issues—and fed the growth of far-right parties—Conservatives have espoused programs to limit immigration and to defend cultural traditions and national patriotism.

Conservatives ■ parties on the center-right that tend to emphasize free markets, "law and order" issues, and upholding traditions; they are often opposed to greater European integration.

Whereas all Conservative parties occupy the Right side of the political spectrum, they do vary, especially in how far they embrace free market principles. The British Conservative Party, especially during and after the reign of Prime Minister Margaret Thatcher, has been most strongly associated with free-market policies, advocating privatization, tax cuts, cuts in government programs, and reforms in fields such as education to get more room for personal choice and non-state initiatives. Whereas the Conservatives succeeded under Thatcher and support for the free market became the new orthodoxy in Britain—breaking with more than three decades of political consensus on the necessity for a strong state role in the economy—by the end of the 1990s they were seen as out of new ideas and out of touch with British voters, and since lost three straight elections (1997, 2001, 2005) to the Labour Party. Elsewhere, the closest party to the British Conservatives is the Czech Civic Democratic Party, led in the 1990s by Václav Klaus, then the prime minister and an open admirer of Margaret Thatcher and other advocates of the free market such as Milton Friedman and Friedrich Hayek. Like Thatcher, Klaus was also critical of what he saw as socialist tendencies in the EU, suggesting at one point that he did not think the Czechs should lower themselves to enter the EU.

Elsewhere, Conservative parties are more accommodating to statist economic policies. For example, in France, the political right is associated with the legacy of Charles de Gaulle who, among other things, advocated a strong state role in the economy (*dirigisme*) to advance the French nationalism and power. Although France has curtailed the state's role in the economy in the past two decades, there has been no Thatcherite revolution. Indeed, the "Right" in France, on questions of the state's role in the economy, has often been more to the "Left" than that of the Labour Party in Britain or the Democratic Party in the US. Indeed, the idea of adopting Anglo-American free-market principles is anathema to many in France, with the center-right government led by the Union for a Popular Majority (UMP) backing away from even tepid reforms in labor policy after widespread protests in 2006. In Scandinavia, Conservative parties have traditionally played by the rules of consensus politics, often cooperating with the political Left and accepting many aspects of the welfare state. However, as the idea of free-market economics has spread in popularity across the globe, they have become more aggressive in attacking some elements of statist policies (e.g., high marginal tax rates) that are not particularly popular with the public. This has proved a winning strategy, as Conservative parties joined coalition governments after elections in Denmark (2001, 2005), Norway (2001), and Sweden (2006, 2010). Conservative parties are also a major political force in Greece, Spain, Ireland, Poland, Croatia, and Hungary, and they do best where they do not have to compete on the Right with Christian Democratic parties.

The Radical Right

Far-right parties, defined by their nationalism and xenophobia (fear of foreigners), have emerged in numerous European states. They emphasize rights for the titular nationality (e.g., France for the French!), and worry deeply about immigration and the erosion of national power thanks to globalization and the growth of the EU. They are in many respects protest parties, galvanized by economic and cultural changes that they feel are causing irreparable harm to the established order. While some of their complaints about immigrants are grounded in economic concern about job loss, many of these parties, such as Hungary's Jobbik mentioned at the outset of this chapter, have a racist edge, attacking the perceived dirtiness, dishonesty, sexual voraciousness, criminality, and inferiority of non-white or non-Christian peoples (e.g., Algerians and Jews in France, Moroccans in the Netherlands, Pakistanis and Africans in Great Britain, Turks and Bosnians in Austria, Jews and Roma in Eastern Europe). They represent, in many people's views, an ugly side of European politics, one that harkens back to fascist movements and earlier incarnations of anti-Semitism and racism.

A few quotes from some prominent leaders of the radical right will suffice. Jean Marie Le Pen, the long-time leader of the FN in France—and who came in second in French Presidential elections in 2002 and whose party has received over 9 percent of the vote in all parliamentary elections since 1986—remarked in 1987 that the gas chambers were a "mere detail" of World War II, complained that the French national soccer team (which won the 1998 World Cup) was made up of too many Arabs and blacks, and that the Islamic veil "protects us from ugly women."[25] He was convicted in 1987 for inciting racial hatred by casting doubt on Nazi persecution of the Jews and in 2000 was banned from political office for a year for assaulting a Socialist opponent. In Italy, Umberto Bossi, head of the *Lega*

Nord—the leading vote-getter in 1994 elections—suggested that "immigration consists of Muslim invaders and common criminals from the Third World." In Austria, Jorg Haidar, former leader of the Freedom Party—which won more votes (27 percent) than any other party in 1999 elections and served in the government—was quoted as saying, "There is something of a problem with the blacks . . . There is just not much of a brain about."[26]

If these parties polled only 1 to 2 percent of the national vote—as has been the case with the British National Party or the German National Democratic Party[27]—one might not have much cause for concern. However, parties of the far right have done well across Europe. In addition to France, Italy—which also has the small Freedom of Action Party that was founded by Mussolini's granddaughter—and Austria, parties and candidates of the far Right have done well in Norway, Switzerland, Denmark, Sweden, Romania, Hungary, and Serbia. For example, in Denmark, the anti-immigrant Danish Peoples' Party won over 12 percent of the vote in three elections in the 2000s and has lent its support to a minority liberal-conservative coalition government. In 2005, one of its parliamentarians was reported to have compared Muslim women who wear a headscarf to bikers who sport swastikas.[28] In Serbia, the Radical Party won the largest number of votes (28.5 percent) of any party in January 2007 elections, despite the fact that the party's leader, Vojislav Seselj, was at the time of the election standing trial for war crimes in The Hague for his actions against Croats and Bosnians during the wars in the former Yugoslavia. In 2007, the Swiss People's Party won the largest share of all Swiss parties (29 percent), running on a platform to expel immigrants and their family members if someone commits a crime. One of the more interesting anti-immigrant parties in Europe was the List Pim Fortuyn, founded in the Netherlands by Pim Forutyn, a gay, formerly left-wing, university professor who objected to Muslim immigration on the grounds that Islam was incompatible with Dutch traditions of liberalism and tolerance. He was killed by an animal rights activist in 2002, and posthumously his party won 17 percent of the vote in 2002, becoming the second largest party in the Dutch parliament. Its anti-Islamic and anti-immigration platform has been picked up by the Dutch Freedom Party, which won 16 percent of the vote in 2010 elections. The Freedom Party is led by Geert Wilders, who has suggested, among other things, that the Koran, the Muslim holy book be banned in the Netherlands.

Why would someone vote for these parties? Aside from appealing to racists, they tap into concerns that countries are being taken over by foreigners or foreign forces that cannot be controlled. To those sympathetic to the far Right, their national leaders—whether on the Right or (especially) on the Left—are sell-outs to the true national interest. These parties do particularly well with the unemployed or economically insecure, who in the past tended to vote for Communists or Social Democrats. Beyond this constituency, many Europeans are quick to blame economic or social ills on immigrants, and thus the idea of curtailing immigration is a political winner, as it has been picked up by more mainstream right-wing parties throughout the continent. As noted later in this text in Chapter 12, after 9/11, 3/11 (Madrid train bombings in 2004), and 7/7 (London transportation bombings in 2005), anti-immigrant, anti-Muslim feelings reached new heights. As much as many Europeans express dismay at statements by some of the leaders of these parties, it is clear that they are not simply going to disappear. They may not win a majority of seats or take over a government, but they will exercise political influence in many states.

Regional Parties and Parties of Ethnic Minorities

Outside of the Left–Right framework, one could also mention parties that try to appeal to voters in a particular region or those belonging to an ethnic minority. Examples include the Scottish National Party (SNP), the *Lega Nord* in Italy, Convergence and Union in Catalonia, the Democratic Union of Hungarians in Romania, the Swedish Peoples' Party in Finland, and the Movement for Rights and Freedoms that is allied with the Turkish minority in Bulgaria. Some (e.g., the SNP) are more closely tied to the Left. Others (e.g., the *Lega Nord*) are aligned with the Right. What they do have in common are arguments for decentralization of power. Most also tend to be pro-EU, seeing the EU as a source of protection against, in their view, national governments that are concerned with augmenting their own power. These parties, almost by definition, cannot win national power. However, they have served in coalition governments in countries such as Italy, Slovakia, Bulgaria, Romania, and Finland.

CAMPAIGNS AND VOTER TURNOUT

Let us now turn to the feature which interests all political parties and is present in all electoral systems: elections themselves. Because they have parliamentary systems, most European countries do not have elections on a regular, predictable cycle as in the US or Mexico, because Prime Ministers may see an advantage in calling for early elections. Thus while there is no fixed four- or six-year term of office, they cannot serve indefinitely without having elections: the maximum time between elections in most European states is four years (as in Germany, Sweden, Spain, Romania, and Poland) or five years (as in France, Great Britain, and Italy).

In addition to selecting members of national, regional, and local governments, Europeans may also participate in referendums.[29] Referendums provide for "direct democracy," allowing citizens to vote directly on a policy question. As noted in the previous chapter, this practice is most common in Switzerland, where it has a history of more than one hundred years. Constitutional questions also require a referendum in Spain, Ireland, Denmark, and Estonia, and in many states governments have the option of putting a question before voters. Referendums have been important on numerous occasions and often receive more attention than normal governmental elections. Examples from recent European history include French voters' approval for a directly elected president (1962), a British referendum affirming its membership in the European Community (1975), rejections of membership in the European Community by Norway (1972, 1994), liberalization of abortion (1992) and divorce (1995) in Catholic Ireland, referendums for devolution in Scotland and Wales (1997), votes for independence from the Soviet Union in Lithuania, Estonia, and Latvia between 1990 and 1991, Italy's change of electoral system (voted on in 1991), narrow French approval of the Maastricht Treaty on EU in 1992, accession to the EU and joining NATO in a number of former communist states in the 1990s and 2000s, Sweden's rejection of the euro (2003), French and

Dutch rejection in 2005 of the proposed EU Constitutional Treaty, and Montenegro's separation from Serbia in 2006. Advocates of direct democracy claim that it reflects the true meaning of democratic government—the people rules themselves and make their own laws—whereas critics claim that the process is unwieldy, favors more mobilized "special interests," and is not the best way to resolve controversial issues.

Regardless of whether candidates, parties, or policy questions are on the ballot, there is certain to be a campaign to mobilize public opinion and ultimately get people to the polls. Campaigns, by their very nature, are idiosyncratic affairs, conditioned upon the nature of the candidates, parties, political culture, and electoral system. A couple of observations about European campaigns, however, generally hold. The first is that the "official" campaign season in most European states is relatively short. Elections are not regularly scheduled. Instead, with a few exceptions, the government announces them only a few weeks in advance. While this period is considered the actual campaign, in reality in Europe (as in every democratic state) campaigning never really stops. In the parliamentary systems of Europe the opposition must be prepared for elections to be called at any time. Rather than going through a long US-presidential primary cycle to choose a challenger, the opposition creates a **shadow cabinet,** a mock cabinet of members of the opposition that signals to voters who will assume positions of leadership should the opposition come to power. The shadow cabinet also provides a means for the opposition to criticize the government, as, for example, the "shadow" finance minister is in charge of explaining why the government's economic plans are ill conceived or not as successful as their proponents claim.

shadow cabinet ■ a group of political figures from the opposition that leads the criticism of the current government and constitutes a sort of mock cabinet, signaling to voters who would serve in government should the opposition win the next election.

Secondly, at least compared to the US, campaigns in Europe are far less expensive. Most countries prohibit widespread television or radio advertising, preferring instead to offer parties a quota of limited advertisements (e.g., in Great Britain the parties get 5 five-minute slots on national television).[30] Several countries do offer parties state-financing, usually tied to their past electoral performance, which of course favors the more established parties. Most countries put caps on party or candidate spending and/or on the amount individuals can contribute to a campaign, although enforcement is frequently a problem, not only in newer democracies in post-communist Europe,[31] but also in Italy, France, Germany, and Great Britain, which were all afflicted by major campaign finance scandals in the 1990s and 2000s. The net result is that spending is much less than in the US. For example, one study concluded that in 2001 a grand total of $1.65 was spent per voter in British elections compared with $13.50 spent in 2000 in the US.[32] Nonetheless, during the time of a political campaign, parties find ways of getting their message across—print advertising, placards, banners, leaflets, and, as I discovered in Austria in 2005, balloons, chocolates, and even free yogurt drinks emblazoned with a party's label.

Notions that one can distinguish between European and US political campaigns may be less true than they used to be. Modern campaign techniques—including polling, use of focus groups, and utilization of the Internet—are now widespread, and even well-known US pollsters such as Stan Greenberg (a Democrat) and Frank Luntz (Republican) regularly work in Europe.[33] Any conception that political campaigning in the US is "dirtier" or "nastier" than in Europe can be dispelled by incidents such as when John Prescott, a deputy prime minister from the

British Labour Party, punched a citizen on the campaign trail in 2001 after the man allegedly threw a tomato at him, or when Prime Minister Silvio Berlusconi in Italy called supporters of his opponents "vampires" and "dickheads" during the 2006 campaign.[34] Ségolène Royal, the first female major party candidate for the French presidency, took a page out of Hillary Clinton's playbook in her 2006–2007 campaign with a well-publicized "listening tour" that included more than 6,000 (many virtual) town meetings.[35] Successful challenges at the European Court of Human Rights by British anti-abortion and animal rights activists may also lead to a loosening of restrictions on political advertising, opening the gates further to mass-media campaigns.

Irrespective of current restrictions on their campaigning, there is little doubt that most European parties outperform their US counterparts in the final result: getting voters to the polls. In general, turnout in European elections is high, particularly when compared with the US. Some states—Austria, Belgium, Cyprus, Italy, Luxembourg, and Turkey—have mandatory voting, although enforcement of this law varies (stronger in Cyprus and Belgium). Turnout tends to be better when voters think there is more at stake, which make explain (in part) why turnout is markedly lower for elections to the European Parliament (discussed in Chapter 4). Continent-wide, there is wide variation in turnout in national elections, as seen in Figures 8.1 and 8.2. The highest turnout in a country without a mandatory voting laws is in Iceland, whereas the lowest turnouts are in Great Britain, Switzerland, Poland, Romania, and Lithuania. The table gives some evidence to support the argument that turnout has declined over time, perhaps

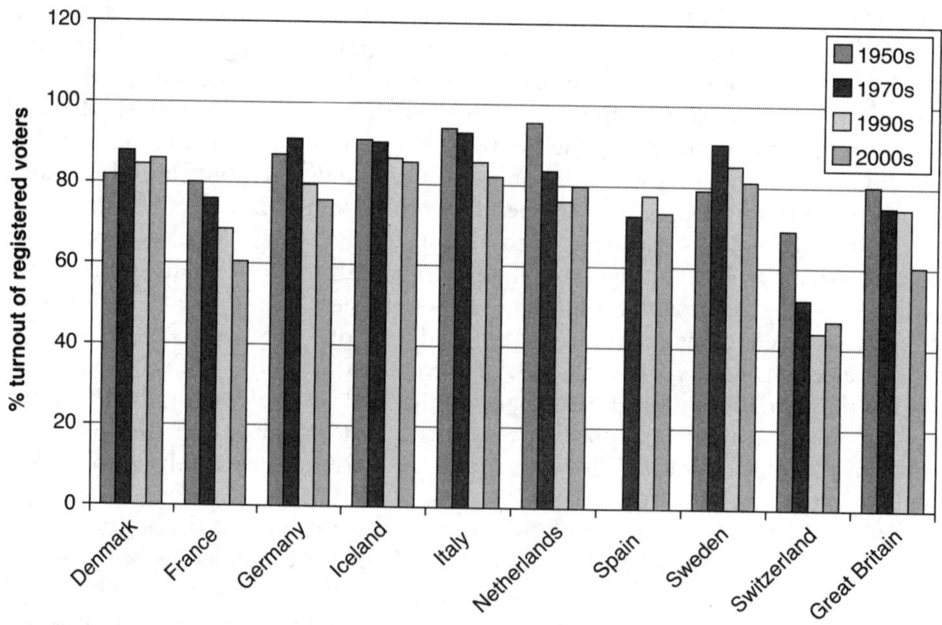

FIGURE 8.1
Trends in Voter Turnout in Western Europe
Source: International Institute for Democracy and Electoral Assistance, http://www.idea.int/vt. Elections refer to national parliamentary elections.

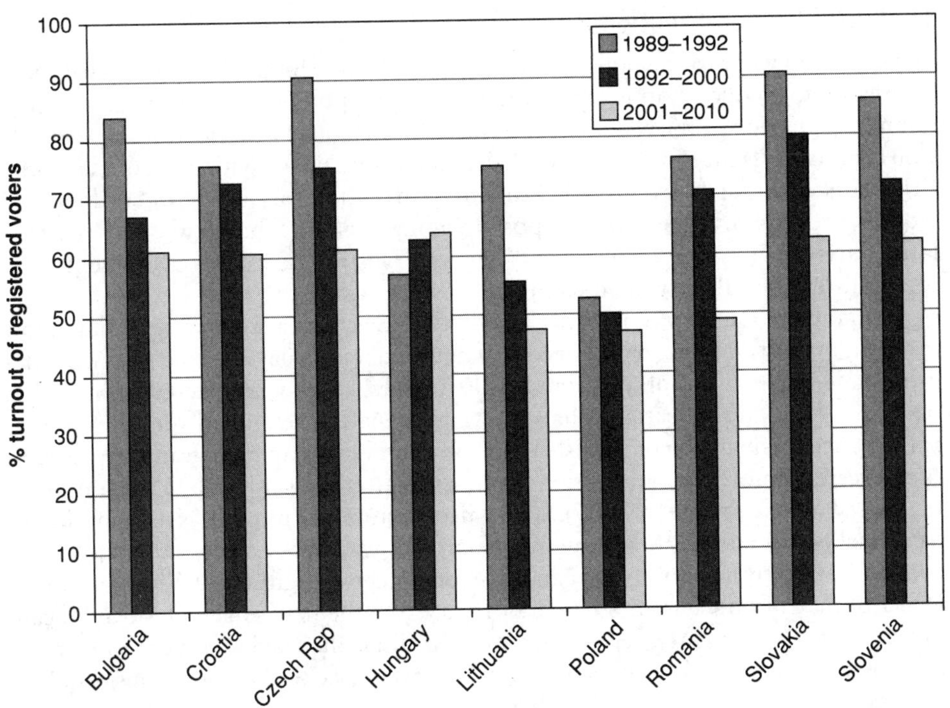

FIGURE 8.2

Trends in Voter Turnout in Post-Communist Europe

Source: International Institute for Democracy and Electoral Assistance, http://www.idea.int/vt. Elections refer to national parliamentary elections.

reflecting a general disengagement with things political. This trend is most marked in post-communist states, as seen in Figure 8.2, where voting turnout has fallen precipitously since the first free, democratic elections in the early 1990s. However, not all European states have seen a decline in voter turnout. As for the question of who votes, older and better-educated citizens tend to vote more. Gender gaps that appeared in the 1950s have now closed, with recent data showing no significant difference in turnout between men and women.[36]

RECENT EUROPEAN ELECTIONS

Thus far, we have discussed parties, elections, and voting primarily in very general terms. In order to get a better grasp of both how political parties and electoral systems actually function as well as learn about some of the issues that concern electorates, let us look at some recent elections in Europe. Obviously, one could choose any number of cases, and arguably each country's elections produce something worthy of discussion. Here we examine elections from 2007 to 2010 in four of the larger countries in Europe, using these cases both to shed light on the individual countries as well as to illustrate some points made earlier in the chapter.

The 2007 French Elections

French voters went to the polls in 2007 in a "collective funk."[37] After twelve years as President, Jacques Chirac, associated with corruption, indecisiveness, and economic stagnation, enjoyed little public confidence. The rejection of the EU Constitutional Treaty in 2005 revealed French uneasiness with the course of the EU. Riots—primarily by French Muslims—in 2005, coupled with student and worker protests in 2006 over proposed changes in the labor laws, showed that large parts of French society were angry and frustrated. Voters overwhelmingly told pollsters that they wanted change.

As noted in Chapter 6, in order to win the French presidency, a candidate must receive a majority of the votes. If no candidate receives a majority, the top two vote-getters advance to a run-off election. In 2007, twelve candidates entered the race, but only four were given a serious chance of advancing to the second round. Nicholas Sarkozy, the serving Interior Minister and son of a Hungarian immigrant, appealed to those desiring more law and order (a big issue after African and Muslim minorities rioted across France in 2005), while also positioning himself as a champion of free-market economic reforms, which he argued was necessary to create jobs and economic growth. He ran as the candidate of the center-right UMP. Ségolène Royal, leader of the Poitou-Charentes region of France and the first female presidential candidate from a major party, represented the Socialists. She tried to appear to be more compassionate—in stark contrast to the more hard-nosed Sarkozy—promising a host of statist economic initiatives (e.g., higher minimum wage, more investments in research and technology) to rejuvenate the economy. Notably, she was not the head of the Socialist Party—that office was occupied by François Holland, Royal's domestic partner and father of her four children—but she was popular due to her charisma and the fact that she, by virtue of her gender if nothing else, clearly represented change. François Bayrou, leader of the center-liberal Union for French Democracy (UDF), fashioned himself as the alternative to the broken-down and "tribal" two-party system.[38] Many saw him as a viable dark-horse candidate. Lastly, as had been the case for over two decades, there was Jean-Marie Le Pen of the FN, who had, to the dismay of many in France and beyond, advanced to the second round in 2002.

The first round in April 2007 produced no great surprise. The two major-party candidates, Sarkozy and Royal, won the most votes, but neither garnered a majority, necessitating a run-off. Bayrou, notably, refused to endorse either candidate, creating added drama and uncertainty to the second round, as the question was where "his" voters would go. Ultimately, Sarkozy prevailed thanks in large measure to his greater experience and his promises to make a break with the past and adopt decisive reforms on the economy, on immigration, and in foreign policy to rekindle French pride and confidence. Given his background, relative youth (fifty-two), and the fact that he openly discussed the necessity for the French to embrace both free-market reforms and a closer relationship with the US, he clearly represented something new. Although some viewed Sarkozy as too dogmatic, he surprised some critics by naming the more consensual François Fillon as prime minister and selecting a diverse cabinet that included seven women (out of fifteen portfolios) and four figures associated with the political Left, including Bernard Kouchner, a well-known humanitarian and founder of *Médecins sans frontières* (Doctors without Borders), who became foreign minister.

TABLE 8.2

2007 Elections in France

Presidential Elections			Parliamentary Elections				
Candidate	% Vote Round 1	% Vote Round 2	Party	% Vote in Round 1	Total Seats	Gain/ Loss	% Seats
N. Sarkozy	31.2	53.1	UMP	39.5	313	–44	54.2
S. Royal	25.9	49.4	Socialists	24.7	186	+46	32.2
F. Bayrou	18.6		MD	7.6	3	n/a	0.5
J.M. Le Pen	10.4		FN	4.3	0	0	0
			Communist	4.3	15	–6	2.6
			Others	19.6	60	–8	10.4

Turnout: 85 percent and 84 percent in the presidential elections; 60 percent in parliamentary elections.

Source: Election results as reported on Wikipedia.

Two months later, the French went to the polls to elect a new National Assembly from among 7,639 candidates vying for 577 seats. Sarkozy, fresh from his victory, urged voters to give him a parliamentary majority so he could implement his reform program. The Socialists ran largely on a platform to deny Sarkozy too much power. Bayrou set up a new centrist party, the Democratic Movement (MD), although most of the erstwhile UDF joined with the UMP or the pro-UMP New Center Party. As shown in Table 8.2, Sarkozy's UMP did get a majority of seats in the National Assembly, although, to the surprise of many, they lost seats compared to the 2002 elections. Note also that it did not get a majority of the votes in the first round (when voters were given a full slate of candidates), making the outcome disproportional. The Socialists did better than expected, even though Royal declined to run for a seat. Bayrou's MD, because it could not make alliances in the second round, could not translate its votes into many seats. Le Pen's FN did worse than it had in any election since the 1980s, arguably showing that the French were tired of his extreme xenophobia, but also, perhaps, because the UMP had appropriated much of his anti-immigrant platform. The fact that "radical" parties on both the right and left won nearly a quarter of the vote, however, shows that a large number of French people are not satisfied with more established, mainstream options.

The 2007 Polish Elections

In the fall of 2007, Poles elected both a new *Sejm* (lower house of parliament) and a Senate, the sixth parliamentary elections since the collapse of communist rule in 1989. Poland obviously does not have venerable traditions of democracy as in Western Europe. Not surprisingly, previous elections in post-communist Poland revealed both a great deal of electoral volatility, with new parties forming in almost every election and power alternating between parties of the left and the right, and volatility in the party system itself, with only one party (the agrarian-based Polish Peoples' Party) surviving from 1991 to 2009. The general issue of the stability and instability of party systems across Europe is taken up in the **In Focus** section.

IN FOCUS

The Stability and Volatility of Party Systems

How stable and dynamic are party systems in Europe? For much of this chapter, we have described the existing spectrum of parties in Europe, but have not explored in depth how they have evolved, how they might be changing, and whether some countries have a more volatile system than others.

In the initial post–World War II period, stability appeared to be the norm. Seymour Lipset and Stein Rokkan, who did much of the pioneering work on political cleavages, maintained that cleavages were frozen, producing stable political alignments and electoral results. One set of authors, writing at the end of the 1960s, maintained that rather than explaining change, the primary need was to explain the absence of change in democratic countries of Western Europe.[39]

It would be difficult to make such an argument today. Already by the 1970s scholars were noting the breakdown of traditional (e.g., class) voting patterns, the formation of new cleavages, and the creation of new political parties.[40] Politics became more volatile and in some cases unpredictable as social structure began to change (e.g., growth of the service sector at the expense of manufacturing and agriculture) and voters switched allegiances and in some cases their identities (e.g., declining prominence of religion). New issues (e.g., the environment, immigration) rose to prominence, and, the realignment of the European party systems around new sets of cleavages (e.g., post-materialism) became a subject of concerted inquiry. Moving the discussion forward in time, in the 1990s and 2000s, new technologies also changed the ways people learned about and participated in politics.

That being said, how dynamic are party systems? The answer is that it depends—both on what one examines and which country is the subject of discussion. Consider, for example, established democracies such as Germany, the Netherlands, and Great Britain. In each, politics since World War II has been dominated by catch-all parties on the center-right (Christian Democrats in Germany and Christian Democrats and Liberals the Netherlands, Conservatives in Britain) and on the center-left (Labour in the Netherlands and Britain, Social Democrats in Germany). Whereas each election has it ups and downs, the results of the major parties in these states have stayed rather similar over several decades. Moreover, continent-wide, if one looks at the overall vote of parties of the left and parties of the center and right over time, there is remarkable stability—parties of the right and center command approximately 55 percent of the vote, parties of the left about 40 percent of the vote.[41]

This statistic, however, may obscure more than it reveals. Within general left/right divides, there have been important changes. On the Left, the Communists have declined in the past two decades, whereas the Greens have established themselves as important political players in several states. On the Right, far-right parties, which emerged mostly on the issue of immigration, are now well entrenched in many states. This is driven by only by changing issues (demand) but also by the electoral system (supply), as the proportional representation system in most European countries facilitates the emergence of new, smaller parties. In other cases, such as Italy's Christian Democrats, volatility has meant their complete disappearance (destroyed by corruption scandals), although they have been replaced by other parties with a different focus or ideology on the right wide of the political spectrum.

Even in countries, with plurality systems, however, there has been volatility and movement away from established parties. For example, in France, there has been an increase in votes for fringe or "anti-system" parties (e.g., the FN, various Trotskyite and other Marxist parties), so that by 2007 the leading center-left and center-right parties commanded only 64 percent of the vote, compared to 77 percent in 1981 and 73 percent in 1988.[42] In Britain, despite the odds against them posited by Duverger's Law, the Liberal-Democrats have become a well-established third party, picking off votes from those disillusioned by the two main parties. As noted below, by 2010 their share of the vote had grown to 23 percent.

However, it is in the eastern half of the continent that we see the most volatility, as parties disappear and are replaced by entirely new creations. This is hardly surprising, as most parties in post-communist Europe are of recent vintage, and thus few command party loyalty of the type that Labour in Britain or the Christian Democrats in Germany might enjoy. What is interesting, however, is how parties in the region have broken up and new parties (or offshoots) take their places and gain electoral traction, a reflection of the dissatisfaction many people feel with the existing political parties. Examples include Jobbik, noted at the outset of this chapter; *Smer* (Direction), which won 2006 elections in Slovakia and had broken from the Party of the Democratic Left in 1999; Law and Justice, which won parliamentary elections in Poland in 2005 after being created by the Kaczynski twins in 2001 as a replacement for the defunct Solidarity Electoral Action bloc; and New Era, which was founded on a platform to combat corruption in 2001 and in elections the following year became the largest party in the Latvian *Saeima* (parliament). The quintessential new party-turned-governing-party, however, was the National Movement for King Simeon II in Bulgaria, which won elections in 2001, the same year it was formed, but whose fortunes (along with the king's) quickly faded, so much so that by 2009 it won only 3 percent of the vote and changed its name to remove reference to its eponymous founder. In other cases, parties (e.g., the Alliance of the Democratic Left in Poland) parties have completely disappeared, even within a few years of when they were leading party in parliament.[43] Elsewhere, as in Albania, the party system is, at best, poorly structured, evidenced by the fact that thirty-six parties contested the 2009 parliamentary elections, although most were in one of four electoral blocs.

Critical Thinking Questions

1. Is the instability of party systems in Eastern Europe a sign that democracy is weak in that region?
2. Many have suggested that recent global changes are more challenging for the Left than the Right? Would you agree? Which side has, in your estimation, changed more since the end of the Cold War?

Poland had both presidential and parliamentary elections only two years before, in 2005. By the time of that vote, the Alliance of the Democratic Left (SLD), a coalition that included the renamed Communist Party, had collapsed as major political force. Alexander Kwasniewski, who was from the SLD and had served as Poland's president since 1995, was barred from seeking a third term. The party itself was in disarray due to corruption scandals, creating auspicious conditions for the return to power of right-wing political parties. Lech Kaczynski, the former mayor of Warsaw and a co-founder in 2001 of the socially conservative, anti-communist, and pro-Catholic Law and Justice Party (PiS in Polish) prevailed in a run-off in the presidential vote. Running on an anti-corruption and nationalist platform, the PiS also became the largest party in the *Sejm*, forming a coalition with other conservative and nationalist-oriented parties. However, personality and policy disputes made management of the coalition difficult, and in July 2006 Jaroslaw Kaczynski, Lech's twin brother and the head of PiS, became Prime Minister, backing away from a pre-election pledge that he would not seek that position. Thus, Poland had the dubious distinction of having twin brothers serving as its head of state and head of government.

The Kaczynskis came to power promising to rid the country of corruption and adopt policies to assist those who felt left behind by the free-market reforms of the 1990s. Soon, however, their style of governance and their policies began to rankle many Poles and other Europeans. Neither spoke a foreign language or liked to travel.

Both seemed uncomfortable around technology. They appointed their political allies to sensitive positions such as head of military counter-intelligence. Their campaigns to rid the country of former spies and ex-communists—implemented as a strategy against corruption—seemed like a witch-hunt. Poland's popular defense minister resigned to protest his displeasure at the government. Populist promises to build more homes went unfulfilled. Support for the US's war in Iraq also did not go down well with Poles. Their demands to refashion EU treaties to their own liking made Poland unpopular with fellow EU members. Lech Kaczynski's suggestion at an EU summit that Poland be granted more votes because it would have had more people if not for Nazi Germany did not meet with support from German chancellor Angela Merkel. The Kaczynskis' nationalist outbursts—including claims that they sought a "pure" Poland (this in the country with the largest concentration camps in World War II) and suggestions that Lech **Walesa**, former president and head of the Solidarity movement, was insufficiently patriotic—struck many as going too far. Critics argued that Poland had become a virtual outcast, a "laughing stock," a "nuisance," due to the rule of the "terrible twins."[44] By 2007, amid various scandals and ongoing government instability, the *Sejm* voted to disband itself and have early elections.

The elections were fought on several issues: foreign policy (involving the EU and the war in Iraq), "moral" concerns such as homosexuality and abortion, and corruption. The main contenders, PiS and the Civic Platform Party (PO in Polish) both hailed from the anti-communist Solidarity movement and are on the political right. The difference, however, was that PO was decidedly more pro-EU and appealed to those voters who felt that they were better off as a result of the reforms of the 1990s. It is more free market in orientation—liberal in European terms—and less ardently pro-Church or anti-gay. In contrast to the more erratic Kaczynskis, Donald Tusk, the leader of the PO, tried to assume an air of competence and a more professional demeanor. The Kaczynskis, thanks to use of questionable tactics in an anti-corruption probe against a PO official, looked more crass and vindictive.

The results, shown in Table 8.3, show a decisive victory for the PO. PiS did gain seats, but its former coalition partners, Self-Defense and the League of Polish Families, each gained less than 2 percent of the vote, far below the 5 percent

TABLE 8.3

Results of 2007 Polish Parliamentary Elections

Party	% Vote	% Seats	Total Seats	+/− from 2005	Seats in Senate
Civic Platform	41.5	45.4	209	+76	60
Law and Justice	32.1	36.1	166	+11	39
SLD	13.1	11.5	53	−2	0
Polish Peoples' Party	8.9	16.7	31	+6	0
Self-Defense	1.5	0	0	−56	0
League Polish Families	1.3	0	0	−34	0
Others	1.5	.2	1	−1	1

Source: Election results as reported on Wikipedia.

threshold needed to win seats in the *Sejm*. The PO won overwhelmingly among younger, urban, and better-educated voters, and it prevailed in the western, wealthier part of the country. It also did extremely well among the roughly one million Poles who were working abroad, mostly in Great Britain and Ireland.[45] Indeed, it was in large measure thanks an unexpectedly high youth vote that PO was able to claim victory.[46] After the election, the PO governed in coalition with the Polish People's Party, and this coalition has the necessary 60 percent of the votes to override any veto by Lech Kaczynski, who remained president until he died in a plane crash in April 2010. Tusk's main task is to tackle chronic problems of corruption and ensure economic growth so that so me of the two million Poles that have since 2004 left for work elsewhere in the EU will return home.

The 2008 Italian Elections

In April 2008 Italians went to the polls to elect members of both chambers of their legislature. They had last been to the polls in 2006, when by a close margin the nine party center-left coalition, The Union, prevailed and selected its leader, Romano Prodi, as Prime Minister. Prodi's tenure in office, however, was difficult, as he enjoyed only a one-seat advantage in the Italian Senate and had to keep his tenuous coalition together. In February 2007, less than a year after taking office, Prodi resigned after communist members of the Senate refused to back his plans for Italian involvement in Afghanistan. He reassembled a coalition, but a year later he resigned for good, after Clemente Massalla, leader of the Popular-UDEUR Party, withdrew his party's support for the government after his wife was put under house arrest for corruption charges. Massalla's party had three seats in the Senate. Thus, while Prodi won a vote of confidence in the lower house of parliament (Chamber of Deputies), where he had a majority of more than fifty seats, he lost in the upper house (the Senate) after the Popular-UDEUR Party left the coalition. Under the Italian system, the prime minister must have the support and confidence of both houses of parliament (this is not true in other countries such as Germany, Spain, or the Netherlands). Prodi resigned, a brief effort to redesign the Italian electoral system failed, and new elections were scheduled.

These elections, like those in 2006, figured to be close. Prodi decided to retire from politics, handing over leadership of the center-left to Walter Veltroni, the mayor of Rome. Veltroni's rival to be prime minister was Silvio Berlusconi, Italy's richest man, head of a giant media empire, and twice former prime minister (1994–1995, 2001–2006). Veltroni tried to form a more stable center-left coalition by abandoning an alliance with smaller far-left parties. Berlusconi put together a center-right coalition, merging his own *Forza Italia* (Forward Italy) party with other parties to create the People of Freedom party, which was the leading party in a three-party center-right coalition. Berlusconi hoped that the inability of the center-left to govern, as well as sluggish economic growth, would catapult him back to the post of prime minister. Berlusconi was (and still is) a highly decisive figure in Italian politics. He has been the subject of numerous corruption investigations and was accused by his critics of using his power as prime minister to change the laws to prevent successful prosecution of his crimes. Others cited his ego (in 2006 he compared himself as a victim of political persecution to Jesus Christ) and his inability to

TABLE 8.4

Results of 2006 and 2008 Elections in Italy

Party/Coalition	% Vote 2006 (C of Dep)	% Vote 2008 (C of Dep)	Seats in C of Dep,	Change, 2006 to 2008	Seats in Senate, 2008	Change, 2006 to 2008
Left (Prodi/Veltroni)	49.8	37.5	246	+9	132	+23
Right (Berlusconi)	49.7	46.8	344	+102	174	+39
Union of the Center	n/a	5.6	36	−3	3	−18

Source: Election results as reported on Wikipedia.

deliver on his promises during his more recent tenure as Prime Minister, when the poor economy prompted some to label Italy the "new sick man of Europe."[47] His defenders pointed to his record as a successful businessman and his personal charisma. As had been the case earlier, Berlusconi counted on his control of private television channels and ownership of the popular AC Milan football club (which fortuitously won the European Champions League in 2007) to boost his image.

The results of the elections are presented in Table 8.4. Because the parties and coalitions have changed their names and composition, the presentation is rather simplified. As can be seen, Berlusconi prevailed. Thanks to changes in the Italian electoral law made in 2005, the winning coalition automatically gets a "bump up" in the Chamber of Deputies to 340 (out of 630 seats), thereby ensuring Berlusconi of a solid majority there. The larger surprise was in the Senate, where Berlusconi and his allies were also able to put together a solid majority. The fact that Berlusconi—who was voted out of office in 2006, who was widely viewed as corrupt, and who advocated unpopular policies such as Italian support for the US invasion of Iraq—won the confidence of Italian voters was surprising to many, and can perhaps be best explained by the failures of Prodi and inability of Veltroni to convince voters that he would fare better or push through reforms needed to jumpstart the economy.

Berlusconi's government is Italy's sixty-second since World War II. He proved from 2001 to 2006 that he could stay in office for a full term—a rare feat in Italy—although his accomplishments in office were, in many ways, meager. Although he pushed through some tax cuts and privatization, he was unable to make such reforms in issues such as the pension system, excessive government bureaucracy, and corruption. His present government depends upon the support of the *Liga Nord*, which won eight percent of the vote and has sixty seats in the Chamber of Deputies and twenty-five in the Senate. Its agenda—decentralization and, potentially, separatism—may clash with that of Berlusconi. Since his election, the Italian economy has slid into a deep recession and Berlusconi has been plagued by numerous corruption and sex scandals, resulting in, among other items, his wife suing for divorce. Thus, it seems highly unlikely that Berlusconi's current turn as prime minister will be any better than his previous ones.

The 2010 British Elections

In May 2010 British voters went to the polls to elect a new House of Commons.[48] Since 1997, Britain had been ruled by the Labour Party, first under Tony Blair

(1997–2007) and then under Gordon Brown (2007–2010). As early as 2005, however, it had become clear that there was decreasing enchantment with Labour, due in large part to Blair taking Britain into war against Iraq. After Blair resigned in 2007, Brown, who had previously served as Chancellor of the Exchequer (Finance Minister), hoped to turn Labour's fortunes around. He lacked, however, Blair's charisma and in 2008 Britain began to experience a severe economic crisis, brought about by the collapse of several banks and housing prices. Some speculated that Brown, because of his low personal standing with voters, would be removed as Labour's leader prior to the 2010 elections. He survived this threat, but managed to create quite a row a week before the elections when a microphone caught him calling a voter he had just spoken with a "bigoted woman." Suffice to say that few were optimistic about Labour's chances.

Meanwhile, the Conservatives, who had been out of power for over a decade, made an effort to remake themselves. Unlike dowdy leaders who ran against Blair, the Conservative standard bearer in 2010 was David Cameron, who many compared to Blair. He was young (forty-three), telegenic, a good public speaker, and embraced new, more moderate issues (e.g., environmentalism) in an attempt to appeal to younger, centrist voters. He described himself as a "compassionate Conservative" and as an "heir to Blair." Eschewing the ideological tenor of previous Conservative leaders, including Margaret Thatcher, he presented himself as a problem-solver, someone capable of leading Britain in the twenty-first century, unlike Brown, who he derided as an "analogue politician in a digital age." During the campaign, one focus of criticism against Cameron was his elite background and his reliance of an "old-boy network" groomed in private schools such as Eton.

Gordon Brown chats with British voter Gillian Duffy, who he later called a "bigoted woman."

The wildcard in the race was the Liberal-Democratic Party, led by Nick Clegg, who had previously worked in the European Commission and served in the European Parliament. A year younger than Cameron, Clegg also presented a fresh face and noted that his party, which had never served in government, was the true party of new ideas. Under Clegg, the Liberal-Democrats embraced market-based economic reforms to public services, but also emphasized the need to invest in education, stronger ties with Europe, and the need to reform the electoral system, the last a constant in the party's program. Clegg performed well in debates prior to the election, with polls two weeks before the elections showing the Liberal-Democrats even with the Conservatives.[49] The strong campaign of the Liberal-Democrats thus added real drama to the campaign, as many speculated that no party would win a majority of the seats in the House of Commons, producing a "hung" parliament that would require either a coalition or minority government.

The final results of the elections are shown in Table 8.5. The Conservatives claimed victory, making their greatest gain in seats between elections since World War II, while Labour suffered its greatest loss of seats since prior to the war. However, the Conservatives were unable to claim a majority of seats, producing the first hung parliament since the 1970s. The day after the election, both David Cameron and Gordon Brown made overtures to the Liberal-Democrats, which, even though the mechanics of the electoral system work against them (compare their percentage of votes with seats won), held the balance of power. It is worth noting as well that despite the anticipation around the election, turnout improved only slightly and remained much lower than the 80 percent–plus figures regularly found in most European countries and in Britain in the first elections after World War II.

Although many Liberal-Democrats feel closer to Labour, math dictated that the more likely coalition was with the Conservatives, which was duly formed after several days of negotiation. As noted in Chapter 5, both David Cameron, the incoming prime minister, and Nick Clegg, who became deputy prime minister, hailed their coalition agreement as historic, ushering in a "new era" in British politics (there had been no

TABLE 8.5

2005 and 2010 British Election Results

	2005 Elections			2010 Elections		
Party	% Vote	Seats Won	% Seats	% Vote	Seats Won	% Seats
Labour	35.2	356	55.1	29.0	258	39.8
Conservative	32.4	199	30.8	36.1	306	47.1
Liberal-Democrats	22.0	62	9.6	23.0	57	8.8
Scottish/Welsh/Irish Parties	4.8	27	4.2	4.2	25	3.9
Independence Party	2.2	0	0	3.1	0	0
Greens	1	0	0	1	1	0
National Party	0.7	0	0	1.9	0	0
Others	1.7	2	0	1.7	1	0
Turnout		61.4			65.1	

Source: Election results as reported on Wikipedia.

coalition government since World War II), and necessary for a strong government in the national interest. The two sides pledged to work together for the full five-year term and made compromises on issues such as taxes and immigration. A national referendum to move to the so-called "alternative vote" system of voting, which is used in Australia, was promised, thus opening up the possibility that electoral reform (albeit not a move to proportional representation), long a top issue for the Liberal-Democrats, would eventually occur. Skeptics, however, suggested that the two parties, which in the past had been sharp critics of each other, were not natural partners, and that governing with a united front, particularly given the need to cut Britain's budget deficit, which had grown to 13 percent of gross domestic product (GDP) (tied with Greece as the highest in Europe), would involve very difficult choices.[50]

As can be seen from the above, elections are among the most important, interesting, and, at times, unpredictable, political phenomena in Europe. What one sees across the continent is that political leaders are under pressure to respond to a variety of issues (e.g., economic worries, foreign policy challenges, immigration, the role of the EU), and that many voters are discontent both with individual politicians and with political institutions as a whole. In some cases, incumbents are reelected, but one trend—seen in the US in 2008—is that "change"—whether in substance, style, or purely as a rhetorical device—is a powerful political mantra. In many respects, of course, this is perfectly understandable as voters look for something new and parties try to respond to voters' preferences. In many countries, this helps create a very dynamic political environment, particularly when more novel, 'protest' parties, such as Jobbik, are on the ballot and capture the public's discontent with more established parties. One problem worth bearing in mind, however, is that "change" can be both for the better or for the worse. In the case of Jobbik and other parties on the political fringes, one might worry that what they represent is less something new and more of a return to an uglier past.

APPLICATION QUESTIONS

1. What are advantages/disadvantages to strong party discipline? Does party discipline undermine or support the basic notions of democracy and representative government?
2. Is there a big difference among political parties in terms of how they are organized and allow for internal democracy? How might parties or other organizations make reforms to prevent the "iron law of oligarchy" from taking hold?
3. What cleavage do you think is most pronounced in your country? Do more traditional lines of cleavage (e.g., class, religion) still matter? What might constitute new forms of political cleavage?
4. Why do you think there is no Socialist or Social Democratic Party in the US? How are Socialist parties in Europe similar to and different from the Democratic Party in the US?
5. How would you explain variance in voter turnout in Figures 8.1 and 8.2?

KEY TERMS

catch-all parties 204
Christian Democrats 213
Communists 208
cosmopolitanism 207
Conservatives 215
dealignment 206
Greens 209
iron law of oligarchy 205
Left 206
Liberals 213
nationalists 207
party discipline 204
political cleavages 206
Right 206
shadow cabinet 219
single-issue parties 204
Social Democrats 210
Third Way 211

ADDITIONAL READING

Briter, Michael, and Deloye, Yves. 2007. *Encyclopedia of European Elections*. New York: Palgrave.

This useful resource that reviews political issues and electoral outcomes throughout Europe.

International Institute for Democracy and Electoral Assistance (IDEA), at http://www.idea.int

An excellent database on electoral systems, voter turnout, and regulations on parties and campaign finance.

Luther, Kurt, and Muller-Rommel, Ferdinand, eds. 2003. *Political Parties in the New Europe: Political and Analytical Challenges*. Oxford: Oxford University Press.

This collection of essays by leading scholars who study political parties includes considerations of how parties are changing organizationally, how they are responding to a new ideological environment, how they maintain bases of support, and how "Europeanization" offers challenges and opportunities.

Mudde, Cas. 2007. *Populist Radical Right Parties in Europe*. Cambridge: Cambridge University Press.

This book examines the factors contributing to the emergence of a "radical right" and how such parties have performed in a number of countries.

Party Politics, journal published by Sage Publishing. Consult http://www.partypolitics.org

This premier scholarly journal publishes research on the theory and practices of political parties, with frequent articles on European political parties.

END NOTES

1. See articles in *The Economist* on June 20, 2009 and April 10, 2010.
2. The full name of the party is Jobbik—The Movement for a Better Hungary (in Hungarian: *Jobbik Magyarországért Mozgalom*).
3. Most countries in the world do have elections—including China, Iran, Cuba, and Iraq under Saddam Hussein. The key point is that these elections must be fair and there must be political competition. The above examples do not meet these criteria.
4. E.E. Schattschneider, *Party Government* (New York: Rinehart, 1942), p. 1.
5. The Whigs and Tories, factions in Britain that date to the eighteenth century, are best thought of as elite factions than as political parties, considering the fact that until 1867 less than 10 percent of Britons enjoyed the right to vote. Nonetheless, today many in the Conservative Party in Britain claim the "Tory" tradition.
6. Party discipline may also be higher because of the nature of parliamentary government, as the members of the party must stick together in order to assure that "their" prime minister and cabinet remain in office.
7. Robert Michels, *Political Parties: A Sociological Study of the Oligarchical Tendencies of Modern Democracy* (New York: Hearst's International Library, 1915).
8. "Political Parties: Empty Vessels," *The Economist*, July 24, 1999.
9. "Party Time," *The Economist*, September 24, 2005.
10. The classic work on political cleavages is Seymour Lipset and Stein Rokkan, eds., *Party Systems and Voter Alignments* (New York: Free Press, 1967). For a more recent presentation of cleavages based upon economic and social changes in Europe, see Ronald Inglehart, *Culture Shift in Advanced Industrial Society* (Princeton: Princeton University Press, 1990).
11. For an obituary on the idea of class voting, see Mark Franklin *et al.*, *Electoral Change: Responses to Evolving Social and Attitudinal Structures in Western Countries* (Cambridge: Cambridge University Press, 1992). For an alternative view, see Geoffrey Evans, *The End of Class Politics?: Class Voting in Comparative Context* (Oxford: Oxford University Press, 1999).
12. Russell Dalton, *Democratic Challenges, Democratic Choices: The Erosion in Political Support in Advanced Industrial Democracies* (Oxford: Oxford University Press, 2004).
13. Good coverage of this theme is in both Inglehart, *Culture Shift*, and in Dalton, *Democratic Challenges*.
14. Lipset and Rokkan, *Party Systems*.
15. For more on the Turkish case, see Serif Mardin, "Center Periphery Relations: A Key to Turkish Politics," *Deadulus* 2:1, 1973, 169–190, and Anna Secor, "Ideologies in Crisis: Political Cleavages and Electoral Politics in Turkey in the 1990s." *Political Geography* 20, 2001, pp. 539–560.
16. Some of these parties went by different names, e.g., the Polish United Workers' Party. Nonetheless, in terms of their orientation, they clearly were "Communist" parties.
17. Herbert Kitschelt, *The Transformation of European Social Democracy* (Cambridge: Cambridge University Press, 1994).

18. Tony Judt, *Postwar: A History of Europe Since 1945* (New York: Penguin, 2005), pp. 553–554.
19. "The Lady in Red," *The Economist*, February 17, 2007.
20. For a view that is more optimistic on the role of the European Parliament in "Europeanizing" political parties, see Amie Kreppel. *The European Parliament and the Supranational Party System* (Cambridge: Cambridge University Press, 2001).
21. Thomas Poguntke, et al., eds. *The Europeanization of National Political Parties: Power and Organizational Adaptation* (London: Routledge, 2007).
22. John Lloyd, "Prepare Ye the Way of the Blair," *The New Statesman*, May 10, 1999, and "Third Way Club Gathers Members," *The Guardian*, May 3, 1999. See also Richard Dunphy, *Contesting Capitalism? Left Parties and European Integration* (Manchester: Manchester University Press, 2004).
23. Ibid.
24. In 1992, the once-dominant Christian Democratic Party in Italy was torn apart by corruption scandals. The Right in Italy is now dominated by explicitly secular parties.
25. *The Guardian*, April 25, 2002.
26. Both of these quotes are from John Lloyd, "Le Pen is Mightier. . ." *New Statesman*, April 29, 2002.
27. Although neither have seats in the national legislature, the British National Party won seats in some local elections in 2006 and the German National Democratic Party won seats in regional elections in 2006. Both have experienced growth in recent years.
28. From a UN anti-discrimination report, quoted in Jason Blau and Mikkel Christensen, "The Denmark Worth Protecting," *Humanity in Action*, June 2006, available at http://www.humanityinaction.org/docs/Mikkel_Jason_Final.doc, assessed on 25 March 2007.
29. A good source on the topic is Mads Qvortrup, *A Comparative Study of Referendums: Government by the People* (Manchester: Manchester University Press, 2002).
30. An excellent source is Lynda Lee Kaid and Christina Holtz-Bacha, eds. *The Sage Handbook of Political Advertising* (Beverly Hills: Sage, 2006).
31. Janis Ikstens, et al., *Campaign Finance in Central and Eastern Europe: Lessons Learned and Challenges Ahead* (Washington DC: IFES, 2002).
32. Patrick Basham, "Campaign Finance Fantasyland," Paper from the Cato Institute, June 9, 2001, at http://www.cato.org/dailys/06-09.01.html, accessed on 31 March 2007. British parties were capped at a measly $28 million for the campaign, the cost of an individual Senate campaign in a large US state.
33. Joe Klein, "The Party's Over," *The Guardian*, May 24, 2001.
34. Berlusconi reference is from "A sad Italian story," *The Economist*, April 8, 2006.
35. "Lady in Red," *The Economist*, February 17, 2007.
36. The best central source on voter turnout can be found at the website of the International Institute for Democracy and Electoral Assistance, http://www.idea.int/vt, accessed on 25 April 2010.
37. Much of the background on the election can be found in "The Race for the Elysée," *The Economist*, April 14, 2007.
38. "Startling Rise of France's Unlikely Revolutionary," *Financial Times*, March 16, 2007.
39. Lipset and Rokkan, *Party Systems*, and Richard Rose and Derek Urwin, "Persistence and Change in Western Party Systems since 1945," *Political Studies* 18, 1970: 287–319. See also *Stefano Bartolini and Peter Mair, Identity, Competition, and Electoral Availability: The Stabilization of European Electorates, 1885–1985* (Cambridge: Cambridge University Press, 1990).
40. The classic source is Mogens Pedersen, "The Dynamics of European Party Systems: Changing Patterns of Electoral Volatility," *European Journal of Political Research* 7:1, 1979, 1–26.
41. Election World, which used to be the premier source for elections, has been replaced by the data on Wikipedia, which I used for this computation.
42. Data from Wikipedia. Votes for the Communist Party were not included as representing the center-left.
43. The SLD was formally disbanded in 2008 after a corruption scandal and sagging electoral fortunes, but it had been the leading party in government as recently as 2001 to 2005.
44. *The Economist*, October 27, 2007, p. 17, p. 59.
45. *The Christian Science Monitor*, November 8, 2007.
46. Total turnout was 53.8 percent, far higher than the 40.6 percent turnout in 2005.
47. "A Sad Italian Story," *The Economist*, April 8, 2006.
48. Much of this section relies on reports from *The Economist*, April 10, April 17, and April 24, 2010.
49. "Getting a Clegg Up," *The Economist*, April 24, 2010, p. 55.
50. For more on the initial reaction to the coalition, see reports on May 12, 2010 in *The Washington Post*, *The New Times*, BBC News, and *The Guardian*.

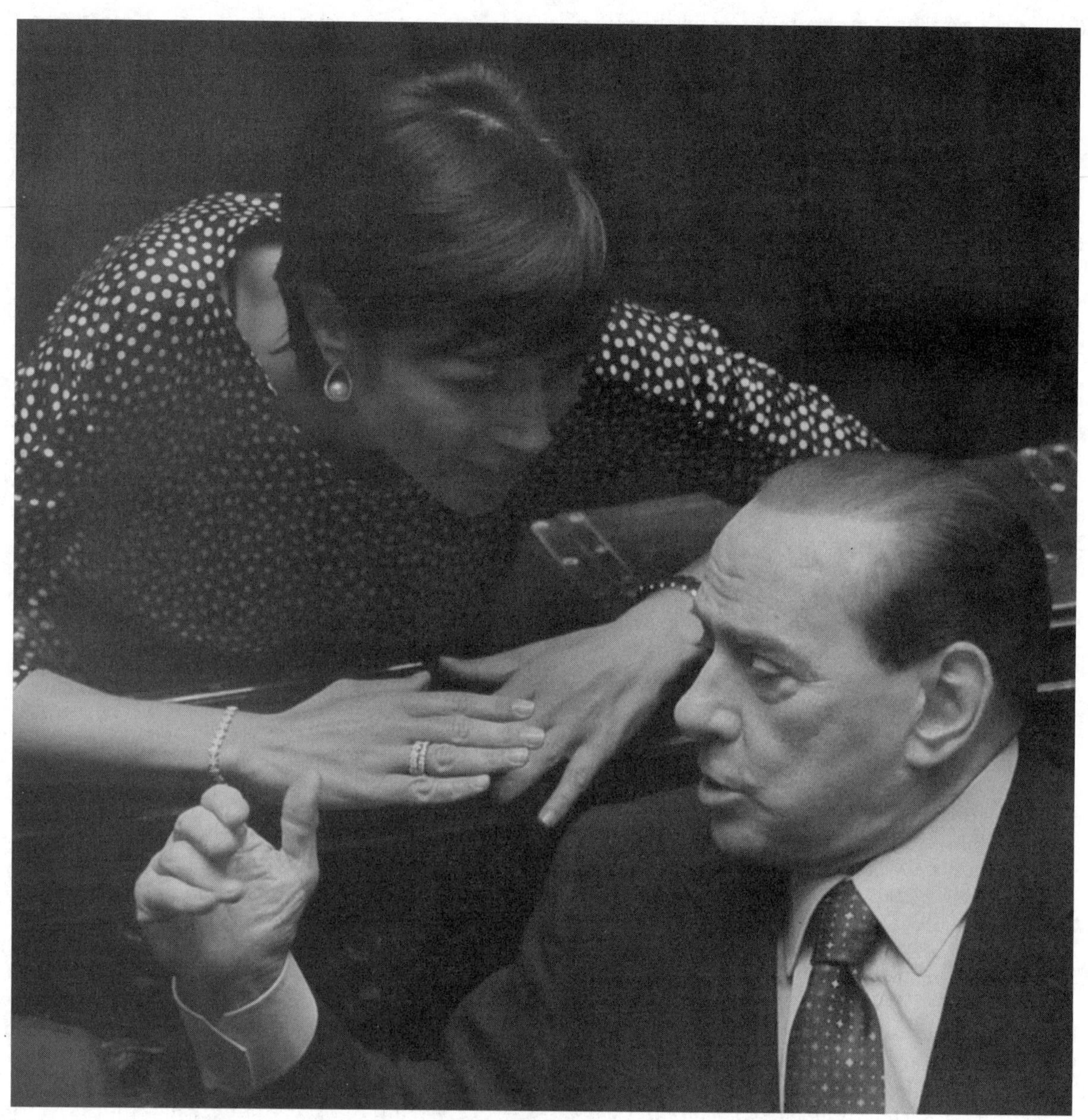

Silvio Berlusconi: An example of Italian-style democracy?

CHAPTER 9

Political Culture and Political Behavior

How can one explain the phenomenon of Silvio Berlusconi? Italy's richest man, he made his fortune as head of a media empire and has served as prime minister three times (1994–1995, 2001–2006, 2008–). Long dogged by allegations of corruption, connections to organized crime, and concerns about his near-monopoly control over Italian television, he has been the consummate political survivor and is Italy's only post-war prime minister to serve a full five-year term of office. Since 2009, however, he has been embroiled in a series of sex scandals, including allegations of an improper relationship with the eighteen-year-old daughter of a political ally and payments to prostitutes who worked parties at his presidential residence, as well as exhibiting what most outsiders would consider bizarre behavior (e.g., nominating showgirls to run from his party for the European Parliament). His wife filed for divorce, but Berlusconi claimed that he was the victim of a plot by the media and communist judges to remove him from office. Critics contend that he has turned Italian politics into a "Mexican soap opera" and a "whore-ocracy."[1] Meanwhile, whereas shenanigans like Berlusconi's would end the career of most political leaders in Europe, he has not only politically survived, but his party even won regional elections in the spring of 2010. How can one account for this?

Perhaps, one could say, his mix of flamboyance and *machismo* is a reflection of Italian culture, some sort of "bizarre Italian anomaly in which sexist macho men and successful businessmen and swindlers are admired rather than villified?"[2] Many Italians, of course, would bristle at such an explanation; lechery and corruption are hardly unique to Italians. However, this type of cultural explanation has a certain resonance: Because governments in Europe are elected by voters, their leaders and their policies must reflect aspects of the country's cultural milieu. Of course, cultural arguments can degenerate into lazy analytical shortcuts and stereotypes (e.g., hardworking Germans are thrifty, slothful Greeks are profligate spenders, "backwards" Eastern Europeans vote for pugnacious nationalists), are often difficult to support with hard evidence, and are often poorly equipped to explain political change. Nonetheless, they are frequently invoked, and the study of political culture figures prominently in political science.

Political culture, and, by extension, various forms of political behavior that are a manifestation of cultural values, are therefore worthy topics of serious consideration. In the previous chapter we looked at political parties and voting patterns among European publics, but this only captures a small part of political behavior or what might also be called citizenship politics. We should also consider peoples' basic political values and orientations, as these core beliefs inform and color their political participation. We should also recognize that citizens engage in political activity in a myriad of ways, and that voting, although certainly the most obvious and perhaps most common form of political participation, is not always the most effective or even important form of political engagement. This chapter therefore serves two purposes: to look at fundamental attributes of political culture across a wide range of European countries and to examine political behavior through interest organizations and social movements, which have at times played crucial roles in shaping political, economic, and social life in Europe.

DEFINING AND REFINING POLITICAL CULTURE

political culture ■ set of attitudes, beliefs, and sentiments that provide the basic assumptions and rules that govern political behavior.

One of the most venerable and popular topics of study in political science is **political culture.** One can define political culture as "the set of attitudes, beliefs and sentiments which give order and meaning to a political process and which provide the underlying assumptions and rules that govern behavior in a political system."[3] As employed by social scientists, it refers to enduring, fundamental sets of beliefs that can be studied across time and across countries. It is thus not the same thing as public opinion *per se*, which is often something more specific and time-bound. For example, asking a rather generic question about trust toward political parties or courts would be tapping into an aspect of political culture. A question more specific to a particular party (e.g., the German Christian Democratic Union) or its leader (Angela Merkel) would be better described as probing public opinion. Put differently, the study of political culture aspires to look at a broader, longer, and moving picture of citizens' values—with more of a psychological or even anthropological aspect—whereas public opinion is often more of a snapshot view, limited in scope and time.

Why study political culture? The basic reason should be obvious, especially when considering democratic political systems. If government is "of the people" and "by the people," the people matter, and their beliefs and values should be reflected in their government. Some invoke a "theory of congruence," meaning that the durability of a political system requires the congruence or resemblance between governmental authority and the values and other authority patterns found within a society.[4] Less prosaically, people get the government they deserve. Aristotle (384–322 BCE), often considered the first political scientist, recognized this, arguing that a successful democracy depended upon the virtue of its citizens.

It is worth mentioning, however, a couple of problems in the study of political culture. One is identifying what aspects of political culture matter most. For example, tolerance and a commitment to equality are usually argued to be an important feature of a democratic political culture. However, sexism, racism, and homophobia have been—and in some cases continue to be—prominent features in democratic polities. A second problem is whether one can isolate political culture as a *cause* of political phenomena. For all the popularity of cultural arguments, they are frequently hard to prove and often end up as tautologies (e.g., Great

IS EUROPE ONE?

How Strong is the Feeling of Europeanness?

European countries are drawing closer and closer together in terms of economic cooperation and political institutions. One of the goals of the EU, however, is social integration, including the development of a broader sense of European identity or European values among various national publics. In other words, on a cultural level, one would think of oneself less and less as German, Swedish, or Romanian and increasingly as simply "European," one who shares common values with citizens in other countries across the continent.

This idea of a European identity has been wrapped up in various projects to fashion a united Europe. True, a prominent theme in European history is the rise of nation-states, but many thinkers saw the nation-state as a stepping-stone to a larger Europe. Jean-Jacques Rousseau, in his *Considerations on the Government of Poland,* suggested—no doubt wishfully—that there "are no more French, German, Spanish, even Englishmen. Whatever one says, there are only Europeans. They all have the same tastes, the same passions, the same habits."[5] Of course, Rousseau's vision has not yet been realized. Identity is based upon symbols, myths of common origins, stirring narratives, and heroes, and, as debates in the late 1990s over whose face should appear on the euro revealed, these are in short-supply on the pan-European level.[6] Yet, identities can be crafted or emerge out of political arrangements. Borrowing from Italian statesman Massimo D'Azeglio, who wrote, "We have made Italy, now we must make Italians," can we say that "Europeans" are being made today?

There are good reasons to be skeptical. Both the World Values Survey (WVS) and the Eurobarometers ask questions about identity, about how "European" people feel as opposed to French, Italian, Swedish, and so on. Not surprisingly, the surveys reveal that people feel primarily local or national identities as opposed to a pan-European identity. For example, in the WVS of 1999 in more than thirty European countries, on average only 3.2 percent of respondents identified primarily with "Europe"—lower than the 6.5 percent who identified with the world as a whole and far less than those citing locality (49.3 percent) or country (27.7 percent). Additionally, only 8.5 percent on average cited Europe as their second choice.[7] In a Eurobarometer survey conducted across all EU countries in 2005, only 17 percent said that they "often" thought of themselves as European in addition to identifying with their own particular nationality.[8]

In addition, there is limited evidence of social interactions that would help support a common European identity. For example, a special Eurobarometer, *The Future of Europe,* carried out in the spring of 2006, found that a minority of Europeans participate in "European" activities: only 43 percent reported they had socialized with people from other EU member states in the past year; only 37 percent said they had visited another EU country; and 23 percent claimed they had read a book or newspaper in a language other than their mother tongue. On all three questions, those in northern European countries (especially Luxembourg, the Netherlands, and Sweden) were more likely to report participation in such activities than those in Southern or Eastern Europe. A separate question revealed only "lukewarm" interest in European affairs—with only 47 percent claiming an interest in European politics, as opposed to 63 percent interested in national-level politics. Knowledge about basic facts of the EU—including the number of countries in the EU, how the European Parliament is elected, and whether their country had a European Commissioner (all countries do)—was also low, with only 22 percent able to answer all three correctly.[9] On all questions, younger respondents, those with more education, those in "white-collar" professions, and those who regularly use the Internet were more likely to be knowledgeable or participate in "European" activities.

(*continued*)

While these data may be disappointing for those hoping to forge a self-conscious citizen of Europe, there are some signs pointing toward the emergence of a growing feeling of "Europeanness." In a Eurobarometer survey in 2008, 54 percent of respondents felt that EU member-states were close in terms of values, an increase of 9 percent from 2006. Younger and better-educated respondents were more likely to claim there are "European values," and, in this case, the highest levels of support for this proposition came from newer members such as Slovakia (71 percent), Cyprus (68 percent), and the Czech Republic (68 percent) with the least support in Austria (39 percent) and Great Britain (45 percent). Most people still identify with a particular country, but people do not necessarily have only one identity. Indeed, the aforementioned Eurobarometer in 2005 finds a large number of respondents (57 percent) anticipated feeling "in the near future" some level of European identity: either solely European (2 percent), European and nationality (7 percent), or nationality and European (48 percent). Among the EU countries surveyed, Europhile Luxembourg reported the highest number of people with multiple identities (72 percent), followed by Malta (71 percent), Cyprus (68 percent), Croatia (66 percent), and the Netherlands (65 percent), whereas the Turks (23 percent) and more Euro-skeptical British (33 percent) were among the least likely to acknowledge some level of European identity. Notably, those who report some level of "Europeanness" were younger, urban, and better educated. Comparing the 2005 data with those from 1996, one set of analysts suggest that the feeling of "Europeanness" should grow over time, thanks in part to generational effects and demographic trends (e.g., rising education) but also to socialization factors such as European media, tourism, and labor mobility.[10] In addition, a Eurobarometer from 2005 finds that a majority of Europeans are "very" (12 percent) or "fairly" (51 percent) proud to be European, with even 43 percent of the British expressing some pride in their "Europeanness." True, the data do not suggest that national-level identity will melt away and be replaced exclusively by a European one, as the vast majority in this survey were either very proud (46 percent) or fairly proud (41 percent) in their own nationality. However, given the fact that many believe one can be both a German, Italian, Dane, and so on, and a good European, one can be somewhat sanguine about the prospects for a more united Europe.

Critical Thinking Questions

1. Does globalization and the spread of various technologies (e.g., Facebook) make the growth of a feeling of "Europeanness" almost inevitable? What might work against the growth of feeling of "Europeanness"?
2. Can you find evidence from contemporary events that there is a pronounced feeling of "Europeanness"? What might bring such feelings out?

Britain is democratic because the British are democratic). Perhaps, culture should be treated as an effect—not a cause, as other factors (e.g., economic development or government policies) help shape political culture. One could take a more agnostic view on causality, maintaining that various factors affect each other in a complex fashion, as pictured in Figure 9.1. Such a perspective would still treat political culture as an important, but not necessarily the only, factor in explaining political phenomena. It would also recognize that political culture can change through **political socialization**, the process through which an individual acquires information, attitudes, and orientations concerning political phenomena. Political socialization can include parental and peer influence, life experiences, education,

political socialization ■ process through which an individual acquires information, attitudes, and orientations about political life.

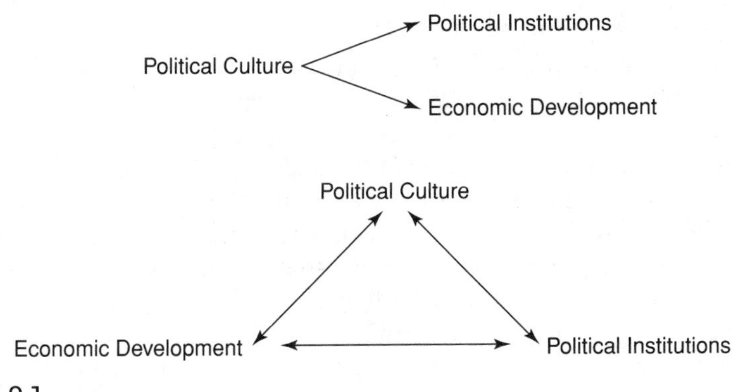

FIGURE 9.1
How Might Political Culture Function?

and exposure to media. The key point from this perspective is that political culture is not an innate characteristic like hair or skin color. One is, in a real sense, not born French, Irish, or Hungarian. One *becomes* these only through political socialization. To the extent that there is a growing pan-European media as well as academic, business, and social networks, one can discuss the emergence of a broader *European* political culture and identity, a topic in this chapter's **Is Europe One?** feature.

ASPECTS OF EUROPEAN POLITICAL CULTURE

Although political culture has a long tradition in political science, until recently it was hard to examination rigorously or systematically. Frequently, assessments of political culture were rooted in impressionistic evidence or travelogues. Hard data, unfortunately, was lacking, although scholars debate aspects of political cultures in historical cases (e.g., how might German political culture explain the rise of Hitler?).

In recent decades, the data problem has been solved thanks to systematic survey research that has been conducted across a number of countries. We can now rely upon broad cross-national research that has traced European values and attitudes for several decades. One source is the WVS, which has completed five iterations in Europe since the early 1980s and is now conducted globally by academic researchers in more than seventy countries. Another is the European Social Survey (ESS), which is similar to the WVS and was conducted in four waves the 2000s in more than twenty different countries. Finally, there is the Eurobarometer series, which is commissioned by the EU and has been conducted for more than thirty years.[11] All are publicly available, and we shall draw upon them in the analysis below. Note that we cannot here present comprehensive data on all measures for all countries. The results are meant to be illustrative, and, if you want to know more about certain countries, you can look up results and/or, in many cases, conduct data analysis online.

A Democratic Political Culture?

One core question would be whether or not there is political culture that is supportive of democracy. To begin, one could define a democratic political culture as one that embraces values generally supportive of democracy, including belief in a democratic system of government, priority on individual rights and freedoms, and confidence in the ability of political competition to produce a well-functioning political system. It should also embrace **political tolerance** and respect for equality, not only in general terms of race and/or gender, but also tolerating the rights of your political opponents or disliked groups, which often can be more trying. In addition, many point to **interpersonal trust**—how much citizens trust each other in the most general terms—as important for democracy because it facilitates the growth of citizens' organizations and makes groups willing to bargain with and cede power to others. Trust is often assumed to be a central component for **social capital**, meaning the skills and attitudes necessary to promote active citizenship and social networks. Lastly, *per* Aristotle, one would expect democratic citizens, given the responsibilities they have within the political system, to take an interest in politics, which, hopefully, contributes to their general political competence as citizens.

political tolerance ■ belief that respects the views and rights of others, even those with whom you disagree or do not identify; considered important for democratic government.

interpersonal trust ■ the degree to which one trusts fellow citizens, often linked to development of associational life and democracy.

social capital ■ skills and attitudes necessary to promote active citizenship and social networks.

What do we find with regards to a democratic political culture? First, among seventeen European countries surveyed between 2005 and 2007 in the WVS,[12] there is near universal acceptance of democracy as a very good or good system of government. For example, when asked directly if they believed having a democratic system was overall good or bad, the vast majority of respondents—92.1 percent—thought having a democracy was good, with the lowest figure being 80 percent in Serbia and the highest of 97.9 percent in Sweden. Similarly, on a scale of one to ten, the majority of respondents (51.1 percent) across the continent thought it was "absolutely important" (a ten) to live in a democracy, with the mean a 8.7, which shows individuals put a high priority on living in a democracy. Similarly, in the 1999 to 2000 round of the WVS, the vast majority of Europeans agreed with the aphorism—usually attributed to Winston Churchill—that democracy may have its problems but it is better than any other form of government. Scores on this variable range from 78 percent agreeing in Romania to 99 percent in Denmark, with not a big difference between the scores for post-communist Europe (88 percent agree) and Western Europe (91.5 percent agree).

These results might give one confidence that the vast majority of Europeans possess democratic values, but these questions tend to produce a positive response to democracy throughout the world, even in non-democratic countries. More telling are questions that ask respondents if a specific alternative might be preferable to democracy. Interestingly, as seen in Table 9.1, despite the fact that Churchill's statement is given a strong endorsement, many Europeans would agree that rule by experts or rule by a strong leader that would not have to bother with elections would be good. On these questions, one sees marked differences between Western and Eastern Europe, a result also present in the 1999–2000 WVS, when majorities across Eastern Europe endorsed one or both alternatives. Indeed, just looking at Table 9.1, it is hard to sanguine about prospects for democracy in Romania and Turkey. How to explain these results? One possible answer is that many Europeans—again, particularly in but not only in Eastern Europe—are not satisfied with the democracy that they have. Thus, while they may not (yet) have soured on democracy in principle, they are more ambivalent about democracy in

TABLE 9.1

Preferences for Non-Democratic Alternatives

	% Saying "Good" or "Fairly Good" to Each Statement							
Statement	Germany	France	Great Britain	Sweden	Poland	Romania	Serbia	Turkey
Having experts, not government, make decisions according to what they think is best for the country	59.4	51.8	44.8	35.9	84.6	76.3	72.4	69.6
Having a strong leader who does not have to bother with parliament and elections	16.9	33.2	28.2	18	30.5	78.3	31.9	58.9

Source: WVS, 2005–2007.

practice, and perhaps in some states that have experienced instability, corruption, or economic crisis—more common in Eastern Europe—the idea of a great leaders or dispassionate experts sounds good. These issues touch upon the broader question of **political legitimacy**, the voluntary acceptance of the validity of a country's political system by its citizens. If citizens feel their system of government is not performing well and another alternative would be preferable, they may seek systemic political change. Whether at present there is a genuine crisis of legitimacy for democracies in Europe is a topic taken up below in the **In Focus** section.

political legitimacy ■ the voluntary acceptance of the validity of a country's political system by its citizens.

Another component of a democratic political culture is valuing rights and freedoms. Surveys in Europe typically do not ask whether people think freedom of speech, religion, assembly, and so on, are important—again, not many would be opposed when questions are asked in such fashion—but some surveys have asked questions that ask respondents how important freedoms are compared to other things. For example, the ESS in 2008 asked respondents about personal freedoms, specifically whether it is important to make one's own decisions and be free or is it important to do what one is told and follow the rules. The results revealed that most Europeans thought it more important to be free (Switzerland 85 percent, Germany 77 percent, Turkey 73 percent, Great Britain 72 percent, Poland 69 percent, Czech Republic 61 percent), although some countries (Bulgaria 54 percent, Portugal 45 percent) did rank lower. In 2005, Eurobarometer surveys asked for respondents to rate the importance of giving people more say in government decisions and freedom of speech as opposed to fighting inflation and maintaining order. When asked to choose two out of these four choices, majorities (e.g., 60 percent in Germany, 53 percent in Poland, 52 percent in Great Britain) or near majorities (46 percent in Czech Republic and in Turkey) listed giving people more say a priority. Fewer (e.g., 26 percent in Germany, 23 percent in Turkey, 12 percent in Poland), however, listed free speech.

What of tolerance, particularly respect for equality and acceptance of differences? Social scientists try to get at this question in various ways. Sometimes they ask about opinions toward certain groups. On this score, one does find discriminatory views toward racial minorities, Jews, immigrants, Muslims, homosexuals, and Roma in many European countries. For the most part, only about 10 to 15 percent of respondents admit to what might be called discriminatory attitudes toward minorities, although this is somewhat more pronounced in Eastern Europe. For example, according to the 1999–2000 WVS, 44 percent of Hungarians, 25 percent of Poles, and 23 percent of Romanians (as opposed to 6 percent of French and 5 percent of Germans) would object to having Jews as neighbors. Another tactic is to ask more general questions about equal treatment of people and respect for differences in opinion. Some data from such questions from the 2008 ESS are presented in Table 9.2. They reveal that most Europeans would rank as tolerant—at least when they answer survey questions—but we also know that anti-immigrant and at times explicitly racist parties have attracted sizeable followings in some countries. Notably, fewer claim it is important to understand different people, although this need not imply that they would suggest banning some groups from exercising rights to express their viewpoints. As to whether or not individuals experience discrimination—for reasons such as gender, race, national origin, or religion—one sees that the figures in many countries are relatively low, although, interestingly, highest in established democracies such as France and Great Britain where immigration and multi-culturalism, issued covered in more detail in Chapter 12, are hot political issues.

Interpersonal trust, as noted above, is also considered an important attribute in a democracy, providing a means for social networks and organizations to form and contributing to a culture of tolerance. Several surveys ask respondents if people can generally be trusted or if one cannot be too careful. Data from the 2008 ESS are

TABLE 9.2

Levels of Tolerance and Discrimination among European Publics

	Figures Are % Agreeing		
Country	Treat People Equally	Need to Understand Different People	I Am a Member of a Group Discriminated Against
Germany	73.8	71.1	5.0
France	77.1	60.7	9.5
Great Britain	70.5	66.0	14.1
Spain	87.2	77.7	5.3
Poland	77.0	62.3	4.7
Czech Republic	62.7	40.6	5.8
Turkey	82.1	75.3	6.5

Source: ESS, 2008. Questions ask whether the respondent identifies with a particular type of person, such as one who believes that everyone should be treated equally and who one believes that one should try to understand others, even if he or she disagrees with that person. Those who say that such a person is "very much like me" or "like me" are included in the table. The question on discrimination asks simply whether the respondent feels him- or herself to be a member of such a group.

TABLE 9.3

Interpersonal Trust in European Countries

Country	% Saying People Can Be Trusted
Germany	40.7
France	29.4
Great Britain	46.5
Netherlands	64.2
Sweden	66.7
Romania	26.7
Poland	25.5
Turkey	14.6

Source: ESS, 2008. Question: "Would you say that most people can be trusted, or that you can't be too careful in dealing with people?" Responses are 0 ("can't be too careful") to 10 ("most people can be trusted"), with responses of 6–10 included in the table.

presented in Table 9.3. Following the pattern already established, we see more trust in countries with longer practice of democracy, although overall levels of trust even in several established democracies (that, also, it is worth mentioning have low crime rates) is not overly high. Those who emphasize the importance of social capital would be disappointed with these data, although one could ask how relevant a question is of this sort since people usually associate, both socially and politically, not with complete strangers but with likeminded people in secure settings. Still, with sufficiently high levels of distrust, one might wonder about the ability of civil society to take root and how different groups will be able to work together for common national goals.

Lastly, how knowledgeable and empowered are citizens about politics? Data from the ESS in 2008, displayed in Table 9.4, reveal sizeable differences in political

TABLE 9.4

Political Interest and Efficacy

	Germany	France	Great Britain	Spain	Sweden	Poland	Czech Republic	Bulgaria
How interested in politics ("Very" or "Quite")	61.7	51.4	56.5	26.1	58.7	41.5	17.9	45.9
Politics is too complicated to understand ("Regularly" or "Frequently" feel that way)	29.3	27.0	39.5	39.1	28.1	43.6	42.6	29.7

Source: ESS 2008.

interest, with majorities throughout Northern Europe (e.g., 71.8 percent in Denmark, 66.8 percent in the Netherlands, 61.7 percent in Germany) asserting they are "very" or "quite" interested in politics. On the other hand, in several countries—both in Eastern Europe (e.g., Poland and the Czech Republic) and in Western Europe (e.g., Spain [74 percent], Portugal [71 percent], Greece [69 percent], even, perhaps surprisingly, Norway [53 percent])—have a majority of respondents who claim they are "hardly" or "not at all" interested in politics. The latter finding does little to support claims of a "civic culture" of political engagement across Europe. Moreover, as seen in Table 9.4, many citizens report that they lack the skills to follow political life, asserting that they regularly or frequently find politics too complicated to understand. These questions get at the idea of **political efficacy**, the feeling that one is capable of participating effectively in political life. If people find politics complicated or, for whatever reason, are not interested, it is hard to imagine them being active, well-informed citizens. If too many citizens withdraw from political life, the crucial link between elected officials and citizens may be very weak, allowing those with greater resources or possessing narrow, particular interests to hold sway over the country.

political efficacy ■ the feeling that one is capable of participating effectively in political life.

What do these numerous data illustrate? Most clearly, one can still see a difference in political culture between Western Europe and Eastern Europe (including Turkey). Whether the years of democratic experience in Western Europe have created more democratic values or whether the values spawned the institutions—a sort of chicken-and-egg argument—cannot be resolved here. What is interesting, though, is that on many measures—social trust, interest in politics, tolerance, political efficacy, and support for democracy itself—there is weak or uncertain evidence of a "democratic political culture" in several countries. Of course, democracy does not require that everyone be the ideal democratic citizen, but the data presented above—and analyzed in detail in other studies[13]—could make one worry about the future of democracy in Europe, a topic examined in more detail in the **In Focus** section.

The Role of the State in the Economy

Another important set of issues is what expectations or preferences people have about the responsibilities of the state on socio-economic questions. This would include items such as whether the state should guarantee people employment, redistribute income, take a role in directing the country's economic life, and provide generous social welfare benefits. While these are not as explicitly political as what was discussed above, they address a fundamental aspect of political economy: How far should the state, as opposed to market forces, go in shaping the direction of the economy? Answers to these questions have been traditionally one of the main lines of cleavage between the Left and Right. Whereas Chapter 10 looks more closely at actual policies, here we can probe values and orientations on this topic.

At first glance, one can find substantial evidence that Europeans support a strong role for the state in the economy. For example, the ESS in 2002 asked whether Europeans agreed that less government interference is good for the economy. Whereas such a statement (at least until the economic crisis of 2008) would be taken as Gospel truth across a wide swath of the American political spectrum,

IN FOCUS

Is There a Crisis of Democracy?

In addition to learning about European political culture in terms of what people consider should be the direction of political, economic, and social policy, we might also ask about how they assess the political systems under which they live. Given our interest in democracy, one might ask about the health of democratic institutions as registered by public attitudes towards their political systems. Charles Maier of Harvard University, in an influential article in 1994, argued that many of the well-established democracies in Europe (and, for that matter, in North America and Japan) were suffering from a "moral crisis," fuelled by resentment about corruption, social inequality, and a perceived abyss between publics and political leaders.[14] While he did not suggest that democratic governments would collapse, he did draw parallels between the 1990s and the 1920s and 1930s, when many European democratic governments failed. Many Europeans, he claimed, suffered from "weariness with politics" (*Politikverdrossenheit* in German) and were either withdrawing from political and social life or turning to more extremist movements, particularly on the xenophobic, nationalist right. Several years later, *The Economist*, drawing upon data from surveys in the late 1990s, suggested that there were genuine signs of worry, pointing to a long-term decline in trust in political leaders and in confidence in political institutions.[15] Ralf Dahrendorf, a prominent German social scientist, wrote in 2000 that "representative government is no longer as compelling a proposition as it once was."[16]

These issues get to the important question of political legitimacy. All political systems, but especially democracies, require political legitimacy.[17] Over the long term, a system that lacks legitimacy will either be removed by one more acceptable to the people or will have to resort to large levels of coercion in order to stay in power. One way of measuring political legitimacy is to ask general questions about the trust or confidence one has in various political and public institutions. Whereas a decline in confidence in generally stable European polities may not mean immediate revolution, it does point to a potential crisis of democracy and may signal that citizens will begin to look for new, possibly more extreme, political groups for remedies and redress of grievances.

Are these exaggerated statements and fears? Almost two decades after Maier's article, do we see signs that this "crisis" is deepening, or, instead, are there more positive signs? One can point to some disturbing developments, some of which were mentioned in previous chapters: the growing emergence of far-right political parties that embrace xenophobic and racist views; lower voter turnout; and fewer members in traditional political parties. One might also mention corruption scandals in the late 1990s and 2000s, which have engulfed not only the new democracies in post-communist Europe (where corruption has been a prominent leitmotif since the fall of communism) but also states such as Great Britain (expense accounts for parliamentarians), Germany (fundraising scandals with the Christian Democratic Union), and, most notoriously, Italy, where Prime Minister Silvio Berlusconi seemed to be under a constant cloud of some financial or sex scandal. One might also suggest that globalization, by forcing the hand of governments to adopt policies that may not represent the will of the people (e.g., think of proposed reforms to the welfare state in Western Europe) has undercut democracy, insofar as international financial actors, not voters, are the primary influence on decision-makers.

Survey evidence confirms a sense of alienation, distrust of political institutions, and widespread dissatisfaction with democratic performance across Europe. For example, in the 2002 ESS, majorities in most countries agreed that "hardly any" or "very few" politicians care about what people like them think. The most disillusioned among the twenty-one countries surveyed were the Slovenes (80 percent, in a country considered one of the most successful in

(*continued*)

post-communist Europe), Greeks (79 percent), and Poles (73 percent). In contrast, a minority of Scandinavians (28 percent of Norwegians, 30 percent of Swedes, 32 percent of Danes, and 37 percent of Finns) expressed this view. This question connects with the aforementioned issue of political efficacy, insofar as people are not likely to feel empowered or that their voice matters if they believe that their elected representatives do not care about their views. One can also ask more specific questions about confidence in institutions, including parties, parliaments, and the courts. The WVS, between 2005 and 2007, asked respondents whether they tended to have confidence in certain institutions. Most did not. Trust in political parties was typically under 20 percent (e.g., 18 percent in Britain, 16 percent in France and Italy, 13 percent in Germany and Romania, 7 percent in Poland), with trust in parliament marginally higher but hardly encouraging (e.g., 36 percent in Britain, 33 percent in Italy, 22 percent in Germany, 17 percent in Romania, 12 percent in Poland).

Most troubling is the fact that many Europeans are not satisfied with their democratic governments. For example, Eurobarometer 65, conducted in the spring of 2006, found that 41 percent of those surveyed in twenty-nine countries were dissatisfied with the way democracy works in their country. The lowest performers tended to be in Eastern Europe (only 22 percent satisfied in Croatia and Bulgaria, 25 percent in Lithuania), but there were also relatively low levels of satisfaction in Portugal (30 percent) and France (45 percent). Denmark (93 percent), Luxembourg (83 percent), and Finland (78 percent) had the highest degree of satisfaction, and overall satisfaction among the older EU members—the pre-2004 EU-15—was 58 percent, compared with a mere 41 percent for the ten new member states.

Are these data capturing a snapshot, or is there a trend at work, one perhaps identified by Maier? Looking back over a decade at previous surveys, one does find—with some variation—similarly low levels of trust in institutions, a sense of alienation, and at best a mixed assessment about democratic performance. The biggest declines have not been in Western Europe, which was Maier's focus, but in Eastern Europe, where many of the high hopes engendered by the collapse of communism have not, at least according to citizens there, been realized. However, since Maier wrote his article, there are, at least in the survey research, some signs of improvement. For example, whereas in 1995 a near majority (49 percent) of respondents in Eurobarometer surveys reported dissatisfaction with their country's democracy, by 2006, only 41 percent felt this way. One could maintain, of course, that 41 percent is too high, and no doubt all governments could do better to empower citizens, respond to their demands, and win their confidence. While one could speculate on how assessments about democracy might evolve in the future or what the consequences of these views will be, it is clear that simply having a democracy does not guarantee that citizens will be satisfied with their governments or that having a democracy leads to a widespread sense of citizen empowerment.

Critical Thinking Questions

1. How serious is the impact of lower voter turnout on the health of a democracy? What can be done to bolster voter turnout?
2. "The problems of today's world are too complex for traditional institutions of democracy." Would you agree? In what way?

in Europe one finds—even in more free-market–oriented Great Britain—minorities endorsing such a view. As seen in Figure 9.2, this holds across both halves of the continent, although arguably for different reasons. Western Europeans equate their post-war welfare states with prosperity. For Eastern Europeans, the first decade of capitalism in the 1990s was so traumatic that many now welcome a larger role for the state in the economy. As for reasons Europeans may support an interventionist

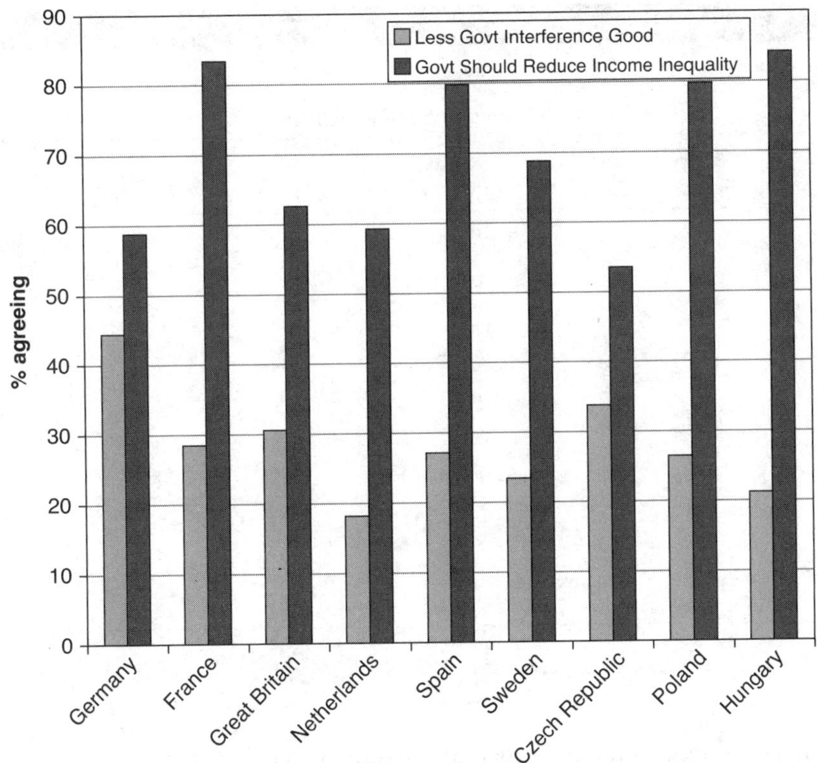

FIGURE 9.2
Views of Role of Government in the Economy
Source: ESS, 2002.

state, one answer is to reduce income inequality, a goal endorsed throughout the continent, although much more so in Poland, Hungary, and France than in Great Britain and the Czech Republic, which have in past decades had more free-market–oriented governments.

This does not mean that Europeans are in favor of communism or a strongly socialist state. Indeed, other evidence shows that Europeans are actually more ambivalent about the role of the state. For example, a Eurobarometer survey in 2006 asked people whether they believed that free competition is the best guarantee of economic prosperity and whether they thought that at present the state intervenes too much in their lives. Results for several countries are presented in Table 9.5. Interestingly, Eastern Europeans tend to endorse free competition more (71 percent on average) than those in the fifteen older EU members (62 percent). France, with a bare majority (52 percent) endorsing competition, is a bit of an outlier, and one can perhaps see from these data why efforts to reform the French political economy in the 2000s (e.g., by making it easier to fire workers) repeatedly evoked protests. The notoriously "socialist" Swedes, in contrast, come off as even more pro-market than the British, and, most surprisingly, perhaps, those Europeans who place themselves on the Left of the political spectrum also tend to agree (61 percent) about the merits of free competition. As for the more general question about

TABLE 9.5

Pro-Market or Pro-State?

	% Agreeing to Each Proposition							
	Germany	France	Great Britain	Italy	Sweden	Hungary	Poland	Romania
Free competition best guarantee of economic prosperity	74	52	64	64	72	55	74	73
State intervenes too much in our lives	66	62	71	67	71	73	56	47
Need more justice and equality, even if freedom is reduced	63	66	55	74	55	73	70	78

Source: Eurobarometer 66, Autumn 2006.

state intervention, again one finds that a majority agrees that the state does intervene too much, and on this question there is little variance across countries. At the same time, however, as seen in Table 9.5, the same Eurobarometer survey finds solid majorities across Europe agreeing to the proposition that more equality and justice is needed even if individual freedom is reduced. This is admittedly puzzling: one finds that Europeans simultaneously aver that free competition is best for the economy while at the same time agreeing that more justice and equality is needed at the expense of freedom. One way of explaining this outcome is that there could be an "agree bias" built into each question. Or, perhaps, one reacts negatively to generic use of intervention but is favorable when the term intervention is eschewed, replaced by the goals of equality and justice.

As one might suspect, these data hide more than they reveal. Clearly there are both pro-market and pro-statist Europeans, just as there are those who are unequivocally democrats and those who are more ambivalent about democracy and democratic values. The more interesting and complicated questions are occupied with assessing what sorts of people harbor what attitudes and, implicitly, what variables or factors account for aspects of political culture. It is to these questions that we now turn.

Parsing the Data

Thus far we have presented national-level data and made comparisons only across countries. However, just as we know that there are identifiable differences among countries, there are important differences among groups of people within countries.

Just as some Germans are Christian Democrats and some are Social Democrats or Greens, one can also, using survey evidence, point to those that are more pro-market, more tolerant, more interested in politics, and so on, as well as to the factors that contribute to or at least help account for the strength or weakness of various attitudes.

Scholars of political culture would point to several prime candidates that lend themselves to cross-national analysis: education, income, age, religion, and gender.[18] Education is generally associated with pro-democratic attitudes and behaviors as well as a stronger belief in a less interventionist role for the state. Income functions similarly, although the precise effects of income versus education—seeing as how the better educated tend to be wealthier—are hard to disentangle. One would imagine that age could matter, although it would be hard to ascertain if it is a reflection of socio-economic status or a distinct generational effect that might divide older and younger citizens. Religion, traditionally at any rate, has been associated with a less democratic orientation and, to the extent that the religious tend to support the political right, arguably more free market. Gender has been found to be significant in some survey research, with males, perhaps because they feel more empowered, tending to support democratic institutions and free-market policies.

What do we find among the issues we have discussed? Tables 9.6 and 9.7 present a simple analysis, identifying how various sub-groups (e.g., the better educated, those older than fifty) rank versus the average across all European countries in the survey on two selected questions: whether one endorses a strong leader that could dispense with parliament and elections (from the 2005–2007 WVS), and whether

TABLE 9.6

Socio-Demographic Factors on Democratic Attitudes

Attribute	% Positively Inclined to Strong Leader Who Does Not Need Elections
Women	34.8
Men	34.5
Higher Education	22.0
Only Primary Education	42.1
High Income	31.8
Low Income	45.1
Over 50	35.8
Under 30	35.4
Very Religious	44.0
Not Religious	29.2
Satisfied with Democracy	27.0
Not Satisfied with Democracy	48.1
Urban	30.4
Rural	43.6
Survey Mean	34.5

Source: WVS, 2005–2007, from seventeen European countries; online analysis.

TABLE 9.7

Socio-Demographic Factors on the Role of the State

Attribute	% Agreeing Less Government Interference Is Good
Women	29.4
Men	34.4
Higher Education	25.5
Only Primary Education	33.0
High Income	32.3
Low Income	27.8
Over 65	38.3
Under 30	26.8
Very Religious	32.6
Not Religious	31.9
Satisfied with Economy	27.0
Not Satisfied with Economy	39.3
Urban	31.8
Rural	31.2
Survey Mean	29.5

Source: ESS 2002 of twenty-one countries, online analysis.

one believes less government intervention is good for the economy (from the 2002 ESS). Note here that we are looking at all European countries in the survey, and that each country could (and probably does) have its own particular pattern and its own, unique cleavage structures that don't lend themselves to cross-national comparison.

A few comments are in order about each figure. First, as seen in Table 9.6, those in big cities, with more education and higher incomes, are *less likely* to endorse this non-democratic alternative, although, as one sees, just because one is in one or more of these categories is no guarantee that that person would reject the idea of a strong leader dispensing with democracy. These three variables are also found to be associated with "democratic attitudes" on a host of measures. Additionally, there are no gender effects on this question, although on other measures, such as interest in politics, there is a very large gender gap (e.g., 53 percent of males compared with 38 percent of females asserting they are interested in politics). Age also does not seem to matter on this question, although in many countries in Eastern Europe younger respondents do tend to be a little less likely to favor ceding control to a strong leader. Older people across Europe, however, are much more interested in politics (49 percent of those older than fifty, compared with 38 percent of those younger than 30), reflecting the widespread observation that young people have other concerns besides politics. Table 9.6 does show a fairly strong effect of religion, with those going to religious services more than once a week—perhaps more "traditional" individuals—more likely to endorse the "law and order," strong leader option than those who do not attend religious services. Not surprisingly, one also finds that general assessment-type variables also matter. For example, those dissatisfied with their democracies are more likely to favor a non-democratic alternative.

Table 9.7 demonstrates some similarities as well as some differences. First, as one would expect, those with more income are more likely to believe government intervention in the economy is harmful, perhaps reflecting the fact that they are less likely to need forms of government support.[19] Interestingly, however, when one looks at education, those with higher education tend to favor more government involvement in the economy more than those with only a primary education do, perhaps reflecting occupational differences (e.g., the former are more likely to be state employees, the latter more likely to be farmers or tradespeople). Men, more likely to have higher incomes, are also more likely to be against government intervention. Place of residence, comparing those in big cities or suburbs of big cities with those in small towns or villages, has no strong effect. Neither does religion. Interestingly, however, older respondents are also more likely to be against government interference. One might ask why: Is it because they have higher incomes than the under-thirty cohort, composed largely of students or those at the beginning of their careers, or are there some sort of generational effects, meaning that the younger generation in Europe will continue to be less pro-market throughout their lifetimes? Lastly, assessment of the country's current economic performance seems to have a significant effect, with those believing things are going poorly more likely to oppose government intervention in the economy, perhaps reflecting a belief on their part that state involvement in the economy is responsible for poor economic performance.

This discussion is by no means meant to be definitive, and one could employ more advanced statistical techniques such as regression analysis to answer some of the questions posed above. The point, however, is to alert you to the fact that there are various cleavages within countries, making it impossible to generalize about "typical" French, Italian, Turkish, and other national attitudes. It also shows that one can demonstrate some effects of economic, social, and demographic factors on various attributes of political culture, allowing one to suggest what might explain differences across countries and changes over time.

POST-MATERIALIST VALUES

As noted briefly in the previous chapter, scholars of European politics in recent decades have noted the emergence of orientations and values that transcend traditional concerns such as physical and economic security. Characterized as **post-materialism**, these orientations focus more on quality of life (not simply economic growth), expansion of rights, and personal expression and empowerment. Post-materialist values were associated with various campaigns and movements in the 1960s and 1970s, including feminism, the student movement, the "sexual revolution," nuclear disarmament, environmentalism, and protests over US policy in Vietnam. What stood out, however, was that the main protagonists in this "movement" were relatively well-to-do, and their primary concerns were not material, economic gains. In the words of Ronald Inglehart, the scholar most associated with the study of post-materialism, "[a]fter a prolonged period of almost uninterrupted economic growth, the principal axis of political cleavage began to shift

post-materialism ■ orientations that focus more on quality of life issues, such as rights and political participation, than economic or security concerns.

from economic issues to life-style issues, entailing a shift in the constituency most interested in obtaining change."[20] In short, what distinguishes a "post-materialist" from a "materialist" is that whereas the latter gives top priority to physical sustenance and safety, the former places emphasis on belonging, self-expression, and quality of life.[21]

Inglehart suggested that the rise of post-materialism was caused by two factors. First, after World War II, Europeans enjoyed peace and prosperity. Having their most basic needs met, Europeans began to aspire to "higher order" needs such as expanding personal freedoms and maintaining a clean and healthy environment.[22] In addition, there was a **socialization effect**.[23] In other words, individuals acquire basic value orientations at a young age. Those that grew up with affluence—as did the initial post-war generation in Western Europe—were more likely to possess a post-materialist orientation than their parents or grandparents that had experienced the Great Depression and World War II. As time wore on, more and more individuals became part of the "post-materialist" generation. Writing in the 1980s, Inglehart maintained that post-materialism had "moved out of the student ghetto" and was being more commonplace among technocrats and the professional class in Western societies.[24]

socialization effect ■ notion that individuals acquire basic political values at a young age and that different environments can therefore produce generational differences.

Inglehart attempted to identify and measure post-materialism through public opinion surveys, in which respondents are asked to state, among several possible priorities, which are the most important to them. Precise measures have varied from survey to survey. In the 2005–2007 wave of the WVS, mentioned earlier in this chapter, respondents were asked:

> If you had to choose among the following things, which are the *two* that seem the most desirable to you?
>
> - A high level of economic growth
> - Strong defense
> - Giving people more say about how things are done
> - Try to make our cities and countryside more beautiful

Those that chose the first and second options were deemed "materialists"; those choosing the third and fourth were "post-materialists"; those with one from each category were labeled "mixed."

Consistent with his hypotheses, Inglehart found that post-materialist attitudes were most prevalent in wealthier states and among the younger generation and became more prevalent over time. By the late 1980s, post-materialist orientations had grown throughout the continent, with the highest levels of post-materialism were in the Netherlands (25 percent), West Germany (24 percent), and Denmark (18 percent), whereas the lowest figures were in the relatively poorer countries of Spain (12 percent), Greece (8 percent), and Portugal (6 percent).[25] Surveys from Eastern Europe in the 1990s revealed, as one might have predicted based upon levels of economic development, fewer numbers of post-materialists. Inglehart's analysis also found that post-materialist orientations were far more prevalent in those younger than thirty-five as opposed to those older than fifty-five. Furthermore, he maintains that the emergence of post-materialism and its concomitant emphasis on individual liberty and expression has been a contributing factor in democratization in Europe and beyond, as there is a strong link between percentage of post-materialists in a country and its level of democracy.[26]

Post-materialist values are often invoked to explain the emergence of "new" political issues in the 1960s and 1970s and a broader "cultural shift," some aspects of which are examined in more detail in Chapter 12. Some post-materialist "causes," such as feminism and environmentalism, have substantially altered the political landscape, especially in Western Europe. Feminism has experienced various waves, beginning with campaigns in the late nineteenth century to give women the vote and improve social welfare benefits for women and children.[27] In the 1960s and 1970s, "second-wave feminism" began mobilizing forces to press for broader cultural and social change. In the 1970s these movements were able to organize literally millions of women, particularly in the large cities, raised public consciousness, and eventually achieved victories on policies such as equal pay, equal rights, maternity leaves, divorce, and abortion. It is worth noting as well that many elements on the feminists' agenda have been enshrined in EU law and directives, including policies on maternal leave (fourteen weeks paid with full job protection), parental leave (three months unpaid with job protection), and recommendations on expanded access to childcare.[28] Today, by most standards, European states rank among the most progressive in the world in terms of protecting women's rights and creating more equality between the sexes. Many of the basic notions underlying feminism are now enshrined in the political culture, but, arguably, there is still progress to be made. For example, in the 2005–2007 WVS, 22.2 percent of Europeans (with 53.3 percent in Turkey and 35.2 percent in Romania) believe that when jobs are scarce men have more right to a job than women and 30.2 percent of Europeans (61.4 percent of Turks and 55 percent of Romanians) believe men make better political leaders than men. Interestingly, in line with what one would expect from ideas about post-materialism, cross-tabulations show that age and education, not gender, is more strongly related to such attitudes, meaning that younger, better-educated individuals tend to adopt the more "feminist" perspective but that one does not see an especially large division between responses from men and women.

Environmentalism is manifest in many ways in contemporary Europe. As noted in the previous chapter, Green parties can be found in a number of countries, and survey research since the 1970s has noticed a growth in environmental consciousness, participation in environmental causes, and a willingness among large sections of the public to favor "green" policies even if they would sacrifice higher economic growth. Data from a 2007 Eurobarometer survey are reported in Table 9.8. Respondents were given a choice about how important they rated environmental protection. The majority across the EU rated it as "very important," with most of the remainder rating it "fairly important"; overall, 96 percent of respondents considered environmental protection "important." Most respondents reported engaging in some sort of environmental activity (e.g., recycling, reducing water or energy use, using eco-friendly means of transport, etc.). Significantly, as seen in Table 9.8, most consider environmental protection more important than economic competitiveness and would endorse governments spending more money on "green" products, although one sees some evidence that those in Eastern Europe are less inclined to rank the environment as a top priority. Lastly, it is worth noting that protection of the environment is one area where there is strong support for EU-level policy, although one can see differences as publics in Euro-skeptic countries such as Denmark and Great Britain are less supportive of granting the EU a say over environmental policy.

TABLE 9.8

Attitudes of Europeans Toward the Environment

Country	Environmental Protection Very Important	Environmental Protection More Important Than Competitiveness of Economy	Government Should Buy "Green" Products Even If Cost Is Higher	Environmental Policy Should be Shared Between EU and Nat'l Govts
Germany	56	75	75	75
France	79	75	78	61
Great Britain	65	60	78	54
Italy	64	65	56	61
Denmark	71	68	88	61
Sweden	89	71	91	69
Poland	58	55	75	66
Czech Republic	63	57	75	67
Bulgaria	72	44	65	50
EU-27	64	64	73	67

Source: Special Eurobarometer, "Attitudes of European Citizens Towards the Environment," November–December 2007, available at http://ec.europa.eu/public_opinion/archives/ebs/ebs_295_en.pdf

Bicycles are a popular form of green transport in the Netherlands.

INTEREST ORGANIZATIONS AND SOCIAL MOVEMENTS

Political culture—defined as attitudes and values—is only one part of what we might call citizen politics. Participation—or what one *does* based upon one's attitudes and values—is also an important topic to study. People can participate in politics in a number of ways. In Chapter 8 we looked at membership in political parties and voting, the latter an important form of political participation. Another type of political engagement is membership in **interest groups**, associations of individuals united around a common goal that organize and express needs or demands to decision-makers. Unlike political parties, they do not nominate candidates for office and typically they are concerned with a narrower set of issues than political parties, which usually attempt to amalgamate a number of various types of interests and groups.

interest groups ■ associations of individuals, united around a common goal, that organize and express needs or demands to decision-makers.

There are different types of interest groups. Anomic interest groups are spontaneous associations that respond to a particular policy or event but do not possess much of an organizational structure (e.g., student protesters, impromptu demonstrators). Institutional groups have more of a structure but are part of organizations that have other functions besides political interest articulation. Examples would be business corporations, bureaucracies, local governments, or the military. Associational groups are organized to represent the interests of a particular collectivity. They have well-developed structures, formal membership, and usually employ professional staff. Associational groups are ones that typically capture the interest of political scientists as interest organizations. Of course, not all associational groups have a political orientation. For example, one could classify chess clubs, flamenco dancing organizations, or Bible-study groups as associational groups, but, except perhaps in exceptional moments, they would not capture the interest of political scientists. Instead, political scientists are more apt to focus on associational groups that frequently engage with political and economic institutions, such as trade unions, business chambers, professional organizations, and environmental groups. In the European context, it is worth noting as well that powerful interest groups seek to influence policy not only at national level but also at the European (EU) level. Thus, for example, the National Federation of Trade Unions in Sweden has to mind not only what transpires in Stockholm but also seek influence in Brussels, insofar as what the EU decides on social policy or labor law can have a significant effect on their Swedish members.

There is a debate in democratic theory about the contribution and functions of interest groups. Traditionally—in writings such as the *Federalist Papers* or Alexis de Tocqueville's *Democracy in America*—interest organizations have been defended as important mechanisms to express and defend the interests of citizens, provide a means of political participation in between elections, educate the population, and check excessive governmental power. Organized groups of citizens that are independent of the government—in other words, civil society—have been lauded as an essential component of democracy, constituting the means through which people acquire democratic norms and can exercise active citizenship.[29]

Some, however, would complain about the activities of such groups, often deriding them as "special interests." In this view, interest organizations, which have a particular agenda to benefit their members, do not represent the common good of the citizenry. Moreover, not all groups are equal, and their political activities may lack transparency. "Special interests" can therefore hijack the political system, using their funds and lobbying ability to craft policy to suit their own interests, weakening both representative democracy and economic performance. For example, the aforementioned National Federation of Trade Unions in Sweden could seek higher wages for their members, making it both difficult for employers to employ workers and pushing up costs of Swedish-made products for Swedish and European consumers. The same could be said for business, agricultural, or other associations that seek policies than would benefit their membership exclusively. To the extent that people believe their political system has been commandeered and compromised by these groups and that their individual votes no longer matter, this feeds public disillusionment with their political system.

How extensive is participation in various organizations among Europeans? The WVS asks about participation in a number of organizations. Some data from the 2005–2007 survey is presented below in Table 9.9. A couple of items stand out. First, participation is significantly higher in Western Europe, which has a longer tradition of independent associational life, than in Turkey or Eastern Europe, where, until 1989, virtually every interest association was controlled by the Communist Party and many of the older, communist-dominated groups collapsed after communist power fell. Second, even within Western Europe there is marked variance, with the British and the Swedes standing out as far more involved in associational life than, say, the Spanish, Germans, and Italians. Moreover, more in-depth analysis of the data reveal that income and education—factors identified

TABLE 9.9

Participation in Various Social/Interest Organizations

Percentage of Respondents Claiming They Were Active or Inactive Members of Such an Organization

Country	Trade Union	Professional Association	Charitable or Humanitarian	Environmental
Great Britain	19.5	23.7	30.7	16.0
France	11.2	10.4	20.6	14.8
Germany	12.1	9.0	10.4	5.0
Netherlands	21.6	12.6	20.7	15.8
Italy	14.2	16.7	21.1	7.8
Spain	7.5	6.7	9.4	4.7
Sweden	58.4	20.6	33.5	10.7
Finland	52.0	13.0	20.9	9.3
Poland	14.3	9.1	10.3	7.5
Romania	6.6	1.7	1.2	0.7
Bulgaria	7.0	2.8	2	1.4
Turkey	2.8	2.8	2.2	1.2

Source: WVS, 2005–2007.

above as strongly linked to more "democratic" values—are positively related to associational membership, meaning that those with higher incomes, more education are more likely to join associations.

Let us look in a bit more detail at some of the largest and politically most important interest organizations in Europe.

Trade Unions

Trade unions grew in strength throughout much of the twentieth century as Europe became more and more industrialized and more and more individuals left the farms and joined the industrial "working class." Postwar reconstruction bolstered the positions of trade unions in many states, and unions dwarfed all other interest groups, at least in terms of membership. Union membership grew throughout the first three decades after World War II, so that, for example, in 1980 union density (the percentage of workers belonging to unions) was 34.8 percent in the Netherlands, 34.9 percent in Germany, 49.6 percent in Italy, 50.7 percent in Great Britain, 54.1 percent in Belgium, and a staggering 78 percent in Sweden.[30] Moreover, union density was near 100 percent in communist Eastern Europe, although unions in these countries were not independent from the authoritarian Party-state and did not truly represent the interests of workers. While some might view unions as primarily economic organizations—concerned first and foremost with wages and working conditions—they were and are often explicitly political. In many European countries, trade unions enjoy close ties with social democratic or left-leaning political parties, influencing party platforms, helping with campaigns, and placing leaders in the party hierarchy. Like all interest organizations, they also lobby the government for policies that would benefit their members, and, with considerable assets and power over the economy, they have often been successful in procuring pro-worker policies.

The way that trade unions interact with political authorities varies from state to state. In some countries, interest mediation is based on **pluralism**, meaning a number of different unions and other interest groups jockey for power and influence over policy-making. The presence of multiple unions may be due to how unions are organized by occupation, with, for example, separate unions for those in blue-collar and white-collar professions or divisions among unions between workers in more competitive export-oriented sectors and domestically protected ones. Such is the case in Hungary, with seven national-level union confederations, and in Great Britain, which, even though it has an umbrella Trade Unions Congress confederation, is usually categorized as a pluralist system due to the divisions among many unions. More typically, however, unions are divided along ideological or party lines. For example, in France and Italy there are union confederations with a communist orientation, more moderate socialist ones, and still others that identify with Catholic social thought. Turkish unions are similarly divided along ideological and religious lines, with different organizations appealing to secular and more Islamic workers. In Poland, the two main union groups are Solidarity, which emerged in 1980 to challenge communist rule and the OPZZ, the formerly "official" unions linked to the communist authorities.

pluralism ■ system of interest mediation in which a number of different interest groups compete for power and influence.

corporatism ■ system of interest mediation in which centralized, singular interest groups, such as a single trade union federation, work closely with the government to coordinate economic policy.

social partnership ■ a feature of a corporatist system, these are bargains among unions, employers, and government designed to foster growth, employment, and peaceful labor relations.

In other European countries, one finds corporatist systems of interest representation. Under **corporatism**, unions enjoy a formal, institutionalized seat at the policymaking table. Rather than just lobbying or competing for influence as in pluralist systems, in corporatist systems unions, together with business organizations and government officials, have a prescribed political role and help set national economic policy. For example, wages are set at a nation-wide or industry-wide level by a bargaining process involving not just unions and employers but the government. In corporatist systems, there is typically one primary or peak interest organization that is centrally organized. This makes negotiations easier, and arguably such an organization, representing a wide swath of workers or employers, is better able to look to common good and oversee enforcement of agreements. Many in the 1970s and 1980s praised the corporatist systems and the resulting "**social partnership**" in such countries as Austria, Sweden, the Netherlands, and Germany as producing economic growth, greater equality, generous welfare states, and being less disruptive and chaotic than the more pluralist systems of Great Britain, Italy, and France, in which multiple competing trade unions did not have guaranteed access to policy-making and often engaged in protests against government policy.[31]

Corporatism's heyday, both in real life and as a subject for study, is long over. Unions, once powerful political forces across much of Europe, have suffered a precipitous decline in membership and in influence in the past three decades, as seen in Table 9.10. One could point to several factors that have negatively affected trade unions: anti-union governments (most notoriously Margaret Thatcher's in Great Britain [1979–1990]), privatization of state-owned industries, the decline of blue-collar manufacturing enterprises, shifts in the nature of work to provision of

TABLE 9.10

Union Decline in European Countries

Union Density in Select Years and Countries

Country	1970	1980	1990	2000	2003
Great Britain	44.8	50.7	39.3	29.7	29.3
France	21.7	18.3	10.1	8.2	8.3
Germany	32	34.9	31.2	25	22.6
Italy	37	49.6	38.8	34.9	33.7
Spain	n/a	12.9	12.5	16.1	16.3
Netherlands	36.5	34.8	24.3	23.1	22.3
Sweden	67.7	78	80.8	79.1	78
Finland	51.3	69.4	72.5	75	74.1
Poland	n/a	n/a	53.1	n/a	14.7[a]
Czech Republic	n/a	n/a	78.8	n/a	27[a]
EU	37.8	39.7	33.1	27.3	26.3[b]

Source: Visser, 2006, p. 45.
[a]Data from 2001.
[b]Data from 2002.

services and more part-time work, and global pressures on European businesses to cut costs. In most European countries, the public sector (e.g., educational and health care establishments, government bureaucracies, state-owned firms) is the strongest redoubt of trade unions. A few states, such as Sweden and Finland, still have sizeable labor organizations, but these are the exception. Across Eastern Europe, for example, the dream of trade union leaders to replicate the "Swedish model" and create powerful corporatist institutions was not realized.[32] As for unions' political influence, many of the unions' chief political allies on the left end of the political spectrum (e.g., the French and Italian Communist and Socialist Parties, the British Labour Party, the German Social Democratic Party, Social Democratic parties throughout post-communist Europe) have either lost much of their former appeal or they have gravitated to the center in the hope of winning more middle-class voters. Notably, a Eurobarometer survey from 2005 found that only 40 percent of European citizens (and only 28 percent in post-communist Europe) trusted trade unions, which placed them lower on the trust scale than the police, army, charitable organizations, the media, and the UN, although, one should note, higher in most cases than political parties or parliaments.[33]

This is not to say that unions are now irrelevant. Strikes, particularly among transportation workers, remain virtually yearly rituals in countries such as France and Italy, and protests by unions in Germany and France have weakened or stopped labor-market reforms in both countries that would have made it easier to fire workers. In Poland, vestiges of the Solidarity labor movement were a major force in Polish politics for over a decade after communism's fall. However, it would be safe to say that the general trend in Europe—and globally, for that matter—has worked against unions, as elements of the welfare state, one of the trade union movement's primary accomplishments, have come under assault and workers, facing both competition from cheap labor overseas and, in many cases, double-digit unemployment rates, are in a poor position vis-à-vis their employers. These issues are taken up in greater detail in the next chapter.

Business Organizations

Trade unions' main rivals—or, in corporatist systems perhaps, partners—are business organizations. Since they represent corporations, they are not mass membership organizations like trade unions, but, nonetheless, thanks to their resources and organizational capacity, they yield considerable influence in many European states. Typically, business associations press for benefits such as lower corporate taxes, fewer protections for workers, start-up monies for investment, and subsidies for business. In some cases, relations between business groups and workers can be very adversarial, and both groups lobby the government for their own cause. In states with corporatist systems, social partnership is the ideal, and business-labor relations, in general, is less conflictual. Even though many business organizations bring together thousands of different enterprises, their corporate-based membership is dwarfed by mass membership organizations such as trade unions.

Like workers, however, not all employers are the same, and thus often—especially in non-corporatist systems—one finds several business associations within a given state. For example, one (e.g., the League of German Industry or the Movement of French Enterprises) might represent large companies, while another (e.g., the National Association of German Employers or the French General Federation of Small and Medium Enterprises) primarily represents small or medium-size enterprises. Whereas most business associations are associated with Conservative (in Great Britain), Christian Democratic (in Germany), or Liberal (in the European sense) parties (as in the Netherlands), they may be divided on other grounds. For example, some business associations may represent older industries and lobby from protection from cheaper foreign imports (e.g., steel producers); others in more competitive industries may favor free trade (e.g., automakers who don't want to pay more for steel). Some businesses are owned in whole or in part by the state (e.g., the giant multinational Airbus) and rely upon state support for their survival, and they may have different agendas from businesses or business associations of privately owned companies that by and large favor more *laissez-faire* policies. In most countries, there are separate business associations on the regional level (e.g., Catalan business groups in Spain, Bavarian ones in Germany, those concentrated around Milan and other industrial centers in northern Italy) that implicitly compete with business associations representing firms in other parts of the country. In Turkey, one finds two main business groups: the Turkish Businessmen and Industrialists' Union that is grounded in the secular establishment and another, the Independent Businessmen and Industrialists' Union that caters to businesses with a more Islamic orientation. Finally, unlike the individual worker, individual large companies (e.g., Shell, Renault, Siemens) can be effective political actors in their own right, either through support of candidates or through lobbying efforts. In post-communist Europe, with its nascent capitalist systems, business organizations are not as well organized, and lobbying of individual firms is more commonplace, although in many countries the close connections between business and politics has fueled political corruption.

Agricultural Associations

Several countries also have sizeable agricultural organizations. The largest ones are the National Federation of Agricultural Enterprises in France and the Italian General Confederation of Agriculture, each of which claims to represent hundreds of thousands of agricultural producers and enterprises. Although the largest number of farmers in Europe today is in poorer post-communist countries such as Poland and Romania, farm associations are weaker there, in part a vestige of the communist experience. As with business groups, there are scores of sector-specific agricultural associations, ranging from those that represent French wine makers to those of Greek olive producers to British beekeepers. Agricultural associations have had a great deal of success in the past in lobbying for financial support from the state. In France, because rural political districts are over-represented, farmers have traditionally been an important lobby, generally connected to parties on the right and, at times, mobilizing to protest government policies. In Italy, the General Confederation of Agriculture, tied to the Christian Democratic Party, enjoyed for years a corporatist type of relationship with the state, becoming almost a quasi-state agency as it administered credits, subsidies, and other services to farmers. Generally speaking, however, as fewer and fewer Europeans are employed in agriculture, agricultural organizations have lost much of their political importance, and, since agricultural policy is now by and large established at the EU level with the Common Agricultural Policy (CAP), more and more of their lobbying efforts concentrate on activities in Brussels.

Other Interest Organizations

Traditionally, most discussions of interest organizations among political scientists center on economic organizations, those representing workers, employers, and farmers. There are, of course, many other interest organizations that are not strictly economic in orientation. Examples would include professional organizations (e.g., medical societies, academic societies), human rights and humanitarian organizations (e.g., Amnesty International and *Médecins sans frontières*, religious organizations, environmental groups, and ethnic organizations. Although some of these organizations are not expressly political, concentrating on items such as maintenance of professional standards, education, and social networking, they can be "political" by lobbying for particular government policies (including, in some cases, higher wages for their members), special "rights," or access to public monies. At times, they can be controversial. For example, ethnic-minority groups such as Basques and Catalans in Spain, Turks in Germany, and ethnic Serbs in Kosovo have their own organizations to advance their particular set of demands, at times creating conflict with the ethnic majority. Some ethnically defined groups go even further, advocating separatism, and a few (e.g., ETA for the Basques in Spain, the PKK for the Kurds in Turkey) engage in terrorist activities.

Social Movements

Citizens can participate in politics in means beyond voting and formal membership or support to an organized interest group. One could assess their level of civic engagement by considering, for example, whether they attempt to have their voice heard by contacting their representatives, signing a petition, or engaging in protests or demonstrations. Such activities might be part of grassroots politics, a more informal, neighborhood or community-based effort to produce some sort of political change. Some grassroots campaigns remain entirely local. Examples might be an effort to secure better funding for the municipality's library or dedicate a monument to some local notable. Others, however, can be transformed into a broader-based **social movement**, meaning "a conscious, collective, organized attempt to bring about or resist large-scale change in the social order by non-institutionalized means."[34]

social movement ■ conscious, collective, organized attempt to bring about or resist large-scale change in the social order by non-institutionalized means.

Social movements can be distinguished from interest groups in various ways. For one, they usually aim for something big; they are less interested in day-to-day, piecemeal change as a permanent, bureaucratic organization might be. Instead, they strive to produce fundamental political change (e.g., think of suffrage, civil rights, labor *movements* as opposed to the more routine and prosaic activities of the typical trade union). They also tend to be more ephemeral than interest organizations; they either run out of energy or achieve their goal, obviating the need for a movement. Moreover, social movements usually are based upon and require active participation (e.g., marches, protests, sit-ins, etc.)—what one scholar identifies as "politically confrontational and socially disruptive tactics"[35]—as opposed to interest organizations that often rely upon people to pay dues in order to hire a professional staff to do the work of the group. Social movements thus seek to gain influence through the power of social mobilization—bringing people out for the cause—as opposed to behind-the-scenes lobbying or campaign donations. True, some social movements can spawn organizations (e.g., the labor movement of the late nineteenth and early twentieth century leading to trade unions), but it is the masses of people in the streets or otherwise gaining exposure in the media that comprise the labor *movement*, peace *movement*, the anti-nuclear *movement*, the women's *movement*, and so on.

In recent European history, one can point to a few prominent social movements, several, as noted above, linked to the rise of post-materialist values. A more contemporary example might be the movement against the war in Iraq in the 2000s in several European countries, which was able to draw millions of people into the streets to protest the actions of the US and several European governments (e.g., Great Britain, Spain, Italy) that sent troops to Iraq. While it is harder at present to identify pan-European social movements, there have been widespread protests in a number of countries focusing on rather specific concerns. Examples include German students protesting higher fees for university attendance, French farmers and workers protesting globalization, Polish workers protesting pro-market policies of their government, and Turkish organizations mobilizing for human rights. Indeed, one could argue that social movements are becoming more and more commonplace, a feature seen, in some form or another, in most European states and around the world.[36]

While protests can often generate headlines, one still might ask how much Europeans participate in social movements or other forms of active citizenship. A precise answer is hard to come by, in large part because people may have different conceptions of what constitute a social movement and surveys typically do not employ the term. However, surveys do regularly ask about different modes of political participation as well as the degree of participation in organizations, including whether one has performed volunteer work. This line of inquiry gets at the idea of active participation, something more than vicarious membership in an association.

Data from the WVS reveal sizeable variance in these forms of political participation. When asked in the 2005–2007 wave if they had participated in the lawful demonstration or protest, 14 percent reported all respondents reported doing so, with the largest figures in Great Britain (54.1 percent) and in Turkey (31.7 percent), the latter of which had seen a variety of protests tied to political causes. The lowest figures were in Poland (4.5 percent), where social mobilization has fallen precipitously since the early 1990s, and in Finland (5.9 percent), where, one might suggest, there may simply be less reason to protest. More people (36.5 percent) reported signing a petition, with the highest figures in Great Britain (81.3 percent) and Sweden (70.5 percent) and the lowest figures in Bulgaria (9.3 percent) and Romania (5.8 percent). Post-communist states also ranked lower in the 1999–2000 WVS when people were queried about unpaid work in a civic association. In Poland and Hungary, for example, fewer than 15 percent of respondents reported such activity, compared to over 50 percent of Swedes and nearly half of the Dutch. If one's "ideal citizen" is one that is *actively* involved in associational life—in other words, a participant in civil society—one finds many countries fall short, especially in post-communist

Europe. Again, the usual variables—the younger city dwellers who are better off and better educated—are associated with non-voting political activity of all types.

What do these data mean? Are too few people engaged in political life? Is democracy the province of the elite, with most people watching passively from the sidelines? Does democracy really require active citizenship? Would politics function better if everyone was constantly protesting, advancing a grassroots initiative, or contacting officials? Can there be "too much" civil society? Many would argue, of course, that Swedish or Dutch democracy functions better than Bulgarian or Romanian democracy, but does that mean that the Swedes or Dutch are better citizens? Are the shortcomings of democratic government in parts of Europe the fault of citizens of those states?

These questions return us to those posed at the beginning of this chapter: How much does political culture matter? Can it be employed to explain specific political outcomes, such as the phenomenon of Berlusconi or a particular Italian style of politics? How can one conclusively isolate political culture from other possible explanatory variables? These are difficult questions, and while it might be easy to make links based on anecdotes or casual observations (e.g., Berlusconi is an outgrowth of various unsavory elements of Italian culture), such positions are often hard to prove with solid evidence and analytical rigor. Learned political scientists frequently debate the overall importance of political culture. As you familiarize yourself with the development and functioning of European governments, you can offer your own hypotheses and assessments.

APPLICATION QUESTIONS

1. Make a simple argument that political culture causes a particular outcome. How can one prove it to be true?
2. At the same time post-materialism, which in many respects is about greater freedom, was appearing in Europe, the welfare state, which created a more pronounced role for the state in many spheres of life, was also expanding. What, if anything, is the relationship between the two phenomena?
3. Based upon your responses to the question (on p. 252) that tries to gauge post-materialism, what are you? Does the causal type of explanation offered by Inglehart seem compelling in your case? In other words, what factors (e.g., family economic status, future expectations, world events) helped produce your values?
4. Despite economic and social problems, why do you think citizens in post-communist states have lower levels of non-voting political behavior? Why do you think Scandinavians have some of the highest?
5. Have unions outlived their usefulness in modern, developed democracies? What explains the varying rates of unionization in European countries?

KEY TERMS

corporatism 258
interest groups 255
interpersonal trust 240
pluralism 257
political culture 236
political efficacy 244
political legitimacy 241
political socialization 238
political tolerance 240
post-materialism 251
social capital 240
social movement 261
social partnership 258
socialization effect 252

ADDITIONAL READING

Dalton, Russell. 2004. *Democratic Challenges, Democratic Choices: The Erosion of Political Support in Advanced Industrial Democracies.* Oxford: Oxford University Press.

Based on examination of survey research, this work looks at various challenges to contemporary democracies, in particular the lack of trust in political institutions.

Inglehart, Ronald, and Welzel, Christian. 2005. *Modernization, Cultural Change, and Democracy.* Cambridge: Cambridge University Press.

This book, building upon previous works by Inglehart, is global in scope and more explicit in linking the emergence of post-materialism and economic growth with democratic development.

Montero, José, and Torcal, Mariano, eds. 2006. *Political Disaffection in Contemporary Democracies: Social Capital, Institutions and Politics.* London: Routledge.

Looking in particular at public attitudes and low levels of civic engagement, this collection of essays takes up the question of whether modern democracies are experiencing some sort of crisis.

Rose, Richard. 2009. *Understanding Post-Communist Transformation: A Bottom Up Approach.* New York: Routledge.

Based upon almost two decades of survey work in post-communist Europe, this book analyzes the role of public opinion and civil society in the transformation to democracy and capitalism.

Tarrow, Sidney. 1998. *Power in Movement: Social Movements and Contentious Politics.* Cambridge: Cambridge University Press.

In this seminal source in the literature on social movements, Tarrow focuses attention both on theories of political activism and on the emergence of "new" social movements in the 1960s and 1970s.

END NOTES

1. Alexander Stille, "The Corrupt Reign of Emperor Silvio," *New York Review of Books*, April 8, 2010, pp. 18–22. See also the film, *Videocracy*, directed by Erik Gandini, which appeared in 2009.
2. Stille, "The Corrupt Reign," p. 18.
3. Lucian Pye, "Political Culture," in *International Encyclopedia of the Social Sciences* (New York: Macmillan, 1968), p. 218.
4. Harry Eckstein, *Regarding Politics* (Berkeley: University of California Press, 1992).
5. Quoted in Ariane Chebel d'Appollonia, "European Nationalism and European Union," in Anthony Pagden, *The Idea of Europe: From Antiquity to the European Union* (Cambridge: Cambridge University Press, 2002), p. 174.
6. Unlike most currencies, the euro notes do not feature a human face. Instead, representative, somewhat banal examples of European architecture appear on the bills, although each country was free to put its own design(s) on euro coins.
7. By far the strongest feeling of Europeanness was in Luxembourg (13.4 percent as first choice, 21.1 percent as second choice); Iceland, not surprisingly, had the lowest such feelings (0.7 percent claiming Europe as their first choice).
8. Eurobarometer 64.2, conducted in October–November 2005, published June 2006. This is from question 39.
9. Only in Cyprus (57 percent) and Malta (51 percent), two small island-nations that joined the EU in 2004, did a majority get all three questions right. In several longstanding EU countries, the results were far worse: Germany (18 percent), Netherlands (18 percent), Great Britain (17 percent), and Italy (14 percent). All from Special Eurobarometer, "The Future of Europe," published in May 2006.
10. Wolfgang Lutz, Sylvia Kritzinger, and Vegard Skirbekk, "The Demography of Growing European Identity," *Science* 314:425, October 20, 2006, pp. 425–426.
11. All of these surveys are conducted according to rigorous social science standards, including selection of a random sample of respondents, face-to-face interviews with trained surveyors, and questions that lend themselves to cross-national and longitudinal (across-time) analysis. The results from all are available online. Data from the World Values Survey can be found at http://www.worldvaluessurvey.org. Data from the ESS are available

at http://ess.nsd.uib.no. Eurobarometers are archived at http://ec.europa.eu/public_opinion/standard_en.htm.

12. These are France, Germany, Italy, Spain, the Netherlands, Great Britain, Cyprus, Turkey, Finland, Sweden, Serbia, Slovenia, Romania, Bulgaria, Andorra, and Switzerland. Other rounds of the WVS surveyed other countries.
13. Russell Dalton, *Democratic Challenges, Democratic Choices: The Erosion of Political Support in Advanced Industrial Democracies* (Oxford: Oxford University Press, 2004).
14. Charles Maier, "Democracy and Its Discontents," *Foreign Affairs* 73:4, July–August 1994: 48–64.
15. *The Economist*, "Public Opinion: Is there a crisis?" July 17, 1999, pp. 49–50.
16. Ralf Dahrendorf, "Afterword," in Susan Pharr and Robert Putnam, eds. *Disaffected Democracies: What's Troubling the Trilateral Countries?* (Princeton: Princeton University Press, 2000), p. 311. See also Russell Dalton, *Democratic Challenges*.
17. The classic treatment of legitimacy is Max Weber, *Economy and Society* (1925). Weber makes a distinction between *Herrschaft* (Rule) and *Macht* (Power or Force), maintaining that a state cannot survive solely on force.
18. This list is by no means exhaustive. Again, the goal is to illustrate some basic patterns, not answer complex issues within political science.
19. The effect for income is less pronounced than it might be as the available measure for income puts income in absolute (e.g., number of euros earned each month) as opposed to relative (e.g., top quarter within each country) terms. The WVS uses a relative measure for income.
20. Ronald Inglehart, *The Silent Revolution: Changing Values and Political Styles Among Western Publics* (Princeton: Princeton University Press, 1977), p. 285.
21. Ronald Inglehart, *Culture Shift in Advanced Industrial Society* (Princeton: Princeton University Press, 1990), p. 66.
22. Central sources for Inglehart are Abraham Maslow, *Motivation and Personality* (New York: Harper, 1954), and Karl Deutsch, *The Nerves of Government* (New York: Free Press, 1963).
23. Inglehart, *Culture Shift*, p. 68.
24. Inglehart, *Culture Shift*, p. 331.
25. Inglehart, *Culture* Shift, p. 93, and Inglehart, *Modernization and Postmodernization: Cultural, Economic and Political Change in 43 Societies* (Princeton, NJ: Princeton: Princeton University Press, 1997), p. 38.
26. Ronald Inglehart and Christian Welzel, *Modernization, Cultural Change, and Democracy*. (Cambridge: Cambridge University Press, 2005), p. 154–155.
27. For an excellent web resource on European feminism, see "Feminism in Europe" at http://www.cddc.vt.edu/feminism/eur.html, accessed October 8, 2009.
28. Catherine Hoskyns, *Integrating Gender: Women, Law, and Politics in the European Union* (London: Verso, 1996).
29. Jean Cohen and Andrew Arato, *Civil Society and Political Theory* (Cambridge: MIT Press, 1992), and Robert Putnam, *Making Democracy Work: Civic Traditions in Modern Italy* (Princeton: Princeton University Press, 1993)
30. Data from Jelle Visser, "Union Membership Statistics in 24 Countries," *Monthly Labor Review*, January 2006, p. 45.
31. Miriam Golden. "The Dynamics of Trade Unionism and National Economic Performance, *American Political Science Review* 87:2, June 1993: 439–454.
32. Paul Kubicek, *Organized Labor in Postcommunist States: From Solidarity to Infirmity* (Pittsburgh: University of Pittsburgh Press, 2004). The one exception may be Slovenia, which inherited a different type of communism that gave greater authority to workers.
33. Eurobarometer 64.2, conducted in October–November 2005 and published in June 2006. Notably, the lowest levels of trust were in Eastern Europe (Bulgaria, 13 percent, Hungary, 20 percent, Poland, 25 percent) and France (31 percent), whereas the highest were in the more "corporatist" countries: Austria (52 percent), Denmark (56 percent), Finland (59 percent), and the Netherlands (62 percent).
34. John Wilson, *Introduction to Social Movements* (New York: Basic Books, 1973) p. 8.
35. Cyrus Zirakzadeh, *Social Movements in Politics: A Comparative Study* (London: Longman, 1997), p. 5.
36. Sidney Tarrow, *Power in Movement: Social Movements and Contentious Politics*, 2nd ed. (New York: Cambridge University Press, 1998).

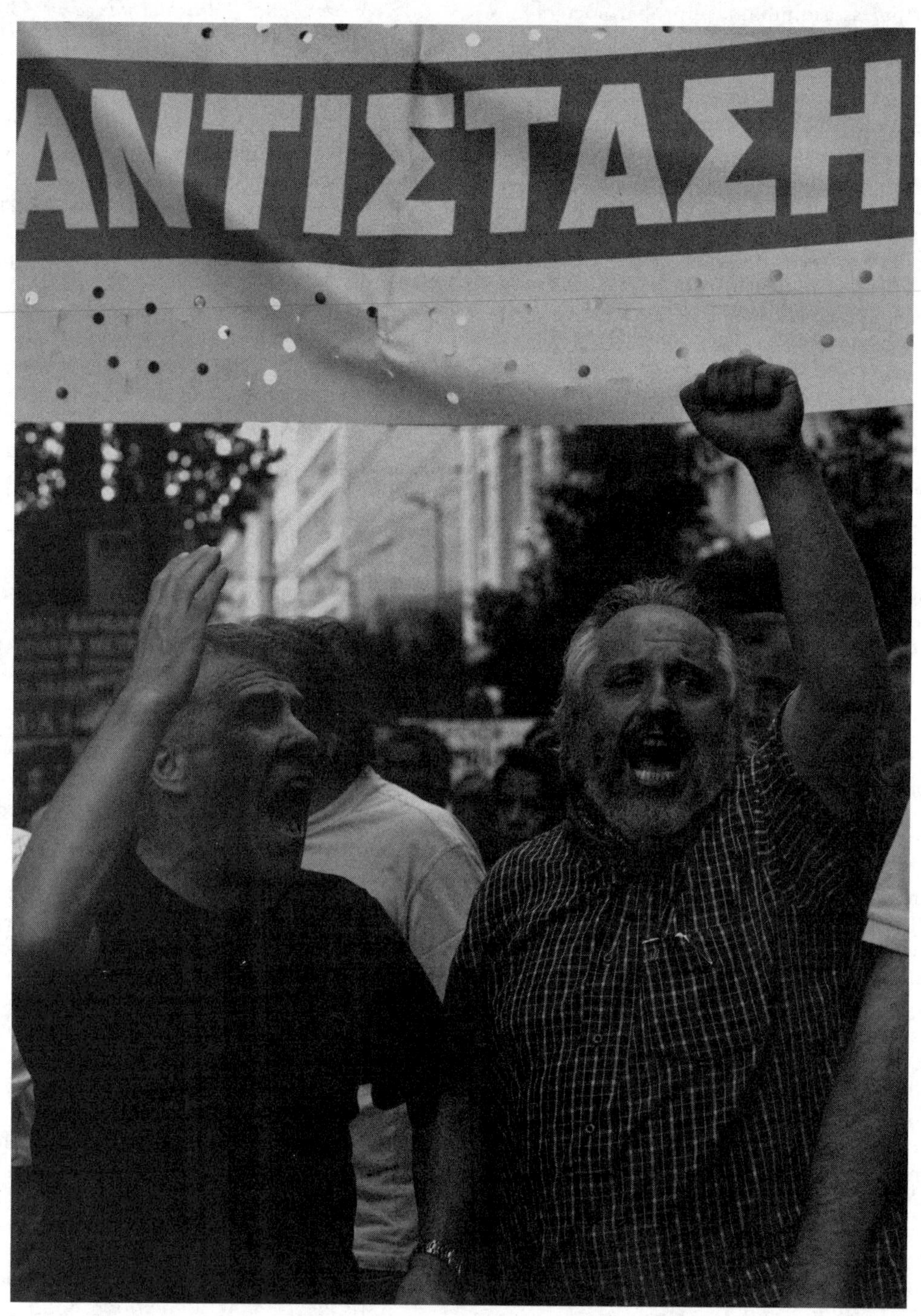

Greeks protest government austerity measures to overcome debt crisis.

CHAPTER 10

Economic and Social Issues in Europe

In 2010, the EU faced perhaps the greatest post-Cold War test of the economic and political unity of the continent. The immediate issue was Greece, which, as a result of years of economic mismanagement and the economic crisis of 2008 to 2010, had run up a massive debt that it could not repay. Greece needed to borrow more money: specifically, €53 billion just to cover its obligations for 2010.[1] The problem, however, was that lenders had little confidence in Greece (whose national accounts had earlier been falsified), and were demanding such high interest rates that borrowing was unaffordable. Greece therefore turned to its European partners for assistance. Many, particularly the Germans, were skeptical, and insisted that Greece had to take measures, such as raising taxes and cutting spending on everything from pensions, civil servant salaries, education, and infrastructure, to get its economic house in order, and perhaps even needed to turn to the International Monetary Fund (IMF) for assistance. Such a response was hardly reassuring, least of all to those who thought that European countries should take the lead in solving European economic problems. Meanwhile, many Greeks mobilized against the impending reforms, with one protest leading to the deaths of three people.

The crisis proved to be at least as much a test for Europe as it was for Greece. Greece by itself, after all, is a relatively small economy. Its importance lay in the fact that it uses the euro, and if it failed it would have reverberations for the entire eurozone. Some believed that failure to act in this case would mean the end of the euro itself, and that "Europe"—the idea of an increasingly united continent—was at stake. Angela Merkel, Germany's chancellor, was reluctant to commit German taxpayer money to the profligate Greeks.[2] In the end, however, with the fear of the Greek "disease" spreading to other heavily indebted countries such as Portugal, Ireland, Spain, and Italy and the specter of steep stock market plunges, European leaders agreed to an ambitious €800 billion ($1 trillion) package that would help guarantee eurozone economies against default. Whereas this decision seems likely to prevent the worst fears from materializing, it remains to be seen both if Greece can politically and economically weather a crisis that will still take years to resolve and if other states fall into a hole as deep as Greece's.

This example dramatically and vividly demonstrates the importance of economic issues, both to individual countries and to Europe as a whole, and it also shows how the economic connections that have developed since World War II—most clearly seen with the euro—can also have negative repercussions. Europe is more tightly connected than ever before, but the flip side of the benefits of greater trade and investment is that each country becomes more vulnerable to events and forces beyond its borders. In this sense, the Greek crisis is a statement not only about Europeanization but also about the more general phenomenon of globalization.

This chapter takes up economic issues in contemporary Europe, looking both at longer-term trends and issues that emerged in the wake of the crisis at the end of the first decade of the 2000s. Although the Greek crisis garnered the headlines in the spring of 2010, economic issues *writ large* always rank as a top concern for citizens and are a major subject of public policy. As noted in Chapter 1, some would contend that the European socio-economic model, which includes a much more developed welfare state than in the US, is one of the cornerstones of European identity. This model took root after World War II and helped ensure economic growth, a high standard of living, and economic security for millions of Europeans. However, in recent decades, as growth in Europe has generally slowed, this model has been challenged on both pragmatic grounds (e.g., can European governments afford it?) and on ideological grounds (e.g., is the high-tax, high-government spending model really the best?). Whether or not European states can maintain this model and what policies or reforms might be more attractive are important questions to consider as we look to the future.

This chapter thus takes up the challenges facing the European economies and the welfare state. Although Europe, compared to other regions of the world, remains rich, many Europeans were concerned about their economic situation even before Greece's collapse in 2010 threatened to spread to other corners of the continent. For years, many European states were plagued by chronically high (10 percent or more) unemployment, economic growth was more sluggish than in the US and in the high-flying emerging economies, and high labor costs and regulations were, arguably, leading to the loss of jobs to other countries such as China and India. Even though the global economic crisis that began in 2007 was rooted primarily in developments in the US, its effects quickly spread to Europe, compounding existing problems and creating dire economic conditions in previously "success stories" such as Iceland, Ireland, Spain, Latvia, and Hungary as well as the aforementioned crisis in Greece. Bailing out heavily indebted countries and generating economic growth and employment across Europe remain major challenges both to European governments and to the efforts of the EU to make Europe globally more competitive and dynamic.

MARGARET THATCHER AND IDEOLOGICAL CHALLENGES TO THE WELFARE STATE

We'll begin our discussion by backing up a bit and continuing the chronological narrative of Chapter 2. One might recall that we ended the discussion of the European welfare state in that chapter in the 1970s, when several states, but especially Great Britain, began to experience lower growth and higher inflation and unemployment. This caused a series of political crises in Britain (e.g., nationwide strikes) and led some to rethink previous assumptions about the "collectivist consensus" that endorsed a strong role for the state in the economy. By the late 1970s, critics of the British welfare state rallied to the Conservative leader, Margaret Thatcher, who became prime minister in 1979. Serving in that post until 1990, Thatcher identified the "nanny state" as the source of Britain's troubles and remade the political economy of Great Britain. She has served a model globally for advocates of less government and market mechanisms.

Britain's Crises in the 1970s and Thatcher's Emergence

As noted earlier in this text, Great Britain was, compared with other European states such as West Germany, a relative poor economic performer in the post-war period. One could list numerous reasons for this development—poor state planning, an aging industrial base, lack of investment in new technologies—but Thatcher and like-minded conservatives saw Britain's economic stagflation in the 1970s—rising unemployment, accelerating inflation (24 percent in 1975), and low growth—as an indication that the big government model of the post-war collectivist consensus needed to be replaced. Her answer was relatively simple: The state needed to get out of the way to let free markets function more efficiently.

Margaret Thatcher had bold and, at the time, controversial, ideas. In the early 1970s, she served as education minister. In order to meet budget targets, she abolished free milk in Britain's schools, earning her the sobriquet "Maggie Thatcher Milk Snatcher."[3] She was ardently committed to principles of smaller government, leading the Conservative Party by proclaiming that it was time to end the quest for political consensus. Although many found her style abrasive, enough Britons believed that she was right, or, at least, offered a more convincing program than the hapless Labour Party. The Conservatives won the 1979 elections and Thatcher became prime minister.

Thatcherism: Freer Markets, Smaller Government

Thatcher came into office with a clear, ideological mission. She did not merely want to reform the welfare state. She intended to scrap many elements of it and remake British culture. Her policies, known as "**Thatcherism**," contained several elements. Taxes were cut to help stimulate investment and spending. The basic tax rate on incomes fell from 33 percent to 25 percent and the highest rate declined from 83 percent to 40 percent. The government also pursued **privatization**, meaning that state-owned assets such as oil companies, mines, public housing, and marquee firms such as British Airways, British Telecom, and Rolls Royce were sold to private investors. Revenue from privatization totaled over $100 billion during her tenure in office. Government regulations, which she viewed as hampering business growth, were scaled back. She sought to cut government spending, particularly on social welfare programs. She attacked the trade unions, ending corporatist tripartite arrangements that gave unions access to policy-making, passing legislation that made it more difficult for workers to strike, and effectively destroying (with great relish) the once-powerful miners' union. She was pro-American and highly skeptical of European integration, claiming that all problems came from

Thatcherism ■ economic philosophy espoused by Margaret Thatcher in Great Britain that argued for lower taxes, freer markets, and less state influence in the economy.

privatization ■ the selling of state-owned enterprises to private owners, pursued in numerous states to promote efficiency and raise revenue.

across the English Channel and all solutions from across the Atlantic. No child of the 1960s, she fought to reestablish traditional values, and, even though she was Britain's first female prime minister, she did not consider herself a feminist.

The overall theme of her program was stress on the individual, freeing the individual from a predatory and paternalistic state and demanding that individuals be responsible for their own fate. In a 1987 interview, she said,

> I think we've been through a period where too many people have been given to understand that if they have a problem, it's the government's job to cope with it. 'I have a problem, I'll get a grant.' 'I'm homeless, the government must house me.' They're casting their problem on society. And, you know, there is no such thing as society. There are individual men and women, and there are families. And no government can do anything except through people, and people must look to themselves first.[4]

Yet, at the same time, she recentralized government, stripping away the powers of local governments and school boards. Presiding over a "remarkable and somewhat disconcerting revival of the British state," Britain under Thatcher, unlike under her predecessors, was "ruled."[5]

It is worth mentioning, however, what Thatcher did not do. While spending was cut for public housing and transport, she did not seek to dismantle the National Health Service, a state-body that dispensed "socialized medicine." British universities remained tuition-free. Total government spending, as percentage of the economy, still remained over 40 percent of gross domestic product (GDP), roughly the same as it was in the late 1970s, in part because unemployment rose—by 1985 twice as many Britons were unemployed as ten years before—and the government was obligated to pay unemployment benefits. Thatcher, then, did not wholly destroy the welfare state, although her policies did refashion both the economy and state-society relations and, perhaps most importantly, changed the political discourse by suggesting that markets, not states, were the best organizers of economic life.

What Did Thatcherism Do for Britain?

Thatcher's rule—in substance and style—was controversial.[6] Former Conservative Prime Minister Harold MacMillan, critical of privatization, accused her of selling "the family silver" and others condemned what they saw as her promotion of greed and "the unacceptable face of capitalism."[7] Her combative style was off-putting to many, and many thought she had no compassion for the less fortunate. Nonetheless, she stuck to her program and won elections in 1983 and 1987.

In part, Thatcher benefited from the weakness of the Labour Party, which was still wedded to an outdated, left-wing program. In addition, however, many would point to positive developments in Britain in the 1980s. After an initial decline from 1979 to 1981, the economy began to rebound, thanks in part to the collapse of inefficient firms, increased competition, and pro-business policies, which attracted needed foreign investment. Millions of British citizens became homeowners and shareholders in privatized firms. Inflation was tamed to single digits, productivity rose, and profits soared. Growth rates in the late 1980s were over 4 percent, led by the burgeoning financial and service sectors.

Critics, however, would point to high social costs of Thatcherism. Unemployment, which was under 5 percent prior to her rule rose to nearly 12 percent by 1986. Although by 1990 unemployment had fallen to under 6 percent, Thatcher's reign tended to favor the "haves" over the "have-nots." Inequality increased, with the wealthiest ten percent of Britons seeing a 65 percent increase in after-tax income in the 1980s, compared to a 14 percent decline for the bottom ten percent.[8] This took on a regional dimension as well as London and southern England prospered in comparison with northern England, Scotland, and Wales. Public services, in particular housing and transport, were squeezed of funds. Private affluence, in the words of one critic, was accompanied by "public squalor."[9]

Thatcher's Impact

Despite these problems and her polarizing personality, the latter of which helped cost her leadership of the Conservative Party in 1990, Thatcher's political legacy is substantial. Old statist approaches were discredited, and, under the leadership of Tony Blair, the opposition Labour Party moved toward the political center. Blair's "New Labour," which came to power in 1997, built on some of Thatcher's successes while trying to be softer around the edges. This is discussed more below. To the extent that Britain, since the late 1980s, has had one of Europe's more successful economies, many would say the Margaret Thatcher laid the groundwork.

Thatcher, however, is a world-historical figure. Her ideas influenced Ronald Reagan, who led a similar campaign against big government during his presidency in the US, and her ideas about markets and privatization became the orthodoxy of the so-called "Washington Consensus" of international development agencies and were pursued in China, India, and Latin America. Within Europe, one can point to her influence in numerous settings. In the 1980s, Francois Mitterrand, the first Socialist president of France, abandoned ideas of state ownership and instead embarked upon his own privatization program. Privatization also featured prominently in government programs in Italy, Spain, and Austria. Criticism of the previously sacrosanct welfare state was heard in Scandinavia. In the 1990s, free market reformers such as Václav Klaus in the Czech Republic and Leszek Balcerowicz in Poland were open admirers of Thatcher and helped make their states more business friendly than most countries in Western Europe. Overall, thanks to Thatcher and, it should be said, the collapse of communism, statist ideas found less and less favor and the Left, which had been the driving force behind many of Europe's welfare states, found itself on the defensive.

IS THE SOCIAL WELFARE STATE DEAD?

Thatcher's "revolution" in Britain demonstrated both that there was an alternative to the post-war European political-economic model and that such an alternative could be, in certain ways, more productive and dynamic. In the early 1990s, much of Europe, including Britain, fell into economic crisis because reunification of West and East Germany dragged down the German economy, whose problems spilled over to other countries. However, some European countries, including Germany, did not vigorously recover, suffering instead from what looked like chronic economic problems.

Some suggested that the old model was in fact obsolete and that other countries in Europe needed their own Thatcher.

The Case for Reform

The "golden days" of high economic growth in Western Europe, discussed in Chapter 2, are now a distant memory. Several countries, including West Germany, France, Italy, Sweden, and the Netherlands, experienced average growth rates of under or only just above 2 percent a year in the 1980s, hardly an impressive accomplishment. Table 10.1 looks at growth patterns since 1993, excluding post-communist Europe, which had uniquely severe economic problems in the aftermath of communism's collapse. These figures are far lower than those seen in the initial post–World War II years, and, as seen in this table, by the end of the 2000s countries across Europe were the victims of a global economic downturn. More interesting, perhaps, are comparisons with the US, as seen in Figure 10.1. Whereas from 1993 to 2000, the US saw more than 3.5 percent average yearly economic growth, many European countries continued to have less dynamic economic performance. Even after the worldwide economic downturn after 9/11, the US recovered faster and stronger than many states in Europe, including France and Germany. The same pattern emerged after the 2007 to 2009 recession. One might wonder what accounts for this difference. There are several possible culprits, including globalization, higher oil prices, immigration, aging infrastructure, and large numbers of retired workers. The contrast between Britain, on the one hand, and France and Germany on the other however, is revealing and suggests another, more politically driven answer: those states with more free-market oriented economies and pro-business policies performed better.

TABLE 10.1

Economic Growth Rates in Western Europe, 1993–2011

	Average Annual Growth of Gross Domestic Product				
Country	1993–2000	2001–2005	2006–2007	2008–2009	2010–2011*
Great Britain	3.1	2.5	2.7	−2.2	1.7
Germany	1.9	.6	2.9	0.4	1.4
France	2.3	1.6	2.3	−0.9	1.4
Italy	1.6	.7	1.8	−3.2	1.1
Spain	3	3.3	4.0	−1.4	.2
Netherlands	3.1	1.2	3.5	−1.9	1.6
Sweden	2.4	2.6	3.8	−2.8	2.2
Finland	3.8	2.5	4.7	−3.3	1.8
Ireland	10.1	5.5	5.7	−5.8	1.0
EU-15	2.4	1.6	3.0	−1.9	1.3

Source: OECD, *Main Economic Indicators* (various issues) and Eurostat, at http://epp.eurostat.ec.europa.eu/portal/page/portal/statistics/themes, accessed on 7 May 2010.
*projected

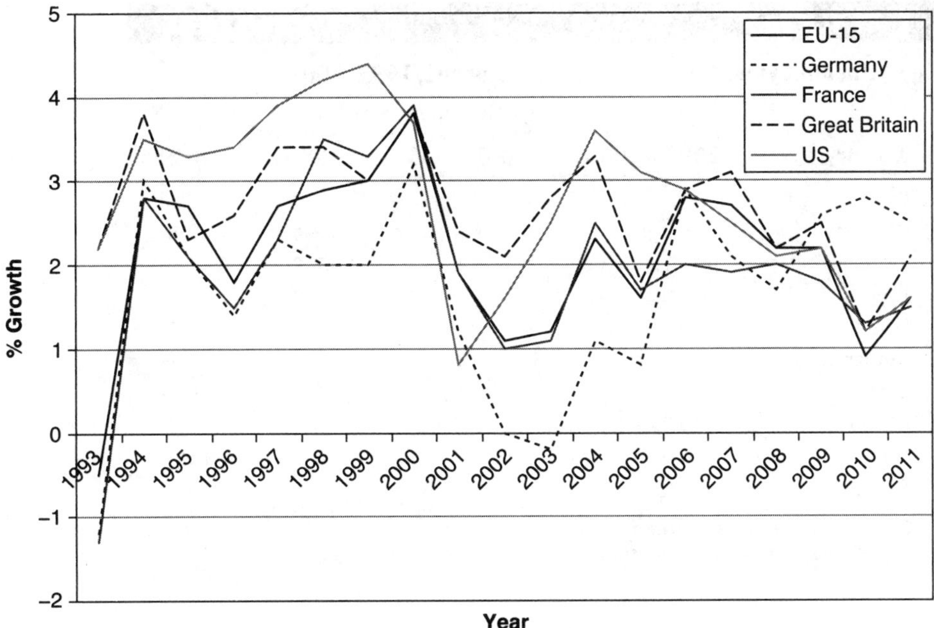

FIGURE 10.1
Economic Growth, Europe versus US
Source: OECD, *Main Economic Indicators* (various issues) and Eurostat, at http://epp.eurostat.ec.europa.eu/portal/page/portal/statistics/themes, accessed on 7 May 2010.

A similar case about European decline can be made with one looks at employment figures, provided in Table 10.2 and Figure 10.2. Whereas several European countries have had chronic unemployment at or near 10 percent, unemployment, at least until the end of the 2000s, has been much lower in the US and in Great Britain. Those who embrace market-oriented reforms would argue that the explanation lies in government policy: lower taxes and less regulation in the US and Britain, arguably, bolster business growth and job creation. Continental Europe's more generous social welfare provisions and less flexible labor markets (e.g., it is very difficult to fire workers in Germany and France) also, arguably, create less incentive for people to look for jobs and for businesses to hire new workers.

In short, "big government" is upheld as the culprit. This raises the following question: How big is "big government" in Europe? Table 10.3 compares the size of government—looking at spending, transfers, and marginal tax rates—in European countries with that in the US. As one sees, with some exceptions (e.g., Ireland), European countries have tended to spend more than the US and to have higher income taxes. Within EU countries, taxes on goods and services (sales or value-added taxes) are also a greater percentage of total taxes (30.7 percent) than in the US (18.3 percent of all taxes). Those who argue against "big government" contend that that these tax and spending policies are harmful to growth and job creation and/or are simply unsustainable, particularly in light of a long-term decline in European birthrates, meaning that there are more and more retirees

TABLE 10.2

Unemployment Rates in Western Europe, 1993–2009

Country	Average Unemployment Rates 1993–2000	2001–2005	2007	2009
Great Britain	7.6	4.9	5.3	7.6
Germany	8.4	9.1	8.4	7.5
France	11.1	8.9	7.9	9.5
Italy	10.9	8.4	5.9	7.8
Spain	17.2	10.5	8.2	18.0
Netherlands	5.1	3.6	4.2	3.4
Sweden	8.5	5.8	5.2	8.3
Finland	13.8	8.9	5.9	8.2
Ireland	10.1	4.4	4.3	11.9
EU-15	9.7	7.8	7.2	9.0

Source: OECD, *Main Economic Indicators* (various issues) and Eurostat at http://epp.eurostat.ec.europa.eu/portal/page/portal/statistics/themes, accessed on 7 May 2010.

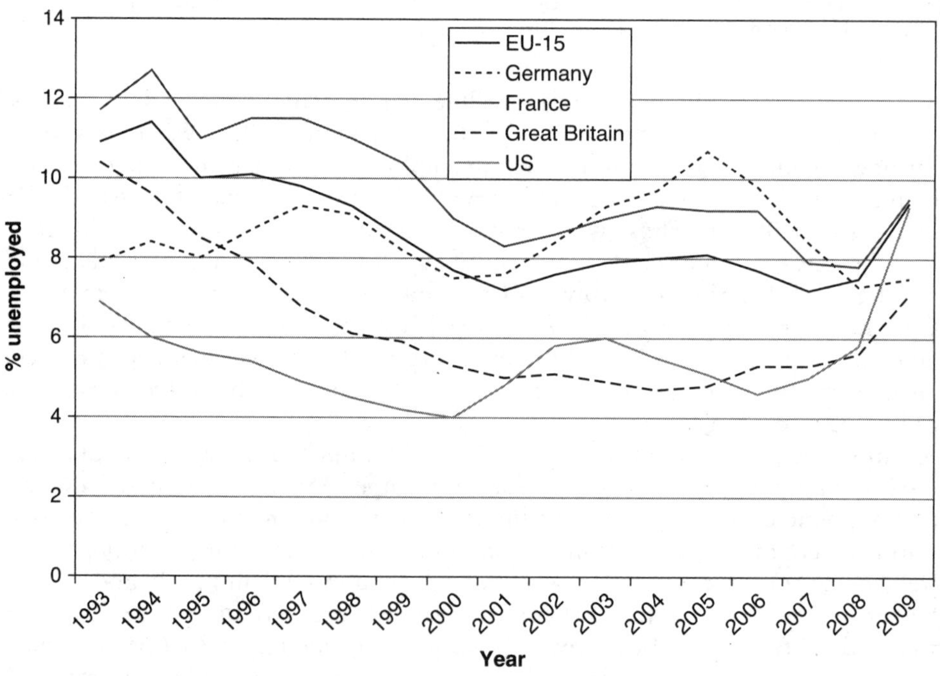

FIGURE 10.2

Unemployment, Europe versus US

Source: OECD, *Main Economic Indicators* (various issues) and Eurostat, at http://epp.eurostat.ec.europa.eu/portal/page/portal/statistics/themes, accessed on 7 May 2010.

TABLE 10.3

Tax Rates and Government Spending in Europe and the US

Country	Highest Rate of Income Tax, 2004	Highest Rate of Corporate Tax, 2004	Gov't Spending as % of GDP, 2006	Social Security Transfer as % of GDP, 2006
Great Britain	40	30	45	13
Germany	47.5	38.9	45.7	18.6
France	36.7	35.4	53.4	17.8
Italy	41.4	33	50.1	17.1
Spain	45	35	38.5	11.6
Netherlands	52	34.5	46.7	11.2
Sweden	56.5	28	55.8	16.7
Greece	33.6	35	36.6	14
Finland	50.3	29	48.6	15.9
Ireland	42	12.5	34.4	8.7
US	41.4	39.3	36.6	12

Source: OECD in Figures, 2007 (Paris, 2007).

taking out of the system and fewer and fewer workers who are paying in. Advocates of these positions—which can be found in virtually every article on European economic issues in *The Economist*, a conservative (in American parlance) British publication—would advise that European governments seriously rethink the large role of the state in the economy, something many Europeans have taken for granted since World War II. The European economic crisis at the end of the 2000s, which resulted in exploding[10] budget deficits in a number of countries, could be the final blow for the welfare state, as many governments now have no choice but to cut back.

Are Things Really That Bad?

This line of argument may not be wholly convincing. True, the crisis of 2008 to 2010 will result in some belt-tightening and additional pressure to trim government expenditures, but this crisis, which had its origins outside of Europe, does not show that all countries are on an unsustainable path. First, as one sees from the Tables 10.1 and 10.2, many European economies were faring well in the early 2000s, and, as of this writing, many were expected to bounce back in the early 2010s and unemployment rates had not mushroomed (with the notable exceptions of Ireland and Spain) as they had in the US. The **In Focus** section will look at Ireland and Finland, two smaller countries that in the 2000s were held up as economic success stories and explore what lessons they may hold for the rest of Europe. Second, matters may not be all that bad. Notably—and surprisingly, perhaps, especially for Americans—some European countries (e.g., Norway, Belgium, Ireland, Germany, France) have greater productivity per worker than the US,[11]

IN FOCUS

The Lessons of Ireland and Finland

Although many European economies have been less-than-impressive performers over the course of the past two decades, some have done quite well. Several Eastern European states, as noted in this chapter, saw solid and steady growth in the 2000s. Norway has taken advantage of oil wealth to become one of the richest countries in the world. Switzerland and Luxembourg are both wealthier, *per capita*, than the US. Two of the most impressive European "success stories," at least until the economic crisis of 2008 to 2010, have been Ireland and Finland.

Ireland, of course, has a history of underdevelopment and poverty. Millions of Irish people left Ireland to find a better life elsewhere. Ireland joined the European Community (EC) in 1973, but, by Western European terms, it was relatively poor, making it a recipient of European regional development funds. Its standard of living lagged well behind than of Great Britain, the country's former master.

Starting in the 1990s, however, Ireland became the "Celtic Tiger," a country that experienced high and sustained economic growth like the so-called "Asian Tigers" of Singapore, Taiwan, and Hong Kong. From 1994 to 2000 economic growth ranged from 6 to 11 percent each year and was more than 5 percent for much of the 2000s. Unemployment dropped from 16 percent in 1993 to less than 5 percent by 2000. By 1997, Ireland had caught up to Great Britain in terms of GDP/capita, and by 2006 its average GDP capita was 44 percent higher than the EU average and even 33 percent higher than that of Great Britain. Among EU states, Ireland ($52,000) in 2007 was the second-wealthiest country in *per capita* income (Luxembourg [$89,700] was first), markedly higher than even the US ($44,000).[12] The Irish diaspora reversed a long historical trend by coming back to Ireland, and thousands of other workers from around the world followed suit.

What accounted for Ireland's success?[13] Some of the answers would warm the heart of Margaret Thatcher: tax reduction, cuts in spending, and opening up of markets, particularly for foreign investment. As seen on Table 10.3, Ireland has, by far, the lowest corporate tax rate in Western Europe and the government spending also accounts a lower percentage of GDP than even in the US. Low taxes, relatively (compared to Britain, say) low labor costs, and, no less crucially, a well-educated labor force whose native language was English, encouraged various companies, particularly in the high tech sector, to set up both production and service sectors in Ireland. Major companies such as Dell, IBM, Microsoft, Google, Intel, and Xerox use Ireland as a base to get into European markets. A quarter of all US foreign investment in Europe is directed to Ireland. According to the UN, Ireland ranks third in the world for foreign investment on a *per capita* basis, and from 1994 to 2003 it was the largest net recipient of foreign investment of any advanced-industrialized state. In 2003, for example, $25 billion in foreign investment came to Ireland (with a population of four and a half million people), more than Great Britain or Germany. Fewer regulations also allowed new, Irish firms to develop. Some flourished, most famously Ryanair, which has become a leading low-cost airline in Europe and provides a great boost to the tourism industry.

These policies were adopted in the 1990s with a large degree of political consensus. Unions signed on to tax cuts and cuts in state spending in return for modest wage increases. The depth of Ireland's crisis in the 1980s—rising debt, slowing growth, high unemployment—made it clear to all parties that reforms were needed. The government worked with interest groups in the National Economic and Social Council on its market-oriented Program for Economic Recovery. Pragmatism and creativity, not ideology, have been the guiding features of Irish political life.

An additional explanation for Irish growth is that Ireland has benefited immensely from EC (later EU) membership. Regional funds in the 1970s and 1980s were devoted to infrastructure development and education. Membership in the EC also meant, however, that Ireland was subjected to competitive pressures from Europe—meaning it could no longer protect failing domestic industries—but also gained access to wider markets. Lacking well-established industrial sectors, it could direct, through the government's Industrial Development Authority, investment and tax incentives into new industries, establishing a niche as a pharmaceutical and high-tech research and development site for Europe. By virtue of being in the EC, production in and export from Ireland made sense for multi-nationals seeking access to the European market.

Finally, one should mention human capital and demographics. Ireland produces more engineers *per capita* than any EU-15 country or the US and was well positioned to capitalize on the growth of high-tech sectors. In addition, years of out-migration meant that were plenty of well-trained Irish workers and managers in multi-national corporations. By European standards, Ireland also had a lot of young workers, with almost half of the population under twenty-five years of age. Growth in the labor force helped drive overall economic growth.

This is not to say that Ireland was free of problems. As the economy grew, prices (particularly for housing) increased dramatically, and inequality, as seen below in Table 10.4, approached US standards. Ireland was also hit very hard by the recession of 2007 to 2010, with growth declining by nearly 10 percent in 2009, twice the average in the eurozone, and unemployment soaring to 12 percent. The popping of the housing bubble and drying up of foreign investment put severe pressure on state finances, putting Ireland the mix with countries such as Greece and Portugal that faced heavy burdens to pay off their debt. In December 2010, the EU approved a €85 billion bailout for Ireland, with Ireland in turn slashing public spending and adopting tax increases to help pay off its debt. While some may question some aspects of the "Irish model" of the 1990s and early 2000s, there seems to be little doubt that the solution to Ireland's crisis will not be to a return to a statist economic model, and economic reformers across the continent will no doubt draw some positive lessons from the Irish experience.

Finland's economic accomplishments are also extremely impressive. In the early 1990s, thanks in large measure to a dramatic drop in trade with Russia, Finland slid into a recession. Unemployment soared to 18 percent in 1993. Since the late 1990s, however, Finnish economic growth has been higher than the European average and its unemployment rate dipped below the EU-15 average in 2007. Average income in Finland now eclipses that in Germany, France, and Great Britain. According to the World Economic Forum in 2005, Finland—not Singapore, South Korea, or some other Asian "tiger"—has the most competitive economy in the world.[14]

What accounts for Finland's success? As one can see from Table 10.3, Finland did not dismantle its welfare state. Its personal income tax rate remains high and, even though its corporate tax rate is lower than the European average, it is still twice as high as Ireland's. Finland has also not been the magnet for foreign investors that Ireland has been. Rather, Finnish growth has been predicated on development of a homegrown technology sector, best exemplified by Nokia (which accounted for over half the value of the Finnish stock market in the early 2000s), but also by literally thousands of smaller companies. By 2005, Finland was the world's *per capita* leader in patent applications.

How did this occur, or, to put it more dramatically, how did the leading industry in Finland change from paper production to high tech? One answer is government policy.[15] Research and development has become an increasingly important part of the state's budget, tripling as a percentage of GDP from the 1980s to the end of the 1990s and reaching 3.5 percent of GDP by 2004, almost twice the European average. Technological development has been furthered by government-business cooperation, exemplified by the government's National Technology

(*continued*)

Agency, which dispenses funds to universities and businesses and helps identify markets and products for companies to develop and manufacture. Finnish firms began reorienting their outputs, and money was provided for spin-offs and start-ups. Market liberalization, in terms of opening the country up to trade and investment, also helped, but there was no Thatcher-like attack on unions or push to eliminate all government regulation. Instead, government, employers, and trade unions have cooperated in focusing on growth in new sectors that provide Finland with high-paying jobs and the funds necessary to maintain a generous social welfare state.

Part of the answer, however, also has to do with Finland's education system, which is ranked among the best in the world.[16] Finnish students consistently score at the top among students globally in math, science, and reading. What is the secret to Finland's educational system, which, in the 1960s and 1970s, was nothing exceptional? Many conventional answers from American debates do not seem to apply. Finns start school at age seven (although most youngsters attend government-subsidized preschools and daycare), go to school on average only five hours a day through elementary school, per-pupil spending ($5,000) is half of that in many US localities, and Finns place little emphasis on national-level student examinations. Instead, answers appear to lie in teaching training (all teachers have masters' degrees), limits on the number of teacher-training programs so that the supply of teachers is low but the quality of teachers is high, and flexibility within the curriculum to encourage innovation.

Does Finland offer a model for other countries? Certainly, Finland, is unique: it is ethnically homogeneous, not hobbled by government or private sector corruption, enjoys a high degree of consensus in political life, and, perhaps more so than the France or Italy, is willing to embrace change. It is also relatively small (five million people), meaning modest investments by French or German standards can go a lot way. Yet, one could argue that aspects of its educational system and research and development policy could easily be adopted elsewhere. Moreover, the Finnish experience illustrates that one does not have to embrace the Anglo-American-Irish reform model in order to succeed.

Critical Thinking Questions

1. Does the Irish crash of 2009 to 2010 undermine the notion that free markets and foreign investment are keys to economic success? If not, what precisely went wrong in Ireland?
2. Finland is a small, very homogeneous country. How successfully can it serve as a "model" for others?

although US workers are still more productive than EU workers on average. Third, it is not apparent that the more free market-oriented American model, even on economic terms, is superior to that of Europe. For example, the US has the world's largest trade deficit (over $600 billion in 2010), is the world's largest debtor nation, and, because of lack of safeguards on loans and poor regulations of complex financial instruments, was the primary source of the global economic crisis at the end of the 2000s. By 2010, unemployment in the US had shot up to over 10 percent, higher than in Germany and France. Finally, and perhaps most significantly, even if Europeans might concede that the US has been more dynamic and efficient, at least measured by aggregate or total growth over the medium and long term, many would still maintain that the European "model" remains more "humane" in various ways and therefore superior to the US system.

Indeed, it is on this point that Europeans and various "Europhiles" defend the European system against the US model.[17] For example, while the top tier of wage earners in the US has fared very well since the 1980s, average wages have been flat. The average European worker, in relative terms, has fared better. At the low end, as illustrated in Table 10.4, poverty rates—defined as those living on less than half of the median income—are under 10 percent in many Western European countries, far lower than the 17 percent found in the US, in large part because European governments more actively pursue **economic redistribution** to provide basic goods and services to those who otherwise would fall into poverty. Such amenities include housing subsidies, free daycare, free higher education, job training, family allowances, guaranteed pensions, and substantial unemployment benefits. Overall, there is more economic equality in Europe: the US has the highest earnings inequality of major western industrialized nations, as seen on Table 10.4, and has the lowest level on income mobility. Consider the following. In 1980, the average American CEO earned forty times the wage of the average workers in manufacturing. In 2000, the ratio was 475:1, compared to 24:1 in Britain, 15:1 in France, and 13:1 in Sweden.[18]

economic redistribution ■ policies, usually based on taxation and government spending, that redistribute money from the wealthy to poorer segments of the population; often a key component of the welfare state.

Most European states have what Americans often deride as "**socialized medicine,**" meaning the government pays for and in some cases provides medical services. All citizens have access to free or very inexpensive health care. Although this is derided as overly costly, the World Health Organization found that the US—not France, Sweden, or Germany—by far spends more on health care *per capita* than any other country, yet ranks only thirty-seventh in the world in terms of public health. Notably, of course, the US does not provide government-run universal health coverage. True, Americans with health insurance have some of the best health care in the world, but, on average, Europeans have higher life expectancies and lower infant mortality, well-established indicators of public health.

socialized medicine ■ term, often used pejoratively, to refer to European governments' payment for, and, in some cases, provision of, health care; in fact, Europeans have universal health coverage and lower health care costs.

Americans are, by most standard measures, wealthier. GDP *per capita* is higher in the US than in most of Europe. Americans tend to own bigger houses, cars, and refrigerators and have more "stuff." Yet, they work far more hours than the typical European—who enjoys four to six weeks of vacation—and, as many Europeans would be sure to remind you, such conspicuous US-style consumption is not environmentally friendly or sustainable.[19] Moreover, GDP figures measure items such as military spending, "wasteful" health insurance, and prisons (far more populated in America than in Europe), factors that do necessarily not reflect a higher quality of life. As seen in Table 10.4, many European countries rank above or near the US on the UN's Human Development Index (HDI), which factors in income, health, and education to determine which countries are the most desirable in which to live.

The Politics of Economic Reform in Western Europe

Given the downturn in growth and debates over the viability and desirability of the tax-and-spend model of the European welfare state, economic reform is now a central political issue in many countries states. Various political parties have put forward various plans to stimulate economic growth and job creation. Some seek to preserve key elements of the welfare state; others seek to overhaul the existing system. Some

TABLE 10.4

Data from the UN Human Development Report, 2007/2008

Country	Rank on HDI	% in Poverty*	Inequality Ratio of Top 20% to Bottom 20%
Iceland	1	n/a	n/a
Norway	2	6.4	3.9
Australia	3	12.2	7.0
Canada	4	11.4	5.5
Ireland	5	16.2	5.6
Sweden	6	6.5	4.0
Switzerland	7	7.6	5.5
Japan	8	11.8	3.4
Netherlands	9	7.3	5.1
France	10	7.3	5.6
Finland	11	5.4	3.8
US	12	17.0	8.4
Spain	13	14.2	6.0
Denmark	14	5.6	4.3
Austria	15	7.7	4.4
Great Britain	16	12.5	7.2
Belgium	17	8.0	4.9
Luxembourg	18	6.0	n/a
New Zealand	19	n/a	6.8
Italy	20	12.7	6.5

Source: UN Human Development Index 2007/2008, at http://hdr.undp.org/en/reports/global/hdr2007-2008, accessed on 28 January 2008.

*defined as earning less than half of the median income, for 2000 to 2004.

reformers can claim success; in other cases, reforms have been resisted both by political actors and by society at large. To understand how debates over economic reform have played out, let us turn to specific cases in Western Europe.

New Labour in Great Britain One of the most interesting developments has occurred in Great Britain, where, after nearly two decades (1979–1997) of rule by the Conservatives, the left-wing Labour Party moved to the political center. Tony Blair, who championed the slogan "New Labour," spearheaded this transformation. Blair pushed through changes in the party's platform, including the abandonment of the goal of state ownership, control over taxes and expenditure, welfare reform, and decreasing the power of trade unions over the party. Blair's moves were both pragmatic and political, bowing to the reality that "Old Labour" was being trounced in elections. Some accused Blair of selling out, that the party had "abandoned virtually all that it had once stood for" and that Blair helped cement the reforms of the 1980s under Thatcher, so that "the economic principles of Thatcherism had become the conventional wisdom."[20]

Blair's defenders did not see things quite this way. As noted in Chapter 8, Blair and New Labour touted the idea of a "**Third Way**," meaning that they hoped to offer an alternative between the excesses of state-led socialism and complete reliance on free markets.[21] Under the "Third Way," the government would not work against marketizing or globalizing economic forces. Rather, the government would help create conditions for economic growth while expanding opportunity for individuals to participate in economic life by supporting education, job retraining, and entrepreneurship. The Third Way thus envisioned a "social investment state," one that focused on human capital, not excessive regulation to constrain markets.

Third Way ■ idea of an economic and social system in-between state-led socialism and reliance on free markets; endorsed by Tony Blair and other center-left politicians in Europe in the 1990s.

Blair's reforms proved to be economically and politically successful. As seen from the tables and figures above, economic growth in Britain was higher than in many European states and unemployment was lower. The stock market soared, and, even though Britain remained outside of the euro zone, London became the unquestioned financial capital of Europe. Taxes, by European standards, remained low, and Blair held the line on public spending, pushing through welfare reform that sought to get people back into the workforce, and, controversially, raising fees at British universities. Not all was well with Britain—many complained of a deterioration in health care, public transport, and school performance, and Blair lost much of his popularity thanks to his support for the invasion of Iraq[22]—but Labour retained its parliamentary majority in 2001 and 2005 elections, reflecting the fact that many middle-class Britons—Thatcher's core constituency—believed that "New Labour" was competent on economic matters. Interestingly, by 2007, the Conservative Party, under the leadership of David Cameron, was seeking to remake itself in Blair's image, emphasizing the notion of competent government, not simply, as under Thatcher, less government. Blair's ideas were also influential to many on the center-left, including US President Bill Clinton and German Chancellor Gerhard Schröder (1998–2005) who had his own "Third Way" slogan (*Der Neue Mitte*, "The New Middle").

Resistance to Reform in France Despite some reforms under President Francois Mitterrand (1981–1995), French economic performance was not particularly impressive. While some French companies have done well, unemployment remained in the double digits throughout the 1990s and the French became increasingly uneasy with the economic costs of globalization. Some began to call for more reform, with *The Economist*, in a magazine cover, suggesting that France needed its own Margaret Thatcher.[23]

Certainly, there was much about France in the 1990s that a person with Thatcher's ideological leanings would not like. The bureaucracy remained large and in many cases stifling. One out of four workers was in the public sector. Taxes and state spending were high; government regulations numerous; pensions and other welfare provisions generous; and the state continued to own or subsidize major industrial enterprises (e.g., Airbus). Whereas in the late 1970s income *per capita* was roughly 25 percent higher in France than in Great Britain, by 2005 the British had overtaken the French.[24]

In the late 1990s and 2000s French leaders began proposing various reforms. One idea, put into effect with much fanfare in 2000, was to mandate a thirty-five-hour work week, under the assumption that firms would hire extra workers to make up the difference. Various programs—including job training and tax break for businesses—were also put into place to help young people find jobs, as a quarter of those younger than 25 years old were unemployed in the late 1990s. The government also tried to get its fiscal house in order, in part to meet the criteria to join the eurozone. The government embarked on privatizations (raising €30 billion from 1997 to 2002), cut income taxes, and trimmed pensions, while investments were made in energy and new technologies (e.g., nuclear power plants, grid computing, high-speed trains).

Nonetheless, the reforms have been rather limited and not overly effective. Unemployment, while down from the highs of the late 1990s, is still above the European average. Rather than hire more workers, many firms made do with what they had. Per worker productivity went up, but many remained unemployed or could find out part-time employment. Much of the problem is with the French labor market, which imposes high **payroll taxes** on employers for social security (25.3 percent of all taxes in France, as opposed to 10.4 percent of the total in Britain or 13.3 percent in the US)[25] and makes it difficult to fire workers. Meanwhile, France's public debt ($1.4 trillion, 66 percent of GDP) is the highest in Western Europe, a reflection that the state spending (53 percent of GDP, from Table 10.3) remains high, even by European standards. The political costs of a relatively stagnant economy—votes for extremist parties, strikes, even riots in poorer, immigrant neighborhoods in 2005 and 2007—were palatable.

payroll taxes ■ taxes put on employers that are used to pay for health insurance, unemployment benefits, and pensions; higher in Europe than in the US.

Nonetheless, it has been difficult to adopt and implement reforms. Lionel Jospin, France's Socialist prime minister (1997–2002) spoke for many French when he declared that capitalism was "unjust and often irrational" and "we reject the market society,"[26] Even though Jacques Chirac campaigned for lower taxes and some reforms in 1995, he was no Margaret Thatcher. In 1995, his proposals to cut welfare payments, raise the retirement age, and increase health-care premiums were abandoned in the wake of nation-wide strikes. Under Chirac, the state bureaucracy and public debt grew, and growth remained under 2 percent a year. When he tried to make changes in the labor market to make it easier to fire (and thus, presumably hire) younger workers, French students and unions launched large-scale protests, compelling Chirac to withdraw the law.[27]

In 2007, Nicholas Sarkozy, who served as interior minister under Chirac, sensed that France was ready for change. Unabashedly pro-US, he campaigned on a platform of reform, urging the French to swallow some bitter pills in order to get the economy moving. His opponent, Socialist Ségolène Royal, promised more state protection and higher wages. Sarkozy prevailed, creating possibilities for economic reform. While no one doubts Sarkozy's energy—he maintains a daily jogging regimen and, after a divorce, has been globe-hopping with his new, ex-supermodel wife—his reform plans, not surprisingly, have encountered opposition. When he proposed cuts in pensions for public sector workers and liberalizing the labor law, there was another round of strikes, shutting down the country's transportation network. Sarkozy, however, appears undaunted, pledging that he will push ahead with more reforms, including reforming the thirty-five-hour workweek law and liberalizing the labor market and thereby eliminating job security for millions of French workers. An ambitious government-commissioned report in 2008 was entitled "300 Decisions for Changing France."[28] It remains to be seen if the government can act upon even a fraction of these ideas.

France's predicament points to the difficulty of reforming an entrenched system by imposing costs on those vested in the system. It was one thing, as under Thatcher, to privatize housing (thereby creating home owners) or large companies (thereby creating shareholders). It is far more difficult to take away people's benefits. Many French are used to job security; they do not want to give it up so somebody else can get a job. They like their health system, which, incidentally, is ranked among the best in the world. They also want to be able to retire—as railway and public transit workers, National Opera employees, and Bank of France officials can—with full pensions as early as the age of fifty.

Can Germany Become Europe's Engine of Growth? Like France, Germany has suffered high unemployment and sagging growth for many years. Germany's more recent economic troubles, of course, stand in contrast with the German "economic miracle" of the 1950s and 1960s. This was built around political consensus, participation of business and labor in important economic decisions, and on a "**conservative welfare state,**" which was managed by semi-public agencies (social security and health funds), was based in part upon worker payments so that those who paid in more received more, and was designed in many respects to support traditional family values (e.g., tax breaks for married couples, family allowances, provisions that discouraged mothers from working).

conservative welfare state ■ used to describe Germany, it rests upon semi-public agencies that administer welfare benefits and are paid into by workers and various "pro-family" provisions.

In the early 1990s, the German economy was put under great strain because of the costs of reunification with East Germany, discussed previously in Chapter 2. The government paid for reunification through a combination of borrowing and higher taxes. Between 1991 and 1996 the proportion of income taken by the government for taxes and social insurance premiums increased from 41 percent to 46 percent. Meanwhile, growth slowed and unemployment—caused by various factors, including high payroll taxes and nonwage labor costs,[29] regulation of the labor market, closures of East German enterprises, and, arguably, immigration—increased, reaching over 9 percent by 1997.

In 1998, thanks in large part to concerns over the economy, Gerhard Schröder returned the Social Democrats to power in coalition with the Greens. As noted, Schröder had been influenced by Blair's ideas of a Third Way and pulled the Social Democratic Party to the center. In 2000, he pushed through major cuts in both income and corporate taxes. The government also pushed measures to give tax breaks to investors and stabilize public spending. The economy, however, did not markedly improve: it experienced no growth from 2002 to 2003, debt soared, Germany became less competitive internationally, and unemployment increased.

In 2003, recognizing that the situation was increasingly dire, Schröder unveiled a more ambitious reform plan, labeled Agenda 2010. Sounding like Margaret Thatcher, he declared, that social welfare programs would be cut and that individuals would have be more responsible and assume more financing of programs such as health insurance and university education. Some benefits, especially unemployment benefits, were to be put on the chopping block. The government also changed the labor laws, making it easier for employers to fire workers. Individuals were encouraged to set up private retirement accounts to make up for cuts in pensions. Agenda 2010 was highly controversial. Unions organized mass protests in opposition, and many within the Social Democratic Party accused

Schröder of betraying long-standing principles. With the help of the opposition Christian Democrats, Schröder got Agenda 2010 through parliament, but he failed to win reelection in 2005, when Angela Merkel of the Christian Democratic Union became Chancellor as part of "Grand Coalition" with the Social Democrats.

Merkel, as a woman on the political right, was compared by some to Margaret Thatcher, but, adopting the slogan *Die Mitte*, she has proven to be a centrist.[30] She has helped push through new laws to create more labor-market flexibility by allowing companies to make local or plant-level agreements with workers and continued some cuts in social programs. However, she was forced to raise both sales taxes and taxes on those with high incomes to ensure that the budget deficits are not excessive. Under her leadership, there were, at least in the first couple of years, some positive developments. Unemployment, nearly 11 percent in 2005, declined to 8.4 percent in 2007; economic growth increased; government debt fell. Germany, which depends heavily on exports, was extremely hard-hit by the 2008–2009 crisis, during which time Merkel showed characteristic flexibility and pragmatism. She resisted calls on the left for a massive stimulus package, but did bail out German banks and large companies such as Opel, angering some on the right who chaffed at such government intervention. Even so, she won reelection in 2009, forming a new coalition with the more free-market oriented Free Democrats, who emphasized the need for tax cuts and cuts in social spending during its campaign.

Swedish model ■ term used to describe the high-tax, extensive welfare state in Sweden, which centered on economic redistribution in an effort to maintain greater economic equality.

Whither the Swedish Model? As noted in Chapter 2, Sweden, as well as other Scandinavian states, developed a very extensive welfare state. The "**Swedish model,**" however, was not predicated on state ownership or government planning. Rather, it was based upon redistribution of resources with the goal of promoting full employment, social security, and greater economic equality. Corporations and individuals paid high taxes, and in return the government devoted resources to health, education, infrastructure, housing, and family allowances. The Social Democrats dominated Swedish politics and corporatist institutions ensured cooperation among the government, business, and unions. Businesses remained privately owned, but employees were granted extensive job security protection and wages were decided through national-level collective bargaining. Swedish politics and society rested upon this consensual model.

Cracks began to appear as early as 1976, with the Social Democrats lost power for the first time since 1932. Part of the reason for their defeat was Sweden's deteriorating economic performance: Growth slowed, unemployment rose, inflation crept up to nearly 10 percent. Non-Socialist leaders tried to stimulate growth by cutting taxes, creating investment incentives, (ironically) socializing the ailing shipbuilding industry, and international borrowing. There was, however, no dramatic improvement in the economy.

The Social Democrats returned to power in 1982, but they began to pursue a more moderate course. Bowing both to domestic and international economic realities, the government announced that while it would seek to maintain the welfare state, it would not add new programs. Taxes would be cut to be more in line with other European states. The government, risking the wrath of the unions, also put a cap on wage increases to limit inflation.

In 1991, amid another economic downturn, another non-Socialist coalition assumed power. It announced its intention to end the "age of collectivism" in

Sweden. Its plans included tax and spending cuts, economic deregulation, and partial privatization of education and social services. However, the government failed to pass many of its proposals, and it was voted out in 1994. Sweden joined the EU in 1995, necessitating some deregulation in favor of market principles. In the latter half of the 1990s, the Social Democrats, again in power, put priority on deficit reduction and price stability, both of which were pursued with an eye to meet the criteria for the euro, which Sweden did not, as it turned out, adopt. The Social Democrats survived (barely) elections in 1998 and 2002, finally succumbing to a center-right coalition in 2006, which has focused its efforts on stimulating job growth by cutting payroll taxes and trimming unemployment benefits, not radically overhauling the system.

Thus, despite some retrenchment, the "Swedish model" is not dead. As seen in Table 10.3, Sweden continues to have high tax rates and greater than average government spending and redistributive policies. Swedish unions remain strong. Yet, Sweden has one of the most competitive economies in the world, boasting world-class companies such as Ericsson, Volvo, and Telia. True, Sweden has experienced economic problems since the 1970s and the once-dominant Social Democrats have been put on the defensive. Immigration—as of 2006 10 percent of the population was born outside of Sweden—has also put strains on the system, and the Swedish economy has some serious problems, including a youth unemployment rate of over 20 percent. Successive Swedish governments have moved to trim the welfare state due to chronic fiscal concerns, but it would be an exaggeration to suggest that there is a broad ideological push to dismantle the "Swedish model." Consensus, which admittedly is less solid than a few decades ago, rests on the idea that much of it should be preserved.

For a non-Swede who might balk at some aspects of this system—particularly the high taxes—one pertinent question might be what explains the resiliency of the Swedish model? There are several possible answers to this query.[31] One is that Swedish society rests on notions of solidarity, meaning reciprocal responsibility or mutual obligation. In other words, the "Swedish model" is grounded in a social commitment. Second, welfare provisions in Sweden are universal in scope, not restricted just to the poor. Students, the elderly, parents, children, and workers—all can take advantage of particular features of state largesse, although, because many universal benefits are taxable, the wealthier in effect receive less than those with low incomes. Thus, while there is without question economic redistribution, most get something. According to one saying, "the richest 90 percent help support the poorest 90 percent." Lastly, considering that Sweden, by virtually any measure, has been politically and economically successful, there is no widespread call to abandon the current system. This is not to say that Sweden is paradise or that there are not potential threats to the current system (e.g., a rise in immigration, an aging population), but, overall, Sweden's continued success shows that the European welfare state is not (yet anyway) passé or good for dead.

THE IMPACT OF GLOBALIZATION

The primary pressure to change the European model, however, has not come from within Europe. Europeans have largely reconciled themselves to the grand bargain: higher taxes but more social welfare and provisions for social protection.

Politically, it has been very difficult to chip away at benefits enjoyed by large segments of society. The argument that these systems are untenable comes less from the fact that voters have grown tired of them than from the fact that they may no longer ensure that Europe can grow and prosper in a global economy. Indeed, it is Europe's need to compete with other countries and regions that is putting pressure on European countries to become more market and business-friendly.[32] Strategies to bolster European competitiveness have been debated at both the national level and in the EU as a whole, which in 2000 unveiled its **Lisbon Strategy** to make the European economy more dynamic and innovative. Whether or not this strategy can bear fruit is discussed in the **Is Europe One?** feature.

Lisbon Strategy ■ adopted in 2000, this is a plan of the EU to bolster economic innovation and competitiveness across Europe.

Economic Challenges of Globalization

Western European countries, starting in the 1950s, took the lead in eliminating barriers to cross-border economic activity. The EU, in many ways, is a leading institution that promotes **globalization**, a multi-faceted process that promotes the flow of goods, information, ideas, and cultures across borders. Today the entire world becoming globalized, whether measured by growth in trade, foreign investment, or even immigration and labor flows. As noted in the next chapter, European countries and the EU as a whole are major actors in the area of international economics. At present, however, we should touch upon real and potential economic consequences of globalization on domestic European economies and societies.

globalization ■ multi-faceted process of growing political, economic, and social connections among countries and individuals; it is putting pressure on Europe to become more economically competitive.

Globalization, without question, poses a challenge to the advanced industrialized states of Western Europe. Labor costs—both in terms of wages and payroll taxes—are high. Government regulations (e.g., on the environment, safety standards, worker protections) are numerous. Other countries or regions may be more business-friendly in terms of lower taxes, fewer regulations, and labor costs that are only a fraction of those in Europe. True, German or Swedish workers may be more productive than their Chinese or Indian counterparts, but, with the difference in labor costs between Western Europe and developing countries up to fifty-fold, are European workers fifty times more productive? If not, there is a real temptation to outsource jobs to lower-costs locales. Consider, for example, the highly successful Danish toymaker LEGO. LEGO maintained design and production plants in Denmark, Switzerland, and the US. In 2006, in a cost-cutting move, LEGO agreed to outsource its production to Flextronics, a Singapore-based firm that has plants in Mexico and the Czech Republic, where wages are much lower than in Denmark or the US. Nine hundred employees in Denmark lost their jobs as a result.[39] This story is not unique. High-end design jobs—for electronics, clothing, furniture, or any number of products—may remain in Europe, but it often makes more economic sense to move production and assembly, which requires less-skilled workers, to other places. As another example, the iconic Swedish furniture firm, IKEA, has most of its production facilities in Asia and Latin America.

In addition to worries about outsourcing, Europeans worry about how they can compete in global markets against low-cost producers. China, in particular, has been a giant exporter, producing a vast variety of goods at low cost. In 2009,

IS EUROPE ONE?

Can the European Union Help Turn European Economies Around?

Until this point, we have primarily discussed individual European economies. While each country has its own unique features, one can nonetheless point to similarities across many European cases, particularly in Western Europe. Whereas one could argue that individual European governments can or should make many reforms to stimulate economic growth, one might also ask what can be done on the European level to strengthen economic performance.

Not surprisingly, the EU has considered this question. Many of the issues discussed in this chapter on a country-by-country basis are included in the EU's Lisbon Strategy, which was adopted in 2000. The Lisbon Strategy recognized that unemployment and declining international competitiveness plague many European states. It declared that EU by 2010 should become "the most dynamic and competitive knowledge-based economy in the world capable of sustainable economic growth with more and better jobs and greater social cohesion and respect for the environment."[33] The Lisbon Strategy placed priority on creating a healthy climate for business, modernizing education, scientific research and development, completion of the internal common market, environmental protection, and combating social exclusion by investing in human capital and putting more Europeans to work. Targets were set for growth, research investments, and employment. The EU defended the need for a broad strategy, noting that

> [o]ur economies are interdependent. Prosperity in one Member State creates prosperity in others. Sluggishness in one Member State holds others back. So Europeans need to work together to achieve economic reform, sharing policies that work. In addition, national policies alone are not enough to allow the Lisbon Growth and Jobs Strategy to succeed. European Union policies are also central to the Strategy. For example, an efficient internal market, the right policies on external trade, the updating and enforcement of EU competition law, well-targeted European research programmes, the effective use of EU Structural and Cohesion funding and the application of EU environmental policies are all crucial to delivering the prosperous and modern society which is the ultimate aim of the Lisbon Strategy.[34]

The goals of the Lisbon Strategy are rather unremarkable. No one would quibble with them. The more difficult question is how the EU and member countries intend to realize these objectives. As a plan that reflected a consensus within the EU, the Lisbon Strategy understandably eschewed radical reforms that would be impossible to adopt and implement. Instead, the idea was that Europeans simply needed to "update" their pre-existing social model. In other words, they could, if they adopted the proper course, avoid tough decisions about reforming the welfare state while redirecting their economies toward the twenty-first century.

The Lisbon Strategy was extremely ambitious, but has it been successful? A mid-term report in 2004, authored by a panel of experts led by former Dutch Prime Minister Wim Kok, was bluntly critical.[35] It noted that the Lisbon Strategy had an "overloaded agenda," "poor coordination," "conflicting priorities," and, most crucially, a "lack of determined political action." While noting that the goals remained worthy, the Kok Report argued that the EU had to do more. At the same time, however, the Kok Report cautioned that reform should not become a code word for deregulation and erosion of workers rights. The EU, in this vision, should not simply adopt the American model and needed to do more to invest in its workers.

Heeding many aspects of the Kok Report, the EU relaunched the Lisbon Strategy in 2005. Highest priority was put on government funding for research and development (the target was 3 percent of GDP)

(*continued*)

and raising employment to 70 percent of the working age population. The opening paragraph of the relevant EU document presented an almost utopian vision:

> Just think what Europe could be. Think of the innate strengths of our enlarged Union. Think of its untapped potential to create prosperity and offer opportunity and justice for all of its citizens. Europe can be a beacon of economic, social, and environmental progress for the rest of the world.[36]

Accompanying such fine words were numerous recommendations, ranging from budgetary policies, cutting red tape to encourage entrepreneurs, lifelong education, and encouraging of competition in all economic areas.

By 2008, the EU noted signs of progress.[37] Growth was up. Six and a half million jobs were created in 2006 and 2007, with employment up to 66 percent of the working-age population. Initiatives have been made in a variety of areas: creation of a European Institute for Technology; streamlining of regulations; encouragement of small and medium-size businesses; liberalization of financial services; and labor-market reforms. The last item is dubbed "flexicurity" by the EU, reflecting again the "we can have it all" idea of combining flexible, more efficient labor markets and with good, secure jobs. Each EU member now submits an annual National Reform Program, which is reviewed by the EU, which in turn issues country-specific reform recommendations. This gives the Lisbon Strategy more focus and direction. Still, there is long list of things to do, including education reform, promotion of energy efficiency, more protection for intellectual property, portability of pensions from country to country, and tax reform, and the economic crisis of 2008 to 2010 will certainly complicate matters.

Again, no one is likely to object to such proposals, but one might still ask if the Lisbon Strategy will really make a difference? The EU can encourage and coordinate all it wants, but it does not have many financial resources at its disposal. As noted in Chapter 4, the EU budget is under great strain. In addition, most of the gains of integration—elimination of trade and investment barriers—have already been made. In other words, the EU has been effective in *removing* obstacles to economic growth. Arguably, it is not so well positioned with respect to *creating* structures that actively promote economic vitality. At present, EU members are not well disposed to a major new round of internal market legislation, preferring to rely upon more informal mechanisms of cooperation.[38]

The EU still has work to do in terms of removing barriers and structures that inhibit the common market from operating to its fullest potential. For example, the EU has adopted a Financial Services Action Plan (FSAP) to facilitate the flow of international capital and remove barriers that block trade in financial services (e.g., banking and insurance). As of 2007, the FSAP was in its consolidation phase, and even though it clearly represents the spirit of the EU—lower barriers to commerce—national governments have dragged their feet in liberalizing financial services because it may threaten "national" banks.

On other fronts, however, the EU's power may be more limited. Labor markets will always be "sticker" than trade or capital movements, for the simple reason that people may be reluctant to leave their home country for the sake of employment. The EU has no jurisdiction to lower payroll taxes to stimulate employment, and one might wonder if "flexicurity" is simply a EU-invented oxymoron. Lastly, its room to maneuver on monetary policy is limited. Although the Kok Report urged the EU to consider a stimulus package to stimulate growth and rethink the Stability and Growth Pact to facilitate government spending to invest in research and new technologies, the European Central Bank's top priority, by statute, is maintaining low inflation, not loosening the purse strings to bolster economic growth.

Critical Thinking Questions

1. If you were a citizen of Germany, would you have supported a bailout of Greece in 2010? Why/why not?
2. What lessons do you think European leaders should learn from the economic crisis at the end of the first decade of the 2000s?

the EU as a whole ran a €130 billion trade deficit with China.[40] European firms that produce similar products to those made overseas will likely, because of labor costs, find their products uncompetitive. They will be unable to sell their products, at home or for export, and thus be put out of business. One answer, of course, is to close Europe off to world markets. As tempting as this may be for some, it would be costly and is not very realistic. Another possibility is to trim labor costs and various regulations, but many fear that this will result in a "race to the bottom," with the lowest wages and standards, prevailing. It is preferable, from the European standpoint, to keep a high-wage, high-productivity economy, but as China and others "catch up," many Europeans feel threatened.

While globalization will, without question, generate "losers" who go out of business or are forced to take salary and benefit cuts, one should be careful not to exaggerate the threat. The challenge is to adjust to a globalized world and finding comparative advantages so that one can compete successfully. Germany is the second-largest trading nation in the world (eclipsed by China in 2009) and numerous countries, including Sweden, the Netherlands, Ireland, and Finland, have embraced globalization and developed high-tech sectors and export-oriented firms. Tourism, which is booming globally, is boosting many European economies, particularly those in Italy, Spain, and France. As noted in Chapter 1, many European firms are global leaders in a variety of sectors ranging from aerospace to publishing to food processing. Expanding global trade can also create jobs. For example, while Chinese imports into the EU have grown five-fold just from 1999 to 2009, exports also grew almost four-fold, meaning that some European firms are selling more to China, which is presumably creating jobs within Europe.

The Political Problem Posed by Globalization

Globalization, however, is more than simply an economic phenomenon or problem. One element of globalization in immigration, an issue dealt with in Chapter 12 and deemed threatening for a host of reasons by many in Europe. Globalization, arguably, also erodes the sovereignty of states. States are compelled to react and adapt to market forces, many of which derive beyond their own national borders. States no longer control their economic borders like they once did, as goods and services flow move from country to country with fewer hindrances. Various international bodies, including the EU and the World Trade Organization (WTO), make rules that states are required to obey.

This has several repercussions. First, to the extent that states are no longer truly sovereign, it means that voters have been stripped of power as well, compromising democracy. In other words, if political actors in Paris, Athens, or Rome no longer have the power to make decisions to affect the country's economic life, then the votes of French, Greek, and Italian citizens become less relevant. Simply put, it matters less who voters elect because elected officials are at times more answerable to or influenced by other actors (e.g., the EU, international markets) than their own citizens. An example might be the euro, which was unpopular in several states. No one directly voted *for* the euro (Swedes, when given a choice in 2003, voted against), and the criteria to join the euro were devised by EU officials. These type of decisions, some might argue, compromise democracy.

One could retort that no one literally forces states to adopt such policies (e.g., Sweden, Denmark, and Britain did not adopt the euro) and that political leaders can resist international market pressures. In other words, leaders do not have to fall lock-step in line with market dictates. They can still do what they (or voters) want. In principle, this is true, but the consequences could be more severe today than in an era with less globalization. Global markets can harshly punish states (e.g., by withdrawing investments) if they do not abide by policies deemed to be most market-friendly. Global capital is extremely mobile. States risk angering markets at their own peril. Thus, what one has seen in a variety of countries is politicians campaigning on populist policies (e.g., maintain or expand the welfare state, workers rights, etc.), but, once in office, they change course and begin to fall into line with expectations from the marketplace. Such was the case with Mitterrand in France in the 1980s, and in Poland, Hungary, and Sweden in the 1990s. During the Greek economic crisis of 2010, it was the Socialist government, not a right-wing Conservative one, that imposed **austerity measures,** including raising the retirement age and cutting salaries. While hardly popular—protesters rallied outside the Greek parliament calling its members a bunch of thieves—the government really had little choice.[41] Similarly, the new British coalition government, elected in 2010 and facing record budget deficits and nervous capital markets, adopted its own austerity program, including defense cuts, a 20 percent reduction in public spending, and up to a tripling of university tuition. Without question, these measures will be politically unpopular—protesters in Demcember 2010 raged through parts of London and even attacked Prince Charles's Rolls Royce—but they may be economically necessary.

austerity measures ■ politically difficult measures, such as tax increases and sharp cuts in public spending, necessary to solve debt crises.

This issue, potentially, creates a problem of public trust and confidence in political leadership. Politicians always campaign on the notion that they can devise policies to improve living standards, create jobs, and so on. Perhaps some can; good policies, as noted in the **In Focus** section, can make a difference. However, national leaders cannot simply roll back globalization. They cannot easily bring back the jobs lost to outsourcing. Thanks to EU and global trade rules, they have lost some of their freedom to maneuver. Finally, it is hard to hold domestic political leaders accountable if the nation's economy suffers because of global economic problems (e.g., a recession in the US, an increase in energy prices, etc.). Globalization suggests the idea that large, structural economic forces, often those beyond the borders of one's own country, have more and more importance in each individual's daily life. Political leaders, arguably, are less and less relevant, less able to make a real difference. While this point remains somewhat speculative, one could, in this way, tie globalization to the lost of confidence in political institutions mentioned in Chapter 9.

Public Attitudes

Public opinion surveys capture European anxiety about globalization. When asked in 2008 about whether they viewed globalization as more of an opportunity or a threat, a plurality (43 percent) of respondents in the EU-27 said they viewed it as a threat, with a smaller number (39 percent) saying it was an opportunity. Responses varied considerably across countries, with Danes (78 percent), Swedes (64 percent), and the Dutch (63 percent) (all of which have relatively competitive economies) all more supportive of globalization, whereas the Greeks (67 percent) and French (66 percent) were more likely to say globalization was a threat.[42]

TABLE 10.5

Public Opinion on Globalization

Country	Globalization Is Opportunity for Economic Growth		Globalization Increases Inequalities		Globalization Profits Large Companies, Not Citizens		Globalization Makes Global Rules Necessary	
	Agree	Disagree	Agree	Disagree	Agree	Disagree	Agree	Disagree
Germany	62	31	65	26	71	24	73	14
France	46	42	74	16	82	12	60	22
Great Britain	53	25	46	28	59	19	55	22
Italy	50	32	51	32	59	24	65	19
Netherlands	79	14	45	44	52	41	62	31
Denmark	85	10	48	44	41	54	73	21
Greece	41	59	76	23	84	15	70	27
Finland	64	30	56	38	60	35	68	24
Ireland	56	16	53	17	58	17	64	9
Poland	59	15	48	26	53	23	62	13
Hungary	58	28	64	22	68	22	65	20
EU-27	56	27	56	26	63	22	64	18

Source: Eurobarometer 69, 2008, available at http://ec.europa.eu/public_opinion/archives/eb/eb69/eb69_globalisation_en.pdf

When asked about how globalization affected different domains, answers were rather mixed, as revealed on Table 10.5. On the one hand, when asked simply if globalization was an opportunity for economic growth (no alternative answer with globalization as a threat, as was the case in the previously mentioned question), most respondents, with the exception of the Greeks, were inclined to agree. One sees, however, significant differences between countries, so that respondents in Denmark and the Netherlands, which are relatively strong economic performers, more pro-globalizaton than those in Italy or France, whose economic performance was not been as strong. However, when asked about different effects of globalization, one sees more skepticism: Most respondents in most countries thought globalization increased inequality and most also thought globalization tended to favor large companies, not individual citizens. On the latter question there is again some variance, with the Greeks and French on one extreme and the Danes at the other. There is more consensus, however, on the idea that globalization requires more global rules, a notion that is regionally applied within the EU itself. In the survey, those who are younger and better educated tend to be more supportive of globalization, although, interestingly, there is little difference between people on the "Left" and "Right" on whether they think globalization is an opportunity or a threat, reflective of the fact that both leftists and rightists share some concerns about globalization's economic and, for the right in particular, cultural impact.

Interestingly, according to data from a 2007 global survey carried out by the Pew Global Attitudes Project, Europeans tend to be less supportive of free trade and foreign companies than publics in developing states such as China, India, Nigeria, and Bangladesh.[43] Eastern Europeans such as the Bulgarians, Czechs, and

Poles, also tended to be more supportive of globalization in this survey than those in Western Europe, particularly the French and Italians. Americans rank as among the least enthusiastic about globalization. Overall, perhaps contrary to some expectations, there is a negative relationship between wealth and support for globalization, with poorer countries more likely to support free trade and activities of foreign companies in their country.

ENVIRONMENTALISM

An increasingly important part of what could be dubbed the European socio-economic model is a focus on the environment and sustainable growth. Chapter 9 included some discussion on the growth of environmentalism, which manifests itself in the programs of political parties across the political spectrum. For example, when Tony Blair's Labour Party came to power in Great Britain in 1997, its election manifesto acknowledged that environmental protection is "not an add-on extra, but informs the whole of government, from housing and energy policy through to global warming and international agreements."[44] Angela Merkel of the center-right Christian Democrats in Germany—whose leader in the 1980s dismissed the Green Party as "the Trojan horse of the Soviet cavalry"[45]—has established herself as a global leader on environmental issues. As noted in the previous chapter, surveys reveal widespread support for green causes, even if they would cause economic growth to slow. Slogans such as "**sustainable development**" are now part of the political mainstream across Europe, as well as a condition for the provision of EU regional funds and development assistance.

sustainable development ■ idea that economic growth must take into account its environmental impact and its consumption of natural resources so that it can be sustained over time.

The impact of environmentalism in Europe is obvious to any American who travels there. The air in most European cities is markedly clearer than in American cities. Higher gas taxes encourage use of public transport. Urban planning stresses the need for more "livable" cities, with a compact core and many pedestrian zones. Environmental regulations (e.g., on air or water pollution) are more restrictive than those in the US. Many Europeans criticize Americans' high energy use (e.g., Americans make up 5 percent of the world's population and consume 25 percent of the world's oil) and uphold their concern for the environment as proof of the superiority of the European "model."

One should note that environmental policies have been enacted on many different levels in Europe. At the European level, as noted in Chapter 4, the EU, since the 1980s, has had an environmental policy. Over the years, the EU has set standards on items ranging from air and water quality to better farming practices and food safety to reduction of noise pollution. EU funds have been used to enhance transportation networks, in particular development of freight and passenger rail. Globally, as will be developed in the next chapter, the EU aspires to environmental leadership, particularly on enacting binding cuts in carbon missions to combat global warming. Because EU environmental policy has been driven by the more environmentally conscious countries (e.g., Denmark, the Netherlands, Germany), EU mandates on the environment have progressively become "greener," compelling national governments to adopt EU standards as their own.

This is not to say that national governments have been forced to adopt "green" policies. On the contrary, many European governments, without prodding from Brussels, have adopted significant legislation to protect the environment.

Much of this stems from the environmental movement itself. For example, Great Britain adopted some laws (e.g., the Protection of Birds Act, the Litter Act) in the 1950s, but in the 1970s and 1980s legislative activity on environmental issues expanded (creation of a Department of the Environment [1970], Deposit of Poisonous Wastes Act [1972], Water Act [1973], Endangered Species Act [1976], Agriculture Act [1985], and Environmental Protection Act [1990]).[46]

Much of the push towards environmentalism, however, occurs and is supported at the local level. Recycling—everything from glass, paper, plastics, and to organic and yard waste (for composting)—is *de rigueur* in Europe, even in smaller towns. Many larger European cities, such as Paris, Vienna, Brussels, and Copenhagen, have public bicycle stations, allowing people rent bicycles at various places around the city at low or no cost. Numerous cities have set their own targets for carbon emission cuts. London, most famously, imposed in 2003 a hefty (£8) surcharge on cars and trucks entering the city, and, in 2008, a variable fee of up to £25 was introduced for SUVs and trucks. Stockholm has followed suit. Munich has launched a major campaign to re-insulate older buildings and hopes to reduce its carbon emissions by 50 percent by 2030. Barcelona has required new buildings to install solar panels to supply at least 60 percent of the energy for hot water, a measure that Swedes, Finns, and Danes could probably not adopt. Nonetheless, perhaps the most environmentally ambitious projects are on the Danish island of Samsø, which is run almost entirely by wind energy, and in Växjö, Sweden, which pledged in 1996 to eventually stop using fossil fuels and has already cut its emissions by 30 percent by using low-emitting, leftover wood chips for heating.[47]

LESSONS FROM EASTERN EUROPE

To this point, we have largely focused our attention on the advanced industrialized states of Western Europe. However, as suggested in the discussion about globalization, the situation may be different in post-communist Eastern Europe. As noted in Chapter 2, in the 1990s these states, with varying enthusiasm and degrees of success, implemented market-oriented reforms to move away from the communist economic system. These reforms included privatization, opening to international trade and finance, freeing of prices, elimination of many state subsidies, and cuts in the social safety net. These reforms were painful, producing inflation, unemployment, and decreasing living standards for many. By the end of the 1990s, however, most countries were experiencing an economic upturn. The purpose here is not to revisit that experience but to make some contemporary comparisons with Western Europe in light of what has been discussed throughout this chapter.

How Are Post-Communist States Faring?

Looking at post-communist Europe today one could argue that many of these states, economically speaking, are on the right track.[48] True, they remain poorer than most West European countries. For example, in 2007, Slovenia, Estonia, and the Czech Republic—three of the wealthiest post-communist countries—each had average GDP *per capita* (at purchasing power parity) of about two-thirds the norm for Western Europe. Other states, such as Romania, Bulgaria, and Macedonia, are much poorer, with GDP *per capita* less than a third of that in Great Britain, France, Italy,

TABLE 10.6

Economic Indicators in Several Post-Communist States

Country	UN Human Development Rank	Unemployment (2009)	Labor Productivity, 2008 (100 = EU Average)	Poverty Rate	Inequality Ratio (Top 20%/ Bottom 20%)
Slovenia	27	5.9	88.4	8.2	3.9
Czech Republic	32	6.7	74.4	4.9	3.5
Hungary	36	10.0	76.0	6.7	3.8
Poland	37	8.2	63.2	8.6	5.6
Slovakia	42	12.0	78.0	7.0	4.0
Estonia	44	13.8	70	12.4	6.4
Romania	60	6.9	40.6	8.1	4.9

Source: UN Human Development Report, 2007/2008, and Eurostat.

or Germany.[49] Nonetheless, for many countries the trend line is up, with growth rates for many post-communist states (e.g., Poland, Estonia, Latvia, Romania) above 6 percent a year in the mid-2000s, three-times the average for Western Europe.

Economic growth may not be everything, of course. Table 10.6 provides additional economic indicators for several post-communist states. Unemployment remains above 10 percent in countries some post-communist countries, although, despite the global economic downturn, the unemployment rate came down in Poland, Romania, the Czech Republic, and Slovakia between 2006 and 2009. Labor productivity lags behind the EU average. Nonetheless, poverty (defined as receiving less than half the median income) and inequality figures compare favorably with that of Western Europe. Moreover, the trend on most indicators—including productivity, employment growth, investment, foreign trade—is up, reflecting that several Eastern European states in the 2000s were showing more signs of economic vitality than larger west European economies such as Germany, France, and Italy.

Are They Doing Anything Differently?

If we accept the notion that post-communist states are looking increasingly economically successful, then the logical next question is what accounts for this success? There are several possible answers. One is simply that they started at a relatively low level. After experiencing decades of problems under communism and then declines in growth in the early 1990s, post-communist states were able to reconfigure their economies, get rid of non-productive enterprises, and employ new technologies to experience high levels of growth, following upon what China, India, and other fast-growing economies have done. Secondly, one could argue that they benefitted from EU largesse in the 1990s, access to European markets, and the enlargement process itself. EU monies helped rebuild infrastructure and offset some costs of reforms; EU markets provided a convenient market for export; and enlargement helped ensure that post-communist states would implement sound

Since the fall of communism, many companies have built factories in Eastern Europe, such as this factory.

economic policies and practice good governance. Finally, Eastern European states, despite years of communist mismanagement of the economy, had a relatively highly skilled workforce. Given that labor costs in Eastern Europe are a fraction of those in Western Europe, some, as noted in the LEGO example above, were able to take advantage of economic globalization to gain foreign investment.

However, one could also make a strong case that many Eastern European countries benefitted themselves by adopting sound policies. In the 1990s, they implemented various reforms to encourage efficient, competitive private enterprise and move out of non-productive sectors. This was economically painful (e.g., thousands of industrial workers lost their jobs), but by the 2000s new jobs were being created. Some policies that encouraged growth and job creation included incentives for foreign investment and low corporate tax rates. For example, corporate taxes in Hungary (16 percent), Poland (19 percent), and Slovakia (19 percent) are well below the EU's average rate (31.1 percent).[50] Foreign investment in most of Eastern Europe—in sectors ranging from automobile production to software engineering to food processing to steel—has grown dramatically in the 2000s, as seen in Table 10.7. Personal income taxes are also lower in post-communist Europe, and many states have adopted a simple flat tax system that some celebrate as much more efficient and growth-friendly.[51]

Is This the New "European Model"?

All of this is not to say that these states have adopted the American or Thatcherite model. Many welfare benefits have been trimmed, but public sector spending as percentage of GDP in the ten post-communist countries that joined the EU averages

TABLE 10.7

Foreign Direct Investment (FDI) in Post-Communist States

Country	Average Annual FDI, 1990–2000	FDI, 2006	FDI as % of Gross Capital Formation, 2006
Poland	3,699	13,922	20.5
Czech Republic	2,131	5957	16.8
Estonia	261	1674	30.1
Hungary	3,244	6098	24.8
Slovakia	634	4165	28.6
Romania	656	11,394	37.9

Source: United Nations Conference on Trade and Development, at http://www.unctad.org. Figures are in millions of dollars.

33.5 percent (ranging from 26 percent in relatively poor Romania to 43 percent in wealthier Hungary), far more than the 21 percent in the US.[52] Politicians in countries such as Poland, Hungary, and Romania have won office on appeals to increase state spending on popular programs such as pensions. The state still provides free or low-cost health care and higher education, although private providers of both exist in many states. By joining the EU, these states have also agreed to a host of regulations over economic activity.

Still, it is probably safe to say that Eastern European countries tend to be more market-oriented and less statist than those in Western Europe, where public sector spending is over 40 percent of GDP in many countries. To the extent that several Eastern European countries in the 2000s outperformed most of Western Europe in terms of economic growth, one question worth considering is whether the recent Eastern European experience holds any lessons for would-be reformers in Western Europe.

Some, of course, would say that the lessons are clear: lower, simpler taxes and incentives for business creation will spur growth. One might wonder, however, if Western European states can simply cut taxes, free markets, and trim spending. As noted, this is politically difficult: unions are more powerful in Western Europe and middle-class voters there do not want their benefits taken away. The ability of a state to lower taxes is constrained in part by the euro's Stability and Growth Pact, which puts limits on a state's budget deficit. For example, Chancellor Angela Merkel won elections in Germany in 2005 on a platform to lower taxes, but, facing an already high budget deficit, she was compelled to *raise* them instead to lower the debt. East European states, with the exception of Slovenia, faced no such constraints in the early 2000s. As for foreign investment, the EU already has a liberal foreign investment regime. Capital can freely move across borders. Eastern Europe, where foreign investment under communism was virtually impossible, has taken advantage of both its "untapped potential" and lower labor costs to draw foreign investment, usually from Western Europe. West European states cannot make similar gains. Additionally, many East European countries (like Ireland and Finland, discussed above) are rather small, meaning that the presence of one or two large investments or companies can make a considerable difference in total economic output; the same cannot be said for larger economies in Western Europe. Finally, most of the growth in Eastern Europe has been with new, "greenfield" investments, not in turning around moribund communist-era enterprises. To the extent that there is less likelihood for various reasons of building "greenfield" projects in Western Europe and that invigorating existing companies is a large priority, the lessons from Eastern Europe may be somewhat limited.

THE 2008 ECONOMIC MELTDOWN AND DEBATES ON REBUILDING CAPITALISM

Since the time of Margaret Thatcher, the common assumption has been that "reform" of European economies should be in a pro-market direction and that the old statist model was an obstacle to Europe's economic revival. Until this point, this chapter has largely followed this logic. In 2008, however, the collapse of the world's financial markets made some question the pro-market model, as governments across the world—including in the US—became more interventionist, even assuming ownership stakes in private companies. Whether these events signal a fundamental shift about how one thinks about markets and government policy remains to be seen, but at minimum they have exacted a great economic toll on Europe.

Even before the meltdown of fall 2008, when many global stock indices lost over 30 percent of their value, many European economies were in trouble. Growth was slowing in a number of states. Higher energy and commodity prices were stoking inflation and lowering domestic demand for many products. An economic slowdown in the US made it harder to export products across the Atlantic. Some European states, especially Ireland, Great Britain, and Spain, experienced a housing crash as well, putting them at risk of recession. Meanwhile, in Eastern Europe, worries about budget deficits, growing wage costs and labor shortages, and diminishing international competitiveness meant that several states that had in the recent past seen double-digit economic growth (e.g., Estonia, Latvia, Slovakia) were dramatically lowering growth forecasts.[53]

Matters became far worse in the fall of 2008, when major American banking and insurance companies collapsed and precipitated a global credit crunch. Some Europeans initially reacted with a bit of *Schadenfreude*, as they felt that America had brought this upon itself due to its financial recklessness. However, many non-US banks, including European ones, also held risky mortgage assets, which, as housing prices dropped and homeowners defaulted on their loans, had less and less value. One of the hardest hit countries was Iceland, which had privatized its banks in 2003. When banks began to fail and credit was cut off, Iceland—the top-tanked country in the 2007 UN's Human Development Report—faced financial collapse, and, after flirting with the idea of securing a loan from Russia, appealed to the IMF for assistance. The banking crisis led to a full-blown recession throughout Europe: the eurozone had a 4 percent economic decline in 2009, and some outside the eurozone such as Latvia and Hungary fared even worse. Unemployment increased in many states, reaching nearly 20 percent in Spain.

European countries scrambled to prevent outright economic collapse and stimulate growth, but in so doing they tested the limits of European unity. Several countries, such as Ireland, Denmark, and Germany, acted unilaterally to guarantee deposits in their own banks. Despite using a common currency, banking supervision remained primarily under national control, and many governments did not want to participate in a collective plan which would, in essence, bail out the more irresponsible. One observer asked how one could "explain to the sturdy burghers in Hamburg [Germany] why it is in their interest to bail out bragging City boys in London or Latvians who overused their credit cards. That's quite a sell."[54] Similarly, countries such as the Netherlands and Germany resisted adopting a massive stimulus program—as was done in the US under Obama and in Great Britain under the Labour government that was voted out in 2010—in part because they already had larger social safety nets, but also for fears of exploding budget deficits as well as concern that the benefits of any national-level stimulus programs would accrue to other states as well.[55] Others, such as the French and Italians, suggested that protectionist measures might be necessary. The French government, for example, extended bailouts to French auto manufacturers, but wanted to require these companies to save jobs in France, not in factories in Slovakia or Slovenia. Other common European policies—including its competition policies, the euro's Stability and Growth Pact, and the commitment to reduce greenhouse gases—also came under assault. Italy's Foreign Minister disparaged market-oriented economists, grouping them together with "bad teachers, exorcists, faith healers, shamans, and witch doctors."[56] East European states, most of whom were not in the eurozone, were hard hit by the crisis, and had to turn to the IMF, rather than the EU, for support.[57]

Interestingly, while the economic crisis did test European unity, some felt, given that the crisis originated in the US, that aspects of the European model were vindicated. One Dutch newspaper crowed, "European capitalism is better suited to meet the challenge of the current financial crisis," and Sarkozy and then–British Prime Minister Gordon Brown suggested in 2008 that there should be a fundamental re-ordering of the global financial system."[58] Brown explicitly denounced the "dogma of unbridled free-market forces."[59] Coming from a British prime minister, such a statement could be taken as recognizing, almost two decades after her fall from office, the end of the Thatcher era. In the end, however, Brown was defeated in the 2010 British elections, and a series of elections throughout Europe at the end of the 2000s (in Germany, in Hungary, in Italy, in Sweden, in the Netherlands) demonstrated that it was parties more favorable to the free market (Conservatives, Christian Democrats, and Liberals) that seemed to politically benefit from the crisis.

As noted at the outset of this chapter, matters became even more serious in 2010, when Greece could no longer make payments on its debt and fears took hold that a "domino effect" might bring down weaker European economies such as Ireland, Spain, and Portugal and possibly lead to the end of the euro.[60] Again, there were political divisions, with France taking the lead for a bailout of Greece, and Germany, the largest EU economy, far more reticent to loan money to the Greeks, who on average worked less and retired earlier than Germans and repeatedly turned a blind eye to corruption, tax evasion, and the doctoring of economic statistics. Eventually, it became clear that the consequences of not assisting Greece would be devastating: collapse of banks across Europe, more countries going under, possibly the end of the euro and the unraveling of much European economic integration. After the initial plan for one-year, €40 billion bailout did little to reassure markets—indeed, interest rates on Greek bonds continued to climb—

in May 2010 European finance ministers agreed, together with the IMF, to supply up to €800 billion to help Greece and other heavily indebted European countries.

Without question, dealing with the fallout of this crisis will have significant repercussions in Greece, which has been forced to raise taxes and slash government spending, and throughout Europe into the 2010s. Indeed, most European governments face difficult choices. Whether governments can muster the political courage to make the necessary reforms (e.g., to the tax system and to reign in state spending) and manage long-term structural problems (e.g., an aging population) to revive their states' economies remains to be seen. Success on these fronts will matter not only on a domestic political level, but will also have repercussions across the continent as Europeans try to preserve and expand economic and political integration.

APPLICATION QUESTIONS

1. Do you think Americans would accept certain elements of the European welfare state if their adoption would mean higher tax rates? Why are Europeans, for the most part, more willing to pay higher taxes than Americans?
2. Sweden has some of the highest taxes and most extensive welfare states anywhere in the world. Yet, Sweden ranks as one of the richest countries in the world. If "tax and spend" is so counter-productive, how does one explain Sweden's success?
3. Do all people benefit equally from globalization? Who "wins"? Who "loses"? Can governments and the EU take action to lessen the negative effects of globalization?
4. How did the Greek economic crisis become a large-scale political and economic crisis for Europe as a whole? What does this crisis say about European political unity and about the future of the euro? What are the larger lessons of the 2008–2010 global economic crisis?
5. Why do you think European states, in general, have embraced more aspects of environmentalism than the US? Can one demonstrate positive or negative impacts of this emphasis on environmentalism?

KEY TERMS

austerity measures 290
privatization 269
Third Way 281
Thatcherism 269
Swedish model 284
conservative welfare state 283
globalization 286
payroll taxes 282
economic redistribution 279
Lisbon Strategy 286
socialized medicine 279
sustainable development 292

ADDITIONAL READING

Cohen-Tanugi, Laurent. 2008. *Beyond Lisbon: A European Strategy for Globalisation*. New York: Peter Lang.

This book provides an overview and assessment of the EU's Lisbon Strategy and suggests how it is inadequate to deal with many of the continent's challenges.

Laqueur, Walter. 2007. *The Last Days of Europe: Epitaph for an Old Continent*. New York: St. Martin's.

Laqueur presents a useful contrast to more positive accounts of contemporary Europe, arguing that Europe faces the prospect of an immense economic crisis because it has declining birth rates and can now longer pay for its welfare system.

Pontusson, Jonas. 2005. *Inequality and Prosperity: Social Europe vs. Liberal America*. Ithaca: Cornell University Press.

This scholarly work provides a comparative overview of the two major models of labor markets and welfare systems in the advanced industrial world: the "liberal capitalist" system of the US and Britain, and the "social market" capitalism of northern Europe. In the 1990s the much-heralded forces of globalization seemed to threaten the very existence of the social-market economies of Europe. Pontusson, however, argues that social-market economies can survive and indeed flourish in the contemporary world economy.

Reid, T.R. 2004. *The US of Europe: The New Superpower and the End of American Supremacy*. New York: Penguin.

Within a larger argument explaining the emergence of Europe as a "superpower," Reid makes a favorable evaluation of European economies in terms of provision of social welfare, technological innovations, and maintenance of equality.

Russell, James. 2006. *Double Standard: Social Policy in Europe and the US*. Latham MD: Rowman and Littlefield.

This book traces the development of the welfare states on both sides of the Atlantic, analyzing why they evolved so differently. It compares policies on issues such as education, health care, and family support, and, although not as one-sided as some treatments, it makes a fairly strong case for the superiority of the European model.

END NOTES

1. Greece's budget deficit as percentage of gross domestic product (GDP) soared to 13 percent in 2010, and the ratio of its public debt to GDP swelled to 130 percent, both far above EU guidelines for the euro zone. Articles from *The Economist*, March 6, 2010, and March 27, 2010.
2. *The Economist*, in its May 1, 2010, issue, featured a cover "Acropolis Now" (a take from the movie *Apocalypse Now*) with Merkel uttering, "the horror, the horror."
3. Tony Judt, *Postwar: A History of Europe since 1945* (New York: Penguin, 2005), p. 540.
4. Interview in *Woman's Own*, September 23, 1987.
5. Judt, *Postwar*, p. 541.
6. For extended discussions, see Earl Reitan, *The Thatcher Revolution* (Lanham MD: Rowman and Littlefield, 2003), and Anthony Seldon and Daniel Collings, *Britain under Thatcher* (New York: Longman, 1999).
7. Judt, *Postwar*, pp. 541–542.
8. Reitan, *The Thatcher Revolution*, pp. 77–78.
9. Judt, *Postwar*, p. 544.
10. For a more scholarly presentation of this position, see Alberto Alesina and Francesco Giavazzi, *The Future of Europe* (Cambridge MA: MIT Press 2008).
11. Jeremy Rifkin, *The European Dream* (New York: Penguin, 2004), p. 46.
12. Data from *OECD in Figures, 2007* (Paris).
13. Good reviews of the turnaround in Ireland can be found in Joseph Harris, "Ireland Unleashed," *Smithsonian*, March 2005, and Sean Dorgan. "How Ireland Became the Celtic Tiger," The Heritage Foundation, June 23, 2006, at http://www.heritage.org/Research/WorldwideFreedom/bg1945.cfm
14. Robert Kaiser, "Innovation Gives Finland a Firm Grasp on Its Future," *Washington Post*, July 14, 2005.
15. Darius Ornston, "Reorganising Adjustment: Finland's Emergence as a High Technology Leader," *West European Politics* 29:4, September 2006: 784–801.
16. See *The New York Times*, April 9, 2004, and *The Economist*, March 25, 2006 and October 18, 2007.
17. Useful sources are Rifkin, *The European Dream*, and T.R. Reid, *The United States of Europe* (New York: Penguin, 2004). More sophisticated treatment is available in Jonas Pontusson, *Inequality and Prosperity: Social Europe vs. Liberal America* (Ithaca: Cornell University Press, 2005). Data used in the text comes from Rifkin, pp. 39–80 and from the UN Human Development Report 2007/2008, available at http://hdr.undp.org/en/reports/global/hdr2007-2008.
18. Tony Judt, "Europe vs. America," *New York Review of Books*, February 10, 2005. See also his book, *Ill Fares the Land* (New York: Penguin, 2010).
19. The UN Human Development Report 2007/2008 notes that per capita electricity consumption in the US is double the rate in France, Germany, Italy, and Great Britain. Scandinavians, with their long and cold winters, use roughly the same as Americans.
20. Reitan, *The Thatcher Revolution*, p. 159, p. 167.
21. Anthony Giddens, *The Third Way: The Renewal of Social Democracy* (London: Polity, 1998). See also James Cronin, *New Labour's Pasts: The Labour Party and Its Discontents* (New York: Pearson, 2004).
22. For a critique of Blair, see Geoffrey Wheatcroft, "The Tragedy of Tony Blair," *The Atlantic Monthly*, June 2004.
23. *The Economist* (European edition), October 28, 2006.
24. "Survey of France," *The Economist*, October 28, 2006.

25. *OECD in Figures, 2007* (Paris, 2007).
26. *New York Times*, November 21, 1999.
27. William Pfaff, "France: The Children's Hour," *New York Review of Books*, May 11, 2006, pp. 40–43.
28. "Attali the Hun," *The Economist*, January 26, 2008.
29. Total tax and nonwage costs of employment (e.g., health and unemployment insurance, sick pay, vacations, pensions) are estimated to add 40 percent to the basic wage earned by a worker.
30. "Merkel Is the Message," *The Economist*, June 27, 2009.
31. Eric Einhorn and John Logue, *Modern Welfare States: Scandinavian Politics and Policy in the Global Age* (Westport CT: Praeger, 2003).
32. See Steven Weber, *Globalization and the European Political Economy* (New York: Columbia University Press, 2001).
33. "Facing the Challenge: The Lisbon strategy for growth and development," Report from high level group chaired by Wim Kok, November 2004, at http://ec.europa.eu/growthandjobs/pdf/kok-report-em.pdf, accessed on 4 February 2008. The general website on the Lisbon Strategy is http://ec.europa.eu/growthandjobs/index-en.htm
34. Taken from EU "Jobs and Growth" website, http://ec.europa.eu/growthandjobs/faqs/background/index_ en.htm
35. "Facing the challenge," 2004.
36. Commission of the European Union, "Working together for growth and jobs: A new start for the Lisbon strategy," COM(2005) 24 final, February 2, 2005.
37. Commission of the European Union, "Strategic report on the renewed Lisbon strategy for growth and jobs: launching the new cycle (2008–2010), COMM(2007) 803 final-Part I, December 11, 2007.
38. Roy Ginsberg, *Demystifying the European Union* (Lanham MD: Rowman and Littlefield, 2007), pp. 240–242.
39. *International Herald Tribune*, June 21, 2006.
40. Data from the EU, available at http://ec.europa.eu/trade/creating-opportunities/bilateral-relations/countries/china/, accessed on 7 May 2010.
41. Some did argue that Greece could default on its debt, announcing more or less that it would not or could not pay. While technically possible, no one would likely lend any more money to Greece, which desperately needed to borrow funds to pay its expenses in 2010.
42. Eurobarometer 69, Spring 2008, accessible at http://ec.europa.eu/public_opinion/archives/eb/eb69/eb69_globalisation_en.pdf, accessed on 10 May 2010.
43. Pew Global Attitudes Project, "Global Views of Life Satisfaction, National Conditions, and the Global Economy," 2007, at http://pewglobal.org/commentary/pdf/1025.pdf, accessed on 7 May 2010.
44. Cited in John Callaghan, "Environmental Politics, the New Left and the New Social Democracy," *The Political Quarterly* 71:3, 2000, p. 301.
45. Franz-Josef Strauss, quoted in Ramachandra Guha, *Environmentalism: A Global History* (New York: Longman, 2000), p. 97.
46. Robert Garner, *Environmental politics: Britain, Europe, and the global environment* (New York: St. Martin's Press, 2000), p. 153.
47. *Christian Science Monitor*, December 12, 2007.
48. Detailed examinations of various countries can be found in Michael Artis et al., eds., *The Central and Eastern European Countries and the European Union* (Cambridge: Cambridge University Press, 2006).
49. Data culled from UN Human Development Report, 2007/2008. Figures are Slovenia ($22,273), Czech Republic ($20,538) and Estonia ($15,478), Romania ($9,060), Bulgaria ($9,032), and Macedonia ($7,200), compared to Great Britain ($33,238), France ($30,386), Germany ($29,461), and Italy ($28,529).
50. *OECD in Figures*, 2007.
51. See debate over this issue in "Flat Taxes," *The Economist Intelligence Unit*, January 18, 2007.
52. Data are from 2005 and come from the World Bank at http://www.worldbank.org.
53. "Dangers ahead," *The Economist*, February 16, 2008, and "The Party Is Nearly Over," *The Economist*, August 16, 2008.
54. "The European Union's Week from Hell," *The Economist*, October 11, 2008.
55. Charlemagne, "Fingers in the Dyke," *The Economist*, March 21, 2009.
56. "Creeping Along," *The Economist*, September 27, 2008.
57. "The whiff of contagion," *The Economist*, February 28, 2009.
58. "Suddenly Europe Look Pretty Smart," *New York Times*, October 19, 2008.
59. "Bagehot: Gordon Brown's 1,001 hours," *The Economist*, September 27, 2008.
60. "In and Out of Each Other's European Wallets," *New York Times*, May 2, 2010, and "Acropolis Now," *The Economist*, May 1, 2010.

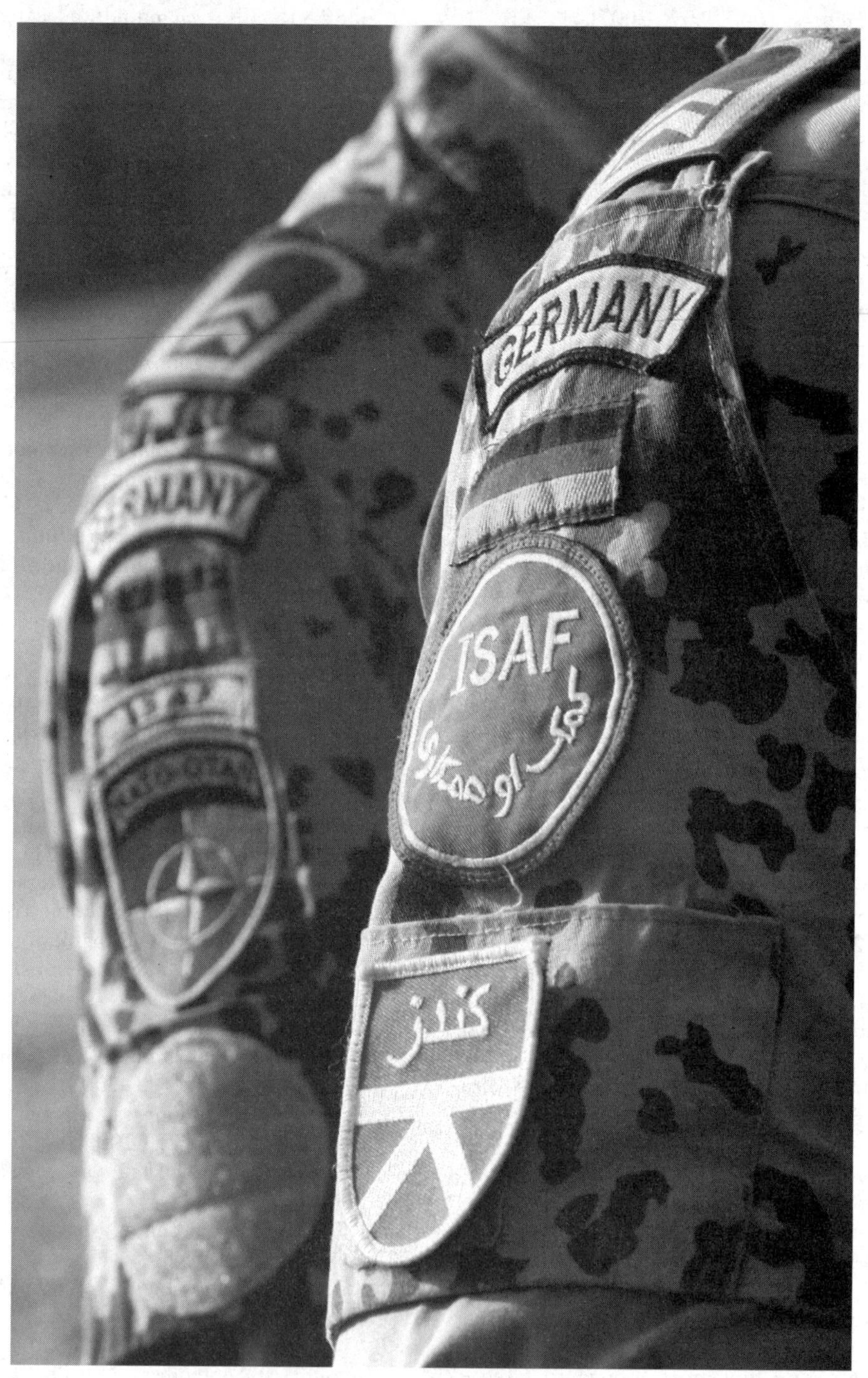

NATO Forces in Afghanistan: Will they stay the course?

CHAPTER 11

Security and Foreign Policy Issues

On February 2010, the government of the Netherlands collapsed as the Labour Party, the second-largest party in the governing coalition, withdrew its support from the government. Such events do occur from time to time in states in states where multi-party systems necessitate coalition governments. What was interesting about this case, however, was that its cause was rooted in a particular foreign policy decision: the Labour Party insisted that the 2,000 Dutch troops in Afghanistan be withdrawn by the previously agreed-upon August 2010 deadline. When Jan Peter Balkenende, the prime minister from the Christian Democratic Party, suggested that they should perhaps stay longer, the Labour Party announced it would not support such a decision and ended its participation in the coalition.

This episode raises many interesting questions, including how to maintain international collective action, what the future holds for Dutch involvement in NATO, what possible rifts may occur in US-European ties as the US pressures Europeans to contribute more troops to Afghanistan, and whether other EU countries will follow the Dutch lead, given that public opinion in many European states has turned against involvement in Afghanistan. For our purposes, however, the most interesting question may be what this demonstrates about European unity and development of a cohesive European foreign policy. Given the hopes of some to turn Europe into a powerful force in international relations, what does it say when in 2010 some European countries, such as Poland, Italy, and Spain, sent more troops to fight in Afghanistan, whereas others, such as the French, balked at calls to increase their troop levels, or, like the Dutch, pulled out completely?

This chapter takes up a host of complex questions concerning security and foreign policy, focusing on united action (or, in some cases, inaction) by European states. The Maastricht Treaty of 1992 introduced a **Common Foreign and Security Policy (CFSP)**, whose goal is the coordination of states' foreign policies and development of a range of policy instruments. The CFSP, perhaps more than any other issue area, remains a work in progress, but its very development is indicative that the goal of a more united Europe is being actively pursued in order to give European states a stronger presence on the world stage. Individual European states, of course, continue to have their own foreign policies and some, particularly larger and more powerful ones such as Great Britain and France,

Common Foreign and Security Policy (CFSP) ■ created by the Maastricht Treaty, its goal is to develop a stronger, united approach on foreign policy and security issues by EU member-states.

have in the past been leading international actors in their own right. This chapter, however, is less concerned about individual state's policies or comparative foreign policy than the development (or lack thereof) of a cohesive European approach in security issues and international affairs more broadly. The rationale is straightforward: For a number of reasons (historical experiences, power imbalances, divergent interests, desires to maintain state sovereignty), foreign policy is the area that arguably should see the *least* amount of integration. Foreign policy thus becomes a crucial case in the examination of the idea of a united Europe. To the extent that one can be sanguine about prospects for creation of a potent and coherent European foreign policy, one would likely think that movement toward "One Europe" could go quite far.

INSTITUTIONAL BASES FOR A "EUROPEAN" FOREIGN POLICY

Origins

The origins of today's CFSP date to the earliest days of European integration, when proponents of a more politically unified Europe tried to create a European Political Community and a European Defence Community. Both of these plans were very ambitious, as they attempted to create supranational political and military organizations. The Treaty on the European Political Community was signed in 1952, but it was rejected by the French parliament, an action that also doomed the European Defence Community. Grandiose plans for European integration thereafter gave way to the more gradualist, functional approach epitomized by the Treaty of Rome.

The founding treaties of the then-European Community (EC) did not delegate to the common European institutions any of the powers of foreign policy–making traditionally exercised by the nation-state. The EC did, however, establish trade agreements with the outside world and offered association agreements to neighboring states such as Turkey and Greece that opened up the possibility of future membership to them. The EC also became an observer in many international organizations and established diplomatic relations with many countries throughout the world. Nonetheless, it was clear that the EC was *not* a state, and to the extent that there was an EC "foreign policy," it was the result of unanimous agreement among the member states. In 1970, the then six members of EC formed the European Political Cooperation (EPC), an informal consultation process on foreign policy matters with the aim of forming common policies. The establishment of the European Council in 1974 contributed to better coordination of EPC because of the role it gave to the heads of state or government in defining the general orientation of Community policy. Early successes for the EPC included the various Lomé Conventions, dating from 1975, which were trade and aid agreements between the EC and former colonies in the developing world, initiation of the Conference on Security and Cooperation in Europe (CSCE), and sanctions against states such as military-ruled Argentina and apartheid South Africa.

Incorporation in the Maastricht Treaty

By the early 1990s, however, there was a sense that the EC could and should do more. Purely inter-governmental consultations were unwieldy. European states had to play second fiddle to the US in the 1991 war to liberate Kuwait from Iraqi occupation and Europe was unprepared to deal with crises closer to home, such as the breakup of Yugoslavia. It is in this context that adding a CFSP was viewed as a logical and necessary extension of the European project.

The Maastricht Treaty established the CFSP. By terms of the Treaty, the CFSP is supposed to safeguard the values and strengthen the security of the EU, preserve international peace in accord with the principles of the UN Charter, promote international cooperation, and develop democracy, rule of law, and respect for human rights. In addition, the Maastricht Treaty envisioned the "progressive framing of a common defence policy, which might in time lead to a common defence." To this end, it brought the **West European Union (WEU)**, which was formed in 1954 but remained largely dormant, into the EU. The WEU was later charged in the 1997 Amsterdam Treaty with humanitarian and rescue missions, peacekeeping, and crisis management. In contrast to NATO, the WEU is purely European and it includes (either as members, associates, or observers) all EU states, including formally "neutral" countries such as Ireland, Austria, and Sweden. As part of the WEU, France, Germany, Belgium, Spain, and Luxembourg have committed 60,000 troops as a Eurocorps, available for humanitarian and peacekeeping missions as well as combat.[1]

West European Union (WEU) ■ defense organization within the EU, which is envisioned to play an important role in peacekeeping and humanitarian missions.

The EU was directed to pursue its CFSP by means of systematic cooperation between member states and the implementation of joint actions in areas where the member states have important interests in common. The individual states, however, retain sovereignty in the conduct of their respective foreign and security policy. In other words, cooperation is inter-governmental, with each state having a final say in policy. Nonetheless, the EU is supposed to ensure that countries refrain from any action that is contrary to the interests of the EU or likely to impair its effectiveness as a cohesive force in international relations. The issue of whether or not this has led to the successful creation of a unified "European" foreign policy is taken up in the **Is Europe One?** section.

Procedures

How does European foreign policy work? This area has evolved rapidly since the 1990s, and the Lisbon Treaty transforms it even more. Under Lisbon, economic aspects of foreign policy (e.g., trade, development assistance) remain under "Community" decision-making principles, meaning that that policy is initiated by the European Commission, debated and voted on (usually by qualified majority voting) in the Council of the EU, and is subject to approval by the European Parliament (EP). CFSP decisions (e.g., use of force, adoption of sanctions) are made in a more inter-governmental fashion, with the European Council, the collection of heads of government, defining the strategic interests and objectives of the EU on the basis of unanimity, which also holds in the Council of the EU, which formally approves EU actions. The requirements of unanimity reflect the fact that foreign policy is an area where concerns about national sovereignty are important.

IS EUROPE ONE?

Is There a Common European Foreign Policy?

The CFSP is an important part of the EU, and over the past two decades European governments have taken a number of steps to give it more substance and teeth. However, one might fairly ask: Can one really speak of a *common* European foreign policy? Does it really make sense to speak of "One Europe" in terms of foreign and defense policies?

The CFSP has a clear rationale. Individually, most European states are too small to have much clout on the world stage. Collectively they can have more of a global role and exercise more influence. In theory, other states would have to deal with "Europe," not France, Spain, Poland, or Estonia. Some, particularly in light of the Iraq war, suggest that Europe needs to band together to balance the hegemonic power of the US.[2] Interestingly, survey data show that majorities across Europe, even in more Euro-skeptical states such as Great Britain and Sweden, endorse multi-level governance in this field, believing that foreign policy decisions should be made not solely by national governments but jointly within the EU.[3]

Has CFSP been effective? In some respects, the answer is yes. Again, Europe has more clout when it works collectively. Sanctions on human rights offenders, for example, are far more likely to be effective if adopted by numerous states than by only a few. The EU has adopted common positions on a number of questions, and functions as a collective whole on a number of issues. As will be highlighted more extensively in this chapter, it has been a leading actor on questions such as human rights, economic development, peacekeeping, removal of land mines and demobilization of combatants, election support, and climate change.[4]

Nonetheless, on many significant questions of international affairs, particularly those involving or requiring hard power, Europe has been less capable of acting with a single voice and/or less than effective in its chosen policy. A prime example was the former Yugoslavia in the early 1990s, where the "hour of Europe," in the words of Luxembourg's foreign minister, turned into four years of bloody fighting and ended thanks to US intervention. Part of the problem in the Yugoslav case was lack of capability, but also lack of will and unity, as European leaders could not agree on a forceful common strategy. In the case of Kosovo in 1999, Greece, a NATO member, lobbied against bombing of Serbia, whereas some European leaders, notably Britain's Tony Blair, argued for a more forceful policy including use of NATO ground troops. Europe remains divided about what to do about Turkey's bid to join the EU. European views on Russia were extremely divided in the 2000s, and policy with respect to China is hampered by the fact that each country wants to make sure that its own businesses grab a piece of the ever-expanding Chinese market. At the UN, France and Great Britain both ardently hold onto their veto powers on the Security Council, rejecting any idea that they should give up their positions in favor of a common "European" seat.

It was in the case of Iraq, however, that notions of a common Europe seemed to fall apart. One writer suggested that Iraq "epitomizes everything that is wrong with the practice and even the concept of the CFSP."[5] The debate over what to do in Iraq, of course, took place in the UN, not within the confines of CSFP, but even there Great Britain was on one side and France and Germany on the other.

Whereas there are signs that after the election of Barack Obama the wounds created within Europe and with the US over Iraq are beginning to heal, the failure of Europe to develop a common policy with respect to Iraq may reveal the limits of CFSP. Yes, Europe can agree on relatively "safe" issues (e.g., sanctions on Myanmar), but it lacks a grand strategic vision (particularly with respect to its relationship with the US) and individual states still have their own interests that they feel obligated to pursue. CFSP remains essentially inter-governmental, revealing the limits of EU integration. Whereas the motives behind the CFSP and Europe's desire to spread its values may be laudable, the effectiveness of the CFSP, as a grand strategy, is another matter. As one French writer dismissingly observes, "If Europe does not speak with a single voice, it is first and foremost because it lacks any strategic concept other than the wish to be friend to all, and notably the protector of widows and orphans."[6]

Critical Thinking Questions

1. Despite European concerns over human rights and genocide in areas such as Bosnia, Rwanda, Darfur, and Congo, European action in these areas has often been minimal or come far too late. Why has Europe been so hamstrung in responding to issues such as these?
2. Does the idea of a Common Foreign Policy for Europe seem attainable or unrealistic to you? Assuming such a policy was a goal, what could be done to realize it?

The European Parliament may debate a given issue and may be consulted, but final approval of any CFSP rests with the Council of the EU.

There is, as one might expect, an elaborate bureaucratic structure for overseeing EU foreign policy and representing Europe to the world. The Amsterdam Treaty of 1997 created the office of the **High Representative** for the CFSP to coordinate the EU's foreign policy. Until the adoption of the Lisbon Treaty, however, the High Representative had to share responsibility for foreign policy with the EU Commissioner for External Affairs. The Lisbon Treaty altered this structure and created a single High Representative of the EU for Foreign Affairs and Security Policy. Catherine Ashton of Great Britain, who had served as EU Trade Commissioner since 2008 but otherwise had little foreign policy experience, was appointed to this post by the European Council. The High Representative, not the European Commission, has the primary responsibility of making foreign policy proposals to the Council of the EU. As noted in Chapter 4, the Lisbon Treaty also created an individual president of the EU (Herman Van Rompuy of Belgium), who is also empowered to represent Europe globally. The Lisbon Treaty also created an EU External Action Force, which will function as an EU diplomatic corps.

High Representative ■ the chief diplomat of the EU, who is given enhanced role under the Lisbon Treaty and empowered to make foreign policy proposals to the EU Council of Ministers.

Instruments of Policy

What can the EU do? The EU has four instruments for its CFSP: Common Positions, Joint Actions, Common Strategies, and Declarations. A Common Position means that EU members are obliged to comply with the EU position with regard to their own foreign policies. Examples include maintenance of sanctions (e.g., on Belarus, Myanmar, Zimbabwe). A Joint Action puts into operation a Common Position. Examples include overseas deployment of police or human rights monitoring forces. A Common Strategy sets out overall policy guidelines with respect to a country or region. For example, the EU has a Common Strategy with both Russia and Ukraine and its European Neighborhood Policy (ENP) with countries to its south and east would fit into this rubric. A Declaration is simply a statement expressing the EU's position (e.g., concern over violence between Russia and Georgia in 2008).

While the EU does have economic and diplomatic muscle to carry out foreign policy, it is relatively lacking when it comes to military capabilities. Individual states and/or NATO were counted on to provide security, and in several instances (e.g., the Italians in Albania in 1997, the British in Sierra Leone in 2000, the French in Ivory Coast in 2002), separate countries have provided the military means to act while the EU has offered only diplomatic or political support. After the Kosovo crisis in 1999, the EU agreed that it must have "the capacity for autonomous action, backed by credible military forces, the means to decide to use them, and the readiness to do so, in order to respond to international crises without prejudice to actions by NATO."[7] To that end, the EU created a **European Strategic Defense Policy (ESDP)**, which included efforts to bolster the EU's military capability. EU members agreed on a "Headline Goal" process that outlined the needs of the EU for its projected peacekeeping and military operations. Some, however, feared that the development of separate EU forces would undermine NATO. In 2002, NATO and EU agreed to cooperate in military affairs, and the EU is allowed to use NATO structures and assets if NATO declines to act in a particular situation. The first EU troops were sent on a peacekeeping mission to Macedonia in 2003, and, as noted below, the EU has participated in several peacekeeping or emergency operations. By 2008, the EU met its 2003 Headline Goal of 60,000 troops that can be deployed for up to a year and also has fifteen multi-national battle groups of 1,500 troops each at its disposal on a rotating basis as part of the ESDP.

European Strategic Defense Policy (ESDP) ■ EU program designed to increase its military capability; has already performed several peacekeeping and humanitarian operations.

The EU has deployed twenty-four military and civilian missions from 2003 to 2010 in order to promote peace and security. The first deployment of EU forces was to Macedonia in 2003, where EU sent 250 troops to keep the peace between the Macedonian government and elements of its ethnic Albanian population. The EU's first mission outside of Europe occurred in 2003, when as part of Operation Artemis it sent 1,800 personnel, mostly French, to the Democratic Republic of Congo for two months to prevent the outbreak of wider violence. As noted more below, EU peacekeepers are still deployed in Bosnia and Kosovo. It also sent a force of more than 4,000 troops to Chad and the Central African Republic to assist in peacekeeping and support of refugees fleeing the Sudanese region of Darfur. EU police and monitoring groups have also been deployed in Georgia, Indonesia, Palestine, Moldova, and Sudan to assist in human rights and peacekeeping operations. While the EU touts such efforts as proof of the organization's positive record in promoting global security, critics would argue that the EU could and should do more (e.g., to stop genocide in Darfur, not simply protecting refugees that have already fled the area) and not confine itself to relatively low-risk peacekeeping or support operations.

OTHER EUROPEAN SECURITY ORGANIZATIONS

The fact that the CFSP is of relatively recent origin can be explained, partially, by the fact that other organizations in Europe focused on security issues. Two of these, NATO and the OSCE, continue to have relevance in the post–Cold War world.

The North Atlantic Treaty Organization (NATO)

NATO (North Atlantic Treaty Organization) ■ military and political alliance of twenty-eight countries in Europe and North America; played key role during Cold War, and has since expanded to new countries and new missions.

The North Atlantic Treaty Organization (**NATO**) arguably remains the most important security institution in Europe. It is headquartered, like the EU, in Brussels, and its top official, the secretary-general, is a European.[8] NATO, however, is not, however, a wholly European organization. Because it includes Canada and the US—indeed, because of US military power, the US is the pre-eminent force in NATO—it is often described as a "trans-Atlantic" institution, one that creates a bond between the US and Europe.

NATO was the key player during the Cold War, serving to deter a possible Soviet attack on Western Europe. Fundamentally, NATO is a military alliance based on a system of collective security, whereby its member states agree to come a member's defense if another actor attacks it. With its initial foe—the Soviet Union—no more, NATO has been compelled to look for a new role in the post–Cold War world.

One recent emphasis of NATO has been the addition of new members. In the 1990s many former communist countries sought NATO membership, less out of explicit security concerns (the possibility of a Soviet attack on Poland or Hungary seemed quite remote) than as recognition that these states were part of the successful West. For their part, NATO states argued that NATO expansion would help consolidate democracy and prevent the emergence of a "security vacuum" in Eastern Europe. Despite objections by Russia, NATO added Poland, the Czech Republic, and Hungary in 1999; Bulgaria, Estonia, Latvia, Lithuania, Romania, Slovakia, and Slovenia in 2004; and Albania and Croatia in 2009. As of 2011, NATO's membership stands at twenty-eight countries, and more countries seek NATO membership. Whether NATO will expand further is an open question. Russia, which has its own special relationship with NATO, has been adamant in its opposition to NATO membership for states such as Ukraine and Georgia, the later of which it invaded in 2008 in a bid, arguably, to reassert control over parts of the post-Soviet space.

NATO has also undertaken military missions outside of its primary responsibility of defending the territory of member states from outside attack. These cases included Bosnia (1994–1995) and Kosovo (1999), where NATO both bombed Serbian positions and took the lead in sending in peacekeepers once the fighting stopped. The intervention in Kosovo was particularly controversial because NATO's own treaty says members must "refrain from the use of force in any manner inconsistent with the purposes of the United Nations" (Article 1) and that the UN Security Council has "primary responsibility" for the maintenance of international peace and security (Article 7). Nonetheless, NATO felt compelled to act, given the juxtaposition of the possibility of another round of mass killing in the Balkans with NATO's fiftieth anniversary celebrations. Indeed, during the fighting NATO approved a new strategic concept that broadened its mission to "stand firm against those who violate human rights, wage war, and conquer territory" and stated that NATO would seek to "contribute to building a stronger and broader Euro-Atlantic community of democracy."[9]

The expansion of the activities and geographical reach of NATO grew even further after the September 11, 2001, attacks on the US. On September 12, 2001,

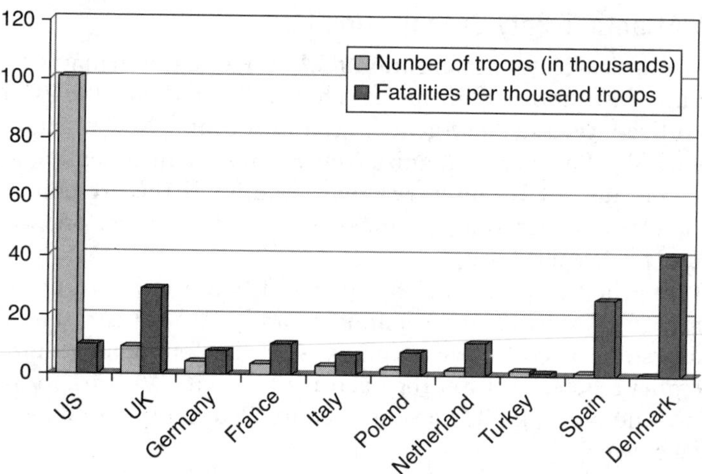

FIGURE 11.1

NATO Forces in Afghanistan.

Sources: ISAF webpage at http://www.isaf.nato.int/en/troop-contributing-nations/index.php and icasualties webpage at http://icasualties.org/oef/, both accessed March 29, 2010. Figures valid through March 2010 and include additional 18,000 US troops still to be deployed. Figure for US troops is for all US troops, not just those attached to ISAF.

NATO, for the first time ever, invoked Article 5, its collective security provision, which declares that any attack on a member state will be considered an attack against the entire group. The US formally asked for and received NATO support for its military operations in Afghanistan against al Qaeda and the Taliban-led Afghan government. In April 2003, NATO agreed to take command of the International Security Assistance Force (ISAF) in Afghanistan, marking the first time NATO took charge of a mission outside of Europe. As of 2010, ISAF is composed of approximately 90,000 troops, over half of which are American. As seen in Figure 11.1, however, numerous European states have contributed to ISAF, and some such as the British and Danes have suffered higher casualties (on a per soldier basis) than the US. Hence European trepidation about adding more troops and desires to pull out those already deployed, as noted in the beginning of the chapter. Given that the Obama administration in the US has committed more troops to Afghanistan and wants NATO allies to follow suit, the hesitancy of European countries to remain committed to what by 2011 was nearly a decade-long conflict has exposed fissures in the alliance.

OSCE (Organization for Security and Cooperation in Europe) ■ pan-European security organization, includes former Soviet states, which has taken a lead in issues such as human rights, democratization, and arms control.

The Organization for Security and Cooperation and Europe (OSCE)

The largest security organization in Europe in terms of member states is the Organization for Security and Cooperation and Europe (**OSCE**). It has fifty-six members, including the US, Canada, all members of the EU, and all the former Soviet states. As the OSCE itself notes, it covers an area from Vancouver to Vladivostok (a Russian city on the Pacific Ocean), making it more than a European organization in the strictest sense of the term and the largest regional security organization in the world.[10]

The OSCE harkens back to the Cold War in the early 1970s, when the pan-European CSCE was created to serve as a multi-lateral forum for dialogue and negotiation between East and West. Meeting over two years in Helsinki and Geneva, the CSCE reached agreement on the Helsinki Final Act, which was signed on August 1, 1975. This document contained a number of key commitments on political, military, economic, environmental, and human rights issues that became central to the so-called "Helsinki process." The Helsinki process was important in many ways, not the least of which was putting human rights on the agenda in Eastern Europe, and many "Helsinki" organizations developed in communist countries to push for political reforms and respect for human rights.

Until 1990, the CSCE functioned mainly as a series of meetings and conferences that built on and extended existing commitments. However, with the end of the Cold War, the members of the CSCE sought to give the organization a stronger institutional basis. Thus, in 1994, it became the OSCE and has permanent headquarters in Vienna, Austria. OSCE decisions have to be taken by consensus. This means that there is no voting on issues. In the case of one or more delegations opposing a decision, the issue goes back into negotiation. If all delegates agree, the decision becomes politically binding for all member states. Unlike the EU, it is therefore an entirely inter-governmental organization.

It has no military of its own, relying upon contributions from member states. The OSCE takes a comprehensive approach to security, however, emphasizing elements such as conflict prevention, early warning, and arms control. In addition, it includes dimensions that include economic development, respect for the environment, human rights, human trafficking, and development of democracy. As such, it works closely with EU efforts in these fields and contributes to the spread of European "soft power" in the global arena, which is discussed later in the chapter. As of 2010, the OSCE has permanent missions or field offices in seventeen different countries, most of which are in the Balkans and former Soviet states. Some of its most visible work is in election monitoring, and in some cases (e.g., Serbia in 2000, Georgia in 2003, Ukraine in 2004), OSCE observers reported irregularities that helped spur local citizens to the streets to demand another round of elections or drive the authorities from office. These efforts, however, are often controversial. Since 2004, Russia has sent observers and certified as free and fair elections in countries with dubious democratic records such as Belarus and Azerbaijan. Citing lack of cooperation on the part of Russia, the OSCE refused to send observers for the 2007 Russian parliamentary elections and 2008 presidential elections.

SECURITY ISSUES IN EUROPE

Post–World War II Europe has often been called a "zone of peace." Indeed, a major, continent-wide war like the two witnessed in the twentieth century seems inconceivable today. This is not to say, however, that there has been no violence in Europe. In the 1970s, terrorism plagued a number of West European states (e.g., the troubles in Northern Ireland, terrorism by the Basque ETA group in Spain, radical groups in Germany and Italy). Military forces were also used to crush challenges to Soviet rule in Eastern Europe, such as the Prague Spring in 1968. Whereas security issues figured prominently in Europe during the Cold War, the collapse of the communist bloc made the fear of a Soviet invasion of Western Europe evaporate.

This is not to say that there are no longer security issues in Europe. There are several, including fears in some quarters (e.g., the Baltic states) of a resurgent Russia, human trafficking, and the still active ETA in Spain. However, we shall focus attention here on two great challenges of wider import: establishing peace and security in the Balkans and Europe as a target in the "global war on terror."

Putting the Balkans Back Together

The collapse of Yugoslavia was briefly covered in Chapter 2. To review, the end of the Cold War created pressures to democratize Yugoslavia. Nationalist politicians gained support in various regions of Yugoslavia. Fighting broke out in several regions, but it was fiercest in Bosnia, which experienced a three-sided conflict among ethnic Serbs, Croats, and Muslims (Bosniacs). After the failure of European diplomacy and UN peacekeepers to stop atrocities, NATO, led by the US, intervened, and the warring parties signed the Dayton Accord to stop the fighting in Bosnia in 1995. When in 1999 there was a risk of more atrocities in the Serb-controlled region of **Kosovo**, which was populated overwhelmingly by ethnic Albanians, NATO again intervened, bombing Serb targets, including the capital, Belgrade. Peacekeepers were sent into both Bosnia and Kosovo, and European monitors were also placed in Macedonia to prevent a major conflict from erupting there. All told, the fighting in the region claimed 200,000 dead and 2 million refugees, as well as, on a continent where most thought such things could never happen again, accusations of genocide.[11]

Since large-scale fighting has stopped, there have been efforts to rebuild and reintegrate formerly war-torn states. International peacekeepers have helped prevent a new round of fighting. In the case of Bosnia, the Dayton Accord established a ceasefire, put a NATO-led force of more than 40,000 international peacekeepers into both Bosnia and Croatia, and established a single Bosnian state with two "entities"—a Muslim-Croat Federation and the *Republika Srpska* (Serb Republic). It also required all governments to cooperate in the hunt for war criminals, allow refugees to return to their homes, and it set up a means for international financial assistance for rebuilding in both Croatia and Bosnia. In Kosovo, after the NATO bombardment the Serbs agreed to pull out of the region and Kosovo became a *de facto* UN protectorate, occupied by 50,000 peacekeepers. In the 2000s, international administrators oversaw reconstruction efforts, helped conduct elections, and prevented large-scale conflict, although ethnic Serbs—perhaps now 5 percent of the population—claim that they have been the targets of violence from Albanians.

Reconstruction and reconciliation among formerly warring parties has been difficult in both Bosnia and Kosovo. Ten years after the Dayton Accord, one observer suggested that Bosnia "barely had a pulse."[12] One EU official in the former Yugoslavia told me in 2007 that Bosnia was basically an "American fiction." Its weak central government exercised little control over its two separate entities and various localities, which were dominated nationalist politicians. Most people live in ethnically segregated communities. Bosnia suffers from corruption and the economy is on international life-support. Cooperation on tracking down war criminals has been spotty. Wartime Bosnia Serb political leader Radovan Karadžić was captured in Belgrade in 2008, but Ratko Mladić, the commander of Bosnian Serb troops during the Srebrenica massacre in 1995, was still at large in 2010. While the number of international peacekeepers has been significantly reduced—down to an EU-led force of approximately 2000 by 2010 from a high of 54,000 in 1996—political reconciliation remains difficult. While Bosnia could, in the long-term qualify for EU membership, it has been slow to adopt reforms and is racked by an "endless tug-of-war" between its ethnic communities. US Vice President Joe Biden traveled to Bosnia in 2009 and exclaimed in a speech before the Bosnian parliament that inflammatory nationalist rhetoric "must stop." Some see the lack of progress in Bosnia as an indication that the EU is incapable of sorting out the country's problems.[13]

Matters are scarcely better in Kosovo. After the war, Kosovo remained, technically, a part of Serbia, even though it was occupied by international peacekeepers. Although Serbia made some progress toward democracy in the 2000s—including a popular uprising that helped remove Serbian wartime leader Slobodan Milošević from office in 2000 and his handing over to international authorities for war crimes in 2001—Serbs insisted that Kosovo should remain part of Serbia. Kosovar Albanians, who made up more than 90 percent of the population in Kosovo, wanted their own country. Kosovo's status remained somewhat ambiguous for much of the 2000s, but in February 2008, Kosovo finally declared its independence from Serbia, reflecting the widely held view that it could not be reintegrated into Serbia. This move was celebrated by Kosovo's Albanian population and was recognized by the US, Canada, and most countries in the EU, although, notably, not Spain, Slovakia, Cyprus, and Romania, each of which worry about existing or potential separatist movements. Russia and China also did not recognize Kosovo's independence, meaning that its formal international status is up in the air. This event provoked outrage among Serbs, and there was violence in regions of northern Kosovo populated by Serbs and mob attacks on the US embassy in Belgrade. NATO and EU forces remain in Kosovo to help stabilize the situation, and, given the debates over Kosovo's status within the EU (let alone among Serbs), it seems clear that some sort of international military presence will have to remain in the region for some time.

Ideally, the EU would like to see reforms in all the countries of the former Yugoslavia, and their future membership in the EU is conditional upon implementation of political and economic reform. However, progress is intermittent at best, even beyond the most troubled regions of Bosnia and Kosovo. While Serbs elected Boris Tadić, pro-European leader as President in 2008—an event that was hailed as "watershed" and a reflection that "Serbia has chosen to join the European family,"[14]—nationalist and anti-EU parties remain powerful, and the acceptance of Kosovo's independence by most of Europe has rankled many in Serbia. By 2009, according to one source, Serbia had "stopped moving on its own path to European integration,"[15] although its apology in 2010 for Srebrenica was generally well received in Europe. Montenegro, which separated from Serbia in 2006, has European aspirations but, like Serbia, is rife with corruption. Macedonia, an EU candidate country, is mired in a dispute with Greece over its name, a quarrel that has complicated its efforts to join NATO and the EU.[16]

Terrorism in Europe after September 11, 2001

Although it occurred in the US, the terrorist attack on September 11, 2001 (9/11), was a global event. The perpetrators were from Arab states. Many of them devised their heinous plot while living in Europe. The victims of 9/11 included peoples from dozens of countries. Europeans rushed to condemn the actions and express sympathy for the US. *Le Monde*, a left-wing French newspaper typically critical of the US, ran a headline, "Nous sommes tous Américains [We are all Americans]" the day after 9/11.[17] Many European states joined the US in its fight in Afghanistan against al Qaeda and the Taliban, although, they all have not agreed with all elements of the American-led "war on terror" (e.g., the prison in Guantanamo Bay, the war in Iraq) and, as noted above, have grown tired and sour of military actions in Afghanistan. As noted in the **In Focus** section, some contend that the US and its European allies have increased diverged in their worldviews in the wake of 9/11.

Europeans cannot, as Americans perhaps can, view radical Islamic terrorists as a faraway threat. The Middle East is, after all, adjacent to Europe, and many residents of Europe come from the Middle East. Soon after 9/11, Europe experienced its own tragedies committed by adherents to radical Islam.

In November 2003, two synagogues, the British Consulate, and a bank headquarters were bombed in Istanbul, Turkey. Fifty-seven people died. A local Turkish group with connections to al Qaeda claimed responsibility for these attacks.

On March 11, 2004 (3/11), bombs exploded on four commuter trains in and around Madrid Spain. One hundred and ninety-one people were killed, and more than 2,000 were wounded. The bombing took place three days before general elections in Spain. The government was accused of withholding or distorting information about the attacks, and, in the ensuing elections, the opposition Socialist Party prevailed. Notably, the Socialists had campaigned on a platform that included removing Spanish troops from Iraq, prompting some to declare that the timing of the attack indicated that the terrorists had achieved their objective of cowing Spanish voters and bringing down a government that had been a staunch ally in the US-led war in Iraq. In subsequent investigations, Spanish police arrested numerous suspects, most of whom are of Moroccan descent.[27]

On July 7, 2005 (7/7), suicide bombers attacked three subway cars and one bus in London. Fifty-two people died and more than 700 were wounded. A group called "al Qaeda in Europe" claimed responsibility for the attacks. Investigators ascertained that the bombers were all British citizens, three of which were of Pakistani descent. Two weeks later, a similar plot to attack public transport in London was not successful, and police arrested the perpetrators, who included Muslim asylum seekers who had lived in Britain for several years.

IN FOCUS

Europe versus America I: Competing Views of the World after September 11, 2001

Anti-Americanism in Europe and anti-European feeling in the US both have long histories. Long before some Americans took to calling French fries "freedom fries," Mark Twain declared, "There is nothing lower than the human race except the French," and the French diplomat Tallyrand (1754–1838) opined that the US is a "land of thirty-two religions and only one dish . . . and even that is inedible." Lest one think this is confined to the French, none other than Sigmund Freud (1856–1939), the famed Austrian psychologist, declared, "America is a mistake, a gigantic mistake."

Humor at the expense of each other and the occasional mean-spirited comments aside, Americans and Europeans also have a history of putting their differences aside during major crises. World War II and the Cold War come to mind, during which both sides affirmed the importance of human liberty. Victory over communism and the emergence of more united Europe based upon democracy and capitalism would seem to bode well for US-European relations.

In the post-9/11 world, however, European-American relations have often been quite complicated and tense. The goodwill and sympathy for the US created by 9/11 had dissipated, with Europeans increasingly critical of the "cowboy"-like unilateralism of US President George W. Bush and many Americans upset at what they viewed as a wimpy and effete Europe. These sentiments were most strongly expressed by the neo-conservative writer Robert Kagan, whose essay "Power and Weakness" was widely read on both sides of the Atlantic. The opening lines of his polemic deserve to be quoted at length:

> It is time to stop pretending that Europeans and Americans share a common view of the world, or even that they occupy the same world. On the all-important question of power—the efficacy of power, the morality of power, the desirability of power—American and European perspectives are diverging. Europe is turning away from power, or, to put it a little differently, it is moving beyond power into a self-contained world of laws and rules and transnational negotiation and cooperation. It is entering a post-historical paradise of peace and relative prosperity, the realization of Immanuel Kant's "perpetual peace." Meanwhile, the United States remains mired in history, exercising power in an anarchic Hobbesian world where international laws and rules are unreliable, and where true security and the defense and promotion of a liberal order still depend on the possession and use of military might. That is why on major strategic and international questions today, Americans are from Mars and Europeans from Venus.[18]

If one is unsure whose side Kagan is on, one only need recall the title of a 1992 book on relationships, *Men Are from Mars, Women Are from Venus.*[19]

While one could argue that several long-term developments are behind the alleged differences in American and European views of the world, the shadow of 9/11 obviously looms large. Although many embraced the notion that the West—Europe *and* America—was embroiled in a "clash of civilizations" against radicalized Islam or "Islamofascism," some, like Kagan, were skeptical that Europe and America would come together against this common enemy.[20] Is it true, with respect to the multi-faceted battle against terrorism, that the US and Europe are living on different planets?

Certainly, there is some evidence to support Kagan's thesis. Differences over the war in Iraq are the most obvious example. The US government, with widespread popular support, attacked Iraq, believing such action was necessary to rid Iraq of weapons of mass destruction. European governments were far more divided on the wisdom of this course. France

(*continued*)

and Germany opposed the US within the UN Security Council. Hence "freedom fries" and *The New York Post* labeling France and Germany as part of the "axis of weasels."[21] Several European states—including Great Britain, Italy, Spain, Denmark, Poland, Romania, and the Czech Republic—sent military forces to Iraq, demonstrating that the division was not, contrary to an assertion made by US Secretary of Defense Donald Rumsfeld, strictly between "old" and "new" Europe. However, it is worth noting that with the exception of Great Britain, where Prime Minister Tony Blair was later accused of "sexing up" the intelligence, European publics were overwhelmingly against military involvement in Iraq. As the conflict continued, several governments (e.g., Spain, Italy, Poland) lost elections and their successors pulled their troops out of Iraq. The revelations of abuse of prisoners at the Abu Ghraib prison in Iraq also generated criticism about how the US was conducting the war. By 2006, a majority of Americans had turned against the war, arguing the invasion was not worth the human and financial costs. Nonetheless, US policy did not change, perhaps lending credence to Kagan's hypothesis.

There are also sharp differences of opinion on other issues related to the struggle against terrorism. As noted above, in Afghanistan, America's NATO allies contributed to efforts to fight the Taliban and al Qaeda, but as the war dragged on and casualties mounted, several countries had lost enthusiasm for this conflict by the end of the 2000s. Some question whether NATO (read: the Europeans) have the will to see the war in Afghanistan through.[22] Europeans have also voiced objections about other anti-terrorist policies adopted by the US. The US detention facility at Guantanamo Bay in Cuba has been roundly condemned by many in Europe both for alleged human rights violations. In November 2006, German lawyers even opened a case accusing Donald Rumsfeld, then the US Defense Secretary, of war crimes over alleged events at Guantanamo. CIA secret prisons in Poland and Romania, whose existence was confirmed in 2005, were also roundly condemned, and the Council of Europe issued a report that noted that they had been sites of torture.[23] Some European citizens have even been picked up by mistake in American anti-terror operations. The most famous was Khalid el Masri, a German of Lebanese descent, who was arrested in Macedonia in December 2003 and later held in US custody in Afghanistan for several months. El Masri, whose name resembles wanted al Qaeda member Khalid *al* Masri, alleges he was tortured by US authorities.[24] He was unceremoniously released in a remote part of Albania in May 2004, and US courts have refused to hear his lawsuit for damages, saying his trial would jeopardize US national security.

On other issues where Europeans and the US profess a common interest, strategies have differed. For example, both sides profess concern about Iran obtaining a nuclear weapon. Europeans, in line with Kagan's hypothesis, have emphasized negotiations and offering Iran a "carrot" (e.g., aid or trade benefits) to allow international inspectors of its nuclear program. The US government, on the other hand, has been far more vocal about possibly using force against the Iranians. The two sides have worked together to impose UN sanctions on Iran, but it is unclear if the Western governments can obtain Iran's compliance to their demands simply by diplomacy. On the question of Arab-Israeli peace talks, the EU and the US have partnered with Russia and the UN (the so-called Quartet) in proposing in 2003 a "road map for peace." Peace, of course, has been elusive, as violence has continued to rage both between Israelis and Palestinians and between different Palestinian groups. As for the issue of homegrown terrorism, some are alarmed at what they see as Europe's excessive tolerance and weak response to would-be terrorists within its own borders.[25] However, as noted above, while individual US and European policies may differ, European countries such as

Great Britain, France, Germany, and Spain have successfully prevented terrorist attacks and prosecuted suspected terrorists.

While Kagan may be right that there are differences in approach, this does not mean that transatlantic ties are doomed to unravel. "Hard" and "soft" power—imagine the "good cop" and "bad cop"—can work together. Despite different points of emphasis, the US and European states have cooperated in many arenas in the struggle against terrorism. By 2007, the disputes over Iraq were far less intense, and elections in Germany in 2005 and France in 2007 brought more pro-US leaders into office. Despite some political opposition, European governments have kept troops in Afghanistan, with pro-US Nicolas Sarkozy pledging to the US Congress (which since 2006 has served "French fries" again) that France "would not let America down."[26] US and European intelligence agencies have worked together to arrest alleged terror plotters in Europe. The election of Barack Obama, who was well received in Europe both during his campaign and as president, also augurs well, as both the style and policies of President Bush, particularly in his first term, rankled many in Europe. Of course, there may still be points of disagreement on various issues or strategies (as there were between Winston Churchill and Franklin Roosevelt in World War II), and Obama may not be able to remove all sources tensions with Europe (e.g., difficulties in closing Guantanamo), but one wonders if Europeans and Americans are really so far apart that we are living on different planets.

Critical Thinking Questions

1. What are acceptable anti-terrorist measures? Are there some things that the government simply should not do in terms of restricting civil liberties?
2. Has the presidency of Barack Obama fundamentally changed US-European relations?

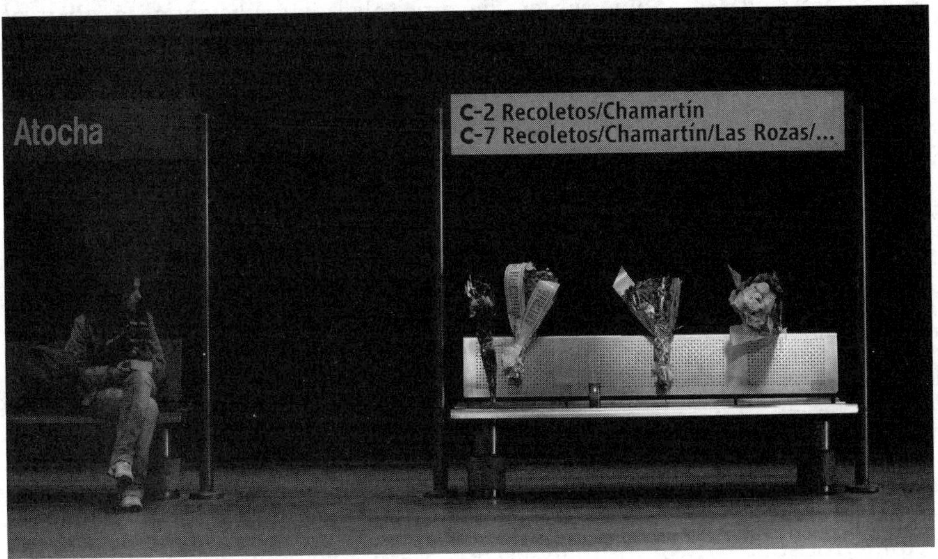

Makeshift memorial to victims of the Madrid train bombing.

Seeking to deflect criticism from his own country, the Pakistani president suggested that Britain was now the primary breeding ground for the next generation of Osama Bin Ladens.[28]

In June 2007, London police discovered two car bombs that, fortunately, did not go off. The next day, two men drove an explosive-laden vehicle into the front entrance of the Glasgow airport in Scotland. Their bombs also did not go off. British police arrested eight individuals, mostly doctors born in the Middle East or India, for these planned attacks.

This list does not include the numerous plots that have been uncovered by police forces and intelligence services across the continent. These include plans to bring down trans-Atlantic airliners, attack soccer stadiums, and blow up government buildings. The common denominator in all, however, has been the fact that the perpetrators are Muslim[29] and most of them were either citizens of European countries or had resided in Europe for many years. The case of 7/7 bombers was perhaps the most disturbing of all, as most of the suicide bombers were British-born and products of the British educational system. The suggestion that some Muslims might be part of an al Qaeda "fifth column" within Europe is far more disturbing and exacerbates concerns over immigration, an issue discussed more fully in the next chapter. One analyst noted, "every single attack carried out or attempted by al Qaeda has [had] some link to Europe, even prior to 9/11."[30]

European governments, of course, have felt compelled to respond to this threat. The issues, however, are more complex than those in the US, where the American Muslim population has posed little threat of political violence. Not only is Europe physically closer to most Muslim countries, but, as examined in more detail in the subsequent chapter, it has its own sizeable Muslim population,[31] many of whom are citizens. Some surveys have revealed that substantial numbers of European Muslims favor introduction of Islamic law or express sympathy with those committing terrorist attacks.[32] To understand their predicament, some Europeans are prone to ask Americans to imagine what the US could or should do if Mexicans had been the perpetrators of 9/11.

Various approaches have been adopted to deal with this security threat. Immigration has been restricted, with some countries such as France even adopting DNA tests for immigrants that want their family members to join them. Britain and the Netherlands, which previously had liberal asylum laws, have been deporting many people who seek political asylum. In Belgium, where Dutch and French speakers agree on very little, there is a consensus that immigration and asylum should be made more difficult. Critics charge that such measures are directed in particular at Muslims, a manifestation of "Islamophobia."[33]

Security measures have also been beefed up. For example, in Great Britain, the government has passed measures that include enhanced powers for the police, more surveillance, and indefinite detention of those suspected of or associated with terrorist activity. British intelligence issued a warning in 2007 that stated that 2000 people in Britain "posed a direct threat to national security" and that terrorists were even recruiting youth as young as fifteen to join their cause.[34]

France, which had its own problems with terrorism committed by Algerians in the 1990s (as part of a civil war in Algeria) has not been so occupied with changes to the legal system. Only a small fraction of the Islamic clerics in France have French citizenship, and many have been put under surveillance and several dozen accused of inflammatory speech have been deported. Germany has proposed a host of measures, including putting spy software on suspects' computers. Spain has arrested hundreds of accused terrorists since 3/11, including one effort that broke up an Internet-based recruiting and propaganda network. Belgium, Italy, Germany, and Denmark all have been the base for alleged al Qaeda "sleeper cells," groups of would-be terrorists that are temporarily lying low while waiting for their assignments. Some intelligence also suggests that terrorists are active in Poland, the Czech Republic, and Bulgaria.[35] Religious education, in many cases sponsored by the government but taught by foreign imams, is also being assessed as a potential source of Islam-inspired violence. Known centers of Islamic political activism, including London's Finsbury Park mosque, Milan's Islamic Cultural Center, and the al-Quds mosque in Hamburg, have been placed under government surveillance.

Finally, and perhaps most importantly, there have been some efforts to try to engage the Muslim community and foster more integration. That is, beyond apprehending the existing "bad guys," governments and societies as a whole are trying to do more to prevent individuals from becoming "bad guys" in the first place. Blatant expressions of racism—such as unprovoked physical attacks on Arabs and Muslims, hostile letters sent to mosques, and rants posted to various websites—are routinely condemned by European leaders. Most European governments have attempted to foster a dialogue with their own Muslim organizations, such as the French National Federation of Muslims and the Muslim Association of Britain.[36] Education and jobs are also seen as ways to improve the lives of many of the poorer immigrants, but how they will be provided is unclear. Some of these issues are taken up more fully in the next chapter.

EUROPE AS A GLOBAL ECONOMIC ACTOR

Whereas the development of a common European security policy is relatively recent, the initial mission of the European project was economic integration. On this front Europe has had its greatest success, both within Europe and beyond. The members of the EU have created a common economic space, the world's largest single market and trading bloc. All members of the EU—even the relatively poorer ones that joined in 2004 and 2007—are wealthy compared to most of the world, and EU countries have great economic resources at its disposal. EU rules define global product safety standards, and its competition rules have affected mighty American companies such as General Electric and Microsoft. To the extent that it can act with a single voice in global trade talks or in the World Trade Organization (WTO), the EU rivals the US in power. Indeed, as noted in Chapter 1, for all the discussion of China and India as rising powers, the size of the Chinese and Indian economies are still dwarfed by the EU. In international economics, Europe is a central actor.

The European Union's Global Trade Policies

The EU has been important in breaking down barriers to international economic activity. Moreover, by many measures, trade liberalization, both within Europe and in the wider world, has been a boon to Europe. However, as noted in Chapter 10, many Europeans are ambivalent or even hostile toward globalization, blaming it for their current economic problems and are unsure if Europe can successfully compete with rising global economic powers such as China. In contrast to free trade, those with these views would prefer to create "Fortress Europe," a walling off of Europe from the rest of world through various protectionist measures. Europe's trade policies reflect this ambivalence. In short, despite the idea that more open markets and freer trade and investment are supposed to spur growth—and indeed, most Europeans have embraced such principles with respect to the development of a common *European* market—Europe's record in promoting global free market is not entirely consistent.

True, Europeans regard themselves as champions for global trade liberalization. After World War II, European countries, together with other advanced industrialized states, embraced the idea of free trade as a measure to prevent economic nationalism and promote economic growth. Individual countries and later the then–EC were major players in various global trade talks that brought down tariffs on manufactured goods from more than 50 percent prior to World War II to less than 4 percent on most products by the 1980s and thereby spurred the growth in world trade in the second half of the twentieth century, which grew on average 8 percent a year from 1945 to 1970. To the extent that the growth in trade eclipsed global economic growth (roughly 5 percent a year from 1945 to 1970), many have argued that freer trade has been a boon to growth across the world.[37]

most-favored nation ■ principle in international trade whereby countries are granted the same level of trade liberalization as the "most-favored" nation; helps to ensure equal treatment of countries and is central idea to lowering barriers to trade.

The EU has concluded various bilateral and multi-lateral trade agreements (e.g., such as those made by the WTO, and, like all WTO members, EU trade agreements are made on the principles of **most-favored nation,** meaning that the EU cannot, with some exceptions, discriminate in favor or against a particular trading partner. Since the 1980s, the EU has worked to facilitate trade by reducing non-tariff barriers (e.g., quotas, regulations), applying WTO principles to trade in services, and securing protection of intellectual property rights. The EU also emphasizes trade as a means to promote sustainable development and regional integration. The EU's leadership on trade issues is underscored by the fact that by the 2000s the EU, as a collective entity, was the world's largest trader, accounting for roughly 20 percent of global imports and exports.

That said, it is worth noting what Europeans have not liberalized. Tariffs on exports of manufactured goods fell, but Europeans continued to protect their textile and agricultural sectors, areas in which Europe did not have a comparative advantage in relation to the developing world. Thus, while touting free trade, "Fortress Europe" blocked—through tariffs, quotas, subsidies—importation of products produced by some of the poorest people on the planet. Noting EU policies on textiles and agriculture, the British charity Oxfam ranked the EU first—ahead of the US, Canada, and Japan—in its "Double Standards League" of free-trade rhetoric and protectionist practice.[38] In 1995, WTO members agreed to reduce quotas on textiles over a ten-year period, but, even so, European tariffs on textiles remain higher than those on other manufactured goods. Trade talks in the 2000s overseen by the WTO had agriculture high on the agenda, but there was no final agreement as many states, not just European ones, were reluctant to open up their markets to cheap food from overseas, despite the fact that well over half the population in the poorest countries in the world work in agriculture and would greatly benefit from trade liberalization.

To be fair, Europeans recognize that not all states are equally ready to embrace or profit from globalization. For several decades the EU managed special trading arrangements with former European colonies, mostly in Africa, the Pacific, and the Caribbean (APC). In 2000, the EU concluded the more ambitious **Cotonou Agreement**(signed in Cotonou, Benin) with seventy-eight APC countries. In addition to providing funds and programs for development and means for a stronger political foundation for APC-EU relations (both discussed more below), the Cotonou Agreement is designed to promote trade cooperation by giving APC special access to the EU market. The EU also grants special trade privileges to those states that meet environmental or social (e.g., labor practice) standards. The Cotonou Agreement will be in effect until 2020, and on balance the EU imports more than it exports to APC countries. However, as seen in Figure 11.2, trade between the EU and APC countries has grown rather modestly between 1999 and 2007, far less than trade with the faster growing economies of China and India.

Contonou Agreement ■ EU agreement, signed with less-developed states in 2000, that provides funds for development and promises to promote trade cooperation.

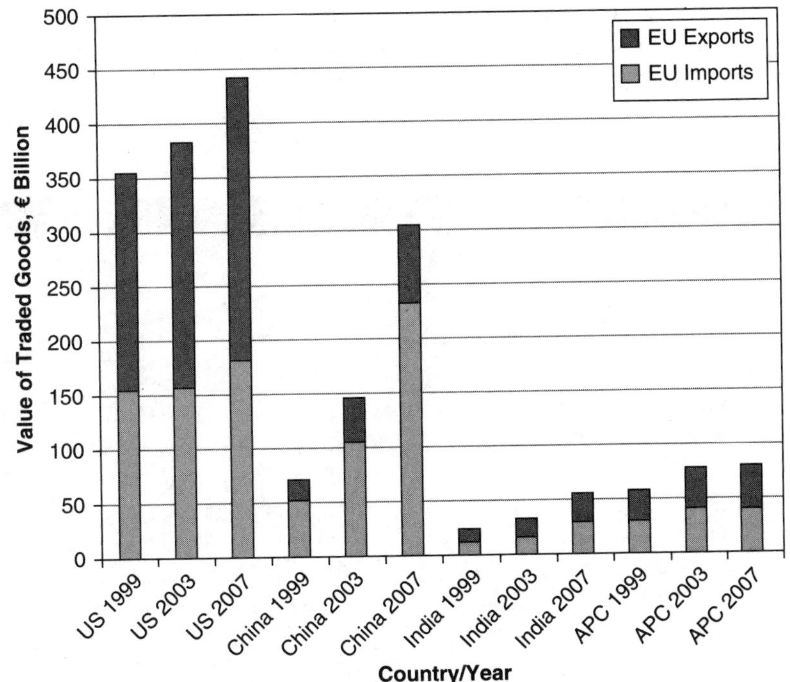

FIGURE 11.2
EU Trade with Selected Countries, 1999–2007.
Source: EU trade data from http://ec.europa.eu/trade/statistics, accessed March 30, 2010.

Under Cotonou, trade relationships are expected to be reciprocal, meaning that the EU provides access to its market to the extent that individual APC countries open up their markets to European goods. However, there are still outcomes that are clearly unfair. For example, the cost of sugar from the developing world is half of that of European produced sugar, which is subsidized through the Common Agricultural Policy (CAP). The EU, until banned from such practices by the WTO, "dumped" its subsidized sugar in markets such as Brazil (!) where it was cheaper than locally produced sugar.[39] Thus, whereas Europeans in trade agreements may gain access to export machinery and other finished or higher-cost goods to developing states, those states do not have unfettered access to export agricultural products—their primary exports—to Europe. With agriculture squarely on the global trade agenda, Europeans now find that their policies are accused of being part of the problem in the global trading regime.[40]

The European Union and Development Assistance

One area of global economic policy that Europeans take great pride in is their relatively generous policy with respect to development assistance to poorer countries. European countries provide over half of the world's development assistance, and, as seen in Table 11.1, spend roughly twice on a *per capita* basis on development assistance than the US. On average, EU member states spend almost $150 a year per citizen on government sponsored overseas development assistance (ODA). Much of the ODA is provided bilaterally, from individual European states to individual donor states. Some European states, notably the Scandinavians, are more generous than others, and they are virtually the only developed states that meet the pledge made to the UN by developed countries to provide 0.7 percent of

Table 11.1

Spending on Overseas Development Assistance (ODA)

Country	Net 2008 ODA, in $ Billion	ODA as % of National Income, 2008	Top Recipients, 2008
US	26.8	0.19	Iraq, Afghanistan, Sudan
Japan	9.6	0.19	Iraq, China, Indonesia
Canada	4.8	0.32	Afghanistan, Haiti, Ethiopia
Great Britain	11.5	0.43	India, Iraq, Afghanistan
France	10.9	0.39	Iraq, Cameroon, Mayotte
Germany	14.0	0.38	Iraq, Cameroon, China
Sweden	4.7	0.98	Tanzania, Mozambique, Sudan
Norway	4.0	0.88	Tanzania, Sudan, Afghanistan
Denmark	2.8	0.82	Tanzania, Uganda, Mozambique
EU Multi-Lateral ODA	14.8	n/a	Turkey, Palestinian Authority, Ethiopia

Source: OECD Development Statistics, available through http://www.oecd.org/countrylist/0,3349,en_2649_34447_1783495_1_1_1_1,00.html, accessed March 30, 2010.

their national income as development assistance.[41] If one takes into account flows of private money to the developing world (e.g., investments) European assistance to the developing world is even more impressive, totaling, for example, $157 billion in 2006 ($91 billion from private sources), compared to $83 billion from the US ($60 billion from private sources).[42]

In addition to bilateral assistance, the EU runs its own development programs, dispensing aid to many regions throughout the world. EU aid totaled over $10 billion in 2006. The largest share of European aid goes to "social infrastructure" (health, education, women's programs), debt relief, and development of economic infrastructure. The EU has embraced the Millennium Development goals of the UN, which are directed at poverty reduction, education, gender equality, health (including AIDS and maternal health), environmental sustainability, and a global partnership for development. Much European development assistance is tied to achievement of "good governance" and respect for human rights. Those states that systematically fall short in these fields (e.g., Zimbabwe, Myanmar) are subject to aid cut-offs and further sanctions. Six of the top ten recipients of European aid are in sub-Saharan Africa (e.g., Cameroon, Congo, Mozambique), but a substantial part of EU "overseas" assistance goes to non-EU European countries such as Turkey, Ukraine, and Serbia and neighbors such as Morocco and the Palestinian Authority.[43]

A more focused comparison between US and European development programs also reveal differences in areas of emphasis. The countries that received the foreign aid, from the United States, since 2001, are Israel, Egypt, Columbia, Afghanistan, Iraq, and Pakistan, all states that are considered strategically valuable by the US, even though, in terms of raw economic need, most do not rank among the poorest countries in the world.[44] In contrast, European aid programs historically have been more directed to poorer African countries, with several countries emphasizing aid programs to their former colonies (e.g., Belgium to Congo, France to Senegal and Cameroon, Britain to Bangladesh, Portugal to Angola). For example, in 2008, over 60 percent of aid from France, Denmark, and Great Britain and almost a third (31.5 percent) of EU development funds went to sub-Saharan Africa, compared to 21.3 percent of aid from the US.[45] Moreover, as noted above, the EU, through the Contonou Agreement, grants privileged access to EU markets to the forty-nine least developed countries (mostly in sub-Saharan Africa), thus supplementing aid with trade incentives to stimulate production and industries in poorer countries.

Although relatively generous foreign aid programs may make Europeans feel good about themselves, it is debatable whether these aid programs are actually effective. Critics of foreign aid note that countries can become dependent on aid, stifling their own development and incentive to adopt better economic policies.[46] Some also allege that European aid is too spread out and is poorly coordinated, and therefore would be better used in countries that either desperately need help or have the political institutions in place to use aid more effectively. As mentioned above, critics of EU would argue that it could do far more to eradicate poverty in the developing world by simply opening up its markets to agricultural imports. The EU and other donors do routinely assess the effectiveness of their aid programs, and have created EuropeAid, another EU bureaucratic organ that is charged with coordinating aid efforts. The Contonou Agreement also stresses the need to build "performance-based partnerships" by channeling aid to those states that on political and economic grounds can be classified as "good performers." This sounds reasonable, but are Europeans therefore to abandon the poorest of the poor? Humanitarians would, of course, say no, but the fact that sub-Saharan Africa, traditionally the largest source of EU has since the 1960s grown on average far less than other regions of the developing world and has done little to diversify exports beyond natural resources may give one pause about the efficacy of EU policies in this area.

Economic Relations with the United States

Europe's economic relationships with the US is worthy of special consideration. The EU and US are the world's two largest markets, and one could argue that "much of what we associate with globalization is very largely the result of expanding economic exchange between Europe and America over the past twenty-five years."[47] The European Commission itself notes that "no other commercial artery in the world is as integrated or fused together" as the transatlantic one.[48]

Statistics bear out these assertions. In 2008, total trade and goods and services between the US and the EU was €700 billion, and in 2006 the EU eclipsed Canada as the US's largest trading partner.[49] The US is also the EU's largest trading partner, accounting for 18.4 percent of total EU trade in 2008, far more than the EU's number-two trade partner, China, which accounted for 9.4 percent of EU trade.[50] Reflecting the levels of integration between the US and EU, up to a third of EU-US trade is trade within firms that have operations on both sides of the Atlantic (e.g., Dell shipping components from its facilities in Ireland to the US or General Motors transferring equipment from the US to Germany). More than 70 percent of EU-US trade is in machinery, chemicals, and other manufactured goods, on which, as noted above, tariffs are quite low. Agriculture, which receives a lot of political attention because each side tries to protect its own farmers, accounts for less than five percent. Significantly, the US runs a trade deficit in trade of goods with the EU. This deficit reached a high of $125 billion in 2005, although it declined (in large part because of recession in the US) to $60 billion in 2009.[51] The largest deficits in 2009 were with Germany ($28 billion), Italy ($14.2 billion), and France ($7.5 billion), substantially less than the US trade deficit with China ($227 billion) and Japan ($45 billion).[52]

Foreign direct investment (FDI) is another important feature of the economic relationship. By 2008, the stocks of FDI held by Europeans in the US and Americans in Europe was €1.89 trillion. This represents approximately three-quarters of total foreign investment in the United States, with Great Britain, Germany, and the Netherlands constituting the largest European sources of investment.[53] Even though foreign-owned firms are at times subjected to political backlash (e.g., consumers are told "Buy American"), foreign firms in the US tend to pay higher wages and are more productive than their US-owned counterparts.[54] Within the EU, the US is by far the largest source of foreign (non-EU) investment, accounting for 25 percent of foreign direct investment in 2008, although annual US investment in the EU in that year (€44 billion) was well down from a €75 billion in 2006 when the US accounted for nearly half (48 percent) of the FDI in the EU.[55] Significantly even given the US's diplomatic row with France over the war in Iraq, in that year US investment in France was still 45 percent higher than total US investment in China, and throughout the early 2000s Europe accounted for 56 percent of all of US foreign investment.[56] The EU estimates that the jobs of between 12 and 14 million people (roughly half in the US, half in the EU) are tied to transatlantic economic ties.[57] Looked at from this perspective, US-European economic ties are complementary, a win-win relationship.

This is not to say, however, that all is harmonious between the US and Europe. Protectionist tendencies are present on both sides, and barriers exist to prevent free trade. This is particularly true in the agricultural sector. American development of genetically modified crops also worries some in Europe, creating a regulatory barrier against US imports. Some trade disputes between the EU and US have been taken to the WTO, which is committed to liberalizing global trade. These include complaints by both the EU and US about subsidies and support offered to Airbus and Boeing, EU action against the US for tariffs on steel, and the so-called "Banana War" in 2004 in which US companies complained of EU policies that favored banana producers in countries that were formerly colonies of EU member states. Given the importance of transatlantic trade and investment, American firms must also be aware of EU policies, and European actions that accused US companies such as Microsoft and Apple of unfair competition policies have been unpopular in the US.

Despite these problems and occasional discussions of a "trade war"—which would be devastating to both the US and the EU—the two sides agree on more than they disagree. Barriers to trade and investment are the exception, not the rule, and both sides have major incentives to cooperate with each other. Without downplaying disputes between the two sides, it is still safe to say that the US and EU "still enjoy an extremely coherent economic relationship."[58]

EUROPEAN EFFORTS TO PROTECT THE GLOBAL ENVIRONMENT

As has been noted in several places in this text, Europeans tend to care very deeply about the environment. Most European countries and publics are far more environmentally conscious than Americans, and support for environmental initiatives comes from across the political spectrum. Europeans, however, have also attempted to take their environmentalism to the global level, and arguably it is in this sphere that Europe is most clearly *the* global leader and even where Europe, as an idea or concept, may seek to carve out part of its identity.

Environmental concerns figure prominently in many European international programs, ranging from bilateral development assistance to help with water quality or deforestation or OSCE programs to foster good stewardship of the environment. However, it is in the most global of all environmental questions—climate change—that Europe hopes to make its mark. *The Economist* writes, "To Europeans, climate change embodies all the trends that will make the European Union exemplary in the next fifty years. The future, they think, will be about solving global problems by pooling sovereignty and setting up a framework of mutually accepted rules. This will be true for trade and conflict resolution as it is for environmental policy." In other words, some in Europe look to set up an international environmental regime modeled, in part, upon the experience of the EU. *The Economist*, with only the slightest sarcasm, concludes, "Europe will rescue the environment from destruction; the environment will rescue Europe from irrelevance."[59]

Kyoto Protocol ■ global agreement signed in 1997 to limit carbon emissions, enthusiastically embraced by many European countries as a first step toward solving the problem of climate change.

Europe has tried to position itself as the "greenest" region in the world. In 1991, the EC issued its first Strategy to limit carbon dioxide emissions. In 2000, it created the European Climate Change Program, which was designed to identify and develop elements of an EU strategy to meet the goals of the 1997 UN's **Kyoto Protocol** on combating climate change. The EU and its member states officially ratified the Kyoto Protocol on global climate change in 2002. Under the terms of Kyoto, the then EU-15 pledged to reduce emissions of greenhouse gases by 2012 by an average of 8 percent from the level of 1990.[60] EU ratification helped the Kyoto Protocol enter into force as an international treaty, but not all countries, such as the US and China, ratified it. Europeans, however, generally embraced Kyoto with enthusiasm. Tony Blair, at that time the British prime minister, claimed that climate change is "probably the greatest long-term challenge facing the human race" and pledged that Britain would cut emissions by 20 percent by 2010, above its commitment through Kyoto.[61] Since 2002, EU members have developed an emission-trading scheme, under which companies get a fixed number of permits to pollute. As they grow, companies must either reduce emissions or buy spare permits from others that have reduced their emissions. Such "cap-and-trade" schemes are upheld by many as a market-based model that could help reduce emissions globally.

Building upon its previous commitments, EU members are attempting to go further. Recognizing that Kyoto expires in 2012, EU members pledged at a 2007 EU summit to cut their emissions by at least 20 percent from 1990 levels by 2020 (and by 30 percent if other rich countries joined in) and to invest in solar, wind, and biofuels so that 20 percent of Europe's energy needs would come from renewable sources. Jacques Chirac, then president of France, hailed this so-called 20/20/20 plan as "a great moment in European history."[62] Much of the impetus for these pledges came from Angela Merkel, Germany's chancellor, who also hosted the 2007 G-8 summit of leading industrialized states to highlight the EU's commitment on climate change. Merkel has made global warming a focal point for German foreign policy. Germany has adopted the world's most comprehensive climate-protection package, which includes measures to boost energy efficiency (including taxing or encouraging trade-ins of gas-guzzling cars) and promote renewable sources of energy. The aim is to reduce greenhouse gases by 36 percent from 1990 levels by 2020. These measures have a clear international orientation. Merkel noted, "We hope that the example set by our decisions will be followed and that we come together internationally to implement ambitious climate goals."[63]

The problem, however, is that Europeans' rhetoric on climate change and various investments (particularly with respect to wind energy) have not led to major accomplishments. Most of the energy used in Europe comes from fossil fuels. Even as governments talk about renewable sources of energy, coal-fired power plants are under construction. In 2006, the British government admitted it would not meet its self-declared Kyoto target, and in 2007 it became apparent that most EU countries would not be able to uphold their own Kyoto commitments, in part because governments gave away too many pollution permits for free. The EU and member governments, concerned over losing credibility on this issue, have proposed increasing regulations to tell businesses not only to cut emissions but how to do so. This has provoked dissension within the EU, with post-communist leaders noting with irony that the EU is coming to resemble communist-era central planners.[64] Targets for production of biofuels have also fallen short. Investment in nuclear power, which is carbon-friendly but anathema for many in Europe, is not widely popular. If trends hold, the EU, after failing to meet its own targets, may have to purchase excess carbon quotas from poorer countries, in effect telling poorer countries that they should not pollute so richer Europe can.

Furthermore, in wake of the 2008 global financial meltdown, Europeans began to revisit the commitments to reduce emissions that they made only a year earlier. A coalition of Eastern European countries, with support from Italy, argued that because they rely heavily on coal-fired power plants, they would have to assume far more costs to meet the 2020 targets than, say, the more wealthy Danes who already get much of their energy from renewable sources. Italy's Silvio Berlusconi suggested that it was not "the moment to push forward on our own like Don Quixote" and Donald Tusk, the Polish Prime Minister, insisted that states should have the right to veto EU environmental agreements.[65] The EU's Commissioner for Environmental Affairs, Stavros Dimas, while insisting that the overall architecture of the 20/20/20 plan will survive, conceded that some concessions to the changed economic conditions will likely be made. For example, whereas the EU envisioned member states spending receipts from carbon permits on improving energy efficiency, he suggested that perhaps they could use the money however they wanted.[66] Some hoped to reboot efforts to reduce carbon emissions in December 2009, when world leaders gathered in Copenhagen to discuss the issue with the aim of drafting a post-Kyoto agreement. Despite agreement that climate change was a problem, however, no binding agreement was reached, leading many to be disappointed with this outcome and the inability of Europe to forge a global consensus on the issue.[67]

Europe is, relatively speaking, only a small part of the climate change problem, producing only a seventh of the world's carbon pollution. It hopes, however, to be a big part of the solution and has very publicly staked its reputation and credibility on this issue.[68] Europe's ability to deliver—on Kyoto and beyond—will be important in determining whether Europe can offer leadership on this issue.

EUROPEAN USE OF "SOFT POWER"

soft power ■ use of non-coercive and non-military instruments of power, such as diplomacy, economic assistance, and power of example, to exert influence in world affairs.

hard power ■ use of the military and other coercive measures such as economic sanctions to exert influence in world affairs.

European governments and the EU are major players on a number of important global issues. However, as should be clear from the above discussion, their international position is not based primarily on military power. Instead, Europeans have attempted to leverage what some have called their "**soft power**"—meaning the ability to get what you want through persuasion and attraction rather than coercion. Instruments of soft power include diplomacy, economic assistance, and the spread of one's values and culture. Soft power is contrasted with "**hard power,**" meaning the use of the military and forceful measures such as economic sanctions to compel others to fall into line. Many actors, of course, engage in both, but in most formulations Europe is held as the main practitioner of soft power, whereas the US, by virtue of its powerful military, is the exemplar of hard power.[69] Noting how European embrace of soft power makes sense given European capabilities and experience of cooperation and integration, a French writer argues that

> [i]n contrast to the "imperialism" attributed to American power, the international ambition of Europe is supposed to consist merely in "humanizing globalization," organizing the "governance" of the planet, helping to resolve crises on the EU's periphery, ensuring the preservation of peace, and attempting to export around the world its model of cooperation and legal and diplomatic resolution of disputes.[70]

Promotion of Human Rights and Democratic Values

A chief example of Europe's use of soft power is in its various efforts to spread its core political values, including respect for human rights and democratic institutions. Of course, the US also has had a longstanding interest in promoting democracy, but often Europeans are more prone to try to influence by example and by persuasion whereas the US is apt to try more direct political pressure and, in extreme cases such as Iraq, military invasion.[71] Several European and transatlantic institutions are interested in democratization, including the EU, OSCE, and the Council of Europe,[72] the last of which drafted the European Convention for the Protection of Human Rights, which is overseen by the **European Court of Human Rights (ECHR)**. The ECHR, which has jurisdiction across Europe, is an important institution through which individuals can take their own governments to court to redress human rights violations (e.g., unlawful imprisonments, discrimination).

European Court of Human Rights (ECHR) ■ body of the Council of Europe, through which individuals can seek redress for alleged human rights violations; the ECHR can issue judgments against states and has been important in upholding human rights.

For the EU, a key element of a democratization strategy is construction of responsive and open political institutions. To this end, the EU gives €100 million a year through its European Initiative for Democracy and Human Rights program as well as trade and other financial incentives to help build democratic institutions and encourage governments to be more respectful of human rights. Part of this push, however, is explicitly values-based, meaning that Europeans hope that various programs (e.g., training of civil servants, monitoring of media) will help spread democratic values to other parts of the world.[73]

How well has this worked out? Without question, the EU's greatest success has been in East-Central Europe. Given the prospect of joining the EU, states adopted the necessary reforms largely in line with EU expectations, although in some states (e.g., Romania) implementation has been a problem and some might question how "deep" or "values-based" these reforms are.[74]

Elsewhere, however, the EU has had, at best, modest success. European encouragement of good governance, respect for human rights, and democracy has found less fertile soil in the Middle East, sub-Saharan Africa, Russia, and China, all of which, in various ways, are major EU trading partners and/or recipients of EU financial assistance. True, there are some success stories (e.g., South Africa, Mozambique, Namibia), but it is very difficult to draw a line and say that EU policy was the "cause," for example, of the end of apartheid in South Africa. Often, when the EU has tried to implement sanctions, such as against Zimbabwe, offending governments can often find other supporters, particularly China, which is becoming more assertive in Africa and the Middle East and is far less particular about dealing with despots. Moreover, frequently Europe's commercial interests (e.g., need for energy, the desire to sell products) conflict with the human rights agenda, as is, for example, the case with China.[75] In short, it is not clear that soft power gives Europe the means to deal with the more recalcitrant dictators who possess their own resources or don't need Europe and have little interest or reason to make political reforms.

Promotion of International Cooperation

Another penchant of European soft power is the emphasis European states place on **multi-lateralism,** meaning cooperative efforts by many states to resolve a particular international problem. As opposed to go-it-alone **unilateralism,** for which many criticized the US, especially during the administration of George W. Bush, Europeans often prefer to take issues to international forums for discussion and development of consensus so that as many actors as possible are committed to a course of action. Examples are numerous: the effort to work out the Iraq crisis through the UN Security Council; international discussions and treaties on climate change and other environmental problems; support for international labor standards to prevent abuse of workers; utilizing the UN to dissuade Iran from building a nuclear weapon. Indeed, one item that is striking is how the UN is viewed quite favorably in Europe whereas the UN is the favorite punching bag for many US politicians.[76] Whereas some Europeans might attempt to explain their inclination for multi-lateralism as proof that they are inherently more "civilized" or disposed toward diplomacy, one can easily explain it by noting that European states, individually, are relatively small and it is only through multi-lateral forums that European countries can hope to exercise global leadership. With few exceptions, Europeans cannot go it alone.

multi-lateralism ■ strategy that relies upon the coordinated efforts of various countries and international institutions to produce a desired outcome; this is a cornerstone of EU policy.

unilateralism ■ strategy in which states pursue their foreign policy aims without cooperation of other states or international institutions.

At times, European efforts to create new international institutions run up against American resistance. A primary example of this is the dispute over the International Criminal Court (ICC). The ICC, which is an outgrowth of *ad hoc* international tribunal for war crimes in the former Yugoslavia and Rwanda, was established in 2002 and is headquartered in The Hague in the Netherlands. As of 2010, 111 nations have ratified the treaty to form the ICC, including all EU states. The ICC is empowered to try individuals for genocide, war crimes, and crimes against humanity, and it has issued warrants of arrest with respect to several conflicts in Africa. Under 2005 revisions of the Cotonou Agreement, ratification of the ICC statues was added as an obligation the EU expects APC states to fulfill. In contrast, the US nullified its signature of ICC treaties in 2002, expressing concerns over violation of national sovereignty and potential for politically motivated prosecutions (e.g., of US soldiers in Iraq). Whereas the EU has pressed over states to cooperate with the ICC, the US linked military assistance to a number of states to an agreement that such states agree that US personnel will be exempt from the jurisdiction of the ICC.

Another means by which Europe attempts to foster international cooperation is by promoting regional integration outside of Europe.[77] Such efforts are an explicit effort to put the "European model" into practice elsewhere. The EU has concluded cooperation agreements with a number of regional organizations, including the Association of Southeast Asian Nations (ASEAN), Mercosur in South America, and the African Union (AU). Promoting regional integration elsewhere coincides with Europe's attempt to define its place in the world. According to Romano Prodi, former head of the European Commission,

> [o]ur European model of integration is the most developed in the world. Imperfect though it is, it nevertheless works on a continental scale . . . I believe we can make a convincing case that it would also work globally.[78]

The influence of the EU is perhaps strongest in Africa, where the EU has tried to foster regional integration through the Cotonou Agreement, a series of reciprocal trade agreements with different regional groupings of African states, and by supporting the AU, which was formally launched in 2002 and includes EU-like institutions such as Commission, Parliament, and Court of Justice. Several West African states have also discussed monetary union, and draft proposals of such a union follow closely the EU practice. Whether or not the AU can realize its stated goals of political integration remains to be seen, and Europe's relations with many African states are frosty given European concern over human rights violations.[79] Nonetheless, one could argue that given the primary successes of the EU—in encouraging economic cooperation and lessening the risk of militarized conflict—give it the potential to be a model for other regions of the world.

REGIONAL POLICIES

The EU and various European governments trade, maintain diplomatic missions, provide humanitarian support, and work to improve global and regional security with countries across the globe. Some regions, by virtue of geography, history, substantial economic ties, and worries over security, might be deemed "high priority" or "high involvement" regions. Leaving aside the US (discussed above), one could easily rank Russia and other former Soviet states, the Middle East, and China as regions of high priority for EU foreign policy.

Russia

Aside from ties with the US, arguably Europe's most important bilateral relationship is that with Russia. Russia, the largest post-Soviet state, threw off communist ideology and in the 1990s moved closer to the West. In 1994, the EU and Russia concluded a Partnership and Cooperation Agreement (PCA), which entered into force in 1997. The PCA foresaw a host of mechanisms to promote Russian-European cooperation on economic, security, political, cultural, energy, and environmental questions. In 2008, Russia was the third-largest trade partner with EU countries, and it is a major source of energy, supplying over 40 percent of the EU's natural gas imports and 30 percent of its crude oil imports. Reflecting the importance of the EU to Russia, Russia's embassy to the EU in Brussels is the largest Russian embassy in the world.

European-Russian ties have produced some significant accomplishments. The EU and its member states provided sizeable economic assistance—both aid (€2.6 billion from 1991–2006) and investment—to Russia to assist in its transition from communism to capitalism. The EU has worked to get Russia accepted into international economic organizations such as the WTO. The EU and Russia have set up dialogues and joint programs to work together on issues such as regional security, energy supplies, the environment, and human trafficking. Former Russian president Vladimir Putin (2000–2008), while not expressing a desire to join the EU, noted that Russia is a "natural member of the European family."[80]

Despite dialogue on a number of fronts, European-Russian ties remain problematic in several areas.[81] Some of the problems are longstanding—for example, the expansion of NATO, failures to solve regional conflicts in Russia's borders, Russian military action in Chechnya—but many are linked to the increasingly authoritarian and nationalistic approach taken by Putin in the 2000s. European governments in the late 2000s became increasingly critical of what they viewed as the erosion of democracy (e.g., rigging elections, banning demonstrations, government control over the media) in Russia. On top of this, Russia and the West in general have a series of policy disagreements, including Kosovo (Russia is steadfastly against Kosovo's independence) and Iran, which is an important trading partner for Russia. The Russian military incursion into Georgia in August 2008, which was designed to support anti-Georgian separatist regions, further complicated Russia's relations with Europe and Western countries more generally, as Georgia had embarked upon a pro-Western orientation and expressed a desire to join NATO. Europe, however, was somewhat divided on how to respond to Russia, as former communist states such as Poland and Lithuania, together with Great Britain, took the lead in criticizing Russia, others, such as Germany and France, were more restrained and sought to mediate between Washington and Moscow, and Italy seemed to endorse Moscow's position.[82] In addition to lack of unity, part of the problem is that Europe has little leverage over Russia, whereas Russia has much over Europe, thanks to European importation of Russian oil and gas.

Other Post-Soviet States

The EU has also sought to engage Ukraine, the second largest of the former Soviet republics. The EU and Ukraine signed a PCA in 1994 and concluded a Common

Strategy in 1999. Despite over €1 billion in EU assistance in the 1990s, relations with Ukraine were undercut by increasingly corrupt and undemocratic Ukrainian authorities, who also wanted to preserve good ties with Russia. In 2004, however, during Ukraine's "Orange Revolution," the EU took a leading role in mediating between rival parties and helping to ensure a third and fair round of voting that brought pro-Western Viktor Yushchenko into the Ukrainian Presidency.[83] Yushchenko claimed that one of his top aims is for Ukraine to join the EU, and the EU has re-negotiated its Action Plan for Ukraine to provide for enhanced co-operation with the EU. However, since the Orange Revolution Ukraine has experienced more instability and political uncertainty, and, with "enlargement fatigue" taking root in the EU, there is, at present, little immediate prospect for Ukraine to join the EU.

Further afield, the EU has attempted to facilitate conflict resolution in breakaway regions such as Abkhazia in Georgia and Transnistria in Moldova. In both cases, EU efforts have been arguably undermined by Russian support for separatist parties, most clearly expressed, as noted above, when Russia invaded Georgian territory in 2008. The EU is also very keen on bringing oil and gas from former Soviet states such as Azerbaijan, Kazakhstan, and Turkmenistan to Europe. European companies have invested heavily in energy fields and in new pipelines, including the Baku-Ceyhan pipeline, which ships oil from the Caspian Sea across Georgia and to a port on Turkey's Mediterranean coast. Other schemes involve pipelines that would ship oil and/or gas directly into Central Europe and Italy or from the Black Sea coast of Ukraine to the Baltic coast of Poland. While ambitious, these are best thought of as long-range plans that will require much political and economic investment and overcoming Russian objections, which at present controls many energy projects and export routes from the region.[84]

The Middle East

Europeans have a long history of involvement in North Africa and the Middle East, including conflicts such as the Crusades and battles with the Ottomans, colonization, and significant trade and cultural ties. North Africans make up a substantial percentage of the immigrant population in Europe, and security concerns since 9/11 have focused global attention on the troubles of the region. Europe, far more than the US, depends upon the Middle East for energy resources. The Middle East, however, is also Europe's backyard, meaning that Europe has been compelled to engage with it to solve common problems and concerns. Many European efforts employ "soft power" and emphasize economic growth, integration, sustainable development, and good governance as factors that can contribute to regional stability.

Although the EU has had disparate elements of a "Mediterranean Strategy" since the 1960s, under the Maastricht Treaty it has attempted to create a more coherent, better-funded instrument to engage the region. This took shape in 1995 with the promulgation of the Euro-Mediterranean Strategy, also known as the

Barcelona Process as it developed out of EU meetings in Barcelona, Spain. The Barcelona Process pledged a sizeable increase in EU assistance to the region—totaling €8.8 billion from the EU from 1995 to 2006 coupled with over €10 billion from the European Development Bank over the same period—in addition to more trade cooperation and regional integration. The EU signed Association Agreements with participating states, which, in addition to receiving privileged access to European markets, pledged to move to free-trade among themselves. The Barcelona Process also created a political dialogue designed to foster institutional reform and promotion of human rights.

In contrast to East-Central Europe, where in the 1990s EU was also deeply committed, the Barcelona Process has been judged a relative failure. Aid and trade are unlikely to be enough to tackle the dire and deeply rooted poverty in the region (North Africa on a *per capita* basis has income levels of approximately 10 percent of the EU average), and the Europe's agricultural markets, as noted above, were not open to free trade. Corruption also undercut much of the aid effort. In addition, the region's burgeoning population eclipses the economic growth that is occurring, meaning that Europe can do little, at least immediately, to improve markedly the region's economies and thereby dampen the allure of immigration. As for political reforms, with EU enlargement to North African and Middle Eastern countries not a possibility, there has arguably been less incentive to engage in political liberalization. With the exception of Israel and Turkey (which *is* a candidate to join the EU and thus treated differently), there is no well-functioning democratic state in the region, and most have serious human rights problems.

In 2003, the EU attempted to upgrade its relations with the Middle East through adoption of the **European Neighborhood Policy (ENP).**[85] The ENP, which includes both the EU's post-Soviet eastern neighbors (e.g., Ukraine, Moldova, Georgia) and North African/Middle Eastern states such as Morocco, Lebanon, Egypt, Israel, and Palestine, is designed to provide a mechanism for enhanced cooperation. Like the Barcelona Process, it has an economic component of trade, investment, and sizeable aid (€12 billion for all sixteen ENP countries from 2007 to 2013), but has a significant security dimension as well, no doubt an outgrowth of both 9/11 and EU expansion in 2004 and 2007. The ENP is also designed to "build on commitments to common values, including democracy, the rule of law, good governance, and respect for human rights, and to the principles of market economy, free trade and sustainable development as well as poverty reduction."[86] Membership in the EU, of course, remains off the table, as Middle Eastern states (unlike, for example, Ukraine) can make no claim to qualify for EU membership. Instead, the EU holds out the prospect of deeper cooperation through individual tailored Action Plans with ENP countries.

European Neighborhood Policy (ENP) ■ EU policy designed to foster stronger ties with neighboring countries in the Middle East, North Africa, and post-Soviet Europe by offering more aid and enhanced cooperation, but not the prospect of EU membership.

What has the ENP delivered in the Middle East? Without question, there has been great attention from the EU and individual European states to the Middle East. The EU notes strengths of the ENP in that it is focused and concrete, rests on "joint ownership" between the EU and other countries, and includes both more and better-used funds. These, however, are more conceptual than on-the-ground accomplishments. Significantly, the EU notes lack of progress on core issues, including trade and economic integration, migration, and resolving regional conflicts. An EU report admits this, but lays much of the blame on lack of response from the targeted countries of the ENP. It states:

> The EU seeks to encourage a very ambitious reform programme in partner countries, with many of the political and economic costs being up-front. Yet an important part of the incentives of the ENP—for instance in terms of market access and integration and other economic benefits—will only bear fruit later. This creates a real difficulty for partner countries in building the necessary domestic support for reform.[87]

More pointedly, one might ask what—if any—success the EU has had in promoting allegedly "shared values" such as democracy to countries, save Israel, that are clearly non-democratic. Indeed, given the aims of the EU to bring good governance and respect for human rights to many states with little tradition of either, one wonders if the ENP can, in fact, succeed in many Middle Eastern states.

China

China's rapid economic development since the 1970s has made it an increasingly important economic partner of European countries. Trade between Europe and China has increased sixty times since 1978, and by 2008 total two-way trade in goods and services as €360 billion, up from €210 billion in 2005. China is Europe's second largest trading partner and EU countries collectively are China's largest trading partner. European investment in China has also been substantial, totaling over €40 billion by 2008.[88] European governments and companies have been eager to sell their goods to China, and several European leaders have travelled to China to conclude trade and purchasing agreements. To complement burgeoning economic ties, the EU has published numerous reports, studies, and policies designed to foster EU-China partnership. In addition to bolstering economic ties and China's integration in the world economy, these reports also highlight the need for political dialogue, development of rule of law and human rights, and cooperation in fields such as the environment, migration, nuclear non-proliferation, and cultural exchange.[89] Negotiations on a PCA with China began in 2007.

Nonetheless, there are some tensions in European-Chinese relations. Like the US, EU countries run a significant trade deficit (€164 billion in 2008) with China. While part of this reflects China's comparative advantage in labor costs, European governments and the EU also complain about market access obstacles, such as price controls and regulatory requirements, as well as problems such as lack of protection for intellectual property rights and restrictive foreign exchange regulations. China's accession to the WTO, which was supported by the EU, is designed to lower some barriers to trade and China has committed itself, in principle, to make reforms on various issues of concern to Europeans. Many in Europe, however, are more skeptical about the benefits of engagement with China, fearing that European investment in China and the flood of Chinese imports—which increased over five-fold from 1999 to 2008—mean European jobs are being lost to low-cost Chinese workers. Public opinion surveys found that 55 percent of Europeans (as opposed to 50 percent of Americans) see China's growing economy as a threat, with fears most pronounced in France, Italy, and Poland.[90] On the environment, a major European concern, China did not sign the Kyoto Protocol and opposed binding measures at the 2009 global summit on the environment in Copenhagen, and increasing Chinese carbon emissions, connected to Chinese economic growth, more than cancel out European reductions.

Human rights have been an important issue as well. In 1989, in response to the violent crackdown on pro-democracy demonstrators in China, the EU imposed an arms embargo on China, hoping that this would demonstrate EU concern about human rights and provide some incentive for China to make political reforms. In the past two decades, progress, as the EU itself acknowledges, has been limited, as the Chinese government continues to repress religious, labor, and human rights organizations. The EU notes that it needs a more "focused and result-oriented" strategy, even though its expectations are "increasingly not being met."[91] The question, as with other cases, is what leverage the Europeans have. Sanctions on China are unfeasible given existing ties and China's size. China has the resources to buy weapons from other states (e.g., Russia) or develop their own. European countries such as France and Germany have expressed an interest in ending the arms embargo in the hope of improving economic ties. European leaders do speak about human rights in China, but, for example, when French president Nicolas Sarkozy goes to China and helps negotiate a multi-billion euro contract for Airbus, what does this action say about European concerns for human rights in China? Despite calls for some sort of protest during the 2008 Beijing Olympics, no country boycotted the Games, although some leaders, including Angela Merkel, Gordon Brown, and Poland's Donald Tusk, boycotted the opening ceremonies.[92]

Many European countries are important individual actors in world politics and, increasingly, the EU is becoming an active player in its own right. However, despite some successes, Europeans continue to face challenges, both with the outside world and among themselves, in constructing an effective, united foreign policy. The CFSP and other instruments are still, in many ways, works in progress, and meanwhile on some issues Europeans disagree about what their priorities or policies should be. On issues as diverse as Kosovo, Russia, the environment, Iraq, and, Afghanistan, Europeans countries continue to have significant disagreements, making the full realization of the CFSP more an aspiration than a reality. Moreover, as in the case with Dutch troops in Afghanistan, European citizens within the same country can be divided among themselves or at odds with their own government. Such phenomena make it even more difficult to coordinate foreign and security policies, particularly those that entail high costs or that are of heightened public concern and scrutiny. As this chapter has suggested, foreign policy is perhaps the hardest area to integrate fully, as individual states have different interests and priorities and are often loathe to surrender sovereignty in this sphere. While one can cite some progress in the past two decades toward a CFSP, it is clear that on this set of issues, those favoring "one Europe" still have much more work to do.

APPLICATION QUESTIONS

1. Does the EU have sufficient power and tools to be a powerful international actor? What factors might work against the emergence of the EU as a "superpower"?
2. Compare and contrast US and European policies toward a particular region or country. Do the policies complement or work against each other? Which one, in your view, is likely to be more successful?
3. How can one measure and assess the costs and benefits of globalization? What can European countries do to maximize benefits and minimize costs?
4. Can you make the case that "soft power" is more effective than "hard power"? Are there limits to the utility of "hard power"?
5. Can the EU model of integration be exported elsewhere? Did Europe have advantages on this front compared to Africa or Asia?

KEY TERMS

Cotonou Agreement 321
Common Foreign and Security Policy (CFSP) 304
European Court of Human Rights (ECHR) 328
European Neighborhood Policy (ENP) 333
European Strategic Defense Policy (ESDP) 308
hard power 328
High Representative 307
Kyoto Protocol 326
most-favored nation 320
multi-lateralism 329
NATO (North Atlantic Treaty Organization) 309
OSCE (Organization for Security and Cooperation in Europe) 310
soft power 328
unilateralism 329
West European Union (WEU) 305

ADDITIONAL READING

Ash, Timothy Garton. 2004. *Free World: America, Europe, and the Surprising Future of the West.* London: Penguin.

Written by a prominent British historian, this book counters European anti-Americanism and calls for renewed transatlantic unity. It offers an optimistic account on how Europe and the US can work together on issues such as global security and democratization.

Bretherton, Charlotte, and Volger, John. 2006. *The European Union as a Global Actor.* London: Routledge.

This book examines the emergence, role, and future of the EU as an actor in world politics. It looks at several areas of European foreign policy, including economy, trade, the environment, development, security, and identity. These are analyzed both theoretically and empirically and draw upon theory both from the development of the EU and from international relations more generally.

Holland, Martin, ed. 2004. *Common Foreign and Security Policy: The First Ten Years*, 2nd edition. London: Continuum.

This book provides a useful review of both the institutional development of the CFSP and case studies of how it has operated in specific circumstances, including Iraq, the developing world, and defense policy.

Kagan. Robert. 2004. *Paradise and Power: America and Europe in the New World Order.* New York: Atlantic Books.

This is a short, oft-cited, and polemical work by a noted conservative American commentator. Kagan's core thesis is that the US and Europe are fundamentally different in their international relations, with former relying on "hard power" and the later establishing an international role based upon "soft power."

Leonard, Mark. 2005. *Why Europe Will Run the Twenty-first Century.* London: Fourth Estate.

A short and provocative book that argues that Europe has a broader and deeper influence on world affairs than the US, and that European power is likely to grow as more and more countries are brought into the "orbit" of Europe. Leonard argues that Europe constitutes a model for the future of international relations, as the growing power of Europe will transform world politics.

END NOTES

1. The Eurocorps dates back to Franco-German military cooperation and was formalized in 1993. See http://www.eurocorps.org
2. For a very passionate argument along these lines, see Juergen Habermas and Jacques Derrida, "February 15th or What Binds Europeans Together," *Constellations* 10:3, September 2003, 291–297.
3. Eurobarometer 60, 2003, available at http://ec.europa.eu/public_opinion/archives/eb/eb60/eb60_en.htm, accessed April 25, 2010.
4. For a review of the EU's accomplishments, see its website dedicated to the CFSP at http://ec.europa.eu/external_relations/cfsp/intro/index.htm
5. Brian Crowe, "A Common European Foreign Policy After Iraq?" *International Affairs* 79:3, May 2003, p. 534.
6. Laurent Cohen-Tanugi, *Alliance at Risk: The United States and Europe Since September 11* (Baltimore: Johns Hopkins University Press, 2003), p. 71.
7. Declaration of the European Council on strengthening the Common European Policy on Security and Defence, June 3, 1999.
8. In 2009, former Danish Prime Minister Anders Fogh Rasmussen was elected to this post by NATO members.
9. Quoted in Jeffrey Simon and Sean Kay, "NATO: European Security and Beyond?" in Ronald Tiersky, ed. *Europe Today: National Politics, European Integration, and European Security*, 2nd ed. (Lanham MD: Rowman and Littlefield, 2004), p. 104.
10. The OSCE maintains an excellent website at http://www.osce.org.
11. Some disputed whether the atrocities in the region, especially in Bosnia, amounted to genocide. A premier source on this issue is Samantha Power, *A Problem from Hell: America and the Age of Genocide* (New York: Basic Books, 2002), Chapters 9 and 11. In 2006, the International Criminal Tribunal for the former Yugoslavia concluded that genocide did occur in Bosnia, at least during the 2005 Srebrenica massacre, but in 2007 the International Court of Justice ruled that the state of Serbia and Montenegro, while failing to prevent genocide, could not held accountable for it.
12. Julie Mertus, "False Dawn: Bosnia Ten Years after Dayton," *Foreign Policy in Focus*, November 23, 2005, available at http://www.fpif.org/articles/false_dawn_bosnia_ten_years_after_dayton, accessed on March 30, 2010. See also Laura Silber, "Dayton, 10 Years After," *New York Times*, November 21, 2005.
13. *The Economist*, May 23, 2009, pp. 51–52.
14. Vladimir Goati of Transparency Serbia in *The Christian Science Monitor*, May 15, 2008.
15. *The Economist*, May 23, 2009, p. 51.
16. Greece claims Macedonia is a region in Greece and that use of the name Macedonia suggests that the country claims dominion over part of Greece. Greece would prefer the name "Former Yugoslav Republic of Macedonia."
17. Jean Marie Colombani, "Nous sommes tous Américains," *Le Monde*, September 12, 2001.
18. Robert Kagan, "Power and Weakness," *Policy Review*, June/July 2002.
19. John Gray, *Men Are from Mars, Women Are from Venus* (New York: HarperCollins, 1992).
20. See both Robert Kagan, *Of Paradise and Power*, and Laurent Cohen-Tanugi, *Alliance at Risk*.
21. *New York Post*, January 24, 2003.
22. "Shadows over NATO," *The Economist*, October 20, 2007.
23. *The Guardian*, June 8, 2007.
24. "America Kidnapped Me," *Los Angeles Times*, December 19, 2005.
25. Bruce Bawer, *While Europe Slept: How Radical Islam Is Destroying the West from Within* (New York: Doubleday, 2006).
26. *The Economist*, November 10, 2007, p. 73.
27. In October 2007, twenty-one of the twenty-eight tried for the attacks were convicted on various charges. Some of the alleged ringleaders, however, were acquitted because of lack of evidence.
28. From Peter Neumann, "Europe's Jihadist Dilemma," *Survival*, 48:2, Summer 2006, p. 71.
29. In the case of the Madrid bombings, some Spaniards were arrested and convicted for supplying the terrorists with explosives, but they themselves were not charged with carrying out the attacks.
30. Lorenzo Vidino, *Al Qaeda in Europe* (Amherst, NY: Prometheus, 2005), p. 368.
31. Precise figures vary, but up to 5 million Muslims reside in France, three million in Germany, nearly 2.5 million in Britain, and more than a million in Spain and the Netherlands.
32. Walter Laqueur, *The Last Days of Europe: Epitaph for an Old Continent* (New York: Thomas Dunne Books, 2007), p. 72. For example, surveys in Britain in 2006 revealed that 40 percent of Muslims favored

introducing Muslim law in parts of Britain and that 13 percent justified al Qaeda style terrorist attacks.
33. "Europe Tightens Immigration Rules," *Christian Science Monitor*, October 17, 2007.
34. *New York Times*, November 6, 2007.
35. Neumann, "Europe's Jihadist Dilemma."
36. These efforts have had mixed success in Britain. See *The Economist*, February 28, 2009, pp. 59–60.
37. Homages to the benefits of free trade can be found at the website of the WTO, http://www.wto.org, as well as that of the International Monetary Fund (IMF), http://www.imf.org.
38. Kevin Watkins and Penny Fowler, *Rigged Rules and Double Standards: Trade, Globalisation, and the Fight Against Poverty* (Oxford: Oxfam Publishing, 2004).
39. See Oxfam Briefing, "The End to EU Sugar Dumping," August 2004, at http://www.oxfam.org/sites/www.oxfam.org/files/dumping_0.pdf, accessed March 29, 2010.
40. For an economic analysis of EU trade policies on the developing world, see Simon Everett, *Do EU Trade Policies Impoverish Developing Countries?* (Washington, DC: Brookings Institution Press, 2006).
41. The Center for Global Development publishes an annual Commitment to Development Index, which utilizes several indicators in addition to aid. In 2009, the top-ranking countries were, in order, Sweden, Denmark, the Netherlands, Norway, New Zealand, and Ireland. Canada. The US, in contrast, ranked seventeenth, just behind Portugal and just ahead of Greece. Taken from http://www.cgdev.org, accessed March 30, 2010.
42. A premier source is the *EU Donor Atlas 2008*, available at http://fs2.bbj.it/#, accessed March 30, 2010.
43. *EU Donor Atlas, 2008*.
44. Israel and Egypt receive most their monies in the form of military aid, which is a provision from the Camp David Peace Accord of 1979.
45. OECD Development Statistics, cited in Table 11.1.
46. See Paul Collier, *The Bottom Billion: Why the Poorest Countries are Failing and What Can be Done about It* (Oxford: Oxford University Press, 2007).
47. John Peterson and Alasdair Young, "Trade and Transatlantic Relations: Old Dogs and New Tricks," in Sophie Meunier and Kathleeen McNamara, *Making History: European Integration and Institutional Change at Fifty, The State of the European Union*, vol. 8 (Oxford: Oxford University Press, 2007), p. 283.
48. European Commission, *Review of the Framework for Relations between the European Union and the United States: An Independent Study*, 2005, p. 13.
49. For EU trade statistics, see http://ec.europa.eu/trade/statistics. According to US Government data, total trade in 2006 with the EU was $544 billion, compared to $533 with Canada. Other major trading partners were Mexico ($332 billion), China ($343 billion), and Japan (($208 billion). Data can be found through the Census Bureau at http://www.census.gov/foreign-trade/balance/c0003.html, accessed March 31, 2010.
50. See EU report on trade with the US at http://trade.ec.europa.eu/doclib/docs/2006/september/tradoc_113465.pdf.
51. Data available from US Census, op cit.
52. US Census Data, op cit.
53. Data from http://ec.europa.eu/trade/statistics.
54. James Jackson, "Foreign Direct Investment in the United States: An Economic Analysis," Congressional Research Service, 2005, available at http://fas.org/sgp/crs/misc/RS21857.pdf.
55. EU Trade statistics at http://ec.europa.eu/trade/statistics and *European Union foreign direct investment yearbook 2008*, available at http://epp.eurostat.ec.europa.eu/cache/ITY_OFFPUB/KS-BK-08-001/EN/KS-BK-08-001-EN.PDF, accessed on 30 March 2010.
56. Peterson and Young, "Trade and Transatlantic Relations," p. 287.
57. European Commission, Bilateral Trade Ties with the United States, at http://ec.europa.eu/trade/issues/bilateral/countries/usa/index_en.htm.
58. Peterson and Young, "Trade and Transatlantic Relations," p. 297.
59. Charlemagne, "Climate control," *The Economist*, March 17, 2007.
60. Precise targets varied from country to country. Germany, for example, pledged to cut gas emissions by 21 percent, France promised they would be at 1990 levels, and some countries such as Greece, Portugal, and Spain were allowed to have higher greenhouse gas emissions than in 1990.
61. "Hot Under the Collar," *The Economist*, April 1, 2006.
62. *The New York Times*, October 17, 2008.
63. "Germany takes dramatic step on climate," *Christian Science Monitor*, December 5, 2007, p. 10.
64. *The Economist*, "Climate Control," 2007.

65. *The New York Times*, October 17, 2008.
66. "Face Value: Climate of Fear," *The Economist*, October 25, 2008.
67. "The Copenhagen climate conference," *The Economist*, December 18, 2009.
68. For more on the EU's vision on this issue, see "The EU's Contribution to Shaping a Future Global Climate Change Regime," at http://ec.europa.eu/environment/climat/future_action.htm.
69. The term "soft power" is most associated with Joseph Nye, a political scientist at Harvard University. See his *Soft Power: The Means to Success in World Politics* (New York: Public Affairs, 2004).
70. Cohen-Tanugi, *An Alliance at Risk*, p. 75.
71. Whether or not the US has been effective or wholly consistent in use of such policies shall not detain us here. For a work analyzing differing US and European approaches, see Jeffrey Kopstein, "The Transatlantic Divide over Democracy Promotion," *The Washington Quarterly* 29:2, Spring 2006, 85–98.
72. Membership in the Council of Europe is open to any European state that agrees to adhere to democratic principles.
73. Sonia Lucarelii and Ian Manners, eds. *Values and Principles in European Union Foreign Policy* (London: Routledge, 2006).
74. A good selection of studies on these issues can be found in Paul Kubicek, ed. *The European Union and Democratization* (London: Routledge, 2003).
75. "Europe's despot dilemma," *The Economist*, October 13, 2007.
76. According to a 2007 global survey, only 48 percent of Americans have favorable views of the UN, compared to 79 percent of Swedes, 68 percent of Poles, 67 percent of Italians, 66 percent of French, 64 percent of Germans, and 58 percent of Britons. Data from Pew Global Attitudes Project, available at http://pewglobal.org/reports/pdf/256.pdf, on 14 November 2009.
77. Mary Farrell, "From EU Model to External Policy? Promoting Regional Integration in the Rest of the World," in Meunier and McNamara, 2007.
78. Prodi, 2000, quoted in Farrell, "From EU Model," p. 299.
79. For example, a planned Europe-Africa Summit was delayed for seven years (until 2007), in large measure because of European opposition to the government of Robert Mugabe in Zimbabwe.
80. "The Bear Necessities of Life," *The Economist*, November 25, 2006.
81. See Michael Emerson, ed. *The Elephant and the Bear Try Again* (Brussels: Centre for European Policy Studies, 2006).
82. *The New York Times*, August 18, 2008, p. A9.
83. Paul Kubicek, "The European Union and democratization in Ukraine," *Communist and Post-Communist Studies* 38:3 (June 2005): 269–292.
84. "Russia Celebrates Its Central Asian Energy Coup," *Eurasianet.org*, 16 May 2007.
85. The ENP grew out of the "Wider Europe—Neighbourhood" Communication of 2003. By 2004, this was transformed into the ENP. For more on the ENP, see its website at http://ec.europa.eu/world/enp/index_en.htm, accessed April 2, 2010.
86. GAER Councils of the ENP, June 14, 2004.
87. EU Commission, "On Strengthening the European Neighbourhood Policy," COMM (2006), December 4, 2006.
88. Data from European Commission, available at http://ec.europa.eu/external_relations/china/index_en.htm, accessed on 1 April 2010.
89. An example would be European Commission, "EU-China: Closer partners, growing responsibilities," COM(2006) 631 final, 2006.
90. Survey of German Marshall Fund, reported in *Christian Science Monitor*, December 6, 2007.
91. "EU-China: Closer partners," 2006.
92. Sarkozy, who earlier said he would boycott the ceremonies, did attend. Italy's Berlusconi was not in Beijing, but cited the hot weather as the reason.

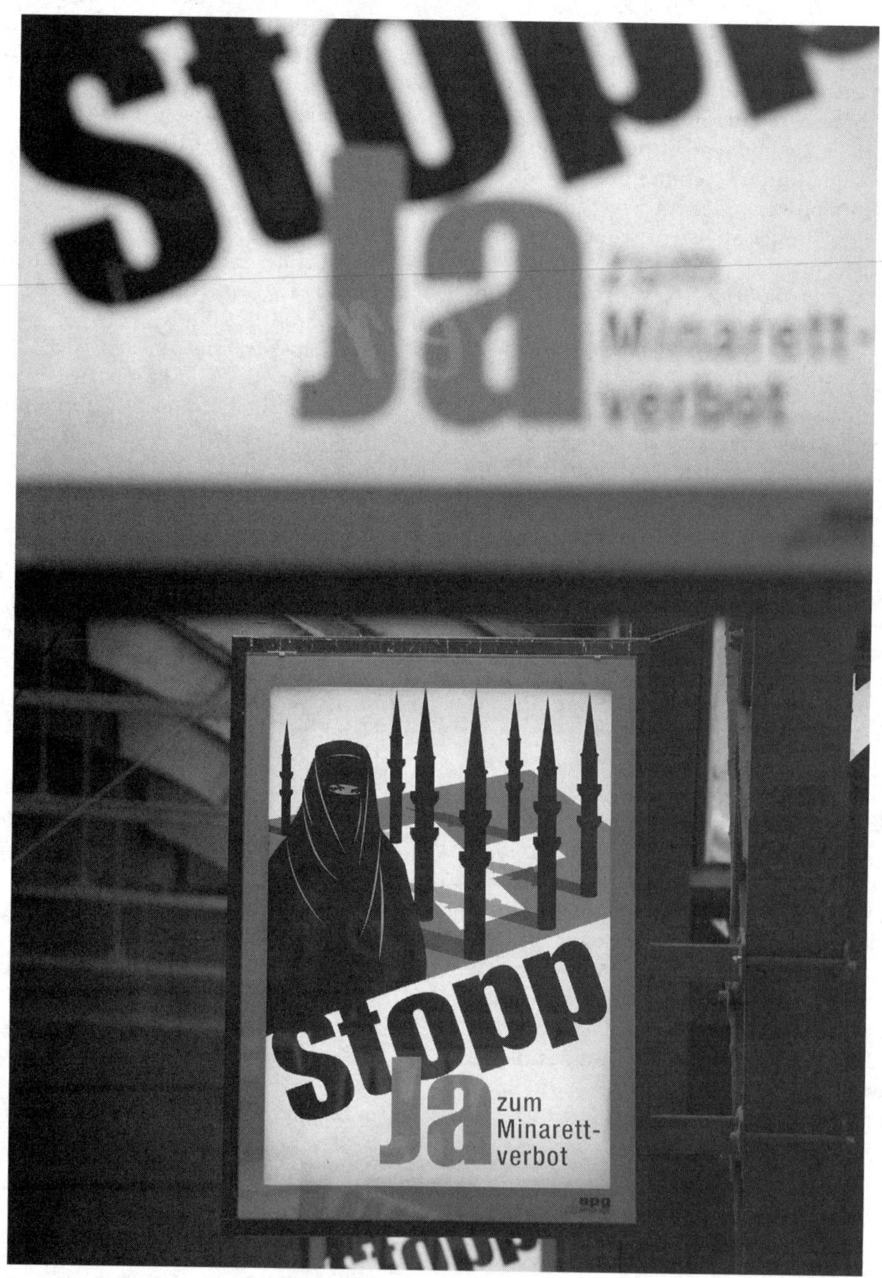

Campaign poster for the anti-minaret campaign in Switzerland.

CHAPTER 12

The Politics of Culture and Multi-Culturalism in Contemporary Europe

On November 29, 2009, in a national referendum in Switzerland, a majority of voters, 57.5 percent, voted to ban the construction of new minarets, towers that are sometimes attached to mosques. Because it was approved both by a majority of voters and in a majority of the Swiss cantons (regions), this measure becomes part of the Swiss constitution and cannot be changed by judicial review. The idea to ban minarets arose from a 2005 controversy involving a Turkish cultural organization that wanted to construct a twenty-foot minaret, and the ban was supported by representatives from anti-immigrant parties and groups, including the Swiss Peoples' Party, which has been accused of harboring a racist platform. The Swiss government and Swiss Catholic bishops both recommended a "no" vote, but not all groups were convinced. The more conservative Society of St. Pius X, based in Ecône, Switzerland, came out in favor of the ban on minarets, arguing that "the Islamic doctrine cannot be accepted when you know what it is all about. How can one expect to condone the propagation of an ideology that encourages husbands to beat their wives, the 'believer" to murder the 'infidel,' a justice that uses body mutilation as punishment, and pushes to reject Jews and Christians?"[1]

The Swiss vote surprised many in Europe and its outcome is sure to be appealed to the European Court of Human Rights (ECHR), but it represents but one of many recent examples of rising tensions in Europe between defenders of more traditional European beliefs and customs and those who welcome or acknowledge the fact that Europe is becoming more multi-cultural. Issues of this sort rank among the most interesting and hotly debated in Europe. As noted in Chapter 1, some define Europe in cultural terms, which could include race, ethnicity, and religion. However, traditional notions of "Europe" and Europeans—the monochromatic vision of Europe's population found in dated films—increasingly bear little resemblance to Europe today. Walk down a street in Paris, Zurich, Hamburg, London, Prague, or Copenhagen, and you will hear a host of non-European languages and see a variety of people who, based upon dress or skin color, would not typically be considered "European." Some may be tourists or business travelers, but many are permanent residents or even citizens, thereby staking a claim that, however they look or pray, they too are now Europeans. Tony Judt, an esteemed historian of modern Europe, argued that issues of immigration and integrating existing minorities, particularly Muslims, constitute Europe's "true dilemmas."[2] More alarmist voices, pointing to high birthrates among Europe's Muslims, fear creation of "**Eurabia**," an Islamic takeover of Europe.[3]

Eurabia ■ term used by those who believe immigration and higher birth rates will lead to an Islamic takeover of Europe.

Europe is changing culturally in other ways as well. Whereas Europe used to be the center for Christianity, religious belief is becoming less and less important. Many European countries have adopted liberal policies on issues such as drug use and sexuality that challenge "traditional values." And, lastly, the prospect of Turkish entry into the EU stretches, unacceptably for some, the geographic and cultural boundaries of Europe. Cultural concerns, broadly understood, constitute important political cleavages in several countries and have fuelled the rise of far-right political parties. Thinking about Europe as a whole, it is easy, as the EU has done, to adopt "Unity in diversity" as a motto. It is far harder to manage diversity in ways that satisfy different groups that have diametrically opposed visions of what constitutes "Europe."

IMMIGRATION AND MULTI-CULTURALISM IN EUROPE

Historical Patterns of Immigration

Although the United States, Canada, and Australia claim some distinctiveness for being immigrant societies, Europe has its own long history of immigration. Germans made up a large percentage of people on "Czech" or "Polish" lands; many Italians, Portuguese, and Spaniards immigrated to France; and a Jewish diaspora lived throughout the continent. Even after the emergence of nationalism in the nineteenth century, migrants continued to settle in new countries. France, for example, became a melting pot for various peoples. By 1881, at roughly the same time that France gave the US its Statue of Liberty to welcome the poor "huddled masses" to America, France had one million immigrants of its own.[4]

Until the later half of the twentieth century, however, most of the immigration in Europe was intra-European immigration. This meant that people from poorer parts of Europe (e.g., Poland, Ireland, Portugal) moved to wealthier countries such as France, the Netherlands, and Great Britain. These immigrants, like the locals, were largely white and Christian. After learning the local language, they could be relatively easily integrated into their new home. Jews would be, of course, somewhat distinctive, and anti-Semitism could be found in all parts of Europe well before Hitler came to power.

Gasarbeiter ■ from German, it literally means "guest worker" and refers to workers, from countries such as Turkey, Algeria, and Morocco, that were allowed to work temporarily in Western Europe after World War II. Many, however, chose not to go back home.

Immigration patterns changed significantly after World War II. Many European states, experiencing a labor shortage, began to look for new sources of workers. Thus, in the 1950s and 1960s, millions of people, mostly young, single males, arrived in Europe as "guest workers" (***Gastarbeiter*** in German). Many came from former European colonies, and frequently laws were very liberal in terms of allowing residents of the colonies to emigrate to the "mother country." Thus, hundreds of thousands of South Asians (e.g., Indians, Pakistanis, Bangladeshis) and blacks from Africa and the Caribbean moved to Britain; Moroccans and Algerians came to France; Surinamese and Indonesians came to the Netherlands, which also invited large numbers of Turks and Moroccans. Germany, which did not have overseas colonies, welcomed Turks and Yugoslavs as *Gastarbeiter*. Suddenly, European countries had millions of new residents, many of whom were not, in traditional terms at any rate, "European." Many were also Muslims.

Initially, this was not viewed as a large problem because these peoples were viewed as temporary guest workers. The plan was that they would eventually move back to their homeland. The problem, however, was that many chose not to move back: they could earn more, for example, in France or Germany, and they did not want to move back to poorer, often unstable or politically repressive states. Some European states began imposing immigration quotas, but, due to policies that allowed family reunification, natural reproduction, and liberal asylum policies, the number of immigrants (particularly Muslims) and those with immigrant background grew. By the 1970s, Islam assumed a larger and more open presence in European countries (e.g., veiled women, new mosques) and an economic downturn led to competition for jobs. Consequently, immigration became a political issue. Far-right political parties advocated more restrictive immigration policies or even expelling non-native peoples, arguing that these newcomers "stole" jobs and threatened "European" culture. By this time, however, many of the "guest workers" had been living in Europe for twenty or more years. In some states, such as France and the Netherlands, many were able to become citizens, and many more in all countries had children born in Europe. Kicking them out was not and is not a realistic option. The challenge then became how to integrate immigrants and their descendents into European societies.

Immigrants in Europe Today

Today Europe is home to millions of immigrants. Overall, approximately 9 percent of residents of the EU are foreign-born, with the figures much higher in countries such as Germany, Austria, and Luxembourg. Figure 12.1 highlights the percentage of foreign-born residents in each country, and Table 12.1 provides a country of origin breakdown for several countries. A few caveats are in order. First, foreign-born is not always the same as immigrant: many European or American expatriates are living in London, Paris, Prague, Brussels, Geneva, Luxembourg, and other cities. These individuals do not intend to seek citizenship or live permanently in their current country of residence and, for the most part, are not viewed in the same manner as immigrants who want to make the host country their permanent home.[5] Second, in the Baltic states, the foreign-born population is mainly ethnic Russians who moved to the region when it was part of the Soviet Union. They do not meet the typical profile of an immigrant. Third, the data do not take into account millions of illegal immigrants, who have been flocking to Europe either through dangerous crossings of the Mediterranean or via overland routes from Turkey, the Middle East, and the former Soviet Union. Finally, while the data do take into account foreign-born individuals who have acquired citizenship in their new country of residence, they do not count the children or grandchildren of immigrants who were born in Europe. If one takes these generations into account, more than 20 percent of the population in many European states has an immigrant background. In some cities, such as Amsterdam, Paris, and London, the number of such "foreigners" is similar to the number of "native" Dutch, French, and English.

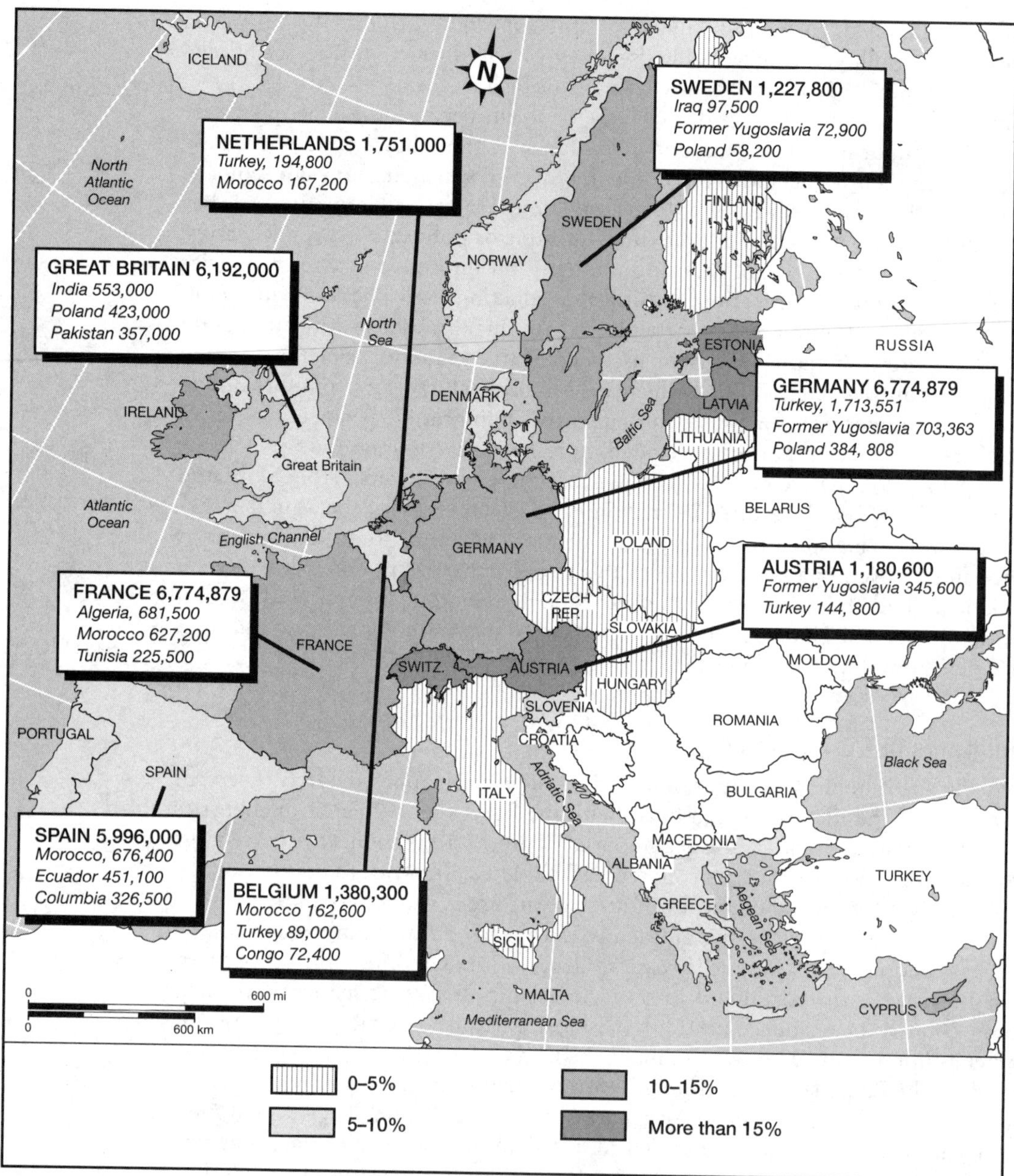

FIGURE 12.1
Foreign-Born Populations in Europe

In 2005, the average net migration into the EU was 3.7 people per 1000 residents—a figure that dwarfed Europe's natural growth rate of 0.7 people per 1000. In other words, Europe is growing mostly due to immigration, with the highest rates of immigration now in Spain, Ireland, and Austria.[6] Great Britain, which opened its borders to workers from East European countries admitted to the EU in

TABLE 12.1

Profiles of Foreign Populations in Selected European Countries, 2007

Country	Total Number of Foreign-Born Population	Homeland of Largest Groups of People from Outside the EU-15 and EEA Countries
Germany	6,744,879	Turkey, 1,713,551 Former Yugoslavia 703,363 Poland, 384,808
France*	4,985,000	Algeria 681,500 Morocco 627,200 Tunisia 225,500
Great Britain	6,192,000	India 553,000 Poland 423,000 Pakistan 357,000
Spain	5,996,000	Morocco 676,400 Ecuador 451,100 Columbia 326,500
Belgium	1,380,300	Morocco, 162,600 Turkey, 89,000 Congo, 72,400
Netherlands	1,751,000	Turkey 194,800 Morocco 167,200
Austria	1,180,600	Former Yugoslavia 345,600 Turkey, 144,800
Sweden	1,227,800	Iraq 97,500 Former Yugoslavia 72,900 Poland 58,200

Source: OECD migration data available at http://www.oecd.org/dataoecd/45/37/43967769.xls, and for Germany from Migration Policy Institute at http://www.migrationinformation.org/DatHub/countrydata/Germany_stcockdata.xls, both accessed on 30 March 2010.

*Data from France are from 2005. EEA (European Economic Association) includes Norway, Switzerland, and Iceland.

2004, has seen a great influx of people from that region, especially from Poland. Immigration trends are thus a reflection of geography (e.g., Spain is relatively easy to reach), economic opportunity, and government policy, which varies markedly to the extent that European states welcome or discourage immigration.

How Are Immigrants Faring?

Most immigrants come to Europe hoping for a better life. They want to live in a safe and secure environment, enjoy personal and civic freedoms, and find suitable employment. Relative to their status in their homelands, one can argue that most succeed, meaning that they enjoy better standards of living and greater freedoms than they would in their native countries.

Nonetheless, the lives of immigrants in Europe are not without difficulties. Leaving one's native country and moving to a place where one does not know the language or culture is always difficult. If one is of a different religion or skin color, meaning one is clearly recognizable as an "outsider," there may be additional problems. Many immigrants, for a host of reasons, feel that they are unwelcome or can live only on the margins of European society. True, all the states of the EU are democracies and all prohibit discrimination and promote, as official policy, tolerance. Many provide generous economic and cultural benefits to immigrants and ethnic minorities. Nonetheless, many immigrants have been unable or even unwilling to embrace policies of **assimilation** or **integration**. Assimilation, usually endorsed by those who dislike immigration, refers to a process whereby immigrants are expected to adopt the practices, manners, customs, and language of the host country. In this process, they are expected to lose many of their own cultural characteristics, which is why most immigrants reject policies of assimilation. Integration suggests less of a transformation and is more a two-way process, in which immigrants make adaptations and governments adopt policies so that newcomers can live easily and productively in their new country. Integration nonetheless suggests, at minimum, that immigrants learn the host country's language and learn to respect the dominant culture. As noted below, even more "hands-off" policies designed to foster **multi-culturalism** and not force either assimilation or integration have not succeeded.

assimilation ■ a process through which immigrants are expected to adopt the practices, customs, and language of their host country.

integration ■ a two-way process through which immigrants make adaptations to life in their new country and in which governments help accommodate the needs of immigrants.

multi-culturalism ■ the acceptance or promotion of multiple identities and cultures in a particular environment, often for practical reasons or for the sake of promoting diversity.

Immigrants point to a number of problems. One is discrimination and prejudice. Political parties have successfully run on anti-immigrant platforms as immigrants are blamed for a number of social and economic problems. Expressions of their culture (e.g., female students wearing the *hijab*, the Islamic headcovering) are viewed by many in Europe as threatening, or, at minimum, inconsistent with traditional secular practices. Extremist "skinhead" groups have also attacked immigrants and ethnic minorities. Pan-European surveys from 2006 show that those who are foreign-born are far more likely (17.1 percent) to report that they have been subjected to discrimination than the native-born (6.5 percent).[7] Among minority groups, both Muslims (37.5 percent) and Jews (39.4 percent) reported high levels of discrimination. Many Europeans openly acknowledge that such discrimination exists. Data from the 1990s in Great Britain reveal that respondents, while generally (roughly 70 percent) claiming that they are not prejudiced at all, acknowledge that there is some or a lot of prejudice against blacks and Asians living in Britain.[8] Comparative data from the 2006 European Social Survey indicate that respondents are more likely to report discrimination in Britain (13.4 percent) and France (10.5 percent) than in Germany (5 percent), Switzerland (3.6 percent), and Denmark (3.4 percent).[9] Nonetheless, polls in Germany have revealed that a sizeable minority—over 20 percent—agree with statements such as "we must preserve the purity of the German people and stop populations from mixing," which has an obvious echo from that country's Nazi past.[10]

Many immigrants, despite living better than they would in their native lands, fare worse economically than the native population. This is, perhaps, not entirely surprising, given the fact that many immigrants are relatively low skilled. Data,

TABLE 12.2

Unemployment Rates Between Native and Foreign-Born Populations

Country	% Unemployed, Native-Born	% Unemployed, Foreign-Born
Austria	4.3	11.2
Belgium	5.6	14.9
Czech Rep	7.0	12.4
Denmark	4.6	11.8
France	8.0	13.8
Germany	10.3	18.3
Great Britain	4.7	7.3
Italy	6.4	6.2
Netherlands	3.6	10.3
Spain	7.8	11.4
Switzerland	2.9	7.5
US	6.9	5.8

Source: From 2004, reported in OECD (Organization for Economic Cooperation and Development) Factbook, 2007 (available through http://www.oecd.org). Data are for males.

presented in Table 12.2, show that throughout Europe foreign-born populations (which, again, includes other Europeans) tend to have higher unemployment rates than the native-born, and these figures probably understate the real issue—unemployment among people with non-European ancestry, which reaches over 20 percent in countries such as France and Germany. Part of the problem is discrimination. Indeed, studies in France—where unemployment among Muslim youth is twice as high as unemployment among non-Muslim immigrants with the same educational qualifications—reveal that, given identical resumes, a man with the name of "Ahmed" is far less likely to get a job interview than one named "Francois."[11] Data on wages are generally harder to come by, although there is little question that since immigrants are over-represented in the least remunerative jobs (e.g., agriculture, hotel and restaurant service, janitors) they earn less than the native-born. Many live in ethnic minority ghettos that have relatively poor housing, social services, and employment opportunities.

Another important issue for immigrants and their descendents is whether they can obtain citizenship in their new countries of residence. Citizenship, of course, confers important political rights (e.g., the right to vote) as well as putting immigrants on equal standing with native citizens for access to welfare provisions. Some countries, such as France and Great Britain, make fairly generous provisions for naturalization, meaning that after a period of residency an immigrant can apply to become a citizen. Moreover, in such countries the children of immigrants are typically granted citizenship based upon the place of their birth (*jus solis*). In other words, if an Algerian immigrant woman gives birth to a child in France, that child is entitled to French citizenship. In other countries, most notably Germany, citizenship has traditionally been based on the principle of *jus sanguinis*, meaning that it was based on a blood relationship. Thus, a son of a Turkish immigrant in Germany, even if he was born in Germany, attended German schools, and spoke better German than Turkish could not become a German citizen. A new law on citizenship came into force in 2000, which specifies that the children of foreigners born in Germany automatically obtain German citizenship if one of the parents has resided in Germany for at least eight years. Similarly, immigrants who have lived in Germany for at least eight years may now apply for German citizenship. Data reveal that rates of **naturalization** for foreign-born populations—meaning those who acquire citizenship in their new countries—vary throughout Europe, with Poland (96 percent) and the Czech Republic (80 percent) having the highest percentage of naturalized foreign-born citizens. Among countries with more sizeable foreign-born populations, the Netherlands (65 percent), Sweden (63 percent), France (53 percent), and, surprisingly perhaps, Germany (46 percent) have some of the highest naturalization rates. Spain, which has seen a more recent wave of immigrants, ranks among the lowest (31 percent), although this is much more than Luxembourg (13 percent naturalized), which is the home to many wealthy expatriates.[12]

naturalization ■ process by which immigrants become citizens of their adopted country; rules governing naturalization vary substantially among European countries.

Coping with Multi-Culturalism

Many European states are now multi-cultural, possessing significant populations of immigrants and their descendents. Their culture—in terms of dress, religion, food, values—may differ from that of native Europeans. The rise of multi-culturalism has presented several challenges to European societies.

Some of these challenges rest with the immigrants, who may resist attempts at assimilation or integration. Many immigrants are confined to ethnic ghettoes and do not feel part of the broader community. Identity is often a question for the children of immigrants: are they, for example, Dutch or Moroccan, Turkish or German? Some attempt to carve out a "third path," building their identities out of elements of both societies, and defend multi-culturalism as a human right.[13] **Hyphenated identity** (e.g., Dutch-Moroccan, Turkish-German), while familiar to American ears, is something new in Europe and challenges many pre-existing formulas. Many may have a more ambivalent attitude about integrating in the host society, a reflection of what one writer calls "ambi-Europeanism" or "ambi-Americanism"—respect for Western economic prosperity and power coupled with disgust over the allegedly spiritual emptiness of the West and how it uses its power.[14] For others, such as the British-born London subway bombers discussed in the previous chapter, the answer is *jihad*, a war to "defend" the true faith against Western culture. At times, there can be a dramatic clash of values, as with the 2006 controversy over anti-Islamic cartoons published in a Danish newspaper, which is discussed in the **Is Europe One** section of this chapter.

hyphenated identity ■ idea that a person can have multiple identities from two cultures or countries, e.g., Turkish-German or Asian-American.

Many "native" Europeans also resist multi-culturalism. **Xenophobia**—fear or contempt of foreigners—is apparent in a number of ways. Immigrants are blamed for crime; accused of being lazy and living off welfare; or are charged with "stealing" jobs. Some accuse them of being insufficiently connected with their new place of residence and believe that they will never become "true" Frenchmen, Germans, Italians, and so on. This type of sentiment ranges from the more frivolous (do British-Indians root for the Indian or English international cricket team?) to the deadly serious (do they owe their fealty to a European state or to *fatwas* issued by Osama Bin Laden?). Far-right

xenophobia ■ fear of foreigners.

IS EUROPE ONE?

Responses to the Danish Cartoon Controversy

The presence of ethnic and religious minorities obviously complicates discussions of a united Europe, as Europe today is arguably more heterogeneous than at any time in its history. The issue, however, goes beyond racial or religious diversity. In some cases, conflicts over the presence of these groups touch upon deeper, philosophical questions and reveal that real tensions exist among the values or priorities that most Europeans hold dear. One concern that has come up repeatedly in Europe is how to balance the rights of free speech against the need and/or expectation for tolerance and respect for diversity.

This was manifested most clearly in the controversy and violence that erupted after the publication on September 30, 2005 of anti-Islamic cartoons in *Jyllands-Posten*, a Danish newspaper. The cartoons made connections between Islam and terrorism, with one depicting Muhammed, the revered prophet of Islam who by Muslim tradition is not to be drawn in any way, with a bomb as his turban. Once these cartoons had been discovered by a wider audience, which occurred months after their original publication when they were republished in newspapers across Europe,[15] there were violent protests against Danish, European, and US facilities in numerous Muslim countries that claimed dozens of lives—leading some to retort that such a backlash affirmed the accuracy of the depictions in the cartoons. In Europe, tens of thousands protested in the streets. Many called for the newspaper to be shut down; some considered lawsuits; many Muslim states boycotted Danish products; still others, mainly outside of Europe, called for the death of the cartoonists and publishers. However, marchers in London who belonged to the extremist al Ghuraba group carried placards that read, "Butcher those who mock Islam" and "Europe, you'll pay, Bin Laden is on his way."[16]

The Danish cartoon controversy has precedents in Europe. The most famous one involved Salman Rushdie, the Indian-born British author of *The Satanic Verses*. In 1989, Iran's leader, Ayatollah Khomeini, declared the book, which is mainly about Muslim immigrants in Europe but, like the Danish cartoons, includes an irreverent depiction of Muhammed, an insult to Muslims and issued a *fatwa* (religious order) enjoining Muslims to kill Rushdie and his publishers. Rushdie went into hiding. In several European states, Muslims burned copies of *The Satanic Verses*, and a terrorist killed himself in London in August 1989 in a failed attempt to assassinate Rushdie.

Then, as now, the issue boils down to limits, if any, on free speech. Is this right absolute, or does the need not to offend (or, in some cases, spark violence) trump speech? If limits are placed on speech, are you not caving into the violent crowd, letting those who want to repress freedoms win? Does freedom carry with it a responsibility? If so, who enforces this responsibility?

As Europeans grappled with these questions, their responses varied.[17] Some fanned the flames. For example, an Italian minister was blamed for sparking riots in Libya, in which eleven people died, for wearing a T-shirt emblazoned with the most controversial cartoon. Others tried to contain the fallout by cracking down on anti-Muslim groups. Sweden's foreign minister, for example, tried to shut down a website that was going to publish more provocative cartoons about Mohammed. Both of these ministers, albeit for different reasons, were forced to resign. The original cartoonist, Kurt Westergaard, who was forced into hiding but was exempt from any legal prosecution, defended the decision to publish the cartoons, maintaining that Islam provided "spiritual ammunition for terrorism" and that Muslims could not simultaneously demand

(*continued*)

toleration for their own practices and then be intolerant of actions that offended them.[18] The editor of *Die Welt*, a German newspaper that published the cartoons, noted that "It is the core of our culture that the most sacred things can be subjected to criticism, laughter, and satire. If we stop using our right to freedom of expression within our legal boundaries then we start to develop an appeasement mentality."[19] An American writer who lives in Oslo argued that Europe had reached a "Weimar moment" in which it had to stand up to Islamic radicals or watch their societies commit cultural suicide.[20] Others took a more measured view. *The Economist*, Britain's foremost newsweekly, rigorously defended the right of free speech, yet, recognizing that publishers must be responsible, opted not to publish the images. Some criticized this, arguing that *The Economist* had been cowed by fears of provoking Islamic extremists. Danish Prime Minister Anders Fogh Rasmussen, while regretting the violence and the offense caused to many Muslims and calling for tolerance, noted that he could not and would not tell newspapers what to print.

The controversy over the crisis has not died. In 2008, Danish police placed Westergaaard under heightened security after they uncovered a plot to kill him. In January 2010, despite these precautions, he was attacked in his home by a Somalian allegedly trained by al Qaeda. The questions that arose from it linger and pose a direct challenge to European values, or at least, to the idea that Europe represents a set of consistent, mutually supporting values. On the one hand, Europe claims to be a land of freedom, and rights of self-expression and dissent are upheld as fundamental. On the other hand, Europe claims to be a land of tolerance, a place upholding "Unity within Diversity." Do expressions that are critical or hateful of others' culture or religion have a place in Europe? What is the line between criticism and hate? Can the tension between the values of freedom and tolerance be reconciled? Should the cartoons have been published? Should the Berlin Opera, as was the case in 2006, have cancelled a performance of Mozart's *Idomeneo* because it featured a scene with the severed heads of Jesus, Muhammed, Buddha, and Poseidon? Questions such as these go beyond anti-Muslim cartoons, statements, or performances. It can include Holocaust denial, a punishable offense in many European countries, openly racist statements, and condemnations of Western culture made by Muslims living in Europe.

The discourse is often shrill, and the choices appear to be stark. Tariq Ramadan, a Swiss Muslim academic (who was denied entry to the United States to teach at Notre Dame), argues, however, that this is not a clash of civilizations, a choice between inalienable freedom of speech and an inviolable sacred sphere. Rather, the lesson he learns from these controversies is that the various sides must have a reasonable and peaceful dialogue, and that extremists on both sides must demonstrate respect for the other and build bridges based upon common values. He writes:

> Disasters threaten that extremists on both sides would not fail to use for their own agendas. If people who cherish freedom, who know the importance of mutual respect and are aware of the imperative necessity to establish a constructive and critical debate, if these people are not ready to speak out, to be more committed and visible, then we can expect sad, painful, tomorrows. The choice is ours.[21]

Critical Thinking Questions

1. Should the publication of material that is intended to offend or provoke be protected? If one can anticipate that publication of such material will lead to negative outcomes such as violence, should the government prevent its publication?
2. After some discussion, the author and editor for this book decided not to reprint any of the anti-Muslim cartoons. Was this the proper decision? Is there anything wrong or anything to be gained by publishing them?

political parties across the continent have called for more restrictive immigration policies and policies to compel immigrants to adapt to the dominant culture. These parties have performed well in countries such as Austria, Denmark, Italy, and the Netherlands. In 2007, the Swiss People's Party, which railed against immigrants, won Swiss national elections with 29 percent of the vote. One if its campaign posters and mailings, which depicted three white sheep kicking out a black one with the tagline "For More Security," was decried by many as "dangerous" and "disgusting," a sign of blatant racism.[22] Some of its leaders, as noted above, were behind the successful campaign in 2009 to change Swiss law to ban the construction of minarets.

Much of the criticism is targeted at Islam as a cultural threat. Noting that mosques are better attended than churches in many parts of Europe, some fear being inundated with Muslims, of Europe turning into "Eurabia." This sentiment is not confined to far-right political parties. Consider the statement in 2000 (before 9/11) of Cardinal Giacomo Biffi of Italy:

> In the vast majority of cases, and with only a few exceptions, Muslims come here with the resolve to remain strangers to our brand of individual or social "humanity" in everything that is most essential, most precious: strangers to what it is most impossible for us to give up as "secularists." More or less openly, they come here with their minds made up to remain fundamentally "different," waiting to make us all become fundamentally like them . . . I believe that Europe must either become Christian again, or else it will become Muslim.[23]

More prosaically, the late Italian journalist and anti-Islamic crusader Oriana Fallaci worries that Muslim men will soon be defecating in the Sistine Chapel.[24]

Public opinion on the issue of immigration is a bit more nuanced than might be inferred from the above quotations. Data on attitudes toward immigration are presented in Tables 12.3 and 12.4. These data, from 2006, reveal that large

TABLE 12.3

Attitudes Toward Immigration in Europe (Percent Agreeing with Each Statement)

Country	Immigrants Make Country Worse to Live	Immigrants Are Bad for the Economy	Allow Many or Some Immigrants from Same Race or Ethnic Group	Allow Many or Some Immigrants of Different Race or Ethnic Group
Belgium	39.2	40.8	74.1	56.5
France	41.9	39.3	62.3	50.8
Germany	41.9	40.0	69.1	49.9
Great Britain	47.1	46.1	59.3	48.0
Poland	15.4	26.7	79.5	69.2
Slovakia	32.8	40.3	69.6	59.5
Spain	36.0	25.0	52.0	48.2
Switzerland	25.5	20.3	81.3	59.9

Source: European Social Survey, Round III, 2006. Data for immigrants being "bad" or "make country worse" are taken from a scale from 0-10, with responses of 0-4 included here as anti-immigrant.

TABLE 12.4

Desired Qualities in Immigrants

Characteristic	% Saying It Is Important
Committed to Way of Life in Host Country	77.6
Know Local Language	69.9
Has Needed Work Skills	69.7
Has Family Living Here	49.5
Christian	26.2
White	13.8

Source: European Social Survey, Round I, 2002. Percent saying important is taken from scale from 0-10, with responses 6-10 included here as agreeing it is important. Data are from a weighted sample from 22 countries.

numbers of Europeans do agree that immigrants make life worse and that they are bad for the economy. Not surprisingly, anti-immigrant sentiment is less widespread in Eastern Europe, where there have been fewer immigrants. Interestingly, the British, where concerns over "Londonistan" have grown since the terror attacks of 7/7 and the far-right British National Party is growing, rank among the most anti-immigrant of all. Generally speaking, these data show that anti-immigrant sentiment has been growing in Europe. For example, compared with results from the 2002 version of the same survey, Germans (41.9 percent vs. 34.3 percent), French (41.9 percent vs. 37.4 percent), the British (47.1 percent vs. 43 percent) were more likely to agree that immigrants made life in the country worse. At the same time, however, at least based upon these data, one cannot claim that the majority of Europeans are completely anti-immigrant. Half or more of respondents in Germany, France, Belgium, and even Switzerland supported more immigration among people of different races or ethnic backgrounds. Racism *per se*, at least judging from this survey, is not the key problem. Rather, as seen in Table 12.4, it is the immigrants' potential to integrate and contribute in a given society that it crucial. Of course, it is usually those coming from poorer countries that do not possess the marketable skills or language ability and will inevitably have more trouble fitting in. EU policies such as "**blue cards**" for skilled immigrants aim to attract, if you will, a different class of immigrants to Europe, which, until now, has been the destination of choice for those with few skills.[25]

blue card ■ a work-visa program that the EU hopes will attract high-skilled immigrants, who are viewed as less burdensome and threatening than lower-skilled immigrants.

Is the backlash against immigrants justified? On the issue of crime, there is evidence that immigrants or those with foreign backgrounds do represent a disproportionate share of those in jails in Europe.[26] The same, of course, could be said for African Americans in the US, and these data by themselves overlook factors such as poor education, high unemployment, and policing and sentencing practices that may be overly or disproportionately applied against immigrants and those with foreign backgrounds. As for the economic effects of immigration, numerous studies have been conducted on this matter. The consensus appears to be that immigration has a negligible effect on native unemployment and on wages, although there is evidence to support the claim that low-wage or low-skilled native workers are harmed by immigration even as total income for the country increases with immigration.[27] Put differently, the benefits of immigration vary. Better-off Europeans can benefit by more maids and restaurants (where many immigrants work), but the low skilled can find themselves competing on the labor market with those willing to work for less. Even in these cases, however, much depends upon factors such as minimum wage laws, enforcement against illegal immigration, and the power of trade unions. Interestingly, Great Britain, which has seen more migration since 2004 than any other EU state—thanks mainly to policies that allow Poles and other East Europeans to come and work—had, prior to the banking and real estate crises of 2008 to 2009, one of the healthiest economies in Europe. Many Britons worry that as Poland becomes wealthier the Poles will move back, creating a labor shortage in many sectors of the economy.[28] On the question of public finances, average immigrants pay more into the system than they take out through social services. Estimates are that the "typical" migrant makes a net contribution of some €50,000 to public finances over her lifetime.[29]

Lastly, the anti-immigrant argument overlooks one essential fact: European needs immigrants. Fertility rates are low in many European countries, with an average in Europe of about 1.4 births per woman. Some countries such as Italy, Germany, Hungary, and Slovenia are already having negative population growth. Immigration and children born to immigrants or those with foreign backgrounds is the major source of population growth in Europe. This is important because whereas Europeans are having fewer children, they are living longer. There is a documented "graying" of Europe and, as noted in Chapter 10, this is putting pressure on the European social-welfare state. Put simply, Europe needs more workers to pay the taxes that fund pensions, health care, education, etc. Europe does not have these workers. It is going to have to either slash provisions of public services—not particularly politically popular—or import more workers. Assuming natural population growth stays the same, studies indicate that the members of the EU will have to have more than two million immigrants a year (roughly six times the present figure) from 2000 to 2050 to maintain the same level of working-age population as in 1995 and even more to maintain the population ratio between older and younger workers.[30]

Case Studies

Policies toward immigrants and individuals' experiences vary widely from country to country. To understand better some of the dilemmas, let us examine in a little more detail the experience of two countries that have taken very different approaches on the question of immigration and multi-culturalism: France and the Netherlands.

France More so than most European countries, France has a tradition of immigration. French policy, however, has always emphasized assimilation, meaning that one could be become French if one learned the language and accepted the ideas of a society of equal citizens. Hyphenated notions of citizenship (e.g., African-French) were explicitly rejected. The French do not even keep census data on race or religion, and "diversity" is not part of French political discourse. Instead, membership in the political community is predicated upon accepting French values. Since the *laïcité* ■ notion dating back to the French Revolution that religion should be precluded from the public sphere; this differs from the American notion of secularism that is open to including diverse public religious displays.

early twentieth century, this has included acceptance of ***laïcité***, secular policies that preclude any role for religion in the public sphere. Even rather innocuous displays of religiosity (e.g., "In God We Trust" on coins, public officials swearing on the Bible) do not occur in France.

For most of French history, this policy worked. Portuguese, Italians, Russians, and Poles became "French." After World War II, however, France became a destination for immigrants from the "Third World," particularly from former French colonies in North Africa. Taking advantage of liberal immigration policy, many Algerians, Tunisians, and Moroccans, many of whom did know French, moved to France. By the late 2000s, it was estimated that over five million Muslims—mainly of North African and sub-Saharan (black) African heritage—lived in France. Half, by virtue of birth or naturalization, are French citizens.

Although far-right political parties in France long complained of the economic effects of immigration, the cultural battle between Islam and traditional French values broke out in earnest in 1989. The issue was whether Muslim schoolgirls could wear the *hijab* to school. Muslims claimed they had a freedom to their religion and that head covering was mandated by their faith. The French pointed to the policy of *laïcité* that prohibited religious symbols in public schools. This issue was dragged through the French courts for over a decade. Finally, in 2004, the French government passed a law banning all conspicuous displays of religious affiliation from the public schools. Although the law could apply to Jewish yarmulkes, Sikh turbans, and even large Christian crosses, few doubted that the target was Muslims.

The ban on the *hijab* generated much controversy both inside and outside of France. The ban was, notably, popular among those both on the political right and the left, and research revealed that even a sizeable population of French Muslims—particularly women—were in favor of the ban.[31] Some Muslim girls, however, shaved their heads in protest. Some parents flatly refused to send their girls to school if they could not wear a *hijab*. Some threatened to sue to the ECHR, which in 2005 upheld a similar ban in Turkey. To many Americans, accustomed to displays of religion, the French law seemed harsh, a violation of rights. The French, however, saw the idea of *laïcité* one of their fundamental values at stake and argued that wearing the *hijab* worked against the overarching goal of assimilation. Interestingly, the French found a backer of their policy in Britain's Tony Blair, who defended a British school for firing a teacher who wore the *hijab*, noting it was a mark of separation.

positive discrimination ■ term from France that is akin to affirmative action in the US, whereby preferences for jobs and university placements would be given to minorities; as in the US, it is highly controversial.

The controversy over the *hijab* launched a broader discussion of the plight of France's Muslims and minorities. Although France celebrated its 1998 World Cup–winning soccer team that featured many Arabs and blacks, the upper echelons of French society remained white. No black or Arab, until 2007, represented mainland France in the National Assembly. The business elite, as well as the students at elite French universities, were, with few exceptions, white. There was not even a black or Arab newscaster until 2006. Many of France's minorities were consigned to live in ghettoes on the edges of large cities such as Paris and Marseilles. These areas featured sub-standard schools and few job opportunities, not to mention the numerous satellite dishes so residents could watch Algerian or Moroccan television. Some politicians began to talk about "**positive discrimination**" (in

American parlance, affirmative action) to give minorities greater educational and employment opportunities. Noting that French law does not recognize any ethnic or group rights and that all citizens are equally legal, President Jacques Chirac rejected such ideas as unacceptable.

Riots in the fall of 2005 across France, carried out largely by black and Arab youths in reaction to two young men dying while attempting to flee police, shocked France and Europe. Cars were burned; stores ransacked; even mosques were targets for vandalism. Some feared that Brussels, Amsterdam, and Berlin would be next. Remarkably, perhaps, some in France began to look at the US as a positive example about how one could integrate racial or religious minorities. Many, however, preferred to view the riots as more of a socio-economic problem than a cultural one. While conceding that much more would have to be done to ensure better, more integrated housing, education, and employment, the French model itself, defenders say, is not broken.[32] France has not seen a terrorist attack like Spain or Britain. Immigrants know or learn French. Data reveal a relatively high rate of inter-marriage between Muslim men and French women (although not the other way around) and that French Muslims (46 percent) in a 2006 survey were far less likely than their British counterparts (81 percent) to say they were Muslim first and French (or British) second.[33]

Still, all is not well in France. In 2006, some French cities saw a spontaneous movement to serve pork soup to the poor, thereby excluding Muslims. There were more violent outbursts directed against French police in some immigrant neighborhoods. Nicolas Sarkozy, the son of a Hungarian immigrant, appropriated part of the far-right National Front's platform in railing against immigration in the 2007 presidential elections. He won, but he conceded that some sort of "positive discrimination" might be necessary. His government created a Ministry for Immigration, Integration, and National Identity, and his cabinet included the daughter of North African immigrants.[34] Companies have been encouraged to set up "diversity charters" and elite French schools to establish special admissions tracks for students from disadvantaged areas.

Sarkozy's commitment to multi-culturalism, however, is clearly limited, as he has spoken out against the *burqa* (a full-length covering of women) as a prison that deprives women of identity. In 2010, the government's commission examining the question of the *burqa* recommended that it be banned in public institutions such as schools, hospitals, public transport, and government offices and that anyone wearing the *burqa* would be ineligible for public services. Amid some controversy, the French National Assembly adopted these recommendations in July 2010, although the law is likely to be challenged in French and perhaps European courts. While such a move is popular among many in French and was even supported by some French imams, it does little to get to socio-economic aspects of the issue. For example, unemployment in parts of Clichy-sous-Bois, where the 2005 riots started, is 50 percent, there is no government-run job center, and residents rarely go to central Paris, nine miles (but 1½ hours by public transport) away. One French author acknowledges that "under the cover of an abstract concept of equality," French society still "practices a pitiless form of apartheid."[35] Clichy-sous-Bois is not likely to be the first place people think of when they think of "Europe." An important part of Europe's future and its identity, however, will be decided in such places.

The Netherlands Unlike the French, the Dutch developed a rather *laissez-faire* policy towards their immigrants, which include sizeable numbers of Moroccans and Turks as well as peoples from former Dutch colonies such as Indonesia and Surinam. While immigrants could become citizens and were assured of their rights to socio-economic equality, political inclusion, and cultural and religious expression, there was no effort to make them "Dutch." While they could partake of social welfare benefits, including free instruction in the Dutch language, they were expected to remain in their own communities, a reflection of the previous Dutch "pillar" system, under which there were separate institutions (e.g., schools, neighborhoods, newspapers, unions, hospitals) for Catholics, Protestants, and the non-religious. Such a scheme did not envision much interaction among the groups, only a minimum of tolerance so that each group was able to do largely what it wanted to do. While such a policy was upheld by its defenders as one respectful of multi-culturalism—after all, the Dutch were not forcing them to assimilate or even integrate into Dutch culture—critics charged that the Netherlands "let its immigrants rot in their own privacy."[36] Few immigrants were able to climb the socioeconomic ladder to achieve economic equality with the native population.

The Dutch model of tolerance was severely tested in the 2000s. First, Pim Fortuyn, a gay formerly Marxist professor who claimed that he understood Moroccans because he had had sex with many Moroccan boys, became the most popular political figure in the country by campaigning against what he believed was Islam's intolerance. In contrast to that of the far-right National Front in France, Fortuyn's attack on immigrants came from the left. Praising Dutch tolerance (e.g., of soft drugs, homosexuality, women's rights), he suggested that Muslim immigrants, because of their culture, were a threat to Dutch values. He was assassinated in 2002 by an animal rights activist, but after his death his party came in second with 17 percent of the vote and compelled the government to adopt more restrictive policies toward immigrants and asylum seekers.

Secondly, Theo van Gogh, a Dutch filmmaker and great-great-grandnephew of Vincent van Gogh, was murdered in November 2004 in broad daylight in Amsterdam by a Dutch-born Moroccan who shot and stabbed him multiple times. Van Gogh was a controversial figure: He had insulted Muslims in very crude terms and produced a film, "Submission," which featured a young Muslim woman who claimed she had been raped by relatives and had words from the Koran (Muslim holy book) superimposed on her beaten and transparently veiled body. His assailant, Mohammed Bouyeri, who had grown up in the Netherlands, had dual Dutch-Moroccan citizenship, had been radicalized after 9/11, and proclaimed that Islamic law had compelled him to chop off the head of anyone who insults Islam. In the aftermath of van Gogh's murder, there were clashes between the native Dutch and Islamic communities, including attacks on mosques and churches, and death threats were directed at Ayaan Hirsi Ali, a Muslim Somali refugee who had wrote "Submission," repudiated Islam as a violent and repressive religion, and been elected to the Dutch parliament.[37] Geert Wilders, another member of parliament, suggested that all Muslim schools be closed and that, "The Netherlands has been too tolerant to intolerant people for too long. We should not import a retarded political Islamic society into our country."[38] He became leader of the Freedom Party. Among other things, he has called the Koran a fascist book and

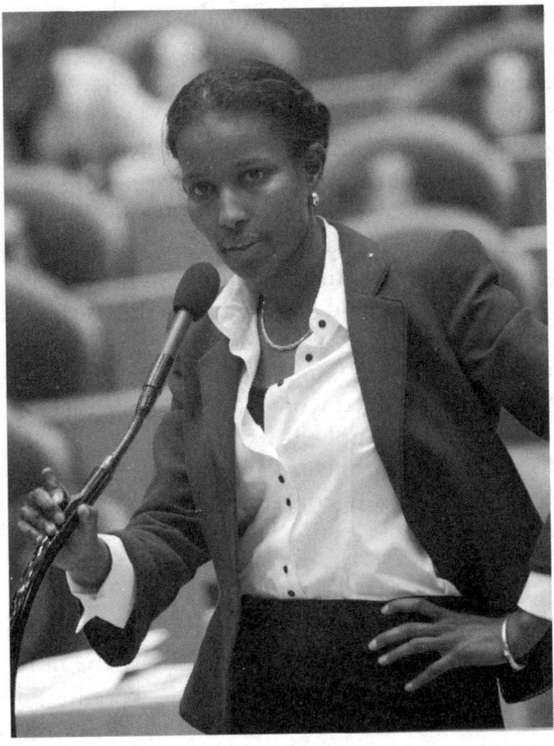

Born a Muslim, Ayaan Hirsi Ali is now an outspoken critic of Islam.

proposed it be banned in the Netherlands, referred to Muhammad as the devil, and in 2008 produced *Fitna*, a short anti-Islamic film.[39]

Since 2004, the Dutch government has adopted a tougher line toward immigration. Prospective immigrants from Muslim countries[40] are now required to pass a test on Dutch language and culture, which costs €350 and includes watching a film on the Netherlands which extols its tolerance for gays (one version features men kissing) and female emancipation (scenes include topless sunbathers) while noting that practices such as Islamic honor killings are not acceptable. While the film is no doubt patronizing and perhaps deliberately offensive, its backers would argue that immigrants need to be informed about Dutch society before they arrive and that the Dutch have every right to defend their cultural and legal traditions. One critic, however, alleged—probably correctly—that the testing program is much more about controlling immigration than promoting integration.[41] Ironically, Ayaan Ali herself got caught up in the anti-immigrant moment, as it was discovered she had lied on her application for political asylum and an unsuccessful attempt was made to strip her of Dutch citizenship. Rita Verdonk, the Minister for Immigration, oversaw a crackdown on asylum seekers (eleven asylum seekers died due to a fire in their holding cell at Amsterdam's airport), proposed banning the wearing of the *hijab* and the *burqa* on security grounds, and the establishment of a national code of conduct that would require Dutch to be spoken on the streets. Immigration played heavily in the 2006 national election, in which Wilders's party won 6 percent of the vote. He improved upon this by winning 15.5 percent in 2010, third among all parties in the Netherlands. For its part, the Dutch government has proposed strengthening blasphemy laws so that inflammatory language could be more easily prosecuted. Thus, one could not, as Ayaan Ali did, call Mohammed a pedophile or suggest Islam is a "nihilistic cult of death." However, as with the Danish cartoon controversy discussed earlier, one might suggest that restrictions on speech run counter to democratic freedoms.

The larger issue, however, is what can be done to integrate the immigrants and those with immigrant backgrounds already in the Netherlands. A proposal to have residents take a Dutch language and culture test is dubious on legal grounds and does not address socio-economic issues or segregated neighborhoods. The Dutch, are, more than ever, discussing issues of multi-culturalism and integration. Neighborhoods with their shrouded women, state-funded Islamic schools, and secretive mosques are no longer upheld as success stories of Dutch tolerance. Moderate Muslims issue calls for civility and understanding. The problem, however, is that it is hard to reach any consensus on what to do amid the shrill discourse on each side.

What Can the European Union Do?

Issues of immigration and cultural change rank among the most important issues discussed at the EU level. The debate over Turkish accession, discussed below, is obviously related to these issues, as one argument against Turkish membership is that hordes of Turks would flood into Europe. The issue, however, is obviously neither entirely about Turkey nor is it wholly new.

Immigration was not originally within the scope of European institutions. However, in the 1980s, as Europe moved towards establishing a common market and some European states adopted the Schengen Agreement creating a free travel area, the need to control and regulate the movement of migrants and third country nationals (e.g., Turkish, Algerian, or Pakistani citizens) became apparent. The Single European Act of 1986 included provisions that cited the need for a common immigration policy, and the Maastricht Treaty foresaw development of a common visa regime and policy toward third country nationals residing in European states under a Justice and Home Affairs pillar.

However, states have been reluctant to cede powers to the EU, preferring that action be taken through inter-governmental means. Border control, citizenship policy, and efforts to promote national integration are, arguably, core policies of a nation-state. Because of the peculiarities of local labor market conditions, cultural concerns about immigration, and historical patterns of immigration, many have argued that it is inappropriate to adopt a common EU immigration policy. However, this argument may be less persuasive today. For example, the external border for Denmark or Sweden is no longer in the Baltic Sea but is now the Mediterranean or the Polish-Ukrainian border, given the fact that, thanks to the Schengen Agreement which by 2009 covered twenty-five countries, once people are inside the EU they can move about with relative ease. A common policy to regulate immigration might therefore make sense. One problem, however, has been that while many member states are interested in above all else in restricting immigration, EU institutions, particularly the technocratic European Commission, look favorably on data that suggest that Europe needs more immigrants. Thus, there has been battle of sorts between the EU and member states over immigration policy, with directives of the EU falling far short of a comprehensive EU immigration policy.[42] Denmark, Great Britain, and Ireland have also opted out of any common EU immigration policies, but this is more an expression of nationalism than a reflection of anti-immigrant sentiment.[43]

This is not to suggest that the EU has been completely inactive on the immigration front. The Amsterdam Treaty of 1997 incorporated the Schengen Agreement into the EU and put priority on the attainment of a European space of freedom, justice, and security. The European Commission was charged with developing a common system for asylum and immigration. While the EU still lacks a comprehensive policy—the key issue of quantitative levels of immigration is still beyond EU control—the EU has adopted a number of directives and laws on immigration, most of which utilize the EU as a means to coordinate exclusion or prohibitions against immigration: a common standard on political asylum to prevent "asylum shopping" whereby asylum seekers would seek asylum in the state with the most liberal asylum laws; bolstering of EU external borders to prevent illegal immigration (estimated to be 500,000 people per year) and cooperation return of illegal migrants; agreements to combat human trafficking, whereby migrants, mostly females, are virtually enslaved in sweatshops or in brothels[44]; a visa information system; rules on family unification; a law on the status of long-term residents; police cooperation; joint initiatives with countries of origin, and monitoring of the status of non-EU citizens within the EU. The EU has also advanced a number of goals with respect to immigrants, including access to employment and education, fostering of entrepreneurship, fighting against discrimination, promotion of social inclusion and protection. The EU has also set up a European Fund for the Integration of Third-Country Nationals and sponsors a Center on Racism and Xenophobia.[45]

In fall 2007, the EU, noting that it was far less successful than the US, Canada, or Australia in attracting skilled immigrants, announced a "blue card" policy that aimed to bring 20 million skilled workers to Europe over a period of twenty years. This broke with previous practice, as EU member states turned to the EU to help determine which and how many migrants should be let into Europe. Whether or not the EU could in fact attract this many migrants—and the "brain drain effect" this might have on their home countries—is, of course, a large question. In this respect, however, EU policy is reflective of policies in many European countries, which has tried to differentiate between "bad" immigration (illegal immigration or immigration of unskilled workers) and "good" immigration that will contribute to the EU's Lisbon Strategy, discussed in Chapter 10, to stimulate European growth and competitiveness. At the same time, however, the EU is aware that immigration is much more than an economic issue, declaring 2008 the European Year for Intercultural Dialogue. The fact that immigration—a "least likely case" for EU supranational policy given traditional concerns over state sovereignty and its political salience—is increasingly subject to EU-level discussions, if not yet comprehensive policy, shows that Europe may make a "radical break with traditional notions of statehood and territorial control."[46]

THE DECLINING IMPORTANCE OF RELIGION

The growth (and perceived threat) of Islam in Europe has been accompanied by another trend: the declining importance of Christianity in many parts of Europe. As noted in Chapter 1, some define Europe in cultural terms and emphasize the continent's Christian heritage. However, whereas in the past religion played a major role both in the lives of individuals and in politics, this is no longer the case today. In terms of policies, the decline of religion has led to more permissive or tolerant views on issues such as divorce, abortion, and homosexuality.

How Religious Are Europeans?

The decline of organized religion in Europe has been commented upon by many observers, and, as noted in the **In Focus** section, distinguishes Europe from the US. Since World War II, religion's role in politics has declined and European Christians, both Catholics and Protestants, have become less and less personally religious. Part of this is due to the rise of post-materialism, discussed in Chapter 9, whereby Europeans began to question traditional authorities. This was accompanied by changes within religious establishments. For example, Tony Judt writes that the Vatican II Council, which began in 1962, was a crucial event, as the Catholic Church began to reconcile itself to liberal democracy, mixed economies, modern science, other religions (including Judaism), and secular politics. Vatican II accelerated movement toward what was already becoming a "post-religious" society, marking the "final divorce between politics and religion in continental Europe" and playing a critical role in "the making of 'the sixties'."[47]

Just how non-religious are Europeans today? Data from the 2006 European Social Survey (ESS) provide some answers, as reported in Figure 12.2. This survey

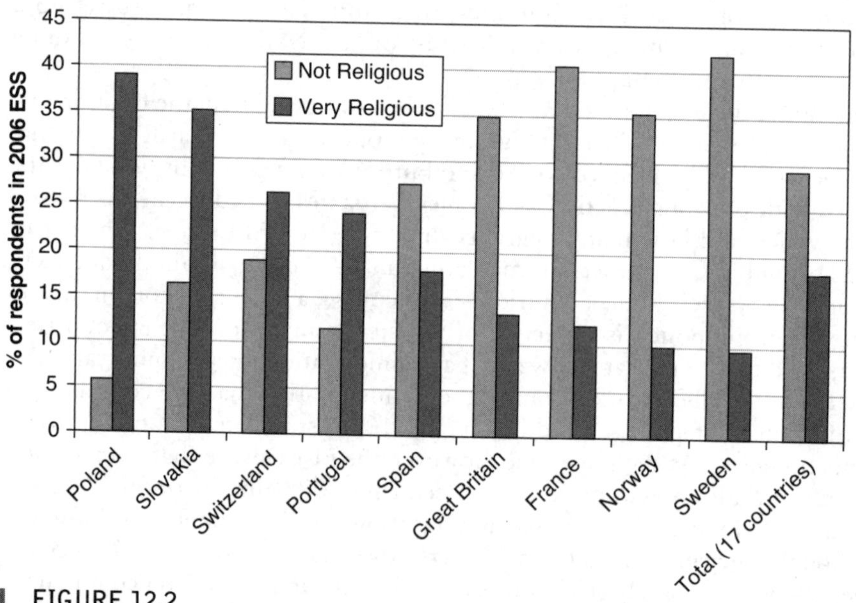

FIGURE 12.2

How Religious Are Europeans?

Source: European Social Survey 2006, available at http://ess.nsd.uib.no. The question asked was, "How religious are you?" On a scale from 0–10, scores from 0–2 are coded "not religious" and those 8–10 are coded "very religious."

IN FOCUS

Europe versus the United States II: The Role of Religion in Politics

The "post-religious" and more permissive orientation of most of Europe offers one of the clearest trans-Atlantic contrasts with the US. American presidents swear an oath on the Bible, start their days with a prayer breakfast, and often pepper their speeches with reference to God. Religious belief—and, in some cases, ardent fealty to Biblical principles—is a necessity to win high political office. Congressional hearings were called after a "wardrobe malfunction" exposed a body part of a pop singer on national television. In contrast, Europeans are used to topless women exposed on the "page threes" of many European tabloid newspapers and their leaders typically do little to draw attention to their own religious beliefs. For example, Tony Blair, who converted to Catholicism after leaving office in 2007, when asked how his faith shaped his politics, responded, "Well I think if you have a religious belief it does, but it's probably best not to take it too far."[48] Elsewhere, European leaders can survive various scandals—such as French President Nicolas Sarkozy divorcing his wife and marrying model Carla Bruni in 2008 and pictures in 2009 depicting topless young women (as well as a naked Czech Prime Minister) at Italian Prime Minister Silvio Berlusconi's villa[49]—that would surely end the career of any American politician. The subject of religion was a subject of debate over the draft EU Constitutional Treaty, with the Poles in particular insisting that it contain some reference to God. In the end, the document referred to Europe's "cultural, religious, and humanist inheritance" but failed to include mention of either the Almighty or Christianity. Its primary author, former French President Valery Giscard d'Estaing, justified this decision, arguing, "Europeans live in a purely secular political system, where religion does not play an important role."[50]

Americans, particularly those critical of what they see as a morally lax Europe, would think such statements and behavior strange. In fact, however, among developed, Western countries, it is the Americans that stand out for their religiosity. For example, surveys typically show that more than 90 percent of Americans believe in God and that over half regularly attend religious services, findings that, among EU members, would only be found in Poland. In a 2002 survey, when asked whether they considered religion very important, a solid majority (59 percent) of Americans said yes, compared with 11 percent of French and Czechs, 21 percent of Germans, 33 percent of Britons, and 36 percent of Poles. Only the Turks (65 percent) considered religion more important than Americans.[51] In a 2007 survey, when given a choice of various freedoms (freedom of speech, freedom of religion, freedom from hunger, freedom from crime and violence), Americans were far more likely (28 percent) to cite freedom of religion as most important; the highest figure among EU members was 12 percent, expressed by Italians and Poles.[52] The US, despite being in many ways the most "modern" society in the world, is the primary outlier on the relationship between religious belief and "modernity."

Why might this be the case? Part of the answer may date back to the founding of the US, when groups fleeing religious persecution in Europe came to the US and made religion a major part of the new social order. Another part of the puzzle may be the freedom of religion enjoyed by Americans. Churches are not tainted by their association with the state, and the freedom of religion has allowed various denominations, mostly Christian, to flourish. Even though He is not mentioned in the Constitution, many Americans see their country's success as something ordained by God, and that the US thus has a godly mission at home and abroad. Others, noting that the US has both more immigration of Christians and is a more mobile society, note the role religion can play in allowing individuals to create new social networks.[53]

What political effect does this have? Certainly, "moral" or "family" values are important political issues in the US, coloring debates over issues ranging

(continued)

from abortion, stem-cell research, gay rights, and the teaching of evolution. All of these issues are far less controversial in most of Europe than in the US. Europeans, for example, will look at Americans with amazement (or lowering and shaking their head) at the idea that creationism or "intelligent design" should be taught along with or instead of Darwin. Alarmists—American and European—invoke Upton Sinclair's quote that when or if fascism arrives in the US, "it will come wrapped in the flag and bearing the cross."

Others, however, would argue that Europe's turn away from religion carries costs. Philip Jenkins links secularization with Europe's falling birthrates, arguing that "modern Europe seems to have embarked on a self-destructive social experiment unprecedented in human history, what some have called slow-motion autogenocide."[54] As noted in the Chapter 10, this has put pressure on the European welfare state. Some, however, go further. One American conservative writer, looking at Europe in the aftermath of the 2005 riots in France conducted by largely by young men of African and Arab descent, maintains:

> The images we recently saw on TV news suggest that Europe has, once again, lost its way . . . having turned away from Jewish and Christian faith, a Europe based solely upon the Enlightenment cannot long survive. The Europe that is declining in population is a Europe more rational than Europe has ever been, more scientific, less religious, less pious, more mundane, wealthier, more consumerist, more universally close to living *etsi Deus non daretur* (as if God does not exist). A very large part of the "European crisis" is the crisis of the Enlightenment. On that ground, a civilization cannot be built, a civilization can only burn down to the last waxed threads of its wick.[55]

Most Europeans, as one would expect, would not embrace such assertions and would defend the values of the Enlightenment. Religious fervor, according to many, was behind recent intra-European conflicts in the Balkans and in Northern Ireland and helps spawn violence across the globe. Europeans, including some of their more secular political leaders, believe they can discuss and embrace values, even if there is no overt reference to religion.[56] While more "permissive" than the US on many questions, Europeans enjoy lower poverty, crime, and teenage pregnancy rates, and there is no evidence that gay marriage in the Netherlands, Belgium, or Spain has destroyed the institution of marriage in those countries. As T.R. Reid puts it, "Yes, Americans put up huge billboards reading 'Love Thy Neighbor,' but they murder and rape their neighbors at rates that would shock any European nation."[57] Bringing aspects of the European welfare state (e.g., free child care, maternal leave, health insurance, etc.) into the debate, one Norwegian official states, "Americans like to talk about family values. We have decided to do more than talk; we use our tax revenues to pay for family values."[58] Finally, given debates over "What is Europe?" and looking at the relative growth of Europe's Muslim population and possible Turkish accession to the EU, a more inclusive, less "Christian" Europe might have more prospects than one that has more strongly anchored to a more traditional embrace of religion.

Critical Thinking Questions

1. Why is there such a divergence between Europe and the US on questions of religious belief?
2. Some suggest that the decline of religiosity in Europe is a cause for concern and that Europe will lose part of its heritage and perhaps its moral compass. Would you agree? Does secularization come at a price?

was conducted in seventeen European nations, and it asked several questions about religious belief and practices. When asked to state how religious they were on a ten-point scale, only 18.1 percent claimed they were very religious (responding 8–10 point on scale) compared to 29.3 percent who said they were not very religious (0–2 on the scale). Whereas most (62.2 percent) claimed they belonged to a religious denomination, a minority from all faiths claimed that they attended religious services once a week or more, whereas a majority claimed they attended services only on special holidays or even more infrequently.[59]

As Figure 12.2 indicates, however, there is significant variation across Europe. Poland, by far, ranks as the most religious country in this survey (Ireland was not included in the survey). Catholic-majority Slovakia, Switzerland, and Portugal are relatively religious, certainly more so than most Protestant-majority countries as well as France, which has a long tradition of secularism. On the question of religious attendance, a majority (53.9 percent) of Poles claim that they attend religious services once a week or more, whereas a majority of the French (50 percent) and the British (51 percent) claim that they *never* attend religious services. No wonder that anecdotal accounts suggest that in any given week more people attend mosques in Great Britain than attend Christian churches.

Available evidence suggests that lack of religious faith has grown over time, a reflection of what Matthew Arnold lamented as early as 1867 in "Dover Beach" as the "long withdrawing roar" of faith. For example, the World Values Survey has conducted several waves of surveys across Europe. Compared with surveys in 1981 and 1982, which, because of political conditions, were conducted primarily in Western Europe, there was less religious belief from 1999 to 2001, with the highest numbers of self-professed atheists in the Czech Republic (52 percent), Sweden (41 percent), the Netherlands (39 percent), Estonia (39 percent), and France (35 percent). Similarly, the numbers of those asserting that God is important in their lives has also declined in most states, so that by 1999 the average score on this question (on a ten-point scale) in the Czech Republic (3.63), Denmark (4.02), Sweden (4.10), and Estonia (4.23) less than half the figure for the US (8.47).[60] Pippa Norris and Ronald Inglehart also report a decline in both religious belief and participation in religious organizations in Western Europe from the 1970s to 2000, and find a strong correlation to individual religious belief to one's socio-economic status, seemingly confirming modernization theory's hypothesis that economic development leads to a decline in religious belief.[61] Longer-term data from surveys in Great Britain is even more striking: whereas in 1957 71 percent of Britons declared that Jesus was the Son of God, only 38 percent claimed so in 2001, and in 2004 only 44 percent of British respondents admitted belief in God.[62]

The relative decline of individuals' religious commitment is reflected as well in a widespread belief that religion should not play a political role. For example, in 2007 surveys conducted by the Pew Global Attitudes Project in nine European countries, there was consensus that religion should be a matter of personal faith and should be kept separate from government policy. Agreement with this statement ranged from a low of 84 percent in Sweden, to 94 percent in very Catholic Poland, with, it is worth adding, a clear majority of Turks (86 percent) also agreeing.[63] It is no wonder then that most European countries do not have the equivalent of groups such as the Moral Majority, Focus on the Family, or Christian Coalition that exist in the US and, despite the presence in several countries of Christian Democratic Parties, religious officials do not exercise significant political influence.

"Values" Issues

The decline of religion and traditional values has manifested itself in policy changes on various "moral" or "values" issues. Here I am referring to a host of issues that, until recently, were considered sinful or immoral by social mores and religious authorities and were often prohibited by state law. These relate to the idea of post-materialism, developed in Chapter 9, in the sense that they do not directly concern economic issues and, insofar as older traditional views, authority structures, and policies are eroding, more liberal practices, as least according to their advocates, strengthen individual rights and autonomy. Since the 1960s, thanks in part to the sexual revolution and its attendant social movements, Europeans tend to be liberal or permissive on previous taboo issues including divorce, sex education, and pre-marital sex. Many European governments have adopted liberal policies on "values" issues, in some cases going well beyond what would be, at present, politically possible in the US.

Abortion Beginning in the 1930s in Protestant countries (e.g., Iceland, Sweden), abortion was legalized. In the 1960s and 1970s, abortion was legalized in most of Western Europe, with Great Britain (1967) adopting one of the most liberal abortion laws. Catholic countries such as France (1975), Italy (1978), and Spain (1985) also legalized abortion, and, more recently, in 2002 and 2007 Switzerland and Portugal, respectively, each of which had some of Europe's more restrictive abortion policies, liberalized their laws after referendums indicated that abortion rights had the support of a majority of voters. In communist Eastern Europe, abortion was legal in all countries except Romania, and it was a popular form of birth control.

Abortion laws vary from state to state.[64] In some countries, such as Germany, Austria, Hungary, and Switzerland, all women are required to undergo counseling before having an abortion. Abortions are paid for under many national health insurance programs. Among European countries, the most restrictive anti-abortion policies are in the two most Catholic countries: Ireland and Poland.

With a few exceptions, however, abortion is not a controversial political issue, as it is in the US. In both Poland and Ireland, pro-choice advocates have attempted to overturn restrictive abortion laws, thus far with little success. On the other side, anti-abortion forces tried to make a case to ban abortion before the ECHR, but, in *Vo v. France* in 2003, the court ruled that the European Convention on Human Rights does not give the fetus legal rights. The Catholic Church continues to lobby for restrictions on abortion in many European countries, but abortion rights have wide support throughout most of the continent,[65] and EU foreign aid even includes funding for abortions in developing countries. The rate of abortions in Europe, as seen in Table 12.5, varies widely, with the highest rates of abortion in Eastern Europe. Although the figures on Table 12.5 may seem high, even alarming to some, it is worth noting that according to studies carried out by the World Health Organization (WHO), Europe, even with its liberal abortion laws, has a lower abortion rate than in Africa and Asia, where laws are more restrictive but where women turn to illegal and often dangerous abortions.[66] Abortion rates have also declined in many countries in recent decades. Nonetheless, there is no denying that the legalization of abortion—together with widespread availability of other forms of contraception—helps account for the fall in European birthrates, which became more marked in the 1960s.[67]

TABLE 12.5

Abortion Rates in Europe

Figures are number of abortions per 1,000 live births.

Country	1980	1990	2000	2006
Great Britain	231	247	291	286
Germany	290	200	176	178
Italy	325	278	258	233*
Denmark	407	325	234	232
Sweden	359	302	343	144
Czech Republic	448	852	381	234
Hungary	544	719	607	464
Romania	1,036	3,153	1,100	685
Bulgaria	1,217	1,375	1,318	504
US	430	387	327	291*

Source: Statistics of the UN Economic Commission for Europe, http://w3.unece.org/pxweb/Dialog/, accessed on 1 April 2010.

* data for 2005.

Drug Policy Ask the typical American college student who has been to Amsterdam something about the city, and the answer, if it is honest, is not likely to be about Rembrandt, van Gogh, Dutch architecture, Anne Frank, or even Amsterdam's famous canals. No, instead you will likely hear something about "coffee shops," a code word of sorts for establishments that sell, in addition to coffee, marijuana (cannabis).

The Dutch amended their drug laws in 1976 to distinguish between "hard" (e.g., heroin, cocaine) and "soft" (e.g., marijuana) drugs. Although the sale of marijuana remains technically illegal in the Netherlands, more than 800 "coffee shops" are tolerated as points of sale, provided they meet certain conditions (e.g., no sales to those under eighteen, no advertising, no alcohol).[68] Several states (e.g., Switzerland, Great Britain, Luxembourg, Spain) have followed the Dutch lead and essentially decriminalized possession of cannabis for personal use, and Portugal went further than any other state by decriminalizing all drug use in 2001. Those caught with drugs—including heroin and cocaine—are sent to treatment and therapy instead of jail. Interestingly, according to studies conducted in the Netherlands, use of marijuana among the Dutch—not taking into account the tourists for whom "legal" marijuana is a novelty—is actually lower than in the US, and drug use in Portugal has also declined since the law was changed.[69]

Not all of Europe is so "soft" on drugs. In France, possession of marijuana can still land one a jail term. Scandinavian countries also have tough drug laws on their books, even if enforcement of the law against individual users is minimal. East European countries, with the exception of the Czech Republic, also maintain stricter drug laws and punishments. European public opinion as a whole has evolved somewhat toward a more "liberal" attitude, but data from a 2006 Eurobarometer found that only 26 percent of respondents favored legalizing marijuana for personal use throughout Europe, with the most support in the Netherlands (49 percent) and the lowest in Finland (8 percent) and Sweden (9 percent).[70]

Prostitution Prostitution is, as the cliché states, the "oldest profession," but, despite almost universal presence, it has usually been met with moral censure. However, it has persisted, if only as part of the "shadow" or "black market" economy. In the 1970s, in part because of the sexual revolution, in part because some women argued they had a right to engage in the trade of their choice, and in part because of worries of the consequences of pushing it underground, some began to argue that it should be legalized. The purported advantages of legalized prostitution were several: legal protections for sex industry workers; improved public health; and tax revenues for the state.

In the Netherlands, prostitution was *de facto* legalized in the 1970s and in 1988 it was recognized as a legal profession. By the 1990s, Amsterdam, the Dutch capital, had become the "sex capital" of Europe. Other states, including Sweden, Great Britain, Denmark, Greece, Austria, and Switzerland, legalized prostitution, and in most cases workers were required to be licensed by the state, be subjected to health exams, and pay income taxes. In 2002, Germany legalized prostitution, which is estimated to bring in €6 billion of revenue a year and "serve" up to a million customers a day.[71] Other states, including the Czech Republic, Bulgaria, the Baltic States, and Norway have considered legalizing prostitution in the 2000s.

These moves have not been without controversy. While traditional moral concerns are no longer paramount, there is great concern in Europe about the problem of human trafficking, especially among young women. Most of these women—there are estimated to be more than 500,000—come from Eastern Europe and the former Soviet Union, and are lured to Germany, the Netherlands, Greece, and elsewhere with promises of a "normal" job. Instead, they are essentially enslaved, subjected to violence, and forced to become prostitutes. For this reason, states such as Bulgaria—a source of many trafficked women—that had considered liberalizing their laws have had second thoughts. In addition, liberalization of prostitution laws in countries such as the Netherlands, Austria, Great Britain, and Denmark has been linked to a growth in the sex industry, and research has shown that a majority of the workers are not native to Western Europe and many are under the age of consent. This has led to widespread concerns that liberal prostitution laws are only abetting human trafficking in women and children, thereby enslaving, not liberating women.[72] Reflective of such concerns, Sweden recriminalized prostitution in 1999, although only the customers will be punished. As a consequence, today's Stockholm, although liberal on many issues, does not have the red-light districts of Amsterdam or Hamburg, although some complain that the sex trade has simply been pushed underground, to the detriment of many women.[73]

Homosexuality and Gay Marriage Homosexuality, throughout most of European history, has been condemned by religious authorities and penalized by state law. Italy (1890) and Poland (1932), interestingly, were the first European countries to decriminalize homosexual behavior, but homosexuals were harshly punished in Mussolini's fascist Italy and in Franco's Spain and were sent to concentration camps in Hitler's Germany.

After World War II, there was more active campaigning to extend legal protections to homosexuals. Inspired in part by activism in the US in the 1960s and 1970s, a European gay rights movement grew in several European countries. Homosexuality was decriminalized throughout most of Europe in the 1960s and 1970s. In 1986, in *Norris v. Ireland*, the ECHR ruled that criminalization of homosexuality violated the European Convention on Human Rights. In 1974, the Netherlands became the first country to allow openly gay people to serve in the military, and in 1999 the ECHR struck down a British law banning gays from military service.[74] Removal of anti-gay legislation has also become a requirement for EU membership, which became an issue when some East European states entered the accession process. In 1989, Denmark was the first state to create registered partnerships for homosexual couples, granting partners inheritance and property rights. In December 2000, the Netherlands, over the objections of the Catholic Church, became the first country to legalize gay marriage. Belgium (2003), Spain (2005), Norway (2008), Sweden (2009), Iceland (2010), and Portugal (2010) have also legalized gay marriage.[75] By the end of 2010, twelve other European countries (including Great Britain, Germany, France, Ireland, and the Czech Republic) have recognized civil unions among gay couples. Some Eastern European countries, such as Latvia, Poland, Bulgaria, and Serbia, have resisted this trend, constitutionally limiting marriage to a union between a man and a woman.

Changes in policy have been accompanied by a shift in the public mood with respect to homosexuality, as seen in Table 12.6. Whereas in the early 1980s homosexuality received wide condemnation, by 2007 there was far greater acceptance, particularly in Western Europe. Eurobarometer surveys from 2006 also found 44 percent of those in the EU favored gay marriage, with 49 percent opposed. In some

TABLE 12.6

Changing Attitudes Toward Homosexuality

Percentage of people who say they accept homosexuality:

Country	1981–1982	2005–2007
Germany[a]	21	60
Great Britain	20	49
France	17	60
Spain	14	63
Sweden	29	82
Poland	n/a	17
Bulgaria	n/a	30
Turkey	n/a	3
US	9	31

Source: Analysis from World Values Survey, at http://www.worldvaluessurvey.org. Figures are those reporting 6-10 on a ten-point scale asking whether they considered homosexuality justifiable, where 10 was always justifiable.

[a] For West Germany only.

countries, such as the Netherlands (82 percent), Sweden (71 percent), Denmark (69 percent), and Belgium (62 percent), solid majorities were in favor of gay marriage.[76] Gay individuals have won political office, serving as mayors of Berlin and Paris and the head of the German Free Democratic Party. In 2009, Johanna Sigurdardottir, a lesbian, became prime minister of Iceland and the first openly gay person to serve as leader of a country.

In contrast, there is far less support for homosexuality and gay marriage in post-communist Europe. Surveys in 2007 found less than 20 percent support for gay marriage in Slovakia, Poland, Bulgaria, and Romania.[77] Sometimes, the expression of anti-homosexual sentiments can be rather comical. For example, in 2007, the top children's rights official in Poland suggested that psychological tests be administered to Tinky Winky, the purple, handbag-carrying character from the BBC's Teletubby program who, allegedly, sends a subversive gay message to preschoolers.[78]

TURKISH ACCESSION TO THE EUROPEAN UNION AND CULTURAL DEFINITIONS OF EUROPE

In Chapter 1, we noted how some define Europe in cultural terms and that by this measure some countries, such as Turkey, may not be truly "European." Turkey has, however, applied to join the EU and since the creation of modern Turkey in the 1920s its leaders have stressed Turkey's European identity. In many ways the question of EU membership for Turkey is a test for how one defines Europe and what Europe will become.

Turkey is eligible to join the EU. This was first affirmed in its 1963 Association Agreement with the (then) European Economic Community and has been repeated in various statements numerous times. However, the proclivity of the Turkish military to intervene against democratically elected governments (in 1960, 1971, 1980, and, albeit more subtly, in 1997), its spotty record in defending civil and human rights, and its economic underdevelopment prompted Brussels to reject its formal bids for membership in 1989 and in 1997. However, in 1999, after the EU agreed to take in several post-communist states as new members, it also declared Turkey a candidate member, offering the Turks the possibility of membership if Ankara could make the necessary political, economic, and legal reforms to meet the Copenhagen Criteria.

In many respects, this decision was the apogee of a decades-long process in Turkey. The Turkish Republic, founded in 1923 as a successor to the Ottoman Empire, embarked on a program of Westernization under its first President, Mustafa Kemal Atatürk (1923–1938). Atatürk wanted to Turkey to break with its past, and he pushed through legal, educational, and social reforms—including legal equality for women, the banning of the fez in favor of a European-style brimmed hat, and adoption of a Latin alphabet—to pull Turkey toward the West and establish a secular state and society. By the 1950s, Turkey had a nascent multiparty democracy and joined NATO.

However, its respect for liberal democratic norms, particularly with respect to freedom of speech and association and rights for its ethnic Kurds, a non-Turkish people that comprise up to 20 percent of the population, maintained problematic. Fighting with separatist Kurdish rebels—labelled terrorists by the Turkish government—claimed more than 30,000 lives in the 1980s and 1990s and was accompanied by numerous human rights abuses on both sides, including torture and the razing of villages. Outspoken journalists and writers were imprisoned. Meanwhile, Islamic political parties, deemed a threat to the secular system enshrined by Atatürk, were banned in the 1990s and many of their leaders sentenced to jail. Critics of the Turkish government could contend that in Turkey old statist habits rooted in past still persisted, which promoted "republicanism over democracy, homogeneity over difference, the military over the civilian, and the state over society."[79] In this context, Turkish membership in the EU looked impossible.

However, the decision by the EU in 1999 to open the door to membership produced a tidal wave of reform in Turkey. The EU put forward several short-term and medium-term goals for Turkey to meet in order for its application to proceed. These demands included legalization of broadcasts in Kurdish, Kurdish-language education, a ban on capital punishment, lifting restrictions on speech and assembly, training for police officials and the judiciary, a reduced role for the military in politics, and progress on resolution of the Cyprus problem. In response, the Turkish government pushed forward a series of reforms in 2001 and 2002, including thirty-four constitutional amendments in line with EU recommendations. Between 2002 and 2004, nine reform packages were passed that substantially liberalized the Turkish state and altered a third of its existing constitution.[80] Most of these measures were passed by a government led by the Justice and Development Party (JDP), which has Islamist roots but a decidedly pro-EU agenda. It was elected to office in 2002 and won re-election in 2007. It has ended the state of emergency in all provinces of the (largely Kurdish) southeast, established an EU Harmonization Commission, and adopted the UN Covenants on Civil and Political Rights and on Economic, Social, and Cultural Rights. The JDP government also pushed through controversial social reforms including a ban on discrimination against homosexuals and harsh punishments for "honor killings."

The EU deserves credit for much of this process. As one Turkish observer noted, Turkey has seen a "period of profound and momentous change in Turkish history . . . [A] change of this magnitude would have been impossible in the absence of a powerful and highly institutionalized EU anchor in the direction of full membership."[81] In 2005, the EU, impressed by the scope of reforms, agreed to open accession talks with Turkey, although all observers expected the process to last for a least a decade.

Turkish membership in the EU, however, is by no means guaranteed and is one of the most controversial issues in Europe. Turkey differs from the post-communist states that joined in 2004 and 2007. Even with its progress toward democracy, it is still too big,[82] too poor,[83] too agricultural,[84] too nationalistic, and too Muslim, some would claim, to fit into today's EU. The prospect of allowing the free movement of millions of Turkish workers across Europe is also unpalatable to many. According to former French President Valery Giscard d'Estaing, Turkish accession to the EU would be "the end of Europe."[85] Both Chancellor Angela Merkel of Germany and President Nicolas Sarkozy of France have suggested that Turkey be given only a "privileged partnership," not full membership, meaning it could participate in many of the EU programs (e.g., the common market) but it would not be formally incorporated into the EU. Eurobarometer surveys in 2005 revealed that only 35 percent of Europeans favored Turkish membership in the EU, lower than support for Croatia (52 percent), Serbia (40 percent), Ukraine (45 percent), and even Albania (36 percent). An additional Eurobarometer in 2006 found that 61 percent of respondents thought that cultural differences between Turkey and the EU are too significant to allow it to join the EU, with the highest support for this view coming from Austria (84 percent), Greece (79 percent), and Germany (74 percent).[86] *The Economist*, noting Brussels's view of impending expansion toward several countries, tersely commented about Turkey, "Good grief, do we have to?"[87]

Turks see such sentiments as racist, a reflection of a desire to keep Europe a "Christian club." Former German Chancellor Helmut Kohl pulled no punches in this regard, arguing in 1997 that the EU is a "civilizational project" in which "Turkey has no place."[88] Turkish Prime Minister Recep T. Erdoğan, however, contends that "the idea of 'Christian Europe' belongs to the Middle Ages. It should be left there . . . There should be no doubt that Turkey's full membership will re-enforce the desire and will for co-habitation between Christians and Muslims."[89] Such arguments have been supported by some in the EU, particularly the British, who see Turkish accession to the EU as, if nothing else, symbolically important in the post-9/11 world. Turks also note how post-communist states—first Central Europeans, then Romania and Bulgaria (both poorer than Turkey), and now Croatia and perhaps other former Yugoslav states—"cut" into the membership queue. They complain that additional criteria—resolution of the thorny Cyprus question, demands for official recognition of genocide against Armenians in 1915, vague pronouncements about the "absorptive capacity of the Union"—are placed on Turkey.

By 2006, the brief honeymoon in Turkish-EU relations was over.[90] As criticism of Turkish membership became more vocal, many Turks believed they were being treated unfairly and that they would never get into the EU. Confidence in EU institutions and support for EU membership fell to just over 50 percent of the population.[91] Pope Benedict XVI's quotation of a Byzantine emperor that Islam only brought things that were "evil and inhuman" cast a shadow over his visit to Turkey. The EU, on its end, also grew increasingly frustrated with Turkey. Implementation of many reforms, particularly with respect to the Kurds, remained a problem. The fact that Turkey's Nobel Prize–winning author, Orhan Pamuk, was put on trial in 2006 for "insulting Turkishness" provoked international outcry. (He was acquitted on a technicality.) Turkish refusal to allow Cypriot planes and ships to enter Turkey led the EU in December 2006 to suspend several chapters of the accession talks. Turkey dodged a bullet in 2008, when, as noted in Chapter 7, the JDP was brought to court for allegedly violating principles of secularism. The Constitutional Court did not ban the JDP, but it did fine it for endorsing certain policies (e.g., allowing the wearing of the Islamic headscarf by university students) that it believes run counter to Turkish principles of secularism. Meanwhile, the government uncovered a plot by elements in the military to launch a coup, which led some to question just how firmly democratic government is established in Turkey.

Turkish-EU accession talks will likely continue for many years, and their outcome remains highly uncertain. However, their results, as noted in Chapter 1, will not only have an impact on Turkey but also say volumes about the EU and Europe itself. Indeed, whether and how Europeans manage growing cultural diversity will go a long away in addressing a key question asked explicitly and implicitly throughout this text: What is Europe? Is Europe about universal democratic values, or is it more about a particular, more narrowly defined culture? Will Europe overcome centuries of conflict with the Islamic world, or will Europe in effect say that pious Muslims have no place in Europe? If Turkish candidacy is rejected on cultural grounds, if other countries prohibit the wearing of the *burqa*, or if others follow Switzerland in banning minarets or taking other actions explicitly directed against Muslims, what will that signal—both to the Muslim world and to the 15 million Muslims already living in the Europe? Cultural issues emanating from immigration and a more visible Muslim presence rank among the most heated concerns in many European countries, and resolving them remains one of the greatest challenges facing Europe today.

APPLICATION QUESTIONS

1. Can one apply lessons from the American "melting pot" and its experience with immigrants to Europe? Why or why not?
2. Consider the campaign poster at the beginning of this chapter as well as the one from the Swiss People's Party in 2007 (available at http://www.dailymail.co.uk/news/article-480493/Proposed-Swiss-immigration-laws-rise-new-racism-xenophobia.html). Do these posters strike you as racist? Does the fact that this party won the largest share of votes in 2007 elections compromise Swiss democracy?
3. Sometimes there is a tension between rights of the individual and rights of the community. When might it be permissible to restrict displays or practices of religion for the sake of order or political harmony?
4. What are the costs and benefits of admitting Turkey to the EU? Should the fact that Turkey is a Muslim-majority country affect its chances for membership?
5. What are the costs and benefits of immigration? Should the religion of an immigrant matter when considering immigrant quotas or eligibility?

KEY TERMS

assimilation 346
blue card 352
Eurabia 342
Gastarbeiter 342
hyphenated identity 348
integration 346
laïcité 354
multi-culturalism 346
naturalization 348
positive discrimination 354
xenophobia 348

ADDITIONAL READING

Buruma, Ian. 2005. *Murder in Amsterdam: Liberal Europe, Islam, and the Limits of Tolerance*. New York: Penguin.

Buruma investigates the context surrounding the murder of Theo van Gogh in Amsterdam. This book does an excellent job in raising questions about how liberal, democratic Europe can respond to the challenges of new immigrants.

Jenkins, Philip. 2007. *God's Continent: Christianity, Islam, and Europe's Religious Crisis*. Oxford: Oxford University Press.

Jenkins presents a well-written and comprehensive account of the decline of Christianity in Europe and how this, together with immigration, is transforming Europe.

Laqueur, Walter. 2007. *The Last Days of Europe: Epitaph for an Old Continent*. New York: St. Martin's.

This book presents an alarmist view of Europe focusing on how low birthrates and high immigration rates create social and economic challenges for European states.

Parson, Craig, and Smeeding, Timothy, eds. 2006. *Immigration and the Transformation of Europe*. Cambridge: Cambridge University Press.

This collection by a variety of writers assesses how immigration is changing Europe economically, socially, and politically.

Ramadan, Tariq. 2004. *Western Muslims and the Future of Islam*. Oxford: Oxford University Press.

A proponent of Euro-Islam who urges tolerance and mutual understanding, Ramadan argues that European Muslims can take the lead in fostering modernization and change throughout the Muslim world.

END NOTES

1. "Switzerland: Constitutional ban on the building of minarets," *Documentation Information Catholique Internationales,* December 23, 2009, at http://www.dici/org/en/?p=4194, accessed on 1 April 2010.
2. Tony Judt, "Europe vs. America," *New York Review of Books,* February 10, 2005.
3. Eurabia itself is a bit of a misnomer, as many of the Muslims in Europe are not Arabs. They are of Turkish, South Asian, or sub-Saharan African origin. For alarmist views of Islam in Europe, see Bat Ye'or, *Eurabia: The Euro-Arab Axis* (Madison NJ: Fairleigh Dickinson University Press, 2005); Oriana Fallaci, *The Rage and the Pride* (New York: Rizzoli International, 2002); and Bruce Bawer, *While Europe Slept: How Radical Islam is Destroying the West from Within* (New York: Doubleday, 2006).
4. Gerard Noiriel, *The French Melting Pot: Immigration, Citizenship, and National Identity* (Minneapolis: University of Minnesota Press, 1996).
5. The percent of non-EU foreign-born varies greatly, from approximately 20 percent in Ireland and 45 percent in Belgium to 63 percent in Great Britain, and 66 percent in France to more than 70 percent of the total of all foreign-born in Italy, the Netherlands, Germany, and Austria. Data from OECD, reported in Jack Citrin and John Sides, "European Immigration in the People's Court," in Craig Parsons and Timothy Smeeding, eds. *Immigration and the Transformation of Europe* (Cambridge: Cambridge University Press, 2006), p. 357.
6. Migration Information Source at http://www.migrationinformation.org, accessed on 13 January 2008.
7. European Social Survey, Round 3, 2006. Data are from a weighted average of surveys conducted in seventeen countries. Data available to registered users at http://ess.nsd.uib.no.
8. National Centre for Social Research, British Social Attitudes, at http://www.britsocat.com.
9. European Social Survey, Round 3, 2006.
10. Hans-Georg Betz, *Radical Right-Wing Populism in Western Europe* (New York: St. Martin's 1994), p. 96.
11. Jocelyne Cesari, *When Islam and Democracy Meet: Muslims in Europe and in the United States* (New York: Palgrave, 2004), p. 22, and Stephanie Giry, "France and Its Muslims," *Foreign Affairs,* 85:5, September/October 2006, p. 93.
12. Migration Information Source, at http://www.migrationinformation.org.
13. Yasemin Nuhoğlu Soysal, *Limits of Citizenship: Migrants and Postnational Membership in Europe* (Chicago: University of Chicago Press, 1994).
14. Zachary Shore, *America, Islam, and the Future of Europe* (Baltimore: Johns Hopkins University Press, 2006), pp. 7–8.
15. When the cartoons were originally published, the controversy was localized to Denmark. It was only later, after some Danish Muslims went to the Middle East and informed others of what had occurred, that the issue acquired global significance. The cartoons can be found at http://www.brusselsjournal.com/node/698 (accessed on 25 March 2010).
16. *The Guardian,* February 7, 2006.
17. A good archive of material, which includes various perspectives and is periodically updated, can be found through the website of The Guardian, at http://www.guardian.co.uk/cartoonprotests, accessed on 1 April 2010.
18. *Glasgow Herald,* February 18, 2006.
19. *The Guardian,* February 6, 2006.
20. Bawer, *While Europe Slept.*
21. *The Guardian,* February 6, 2006.
22. *New York Times,* October 8, 2007. A copy of the campaign poster was re-printed in the Daily Mail (London) and can be found http://www.dailymail.co.uk/news/article-480493/Proposed-Swiss-immigration-laws-rise-new-racism-xenophobia.html. One can also view their campaign video, "Heaven or Hell," which contrasts the lives of immigrants with those of "real" Swiss. I found it at http://www.youtube.com/watch?v=3VSguNay8Ys&eurl=http://viz.cwrl.utexas.edu/node/160&feature=player_embedded (accessed January 27, 2009).
23. Quoted in Cesari, *The Rage and the Pride,* p. 33.
24. See obituary for Fallaci in *The Economist,* September 21, 2006.
25. *New York Times,* October 24, 2007.
26. For example, in Switzerland 70 percent of those in prison are non-Swiss. See *New York Times,* October 8, 2007.
27. For more discussion on these themes, see Herbert Brücker, Joachim Frick, and Gert Wagner, "Economic consequences of immigration in Europe," in Parsons and Smeeding, *Immigration and the Transformation of Europe* 2006.
28. *New York Times,* October 19, 2007.
29. Brücker et al., "Economic consequences of immigration," p. 137.

30. Craig Parsons and Timothy Smeeding, "What's Unique about Immigration in Europe?" and Paul Demeny, "Europe's Immigration Challenge in Demographic Perspective," both in Parsons and Smeeding, *Immigration and the Transformation of Europe.*
31. *The Economist,* February 7, 2004, p. 25.
32. Giry, "France and Its Muslims."
33. Pew Research poll cited in Jonathan Paris, "Europe and Its Muslims," *Foreign Affairs* 86:1, January/February 2007, p. 182.
34. Rachida Dati served as Minister of Justice from 2008 to 2009. She resigned in 2009 to take up a seat in the European Parliament.
35. "Survey: France 'Minority Report'," *The Economist,* October 26, 2006.
36. Jane Kramer, "The Dutch Model," *The New Yorker,* April 3, 2006, p. 63.
37. The premier source on the murder and its aftermath is Ian Buruma, *Murder in Amsterdam: Liberal Europe, Islam, and the Limits of Tolerance* (New York: Penguin, 2006).
38. Associated Press, November 19, 2004.
39. Over fears of possible violence, Wilders was denied entry into Great Britain in 2008.
40. Those wishing to immigrate to the Netherlands from Western states, including Canada, the US, Australia, and Japan, are exempt. One can find a version of the film at http://www.spike.com/video/to-netherlands/2710876, accessed on 1 April 2010.
41. Kees Groenendijk, head of Center for Migration Law at University of Nijmegen, in *RFE/RL Newsline,* April 5, 2006.
42. Adam Luedtke, "The European Union Dimension: Supranational Integration, Free Movement of Persons, and Immigration Politics," in Parsons and Smeeding, *Immigration and the Transformation of Europe,* pp. 419–441.
43. Ireland and Great Britain, for example, have allowed workers from new members states in Eastern Europe to come and work, and Denmark allows members of a refugee's family up to the age of twenty-four to relocate to Denmark, whereas the EU norm in 21.
44. This is a major problem in both Western and Eastern Europe. See Caroline Moorehead, "Women and Children for Sale," *New York Review of Books,* October 11, 2007, pp. 15–18.
45. European Commission. "Third Annual Report on Migration and Integration," COM (2007) 512, September 11, 2007.
46. Luedtke, "The European Union dimension," p. 438.
47. Tony Judt, *Postwar: A History of Europe Since 1945* (New York: Penguin, 2005), p. 375.
48. Philip Jenkins, *God's Continent: Christianity, Islam, and Europe's Religious Crisis* (Oxford: Oxford University Press, 2007), p. 41.
49. Berlusconi's wife announced in 2009 that she was divorcing him after he was linked with an eighteen-year-old model (he was seventy-two at the time). His standing among Italians, however, barely declined, and in 2010 his party prevailed in regional elections.
50. Quoted in Jenkins, *God's Continent,* p. 39.
51. Pew Global Attitudes Project, "Among Wealthy Nations, US Stands Alone in Its Embrace of Religion," 2002.
52. Pew Global Attitudes, "World Publics Welcome Global Trade—But Not Immigration," October 4, 2007, available at http://pewglobal.org/reports/pdf/258.pdf, accessed March 30, 2010.
53. Jenkins, *God's Continent,* pp. 47–54.
54. Jenkins, *God's Continent,* p. 6.
55. Michael Novak, quoted in Jenkins, *God's Continent,* p. 9.
56. Charlemagne, "A European values debate," *The Economist,* December 9, 2006.
57. T.R. Reid, *The United States of Europe* (New York: Penguin, 2004), p. 218.
58. Valgard Haugland, quoted in Judt, "Europe vs. America."
59. The figures are as follows: 31 percent of Catholics, 28 percent of Muslims, 14 percent of Jews, and 12 percent of Protestants attended services once a week or more. In contrast, 51 percent of Catholics, 60 percent of Muslims, 76 percent of Protestants, and 79 percent of Jews claimed they went only on major holidays or more infrequently. Analysis from 2006 European Social Survey.
60. World Value Survey (WVS), online analysis at http://www.worldvaluessurvey.org
61. Pippa Norris and Ronald Inglehart, *Sacred and Secular: Religion and Politics Worldwide* (Cambridge: Cambridge University Press, 2004).
62. Data reported in Jenkins, *God's Continent,* p. 27.
63. Pew Global Attitudes Project, "World Publics."
64. See BBC News, "Europe's Abortion Rules," February 12, 2007, at http://news.bbc.co.uk/2/hi/europe/6235557.stm, accessed on 30 March 2010.
65. Analysis from data from the 1999–2001 WVS show that in Europe the percentage of people saying abortions are never justified is largest in Ireland (49.7 percent), Croatia (42.8 percent),

Poland (41.7 percent), all of which are overwhelmingly Catholic, and in Turkey (63.9 percent).

66. "Safe, Legal, and Falling," *The Economist*, October 20, 2007.
67. Tony Judt, *Postwar* p. 490.
68. The best source by far on drug policies in Europe is the European Legal Database on Drugs, available at http://eldd.emcdda.europa.eu, accessed on 30 March 2010. In particular, see its 2005 report, "Illicit Drug Use in the EU's Legislative Approaches."
69. *International Herald Tribune,* November 7, 2007. The Netherlands has not actually legalized cannabis, a move that would cause trouble within the EU and arguably be against existing UN agreements on combating controlled substances. On Portugal, see "Drugs in Portugal: Did Decriminalization Work?" *Time,* April 26, 2009.
70. Standard Eurobarometer 66, conducted in September and October 2006, reported in http://ec.europa.eu/public_opinion/archives/eb/eb66/eb66_en.pdf, accessed on 1 April 2010.
71. *Christian Science Monitor,* May 11, 2005.
72. See *International Herald Tribune,* October 5, 2007, and Richard Poulin, "The Legalization of Prostitution and Its Impact on Trafficking in Women and Children," February 6, 2005, at http://sisyphe.org/spip.php?article1596, accessed March 30, 2010.
73. *Christian Science Monitor,* January 10, 2008.
74. By 2005, the British government was actively working to recruit more gays into the service. See *International Herald Tribune,* February 23, 2005.
75. As of 2010, these six countries, together with Canada (2005), South Africa (2006), and Argentina (2010) are the only ones to recognize gay marriage.
76. Standard Eurobarometer 66, conducted in September and October 2006, reported in http://ec.europa.eu/public_opinion/archives/eb/eb66/eb66_en.pdf, accessed April 1, 2010.
77. See Pew Forum on Religion and Public Life, "Same-Sex Marriage: Redefining Marriage Around the World," July 11, 2007, at http://pewforum.org/docs/?DocID=235, accessed March 30, 2010.
78. *Financial Times,* May 30, 2007, p. 10.
79. M. Hakan Yavuz, "Turkey's Fault Lines and the Crisis of Kemalism," *Current History* 99, January 2000, p. 34.
80. Ergun Özbudun, "Democratization Reforms in Turkey, 1993–2004," *Turkish Studies* 8:2, June 2007, p. 195.
81. Ziya Öniş, "Domestic Politics, International Norms and Challenges to the State: Turkey-EU Relations in the post-Helsinki Era," in Ali Çarkoglu and Barry Rubin, eds. *Turkey and the European Union* (London: Frank Cass, 2003), p. 13.
82. With a population of approximately 70 million people, Turkey is almost twice as large as Poland, the largest state to join the EU in 2004, and will become larger than any other EU country EU within twenty years.
83. According to the World Bank, in 2008 per capita income in Turkey was $9340, well below the eurozone average ($38821) and lower than all countries that joined the EU in 2004, although it is higher than Romania ($7930) and Bulgaria ($5490), which joined the EU in 2007. Data available at http://www.worldbank.org
84. The CIA World Fact Book reports that as of 2005 29.5 percent of employment in Turkey is in agriculture, compared with 29.7 percent in Romania and 17.4 percent in Poland, the post-communist EU members with the largest agricultural sectors. See https://www.cia.gov/library/publications/the-world-factbook/fields/2048.html, accessed on 30 March 2010.
85. *Le Monde,* November 8, 2002.
86. Standard Eurobarometer 63, conducted May-June 2005, available at http://ec.europa.eu/public_opinion/archives/eb/eb63/eb63_en.htm. Only 10 percent were in favor in Austria, 16 percent in Cyprus, and only 21 percent in France and Germany. Only in Poland (54 percent), Slovenia (53 percent), Hungary (51 percent), and Sweden (50 percent) did majorities favor Turkish membership. For the 2006 survey, see Standard Eurobarometer 66, conducted reported in http://ec.europa.eu/public_opinion/archives/eb/eb66/eb66_en.pdf. Both surveys accessed on 1 April 2010.
87. *The Economist,* November 17, 2001, p. 47.
88. *The Guardian,* March 7, 1997.
89. R.T. Erdoğan, "Why the EU Needs Turkey," Speech at Oxford University, 28 May 2004, available at http://www.sant.ox.ac.uk/esc/docs/Erdogan1.pdf, accessed on 30 March 2010.
90. Soli Özel, "Turkey Faces West," *Wilson Quarterly,* Winter 2007, pp. 18–25, and Ziya Öniş, "Turkey-EU Relations: Beyond the Current Stalemate," *Insight Turkey* 10:4, Summer 2008, pp. 35–50.
91. Standard Eurobarometer 66, available at http://ec.europa.eu/public_opinion/archives/eb/eb66/eb66_en.pdf

FINAL QUESTIONS AND POSSIBLE TRAJECTORIES

This book has offered a broad introduction to European politics, covering history, domestic political institutions, social actors, public policies, the EU, and Europe's place in the world. It has tried to relate where Europe and Europeans have been, what their concerns are at present, and the possible directions for future development. In order to make the last set of issues more explicit and in lieu of a final chapter, we conclude with a list of questions, suitable for reflection upon finishing this text, class discussion, a final exam, and/or further research.

1. Has Europe really overcome its history? Which historical attributes—for better or for worse—continue to color European politics?
2. How important do you think the old division between West and East is in Europe today?
3. What is the biggest threat to democracy in Europe today? How healthy do you think the state of democracy in Europe is?
4. The European project has made much progress in integrating states. Can it do the same in terms of integrating peoples? Can it do so without a strong notion of European "peoplehood" or citizenship?
5. The mission of the 1957 Treaty of Rome is largely complete with economic integration of the continent. After the failure of the Constitutional Treaty, can Europe regain its collective purpose? What will be the next big "narrative" for European integration?
6. Will Europe be able to compete the rising powers such as China and India? What must Europe do in order to be better served by globalization?
7. What is the future of US-European relations? Will the two sides continue to drift apart, or can rifts in the relationship be easily healed?
8. Can European states and societies adjust to their increasing multi-culturalism? Is immigration a threat to Europe? How is immigration changing the idea of what "Europe" is?
9. Does the success of more free-market policies in many European countries (Great Britain, Czech Republic, Estonia) point the way forward for Europe?
10. Are the European welfare states and the much-vaunted European social model dead? If so, what, perhaps, might be retained or salvaged?
11. How seriously do the Greek and Irish economic crises threaten Europe? Does it show that the idea of the euro or of Europe becoming a cohesive political community is illusionary?
12. What are the limits of European integration? Can the European Union really live up to its motto, "Unity in Diversity"?
13. Given the differences within Europe, does it even make sense to speak of "One Europe"?

CREDITS

Chapter 1: *p. 2:* Lionel Cironneau/AP Images.
p. 8: EyesWideOpen/Getty Images.

Chapter 2: *p. 24:* Joe Klamar/AFP/Getty Images.
p. 48: Alik Keplicz/AP Images.

Chapter 3: *p. 64:* Peter Morrison/AP Images.
p. 89: Giuseppe Cacace/Getty Images.

Chapter 4: *p. 96:* © Eric Lalmand/epa/Corbis.
p. 119: © EPA/Corbis.

Chapter 5: *p. 126:* © Matt Cardy/Getty Images.
p. 143: © Michael Gottschalk/AFP/Getty Images.

Chapter 6: *p. 152:* © David W Cerny/Reuters/Corbis.
p. 169: © Paulo Carrico/epa/Corbis.

Chapter 7: *p. 180:* Yoray Liberman/Getty images.
p. 195: Michael Latz/AFP/Getty Images.

Chapter 8: *p. 202:* Atilla Kisbenedik/AFP/Getty Images.
p. 229: Lewis Whyld/PA Wire/AP Images.

Chapter 9: *p. 234:* Tiziana Fabi/AFP/Getty Images.
p. 254: © Helen King/Corbis.

Chapter 10: *p. 266:* Nikolas Glakoumidis/AP Images.
p. 295: AP Images.

Chapter 11: *p. 302:* © Fabrizio Bensen/Reuters/Corbis.
p. 317: © Susana Vera/Reuters/Corbis.

Chapter 12: *p. 340:* Fabrice Coffrini/AFP/Getty Images.
p. 357: Bas Czerwinski/AP Images.

INDEX